UNIX™ SYSTEMS PROGRAMMING

Communication, Concurrency, and Threads

Kay A. Robbins · **Steven Robbins**

PRENTICE
HALL
PTR

Prentice Hall PTR
Upper Saddle River, NJ 07458
www.phptr.com

Library of Congress Cataloging-in-Publication Data

Robbins, Steven, 1947-
   UNIX systems programming : communication, concurrency, and threads / Steven Robbins, Kay Robbins.
      p. cm.
   Previously published under the title: Practical UNIX Programming / Kay Robbins. Upper Saddle River, NJ : Prentice Hall, c1996.
   ISBN 0-13-042411-0
      1. UNIX (Computer file) 2. Operating systems (Computers) I. Robbins, Kay A. II. Robbins, Kay A. Practical UNIX programming. III. Title.

Production Supervisor: Wil Mara
Acquisitions Editor: Greg Doench
Cover Design: Nina Scuderi and Talar Boorujy
Cover Design Director: Jerry Votta
Editorial Assistant: Brandt Kenna
Marketing Manager: Dan DePasquale
Manufacturing Manager: Alexis Heydt-Long

© 2003 Pearson Education, Inc.
Publishing as Prentice Hall Professional Technical Rereference
Upper Saddle River, New Jersey 07458

Prentice Hall books are widely used by corporations and government agencies for training, marketing, and resale.

Prentice Hall PTR offers excellent discounts on this book when ordered in quantity for bulk purchases or special sales. For more information, please contact: U.S. Corporate and Government Sales, 1-800-382-3419, corpsales@pearsontechgroup.com. For sales outside of the U.S., please contact: International Sales, 1-317-581-3793, international@pearsontechgroup.com.

Company and product names mentioned herein are the trademarks or registered trademarks of their respective owners.

Printed in the United States of America

3rd Printing

ISBN 0-13-042411-0

Pearson Education LTD.
Pearson Education Australia PTY, Limited
Pearson Education Singapore, Pte. Ltd.
Pearson Education North Asia Ltd.
Pearson Education Canada, Ltd.
Pearson Educación de Mexico, S.A. de C.V.
Pearson Education—Japan
Pearson Education Malaysia, Pte. Ltd.

To Nicole and Thomas

About the Web Site

The *http://usp.cs.utsa.edu/usp* web site offers additional resources for the book, including all of the programs in downloadable form. These programs are freely available with no restrictions other than acknowledgment of their source. The site also has links to simulators, testing tools, course material prepared by the authors, and an errata list.

Contents

IV Communication   607

Contents

Preface

UNIX Systems Programming: Communication, Concurrency and Threads is the second edition of *Practical UNIX Programming: A Guide to Communication, Concurrency and Multithreading*, which was published by Prentice Hall in 1995. We changed the title to better convey what the book is about. Several things have changed, besides the title, since the last edition.

The Internet has become a dominant aspect of computing and of society. Our private information is online; our software is under constant attack. Never has it been so important to write correct code. In the new edition of the book, we tried to produce code that correctly handles errors and special situations. We realized that saying *handle all errors* but giving code examples with the error handling omitted was not effective. Unfortunately, error handling makes code more complex. We have worked hard to make the code clear.

Another important development since the last edition is the adoption of a Single UNIX Specification, which we refer to as POSIX in the book. We no longer have to decide which vendor's version of a library function to use—there is an official version. We have done our best to comply with the standard.

The exercises and projects make this book unique. In fact, the book began as a project workbook developed as part of a National Science Foundation Grant. It became clear to us, after preliminary development, that the material needed to do the projects was scattered in many places—often found in reference books that provide many details but little conceptual overview. The book has since evolved into a self-contained reference that relies on the latest UNIX standards.

The book is organized into four parts, each of which contains topic chapters and project chapters. A topic chapter covers the specified material in a work-along fashion. The topic chapters have many examples and short exercises of the form "try this" or "what happens if." The topic chapters close with one or more exercise sections. The book provides programming exercises for many fundamental concepts in process management, concurrency and communication. These programming exercises satisfy the same need as do laboratory experiments in a traditional science course. You must use the concepts in practice to have real understanding. Exercises are specified for step-by-step development, and many can be implemented in under 100 lines of code.

The table below summarizes the organization of the book—twenty two chapters grouped into four parts. The fifteen topic chapters do not rely on the eight project chapters. You can skip the projects on the first pass through the book.

Part	Topic Chapter	#	Project Chapter	#
I **Fundamentals**	Technology's Impact	1		
	Programs	2		
	Processes in UNIX	3		
	UNIX I/O	4		
	Files and Directories	5		
	UNIX Special Files	6		
			The Token Ring	7
II **Asynchronous Events**	Signals	8		
	Times and Timers	9		
			Virtual Timers	10
			Cracking Shells	11
III **Concurrency**	POSIX Threads	12		
	Thread Synchronization	13		
	Semaphores	14		
	POSIX IPC	15		
			Producer Consumer	16
			Virtual Machine	17
IV **Communication**	Connection-Oriented Commun.	18	*WWW Redirection*	19
	Connectionless Commun.	20		
			Internet Radio	21
			Server Performance	22

Project chapters integrate material from several topic chapters by developing a more extensive application. The projects work on two levels. In addition to illustrating the programming ideas, the projects lead to understanding of an advanced topic related to the application. These projects are designed in stages, and most full implementations are a few hundred lines long. Since you don't have to write a large amount of code, you can concentrate on understanding concepts rather than debugging. To simplify the programming, we make libraries available for network communication and logging of output. For a professional programmer, the exercises at the end of the topic chapters provide a minimal hands-on introduction to the material. Typically, an instructor using this book in a course would select several exercises plus one of the major projects for implementation during a semester course. Each project has a number of variations, so the projects can be used in multiple semesters.

There are many paths through this book. The topic chapters in Part I are prerequisites for the rest of the book. Readers can cover Parts II through IV in any order after the topic chapters of Part I. The exception is the discussion at the end of later chapters about interactions (e.g., how threads interact with signals).

We have assumed that you are a good C programmer though not necessarily a UNIX C programmer. You should be familiar with C programming and basic data structures. Appendix A covers the bare essentials of program development if you are new to UNIX.

This book includes synopsis boxes for the standard functions. The relevant standards that specify the function appear in the lower-right corner of the synopsis box.

A book like this is never done, but we had to stop somewhere. We welcome your comments and suggestions. You can send email to us at `authors@usp.cs.utsa.edu`. We have done our best to produce an error-free book. However, should you be the first to report an error, we will gratefully acknowledge you on the book web site. Information on the book is available on the WWW site `http://usp.cs.utsa.edu/usp`. All of the code included in the book can be downloaded from the WWW site.

Acknowledgments

We are very grateful to Mike Speciner and Bob Lynch for reading the entire manuscript and making many useful suggestions. We are especially grateful to Mary Lou Nohr for her careful and intelligent copy-editing. We would also like to express our appreciation to Neal Wagner and Radia Perlman for their encouragement and suggestions.

We have taught undergraduate and graduate operating systems courses from 1988 to date (2003), and much of the material in the book has been developed as part of teaching these courses. The students in these courses have suffered through drafts in various stages of development and have field-tested emerging projects. Their program bugs, comments, complaints, and suggestions made the book a lot better and gave us insight into how these topics interrelate. Some of the students who found errors in an early draft include Joseph Bell, Carlos Cadenas, Igor Grinshpan, Jason Jendrusch and James Manion. We would like to acknowledge the National Science Foundation for providing support through the NSF-ILI grant USE-0950497 to build a laboratory so that we had the opportunity to develop the original curriculum upon which this book is based. NSF (DUE-975093, DUE-9752165 and DUE-0088769) also supported development of tools for exploration and analysis of OS concepts.

We would like to thank Greg Doench, our editor at Prentice Hall, for guiding us through the process and William Mara our production editor, for bringing the book to publication. We typeset the book using LaTeX 2_ε, and we would like to express our appreciation to its producers for making this software freely available.

Special thanks go to our families for their unfailing love and support and especially to our children, Nicole and Thomas, who have dealt with this arduous project with enthusiasm and understanding.

Part I

Fundamentals

Chapter 1

Technology's Impact on Programs

This chapter introduces the ideas of communication, concurrency and asynchronous operation at the operating system level and at the application level. Handling such program constructs incorrectly can lead to failures with no apparent cause, even for input that previously seemed to work perfectly. Besides their added complexity, many of today's applications run for weeks or months, so they must properly release resources to avoid waste (so-called leaks of resources). Applications must also cope with outrageously malicious user input, and they must recover from errors and continue running. The Portable Operating System Interface (POSIX) standard is an important step toward producing reliable applications. Programmers who write for POSIX-compliant systems no longer need to contend with small but critical variations in the behavior of library functions across platforms. Most popular UNIX versions (including Linux and Mac OS X) are rapidly moving to support the base POSIX standard and various levels of its extensions.

Objectives
- Learn how an operating system manages resources
- Experiment with buffer overflows
- Explore concurrency and asynchronous behavior
- Use basic operating systems terminology
- Understand the serious implications of incorrect code

1.1 Terminology of Change

Computer power has increased exponentially for nearly fifty years [73] in many areas including processor, memory and mass-storage capacity, circuit density, hardware reliability and I/O bandwidth. The growth has continued in the past decade, along with sophisticated instruction pipelines on single CPUs, placement of multiple CPUs on the desktop and an explosion in network connectivity.

The dramatic increases in communication and computing power have triggered fundamental changes in commercial software.

- Large database and other business applications, which formerly executed on a mainframe connected to terminals, are now distributed over smaller, less expensive machines.

- Terminals have given way to desktop workstations with graphical user interfaces and multimedia capabilities.

- At the other end of the spectrum, standalone personal computer applications have evolved to use network communication. For example, a spreadsheet application is no longer an isolated program supporting a single user because an update of the spreadsheet may cause an automatic update of other linked applications. These could graph the data or perform sales projections.

- Applications such as cooperative editing, conferencing and common whiteboards facilitate group work and interactions.

- Computing applications are evolving through sophisticated data sharing, real-time interaction, intelligent graphical user interfaces and complex data streams that include audio and video as well as text.

These developments in technology rely on communication, concurrency and asynchronous operation within software applications.

Asynchronous operation occurs because many computer system events happen at unpredictable times and in an unpredictable order. For example, a programmer cannot predict the exact time at which a printer attached to a system needs data or other attention. Similarly, a program cannot anticipate the exact time that the user presses a key for input or interrupts the program. As a result, a program must work correctly for all possible timings in order to be correct. Unfortunately, timing errors are often hard to repeat and may only occur once every million executions of a program.

Concurrency is the sharing of resources in the same time frame.When two programs execute on the same system so that their execution is interleaved in time, they share processor resources. Programs can also share data, code and devices. The concurrent entities can be threads of execution within a single program or other abstract objects. Concurrency can occur in a system with a single CPU, multiple CPUs sharing the same memory, or independent systems running over a network. A major job of a modern operating system is to manage the concurrent operations of a computer system and its running applications. However, concurrency control has also become an integral part of applications. Concurrent and asynchronous operations share the same problems—they cause bugs that are often hard to reproduce and create unexpected side effects.

Communication is the conveying of information by one entity to another. Because of the World Wide Web and the dominance of network applications, many programs must deal with I/O over the network as well as from local devices such as disks. Network communication introduces a myriad of new problems resulting from unpredictable timings and the possibility of undetected remote failures.

The remainder of this chapter describes simplified examples of asynchronous operation, concurrency and communication. The buffer overflow problem illustrates how careless programming and lack of error checking can cause serious problems and security breaches. This chapter also provides a brief overview of how operating systems work and summarizes the operating system standards that are used in the book.

1.2 Time and Speed

Operating systems manage system resources: processors, memory and I/O devices including keyboards, monitors, printers, mouse devices, disks, tapes, CD-ROMs and network interfaces. The convoluted way operating systems appear to work derives from the characteristics of peripheral devices, particularly their speed relative to the CPU or processor. Table 1.1 lists typical processor, memory and peripheral times in nanoseconds. The third column shows these speeds slowed down by a factor of 2 billion to give the time scaled in human terms. The scaled time of one operation per second is roughly the rate of the old mechanical calculators from fifty years ago.

item	time		scaled time in human terms (2 billion times slower)
processor cycle	0.5 ns	(2 GHz)	1 second
cache access	1 ns	(1 GHz)	2 seconds
memory access	15 ns		30 seconds
context switch	5,000 ns	(5 μs)	167 minutes
disk access	7,000,000 ns	(7 ms)	162 days
quantum	100,000,000 ns	(100 ms)	6.3 years

Table 1.1: Typical times for components of a computer system. One nanosecond (ns) is 10^{-9} seconds, one microsecond (μs) is 10^{-6} seconds, and one millisecond (ms) is 10^{-3} seconds.

Disk drives have improved, but their rotating mechanical nature limits their performance. Disk access times have not decreased exponentially. The disparity between processor and disk access times continues to grow; as of 2003 the ratio is roughly 1 to 14,000,000 for a 2-GHz processor. The cited speeds are a moving target, but the trend is that processor speeds are increasing exponentially, causing an increasing performance gap between processors and peripherals.

The *context-switch time* is the time it takes to switch from executing one process to another. The *quantum* is roughly the amount of CPU time allocated to a process before it has to let another process run. In a sense, a user at a keyboard is a peripheral device. A fast typist can type a keystroke every 100 milliseconds. This time is the same order of magnitude as the process scheduling quantum, and it is no coincidence that these numbers are comparable for interactive timesharing systems.

☐ Exercise 1.1

A modem is a device that permits a computer to communicate with another computer over a phone line. A typical modem is rated at 57,600 bps, where bps means "bits per second." Assuming it takes 8 bits to transmit a byte, estimate the time needed for a 57,600 bps modem to fill a computer screen with 25 lines of 80 characters. Now consider a graphics display that consists of an array of 1024 by 768 pixels. Each pixel has a color value that can be one of 256 possible colors. Assume such a pixel value can be transmitted by modem in 8 bits. What compression ratio is necessary for a 768-kbps DSL line to fill a screen with graphics as fast as a 57,600-bps modem can fill a screen with text?

Answer:

Table 1.2 compares the times. The text display has $80 \times 25 = 2000$ characters so 16,000 bits must be transmitted. The graphics display has $1024 \times 768 = 786,432$ pixels so 6,291,456 bits must be transmitted. The estimates do not account for compression or for communication protocol overhead. A compression ratio of about 29 is necessary!

modem type	bits per second	time needed to display	
		text	graphics
1979 telephone modem	300	1 minute	6 hours
1983 telephone modem	2,400	6 seconds	45 minutes
current telephone modem	57,600	0.28 seconds	109 seconds
current DSL modem	768,000	0.02 seconds	8 seconds

Table 1.2: Comparison of time estimates for filling a screen.

1.3 Multiprogramming and Time Sharing

Observe from Table 1.1 that processes performing disk I/O do not use the CPU very efficiently: 0.5 nanoseconds versus 7 milliseconds, or in human terms, 1 second versus 162 days. Because of the time disparity, most modern operating systems do multiprogramming. *Multiprogramming* means that more than one process can be ready to execute. The operating system chooses one of these ready processes for execution. When that process needs to wait for a resource (say, a keystroke or a disk access), the operating system saves all the information needed to resume that process where it left off and chooses another ready process to execute. It is simple to see how multiprogramming might be implemented. A resource request (such as `read` or `write`) results in an operating system request (i.e., a system call). A *system call* is a request to the operating system for service that causes the normal CPU cycle to be interrupted and control to be given to the operating system. The operating system can then switch to another process.

◻ Exercise 1.2

Explain how a disk I/O request might allow the operating system to run another process.

Answer:

Most devices are handled by the operating system rather than by applications. When an application executes a disk read, the call issues a request for the operating system to actually perform the operation. The operating system now has control. It can issue commands to the disk controller to begin retrieving the disk blocks requested by the application. However, since the disk retrieval does not complete for a long time (162 days in relative time), the operating system puts the application's process on a queue of processes that are waiting for I/O to complete and starts another process that is ready to run. Eventually, the disk controller interrupts the CPU instruction cycle when the results are available. At that time, the operating system regains control and can choose whether to continue with the currently running process or to allow the original process to run.

UNIX does *timesharing* as well as multiprogramming. Timesharing creates the illusion that several processes execute simultaneously, even though there may be only one physical CPU. On a single processor system, only one instruction from one process can be executing at any particular time. Since the human time scale is billions of times slower than that of modern computers, the operating system can rapidly switch between processes to give the appearance of several processes executing at the same time.

Consider the following analogy. Suppose a grocery store has several checkout counters (the processes) but only one checker (the CPU). The checker checks one item from a customer (the instruction) and then does the next item for that same customer. Checking continues until a price check (a resource request) is needed. Instead of waiting for the price check and doing nothing, the checker moves to another checkout counter and checks items from another customer. The checker (CPU) is always busy as long as there are customers (processes) ready to check out. This is multiprogramming. The checker is efficient, but customers probably would not want to shop at such a store because of the long wait when someone has a large order with no price checks (a CPU-bound process).

Now suppose that the checker starts a 10-second timer and processes items for one customer for a maximum of 10 seconds (the quantum). If the timer expires, the checker moves to another customer even if no price check is needed. This is timesharing. If the checker is sufficiently fast, the situation is almost equivalent to having one slower checker at each checkout stand. Consider making a video of such a checkout stand and playing it back at 100 times its normal speed. It would look as if the checker were handling several customers simultaneously.

❑ Exercise 1.3

Suppose that the checker can check one item per second (a one-second processor cycle time in Table 1.1). According to this table, what would be the maximum time the checker would spend with one customer before moving to a waiting customer?

Answer:

The time is the quantum that is scaled in the table to 6.3 years. A program may execute billions of instructions in a quantum—a bit more than the number of grocery items purchased by the average customer.

If the time to move from one customer to another (the context-switch time) is small compared with the time between switches (the CPU burst time), the checker handles customers efficiently. Timesharing wastes processing cycles by switching between customers, but it has the advantage of not wasting the checker resources during a price check. Furthermore, customers with small orders are not held in abeyance for long periods while waiting for customers with large orders.

The analogy would be more realistic if instead of several checkout counters, there were only one, with the customers crowded around the checker. To switch from customer A to customer B, the checker saves the contents of the register tape (the context) and restores it to what it was when it last processed customer B. The context-switch time can be reduced if the cash register has several tapes and can hold the contents of several customers' orders simultaneously. In fact, some computer systems have special hardware to hold many contexts at the same time.

Multiprocessor systems have several processors accessing a shared memory. In the checkout analogy for a multiprocessor system, each customer has an individual register tape and multiple checkers rove the checkout stands working on the orders for unserved customers. Many grocery stores have packers who do this.

1.4 Concurrency at the Applications Level

Concurrency occurs at the hardware level because multiple devices operate at the same time. Processors have internal parallelism and work on several instructions simultaneously, systems have multiple processors, and systems interact through network communication. Concurrency is visible at the applications level in signal handling, in the overlap of I/O and processing, in communication, and in the sharing of resources between processes or among threads in the same process. This section provides an overview of concurrency and asynchronous operation.

1.4.1 Interrupts

The execution of a single instruction in a program at the *conventional machine level* is the result of the *processor instruction cycle*. During normal execution of its instruction cycle, a processor retrieves an address from the program counter and executes the instruction at that address. (Modern processors have internal parallelism such as pipelines to reduce execution time, but this discussion does not consider that complication.) Concurrency arises at the conventional machine level because a peripheral device can generate an electrical signal, called an *interrupt*, to set a hardware flag within the processor. The detection of an interrupt is part of the instruction cycle itself. On each instruction cycle, the processor checks hardware flags to see if any peripheral devices need attention. If the processor detects that an interrupt has occurred, it saves the current value of the program counter and loads a new value that is the address of a special function called an *interrupt service routine* or *interrupt handler*. After finishing the interrupt service routine, the processor must be able to resume execution of the previous instruction where it left off.

An event is *asynchronous* to an entity if the time at which it occurs is not determined by that entity. The interrupts generated by external hardware devices are generally *asynchronous* to programs executing on the system. The interrupts do not always occur at the same point in a program's execution, but a program should give a correct result regardless of where it is interrupted. In contrast, an error event such as division by zero is *synchronous* in the sense that it always occurs during the execution of a particular instruction if the same data is presented to the instruction.

Although the interrupt service routine may be part of the program that is interrupted, the processing of an interrupt service routine is a distinct entity with respect to concurrency. Operating-system routines called *device drivers* usually handle the interrupts generated by peripheral devices. These drivers then notify the relevant processes, through a software mechanism such as a signal, that an event has occurred.

Operating systems also use interrupts to implement timesharing. Most machines have a device called a *timer* that can generate an interrupt after a specified interval of time. To execute a user program, the operating system starts the timer before setting the program counter. When the timer expires, it generates an interrupt that causes the CPU to execute the timer interrupt service routine. The interrupt service routine writes the address of the operating system code into the program counter, and the operating system is back in control. When a process loses the CPU in the manner just described, its quantum is said to have *expired*. The operating system puts the process in a queue of processes that are ready to run. The process waits there for another turn to execute.

1.4.2 Signals

A *signal* is a software notification of an event. Often, a signal is a response of the operating system to an interrupt (a hardware event). For example, a keystroke such as Ctrl-C generates an interrupt for the device driver handling the keyboard. The driver recognizes the character as the interrupt character and notifies the processes that are associated with this terminal by sending a signal. The operating system may also send a signal to a process to notify it of a completed I/O operation or an error.

A signal is *generated* when the event that causes the signal occurs. Signals can be generated either synchronously or asynchronously. A signal is generated synchronously if it is generated by the process or thread that receives it. The execution of an illegal instruction or a divide-by-zero may generate a synchronous signal. A Ctrl-C on the keyboard generates an asynchronous signal. Signals (Chapter 8) can be used for timers (Chapter 10), terminating programs (Section 8.2), job control (Section 11.7) or asynchronous I/O (Section 8.8).

A process *catches* a signal when it executes a handler for the signal. A program that catches a signal has at least two concurrent parts, the main program and the signal handler. Potential concurrency restricts what can be done inside a signal handler (Section 8.6). If the signal handler modifies external variables that the program can modify elsewhere, then proper execution may require that those variables be protected.

1.4.3 Input and output

A challenge for operating systems is to coordinate resources that have greatly differing characteristic access times. The processor can perform millions of operations on behalf of other processes while a program waits for a disk access to complete. Alternatively, the process can avoid blocking by using asynchronous I/O or dedicated threads instead of ordinary blocking I/O. The tradeoff is between the additional performance and the extra programming overhead in using these mechanisms.

A similar problem occurs when an application monitors two or more input channels such as input from different sources on a network. If standard blocking I/O is used, an application that is blocked waiting for input from one source is not able to respond if input from another source becomes available.

1.4.4 Processes, threads and the sharing of resources

A traditional method for achieving concurrent execution in UNIX is for the user to create multiple processes by calling the `fork` function. The processes usually need to coordinate their operation in some way. In the simplest instance they may only need to coordinate their termination. Even the termination problem is more difficult than it might seem. Chapter 3 addresses process structure and management and introduces the UNIX `fork`, `exec` and `wait` system calls.

Processes that have a common ancestor can communicate through *pipes* (Chapter 6). Processes without a common ancestor can communicate by signals (Chapter 8), FIFOs (Section 6.3), semaphores (Sections 14.2 and 15.2), shared address space (Section 15.3) or messages (Section 15.4 and Chapter 18).

Multiple threads of execution can provide concurrency within a process. When a program executes, the CPU uses the program counter to determine which instruction to execute next. The resulting stream of instructions is called the program's *thread of execution*. It is the flow of control for the process. If two distinct threads of execution share a resource within a time frame, care must be taken that these threads do not interfere with each other. Multiprocessor systems expand the opportunity for concurrency and sharing among applications and within applications. When a multithreaded application has more than one thread of execution concurrently active on a multiprocessor system, multiple instructions from the same process may be executed at the same time.

Until recently there has not been a standard for using threads, and each vendor's thread package behaved differently. A thread standard has now been incorporated into the POSIX standard. Chapters 12 and 13 discuss this new standard.

1.4.5 Multiple processors with shared memory

How many CPUs does a typical home computer have? If you think the answer is one, think again. In early machines, the main CPU handled most of the decision making. As machine design evolved, I/O became more complicated and placed more demands on the CPU. One way of enhancing the performance of a system is to determine which components are the bottlenecks and then improve or replicate these components. The main I/O controllers such as the video controller and disk controller took over some of the processing related to these peripherals, relieving the CPU of this burden. In modern machines, these controllers and other I/O controllers have their own special purpose CPUs.

What if after all this auxiliary processing has been offloaded, the CPU is still the bottleneck? There are two approaches to improving the performance. Admiral Grace Murray Hopper, a pioneer in computer software, often compared computing to the way fields were plowed in the pioneer days: "If one ox could not do the job, they did not try to grow a bigger ox, but used two oxen." It was usually cheaper to add another processor or two than to increase the speed of a single processor. Some problems do not lend themselves to just increasing the number of processors indefinitely. Seymour Cray, a pioneer in computer hardware, is reported to have said, "If you were plowing a field, which would you rather use? Two strong oxen or 1024 chickens?"

The optimal tradeoff between more CPUs and better CPUs depends on several factors, including the type of problem to be solved and the cost of each solution. Machines with multiple CPUs have already migrated to the desktop and are likely to become more common as prices drop. Concurrency issues at the application level are slightly different when there are multiple processors, but the methods discussed in this book are equally applicable in a multiprocessor environment.

1.4.6 The network as the computer

Another important trend is the distribution of computation over a network. Concurrency and communication meet to form new applications. The most widely used model of distributed computation is the *client-server model*. The basic entities in this model are server processes that manage resources, and client processes that require access to shared resources. (A process can be both a server and a client.) A client process shares a resource by sending a request to a server. The server performs the request on behalf of the client and sends a reply to the client. Examples of applications based on the client-server model include file transfer (`ftp`), electronic mail, file servers and the World Wide Web. Development of client-server applications requires an understanding of concurrency and communication.

The *object-based model* is another model for distributed computation. Each resource in the system is viewed as an object with a message-handling interface, allowing all resources to be accessed in a uniform way. The object-based model allows for controlled incremental development and code reuse. Object frameworks define interactions between code modules, and the object model naturally expresses notions of protection. Many of the experimental distributed operating systems such as Argus [74], Amoeba [124], Mach [1], Arjuna [106], Clouds [29] and Emerald [11] are object based. Object-based models require object managers to track the location of the objects in the system.

An alternative to a truly distributed operating system is to provide application layers that run on top of common operating systems to exploit parallelism on the network. The Parallel Virtual Machine (PVM) and its successor, Message Passing Interface (MPI), are software libraries [10, 43] that allow a collection of heterogeneous workstations to function as a parallel computer for solving large computational problems. PVM manages and monitors tasks that are distributed on workstations across the network. Chapter 17 develops a dispatcher for a simplified version of PVM. CORBA (Common Object Request Broker Architecture) is another type of software layer that provides an object-oriented interface to a set of generic services in a heterogeneous distributed environment [104].

1.5 Security and Fault Tolerance

The 1950s and early 1960s brought batch processing, and the mid-to-late 1960s saw deployment of operating systems that supported multiprogramming. Time-sharing and real-time programming gained popularity in the 1970s. During the 1980s, parallel processing moved from the supercomputer arena to the desktop. The 1990s was the decade of the network—with the widespread use of distributed processing, email and the World Wide Web. The 2000s appears to be the decade of security and fault-tolerance. The rapid computerization and the distribution of critical infrastructure (banking, transportation, communication, medicine and government) over networks has exposed enormous vulnerabilities. We have come to rely on programs that were not adequately designed or tested for a concurrent environment, written by programmers who may not have understood the implications of incorrectly working programs. The liability disclaimers distributed with most software attempts to absolve the manufacturers of responsibility for damage—software is distributed *as is*.

But, lives now depend on software, and each of us has a responsibility to become attuned to the implications of bad software. With current technology, it is almost impossible to write completely error-free code, but we believe that programmer awareness can greatly reduce the scope of the problem. Unfortunately, most people learn to program for an environment in which programs are presented with correct or almost correct input. Their ideal users behave graciously, and programs are allowed to exit when they encounter an error.

Real-world programs, especially systems programs, are often long-running and are expected to continue running after an error (no blue-screen of death or reboot allowed). Long-running programs must release resources, such as memory, when these resources are no longer needed. Often, programmers release resources such as buffers in the obvious places but forget to release them if an error occurs.

Most UNIX library functions indicate an error by a return value. However, C makes no requirement that return values be checked. If a program doesn't check a return value, execution can continue well beyond the point at which a critical error occurs. The consequence of the function error may not be apparent until much later in the execution. C also allows programs to write out of the bounds of variables. For example, the C runtime system does not complain if you modify a nonexistent array element—it writes values into that memory (which probably corresponds to some other variable). Your program may not detect the problem at the time it happened, but the overwritten variable may present a problem later. Because overwritten variables are so difficult to detect and so dangerous, newer programming languages, such as Java, have runtime checks on array bounds.

Even software that has been in distribution for years and has received heavy scrutiny is riddled with bugs. For example, an interesting study by Chou et al. [23] used a modified compiler to look for 12 types of bugs in Linux and OpenBSD source code. They examined 21 snapshots of Linux spanning seven years and one snapshot of OpenBSD. They found 1025 bugs in the code by using automatic scanning techniques. One of the most common bugs was the failure to check for a NULL return on functions that return pointers. If the code later uses the returned pointer, a core dump occurs.

Commercial software is also prone to bugs. Software problems with the Therac-25 [71], a medical linear accelerator used to destroy tumors, resulted in serious accidents.

Another problem is the exponential growth in the number of truly malicious users who launch concerted attacks on servers and user computers. The next section describes one common type of attack, the buffer overflow.

1.6 Buffer Overflows for Breaking and Entering

This section presents a simplified explanation of buffer overflows and how they might be used to attack a computer system. A *buffer overflow* occurs when a program copies data into a variable for which it has not allocated enough space.

Example 1.4 shows a code segment that may have a buffer overflow. A user types a name in response to the prompt. The program stores the input in a char array called buf. If the user enters more than 79 bytes, the resulting string and string terminator do not fit in the allocated variable.

■ Example 1.4

The following code segment has the possibility of a buffer overflow.

```
char buf[80];

printf("Enter your first name:");
scanf("%s", buf);
```

Your first thought in fixing this potential overflow might be to make buf bigger, say, 1000 bytes. What user's first name could be that long? Even if a user decides to type in a very long string of characters, 1000 bytes should be large enough to handle all but the most persistent user. However, regardless of the ultimate size that you choose, the code segment is still susceptible to a buffer overflow. The user simply needs to redirect standard input to come from an arbitrarily large file.

Example 1.5 shows a simple way to fix this problem. The format specification limits the input string to one less than the size of the variable, allowing room for the string terminator. The program reads at most 79 characters into buf but stops when it encounters a white space character. If the user enters more than 79 characters, the program reads the additional characters in subsequent input statements.

■ **Example 1.5**

The following code segment does not have a buffer overflow.

```
char buf[80];

printf("Enter your first name:");
scanf("%79s", buf);
```

1.6.1 Consequences of buffer overflows

To understand what happens when a buffer overflow occurs, you need to understand how programs are laid out in memory. Most program code is executed in functions with local variables that are automatic. While the details differ from machine to machine, programs generally allocate automatic variables on the program stack.

In a typical system, the stack grows from high memory to low memory. When a function is called, the lower part of the stack contains the passed parameters and the return address. Higher up on the stack (lower memory addresses) are the local automatic variables. The stack may store other values and have gaps that are not used by the program at all. One important fact is that the return address for each function call is usually stored in memory after (with larger address than) the automatic variables.

When a program writes beyond the limits of a variable on the stack, a buffer overflow occurs. The extra bytes may write over unused space, other variables, the return address or other memory not legally accessible to your program. The consequences can range from none, to a program crash and a core dump, to unpredictable behavior.

Program 1.1 shows a function that can have a buffer overflow. The `checkpass` function checks whether the entered string matches `"mypass"` and returns 1 if they match, and 0 otherwise.

Program 1.1 ————————————————————————————— `checkpass.c`

  A function that checks a password. This function is susceptible to buffer overflow.

```c
#include <stdio.h>
#include <string.h>

int checkpass(void){
   int x;
   char a[9];
   x = 0;
   fprintf(stderr,"a at %p and\nx at %p\n", (void *)a, (void *)&x);
   printf("Enter a short word: ");
   scanf("%s", a);
   if (strcmp(a, "mypass") == 0)
      x = 1;
   return x;
}
```

Program 1.1 ————————————————————————————— `checkpass.c`

Figure 1.1 shows a possible organization of the stack for a call to checkpass. The diagram assumes that integers and pointers are 4 bytes. Note that the compiler allocates 12 bytes for array a, even though the program specifies only 9 bytes, so that the system can maintain a stack pointer that is aligned on a word boundary.

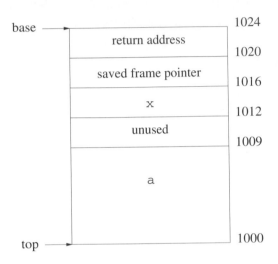

Figure 1.1: Possible stack layout for the checkpass function of Program 1.1.

If the character array a is stored on the stack in lower memory than the integer x, a buffer overflow of a may change the value of x. If the user enters a word that is slightly longer than the array a, the overflow changes the value of x, but there is no other effect. Exactly how long the entered string needs to be to cause a problem depends on the system. With the memory organization of Figure 1.1, if the user enters 12 characters, the string terminator overwrites one byte of x without changing its value. If the user enters more than 12 characters, some of them overwrite x, changing its value. If the user enters 13 characters, x changes to a nonzero value and the function returns 1, no matter what characters are entered.

If the user enters a long password, the return address is overwritten, and most likely the function will try to return to a location outside the address space of the program, generating a segmentation fault and core dump. Buffer overflows that cause an application program to exit with a segmentation fault can be annoying and can cause the program to lose unsaved data. The same type of overflow in an operating system function can cause the operating system to crash.

Buffer overflows in dynamically allocated buffers or buffers with static storage can also behave unpredictably. One of our students wrote a program that appeared to show an error in the C library. He traced a segmentation fault to a call to malloc and was able to show that the program was working until the call to `malloc`. The program had a segmentation fault before the call to `malloc` returned. He eventually traced the problem to a type of buffer overflow in which the byte before a buffer dynamically allocated by a previous `malloc` call was overwritten. (This can easily happen if a buffer is being filled from the back and a count is off by one.) Overwriting control information stored in the heap caused the next call to `malloc` to crash the program.

1.6.2 Buffer overflows and security

Security problems related to buffer overflows have been known for over a decade. They first acquired national attention when on November 2, 1988, Robert Morris released a worm on the Internet. A worm is a self-replicating, self-propagating program. This program forced many system administrators to disconnect their sites from the Internet so that they would not be continually reinfected. It took several days for the Internet to return to normal. One of the methods used by the Morris worm was to exploit a buffer overflow in the `finger` daemon. This daemon ran on most UNIX machines to allow the display of information about users.

In response to this worm, CERT, the Computer Emergency Response Team, was created [24]. The CERT Coordination Center is a federally funded center of Internet security expertise that regularly publishes computer security alerts.

Programs that are susceptible to buffer overflow are still being written, in spite of past experiences. The first six CERT advisories in 2002 describe buffer overflow flaws in various computer systems, including Common Desktop Environment for the Sun Solaris operating environment (a windowing system), ICQ from AOL (an instant messaging program used by over 100 million users), Simple Network Management Protocol (a network management protocol used by many vendors), and Microsoft Internet Explorer. In 1999 Steve Ballmer, the CEO of Microsoft, was quoted as saying, "You would think we could figure out how to fix buffer overflows by now." The problem is not that we do not know how to write correct code, the problem is that writing correct code takes more care than writing sloppy code. As long as priorities are to produce code quickly, sloppy code will be produced. The effects of poor coding are exacerbated by compilers and runtime systems that don't enforce range checking.

There are many ways in which buffer overflows have been used to compromise a system. Here is a possible scenario. The `telnet` program allows a user to remotely log in to a machine. It communicates over the network with a `telnet` daemon running on the remote machine. One of the functions of the `telnet` daemon is to query for a user name and password and then to create a shell for the user if the password is correct.

Suppose the function in the `telnet` daemon that requests and checks a password returns 1 if the password is correct and 0 otherwise, similar to the `checkpass` function of Program 1.1. Suppose the function allocates a buffer of size 100 for the password. This might seem reasonable, since passwords in UNIX are at most 8 bytes long. If the program does not check the length of the input, it might be possible to have input that writes over the return value (x in Program 1.1), causing a shell to be created even if the password is incorrect.

Any application that runs with root privileges and is susceptible to a buffer overflow might be used to create a shell with root privileges. The implementation is technical and depends on the system, but the idea is relatively simple. First, the user compiles code to create a shell, something like the following code.

```
execvl("/bin/sh", "/bin/sh", NULL);
exit(0);
```

The user then edits the compiled code file so that the compiled code appears at exactly the correct relative position in the file. When the user redirects standard input to this file, the contents of the file overwrite the return address. If the bytes that overwrite the return address happen to correspond to the address of the execvl code, the function return creates a new user shell. Since the program is already running with the user ID of root, the new shell also runs with this user ID, and the ordinary user now has root privileges. The vulnerability depends on getting the bytes in the input file exactly right. Finding the address of the execvl is not as difficult as it might first appear, because most processor instruction sets support a relative addressing mode.

1.7 UNIX Standards

Not too long ago, two distinct and somewhat incompatible "flavors" of UNIX, System V from AT&T and BSD from Berkeley coexisted. Because no official standard existed, there were major and minor differences between the versions from different vendors, even within the same flavor. Consequently, programs written for one type of UNIX would not run correctly or sometimes would not even compile under a UNIX from another vendor.

The IEEE (Institute of Electronic and Electrical Engineers) decided to develop a standard for the UNIX libraries in an initiative called POSIX. POSIX stands for Portable Operating System Interface and is pronounced *pahz-icks*, as stated explicitly by the standard. IEEE's first attempt, called POSIX.1, was published in 1988. When this standard was adopted, there was no known historical implementation of UNIX that would not have to change to meet the standard. The original standard covered only a small subset of UNIX. In 1994, the X/Open Foundation published a more comprehensive standard called Spec 1170, based on System V. Unfortunately, inconsistencies between Spec 1170 and POSIX made it difficult for vendors and application developers to adhere to both standards.

In 1998, after another version of the X/Open standard, many additions to the POSIX standard, and the threat of world-domination by Microsoft, the Austin Group was formed. This group included members from The Open Group (a new name for the X/Open Foundation), IEEE POSIX and the ISO/IEC Joint Technical Committee. The purpose of the group was to revise, combine and update the standards. Finally, at the end of 2001, a joint document was approved by the IEEE and The Open Group. The ISO/IEC approved this document in November of 2002. This specification is referred to as the Single UNIX Specification, Version 3, or IEEE Std. 1003.1-2001, POSIX. In this book we refer to this standard merely as POSIX.

Each of the standards organizations publishes copies of the standard. Print and electronic versions of the standard are available from IEEE and ISO/IEC. The Open Group publishes the standard on CD-ROM. It is also freely available on their web site [89]. The copy of the standard published by the IEEE is in four volumes: Base Definitions [50], Shell and Utilities [52], System Interfaces [49] and Rationale [51] and is over 3600 pages in length.

The code for this book was tested on three systems: Solaris 9, Redhat Linux 8 and Mac OS 10.2. Table 1.3 lists the extensions of POSIX discussed in the book and the status of implementation of each on the tested systems. This indication is based on the man pages and on running the programs from the book, not on any official statement of compliance.

code	extension	Solaris 9	Redhat 8	Mac OS 10.2
AIO	asynchronous input and output	yes	yes	no
CX	extension to the ISO C standard	yes	yes	yes
FSC	file synchronization	yes	yes	yes
RTS	realtime signals extension	yes	yes	no
SEM	semaphores	yes	unnamed only	named only
THR	threads	yes	almost	yes
TMR	timers	yes	yes	no
TPS	thread execution scheduling	yes	yes	yes
TSA	thread stack address attribute	no	no	no
TSF	thread-safe functions	yes	`strtok_r` only	yes
XSI	XSI extension	yes	yes	timers, `getsid`, `ftok`, no IPC
`_POSIX_VERSION`		199506	199506	198808

Table 1.3: POSIX extensions supported by our test systems.

A POSIX-compliant implementation must support the POSIX base standard. Many of the interesting aspects of POSIX are not part of the base standard but rather are defined as extensions to the base standard. Table E.1 of Appendix E gives a complete list of the extensions in the 2001 version of POSIX. Appendix E applies only to implementations that claim compliance with the 2001 version base standard. These implementations set the symbol `_POSIX_VERSION` defined in `unistd.h` to 200112L. As of the writing of this book, none of the systems we tested used this value. Systems that support the previous version of POSIX have a value of 199506L. Differences between the 1995 and 2001 standards for features supported by both are minor.

The new POSIX standard also incorporates the ISO/IEC International Standard 9899, also referred to as ISO C. In the past, minor differences between the POSIX and ISO C standards have caused confusion. Often, these differences were unintentional, but differences in published standards required developers to choose between them. The current POSIX standard makes it clear that any differences between the published POSIX standard and the ISO C standard are unintentional. If any discrepancies occur, the ISO C standard takes precedence.

1.8 Additional Reading

Most general operating systems books present an overview and history of operating systems. Recommended introductions include Chapter 1 of *Modern Operating Systems* by Tanenbaum [122] or Chapters 1 to 3 of *Operating Systems Concepts* by Silberschatz et al. [107]. Chapters 1 and 2 of *Distributed Systems: Concepts and Design* by Coulouris et al. discuss design issues for distributed systems [26]. *Distributed Operating Systems* by Tanenbaum [121] also has a good overview of distributed systems issues, but it provides fewer details about specific distributed systems than does [26]. See also *Distributed Systems: Principles and Paradigms* by Van Steen and Tanenbaum [127].

Advanced Programming in the UNIX Environment by Stevens [112] is a key technical reference on the UNIX interface to use in conjunction with this book. Serious systems programmers should acquire the *POSIX Std. 1003.1* from the IEEE [50] or the Open Group web site [89]. The standard is surprisingly readable and thorough. The rationale sections included with each function provide a great deal of insight into the considerations that went into the standard. The final arbiter of C questions is the ISO C standard [56].

The CERT web site [24] is a good source for current information on recently discovered bugs, ongoing attacks and vulnerabilities. The book *Know Your Enemy: Revealing the Security Tools, Tactics, and Motives of the Blackhat Community* edited by members of the Honeynet Project [48] is an interesting glimpse into the realm of the malicious.

Chapter 2

Programs, Processes and Threads

One popular definition of a process is an instance of a program whose execution has started but has not yet terminated. This chapter discusses the differences between programs and processes and the ways in which the former are transformed into the latter. The chapter addresses issues of program layout, command-line arguments, program environment and exit handlers.

Objectives
- Learn about programs, processes and threads
- Experiment with memory allocation and manipulation
- Explore implications of static objects
- Use environment variables for context
- Understand program structure and layout

2.1 How a Program Becomes a Process

A *program* is a prepared sequence of instructions to accomplish a defined task. To write a C source program, a programmer creates disk files containing C statements that are organized into functions. An individual C source file may also contain variable and function declarations, type and macro definitions (e.g., `typedef`) and preprocessor commands (e.g., `#ifdef`, `#include`, `#define`). The source program contains exactly one `main` function.

Traditionally, C source filenames have a `.c` extension, and header filenames have a `.h` extension. Header files usually only contain macro and type definitions, defined constants and function declarations. Use the `#include` preprocessor command to insert the contents of a header file into the source.

The C compiler translates each source file into an object file. The compiler then links the individual object files with the necessary libraries to produce an *executable module*. When a program is run or *executed*, the operating system copies the executable module into a *program image* in main memory.

A *process* is an instance of a program that is executing. Each instance has its own address space and execution state. When does a program become a process? The operating system reads the program into memory. The allocation of memory for the program image is not enough to make the program a process. The process must have an ID (the *process ID*) so that the operating system can distinguish among individual processes. The *process state* indicates the execution status of an individual process. The operating system keeps track of the process IDs and corresponding process states and uses the information to allocate and manage resources for the system. The operating system also manages the memory occupied by the processes and the memory available for allocation.

When the operating system has added the appropriate information in the kernel data structures and has allocated the necessary resources to run the program code, the program has become a process. A process has an address space (memory it can access) and at least one flow of control called a *thread*. The variables of a process can either remain in existence for the life of the process (static storage) or be automatically allocated when execution enters a block and deallocated when execution leaves the block (automatic storage). Appendix A.5 discusses C storage classes in detail.

A process starts with a single flow of control that executes a sequence of instructions. The processor program counter keeps track of the next instruction to be executed by that processor (CPU). The CPU increments the program counter after fetching an instruction and may further modify it during the execution of the instruction, for example, when a branch occurs. Multiple processes may reside in memory and execute concurrently, almost independently of each other. For processes to communicate or cooperate, they must explicitly interact through operating system constructs such as the filesystem (Section 5.1), pipes (Section 6.1), shared memory (Section 15.3) or a network (Chapters 18-22).

2.2 Threads and Thread of Execution

When a program executes, the value of the process program counter determines which process instruction is executed next. The resulting stream of instructions, called a *thread of execution*, can be represented by the sequence of instruction addresses assigned to the program counter during the execution of the program's code.

■ **Example 2.1**

Process 1 executes statements 245, 246 and 247 in a loop. Its thread of execution can be represented as 245_1, 246_1, 247_1, 245_1, 246_1, 247_1, 245_1, 246_1, 247_1 ..., where the subscripts identify the thread of execution as belonging to process 1.

The sequence of instructions in a thread of execution appears to the process as an uninterrupted stream of addresses. From the point of view of the processor, however, the threads of execution from different processes are intermixed. The point at which execution switches from one process to another is called a *context switch*.

■ **Example 2.2**

Process 1 executes its statements 245, 246 and 247 in a loop as in Example 2.1, and process 2 executes its statements 10, 11, 12 .... The CPU executes instructions in the order 245_1, 246_1, 247_1, 245_1, 246_1, [context-switch instructions], 10_2, 11_2, 12_2, 13_2, [context-switch instructions], 247_1, 245_1, 246_1, 247_1 .... Context switches occur between 246_1 and 10_2 and between 13_2 and 247_1. The processor sees the threads of execution interleaved, whereas the individual processes see uninterrupted sequences.

A natural extension of the process model allows multiple threads to execute within the same process. Multiple threads avoid context switches and allow sharing of code and data. The approach may improve program performance on machines with multiple processors. Programs with natural parallelism in the form of independent tasks operating on shared data can take advantage of added execution power on these multiple-processor machines. Operating systems have significant natural parallelism and perform better by having multiple, simultaneous threads of execution. Vendors advertise *symmetric multiprocessing* support in which the operating system and applications have multiple undistinguished threads of execution that take advantage of parallel hardware.

A *thread* is an abstract data type that represents a thread of execution within a process. A thread has its own execution stack, program counter value, register set and state. By declaring many threads within the confines of a single process, a programmer can write programs that achieve parallelism with low overhead. While these threads provide low-overhead parallelism, they may require additional synchronization because they reside in the same process address space and therefore share process resources. Some people call processes *heavyweight* because of the work needed to start them. In contrast, threads are sometimes called *lightweight processes*.

2.3 Layout of a Program Image

After loading, the program executable appears to occupy a contiguous block of memory called a *program image*. Figure 2.1 shows a sample layout of a program image in its logical address space [112]. The program image has several distinct sections. The program text or code is shown in low-order memory. The initialized and uninitialized static variables have their own sections in the image. Other sections include the heap, stack and environment.

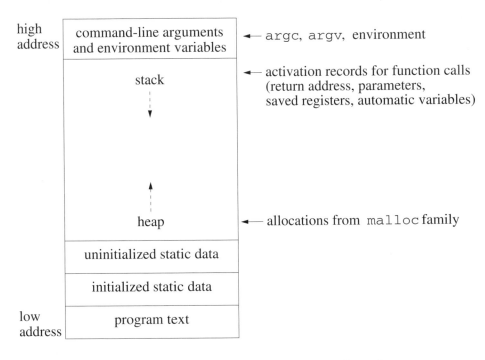

Figure 2.1: Sample layout for a program image in main memory.

An *activation record* is a block of memory allocated on the top of the process stack to hold the execution context of a function during a call. Each function call creates a new activation record on the stack. The activation record is removed from the stack when the function returns, providing the last-called-first-returned order for nested function calls.

The activation record contains the return address, the parameters (whose values are copied from the corresponding arguments), status information and a copy of some of the CPU register values at the time of the call. The process restores the register values on return from the call represented by the record. The activation record also contains automatic variables that are allocated within the function while it is executing. The particular format for an activation record depends on the hardware and on the programming language.

In addition to the static and automatic variables, the program image contains space for `argc` and `argv` and for allocations by `malloc`. The `malloc` family of functions allocates storage from a free memory pool called the *heap*. Storage allocated on the heap persists until it is freed or until the program exits. If a function calls `malloc`, the storage remains allocated after the function returns. The program cannot access the storage after the return unless it has a pointer to the storage that is accessible after the function returns.

Static variables that are not explicitly initialized in their declarations are initialized to 0 at run time. Notice that the initialized static variables and the uninitialized static variables occupy different sections in the program image. Typically, the initialized static variables are part of the executable module on disk, but the uninitialized static variables are not. Of course, the automatic variables are not part of the executable module because they are only allocated when their defining block is called. The initial values of automatic variables are undetermined unless the program explicitly initializes them.

☐ Exercise 2.3

Use `ls -l` to compare the sizes of the executable modules for the following two C programs. Explain the results.
Version 1:

```
int myarray[50000] = {1, 2, 3, 4};

int main(void) {
    myarray[0] = 3;
    return 0;
}
```

—— **largearrayinit.c**

Version 2:

```
int myarray[50000];

int main(void) {
    myarray[0] = 3;
    return 0;
}
```

—— **largearray.c**

Answer:
The executable module for Version 1 should be about 200,000 bytes larger than that of Version 2 because the `myarray` of Version 1 is initialized static data and is therefore part of the executable module. The `myarray` of Version 2 is not allocated until the program is loaded in memory, and the array elements are initialized to 0 at that time.

Static variables can make a program unsafe for threaded execution. For example, the C library function `readdir` and its relatives described in Section 5.2 use static variables to hold return values. The function `strtok` discussed in Section 2.6 uses a static variable to keep track of its progress between calls. Neither of these functions can be safely called by multiple threads within a program. In other words, they are not *thread-safe*. External static variables also make code more difficult to debug because successive invocations of a function that references a static variable may behave in unexpected ways. *For these reasons, avoid using static variables except under controlled circumstances.* Section 2.9 presents an example of when to use variables with static storage class.

Although the program image appears to occupy a contiguous block of memory, in practice, the operating system maps the program image into noncontiguous blocks of physical memory. A common mapping divides the program image into equal-sized pieces, called *pages*. The operating system loads the individual pages into memory and looks up the location of the page in a table when the processor references memory on that page. This mapping allows a large logical address space for the stack and heap without actually using physical memory unless it is needed. The operating system hides the existence of such an underlying mapping, so the programmer can view the program image as logically contiguous even when some of the pages do not actually reside in memory.

2.4 Library Function Calls

We introduce most library functions by a condensed version of its specification, and you should always refer to the man pages for more complete information.

The summary starts with a brief description of the function and its parameters, followed by a SYNOPSIS box giving the required header files and the function prototype. (Unfortunately, some compilers do not give warning messages if the header files are missing, so be sure to use `lint` as described in Appendix A to detect these problems.) The SYNOPSIS box also names the POSIX standard that specifies the function. A description of the function return values and a discussion of how the function reports errors follows the SYNOPSIS box. Here is a typical summary.

The `close` function deallocates the file descriptor specified by `fildes`.

SYNOPSIS

```
#include <unistd.h>

int close(int fildes);
```
POSIX

If successful, `close` returns 0. If unsuccessful, `close` returns −1 and sets `errno`. The following table lists the mandatory errors for `close`.

errno	cause
EBADF	`fildes` is not valid
EINTR	`close` was interrupted by a signal

This book's summary descriptions generally include the mandatory errors. These are the errors that the standard requires that every implementation detect. We include these particular errors because they are a good indication of the major points of failure. *You must handle all errors, not just the mandatory ones.* POSIX often defines many other types of optional errors. If an implementation chooses to treat the specified condition as an error, then it should use the specified error value. Implementations are free to define other errors as well. When there is only one mandatory error, we describe it in a sentence. When the function has more than one mandatory error, we use a table like the one for close.

Traditional UNIX functions usually return −1 (or sometimes NULL) and set errno to indicate the error. The POSIX standards committee decided that all new functions would not use errno and would instead directly return an error number as a function return value. We illustrate both ways of handling errors in examples throughout the text.

■ Example 2.4

The following code segment demonstrates how to call the close function.

```
int fildes;

if (close(fildes) == -1)
   perror("Failed to close the file");
```

The code assumes that the unistd.h header file has been included in the source. In general, we do not show the header files for code segments.

The perror function outputs to standard error a message corresponding to the current value of errno. If s is not NULL, perror outputs the string (an array of characters terminated by a null character) pointed to by s and followed by a colon and a space. Then, perror outputs an error message corresponding to the current value of errno followed by a newline.

```
SYNOPSIS

   #include <stdio.h>

   void perror(const char *s);
                                                    POSIX:CX
```

No return values and no errors are defined for perror.

■ Example 2.5

The output produced by Example 2.4 might be as follows.

```
Failed to close the file: invalid file descriptor
```

The strerror function returns a pointer to the system error message corresponding to the error code errnum.

```
SYNOPSIS

   #include <string.h>

   char *strerror(int errnum);
                                                                    POSIX:CX
```

If successful, `strerror` returns a pointer to the error string. No values are reserved for failure.

Use `strerror` to produce informative messages, or use it with functions that return error codes directly without setting `errno`.

■ Example 2.6

The following code segment uses `strerror` to output a more informative error message when `close` fails.

```
int fildes;

if (close(fildes) == -1)
    fprintf(stderr, "Failed to close file descriptor %d: %s\n",
                    fildes, strerror(errno));
```

The `strerror` function may change `errno`. *You should save and restore* `errno` *if you need to use it again.*

■ Example 2.7

The following code segment illustrates how to use `strerror` and still preserve the value of `errno`.

```
int error;
int fildes;

if (close(fildes) == -1) {
    error = errno;                                /* temporarily save errno */
    fprintf(stderr, "Failed to close file descriptor %d: %s\n",
                    fildes, strerror(errno));
    errno = error;     /* restore errno after writing the error message */
}
```

Correctly handing `errno` is a tricky business. Because its implementation may call other functions that set `errno`, a library function may change `errno`, even though the man page doesn't explicitly state that it does. Also, applications cannot change the string returned from `strerror`, but subsequent calls to either `strerror` or `perror` may overwrite this string.

Another common problem is that many library calls abort if the process is interrupted by a signal. Functions generally report this type of return with an error code of `EINTR`. For example, the `close` function may be interrupted by a signal. In this case, the error was not due to a problem with its execution but was a result of some external factor. Usually the program should not treat this interruption as an error but should restart the call.

■ **Example 2.8**

The following code segment restarts the `close` function if a signal occurs.

```
int error;
int fildes;

while (((error = close(fildes)) == -1) && (errno == EINTR))   ;
if (error == -1)
   perror("Failed to close the file"); /* a real close error occurred */
```

The `while` loop of Example 2.8 has an empty statement clause. It simply calls `close` until it either executes successfully or encounters a real error. The problem of restarting library calls is so common that we provide a library of restarted calls with prototypes defined in `restart.h`. The functions are designated by a leading `r_` prepended to the regular library name. For example, the restart library designates a restarted version of `close` by the name `r_close`.

■ **Example 2.9**

The following code segment illustrates how to use a version of `close` from the restart library.

```
#include "restart.h"     /* user-defined library not part of standard */
int fildes;

if (r_close(fildes) == -1)
   perror("Failed to close the file"); /* a true close error occurred */
```

2.5 Function Return Values and Errors

Error handling is a key issue in writing reliable systems programs. When you are writing a function, think in terms of that function being called millions of times by the same application. How do you want the function to behave? In general, functions should never exit on their own, but rather should always indicate an error to the calling program. This strategy gives the caller an opportunity to recover or to shut down gracefully.

Functions should also not make unexpected changes to the process state that persist beyond the return from the function. For example, if a function blocks signals, it should restore the signal mask to its previous value before returning.

Finally, the function should release all the hidden resources that it uses during its execution. Suppose a function allocates a temporary buffer by calling `malloc` and does not free it before returning. One call to this function may not cause a problem, but hundreds or thousands of successive calls may cause the process memory usage to exceed its limits. Usually, a function that allocates memory should either free the memory or make a pointer available to the calling program. Otherwise, a long-running program may have a *memory leak*; that is, memory "leaks" out of the system and is not available until the process terminates.

You should also be aware that the failure of a library function usually does not cause your program to stop executing. Instead, the program continues, possibly using inconsistent or invalid data. *You must examine the return value of every library function that can return an error that affects the running of your program, even if you think the chance of such an error occurring is remote.*

Your own functions should also engage in careful error handling and communication. Standard approaches to handling errors in UNIX programs include the following.

- Print out an error message and exit the program (*only* in `main`).
- Return −1 or `NULL`, and set an error indicator such as `errno`.
- Return an error code.

In general, functions should never exit on their own but should always report an error to the calling program. Error messages within a function may be useful during the debugging phase but generally should not appear in the final version. A good way to handle debugging is to enclose debugging print statements in a conditional compilation block so that you can reactivate them if necessary.

■ **Example 2.10**

The following code segment shows an example of how to use conditional compilation for error messages in functions.

```
#define DEBUG    /* comment this line out for no error messages */

int myfun(int x) {
   x++;
#ifdef DEBUG
   fprintf(stderr, "The current value of x is %d\n", x);
#endif
}
```

If you comment the `#define` line out, the `fprintf` statement is not compiled and `myfun` does no printing. Alternatively, you can leave the `#define` out of the code completely and define `DEBUG` on the compiler line as follows.

```
cc -DDEBUG ...
```

Most library functions provide good models for implementing functions. Here are guidelines to follow.

1. Make use of return values to communicate information and to make error trapping easy for the calling program.
2. Do not exit from functions. Instead, return an error value to allow the calling program flexibility in handling the error.
3. Make functions general but usable. (Sometimes these are conflicting goals.)
4. Do not make unnecessary assumptions about sizes of buffers. (This is often hard to implement.)

   5.   When it is necessary to use limits, use standard system-defined limits rather than arbitrary constants.
   6.   Do not reinvent the wheel—use standard library functions when possible.
   7.   Do not modify input parameter values unless it makes sense to do so.
   8.   Do not use static variables or dynamic memory allocation if automatic allocation will do just as well.
   9.   Analyze all the calls to the `malloc` family to make sure the program frees the memory that was allocated.
   10. Consider whether a function is ever called recursively or from a signal handler or from a thread. Functions with variables of static storage class may not behave in the desired way. (The error number can cause a big problem here.)
   11. Analyze the consequences of interruptions by signals.
   12. Carefully consider how the entire program terminates.

2.6 Argument Arrays

A command line consists of tokens (the arguments) that are separated by white space: blanks, tabs or a backslash (\) at the end of a line. Each token is a string of characters containing no white space unless quotation marks are used to group tokens. When a user enters a command line corresponding to a C executable program, the shell parses the command line into tokens and passes the result to the program in the form of an argument array. An *argument array* is an array of pointers to strings. The end of the array is marked by an entry containing a `NULL` pointer. Argument arrays are also useful for handling a variable number of arguments in calls to `execvp` and for handling environment variables. (Refer to Section 3.5 for an example of their application.)

■ **Example 2.11**

The following command line contains the four tokens: `mine`, `-c`, `10` and `2.0`.

```
mine -c 10 2.0
```

The first token on a command line is the name of the command or executable. Figure 2.2 shows the argument array for the command line of Example 2.11.

■ **Example 2.12**

The `mine` program of Example 2.11 might start with the following line.

```
int main(int argc, char *argv[])
```

In Example 2.12, the `argc` parameter contains the number of command-line tokens or arguments (four for Example 2.11), and `argv` is an array of pointers to the command-line tokens. The `argv` is an example of an argument array.

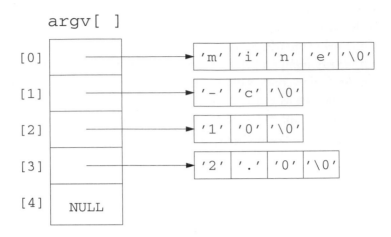

Figure 2.2: The `argv` array for the call `mine -c 10 2.0`.

2.6.1 Creating an argument array with `makeargv`

This section develops a function, `makeargv`, that creates an argument array from a string of tokens. The `makeargv` function illustrates some complications introduced by static variables. We use this function in several projects and exercises of subsequent chapters.

■ **Example 2.13**

Here is a prototype for a `makeargv` function that creates an argument array from a string of tokens.

```
char **makeargv(char *s);
```

The `makeargv` of Example 2.13 has a string input parameter and returns a pointer to an `argv` array. If the call fails, `makeargv` returns a `NULL` pointer.

■ **Example 2.14**

The following code segment illustrates how the `makeargv` function of Example 2.13 might be invoked.

```
int i;
char **myargv;
char mytest[] = "This is a test";

if ((myargv = makeargv(mytest)) == NULL)
    fprintf(stderr, "Failed to construct an argument array\n");
else
    for (i = 0; myargv[i] != NULL; i++)
        printf("%d:%s\n", i, myargv[i]);
```

■ Example 2.15

The following alternative prototype specifies that `makeargv` should pass the argument array as a parameter. This alternative version of `makeargv` returns an integer giving the number of tokens in the input string. In this case, `makeargv` returns −1 to indicate an error.

```
int makeargv(char *s, char ***argvp);
```

■ Example 2.16

The following code segment calls the `makeargv` function defined in Example 2.15.

```
int i;
char **myargv;
char mytest[] = "This is a test";
int numtokens;

if ((numtokens = makeargv(mytest, &myargv)) == -1)
   fprintf(stderr, "Failed to construct an argument array\n");
else
   for (i = 0; i < numtokens; i++)
      printf("%d:%s\n", i, myargv[i]);
```

Because C uses call-by-value parameter passing, Example 2.15 shows one more level of indirection (*) when the address of `myargv` is passed. A more general version of `makeargv` allows an extra parameter that represents the set of delimiters to use in parsing the string.

■ Example 2.17

The following prototype shows a `makeargv` function that has a delimiter set parameter.

```
int makeargv(const char *s, const char *delimiters, char ***argvp);
```

The `const` qualifier means that the function does not modify the memory pointed to by the first two parameters.

Program 2.1 calls the `makeargv` function of Example 2.17 to create an argument array from a string passed on the command line. The program checks that it has exactly one command-line argument and outputs a usage message if that is not the case. The `main` program returns 1 if it fails, and 0 if it completes successfully. The call to `makeargv` uses blank and tab as delimiters. The shell also uses the same delimiters, so be sure to enclose the command-line arguments in double quotes as shown in Example 2.18.

■ Example 2.18

If the executable for Program 2.1 is called `argtest`, the following command creates and prints an argument array for `This is a test`.

```
argtest "This is a test"
```

Program 2.1 ──────────────────────────────── `argtest.c`

A program that takes a single string as its command-line argument and calls `makeargv` *to create an argument array.*

```c
#include <stdio.h>
#include <stdlib.h>
int makeargv(const char *s, const char *delimiters, char ***argvp);

int main(int argc, char *argv[]) {
   char delim[] = " \t";
   int i;
   char **myargv;
   int numtokens;

   if (argc != 2) {
      fprintf(stderr, "Usage: %s string\n", argv[0]);
      return 1;
   }
   if ((numtokens = makeargv(argv[1], delim, &myargv)) == -1) {
      fprintf(stderr, "Failed to construct an argument array for %s\n", argv[1]);
      return 1;
   }
   printf("The argument array contains:\n");
   for (i = 0; i < numtokens; i++)
      printf("%d:%s\n", i, myargv[i]);
   return 0;
}
```

Program 2.1 ──────────────────────────────── `argtest.c`

2.6.2 Implementation of `makeargv`

This section develops an implementation of `makeargv` based on the prototype of Example 2.17 as follows.

```c
int makeargv(const char *s, const char *delimiters, char ***argvp);
```

The `makeargv` function creates an argument array pointed to by `argvp` from the string `s`, using the delimiters specified by `delimiters`. If successful, `makeargv` returns the number of tokens. If unsuccessful, `makeargv` returns −1 and sets `errno`.

The `const` qualifiers on `s` and `delimiters` show that `makeargv` does not modify either `s` or `delimiters`. The implementation does not make any a priori assumptions about the length of `s` or of `delimiters`. The function also releases all memory that it dynamically allocates except for the actual returned array, so `makeargv` can be called multiple times without causing a memory leak.

In writing general library programs, you should avoid imposing unnecessary a priori limitations on sizes (e.g., by using buffers of predefined size). Although the system-defined constant MAX_CANON is a reasonable buffer size for handling command-line arguments, the `makeargv` function might be called to make an environment list or to parse an arbitrary command string read from a file. This implementation of `makeargv` allocates all buffers dynamically by calling `malloc` and uses the C library function `strtok` to split off individual tokens. To preserve the input string `s`, `makeargv` does not apply `strtok` directly to `s`. Instead, it creates a scratch area of the same size pointed to by `t` and copies `s` into it. The overall implementation strategy is as follows.

1. Use `malloc` to allocate a buffer `t` for parsing the string in place. The `t` buffer must be large enough to contain `s` and its terminating `'\0'`.
2. Copy `s` into `t`. Figure 2.3 shows the result for the string `"mine -c 10 2.0"`.
3. Make a pass through the string `t`, using `strtok` to count the tokens.
4. Use the count (`numtokens`) to allocate an `argv` array.
5. Copy `s` into `t` again.
6. Use `strtok` to obtain pointers to the individual tokens, modifying `t` and effectively parsing `t` in place. Figure 2.4 shows the method for parsing the tokens in place.

The implementation of `makeargv` discussed here uses the C library function `strtok` to split a string into tokens. The first call to `strtok` is different from subsequent calls. On the first call, pass the address of the string to parse as the first argument, `s1`. On subsequent calls for parsing the same string, pass a NULL for `s1`. The second argument to `strtok`, `s2`, is a string of allowed token delimiters.

SYNOPSIS

```
#include <string.h>

char *strtok(char *restrict s1, const char *restrict s2);
```
                                                                        POSIX:CX

Each successive call to `strtok` returns the start of the next token and inserts a `'\0'` at the end of the token being returned. The `strtok` function returns NULL when it reaches the end of `s1`.

It is important to understand that `strtok` does not allocate new space for the tokens, but rather it tokenizes `s1` in place. Thus, if you need to access the original `s1` after calling `strtok`, you should pass a copy of the string.

The `restrict` qualifier on the two parameters requires that any object referenced by `s1` in this function cannot also be accessed by `s2`. That is, the tail end of the string being parsed cannot be used to contain the delimiters. This restriction, one that would normally be satisfied in any conceivable application, allows the compiler to perform optimizations on the code for `strtok`. The `const` qualifier on the second parameter indicates that the `strtok` function does not modify the delimiter string.

Program 2.2 shows an implementation of `makeargv`. Since `strtok` allows the caller to specify which delimiters to use for separating tokens, the implementation includes a `delimiters` string as a parameter. The program begins by using `strspn` to skip over leading delimiters. This ensures that `**argvp`, which points to the first token, also points

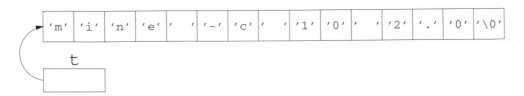

Figure 2.3: The `makeargv` makes a working copy of the string `s` in the buffer `t` to avoid modifying that input parameter.

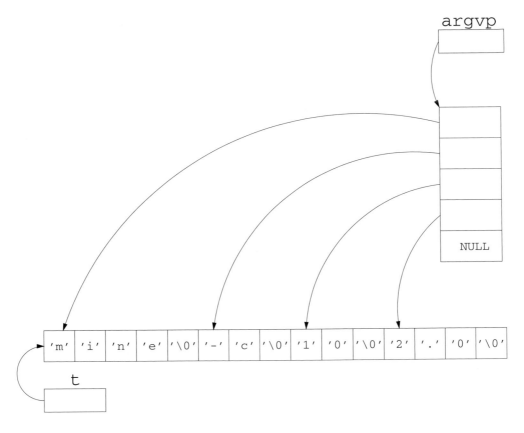

Figure 2.4: The `makeargv` parses the tokens in place by using `strtok`.

to the start of the scratch buffer, called `t` in the program. If an error occurs, this scratch buffer is explicitly freed. Otherwise, the calling program can free this buffer. The call to `free` may not be important for most programs, but if `makeargv` is called frequently from a shell or a long-running communication program, the unfreed space from failed calls to `makeargv` can accumulate. *When using* `malloc` *or a related call, analyze whether to free the memory if an error occurs or when the function returns.*

Program 2.2 ──────────────────────────── `makeargv.c`

An implementation of `makeargv`.

```c
#include <errno.h>
#include <stdlib.h>
#include <string.h>

int makeargv(const char *s, const char *delimiters, char ***argvp) {
   int error;
   int i;
   int numtokens;
   const char *snew;
   char *t;

   if ((s == NULL) || (delimiters == NULL) || (argvp == NULL)) {
      errno = EINVAL;
      return -1;
   }
   *argvp = NULL;
   snew = s + strspn(s, delimiters);            /* snew is real start of string */
   if ((t = malloc(strlen(snew) + 1)) == NULL)
      return -1;
   strcpy(t, snew);
   numtokens = 0;
   if (strtok(t, delimiters) != NULL)      /* count the number of tokens in s */
      for (numtokens = 1; strtok(NULL, delimiters) != NULL; numtokens++) ;

                              /* create argument array for ptrs to the tokens */
   if ((*argvp = malloc((numtokens + 1)*sizeof(char *))) == NULL) {
      error = errno;
      free(t);
      errno = error;
      return -1;
   }
                     /* insert pointers to tokens into the argument array */
   if (numtokens == 0)
      free(t);
   else {
      strcpy(t, snew);
      **argvp = strtok(t, delimiters);
      for (i = 1; i < numtokens; i++)
         *((*argvp) + i) = strtok(NULL, delimiters);
   }
   *((*argvp) + numtokens) = NULL;                 /* put in final NULL pointer */
   return numtokens;
}
```

Program 2.2 ──────────────────────────── `makeargv.c`

■ **Example 2.19**

The following function frees all the memory associated with an argument array that was allocated by makeargv. If the first entry in the array is not NULL, freeing the entry also frees the memory allocated for all the strings. The argument array is freed next. Notice that it would be incorrect to free the argument array and then access the first entry.

```
#include <stdlib.h>

void freemakeargv(char **argv) {
   if (argv == NULL)
      return;
   if (*argv != NULL)
      free(*argv);
   free(argv);
}
```

                                                          freemakeargv.c

2.7   Thread-Safe Functions

The strtok function is not a model that you should emulate in your programs. Because of its definition (page 35), it must use an internal static variable to keep track of the current location of the next token to parse within the string. However, when calls to strtok with different parse strings occur in the same program, the parsing of the respective strings may interfere because there is only one variable for the location.

Program 2.3 shows an incorrect way to determine the average number of words per line by using strtok. The wordaverage function determines the average number of words per line by using strtok to find the next line. The function then calls wordcount to count the number of words on this line. Unfortunately, wordcount also uses strtok, this time to parse the words on the line. Each of these functions by itself would be correct if the other one did not call strtok. The wordaverage function works correctly for the first line, but when wordaverage calls strtok to parse the second line, the internal state information kept by strtok has been reset by wordcount.

The behavior that causes wordaverage to fail also prevents strtok from being used safely in programs with multiple threads. If one thread is in the process of using strtok and a second thread calls strtok, subsequent calls may not behave properly. POSIX defines a thread-safe function, strtok_r, to be used in place of strtok. The _r stands for *reentrant*, an obsolescent term indicating the function can be reentered (called again) before a previous call finishes.

Program 2.3 ———————————————————————— `wordaveragebad.c`

An incorrect use of `strtok` *to determine the average number of words per line.*

```c
#include <string.h>
#define LINE_DELIMITERS "\n"
#define WORD_DELIMITERS " "

static int wordcount(char *s) {
   int count = 1;

   if (strtok(s, WORD_DELIMITERS) == NULL)
      return 0;
   while (strtok(NULL, WORD_DELIMITERS) != NULL)
      count++;
   return count;
}

double wordaverage(char *s) {        /* return average size of words in s */
   int linecount = 1;
   char *nextline;
   int words;

   nextline = strtok(s, LINE_DELIMITERS);
   if (nextline == NULL)
      return 0.0;
   words = wordcount(nextline);
   while ((nextline = strtok(NULL, LINE_DELIMITERS)) != NULL) {
      words += wordcount(nextline);
      linecount++;
   }
   return (double)words/linecount;
}
```

Program 2.3 ———————————————————————— `wordaveragebad.c`

The `strtok_r` function behaves similarly to `strtok` except for an additional parameter, `lasts`, a user-provided pointer to a location that `strtok_r` uses to store the starting address for the next parse.

SYNOPSIS

```c
   #include <string.h>

   char *strtok_r(char *restrict s, const char *restrict sep,
             char **restrict lasts);
```

POSIX:TSF

Each successive call to `strtok_r` returns the start of the next token and inserts a '`\0`' at the end of the token being returned. The `strtok_r` function returns NULL when it reaches the end of `s`.

Program 2.4 corrects Program 2.3 by using `strtok_r`. Notice that the identifier `lasts` used by each function has no linkage, so each invocation accesses a distinct object. Thus, the two functions use different variables for the third parameter of `strtok_r` and do not interfere.

Program 2.4 ──────────────────────────────── **wordaverage.c** ┐
  A correct use of `strtok_r` *to determine the average number of words per line.*

```c
#include <string.h>
#define LINE_DELIMITERS "\n"
#define WORD_DELIMITERS " "

static int wordcount(char *s) {
   int count = 1;
   char *lasts;

   if (strtok_r(s, WORD_DELIMITERS, &lasts) == NULL)
      return 0;
   while (strtok_r(NULL, WORD_DELIMITERS, &lasts) != NULL)
      count++;
   return count;
}

double wordaverage(char *s) {      /* return average size of words in s */
   char *lasts;
   int linecount = 1;
   char *nextline;
   int words;

   nextline = strtok_r(s, LINE_DELIMITERS, &lasts);
   if (nextline == NULL)
      return 0.0;
   words = wordcount(nextline);
   while ((nextline = strtok_r(NULL, LINE_DELIMITERS, &lasts)) != NULL) {
      words += wordcount(nextline);
      linecount++;
   }
   return (double)words/linecount;
}
```

└ **Program 2.4** ──────────────────────────────── **wordaverage.c** ┘

2.8 Use of Static Variables

While care must be taken in using static variables in situations with multiple threads, static variables are useful. For example, a static variable can hold internal state information between calls to a function.

Program 2.5 shows a function called `bubblesort` along with auxiliary functions for keeping track of the number of interchanges made. The variable count has a static storage class because it is declared outside any block. The static qualifier forces this variable to have internal linkage, guaranteeing that the count variable cannot be directly accessed by any function aside from bubblesort.c. The clearcount function and the interchange in the onepass function are the only code segments that modify count. The internal linkage allows other files linked to bubblesort.c to use an identifier, count, without interfering with the integer count in this file.

The three functions clearcount, getcount and bubblesort have external linkage and are accessible from outside. Notice that the static qualifier for onepass gives this function internal linkage so that it is not accessible from outside this file. By using appropriate storage and linkage classes, bubblesort hides its implementation details from its callers.

Program 2.5 ──────────────────────────── **bubblesort.c**

A function that sorts an array of integers and counts the number of interchanges made in the process.

```c
static int count = 0;

static int onepass(int a[], int n) { /* return true if interchanges are made */
    int i;
    int interchanges = 0;
    int temp;

    for (i = 0; i < n - 1; i++)
        if (a[i] > a[i+1]) {
            temp = a[i];
            a[i] = a[i+1];
            a[i+1] = temp;
            interchanges = 1;
            count++;
        }
    return interchanges;
}

void clearcount(void) {
    count = 0;
}

int getcount(void) {
    return count;
}

void bubblesort(int a[], int n) {                    /* sort a in ascending order */
    int i;
    for (i = 0; i < n - 1; i++)
        if (!onepass(a, n - i))
            break;
}
```

Program 2.5 ──────────────────────────── **bubblesort.c**

☐ **Exercise 2.20**

For each object and function in Program 2.5 give the storage and linkage class where appropriate.

Answer:

The function `onepass` has internal linkage. The other functions have external linkage. Functions do not have a storage class. The `count` identifier has internal linkage and static storage. All other variables have no linkage and automatic storage. (See Section A.5 for additional discussion about linkage.)

Section 2.9 discusses a more complex use of static variables to approximate object-oriented behavior in a C program.

2.9   Structure of Static Objects

Static variables are commonly used in the C implementation of a data structure as an object. The data structure and all the functions that access it are placed in a single source file, and the data structure is defined outside any function. The data structure has the `static` attribute, giving it internal linkage: it is private to that source file. Any references to the data structure outside the file are made through the access functions (methods, in object-oriented terminology) defined within the file. The actual details of the data structure should be invisible to the outside world so that a change in the internal implementation does not require a change to the calling program. You can often make an object thread-safe by placing locking mechanisms in its access functions without affecting outside callers.

This section develops an implementation of a list object organized according to the type of static structure just described. Each element of the list consists of a time and a string of arbitrary length. The user can store items in the list object and traverse the list object to examine the contents of the list. The user may not modify data that has already been put in the list. This list object is useful for logging operations such as keeping a list of commands executed by a program.

The requirements make the implementation of the list both challenging and interesting. Since the user cannot modify data items once they are inserted, the implementation must make sure that no caller has access to a pointer to an item stored in the list. To satisfy this requirement, the implementation adds to the list a pointer to a *copy* of the string rather than a pointer to the original string. Also, when the user retrieves data from the list, the implementation returns a pointer to a copy of the data rather than a pointer to the actual data. In the latter case, the caller is responsible for freeing the memory occupied by the copy.

The trickiest part of the implementation is the traversal of the list. During a traversal, the list must save the current position to know where to start the next request. We do not want to do this the way `strtok` does, since this approach would make the list object unsafe for multiple simultaneous traversals. We also do not want to use the strtok_r strategy, which requires the calling program to provide a location for storing a pointer to the next entry in the list. This pointer would allow the calling program to modify entries in the list, a feature we have ruled out in the specification.

We solve this problem by providing the caller with a key value to use in traversing the list. The list object keeps an array of pointers to items in the list indexed by the key. The memory used by these pointers should be freed or reused when the key is no longer needed so that the implementation does not consume unnecessary memory resources.

Program 2.6 shows the listlib.h file containing the prototypes of the four access functions: accessdata, adddata, getdata and freekey. The data_t structure holds a time_t value (time) and a pointer to a character string of undetermined length (string). Programs that use the list must include the listlib.h header file.

Program 2.6 ——————————————————————— **listlib.h**

The header file listlib.h.

```
#include <time.h>

typedef struct data_struct {
    time_t time;
    char *string;
} data_t;

int accessdata(void);
int adddata(data_t data);
int freekey(int key);
int getdata(int key, data_t *datap);
```

Program 2.6 ——————————————————————— **listlib.h**

Program 2.7 shows an implementation of the list object. The adddata function inserts a copy of the data item at the end of the list. The getdata function copies the next item in the traversal of the list into a user-supplied buffer of type data_t. The getdata function allocates memory for the copy of the string field of this data buffer, and the caller is responsible for freeing it.

The accessdata function returns an integer key for traversing the data list. Each key value produces an independent traversal starting from the beginning of the list. When the key is no longer needed, the caller can free the key resources by calling freekey. The key is also freed when the getdata function gives a NULL pointer for the string field of *datap to signify that there are no more entries to examine. *Do not call* freekey *once you have reached the end of the list.*

If successful, accessdata returns a valid nonnegative key. The other three functions return 0 if successful. If unsuccessful, these functions return −1 and set errno.

Program 2.7 ———————————————————————— `listlib.c`

A list object implementation.

```c
#include <errno.h>
#include <stdlib.h>
#include <string.h>
#include "listlib.h"
#define TRAV_INIT_SIZE 8

typedef struct list_struct {
     data_t item;
     struct list_struct *next;
} list_t;

static list_t endlist;
static list_t *headptr = NULL;
static list_t *tailptr = NULL;
static list_t **travptrs = NULL;
static int travptrs_size = 0;

int accessdata(void) {               /* return a nonnegative key if successful */
   int i;
   list_t **newptrs;
   if (headptr == NULL) {             /* can't access a completely empty list */
      errno = EINVAL;
      return -1;
   }
   if (travptrs_size == 0) {                            /* first traversal */
      travptrs = (list_t **)calloc(TRAV_INIT_SIZE, sizeof(list_t *));
      if (travptrs == NULL)    /* couldn't allocate space for traversal keys */
         return -1;
      travptrs[0] = headptr;
      travptrs_size = TRAV_INIT_SIZE;
      return 0;
   }
   for (i = 0; i < travptrs_size; i++) {    /* look for an empty slot for key */
      if (travptrs[i] == NULL) {
         travptrs[i] = headptr;
         return i;
      }
   }
   newptrs = realloc(travptrs, 2*travptrs_size*sizeof(list_t *));
   if (newptrs == NULL)         /* couldn't expand the array of traversal keys */
      return -1;
   travptrs = newptrs;
   travptrs[travptrs_size] = headptr;
   travptrs_size *= 2;
   return travptrs_size/2;
}

int adddata(data_t data) {   /* allocate node for data and add to end of list */
   list_t *newnode;
   int nodesize;

   nodesize = sizeof(list_t) + strlen(data.string) + 1;
   if ((newnode = (list_t *)(malloc(nodesize))) == NULL) /* couldn't add node */
      return -1;
```

```
      newnode->item.time = data.time;
      newnode->item.string = (char *)newnode + sizeof(list_t);
      strcpy(newnode->item.string, data.string);
      newnode->next = NULL;
      if (headptr == NULL)
         headptr = newnode;
      else
         tailptr->next = newnode;
      tailptr = newnode;
      return 0;
   }

   int getdata(int key, data_t *datap) { /* copy next item and set datap->string */
      list_t *t;

      if ( (key < 0) || (key >= travptrs_size) || (travptrs[key] == NULL) ) {
         errno = EINVAL;
         return -1;
      }
      if (travptrs[key] == &endlist) { /* end of list, set datap->string to NULL */
         datap->string = NULL;
         travptrs[key] = NULL;
         return 0;          /* reaching end of list natural condition, not an error */
      }
      t = travptrs[key];
      datap->string = (char *)malloc(strlen(t->item.string) + 1);
      if (datap->string == NULL) /* couldn't allocate space for returning string */
         return -1;
      datap->time = t->item.time;
      strcpy(datap->string, t->item.string);
      if (t->next == NULL)
         travptrs[key] = &endlist;
      else
         travptrs[key] = t->next;
      return 0;
   }

   int freekey(int key) {                    /* free list entry corresponding to key */
      if ( (key < 0) || (key >= travptrs_size) ) {          /* key out of range */
         errno = EINVAL;
         return -1;
      }
      travptrs[key] = NULL;
      return 0;
   }
```

Program 2.7 ———————————————————————————————————— `listlib.c`

   The implementation of Program 2.7 does not assume an upper bound on the length of
the `string` field of `data_t`. The `adddata` function appends to its internal list structure a
node containing a copy of `data`. The `malloc` function allocates space for both the `list_t`
and its string data in a contiguous block. The only way that `adddata` can fail is if `malloc`
fails. The `accessdata` function also fails if there are not sufficient resources to provide

an additional access stream. The `freekey` function fails if the key passed is not valid or
has already been freed. Finally, `getdata` fails if the key is not valid. Reaching the end of
a list during traversal is a natural occurrence rather than an error. The `getdata` function
sets the `string` field of `*datap` to `NULL` to indicate the end.

The implementation in Program 2.7 uses a key that is just an index into an array of
traversal pointers. The implementation allocates the array dynamically with a small initial
size. When the number of traversal streams exceeds the size of the array, `accessdata`
calls `realloc` to expand the array.

The data structures for the object and the code for the access functions of `listlib` are
in a single file. Several later projects use this list object or one that is similar. In an object
representation, outside callers should not have access to the internal representation of the
object. For example, they should not be aware that the object uses a linked list rather than
an array or other implementation of the abstract data structure.

The implementation of Program 2.7 allows nested or recursive calls to correctly add
data to the list or to independently traverse the list. However, the functions have critical
sections that must be protected in a multithreaded environment. Sections 13.2.3 and 13.6
discuss how this can be done.

☐ Exercise 2.21

What happens if you try to access an empty list in Program 2.7?

Answer:

The `accessdata` returns −1, indicating an error.

Program 2.8 executes commands and keeps an internal history, using the list data
object of Program 2.7. The program takes an optional command-line argument, `history`.
If `history` is present, the program outputs a history of commands run thus far whenever
the program reads the string `"history"` from standard input.

Program 2.8 calls `runproc` to run the command and `showhistory` to display the
history of commands that were run. The program uses `fgets` instead of `gets` to prevent
a buffer overrun on input. `MAX_CANON` is a constant specifying the maximum number
of bytes in a terminal input line. If `MAX_CANON` is not defined in `limits.h`, then the
maximum line length depends on the particular device and the program sets the value to
8192 bytes.

Program 2.9 shows the source file containing the `runproc` and `showhistory` functions. When `runproc` successfully executes a command, it adds a node to the history list by calling `adddata`. The `showhistory` function displays the contents of each
node in the list by calling the `getdata` function. After displaying the string in a data
item, `showhistory` function frees the memory allocated by the `getdata` call. The
`showhistory` function does not call `freekey` explicitly because it does a complete
traversal of the list.

Program 2.8 ──────────────────────────────── `keeplog.c`

A main program that reads commands from standard input and executes them.

```c
#include <limits.h>
#include <stdio.h>
#include <stdlib.h>
#include <string.h>

#ifndef MAX_CANON
#define MAX_CANON 8192
#endif

int runproc(char *cmd);
void showhistory(FILE *f);

int main(int argc, char *argv[]) {
   char cmd[MAX_CANON];
   int history = 1;

   if (argc == 1)
      history = 0;
   else if ((argc > 2) || strcmp(argv[1], "history")) {
      fprintf(stderr, "Usage: %s [history]\n", argv[0]);
      return 1;
   }
   while(fgets(cmd, MAX_CANON, stdin) != NULL) {
      if (*(cmd + strlen(cmd) - 1) == '\n')
         *(cmd + strlen(cmd) - 1) = 0;
      if (history && !strcmp(cmd, "history"))
         showhistory(stdout);
      else if (runproc(cmd)) {
         perror("Failed to execute command");
         break;
      }
   }
   printf("\n\n>>>>>>The list of commands executed is:\n");
   showhistory(stdout);
   return 0;
}
```

Program 2.8 ──────────────────────────────── `keeplog.c`

The `runproc` function of Program 2.9 calls the `system` function to execute a command. The `runproc` function returns 0 if the command can be executed. If the command cannot be executed, `runproc` returns −1 with `errno` set.

The `system` function passes the `command` parameter to a command processor for execution. It behaves as if a child process were created with `fork` and the child process invoked `sh` with `execl`.

SYNOPSIS

```c
#include <stdlib.h>

int system(const char *command);
```

POSIX:CX

If `command` is `NULL`, the `system` function always returns a nonzero value to mean that a command language interpreter is available. If `command` is not `NULL`, `system` returns the termination status of the command language interpreter after the execution of `command`. If `system` could not fork a child or get the termination status, it returns –1 and sets `errno`. A zero termination status generally indicates successful completion.

Program 2.9 ────────────────────────────────────── `keeploglib.c`

The file `keeploglib.c`.

```
#include <stdio.h>
#include <stdlib.h>
#include "listlib.h"

int runproc(char *cmd) { /* execute cmd; store cmd and time in history list */
   data_t execute;

   if (time(&(execute.time)) == -1)
      return -1;
   execute.string = cmd;
   if (system(cmd) == -1)              /* command could not be executed at all */
      return -1;
   return adddata(execute);
}

void showhistory(FILE *f) {          /* output the history list of the file f */
   data_t data;
   int key;

   key = accessdata();
   if (key == -1) {
      fprintf(f, "No history\n");
      return;
   }
   while (!getdata(key, &data) && (data.string != NULL)) {
      fprintf(f, "Command: %s\nTime: %s\n", data.string, ctime(&(data.time)));
      free(data.string);
   }
}
```

Program 2.9 ────────────────────────────────────── `keeploglib.c`

2.10 Process Environment

An *environment list* consists of an array of pointers to strings of the form *name = value*. The *name* specifies an *environment variable*, and the *value* specifies a string value associated with the environment variable. The last entry of the array is `NULL`.

The external variable `environ` points to the process environment list when the process begins executing. The strings in the process environment list can appear in any order.

```
SYNOPSIS

   extern char **environ
```
ISO C

If the process is initiated by execl, execlp, execv or execvp, then the process inherits the environment list of the process just before the execution of exec. The execle and execve functions specifically set the environment list as discussed in Section 3.5.

■ Example 2.22

The following C program outputs the contents of its environment list and exits.

```
#include <stdio.h>

extern char **environ;

int main(void) {
   int i;

   printf("The environment list follows:\n");
   for(i = 0; environ[i] != NULL; i++)
     printf("environ[%d]: %s\n", i, environ[i]);
   return 0;
}
```
———————————————————————————————————— **environ.c**

Environment variables provide a mechanism for using system-specific or user-specific information in setting defaults within a program. For example, a program may need to write status information in the user's home directory or may need to find an executable file in a particular place. The user can set the information about where to look for executables in a single variable. Applications interpret the value of an environment variable in an application-specific way. Some of the environment variables described by POSIX are shown in Table 2.1. These environment variables are not required, but if one of these variables is present, it must have the meaning specified in the table.

Use getenv to determine whether a specific variable has a value in the process environment. Pass the name of the environment variable as a string.

```
SYNOPSIS

  #include <stdlib.h>

  char *getenv(const char *name);
```
POSIX:CX

The getenv function returns NULL if the variable does not have a value. If the variable has a value, getenv returns a pointer to the string containing that value. *Be careful about calling* getenv *more than once without copying the first return string into a buffer.* Some implementations of getenv use a static buffer for the return strings and overwrite the buffer on each call.

variable	meaning
COLUMNS	preferred width in columns for terminal
HOME	user's home directory
LANG	locale when not specified by LC_ALL or LC_*
LC_ALL	overriding name of locale
LC_COLLATE	name of locale for collating information
LC_CTYPE	name of locale for character classification
LC_MESSAGES	name of locale for negative or affirmative responses
LC_MONETARY	name of locale for monetary editing
LC_NUMERIC	name of locale for numeric editing
LC_TIME	name of locale for date/time information
LINES	preferred number of lines on a page or vertical screen
LOGNAME	login name associated with a process
PATH	path prefixes for finding executables
PWD	absolute pathname of the current working directory
SHELL	pathname of the user's preferred command interpreter
TERM	terminal type for output
TMPDIR	pathname of directory for temporary files
TZ	time zone information

Table 2.1: POSIX environment variables and their meanings.

■ **Example 2.23**

POSIX specifies that the shell sh should use the environment variable MAIL as the pathname of the mailbox for incoming mail, provided that the MAILPATH variable is not set. The following code segment sets mailp to the value of the environment variable MAIL if this variable is defined and MAILPATH is not defined. Otherwise, the segment sets mailp to a default value.

```
#define MAILDEFAULT "/var/mail"
char *mailp = NULL;

if (getenv("MAILPATH") == NULL)
   mailp = getenv("MAIL");
if (mailp == NULL)
    mailp = MAILDEFAULT;
```

The first call to getenv in Example 2.23 merely checks for the existence of MAILPATH, so it is not necessary to copy the return value to a separate buffer before calling getenv again.

Do not confuse environment variables with predefined constants like MAX_CANON. The predefined constants are defined in header files with #define. Their values are constants and known at compile time. To see whether a definition of such a constant exists, use the `#ifndef` compiler directive as in Program 2.8. In contrast, environment variables are dynamic, and their values are not known until run time.

☐ **Exercise 2.24**

Write a function to produce an argument array containing the components of the `PATH` environment variable.

Answer:

```
#include <stdlib.h>
#define PATH_DELIMITERS ":"

int makeargv(const char *s, const char *delimiters, char ***argvp);

char **getpaths(void) {
   char **myargv;
   char *path;

   path = getenv("PATH");
   if (makeargv(path, PATH_DELIMITERS, &myargv) == -1)
      return NULL;
   else
      return myargv;
}
```

── **getpaths.c**

2.11 Process Termination

When a process terminates, the operating system deallocates the process resources, updates the appropriate statistics and notifies other processes of the demise. The termination can either be *normal* or *abnormal*. The activities performed during process termination include canceling pending timers and signals, releasing virtual memory resources, releasing other process-held system resources such as locks, and closing files that are open. The operating system records the process status and resource usage, notifying the parent in response to a `wait` function.

In UNIX, a process does not completely release its resources after termination until the parent waits for it. If its parent is not waiting when the process terminates, the process becomes a *zombie*. A *zombie* is an inactive process whose resources are deleted later when its parent waits for it. When a process terminates, its orphaned children and zombies are adopted by a special system process. In traditional UNIX systems, this special process is called the `init` process, a process with process ID value 1 that periodically waits for children.

A normal termination occurs under the following conditions.

- `return` from `main`
- Implicit return from `main` (the `main` function falls off the end)
- Call to `exit`, `_Exit` or `_exit`

The C exit function calls user-defined exit handlers that were registered by atexit in the reverse order of registration. After calling the user-defined handlers, exit flushes any open streams that have unwritten buffered data and then closes all open streams. Finally, exit removes all temporary files that were created by tmpfile() and then terminates control. Using the return statement from main has the same effect as calling exit with the corresponding status. Reaching the end of main has the same effect as calling exit(0).

The _Exit and _exit functions do not call user-defined exit handlers before terminating control. The POSIX standard does not specify what happens when a program calls these functions: that is, whether open streams are flushed or temporary files are removed.

The functions exit, _Exit and _exit take a small integer parameter, status, indicating the termination status of the program. Use a status value of 0 to report a successful termination. Programmer-defined nonzero values of status report errors. Example 3.22 on page 77 illustrates how a parent can determine the value of status when it waits for the child. Only the low-order byte of the status value is available to the parent process.

```
SYNOPSIS

    #include <stdlib.h>

    void exit(int status);
    void _Exit(int status);
                                                              ISO C
```

```
SYNOPSIS

    #include <unistd.h>

    void _exit(int status);
                                                              POSIX
```

The C atexit function installs a user-defined exit handler. Exit handlers are executed on a last-installed-first-executed order when the program returns from main or calls exit. Use multiple calls to atexit to install several handlers. The atexit function takes a single parameter, the function to be executed as a handler.

```
SYNOPSIS

    #include <stdlib.h>

    int atexit(void (*func)(void));
                                                              ISO C
```

If successful, atexit returns 0. If unsuccessful, atexit returns a nonzero value.

Program 2.10 has an exit handler, showtimes, that causes statistics about the time used by the program and its children to be output to standard error before the program terminates. The times function returns timing information in the form of the number of clock ticks. The showtimes function converts the time to seconds by dividing by the number of clock ticks per second (found by calling sysconf). Chapter 9 discusses time more completely.

Program 2.10 ———————————————————————— `showtimes.c`

A program with an exit handler that outputs CPU usage.

```c
#include <limits.h>
#include <stdio.h>
#include <stdlib.h>
#include <unistd.h>
#include <sys/times.h>

static void showtimes(void) {
   double ticks;
   struct tms tinfo;

   if ((ticks = (double) sysconf(_SC_CLK_TCK)) == -1)
      perror("Failed to determine clock ticks per second");
   else if (times(&tinfo) == (clock_t)-1)
      perror("Failed to get times information");
   else {
      fprintf(stderr, "User time:              %8.3f seconds\n",
         tinfo.tms_utime/ticks);
      fprintf(stderr, "System time:            %8.3f seconds\n",
         tinfo.tms_stime/ticks);
      fprintf(stderr, "Children's user time:   %8.3f seconds\n",
         tinfo.tms_cutime/ticks);
      fprintf(stderr, "Children's system time: %8.3f seconds\n",
         tinfo.tms_cstime/ticks);
   }
}

int main(void) {
   if (atexit(showtimes))  {
      fprintf(stderr, "Failed to install showtimes exit handler\n");
      return 1;
   }
    /*  rest of main program goes here */
   return 0;
}
```

Program 2.10 ———————————————————————— `showtimes.c`

A process can also terminate abnormally either by calling abort or by processing a signal that causes termination. The signal may be generated by an external event (like Ctrl-C from the keyboard) or by an internal error such as an attempt to access an illegal memory location. An abnormal termination may produce a core dump, and user-installed exit handlers are not called.

2.12 Exercise: An `env` Utility

The `env` utility examines the environment and modifies it to execute another command. When called without arguments, the `env` command writes the current environment to standard output. The optional `utility` argument specifies the command to be executed under the modified environment. The optional `-i` argument means that `env` should ignore the environment inherited from the shell when executing `utility`. Without the `-i` option, `env` uses the `[name=value]` arguments to modify rather than replace the current environment to execute `utility`. The `env` utility does not modify the environment of the shell that executes it.

```
SYNOPSIS

    env [-i] [name=value] ... [utility [argument ...]]
                                              POSIX:Shell and Utilities
```

■ Example 2.25

Calling `env` from the C shell on a machine running Sun Solaris produced the following output.

```
HOME=/users/srobbins
USER=srobbins
LOGNAME=srobbins
PATH=/bin:/usr/bin:/usr/ucb:/usr/bin/X11:/usr/local/bin
MAIL=/var/mail/srobbins
TZ=US/Central
SSH2_CLIENT=129.115.12.131 41064 129.115.12.131 22
TERM=sun-cmd
DISPLAY=sqr3:12.0
SSH2_SFTP_LOG_FACILITY=-1
PWD=/users/srobbins
```

Write a program called `doenv` that behaves in the same way as the `env` utility when executing another program.

1. When called with no arguments, the `doenv` utility calls the `getenv` function and outputs the current environment to standard output.

2. When `doenv` is called with the optional `-i` argument, the entire environment is replaced by the `name=value` pairs. Otherwise, the pairs modify or add to the current environment.

3. If the `utility` argument is given, use `system` to execute `utility` after the environment has been appropriately changed. Otherwise, print the changed environment to standard output, one entry per line.

4. One way to change the current environment in a program is to overwrite the value of the `environ` external variable. If you are completely replacing the old environment (`-i` option), count the number of `name=value` pairs, allocate

enough space for the argument array (don't forget the extra NULL entry), copy the pointers from argv into the array, and set environ.

5. If you are modifying the current environment by overwriting environ, allocate enough space to hold the old entries and any new entries to be added. Copy the pointers from the old environ into the new one. For each name=value pair, determine whether the name is already in the old environment. If name appears, just replace the pointer. Otherwise, add the new entry to the array.

6. Note that it is not safe to just append new entries to the old environ, since you cannot expand the old environ array with realloc. If all name=value pairs correspond to entries already in the environment, just replace the corresponding pointers in environ.

2.13 Exercise: Message Logging

The exercise in this section describes a logging library that is similar to the list object defined in listlib.h and listlib.c of Program 2.6 and Program 2.7, respectively. The logging utility allows the caller to save a message at the end of a list. The logger also records the time that the message was logged. Program 2.11 shows the log.h file for the logger.

Program 2.11 ──────────────────────────────── **log.h**

The header file log.h for the logging facility.

```
#include <time.h>

typedef struct data_struct {
    time_t time;
    char *string;
} data_t;

int addmsg(data_t data);
void clearlog(void);
char *getlog(void);
int savelog(char *filename);
```

Program 2.11 ──────────────────────────────── **log.h**

The data_t structure and the addmsg function have the same respective roles as the list_t structure and adddata function of listlib.h. The savelog function saves the logged messages to a disk file. The clearlog function releases all the storage that has been allocated for the logged messages and empties the list of logged messages. The getlog function allocates enough space for a string containing the entire log, copies the log into this string, and returns a pointer to the string. It is the responsibility of the calling program to free this memory when necessary.

If successful, `addmsg` and `savelog` return 0. A successful `getlog` call returns a pointer to the log string. If unsuccessful, `addmsg` and `savelog` return −1. An unsuccessful `getlog` call returns `NULL`. These three functions also set `errno` on failure.

Program 2.12 contains templates for the four functions specified in `log.h`, as well as the static structures for the list itself. Complete the implementation of `loglib.c`. Use the logging facility to save the messages that were printed by some of your programs. How might you use this facility for program debugging and testing?

Program 2.12 ──────────────────────────────────── `loglib.c`

A template for a simple logging facility.

```c
#include <stdlib.h>
#include <string.h>
#include "log.h"

typedef struct list_struct {
    data_t item;
    struct list_struct *next;
} log_t;

static log_t *headptr = NULL;
static log_t *tailptr = NULL;

int addmsg(data_t data) {
    return 0;
}

void clearlog(void) {
}

char *getlog(void) {
    return NULL;
}

int savelog(char *filename) {
    return 0;
}
```

Program 2.12 ──────────────────────────────────── `loglib.c`

2.14 Additional Reading

The prerequisite programming background for doing the projects in this text includes a general knowledge of UNIX and C. Appendix A summarizes the basics of developing programs in a UNIX environment. *UNIX in a Nutshell: A Desktop Quick Reference for System V* by Robbins and Gilly is a good user's reference [94]. *A Practical Guide to the UNIX System*, 3rd ed. by Sobell [108] gives an overview of UNIX and its utilities from the user perspective. The classic reference to C is *The C Programming Language*, 2nd ed. by

Kernighan and Ritchie [62]. *C: A Reference Manual*, 4th ed. by Harbison and Steele [46] provides a detailed discussion of many of the C language issues that you might encounter in programming the projects for this text. Finally, *Standard C Library* by Plauger is an interesting, but ultimately detailed, look at C library function implementation [91]. The final arbiter of C questions is the ISO C Standard [56].

Chapter 3

Processes in UNIX

A *process* is the basic active entity in most operating-system models. This chapter covers the UNIX process model, including process creation, process destruction and daemon processes. The chapter uses process fans and process chains to illustrate concepts of parentage, inheritance and other process relationships. The chapter also looks at the implications of critical sections in concurrent processes.

Objectives

- Learn how to create processes
- Experiment with `fork` and `exec`
- Explore the implications of process inheritance
- Use `wait` for process cleanup
- Understand the UNIX process model

3.1 Process Identification

UNIX identifies processes by a unique integral value called the *process ID*. Each process also has a *parent process ID*, which is initially the process ID of the process that created it. If this *parent process* terminates, the process is adopted by a system process so that the parent process ID always identifies a valid process.

The `getpid` and `getppid` functions return the process ID and the parent process ID, respectively. The `pid_t` is an unsigned integer type that represents a process ID.

```
SYNOPSIS

   #include <unistd.h>

   pid_t getpid(void);
   pid_t getppid(void);
                                                                              POSIX
```

Neither the `getpid` nor the `getppid` functions can return an error.

■ Example 3.1

The following program outputs its process ID and its parent process ID. Notice that the return values are cast to `long` for printing since there is no guarantee that a `pid_t` will fit in an `int`.

```
#include <stdio.h>
#include <unistd.h>

int main (void) {
   printf("I am process %ld\n", (long)getpid());
   printf("My parent is %ld\n", (long)getppid());
   return 0;
}
                                                          outputPID.c
```

System administrators assign a unique integral *user ID* and an integral *group ID* to each user when creating the user's account. The system uses the user and group IDs to retrieve from the system database the privileges allowed for that user. The most privileged user, *superuser* or *root*, has a user ID of 0. The root user is usually the system administrator.

A UNIX process has several user and group IDs that convey privileges to the process. These include the real user ID, the real group ID, the effective user ID and the effective group ID. Usually, the real and effective IDs are the same, but under some circumstances the process can change them. The process uses the effective IDs for determining access permissions for files. For example, a program that runs with root privileges may want to create a file on behalf of an ordinary user. By setting the process's effective user ID to be that of this user, the process can create the files "as if" the user created them. For the most part, we assume that the real and effective user and group IDs are the same.

The following functions return group and user IDs for a process. The `gid_t` and `uid_t` are integral types representing group and user IDs, respectively. The `getgid` and `getuid` functions return the real IDs, and `getegid` and `geteuid` return the effective IDs.

```
SYNOPSIS

    #include <unistd.h>

    gid_t getegid(void);
    uid_t geteuid(void);
    git_t getgid(void);
    uid_t getuid(void);
                                                              POSIX
```

None of these functions can return an error.

■ Example 3.2

The following program prints out various user and group IDs for a process.

```
#include <stdio.h>
#include <unistd.h>

int main(void) {
    printf("My real user ID is       %5ld\n", (long)getuid());
    printf("My effective user ID is  %5ld\n", (long)geteuid());
    printf("My real group ID is      %5ld\n", (long)getgid());
    printf("My effective group ID is %5ld\n", (long)getegid());
    return 0;
}
```
———————————————————————————————— **outputIDs.c**

3.2 Process State

The *state* of a process indicates its status at a particular time. Most operating systems allow some form of the states listed in Table 3.1. A *state diagram* is a graphical representation of the allowed states of a process and the allowed transitions between states. Figure 3.1 shows such a diagram. The nodes of the graph in the diagram represent the possible states, and the edges represent possible transitions. A directed arc from state *A* to state *B* means that a process can go directly from state *A* to state *B*. The labels on the arcs specify the conditions that cause the transitions between states to occur.

While a program is undergoing the transformation into an active process, it is said to be in the *new* state. When the transformation completes, the operating system puts the process in a queue of processes that are ready to run. The process is then in the *ready* or *runnable* state. Eventually the component of the operating system called the process scheduler selects a process to run. The process is in the *running* state when it is actually executing on the CPU.

state	meaning
new	being created
running	instructions are being executed
blocked	waiting for an event such as I/O
ready	waiting to be assigned to a processor
done	finished

Table 3.1: Common process states.

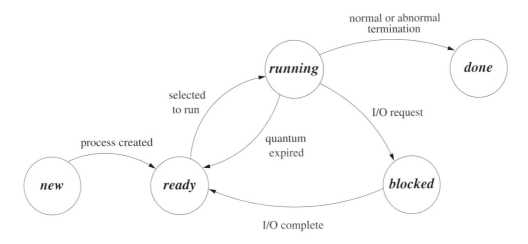

Figure 3.1: State diagram for a simple operating system.

A process in the *blocked* state is waiting for an event and is not eligible to be picked for execution. A process can voluntarily move to the *blocked* state by executing a call such as `sleep`. More commonly, a process moves to the *blocked* state when it performs an I/O request. As explained in Section 1.2, input and output can be thousands of times slower than ordinary instructions. A process performs I/O by requesting the service through a library function that is sometimes called a *system call*. During the execution of a system call, the operating system regains control of the processor and can move the process to the *blocked* state until the operation completes.

A *context switch* is the act of removing one process from the *running* state and re-placing it with another. The *process context* is the information that the operating systems needs about the process and its environment to restart it after a context switch. Clearly, the executable code, stack, registers and program counter are part of the context, as is the memory used for static and dynamic variables. To be able to transparently restart a process, the operating system also keeps track of the process state, the status of program I/O, user and process identification, privileges, scheduling parameters, accounting information and memory management information. If a process is waiting for an event or has caught a signal, that information is also part of the context. The context also contains information about other resources such as locks held by the process.

The `ps` utility displays information about processes. By default, `ps` displays information about processes associated with the user. The `-a` option displays information for processes associated with terminals. The `-A` option displays information for all processes. The `-o` option specifies the format of the output.

SYNOPSIS

```
ps [ aA] [-G grouplist] [-o format]...[-p proclist]
   [-t termlist] [-U userlist]
```

POSIX Shells and Utilities

■ Example 3.3

The following is sample output from the `ps -a` command.

```
>% ps -a
  PID TTY      TIME CMD
20825 pts/11   0:00 pine
20205 pts/11   0:01 bash
20258 pts/16   0:01 telnet
20829 pts/2    0:00 ps
20728 pts/4    0:00 pine
19086 pts/12   0:00 vi
```

The POSIX:XSI Extension provides additional arguments for the `ps` command. Among the most useful are the full (`-f`) and the long (`-l`) options. Table 3.2 lists the fields that are printed for each option. An (all) in the option column means that the field appears in all forms of `ps`.

■ Example 3.4

The execution of the `ps -la` command on the same system as for Example 3.3 produced the following output.

```
F S   UID   PID  PPID  C PRI NI ADDR   SZ WCHAN TTY       TIME CMD
8 S  4228 20825 20205  0  40 20   ?   859     ? pts/11   0:00 pine
8 S  4228 20205 19974  0  40 20   ?   321     ? pts/11   0:01 bash
8 S  2852 20258 20248  0  40 20   ?   328     ? pts/16   0:01 telnet
8 O   512 20838 18178  0  50 20   ?   134       pts/2    0:00 ps
8 S  3060 20728 20719  0  40 20   ?   845     ? pts/4    0:00 pine
8 S  1614 19086 18875  0  40 20   ?   236     ? pts/12   0:00 vi
```

header	option	meaning
F	-l	flags (octal and additive) associated with the process
S	-l	process state
UID	-f, -l	user ID of the process owner
PID	(all)	process ID
PPID	-f, -l	parent process ID
C	-f, -l	processor utilization used for scheduling
PRI	-l	process priority
NI	-l	nice value
ADDR	-l	process memory address
SZ	-l	size in blocks of the process image
WCHAN	-l	event on which the process is waiting
TTY	(all)	controlling terminal
TIME	(all)	cumulative execution time
CMD	(all)	command name (arguments with -f option)

Table 3.2: Fields reported for various options of the ps command in the POSIX:XSI Extension.

3.3 UNIX Process Creation and `fork`

A process can create a new process by calling fork. The calling process becomes the *parent*, and the created process is called the *child*. The fork function copies the parent's memory image so that the new process receives a copy of the address space of the parent. Both processes continue at the instruction after the fork statement (executing in their respective memory images).

SYNOPSIS

```
#include <unistd.h>

pid_t fork(void);
```
                                                                                POSIX

Creation of two completely identical processes would not be very useful. The fork function return value is the critical characteristic that allows the parent and the child to distinguish themselves and to execute different code. The fork function returns 0 to the child and returns the child's process ID to the parent. When fork fails, it returns –1 and sets the errno. If the system does not have the necessary resources to create the child or if limits on the number of processes would be exceeded, fork sets errno to EAGAIN. In case of a failure, the fork does not create a child.

■ Example 3.5

In the following program, both parent and child execute the $x = 1$ assignment statement after returning from `fork`.

```c
#include <stdio.h>
#include <unistd.h>

int main(void) {
   int x;

   x = 0;
   fork();
   x = 1;
   printf("I am process %ld and my x is %d\n", (long)getpid(), x);
   return 0;
}
```

——————————————————————————— **`simplefork.c`**

Before the fork of Example 3.5, one process executes with a single x variable. After the fork, two independent processes execute, each with its own copy of the x variable. Since the parent and child processes execute independently, they do not execute the code in lock step or modify the same memory locations. Each process prints a message with its respective process ID and x value.

The parent and child processes execute the same instructions because the code of Example 3.5 did not test the return value of `fork`. Example 3.6 demonstrates how to test the return value of `fork`.

■ Example 3.6

After `fork` in the following program, the parent and child output their respective process IDs.

```c
#include <stdio.h>
#include <unistd.h>
#include <sys/types.h>

int main(void) {
   pid_t childpid;

   childpid = fork();
   if (childpid == -1) {
      perror("Failed to fork");
      return 1;
   }
   if (childpid == 0)                              /* child code */
      printf("I am child %ld\n", (long)getpid());
   else                                            /* parent code */
      printf("I am parent %ld\n", (long)getpid());
   return 0;
}
```

——————————————————————————— **`twoprocs.c`**

The original process in Example 3.6 has a nonzero value of the `childpid` variable, so it executes the second `printf` statement. The child process has a zero value of `childpid` and executes the first `printf` statement. The output from these processes can appear in either order, depending on whether the parent or the child executes first. If the program is run several times on the same system, the order of the output may or may not always be the same.

☐ Exercise 3.7

What happens when the following program executes?

```
#include <stdio.h>
#include <unistd.h>
#include <sys/types.h>

int main(void) {
   pid_t childpid;
   pid_t mypid;

   mypid = getpid();
   childpid = fork();
   if (childpid == -1) {
      perror("Failed to fork");
      return 1;
   }
   if (childpid == 0)                                        /* child code */
      printf("I am child %ld, ID = %ld\n", (long)getpid(), (long)mypid);
   else                                                      /* parent code */
      printf("I am parent %ld, ID = %ld\n", (long)getpid(), (long)mypid);
   return 0;
}
```
———————————————————————————————————— **badprocessID.c**

Answer:
The parent sets the `mypid` value to its process ID before the fork. When `fork` executes, the child gets a copy of the process address space, including all variables. Since the child does not reset `mypid`, the value of `mypid` for the child does not agree with the value returned by `getpid`.

Program 3.1 creates a chain of n processes by calling `fork` in a loop. On each iteration of the loop, the parent process has a nonzero `childpid` and hence breaks out of the loop. The child process has a zero value of `childpid` and becomes a parent in the next loop iteration. In case of an error, `fork` returns –1 and the calling process breaks out of the loop. The exercises in Section 3.8 build on this program.

Figure 3.2 shows a graph representing the chain of processes generated for Program 3.1 when n is 4. Each circle represents a process labeled by its value of i when it leaves the loop. The edges represent the *is-a-parent* relationship. A → B means process A is the parent of process B.

Program 3.1 ———————————————————— `simplechain.c`
A program that creates a chain of n *processes, where* n *is a command-line argument.*

```c
#include <stdio.h>
#include <stdlib.h>
#include <unistd.h>

int main (int argc, char *argv[]) {
   pid_t childpid = 0;
   int i, n;

   if (argc != 2){    /* check for valid number of command-line arguments */
      fprintf(stderr, "Usage: %s processes\n", argv[0]);
      return 1;
   }
   n = atoi(argv[1]);
   for (i = 1; i < n; i++)
      if (childpid = fork())
         break;

   fprintf(stderr, "i:%d  process ID:%ld  parent ID:%ld  child ID:%ld\n",
           i, (long)getpid(), (long)getppid(), (long)childpid);
   return 0;
}
```

Program 3.1 ———————————————————— `simplechain.c`

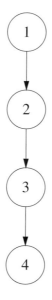

Figure 3.2: Chain of processes generated by Program 3.1 when called with a command-line argument of 4.

❑ Exercise 3.8

Run Program 3.1 for large values of n. Will the messages always come out ordered by increasing i?

Answer:

The exact order in which the messages appear depends on the order in which the processes are selected by the process scheduler to run. If you run the program several times, you should notice some variation in the order.

❑ Exercise 3.9

What happens if Program 3.1 writes the messages to stdout, using printf, instead of to stderr, using fprintf?

Answer:

By default, the system buffers output written to stdout, so a particular message may not appear immediately after the printf returns. Messages to stderr are not buffered, but instead written immediately. For this reason, you should always use stderr for your debugging messages.

Program 3.2 creates a fan of n processes by calling fork in a loop. On each iteration, the newly created process breaks from the loop while the original process continues. In contrast, the process that calls fork in Program 3.1 breaks from the loop while the newly created process continues for the next iteration.

Program 3.2 ────────────────────────────────── **simplefan.c**

A program that creates a fan of n processes where n is passed as a command-line argument.

```
#include <stdio.h>
#include <stdlib.h>
#include <unistd.h>

int main (int argc, char *argv[]) {
   pid_t childpid = 0;
   int i, n;

   if (argc != 2){    /* check for valid number of command-line arguments */
      fprintf(stderr, "Usage: %s processes\n", argv[0]);
      return 1;
   }
   n = atoi(argv[1]);
   for (i = 1; i < n; i++)
      if ((childpid = fork()) <= 0)
         break;

   fprintf(stderr, "i:%d  process ID:%ld  parent ID:%ld  child ID:%ld\n",
           i, (long)getpid(), (long)getppid(), (long)childpid);
   return 0;
}
```

Program 3.2 ────────────────────────────────── **simplefan.c**

Figure 3.3 shows the process fan generated by Program 3.2 when n is 4. The processes are labeled by the value of i at the time they leave the loop. The original process creates n–1 children. The exercises in Section 3.9 build on this example.

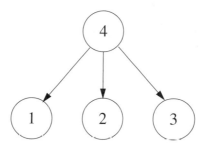

Figure 3.3: Fan of processes generated by Program 3.2 with a command-line argument of 4.

☐ **Exercise 3.10**

Explain what happens when you replace the test

```
(childpid = fork()) <= 0
```

of Program 3.2 with

```
(childpid = fork()) == -1
```

Answer:
In this case, all the processes remain in the loop unless the fork fails. Each iteration of the loop doubles the number of processes, forming a tree configuration illustrated in Figure 3.4 when n is 4. The figure represents each process by a circle labeled with the i value at the time it was created. The original process has a 0 label. The lowercase letters distinguish processes that were created with the same value of i. Although this code appears to be similar to that of Program 3.1, it does not distinguish between parent and child after `fork` executes. Both the parent and child processes go on to create children on the next iteration of the loop, hence the population explosion.

☐ **Exercise 3.11**

Run Program 3.1, Program 3.2, and a process tree program based on the modification suggested in Exercise 3.10. Carefully examine the output. Draw diagrams similar to those of Figure 3.2 through Figure 3.4, labeling the circles with the actual process IDs. Use → to designate the *is-a-parent* relationship. Do not use large values of the command-line argument unless you are on a dedicated system.

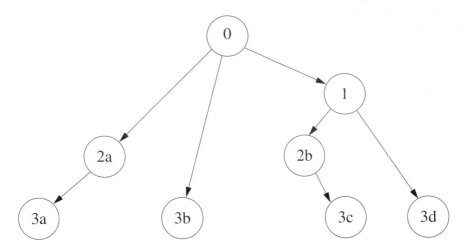

Figure 3.4: Tree of processes produced by the modification of Program 3.2 suggested in Exercise 3.10.

How can you modify the programs so that you can use ps to see the processes that are created?

Answer:

In their current form, the programs complete too quickly for you to view them with ps. Insert the sleep(30); statement immediately before return in order to have each process block for 30 seconds before exiting. In another command window, continually execute ps -l. Section 3.4 explains why some of the processes may report a parent ID of 1 when sleep is omitted.

The fork function creates a new process by making a copy of the parent's image in memory. The child *inherits* parent attributes such as environment and privileges. The child also inherits some of the parent's resources such as open files and devices.

Not every parent attribute or resource is inherited by the child. For instance, the child has a new process ID and of course a different parent ID. The child's times for CPU usage are reset to 0. The child does not get locks that the parent holds. If the parent has set an alarm, the child is not notified when the parent's alarm expires. The child starts with no pending signals, even if the parent had signals pending at the time of the fork.

Although a child inherits its parent's process priority and scheduling attributes, it competes for processor time with other processes as a separate entity. A user running on a crowded time-sharing system can obtain a greater share of the CPU time by creating more processes. A system manager on a crowded system might restrict process creation to prevent a user from creating processes to get a bigger share of the resources.

3.4 The `wait` Function

When a process creates a child, both parent and child proceed with execution from the point of the fork. The parent can execute `wait` or `waitpid` to block until the child finishes. The `wait` function causes the caller to suspend execution until a child's status becomes available or until the caller receives a signal. A process status most commonly becomes available after termination, but it can also be available after the process has been stopped. The `waitpid` function allows a parent to wait for a particular child. This function also allows a parent to check whether a child has terminated without blocking.

The `waitpid` function takes three parameters: a `pid`, a pointer to a location for returning the status and a flag specifying options. If `pid` is −1, `waitpid` waits for any child. If `pid` is greater than 0, `waitpid` waits for the specific child whose process ID is `pid`. Two other possibilities are allowed for the `pid` parameter. If `pid` is 0, `waitpid` waits for any child in the same process group as the caller. Finally, if `pid` is less than −1, `waitpid` waits for any child in the process group specified by the absolute value of `pid`. Process groups are discussed in Section 11.5.

The `options` parameter of `waitpid` is the bitwise inclusive OR of one or more flags. The WNOHANG option causes `waitpid` to return even if the status of a child is not immediately available. The WUNTRACED option causes `waitpid` to report the status of unreported child processes that have been stopped. Check the man page on `waitpid` for a complete specification of its parameters.

SYNOPSIS

```
#include <sys/wait.h>

pid_t wait(int *stat_loc);
pid_t waitpid(pid_t pid, int *stat_loc, int options);
```
                                                                          POSIX

If `wait` or `waitpid` returns because the status of a child is reported, these functions return the process ID of that child. If an error occurs, these functions return −1 and set `errno`. If called with the WNOHANG option, `waitpid` returns 0 to report that there are possible unwaited-for children but that their status is not available. The following table lists the mandatory errors for `wait` and `waitpid`.

errno	cause
ECHILD	caller has no unwaited-for children (`wait`), or process or process group specified by `pid` does not exist (`waitpid`), or process group specified by `pid` does not have a member that is a child of caller (`waitpid`)
EINTR	function was interrupted by a signal
EINVAL	`options` parameter of `waitpid` was invalid

■ **Example 3.12**

The following code segment waits for a child.

```
pid_t childpid;

childpid = wait(NULL);
if (childpid != -1)
    printf("Waited for child with pid %ld\n", childpid);
```

The r_wait function shown in Program 3.3 restarts the wait function if it is interrupted by a signal. Program 3.3 is part of the *restart library* developed in this book and described in Appendix B. The restart library includes wrapper functions for many standard library functions that should be restarted if interrupted by a signal. Each function name starts with r_ followed by the name of the function. Include the restart.h header file when you use functions from the restart library in your programs.

┌─ **Program 3.3** ──────────────────────────────── **r_wait.c** ─┐

A function that restarts wait *if interrupted by a signal.*

```
#include <errno.h>
#include <sys/wait.h>

pid_t r_wait(int *stat_loc) {
    int retval;

    while (((retval = wait(stat_loc)) == -1) && (errno == EINTR)) ;
    return retval;
}
```

└─ **Program 3.3** ──────────────────────────────── **r_wait.c** ─┘

■ **Example 3.13**

The following code segment waits for all children that have finished but avoids blocking if there are no children whose status is available. It restarts waitpid if that function is interrupted by a signal or if it successfully waited for a child.

```
pid_t childpid;

while (childpid = waitpid(-1, NULL, WNOHANG))
    if ((childpid == -1) && (errno != EINTR))
        break;
```

□ **Exercise 3.14**

What happens when a process terminates, but its parent does not wait for it?

Answer:

It becomes a *zombie* in UNIX terminology. Zombies stay in the system until they are waited for. If a parent terminates without waiting for a child, the child becomes an *orphan* and is adopted by a special system process. Traditionally, this process is called init and has process ID equal to 1, but POSIX does not require this designation. The init process periodically waits for children, so eventually orphaned zombies are removed.

■ **Example 3.15**

The following modification of the process fan of Program 3.2 causes the original process to print out its information after all children have exited.

```
#include <stdio.h>
#include <stdlib.h>
#include <unistd.h>
#include <sys/wait.h>
#include "restart.h"

int main(int argc, char *argv[]) {
   pid_t childpid;
   int i, n;

   if (argc != 2) {
      fprintf(stderr, "Usage: %s n\n", argv[0]);
      return 1;
   }
   n = atoi(argv[1]);
   for (i = 1; i < n; i++)
      if ((childpid = fork()) <= 0)
         break;

   while(r_wait(NULL) > 0) ;    /* wait for all of your children */
   fprintf(stderr, "i:%d  process ID:%ld  parent ID:%ld  child ID:%ld\n",
           i, (long)getpid(), (long)getppid(), (long)childpid);
   return 0;
}
```

── `fanwait.c`

□ **Exercise 3.16**

What happens if you interchange the `while` loop and `fprintf` statements in Example 3.15?

Answer:

The original process still exits last, but it may output its ID information before some of its children output theirs.

□ **Exercise 3.17**

What happens if you replace the `while` loop of Example 3.15 with the statement `wait(NULL);`?

Answer:

The parent waits for at most one process. If a signal happens to come in before the first child completes, the parent won't actually wait for any children.

□ Exercise 3.18

Describe the possible forms of the output from the following program.

```c
#include <stdio.h>
#include <unistd.h>
#include <sys/types.h>
#include <sys/wait.h>

int main (void) {
   pid_t childpid;
                                  /* set up signal handlers here ... */
   childpid = fork();
   if (childpid == -1) {
      perror("Failed to fork");
      return 1;
   }
   if (childpid == 0)
      fprintf(stderr, "I am child %ld\n", (long)getpid());
   else if (wait(NULL) != childpid)
      fprintf(stderr, "A signal must have interrupted the wait!\n");
   else
      fprintf(stderr, "I am parent %ld with child %ld\n", (long)getpid(),
            (long)childpid);
   return 0;
}
```
—— **parentwaitpid.c**

Answer:

The output can have several forms, depending on exact timing and errors.

1. If `fork` fails (unlikely unless some other program has generated a runaway tree of processes and exceeded the system limit), the `"Failed to fork"` message appears. Otherwise, if there are no signals, something similar to the following appears.

   ```
   I am child 3427
   I am parent 3426 with child 3427
   ```

2. If the parent catches a signal after the child executes `fprintf` but before the child's `return`, the following appears.

   ```
   I am child 3427
   A signal must have interrupted the wait!
   ```

3. If the parent catches a signal after the child terminates and `wait` returns successfully, the following appears.

   ```
   I am child 3427
   I am parent 3426 with child 3427
   ```

4. If the parent catches a signal between the time that the child terminates and `wait` returns, either of the previous two results is possible, depending on when the signal is caught.

5. If the parent catches a signal before the child executes `fprintf` and if the parent executes its `fprintf` first, the following appears.

```
A signal must have interrupted the wait!
I am child 3427
```

6. Finally, if the parent catches a signal before the child executes `fprintf` and the child executes its `fprintf` first, the following appears.

```
I am child 3427
A signal must have interrupted the wait!
```

☐ Exercise 3.19

For the child of Exercise 3.18 to always print its message first, the parent must run `wait` repeatedly until the child exits before printing its own message. What is wrong with the following?

```
while(childpid != wait(&status)) ;
```

Answer:

The loop fixes the problem of interruption by signals, but `wait` can fail to return the `childpid` because it encounters a real error. You should always test `errno` as demonstrated in the `r_wait` of Program 3.3.

☐ Exercise 3.20

The following program creates a process fan. All the forked processes are children of the original process. How are the output messages ordered?

```c
#include <errno.h>
#include <stdio.h>
#include <stdlib.h>
#include <unistd.h>
#include <sys/wait.h>

int main (int argc, char *argv[]) {
   pid_t childpid = 0;
   int i, n;

   if (argc != 2){       /* check number of command-line arguments */
      fprintf(stderr, "Usage: %s processes\n", argv[0]);
      return 1;
   }
   n = atoi(argv[1]);
   for (i = 1; i < n; i++)
      if ((childpid = fork()) <= 0)
         break;
   for( ; ; ) {
      childpid = wait(NULL);
      if ((childpid == -1) && (errno != EINTR))
         break;
   }
   fprintf(stderr, "I am process %ld, my parent is %ld\n",
                   (long)getpid(), (long)getppid());
   return 0;
}
```

fanwaitmsg.c

Answer:

Because none of the forked children are parents, their `wait` function returns −1 and sets `errno` to `ECHILD`. They are not blocked by the second `for` loop. Their identification messages may appear in any order. The message from the original process comes out at the very end after it has waited for all of its children.

❏ Exercise 3.21

The following program creates a process chain. Only one forked process is a child of the original process. How are the output messages ordered?

```c
#include <errno.h>
#include <stdio.h>
#include <stdlib.h>
#include <unistd.h>
#include <sys/wait.h>

int main (int argc, char *argv[]) {
   pid_t childpid;
   int i, n;
   pid_t waitreturn;

   if (argc != 2){    /* check number of command-line arguments */
      fprintf(stderr, "Usage: %s processes\n", argv[0]);
      return 1;
   }
   n = atoi(argv[1]);
   for (i = 1; i < n; i++)
      if (childpid = fork())
         break;
   while(childpid != (waitreturn = wait(NULL)))
      if ((waitreturn == -1) && (errno != EINTR))
         break;
   fprintf(stderr, "I am process %ld, my parent is %ld\n",
                   (long)getpid(), (long)getppid());
   return 0;
}
```
————————————————————————————————————— `chainwaitmsg.c`

Answer:

Each forked child waits for its own child to complete before outputting a message. The messages appear in reverse order of creation.

3.4.1 Status values

The `stat_loc` argument of `wait` or `waitpid` is a pointer to an integer variable. If it is not `NULL`, these functions store the return status of the child in this location. The child returns its status by calling `exit`, `_exit`, `_Exit` or `return` from main. A zero return value indicates `EXIT_SUCCESS`; any other value indicates `EXIT_FAILURE`. The parent can only access the 8 least significant bits of the child's return status.

POSIX specifies six macros for testing the child's return status. Each takes the status value returned by a child to `wait` or `waitpid` as a parameter.

```
SYNOPSIS

   #include <sys/wait.h>

   WIFEXITED(int stat_val)
   WEXITSTATUS(int stat_val)
   WIFSIGNALED(int stat_val)
   WTERMSIG(int stat_val)
   WIFSTOPPED(int stat_val)
   WSTOPSIG(int stat_val)

                                                              POSIX
```

The six macros are designed to be used in pairs. The WIFEXITED evaluates to a nonzero value when the child terminates normally. If WIFEXITED evaluates to a nonzero value, then WEXITSTATUS evaluates to the low-order 8 bits returned by the child through _exit(), exit() or return from main.

The WIFSIGNALED evaluates to a nonzero value when the child terminates because of an uncaught signal (see Chapter 8). If WIFSIGNALED evaluates to a nonzero value, then WTERMSIG evaluates to the number of the signal that caused the termination.

The WIFSTOPPED evaluates to a nonzero value if a child is currently stopped. If WIFSTOPPED evaluates to a nonzero value, then WSTOPSIG evaluates to the number of the signal that caused the child process to stop.

■ Example 3.22

The following function determines the exit status of a child.

```c
#include <errno.h>
#include <stdio.h>
#include <sys/types.h>
#include <sys/wait.h>
#include "restart.h"

void show_return_status(void) {
   pid_t childpid;
   int status;

   childpid = r_wait(&status);
   if (childpid == -1)
     perror("Failed to wait for child");
   else if (WIFEXITED(status) && !WEXITSTATUS(status))
     printf("Child %ld terminated normally\n", (long)childpid);
   else if (WIFEXITED(status))
     printf("Child %ld terminated with return status %d\n",
            (long)childpid, WEXITSTATUS(status));
   else if (WIFSIGNALED(status))
     printf("Child %ld terminated due to uncaught signal %d\n",
            (long)childpid, WTERMSIG(status));
   else if (WIFSTOPPED(status))
     printf("Child %ld stopped due to signal %d\n",
            (long)childpid, WSTOPSIG(status));
}
```

`showreturnstatus.c`

3.5 The `exec` Function

The `fork` function creates a copy of the calling process, but many applications require the child process to execute code that is different from that of the parent. The `exec` family of functions provides a facility for overlaying the process image of the calling process with a new image. The traditional way to use the `fork–exec` combination is for the child to execute (with an `exec` function) the new program while the parent continues to execute the original code.

```
SYNOPSIS

   #include <unistd.h>

   extern char **environ;
   int execl(const char *path, const char *arg0, ... /*, char *(0) */);
   int execle (const char *path, const char *arg0, ... /*, char *(0),
              char *const envp[] */);
   int execlp (const char *file, const char *arg0, ... /*, char *(0) */);
   int execv(const char *path, char *const argv[]);
   int execve (const char *path, char *const argv[], char *const envp[]);
   int execvp (const char *file, char *const argv[]);
                                                                      POSIX
```

All `exec` functions return −1 and set `errno` if unsuccessful. In fact, if any of these functions return at all, the call was unsuccessful. The following table lists the mandatory errors for the `exec` functions.

errno	cause
E2BIG	size of new process's argument list and environment list is greater than system-imposed limit of `ARG_MAX` bytes
EACCES	search permission on directory in path prefix of new process is denied, new process image file execution permission is denied, or new process image file is not a regular file and cannot be executed
EINVAL	new process image file has appropriate permission and is in a recognizable executable binary format, but system cannot execute files with this format
ELOOP	a loop exists in resolution of `path` or `file` argument
ENAMETOOLONG	the length of `path` or `file` exceeds `PATH_MAX`, or a pathname component is longer than `NAME_MAX`
ENOENT	component of `path` or `file` does not name an existing file, or `path` or `file` is an empty string
ENOEXEC	image file has appropriate access permission but has an unrecognized format (does not apply to `execlp` or `execvp`)
ENOTDIR	a component of the image file path prefix is not a directory

The six variations of the exec function differ in the way command-line arguments and the environment are passed. They also differ in whether a full pathname must be given for the executable. The execl (execl, execlp and execle) functions pass the command-line arguments in an explicit list and are useful if you know the number of command-line arguments at compile time. The execv (execv, execvp and execve) functions pass the command-line arguments in an argument array such as one produced by the makeargv function of Section 2.6. The arg$_i$ parameter represents a pointer to a string, and argv and envp represent NULL-terminated arrays of pointers to strings.

The path parameter to execl is the pathname of a process image file specified either as a fully qualified pathname or relative to the current directory. The individual command-line arguments are then listed, followed by a (char *)0 pointer (a NULL pointer).

Program 3.4 calls the ls shell command with a command-line argument of -l. The program assumes that ls is located in the /bin directory. The execl function uses its character-string parameters to construct an argv array for the command to be executed. Since argv[0] is the program name, it is the second argument of the execl. Notice that the first argument of execl, the pathname of the command, also includes the name of the executable.

Program 3.4 ————————————————————————————————— **execls.c**

A program that creates a child process to run ls -l.

```
#include <stdio.h>
#include <stdlib.h>
#include <unistd.h>
#include <sys/wait.h>

int  main(void) {
   pid_t childpid;

   childpid = fork();
   if (childpid == -1)  {
      perror("Failed to fork");
      return 1;
   }
   if (childpid == 0) {                            /* child code */
      execl("/bin/ls", "ls", "-l", NULL);
      perror("Child failed to exec ls");
      return 1;
   }
   if (childpid != wait(NULL)) {                   /* parent code */
      perror("Parent failed to wait due to signal or error");
      return 1;
   }
   return 0;
}
```

Program 3.4 ————————————————————————————————— **execls.c**

An alternative form is `execlp`. If the first parameter (`file`) contains a slash, then `execlp` treats `file` as a pathname and behaves like `execl`. On the other hand, if `file` does not have a slash, `execlp` uses the `PATH` environment variable to search for the executable. Similarly, the shell tries to locate the executable file in one of the directories specified by the `PATH` variable when a user enters a command.

A third form, `execle`, takes an additional parameter representing the environment of the new process. For the other forms of `execl`, the new process inherits the environment of the calling process through the `environ` variable.

The `execv` functions use a different form of the command-line arguments. Use an `execv` function with an argument array constructed at run time. The `execv` function takes exactly two parameters, a pathname for the executable and an argument array. (The `makeargv` function of Program 2.2 is useful here.) The `execve` and `execvp` are variations on `execv`; they are similar in structure to `execle` and `execlp`, respectively.

Program 3.5 shows a simple program to execute one program from within another program. The program forks a child to execute the command. The child performs an `execvp` call to overwrite its process image with an image corresponding to the command. The parent, which retains the original process image, waits for the child, using the `r_wait` function of Program 3.3 from the restart library. The `r_wait` restarts its `wait` function if interrupted by a signal.

■ Example 3.23

The following command line to Program 3.5 causes `execcmd` to create a new process to execute the `ls -l` command.

```
execcmd ls -l
```

Program 3.5 avoids constructing the `argv` parameter to `execvp` by using a simple trick. The original `argv` array produced in Example 3.23 contains pointers to three tokens: `myexec`, `ls` and `-l`. The argument array for the `execvp` starts at `&argv[1]` and contains pointers to the two tokens `ls` and `-l`.

☐ Exercise 3.24

How big is the argument array passed as the second argument to `execvp` when you execute `execcmd` of Program 3.5 with the following command line?

```
execcmd ls -l *.c
```

Answer:
The answer depends on the number of `.c` files in the current directory because the shell expands `*.c` before passing the command line to `execcmd`.

Program 3.6 creates an argument array from the first command-line argument and then calls `execvp`. Notice that `execcmdargv` calls the `makeargv` function only in the child process. Program 2.2 on page 37 shows an implementation of the `makeargv` function.

┌─ **Program 3.5** ─────────────────────────────────── **execcmd.c** ─┐

A program that creates a child process to execute a command. The command to be executed is passed on the command line.

```c
#include <errno.h>
#include <stdio.h>
#include <unistd.h>
#include <sys/types.h>
#include <sys/wait.h>
#include "restart.h"

int main(int argc, char *argv[]) {
   pid_t childpid;

   if (argc < 2){       /* check for valid number of command-line arguments */
      fprintf (stderr, "Usage: %s command arg1 arg2 ...\n", argv[0]);
      return 1;
   }
   childpid = fork();
   if (childpid == -1) {
      perror("Failed to fork");
      return 1;
   }
   if (childpid == 0) {                                     /* child code */
      execvp(argv[1], &argv[1]);
      perror("Child failed to execvp the command");
      return 1;
   }
   if (childpid != r_wait(NULL)) {                          /* parent code */
      perror("Parent failed to wait");
      return 1;
   }
   return 0;
}
```

└─ **Program 3.5** ─────────────────────────────────── **execcmd.c** ─┘

□ **Exercise 3.25**

How would you pass a string containing multiple tokens to execcmdargv of Program 3.6?

Answer:

Place the command string in double quotes so that the command line interpreter treats the string as a single token. For example, to execute ls -l, call execcmdargv with the following command line.

```
execcmdargv "ls -l"
```

□ **Exercise 3.26**

Program 3.6 only calls the makeargv function in the child process after the fork. What happens if you move the makeargv call before the fork?

Answer:

A parent call to makeargv before the fork allocates the argument array on the heap in the parent process. The fork function creates a copy of the parent's process image for the child. After fork executes, both parent and child have copies of the argument array. A single call to makeargv does not present a problem. However, when the parent represents a shell process, the allocation step might be repeated hundreds of times. Unless the parent explicitly frees the argument array, the program will have a memory leak.

Program 3.6 ─────────────────────────────── **execcmdargv.c** ─

A program that creates a child process to execute a command string passed as the first command-line argument.

```c
#include <errno.h>
#include <stdio.h>
#include <stdlib.h>
#include <unistd.h>
#include <sys/wait.h>
#include "restart.h"

int makeargv(const char *s, const char *delimiters, char ***argvp);

int main(int argc, char *argv[]) {
   pid_t childpid;
   char delim[] = " \t";
   char **myargv;

   if (argc != 2) {
      fprintf(stderr, "Usage: %s string\n", argv[0]);
      return 1;
   }
   childpid = fork();
   if (childpid == -1) {
      perror("Failed to fork");
      return 1;
   }
   if (childpid == 0) {                               /* child code */
      if (makeargv(argv[1], delim, &myargv) == -1) {
         perror("Child failed to construct argument array");
      } else {
         execvp(myargv[0], &myargv[0]);
         perror("Child failed to exec command");
      }
      return 1;
   }
   if (childpid != r_wait(NULL)) {                    /* parent code */
      perror("Parent failed to wait");
      return 1;
   }
   return 0;
}
```

Program 3.6 ──────────────────────────────────── **execcmdargv.c** ─

The `exec` function copies a new executable into the process image. The program text, variables, stack and heap are overwritten. The new process inherits the environment (meaning the list of environment variables and their associated values) unless the original process called `execle` or `execve`. Files that are open at the time of the `exec` call are usually still open afterward.

Table 3.3 summarizes the attributes that are inherited by processes after `exec`. The second column of the table gives library functions related to the items. The IDs associated with the process are intact after `exec` runs. If a process sets an alarm before calling `exec`, the alarm still generates a signal when it expires. Pending signals are also carried over on `exec` in contrast to `fork`. The process creates files with the same permissions as before `exec` ran, and accounting of CPU time continues without being reinitialized.

attribute	relevant library function
process ID	`getpid`
parent process ID	`getppid`
process group ID	`getpgid`
session ID	`getsid`
real user ID	`getuid`
real group ID	`getgid`
supplementary group IDs	`getgroups`
time left on an alarm signal	`alarm`
current working directory	`getcwd`
root directory	
file mode creation mask	`umask`
file size limit*	`ulimit`
process signal mask	`sigprocmask`
pending signals	`sigpending`
time used so far	`times`
resource limits*	`getrlimit, setrlimit`
controlling terminal*	`open, tcgetpgrp`
interval timers*	`ualarm`
nice value*	`nice`
`semadj` values*	`semop`

Table 3.3: Attributes that are preserved after calls to `exec`. The second column lists some library functions relevant to these attributes. A * indicates an attribute inherited in the POSIX:XSI Extension.

3.6 Background Processes and Daemons

The shell is a command interpreter that prompts for commands, reads the commands from standard input, forks children to execute the commands and waits for the children to finish. When standard input and output come from a terminal type of device, a user can terminate an executing command by entering the interrupt character. (The interrupt character is settable, but many systems assume a default value of Ctrl-C.)

☐ **Exercise 3.27**

What happens when you execute the following commands?

```
cd /etc
ls -l
```

Now execute the `ls -l` command again, but enter a Ctrl-C as soon as the listing starts to display. Compare the results to the first case.

Answer:
In the first case, the prompt appears after the directory listing is complete because the shell waits for the child before continuing. In the second case, the Ctrl-C terminates the `ls`.

Most shells interpret a line ending with & as a command that should be executed by a background process. When a shell creates a background process, it does not wait for the process to complete before issuing a prompt and accepting additional commands. Furthermore, a Ctrl-C from the keyboard does not terminate a background process.

☐ **Exercise 3.28**

Compare the results of Exercise 3.27 with the results of executing the following command.

```
ls -l  &
```

Reenter the `ls -l &` command and try to terminate it by entering Ctrl-C.

Answer:
In the first case, the prompt appears before the listing completes. The Ctrl-C does not affect background processes, so the second case behaves in the same way as the first.

A *daemon* is a background process that normally runs indefinitely. The UNIX operating system relies on many daemon processes to perform routine (and not so routine) tasks. Under the Solaris operating environment, the `pageout` daemon handles paging for memory management. The `in.rlogind` handles remote login requests. Other daemons handle mail, file transfer, statistics and printer requests, to name a few.

The `runback` program in Program 3.7 executes its first command-line argument as a background process. The child calls `setsid` so that it does not get any signals because of a Ctrl-C from a controlling terminal. (See Section 11.5.) The `runback` parent does not wait for its child to complete.

Program 3.7 ————————————————————— **runback.c**

The `runback` program creates a child process to execute a command string in the background.

```c
#include <stdio.h>
#include <stdlib.h>
#include <unistd.h>
#include <sys/wait.h>
#include "restart.h"

int makeargv(const char *s, const char *delimiters, char ***argvp);

int main(int argc, char *argv[]) {
   pid_t childpid;
   char delim[] = " \t";
   char **myargv;

   if (argc != 2) {
      fprintf(stderr, "Usage: %s string\n", argv[0]);
      return 1;
   }
   childpid = fork();
   if (childpid == -1) {
      perror("Failed to fork");
      return 1;
   }
   if (childpid == 0) {                    /* child becomes a background process */
     if (setsid() == -1)
        perror("Child failed to become a session leader");
     else if (makeargv(argv[1], delim, &myargv) == -1)
         fprintf(stderr, "Child failed to construct argument array\n");
     else {
        execvp(myargv[0], &myargv[0]);
        perror("Child failed to exec command");
     }
     return 1;                             /* child should never return */
   }
   return 0;                               /* parent exits */
}
```

Program 3.7 ————————————————————— **runback.c**

■ **Example 3.29**

The following command is similar to entering `ls -l &` directly from the shell.

```
runback "ls -l"
```

3.7 Critical Sections

Imagine a scenario in which a computer system has a printer that can be directly accessed by all the processes in the system. Each time a process wants to print something, it writes to the printer device. How would the printed output look if several processes wrote to the printer simultaneously? The individual processes are allowed only a fixed quantum of processor time. If the quantum expires before a process completes writing, another process might send output to the printer. The resulting printout would have the output from the processes interspersed—an undesirable feature.

The problem with the previous scenario is that the processes are "simultaneously" attempting to access a shared resource—a resource that should be used by only one process at a time. That is, the printer requires *exclusive access* by the processes in the system. The portion of code in which each process accesses such a shared resource is called a *critical section*. Programs with critical sections must be sure not to violate the *mutual exclusion* requirement.

One method of providing mutual exclusion uses a locking mechanism. Each process acquires a lock that excludes all other processes before entering its critical section. When the process finishes the critical section, it releases the lock. Unfortunately, this approach relies on the cooperation and correctness of all participants. If one process fails to acquire the lock before accessing the resource, the system fails.

A common approach is to encapsulate shared resources in a manner that ensures exclusive access. Printers are usually handled by having only one process (the printer daemon) with permissions to access the actual printer. Other processes print by sending a message to the printer daemon process along with the name of the file to be printed. The printer daemon puts the request in a queue and may even make a copy of the file to print in its own disk area. The printer daemon removes request messages from its queue one at a time and prints the file corresponding to the message. The requesting process returns immediately after writing the request or after the printer daemon acknowledges receipt, not when the printing actually completes.

Operating systems manage many shared resources besides the obvious devices, files and shared variables. Tables and other information within the operating system kernel code are shared among processes managing the system. A large operating system has many diverse parts with possibly overlapping critical sections. When one of these parts is modified, you must understand the entire operating system to reliably determine whether the modification adversely affects other parts. To reduce the complexity of internal interactions, some operating systems use an *object-oriented* design. Shared tables and other resources are encapsulated as objects with well-defined access functions. The only way to access such a table is through these functions, which have appropriate mutual exclusion built in. In a distributed system, the object interface uses messages. Changes to modules in a properly designed object-oriented system do not have the same impact as they do for uncontrolled access.

On the surface, the object-oriented approach appears to be similar to the daemons described in Section 3.6, but structurally these approaches can be very different. There is no requirement that daemons encapsulate resources. They can fight over shared data structures in an uncontrolled way. Good object-oriented design ensures that data structures are encapsulated and accessed only through carefully controlled interfaces. Daemons can be implemented with an object-oriented design, but they do not have to be.

3.8 Exercise: Process Chains

This section expands on the process chain of Program 3.1. The chain is a vehicle for experimenting with `wait` and with sharing of devices. All of the processes in the chain created by Program 3.1 share standard input, standard output and standard error. The `fprintf` to standard error is a critical section of the program. This exercise explores some implications of critical sections. Later chapters extend this exercise to critical sections involving other devices (Chapter 6) and a token-ring simulation (Chapter 7).

Program 3.1 creates a chain of processes. It takes a single command-line argument that specifies the number of processes to create. Before exiting, each process outputs its `i` value, its process ID, its parent process ID and the process ID of its child. The parent does not execute `wait`. If the parent exits before the child, the child becomes an orphan. In this case, the child process is adopted by a special system process (which traditionally is a process, `init`, with process ID of 1). As a result, some of the processes may indicate a parent process ID of 1.

Do not attempt this exercise on a machine with other users because it strains the resources of the machine.

1. Run Program 3.1 and observe the results for different numbers of processes.
2. Fill in the actual process IDs of the processes in the diagram of Figure 3.2 for a run with command-line argument value of 4.
3. Experiment with different values for the command-line argument to find out the largest number of processes that the program can generate. Observe the fraction that are adopted by `init`.
4. Place `sleep(10);` directly before the final `fprintf` statement in Program 3.1. What is the maximum number of processes generated in this case?
5. Put a loop around the final `fprintf` in Program 3.1. Have the loop execute `k` times. Put `sleep(m);` inside this loop after the `fprintf`. Pass `k` and `m` on the command line. Run the program for several values of `n`, `k` and `m`. Observe the results.
6. Modify Program 3.1 by putting a `wait` function call before the final `fprintf` statement. How does this affect the output of the program?

7. Modify Program 3.1 by replacing the final `fprintf` statement with four `fprintf` statements, one each for the four integers displayed. Only the last one should output a newline. What happens when you run this program? Can you tell which process generated each part of the output? Run the program several times and see if there is a difference in the output.

8. Modify Program 3.1 by replacing the final `fprintf` statement with a loop that reads `nchars` characters from standard input, one character at a time, and puts them in an array called `mybuf`. The values of `n` and `nchars` should be passed as command-line arguments. After the loop, put a `'\0'` character in entry `nchars` of the array so that it contains a string. Output to standard error in a single `fprintf` the process ID followed by a colon followed by the string in `mybuf`. Run the program for several values of `n` and `nchars`. Observe the results. Press the Return key often and continue typing at the keyboard until all of the processes have exited.

3.9 Exercise: Process Fans

The exercises in this section expand on the fan structure of Program 3.2 through the development of a simple batch processing facility, called `runsim`. (Modifications in Section 14.6 lead to a license manager for an application program.) The `runsim` program takes exactly one command-line argument specifying the maximum number of simultaneous executions. Follow the outline below for implementing `runsim`. Write a test program called `testsim` to test the facility. Suggested library functions appear in parentheses.

1. Write a program called `runsim` that takes one command-line argument.
2. Check for the appropriate command-line argument and output a usage message if the command line is incorrect.
3. Initialize `pr_limit` from the command line. The `pr_limit` variable specifies the maximum number of children allowed to execute at a time.
4. Initialize the `pr_count` variable to 0. The `pr_count` variable holds the number of active children.
5. Execute the following main loop until end-of-file is reached on standard input.
    a) If `pr_count` is `pr_limit`, wait for a child to finish (`wait`) and decrement `pr_count`.
    b) Read a line from standard input (`fgets`) of up to `MAX_CANON` characters and execute a program corresponding to that command line by forking a child (`fork`, `makeargv`, `execvp`).
    c) Increment `pr_count` to track the number of active children.
    d) Check to see if any of the children have finished (`waitpid` with the `WNOHANG` option). Decrement `pr_count` for each completed child.

6. After encountering an end-of-file on standard input, wait for all the remaining children to finish (`wait`) and then exit.

Write a test program called `testsim` that takes two command-line arguments: the sleep time and the repeat factor. The repeat factor is the number of times `testsim` iterates a loop. In the loop, `testim` sleeps for the specified sleep time and then outputs a message with its process ID to standard error. Use `runsim` to run multiple copies of the `testsim` program.

Create a test file called `testing.data` that contains commands to run. For example, the file might contain the following lines.

```
testsim 5 10
testsim 8 10
testsim 4 10
testsim 13 6
testsim 1 12
```

Run the program by entering a command such as the following.

```
runsim 2 < testing.data
```

3.10 Additional Reading

The Design of the UNIX Operating System by Bach [9] discusses process implementation under System V. *The Design and Implementation of the 4.3BSD UNIX Operating System* by Leffler et al. [70] discusses process implementation for BSD UNIX. Both of these books provide detailed examinations of how real operating systems are implemented. *Operating Systems: Design and Implementation, 2nd ed.* by Tanenbaum and Woodhull [125] develops a full implementation of a UNIX-like operating system called MINIX. *Solaris Internals: Core Kernel Architecture* by Mauro and McDougall [79] is another detailed book on a UNIX implementation.

There are many books that discuss Linux implementation. For example, *Linux Device Drivers, 2nd ed.* by Rubini and Corbet [102] provides a detailed guide to writing device drivers for Linux. *IA-64 Linux Kernel: Design and Implementation* by Mossberger et al. [83] discusses the implementation of Linux on the Itanium processor.

Most general operating systems books such as *Operating Systems Concepts*, 6th ed. by Silberschatz et al. [107] and *Modern Operating Systems* by Tanenbaum [122] address the process model. Both of these references have case studies on UNIX and on Mach, a well-known microkernel operating system. Comparing these two systems would be useful at this point. *P.S. to Operating Systems* by Dowdy and Lowery [31] focuses on performance issues and analytical models.

Chapter 4

UNIX I/O

UNIX uses a uniform device interface, through file descriptors, that allows the same I/O calls to be used for terminals, disks, tapes, audio and even network communication. This chapter explores the five functions that form the basis for UNIX device-independent I/O. The chapter also examines I/O from multiple sources, blocking I/O with timeouts, inheritance of file descriptors and redirection. The code carefully handles errors and interruption by signals.

Objectives

- Learn the basics of device-independent I/O
- Experiment with `read` and `write`
- Explore ways to monitor multiple descriptors
- Use correct error handling
- Understand inheritance of file descriptors

4.1 Device Terminology

A *peripheral device* is piece of hardware accessed by a computer system. Common peripheral devices include disks, tapes, CD-ROMs, screens, keyboards, printers, mouse devices and network interfaces. User programs perform control and I/O to these devices through system calls to operating system modules called *device drivers*. A device driver hides the details of device operation and protects the device from unauthorized use. Devices of the same type may vary substantially in their operation, so to be usable, even a single-user machine needs device drivers. Some operating systems provide *pseudodevice drivers* to simulate devices such as terminals. Pseudoterminals, for example, simplify the handling of remote login to computer systems over a network or a modem line.

Some operating systems provide specific system calls for each type of supported device, requiring the systems programmer to learn a complex set of calls for device control. UNIX has greatly simplified the programmer device interface by providing uniform access to most devices through five functions—open, close, read, write and ioctl. All devices are represented by files, called *special files*, that are located in the /dev directory. Thus, disk files and other devices are named and accessed in the same way. A *regular file* is just an ordinary data file on disk. A *block special file* represents a device with characteristics similar to a disk. The device driver transfers information from a block special device in blocks or chunks, and usually such devices support the capability of retrieving a block from anywhere on the device. A *character special file* represents a device with characteristics similar to a terminal. The device appears to represent a stream of bytes that must be accessed in sequential order.

4.2 Reading and Writing

UNIX provides sequential access to files and other devices through the read and write functions. The read function attempts to retrieve nbyte bytes from the file or device represented by fildes into the user variable buf. You must actually provide a buffer that is large enough to hold nbyte bytes of data. (A common mistake is to provide an uninitialized pointer, buf, rather than an actual buffer.)

```
SYNOPSIS

   #include <unistd.h>

   ssize_t read(int fildes, void *buf, size_t nbyte);
                                                              POSIX
```

If successful, read returns the number of bytes actually read. If unsuccessful, read returns −1 and sets errno. The following table lists the mandatory errors for read.

errno	cause
ECONNRESET	read attempted on a socket and connection was forcibly closed by its peer
EAGAIN	O_NONBLOCK is set for file descriptor and thread would be delayed
EBADF	fildes is not a valid file descriptor open for reading
EINTR	read was terminated due to receipt of a signal and no data was transferred
EIO	process is a member of a background process group attempting to read from its controlling terminal and either process is ignoring or blocking SIGTTIN or process group is orphaned
ENOTCONN	read attempted on socket that is not connected
EOVERFLOW	the file is a regular file, nbyte is greater than 0, and the starting position exceeds offset maximum
ETIMEDOUT	read attempted on socket and transmission timeout occurred
EWOULDBLOCK	file descriptor is for socket marked O_NONBLOCK and no data is waiting to be received (EAGAIN is alternative)

A read operation for a regular file may return fewer bytes than requested if, for example, it reached end-of-file before completely satisfying the request. A read operation for a regular file returns 0 to indicate end-of-file. When special files corresponding to devices are read, the meaning of a read return value of 0 depends on the implementation and the particular device. A read operation for a pipe returns as soon as the pipe is not empty, so the number of bytes read can be less than the number of bytes requested. (Pipes are a type of communication buffer discussed in Chapter 6.) When reading from a terminal, read returns 0 when the user enters an end-of-file character. On many systems the default end-of-file character is Ctrl-D.

The ssize_t data type is a signed integer data type used for the number of bytes read, or –1 if an error occurs. On some systems, this type may be larger than an int. The size_t is an unsigned integer data type for the number of bytes to read.

■ Example 4.1

The following code segment reads at most 100 bytes into buf from standard input.

```
char buf[100];
ssize_t bytesread;

bytesread = read(STDIN_FILENO, buf, 100);
```

This code does no error checking.

The file descriptor, which represents a file or device that is open, can be thought of as an index into the process file descriptor table. The file descriptor table is in the process user area and provides access to the system information for the associated file or device.

When you execute a program from the shell, the program starts with three open streams associated with file descriptors `STDIN_FILENO`, `STDOUT_FILENO` and `STDERR_FILENO`. `STDIN_FILENO` and `STDOUT_FILENO` are standard input and standard output, respectively. By default, these two streams usually correspond to keyboard input and screen output. Programs should use `STDERR_FILENO`, the standard error device, for error messages and should never close it. In legacy code standard input, standard output and standard error are represented by 0, 1 and 2, respectively. However, you should always use their symbolic names rather than these numeric values. Section 4.6 explains how file descriptors work.

☐ Exercise 4.2

What happens when the following code executes?

```
char *buf;
ssize_t bytesread;

bytesread = read(STDIN_FILENO, buf, 100);
```

Answer:
The code segment, which may compile without error, does not allocate space for `buf`. The result of `read` is unpredictable, but most probably it will generate a memory access violation. If `buf` is an automatic variable stored on the stack, it is not initialized to any particular value. Whatever that memory happens to hold is treated as the address of the buffer for reading.

The `readline` function of Program 4.1 reads bytes, one at a time, into a buffer of fixed size until a newline character (`'\n'`) or an error occurs. The function handles end-of-file, limited buffer size and interruption by a signal. The `readline` function returns the number of bytes read or –1 if an error occurs. A return value of 0 indicates an end-of-file before any characters were read. A return value greater than 0 indicates the number of bytes read. In this case, the buffer contains a string ending in a newline character. A return value of –1 indicates that `errno` has been set and one of the following errors occurred.

- An error occurred on `read`.
- At least one byte was read and an end-of-file occurred before a newline was read.
- `nbytes-1` bytes were read and no newline was found.

Upon successful return of a value greater than 0, the buffer contains a string ending in a newline character. If `readline` reads from a file that does not end with a newline character, it treats the last line read as an error. The `readline` function is available in the restart library, of Appendix B.

Program 4.1 ──────────────────────────────────── `readline.c`

The `readline` *function returns the next line from a file.*

```
#include <errno.h>
#include <unistd.h>

int readline(int fd, char *buf, int nbytes) {
   int numread = 0;
   int returnval;

   while (numread < nbytes - 1) {
      returnval = read(fd, buf + numread, 1);
      if ((returnval == -1) && (errno == EINTR))
         continue;
      if ( (returnval == 0) && (numread == 0) )
         return 0;
      if (returnval == 0)
         break;
      if (returnval == -1)
         return -1;
      numread++;
      if (buf[numread-1] == '\n') {
         buf[numread] = '\0';
         return numread;
      }
   }
   errno = EINVAL;
   return -1;
}
```

Program 4.1 ──────────────────────────────────── `readline.c`

■ **Example 4.3**

The following code segment calls the `readline` function of Program 4.1 to read a line of at most 99 bytes from standard input.

```
int bytesread;
char mybuf[100];

bytesread = readline(STDIN_FILENO, mybuf, sizeof(mybuf));
```

□ **Exercise 4.4**

Under what circumstances does the `readline` function of Program 4.1 return a buffer with no newline character?

Answer:

This can only happen if the return value is 0 or –1. The return value of 0 indicates that nothing was read. The return of –1 indicates some type of error. In either case, the buffer may not contain a string.

The `write` function attempts to output `nbyte` bytes from the user buffer `buf` to the file represented by file descriptor `fildes`.

```
SYNOPSIS

  #include <unistd.h>

  ssize_t write(int fildes, const void *buf, size_t nbyte);
```
                                                                                    POSIX

If successful, `write` returns the number of bytes actually written. If unsuccessful, `write`
returns −1 and sets `errno`. The following table lists the mandatory errors for `write`.

errno	cause
ECONNRESET	write attempted on a socket that is not connected
EAGAIN	O_NONBLOCK is set for file descriptor and thread would be delayed
EBADF	fildes is not a valid file descriptor open for writing
EFBIG	attempt to write a file that exceeds implementation-defined maximum; file is a regular file, nbyte is greater than 0, and starting position exceeds offset maximum
EINTR	write was terminated due to receipt of a signal and no data was transferred
EIO	process is a member of a background process group attempting to write to controlling terminal, TOSTOP is set, process is neither blocking nor ignoring SIGTTOU and process group is orphaned
ENOSPC	no free space remaining on device containing the file
EPIPE	attempt to write to a pipe or FIFO not open for reading or that has only one end open (thread may also get SIGPIPE), or write attempted on socket shut down for writing or not connected (if not connected, also generates SIGPIPE signal)
EWOULDBLOCK	file descriptor is for socket marked O_NONBLOCK and write would block (EAGAIN is alternative)

◻ Exercise 4.5

What can go wrong with the following code segment?

```
#define BLKSIZE 1024
char buf[BLKSIZE];

read(STDIN_FILENO, buf, BLKSIZE);
write(STDOUT_FILENO, buf, BLKSIZE);
```

Answer:

The `write` function assumes that the `read` has filled `buf` with `BLKSIZE` bytes.
However, `read` may fail or may not read the full `BLKSIZE` bytes. In these two
cases, `write` outputs garbage.

❑ Exercise 4.6

What can go wrong with the following code segment to read from standard input and write to standard output?

```
#define BLKSIZE 1024
char buf[BLKSIZE];
ssize_t bytesread;

bytesread = read(STDIN_FILENO, buf, BLKSIZE);
if (bytesread > 0)
   write(STDOUT_FILE, buf, bytesread);
```

Answer:

Although `write` uses `bytesread` rather than `BLKSIZE`, there is no guarantee that `write` actually outputs all of the bytes requested. Furthermore, either `read` or `write` can be interrupted by a signal. In this case, the interrupted call returns a −1 with `errno` set to `EINTR`.

Program 4.2 copies bytes from the file represented by `fromfd` to the file represented by `tofd`. The function restarts `read` and `write` if either is interrupted by a signal. Notice that the `write` statement specifies the buffer by a pointer, `bp`, rather than by a fixed address such as `buf`. If the previous `write` operation did not output all of `buf`, the next `write` operation must start from the end of the previous output. The `copyfile` function returns the number of bytes read and does not indicate whether or not an error occurred.

■ Example 4.7

The following program calls `copyfile` to copy a file from standard input to standard output.

```
#include <stdio.h>
#include <unistd.h>

int copyfile(int fromfd, int tofd);

int main (void) {
   int numbytes;

   numbytes = copyfile(STDIN_FILENO, STDOUT_FILENO);
   fprintf(stderr, "Number of bytes copied: %d\n", numbytes);
   return 0;
}
```

———————————————————————————— **simplecopy.c**

❑ Exercise 4.8

What happens when you run the program of Example 4.7?
Answer:
Standard input is usually set to read one line at a time, so I/O is likely be entered and echoed on line boundaries. The I/O continues until you enter the end-of-file character (often Ctrl-D by default) at the start of a line or you interrupt the

program by entering the interrupt character (often Ctrl-C by default). Use the
`stty -a` command to find the current settings for these characters.

Program 4.2 ── `copyfile1.c`

The `copyfile.c` function copies a file from `fromfd` to `tofd`.

```
#include <errno.h>
#include <unistd.h>
#define BLKSIZE 1024

int copyfile(int fromfd, int tofd) {
   char *bp;
   char buf[BLKSIZE];
   int bytesread, byteswritten;
   int totalbytes = 0;

   for (  ;  ;  ) {
      while (((bytesread = read(fromfd, buf, BLKSIZE)) == -1) &&
            (errno == EINTR)) ;         /* handle interruption by signal */
      if (bytesread <= 0)           /* real error or end-of-file on fromfd */
         break;
      bp = buf;
      while (bytesread > 0) {
         while(((byteswritten = write(tofd, bp, bytesread)) == -1 ) &&
               (errno == EINTR)) ;       /* handle interruption by signal */
         if (byteswritten <= 0)                    /* real error on tofd */
            break;
         totalbytes += byteswritten;
         bytesread -= byteswritten;
         bp += byteswritten;
      }
      if (byteswritten == -1)                      /* real error on tofd */
         break;
   }
   return totalbytes;
}
```

Program 4.2 ── `copyfile1.c`

◻ Exercise 4.9

How would you use the program of Example 4.7 to copy the file `myin.dat` to
`myout.dat`?

Answer:

Use redirection. If the executable of Example 4.7 is called `simplecopy`, the line
would be as follows.

```
simplecopy < myin.dat > myout.dat
```

The problems of restarting `read` and `write` after signals and of writing the entire
amount requested occur in nearly every program using `read` and `write`. Program 4.3
shows a separate `r_read` function that you can use instead of `read` when you want to

restart after a signal. Similarly, Program 4.4 shows a separate r_write function that restarts after a signal and writes the full amount requested. For convenience, a number of functions, including r_read, r_write, copyfile and readline, have been collected in a library called restart.c. The prototypes for these functions are contained in restart.h, and we include this header file when necessary. Appendix B presents the complete restart library implementation.

Program 4.3 ──────────────────────────────── **r_read.c**

The r_read.c *function is similar to* read *except that it restarts itself if interrupted by a signal.*

```
#include <errno.h>
#include <unistd.h>

ssize_t r_read(int fd, void *buf, size_t size) {
   ssize_t retval;

   while (retval = read(fd, buf, size), retval == -1 && errno == EINTR) ;
   return retval;
}
```

Program 4.3 ──────────────────────────────── **r_read.c**

Program 4.4 ──────────────────────────────── **r_write.c**

The r_write.c *function is similar to* write *except that it restarts itself if interrupted by a signal and writes the full amount requested.*

```
#include <errno.h>
#include <unistd.h>

ssize_t r_write(int fd, void *buf, size_t size) {
   char *bufp;
   size_t bytestowrite;
   ssize_t byteswritten;
   size_t totalbytes;

   for (bufp = buf, bytestowrite = size, totalbytes = 0;
        bytestowrite > 0;
        bufp += byteswritten, bytestowrite -= byteswritten) {
      byteswritten = write(fd, bufp, bytestowrite);
      if ((byteswritten) == -1 && (errno != EINTR))
         return -1;
      if (byteswritten == -1)
         byteswritten = 0;
      totalbytes += byteswritten;
   }
   return totalbytes;
}
```

Program 4.4 ──────────────────────────────── **r_write.c**

The functions `r_read` and `r_write` can greatly simplify programs that need to read and write while handling signals.

Program 4.5 shows the `readwrite` function that reads bytes from one file descriptor and writes all of the bytes read to another one. It uses a buffer of size `PIPE_BUF` to transfer at most `PIPE_BUF` bytes. This size is useful for writing to pipes since a write to a pipe of `PIPE_BUF` bytes or less is atomic. Program 4.6 shows a version of `copyfile` that uses the `readwrite` function. Compare this with Program 4.2.

Program 4.5 ──────────────────────────────────── **readwrite.c**

A program that reads from one file descriptor and writes all the bytes read to another file descriptor.

```c
#include <limits.h>
#include "restart.h"
#define BLKSIZE PIPE_BUF

int readwrite(int fromfd, int tofd) {
   char buf[BLKSIZE];
   int bytesread;

   if ((bytesread = r_read(fromfd, buf, BLKSIZE)) == -1)
      return -1;
   if (bytesread == 0)
      return 0;
   if (r_write(tofd, buf, bytesread) == -1)
      return -1;
   return bytesread;
}
```

Program 4.5 ──────────────────────────────────── **readwrite.c**

Program 4.6 ──────────────────────────────────── **copyfile.c**

A simplified implementation of `copyfile` that uses `r_read` and `r_write`.

```c
#include <unistd.h>
#include "restart.h"
#define BLKSIZE 1024

int copyfile(int fromfd, int tofd) {
   char buf[BLKSIZE];
   int bytesread, byteswritten;
   int totalbytes = 0;

   for ( ; ; ) {
      if ((bytesread = r_read(fromfd, buf, BLKSIZE)) <= 0)
         break;
      if ((byteswritten = r_write(tofd, buf, bytesread)) == -1)
         break;
      totalbytes += byteswritten;
   }
   return totalbytes;
}
```

Program 4.6 ──────────────────────────────────── **copyfile.c**

The r_write function writes all the bytes requested and restarts the write if fewer bytes are written. The r_read only restarts if interrupted by a signal and often reads fewer bytes than requested. The readblock function is a version of read that continues reading until the requested number of bytes is read or an error occurs. Program 4.7 shows an implementation of readblock. The readblock function is part of the restart library. It is especially useful for reading structures.

Program 4.7 ──────────────────────────────── **readblock.c**

A function that reads a specific number of bytes.

```c
#include <errno.h>
#include <unistd.h>

ssize_t readblock(int fd, void *buf, size_t size) {
   char *bufp;
   size_t bytestoread;
   ssize_t bytesread;
   size_t totalbytes;

   for (bufp = buf, bytestoread = size, totalbytes = 0;
        bytestoread > 0;
        bufp += bytesread, bytestoread -= bytesread) {
      bytesread = read(fd, bufp, bytestoread);
      if ((bytesread == 0) && (totalbytes == 0))
         return 0;
      if (bytesread == 0) {
         errno = EINVAL;
         return -1;
      }
      if ((bytesread) == -1 && (errno != EINTR))
         return -1;
      if (bytesread == -1)
         bytesread = 0;
      totalbytes += bytesread;
   }
   return totalbytes;
}
```

Program 4.7 ──────────────────────────────── **readblock.c**

There are only three possibilities for the return value of readblock. The readblock function returns 0 if an end-of-file occurs before any bytes are read. This happens if the first call to read returns 0. If readblock is successful, it returns size, signifying that the requested number of bytes was successfully read. Otherwise, readblock returns −1 and sets errno. If readblock reaches the end-of-file after some, but not all, of the needed bytes have been read, readblock returns −1 and sets errno to EINVAL.

■ **Example 4.10**

The following code segment can be used to read a pair of integers from an open file descriptor.

```
        struct {
            int x;
            int y;
        } point;
        if (readblock(fd, &point, sizeof(point)) <= 0)
            fprintf(stderr, "Cannot read a point.\n");
```

Program 4.8 combines `readblock` with `r_write` to read a fixed number of bytes from one open file descriptor and write them to another open file descriptor.

Program 4.8 ───────────────────────────────── **readwriteblock.c**
   A program that copies a fixed number of bytes from one file descriptor to another.

```
#include "restart.h"

int readwriteblock(int fromfd, int tofd, char *buf, int size) {
    int bytesread;

    bytesread = readblock(fromfd, buf, size);
    if (bytesread != size)                         /* can only be 0 or -1 */
        return bytesread;
    return r_write(tofd, buf, size);
}
```

Program 4.8 ───────────────────────────────── **readwriteblock.c**

4.3 Opening and Closing Files

The `open` function associates a file descriptor (the handle used in the program) with a file or physical device. The `path` parameter of `open` points to the pathname of the file or device, and the `oflag` parameter specifies status flags and access modes for the opened file. You must include a third parameter to specify access permissions if you are creating a file.

SYNOPSIS

```
    #include <fcntl.h>
    #include <sys/stat.h>

    int open(const char *path, int  oflag, ...);
```
                                                                          POSIX

If successful, `open` returns a nonnegative integer representing the open file descriptor. If unsuccessful, `open` returns −1 and sets `errno`. The following table lists the mandatory errors for `open`.

errno	cause
EACCES	search permission on component of path prefix denied, or file exists and permissions specified by oflag denied, or file does not exist and write permission on parent directory denied, or O_TRUNC specified and write permission denied
EEXIST	O_CREAT and OEXCL are set and named file already exists
EINTR	signal was caught during open
EISDIR	named file is directory and oflag includes O_WRONLY or O_RDWR
ELOOP	a loop exists in resolution of path
EMFILE	OPEN_MAX file descriptors currently open in calling process
ENAMETOOLONG	the length of path exceeds PATH_MAX, or a pathname component is longer than NAME_MAX
ENFILE	maximum allowable number of files currently open in system
ENOENT	O_CREAT not set and name file does not exist, or O_CREAT is set and either path prefix does not exist or or path is an empty string
ENOSPC	directory or file system for new file cannot be expanded, the file does not exist and O_CREAT is specified
ENOTDIR	a component of the path prefix is not a directory
ENXIO	O_NONBLOCK is set, the named file is a FIFO, O_WRONLY is set, no process has file open for reading; file is a special file and device associated with file does not exist
EOVERFLOW	named file is a regular file and size cannot be represented by an object of type off_t
EROFS	the named file resides on a read-only file system and one of O_WRONLY, O_RDWR, O_CREAT (if the file does not exist), or O_TRUNC is set in oflag

Construct the oflag argument by taking the bitwise OR (|) of the desired combination of the access mode and the additional flags. The POSIX values for the access mode flags are O_RDONLY, O_WRONLY and O_RDWR. You must specify exactly one of these designating read-only, write-only or read-write access, respectively.

The additional flags include O_APPEND, O_CREAT, O_EXCL, O_NOCTTY, O_NONBLOCK and O_TRUNC. The O_APPEND flag causes the file offset to be moved to the end of the file before a write, allowing you to add to an existing file. In contrast, O_TRUNC truncates the length of a regular file opened for writing to 0. The O_CREAT flag causes a file to be created if it doesn't already exist. If you include the O_CREAT flag, you must also pass a third argument to open to designate the permissions. If you want to avoid writing over an existing file, use the combination O_CREAT | O_EXCL. This combination returns an error if the file already exists. The O_NOCTTY flag prevents an opened device from becoming a controlling terminal. Controlling terminals are discussed in Section 11.5. The O_NONBLOCK flag controls whether the open returns immediately or blocks until the device is ready. Section 4.8 discusses how the O_NONBLOCK flag affects the behavior of read and write. Certain POSIX extensions specify additional flags. You can find the flags in fcntl.h.

■ Example 4.11

The following code segment opens the file /home/ann/my.dat for reading.

```
int myfd;
myfd = open("/home/ann/my.dat", O_RDONLY);
```

This code does no error checking.

☐ Exercise 4.12

How can the call to open of Example 4.11 fail?

Answer:

The open function returns −1 if the file doesn't exist, the open call was interrupted by a signal or the process doesn't have the appropriate access permissions. If your code uses myfd for a subsequent read or write operation, the operation fails.

■ Example 4.13

The following code segment restarts open after a signal occurs.

```
int myfd;
while((myfd = open("/home/ann/my.dat", O_RDONLY)) == -1 &&
      errno == EINTR) ;
if (myfd == -1)                       /* it was a real error, not a signal */
   perror("Failed to open the file");
else                                                      /* continue on */
```

☐ Exercise 4.14

How would you modify Example 4.13 to open /home/ann/my.dat for non-blocking read?

Answer:

You would OR the O_RDONLY and the O_NONBLOCK flags.

```
myfd = open("/home/ann/my.dat", O_RDONLY | O_NONBLOCK);
```

Each file has three classes associated with it: a user (or owner), a group and everybody else (others). The possible permissions or privileges are read(r), write(w) and execute(x). These privileges are specified separately for the user, the group and others. When you open a file with the O_CREAT flag, you must specify the permissions as the third argument to open in a mask of type mode_t.

Historically, the file permissions were laid out in a mask of bits with 1's in designated bit positions of the mask, signifying that a class had the corresponding privilege. Figure 4.1 shows an example of a typical layout of such a permission mask. *Although numerically coded permission masks frequently appear in legacy code, you should avoid using numerical values in your programs.*

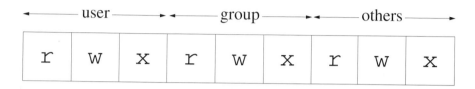

Figure 4.1: Historical layout of the permissions mask.

POSIX defines symbolic names for masks corresponding to the permission bits so that you can specify file permissions independently of the implementation. These names are defined in `sys/stat.h`. Table 4.1 lists the symbolic names and their meanings. To form the permission mask, bitwise OR the symbols corresponding to the desired permissions.

symbol	meaning
S_IRUSR	read by owner
S_IWUSR	write by owner
S_IXUSR	execute by owner
S_IRWXU	read, write, execute by owner
S_IRGRP	read by group
S_IWGRP	write by group
S_IXGRP	execute by group
S_IRWXG	read, write, execute by group
S_IROTH	read by others
S_IWOTH	write by others
S_IXOTH	execute by others
S_IRWXO	read, write, execute by others
S_ISUID	set user ID on execution
S_ISGID	set group ID on execution

Table 4.1: POSIX symbolic names for file permissions.

■ Example 4.15

The following code segment creates a file, `info.dat`, in the current directory. If the `info.dat` file already exists, it is overwritten. The new file can be read or written by the user and only read by everyone else.

```
int fd;
mode_t fdmode = (S_IRUSR | S_IWUSR | S_IRGRP | S_IROTH);

if ((fd = open("info.dat", O_RDWR | O_CREAT, fdmode)) == -1)
   perror("Failed to open info.dat");
```

Program 4.9 copies a source file to a destination file. Both filenames are passed as command-line arguments. Because the `open` function for the destination file has `O_CREAT | O_EXCL`, the file copy fails if that file already exists.

Program 4.9 ———————————————————————— **copyfilemain.c**

A program to copy a file.

```
#include <fcntl.h>
#include <stdio.h>
#include <unistd.h>
#include <sys/stat.h>
#include "restart.h"

#define READ_FLAGS O_RDONLY
#define WRITE_FLAGS (O_WRONLY | O_CREAT | O_EXCL)
#define WRITE_PERMS (S_IRUSR | S_IWUSR)

int main(int argc, char *argv[]) {
   int bytes;
   int fromfd, tofd;

   if (argc != 3) {
      fprintf(stderr, "Usage: %s from_file to_file\n", argv[0]);
      return 1;
   }

   if ((fromfd = open(argv[1], READ_FLAGS)) == -1) {
      perror("Failed to open input file");
      return 1;
   }

   if ((tofd = open(argv[2], WRITE_FLAGS, WRITE_PERMS)) == -1) {
      perror("Failed to create output file");
      return 1;
   }

   bytes = copyfile(fromfd, tofd);
   printf("%d bytes copied from %s to %s\n", bytes, argv[1], argv[2]);
   return 0;                                    /* the return closes the files */
}
```

Program 4.9 ———————————————————————— **copyfilemain.c**

Program 4.9 returns immediately after performing the copy and does not explicitly close the file. The return from main causes the necessary cleanup to release the resources associated with open files. In general, however, you should be careful to release open file descriptors by calling close.

The close function has a single parameter, fildes, representing the open file whose resources are to be released.

```
SYNOPSIS

   #include <unistd.h>

   int close(int fildes);
                                                                    POSIX
```

If successful, close returns 0. If unsuccessful, close returns −1 and sets errno. The following table lists the mandatory errors for close.

errno	cause
EBADF	fildes is not a valid file descriptor
EINTR	the close function was interrupted by a signal

Program 4.10 shows an r_close function that restarts itself after interruption by a signal. Its prototype is in the header file restart.h.

Program 4.10 ———————————————————— **r_close.c**

The r_close.c function is similar to close except that it restarts itself if interrupted by a signal.

```
#include <errno.h>
#include <unistd.h>

int r_close(int fd) {
   int retval;

   while (retval = close(fd), retval == -1 && errno == EINTR) ;
   return retval;
}
```

Program 4.10 ———————————————————— **r_close.c**

4.4 The select Function

The handling of I/O from multiple sources is an important problem that arises in many different forms. For example, a program may want to overlap terminal I/O with reading input from a disk or with printing. Another example occurs when a program expects input from two different sources, but it doesn't know which input will be available first. If the program tries to read from source A, and in fact, input was only available from source B, the program blocks. To solve this problem, we need to block until input from *either* source becomes available. Blocking until at least one member of a set of conditions becomes true is called *OR synchronization*. The condition for the case described is "input available" on a descriptor.

One method of monitoring multiple file descriptors is to use a separate process for each one. Program 4.11 takes two command-line arguments, the names of two files to monitor. The parent process opens both files before creating the child process. The parent monitors the first file descriptor, and the child monitors the second. Each process echoes the contents of its file to standard output. If two named pipes are monitored, output appears as input becomes available.

Program 4.11 ———————————————————————— `monitorfork.c`

A program that monitors two files by forking a child process.

```c
#include <errno.h>
#include <fcntl.h>
#include <stdio.h>
#include <string.h>
#include <unistd.h>
#include "restart.h"

int main(int argc, char *argv[]) {
    int bytesread;
    int childpid;
    int fd, fd1, fd2;

    if (argc != 3) {
        fprintf(stderr, "Usage: %s file1 file2\n", argv[0]);
        return 1;
    }
    if ((fd1 = open(argv[1], O_RDONLY)) == -1) {
        fprintf(stderr, "Failed to open file %s:%s\n", argv[1], strerror(errno));
        return 1;
    }
    if ((fd2 = open(argv[2], O_RDONLY)) == -1) {
        fprintf(stderr, "Failed to open file %s:%s\n", argv[2], strerror(errno));
        return 1;
    }
    if ((childpid = fork()) == -1) {
        perror("Failed to create child process");
        return 1;
    }
    if (childpid > 0)                                        /* parent code */
        fd = fd1;
    else
        fd = fd2;
    bytesread = copyfile(fd, STDOUT_FILENO);
    fprintf(stderr, "Bytes read: %d\n", bytesread);
    return 0;
}
```

Program 4.11 ———————————————————————— `monitorfork.c`

While using separate processes to monitor two file descriptors can be useful, the two processes have separate address spaces and so it is difficult for them to interact.

◻ Exercise 4.16

How would you modify Program 4.11 so that it prints the total number of bytes read from the two files?

Answer:

Set up some form of interprocess communication before creating the child. For example, the parent process could create a pipe and the child could send its byte count to the pipe when it has finished. After the parent has processed its file, the parent could wait for the child and read the byte count from the pipe.

The `select` call provides a method of monitoring file descriptors from a single process. It can monitor for three possible conditions—a read can be done without blocking, a write can be done without blocking, or a file descriptor has error conditions pending. Older versions of UNIX defined the `select` function in `sys/time.h`, but the POSIX standard now uses `sys/select.h`.

The `nfds` parameter of `select` gives the range of file descriptors to be monitored. The value of `nfds` must be at least one greater than the largest file descriptor to be checked. The `readfds` parameter specifies the set of descriptors to be monitored for reading. Similarly, `writefds` specifies the set of descriptors to be monitored for writing, and `errorfds` specifies the file descriptors to be monitored for error conditions. The descriptor sets are of type `fd_set`. Any of these parameters may be NULL, in which case `select` does not monitor the descriptor for the corresponding event. The last parameter is a timeout value that forces a return from `select` after a certain period of time has elapsed, even if no descriptors are ready. When `timeout` is NULL, `select` may block indefinitely.

SYNOPSIS

```
#include <sys/select.h>

int select(int nfds, fd_set *restrict readfds,
          fd_set *restrict writefds, fd_set *restrict errorfds,
          struct timeval *restrict timeout);

void FD_CLR(int fd, fd_set *fdset);
int FD_ISSET(int fd, fd_set *fdset);
void FD_SET(int fd, fd_set *fdset);
void FD_ZERO(fd_set *fdset);
```

POSIX

On successful return, `select` clears all the descriptors in each of `readfds`, `writefds` and `errorfds` except those descriptors that are ready. If successful, the `select` function returns the number of file descriptors that are ready. If unsuccessful, `select` returns −1 and sets `errno`. The following table lists the mandatory errors for `select`.

errno	cause
EBADF	one or more file descriptor sets specified an invalid file descriptor
EINTR	the select was interrupted by a signal before
	timeout or selected event occurred
EINVAL	an invalid timeout interval was specified, or
	nfds is less than 0 or greater than FD_SETSIZE

Historically, systems implemented the descriptor set as an integer bit mask, but that implementation does not work for more than 32 file descriptors on most systems. The descriptor sets are now usually represented by bit fields in arrays of integers. Use the macros FD_SET, FD_CLR, FD_ISSET and FD_ZERO to manipulate the descriptor sets in an implementation-independent way as demonstrated in Program 4.12.

The FD_SET macro sets the bit in *fdset corresponding to the fd file descriptor, and the FD_CLR macro clears the corresponding bit. The FD_ZERO macro clears all the bits in *fdset. Use these three macros to set up descriptor masks before calling select. Use the FD_ISSET macro after select returns, to test whether the bit corresponding to the file descriptor fd is set in the mask.

Program 4.12 ────────────────────────────── **whichisready.c**

A function that blocks until one of two file descriptors is ready.

```
#include <errno.h>
#include <string.h>
#include <sys/select.h>

int whichisready(int fd1, int fd2) {
   int maxfd;
   int nfds;
   fd_set readset;

   if ((fd1 < 0) || (fd1 >= FD_SETSIZE) ||
       (fd2 < 0) || (fd2 >= FD_SETSIZE)) {
      errno = EINVAL;
      return -1;
   }
   maxfd = (fd1 > fd2) ? fd1 : fd2;
   FD_ZERO(&readset);
   FD_SET(fd1, &readset);
   FD_SET(fd2, &readset);
   nfds = select(maxfd+1, &readset, NULL, NULL, NULL);
   if (nfds == -1)
      return -1;
   if (FD_ISSET(fd1, &readset))
      return fd1;
   if (FD_ISSET(fd2, &readset))
      return fd2;
   errno = EINVAL;
   return -1;
}
```

Program 4.12 ────────────────────────────── **whichisready.c**

The function `whichisready` blocks until at least one of the two file descriptors passed as parameters is ready for reading and returns that file descriptor. If both are ready, it returns the first file descriptor. If unsuccessful, `whichisready` returns −1 and sets `errno`.

Program 4.13 ———————————————————— **copy2files.c**

A function that uses `select` to do two concurrent file copies.

```c
#include <errno.h>
#include <stdio.h>
#include <string.h>
#include <sys/time.h>
#include "restart.h"

int copy2files(int fromfd1, int tofd1, int fromfd2, int totd2) {
   int bytesread;
   int maxfd;
   int num;
   fd_set readset;
   int totalbytes = 0;

   if ((fromfd1 < 0) || (fromfd1 >= FD_SETSIZE) ||
       (tofd1 < 0) || (tofd1 >= FD_SETSIZE) ||
       (fromfd2 < 0) || (fromfd2 >= FD_SETSIZE) ||
       (tofd2 < 0) || (tofd2 >= FD_SETSIZE))
      return 0;
   maxfd = fromfd1;                      /* find the biggest fd for select */
   if (fromfd2 > maxfd)
      maxfd = fromfd2;

   for ( ; ; ) {
      FD_ZERO(&readset);
      FD_SET(fromfd1, &readset);
      FD_SET(fromfd2, &readset);
      if (((num = select(maxfd+1, &readset, NULL, NULL, NULL)) == -1) &&
          (errno == EINTR))
         continue;
      if (num == -1)
         return totalbytes;
      if (FD_ISSET(fromfd1, &readset)) {
         bytesread = readwrite(fromfd1, tofd1);
         if (bytesread <= 0)
            break;
         totalbytes += bytesread;
      }
      if (FD_ISSET(fromfd2, &readset)) {
         bytesread = readwrite(fromfd2, tofd2);
         if (bytesread <= 0)
            break;
         totalbytes += bytesread;
      }
   }
   return totalbytes;
}
```

Program 4.13 ———————————————————— **copy2files.c**

The `whichisready` function of Program 4.12 is problematic because it always chooses `fd1` if both `fd1` and `fd2` are ready. The `copy2files` function copies bytes from `fromfd1` to `tofd1` and from `fromfd2` to `tofd2` without making any assumptions about the order in which the bytes become available in the two directions. The function returns if either copy encounters an error or end-of-file.

The `copy2files` function of Program 4.13 can be generalized to monitor multiple file descriptors for input. Such a problem might be encountered by a command processor that was monitoring requests from different terminals. The program cannot predict which source will produce the next input, so it must use a method such as `select`. In addition, the set of monitored descriptors is dynamic—the program must remove a source from the monitoring set if an error condition arises on that source's descriptor.

The `monitorselect` function in Program 4.14 monitors an array of open file descriptors `fd`. When input is available on file descriptor `fd[i]`, the program reads information from `fd[i]` and calls `docommand`. The `monitorselect` function has two parameters: an array of open file descriptors and the number of file descriptors in the array. The function restarts the `select` or `read` if either is interrupted by a signal. When `read` encounters other types of errors or an end-of-file, `monitorselect` closes the corresponding descriptor and removes it from the monitoring set. The `monitorselect` function returns when all descriptors have indicated an error or end-of-file.

The `waitfdtimed` function in Program 4.15 takes two parameters: a file descriptor and an ending time. It uses `gettimeout` to calculate the timeout interval from the end time and the current time obtained by a call to `gettimeofday`. (See Section 9.1.3.) If `select` returns prematurely because of a signal, `waitfdtimed` recalculates the timeout and calls `select` again. The standard does not say anything about the value of the `timeout` parameter or the `fd_set` parameters of `select` when it is interrupted by a signal, so we reset them inside the `while` loop.

You can use the `select` timeout feature to implement a timed read operation, as shown in Program 4.16. The `readtimed` function behaves like `read` except that it takes an additional parameter, `seconds`, specifying a timeout in seconds. The `readtimed` function returns −1 with `errno` set to `ETIME` if no input is available in the next `seconds` interval. If interrupted by a signal, `readtimed` restarts with the remaining time. Most of the complication comes from the need to restart `select` with the remaining time when `select` is interrupted by a signal. The `select` function does not provide a direct way of determining the time remaining in this case. The `readtimed` function in Program 4.16 sets the end time for the timeout by calling `add2currenttime` in Program 4.15. It uses this value when calling `waitfdtimed` from Program 4.15 to wait until the file descriptor can be read or the time given has occurred.

Program 4.14 ————————————————— **monitorselect.c**

A function to monitor file descriptors using select.

```c
#include <errno.h>
#include <string.h>
#include <unistd.h>
#include <sys/select.h>
#include <sys/types.h>
#include "restart.h"
#define BUFSIZE 1024
void docommand(char *, int);

void monitorselect(int fd[], int numfds) {
    char buf[BUFSIZE];
    int bytesread;
    int i;
    int maxfd;
    int numnow, numready;
    fd_set readset;

    maxfd = 0;                      /* set up the range of descriptors to monitor */
    for (i = 0; i < numfds; i++) {
        if ((fd[i] < 0) || (fd[i] >= FD_SETSIZE))
            return;
        if (fd[i] >= maxfd)
            maxfd = fd[i] + 1;
    }
    numnow = numfds;
    while (numnow > 0) {            /* continue monitoring until all are done */
        FD_ZERO(&readset);                  /* set up the file descriptor mask */
        for (i = 0; i < numfds; i++)
            if (fd[i] >= 0)
                FD_SET(fd[i], &readset);
        numready = select(maxfd, &readset, NULL, NULL, NULL);  /* which ready? */
        if ((numready == -1) && (errno == EINTR))     /* interrupted by signal */
            continue;
        else if (numready == -1)                          /* real select error */
            break;
        for (i = 0; (i < numfds) && (numready > 0); i++) { /* read and process */
            if (fd[i] == -1)                           /* this descriptor is done */
                continue;
            if (FD_ISSET(fd[i], &readset)) {        /* this descriptor is ready */
                bytesread = r_read(fd[i], buf, BUFSIZE);
                numready--;
                if (bytesread > 0)
                    docommand(buf, bytesread);
                else {           /* error occurred on this descriptor, close it */
                    r_close(fd[i]);
                    fd[i] = -1;
                    numnow--;
                }
            }
        }
    }
    for (i = 0; i < numfds; i++)
        if (fd[i] >= 0)
            r_close(fd[i]);
}
```

Program 4.14 ————————————————— **monitorselect.c**

A function that waits for a given time for input to be available from an open file descriptor.

```
#include <errno.h>
#include <string.h>
#include <sys/select.h>
#include <sys/time.h>
#include "restart.h"
#define MILLION 1000000L
#define D_MILLION 1000000.0

static int gettimeout(struct timeval end,
                                 struct timeval *timeoutp) {
   gettimeofday(timeoutp, NULL);
   timeoutp->tv_sec = end.tv_sec - timeoutp->tv_sec;
   timeoutp->tv_usec = end.tv_usec - timeoutp->tv_usec;
   if (timeoutp->tv_usec >= MILLION) {
      timeoutp->tv_sec++;
      timeoutp->tv_usec -= MILLION;
   }
   if (timeoutp->tv_usec < 0) {
      timeoutp->tv_sec--;
      timeoutp->tv_usec += MILLION;
   }
   if ((timeoutp->tv_sec < 0) ||
       ((timeoutp->tv_sec == 0) && (timeoutp->tv_usec == 0))) {
      errno = ETIME;
      return -1;
   }
   return 0;
}

struct timeval add2currenttime(double seconds) {
   struct timeval newtime;

   gettimeofday(&newtime, NULL);
   newtime.tv_sec += (int)seconds;
   newtime.tv_usec += (int)((seconds - (int)seconds)*D_MILLION + 0.5);
   if (newtime.tv_usec >= MILLION) {
      newtime.tv_sec++;
      newtime.tv_usec -= MILLION;
   }
   return newtime;
}

int waitfdtimed(int fd, struct timeval end) {
   fd_set readset;
   int retval;
   struct timeval timeout;

   if ((fd < 0) || (fd >= FD_SETSIZE)) {
      errno = EINVAL;
      return -1;
   }
   FD_ZERO(&readset);
   FD_SET(fd, &readset);
   if (gettimeout(end, &timeout) == -1)
```

```
        return -1;
    while (((retval = select(fd + 1, &readset, NULL, NULL, &timeout)) == -1)
            && (errno == EINTR)) {
        if (gettimeout(end, &timeout) == -1)
            return -1;
        FD_ZERO(&readset);
        FD_SET(fd, &readset);
    }
    if (retval == 0) {
        errno = ETIME;
        return -1;
    }
    if (retval == -1)
        return -1;
    return 0;
}
```
─ **Program 4.15** ──────────────────────────────────── **waitfdtimed.c** ─

┌─ **Program 4.16** ──────────────────────────────────── **readtimed.c** ─
                A function do a timed read from an open file descriptor.

```
#include <sys/time.h>
#include "restart.h"

ssize_t readtimed(int fd, void *buf, size_t nbyte, double seconds) {
    struct timeval timedone;

    timedone = add2currenttime(seconds);
    if (waitfdtimed(fd, timedone) == -1)
        return (ssize_t)(-1);
    return r_read(fd, buf, nbyte);
}
```
─ **Program 4.16** ──────────────────────────────────── **readtimed.c** ─

☐ Exercise 4.17

Why is it necessary to test whether `newtime.tv_usec` is greater than or equal to a million when it is set from the fractional part of `seconds`? What are the consequences of having that value equal to one million?

Answer:

Since the value is rounded to the nearest microsecond, a fraction such as 0.999999999 might round to one million when multiplied by `MILLION`. The action of functions that use `struct timeval` values are not specified when the `tv_usec` field is not strictly less than one million.

☐ Exercise 4.18

One way to simplify Program 4.15 is to just restart the `select` with the same timeout whenever it is interrupted by a signal. What is wrong with this?

Answer:
If your program receives signals regularly and the time between signals is smaller than the timeout interval, `waitfdtimed` never times out.

The 2000 version of POSIX introduced a new version of `select` called `pselect`. The `pselect` function is identical to the `select` function, but it uses a more precise timeout structure, `struct timespec`, and allows for the blocking or unblocking of signals while it is waiting for I/O to be available. The `struct timespec` structure is discussed in Section 9.1.4. However, at the time of writing, (March 2003), none of the our test operating systems supported `pselect`.

4.5 The `poll` Function

The `poll` function is similar to `select`, but it organizes the information by file descriptor rather than by type of condition. That is, the possible events for one file descriptor are stored in a `struct pollfd`. In contrast, `select` organizes information by the type of event and has separate descriptor masks for read, write and error conditions. The `poll` function is part of the POSIX:XSI Extension and has its origins in UNIX System V.

The `poll` function takes three parameters: `fds`, `nfds` and `timeout`. The `fds` is an array of `struct pollfd`, representing the monitoring information for the file descriptors. The `nfds` parameter gives the number of descriptors to be monitored. The `timeout` value is the time in milliseconds that the `poll` should wait without receiving an event before returning. If the `timeout` value is −1, `poll` never times out. If integers are 32 bits, the maximum timeout period is about 30 minutes.

SYNOPSIS

```
#include <poll.h>

int poll(struct pollfd fds[], nfds_t nfds, int timeout);
```
                                                                            POSIX:XSI

The `poll` function returns 0 if it times out. If successful, `poll` returns the number of descriptors that have events. If unsuccessful, `poll` returns −1 and sets `errno`. The following table lists the mandatory errors for `poll`.

errno	cause
EAGAIN	allocation of internal data structures failed, but a subsequent request may succeed
EINTR	a signal was caught during `poll`
EINVAL	`nfds` is greater than OPEN_MAX

The `struct pollfd` structure includes the following members.

```
int fd;          /* file descriptor */
short events;    /* requested events */
short revents;   /* returned events */
```

The `fd` is the file descriptor number, and the `events` and `revents` are constructed by taking the logical OR of flags representing the various events listed in Table 4.2. Set `events` to contain the events to monitor; `poll` fills in the `revents` with the events that have occurred. The `poll` function sets the POLLHUP, POLLERR and POLLNVAL flags in `revents` to reflect the existence of the associated conditions. You do not need to set the corresponding bits in `events` for these. If `fd` is less than zero, the `events` field is ignored and `revents` is set to zero. The standard does not specify how end-of-file is to be handled. End-of-file can either be communicated by an `revents` flag of POLLHUP or a normal read of 0 bytes. It is possible for POLLHUP to be set even if POLLIN or POLLRDNORM indicates that there is still data to read. Therefore, normal reading should be handled before error checking.

event flag	meaning
POLLIN	read other than high priority data without blocking
POLLRDNORM	read normal data without blocking
POLLRDBAND	read priority data without blocking
POLLPRI	read high-priority data without blocking
POLLOUT	write normal data without blocking
POLLWRNORM	same as POLLOUT
POLLERR	error occurred on the descriptor
POLLHUP	device has been disconnected
POLLNVAL	file descriptor invalid

Table 4.2: Values of the event flags for the `poll` function.

Program 4.17 implements a function to process commands from multiple file descriptors by using the `poll` function. Compare the implementation with that of Program 4.14. The `select` call modifies the file descriptor sets that are passed to it, and the program must reset these descriptor sets each time it calls `select`. The `poll` function uses separate variables for input and return values, so it is not necessary to reset the list of monitored descriptors after each call to `poll`. The `poll` function has a number of advantages. The masks do not need to be reset after each call. Unlike `select`, the `poll` function treats errors as events that cause `poll` to return. The `timeout` parameter is easier to use, although its range is limited. Finally, `poll` does not need a `max_fd` argument.

Program 4.17 ────────────────────────────────────── `monitorpoll.c`

A function to monitor an array of file descriptors by using `poll`.

```c
#include <errno.h>
#include <poll.h>
#include <stdlib.h>
#include <stropts.h>
#include <unistd.h>
#include "restart.h"
#define BUFSIZE 1024

void docommand(char *, int);

void monitorpoll(int fd[], int numfds)  {
   char buf[BUFSIZE];
   int bytesread;
   int i;
   int numnow = 0;
   int numready;
   struct pollfd *pollfd;

   for (i=0; i< numfds; i++)            /* initialize the polling structure */
      if (fd[i] >= 0)
         numnow++;
   if ((pollfd = (void *)calloc(numfds, sizeof(struct pollfd))) == NULL)
      return;
   for (i = 0; i < numfds; i++) {
      (pollfd + i)->fd = *(fd + i);
      (pollfd + i)->events = POLLRDNORM;
   }
   while (numnow > 0) {          /* Continue monitoring until descriptors done */
      numready = poll(pollfd, numfds, -1);
      if ((numready == -1) && (errno == EINTR))
         continue;                   /* poll interrupted by a signal, try again */
      else if (numready == -1)            /* real poll error, can't continue */
         break;
      for (i = 0; i < numfds && numready > 0; i++)  {
         if ((pollfd + i)->revents) {
            if ((pollfd + i)->revents & (POLLRDNORM | POLLIN) ) {
               bytesread = r_read(fd[i], buf, BUFSIZE);
               numready--;
               if (bytesread > 0)
                  docommand(buf, bytesread);
               else
                  bytesread = -1;                                 /* end of file */
            } else if ((pollfd + i)->revents & (POLLERR | POLLHUP))
               bytesread = -1;
            else                   /* descriptor not involved in this round */
               bytesread = 0;
            if (bytesread == -1) {     /* error occurred, remove descriptor */
               r_close(fd[i]);
               (pollfd + i)->fd = -1;
               numnow--;
            }
         }
      }
   }
   for (i = 0; i < numfds; i++)
      r_close(fd[i]);
   free(pollfd);
}
```

Program 4.17 ────────────────────────────────────── `monitorpoll.c`

4.6 File Representation

Files are designated within C programs either by file pointers or by file descriptors. The standard I/O library functions for ISO C (fopen, fscanf, fprintf, fread, fwrite, fclose and so on) use file pointers. The UNIX I/O functions (open, read, write, close and ioctl) use file descriptors. File pointers and file descriptors provide logical designations called *handles* for performing device-independent input and output. The symbolic names for the file pointers that represent standard input, standard output and standard error are stdin, stdout and stderr, respectively. These symbolic names are defined in stdio.h. The symbolic names for the file descriptors that represent standard input, standard output and standard error are STDIN_FILENO, STDOUT_FILENO and STDERR_FILENO, respectively. These symbolic names are defined in unistd.h.

◻ Exercise 4.19

Explain the difference between a library function and a system call.

Answer:

The POSIX standard does not make a distinction between library functions and system calls. Traditionally, a library function is an ordinary function that is placed in a collection of functions called a library, usually because it is useful, widely used or part of a specification, such as C. A system call is a request to the operating system for service. It involves a trap to the operating system and often a context switch. System calls are associated with particular operating systems. Many library functions such as read and write are, in fact, jackets for system calls. That is, they reformat the arguments in the appropriate system-dependent form and then call the underlying system call to perform the actual operation.

Although the implementation details differ, versions of UNIX follow a similar implementation model for handling file descriptors and file pointers within a process. The remainder of this section provides a schematic model of how file descriptors (UNIX I/O) and file pointers (ISO C I/O) work. We use this model to explain redirection (Section 4.7) and inheritance (Section 4.6.3, Section 6.2 and Chapter 7).

4.6.1 File descriptors

The open function associates a file or physical device with the logical handle used in the program. The file or physical device is specified by a character string (e.g., /home/johns/my.dat or /dev/tty). The handle is an integer that can be thought of as an index into a *file descriptor table* that is specific to a process. It contains an entry for each open file in the process. The file descriptor table is part of the process user area, but the program cannot access it except through functions using the file descriptor.

◾ Example 4.20

Figure 4.2 shows a schematic of the file descriptor table after a program executes the following.

```
myfd = open("/home/ann/my.dat", O_RDONLY);
```

The `open` function creates an entry in the file descriptor table that points to an entry in the system file table. The `open` function returns the value 3, specifying that the file descriptor entry is in position three of the process file descriptor table.

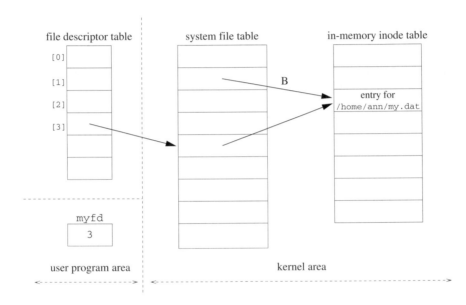

Figure 4.2: Schematic diagram of the relationship between the file descriptor table, the system file table and the in-memory inode table in a UNIX-like operating system after the code of Example 4.20 executes.

The *system file table*, which is shared by all the processes in the system, has an entry for each active `open`. Each system file table entry contains the file offset, an indication of the access mode (i.e., read, write or read-write) and a count of the number of file descriptor table entries pointing to it.

Several system file table entries may correspond to the same physical file. Each of these entries points to the same entry in the *in-memory inode table*. The in-memory inode table contains an entry for each active file in the system. When a program opens a particular physical file that is not currently open, the call creates an entry in this inode table for that file. Figure 4.2 shows that the file `/home/ann/my.dat` had been opened before the code of Example 4.20 because there are two entries in the system file table with pointers to the entry in the inode table. (The label B designates the earlier pointer in the figure.)

◻ **Exercise 4.21**

What happens when the process whose file descriptor table is shown in Figure 4.2 executes the `close(myfd)` function?

Answer:

The operating system deletes the fourth entry in the file descriptor table and the corresponding entry in the system file table. (See Section 4.6.3 for a more complete discussion.) If the operating system also deleted the inode table entry, it would leave pointer B hanging in the system file table. Therefore, the inode table entry must have a count of the system file table entries that are pointing to it. When a process executes the `close` function, the operating system decrements the count in the inode entry. If the inode entry has a 0 count, the operating system deletes the inode entry from memory. (The operating system might not actually delete the entry right away on the chance that it will be accessed again in the immediate future.)

◻ **Exercise 4.22**

The system file table entry contains an offset that gives the current position in the file. If two processes have each opened a file for reading, each process has its own offset into the file and reads the entire file independently of the other process. What happens if each process opens the same file for write? What would happen if the file offset were stored in the inode table instead of the system file table?

Answer:

The writes are independent of each other. Each user can write over what the other user has written because of the separate file offsets for each process. On the other hand, if the offsets were stored in the inode table rather than in the system file table, the writes from different active opens would be consecutive. Also, the processes that had opened a file for reading would only read parts of the file because the file offset they were using could be updated by other processes.

◻ **Exercise 4.23**

Suppose a process opens a file for reading and then forks a child process. Both the parent and child can read from the file. How are reads by these two processes related? What about writes?

Answer:

The child receives a copy of the parent's file descriptor table at the time of the fork. The processes share a system file table entry and therefore also share the file offset. The two processes read different parts of the file. If no other processes have the file open, writes append to the end of the file and no data is lost on writes. Subsection 4.6.3 covers this situation in more detail.

4.6.2 File pointers and buffering

The ISO C standard I/O library uses file pointers rather than file descriptors as handles for
I/O. A *file pointer* points to a data structure called a FILE structure in the user area of the
process.

■ **Example 4.24**

The following code segment opens the file /home/ann/my.dat for output and
then writes a string to the file.

```
FILE *myfp;

if ((myfp = fopen("/home/ann/my.dat", "w")) == NULL)
    perror("Failed to open /home/ann/my.dat");
else
    fprintf(myfp, "This is a test");
```

Figure 4.3 shows a schematic of the FILE structure allocated by the fopen call of Example 4.24. The FILE structure contains a buffer and a file descriptor value. The file
descriptor value is the index of the entry in the file descriptor table that is actually used to
output the file to disk. In some sense the file pointer is a handle to a handle.

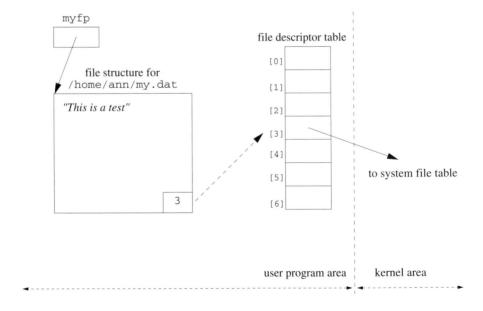

Figure 4.3: Schematic handling of a file pointer after fopen.

What happens when the program calls fprintf? The result depends on the type of
file that was opened. Disk files are usually fully buffered, meaning that the fprintf

does not actually write the *This is a test* message to disk, but instead writes the bytes to a buffer in the `FILE` structure. When the buffer fills, the I/O subsystem calls `write` with the file descriptor, as in the previous section. The delay between the time when a program executes `fprintf` and the time when the writing actually occurs may have interesting consequences, especially if the program crashes. Buffered data is sometimes lost on system crashes, so it is even possible for a program to appear to complete normally but its disk output could be incomplete.

How can a program avoid the effects of buffering? An `fflush` call forces whatever has been buffered in the `FILE` structure to be written out. A program can also call `setvbuf` to disable buffering.

Terminal I/O works a little differently. Files associated with terminals are line buffered rather than fully buffered (except for standard error, which by default, is not buffered). On output, line buffering means that the line is not written out until the buffer is full or until a newline symbol is encountered.

□ Exercise 4.25

How does the output appear when the following program executes?

```c
#include <stdio.h>

int main(void) {
   fprintf(stdout, "a");
   fprintf(stderr, "a has been written\n");
   fprintf(stdout, "b");
   fprintf(stderr, "b has been written\n");
   fprintf(stdout, "\n");
   return 0;
}
```
── **bufferout.c**

Answer:

The messages written to standard error appear before the `'a'` and `'b'` because standard output is line buffered, whereas standard error is not buffered.

□ Exercise 4.26

How does the output appear when the following program executes?

```c
#include <stdio.h>

int main(void) {
   int i;
   fprintf(stdout, "a");
   scanf("%d", &i);
   fprintf(stderr, "a has been written\n");
   fprintf(stdout, "b");
   fprintf(stderr, "b has been written\n");
   fprintf(stdout, "\n");
   return 0;
}
```
── **bufferinout.c**

Answer:
The `scanf` function flushes the buffer for `stdout`, so `'a'` is displayed before the
number is read in. After the number has been entered, `'b'` still appears after the
`b has been written` message.

The issue of buffering is more subtle than the previous discussion might lead you to
believe. If a program that uses file pointers for a buffered device crashes, the last partial
buffer created from the `fprintf` calls may never be written out. When the buffer is full,
a `write` operation is performed. Completion of a `write` operation does not mean that
the data actually made it to disk. In fact, the operating system copies the data to a system
buffer cache. Periodically, the operating system writes these *dirty blocks* to disk. If the
operating system crashes before it writes the block to disk, the program still loses the data.
Presumably, a system crash is less likely to happen than an individual program crash.

4.6.3 Inheritance of file descriptors

When `fork` creates a child, the child inherits a copy of most of the parent's environment
and context, including the signal state, the scheduling parameters and the file descriptor
table. The implications of inheritance are not always obvious. Because children receive a
copy of their parent's file descriptor table at the time of the fork, the parent and children
share the same file offsets for files that were opened by the parent prior to the fork.

■ **Example 4.27**

In the following program, the child inherits the file descriptor for `my.dat`. Each
process reads and outputs one character from the file.

```c
#include <fcntl.h>
#include <stdio.h>
#include <unistd.h>
#include <sys/stat.h>

int main(void) {
   char c = '!';
   int myfd;

   if ((myfd = open("my.dat", O_RDONLY)) == -1) {
      perror("Failed to open file");
      return 1;
   }
   if (fork() == -1) {
      perror("Failed to fork");
      return 1;
   }
   read(myfd, &c, 1);
   printf("Process %ld got %c\n", (long)getpid(), c);
   return 0;
}
```

———————————————————————————————————— **openfork.c**

Figure 4.4 shows the parent and child file descriptor tables for Example 4.27. The file descriptor table entries of the two processes point to the same entry in the system file table. The parent and child therefore share the file offset, which is stored in the system file table.

□ Exercise 4.28

Suppose the first few bytes in the file `my.dat` are `abcdefg`. What output would be generated by Example 4.27?

Answer:

Since the two processes share the file offset, the first one to read gets `a` and the second one to read gets `b`. Two lines are generated in the following form.

```
Process nnn got a
Process mmm got b
```

In theory, the lines could be output in either order but most likely would appear in the order shown.

□ Exercise 4.29

When a program closes a file, the entry in the file descriptor table is freed. What about the corresponding entry in the system file table?

Answer:

The system file table entry can only be freed if no more file descriptor table entries are pointing to it. For this reason, each system file table entry contains a count of the number of file descriptor table entries that are pointing to it. When a process closes a file, the operating system decrements the count and deletes the entry only when the count becomes 0.

□ Exercise 4.30

How does `fork` affect the system file table?

Answer:

The system file table is in system space and is not duplicated by `fork`. However, each entry in the system file table keeps a count of the number of file descriptor table entries pointing to it. These counts must be adjusted to reflect the new file descriptor table created for the child.

■ Example 4.31

In the following program, the parent and child each open `my.dat` for reading, read one character, and output that character.

```
#include <fcntl.h>
#include <stdio.h>
#include <unistd.h>
#include <sys/stat.h>
```

```
int main(void) {
   char c = '!';
   int myfd;

   if (fork() == -1) {
      perror("Failed to fork");
      return 1;
   }
   if ((myfd = open("my.dat", O_RDONLY)) == -1) {
      perror("Failed to open file");
      return 1;
   }
   read(myfd, &c, 1);
   printf("Process %ld got %c\n", (long)getpid(), c);
   return 0;
}
```
_____ **forkopen.c**

parent's file descriptor table   system file table (SFT)

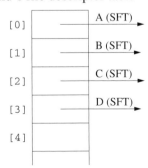

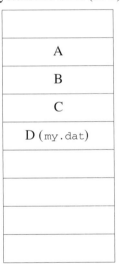

child's file descriptor table

Figure 4.4: If the parent opens my.dat before forking, both parent and child share the system file table entry.

Figure 4.5 shows the file descriptor tables for Example 4.31. The file descriptor table entries corresponding to `my.dat` point to different system file table entries. Consequently, the parent and child do not share the file offset. The child does not inherit the file descriptor, because each process opens the file after the fork and each `open` creates a new entry in the system file table. The parent and child still share system file table entries for standard input, standard output and standard error.

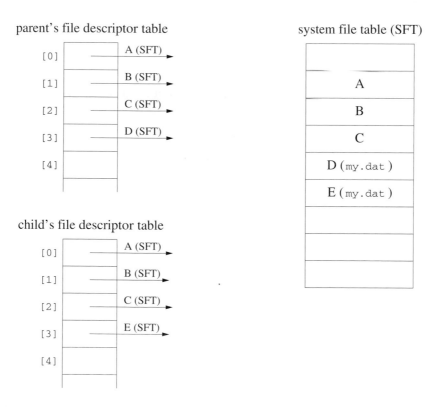

Figure 4.5: If the parent and child open `my.dat` after the `fork` call, their file descriptor table entries point to different system file table entries.

□ **Exercise 4.32**

Suppose the first few bytes in the file `my.dat` are `abcdefg`. What output would be generated by Example 4.31?

Answer:

Since the two processes use different file offsets, each process reads the first byte of the file. Two lines are generated in the following form.

```
Process nnn got a
Process mmm got a
```

❑ **Exercise 4.33**

What output would be generated by the following program?

```
#include <stdio.h>
#include <unistd.h>

int main(void) {
   printf("This is my output.");
   fork();
   return 0;
}
```
── **fileiofork.c**

Answer:

Because of buffering, the output of `printf` is likely to be written to the buffer corresponding to `stdout`, but not to the actual output device. Since this buffer is part of the user space, it is duplicated by `fork`. When the parent and the child each terminate, the return from `main` causes the buffers to be flushed as part of the cleanup. The output appears as follows.

```
This is my output.This is my output.
```

❑ **Exercise 4.34**

What output would be generated by the following program?

```
#include <stdio.h>
#include <unistd.h>

int main(void) {
   printf("This is my output.\n");
   fork();
   return 0;
}
```
── **fileioforkline.c**

Answer:

The buffering of standard output is usually line buffering. This means that the buffer is flushed when it contains a newline. Since in this case a newline is output, the buffer will probably be flushed before the `fork` and only one line of output will appear.

4.7 Filters and Redirection

UNIX provides a large number of utilities that are written as filters. A *filter* reads from standard input, performs a transformation, and outputs the result to standard output. Filters write their error messages to standard error. All of the parameters of a filter are communicated as command-line arguments. The input data should have no headers or trailers, and a filter should not require any interaction with the user.

Examples of useful UNIX filters include `head`, `tail`, `more`, `sort`, `grep` and `awk`. The `cat` command takes a list of filenames as command-line arguments, reads each of the files in succession, and echoes the contents of each file to standard output. However, if no input file is specified, `cat` takes its input from standard input and writes its results to standard output. In this case, `cat` behaves like a filter.

Recall that a file descriptor is an index into the file descriptor table of that process. Each entry in the file descriptor table points to an entry in the system file table, which is created when the file is opened. A program can modify the file descriptor table entry so that it points to a different entry in the system file table. This action is known as *redirection*. Most shells interpret the greater than character (>) on the command line as redirection of standard output and the less than character (<) as redirection of standard input. (Associate > with output by picturing it as an arrow pointing in the direction of the output file.)

■ Example 4.35

The `cat` command with no command-line arguments reads from standard input and echoes to standard output. The following command redirects standard output to `my.file` with >.

```
cat > my.file
```

The `cat` command of Example 4.35 gathers what is typed from the keyboard into the file `my.file`. Figure 4.6 depicts the file descriptor table for Example 4.35. Before redirection, entry `[1]` of the file descriptor table points to a system file table entry corresponding to the usual standard output device. After the redirection, entry `[1]` points to a system file table entry for `my.file`.

The redirection of standard output in `cat > my.file` occurs because the shell changes the standard output entry of the file descriptor table (a pointer to the system file table) to reference a system file table entry associated with `my.file`. To accomplish this redirection in a C program, first open `my.file` to establish an appropriate entry in the system file table. After the `open` operation, copy the pointer to `my.file` into the entry for standard output by executing the `dup2` function. Then, call `close` to eliminate the extra file descriptor table entry for `my.file`.

The `dup2` function takes two parameters, `fildes` and `fildes2`. It closes entry `fildes2` of the file descriptor table if it was open and then copies the pointer of entry `fildes` into entry `fildes2`.

SYNOPSIS

```
#include <unistd.h>

int dup2(int fildes, int fildes2);
```
POSIX

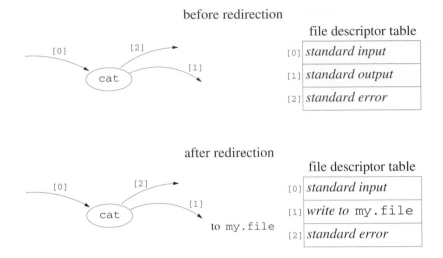

Figure 4.6: Status of the file descriptor table before and after redirection for the process that is executing `cat > my.file`.

On success, dup2 returns the file descriptor value that was duplicated. On failure, dup2 returns −1 and sets errno. The following table lists the mandatory errors for dup2.

errno	cause
EBADF	fildes is not a valid open file descriptor, or fildes2 is negative or greater than or equal to OPEN_MAX
EINTR	dup2 was interrupted by a signal

■ Example 4.36

Program 4.18 redirects standard output to the file my.file and then appends a short message to that file.

Figure 4.7 shows the effect of the redirection on the file descriptor table of Program 4.18. The open function causes the operating system to create a new entry in the system file table and to set entry [3] of the file descriptor table to point to this entry. The dup2 function closes the descriptor corresponding to the second parameter (standard output) and then copies the entry corresponding to the first parameter (fd) into the entry corresponding to the second parameter (STDOUT_FILENO). From that point on in the program, a write to standard output goes to my.file.

Figure 4.7: Status of the file descriptor table during the execution of Program 4.18.

Program 4.18 ——————————————— **redirect.c**

A program that redirects standard output to the file my.file.

```c
#include <fcntl.h>
#include <stdio.h>
#include <sys/stat.h>
#include <unistd.h>
#include "restart.h"
#define CREATE_FLAGS (O_WRONLY | O_CREAT | O_APPEND)
#define CREATE_MODE (S_IRUSR | S_IWUSR | S_IRGRP | S_IROTH)

int main(void) {
   int fd;

   fd = open("my.file", CREATE_FLAGS, CREATE_MODE);
   if (fd == -1) {
      perror("Failed to open my.file");
      return 1;
   }
   if (dup2(fd, STDOUT_FILENO) == -1) {
      perror("Failed to redirect standard output");
      return 1;
   }
   if (r_close(fd) == -1) {
      perror("Failed to close the file");
      return 1;
   }
   if (write(STDOUT_FILENO, "OK", 2) == -1) {
      perror("Failed in writing to file");
      return 1;
   }
   return 0;
}
```

Program 4.18 ——————————————— **redirect.c**

4.8 File Control

The `fcntl` function is a general-purpose function for retrieving and modifying the flags associated with an open file descriptor. The `fildes` argument of `fcntl` specifies the descriptor, and the `cmd` argument specifies the operation. The `fcntl` function may take additional parameters depending on the value of `cmd`.

SYNOPSIS

```
#include <fcntl.h>
#include <unistd.h>
#include <sys/types.h>

int fcntl(int fildes, int cmd, /* arg */ ...);
```
                                                                                    POSIX

The interpretation of the return value of `fcntl` depends on the value of the `cmd` parameter. However, if unsuccessful, `fcntl` returns −1 and sets `errno`. The following table lists the mandatory errors for `fcntl`.

errno	cause
EACCES	cmd is F_SETLK and locking not allowed
EBADF	fildes is not a valid open file descriptor or file is not opened properly for type of lock
EINTR	cmd is F_SETLKW and function interrupted by a signal
EINVAL	cmd is invalid, or cmd is F_DUPFD and arg is negative or greater than or equal to OPEN_MAX, or cmd is a locking function and arg is invalid, or fildes refers to a file that does not support locking
EMFILE	cmd is F_DUPFD and OPEN_MAX descriptors for process are open, or no file descriptors greater than or equal to arg are available
ENOLCK	cmd is F_SETLK or F_SETLKW and locks would exceed limit
EOVERFLOW	one of values to be returned cannot be represented correctly, or requested lock offset cannot be represented in off_t

The `fcntl` function may only be interrupted by a signal when the `cmd` argument is `F_SETLKW` (block until the process acquires an exclusive lock). In this case, `fcntl` returns −1 and sets `errno` to `EINTR`. Table 4.3 lists the POSIX values of the `cmd` parameter for `fcntl`.

An important example of the use of file control is to change an open file descriptor to use nonblocking I/O. When a file descriptor has been set for nonblocking I/O, the `read` and `write` functions return −1 and set `errno` to `EAGAIN` to report that the process would be delayed if a blocking I/O operation were tried. Nonblocking I/O is useful for monitoring multiple file descriptors while doing other work. Section 4.4 and Section 4.5 discuss the `select` and `poll` functions that allow a process to block until any of a set of descriptors

cmd	meaning
F_DUPFD	duplicate a file descriptor
F_GETFD	get file descriptor flags
F_SETFD	set file descriptor flags
F_GETFL	get file status flags and access modes
F_SETFL	set file status flags and access modes
F_GETOWN	if fildes is a socket, get process or group ID for out-of-band signals
F_SETOWN	if fildes is a socket, set process or group ID for out-of-band signals
F_GETLK	get first lock that blocks description specified by arg
F_SETLK	set or clear segment lock specified by arg
F_SETLKW	same as FSETLK except it blocks until request satisfied

Table 4.3: POSIX values for cmd as specified in fcntl.h.

becomes available. However, both of these functions block while waiting for I/O, so no other work can be done during the wait.

To perform nonblocking I/O, a program can call open with the O_NONBLOCK flag set. A program can also change an open descriptor to be nonblocking by setting the O_NONBLOCK flag, using fcntl. To set an open descriptor to perform nonblocking I/O, use the F_GETFL command with fcntl to retrieve the flags associated with the descriptor. Use inclusive bitwise OR of O_NONBLOCK with these flags to create a new flags value. Finally, set the descriptor flags to this new value, using the F_SETFL command of fcntl.

■ **Example 4.37**

The following function sets an already opened file descriptor fd for nonblocking I/O.

```c
#include <fcntl.h>
#include <stdio.h>
#include <unistd.h>

int setnonblock(int fd) {
   int fdflags;

   if ((fdflags = fcntl(fd, F_GETFL, 0)) == -1)
      return -1;
   fdflags |= O_NONBLOCK;
   if (fcntl(fd, F_SETFL, fdflags) == -1)
      return -1;
   return 0;
}
```

setnonblock.c

If successful, `setnonblock` returns 0. Otherwise, `setnonblock` returns −1 and sets `errno`.

The `setnonblock` function of Example 4.37 reads the current value of the flags associated with `fd`, performs a bitwise OR with `O_NONBLOCK`, and installs the modified flags. After this function executes, a `read` from `fd` returns immediately if no input is available.

∎ Example 4.38

The following function changes the I/O mode associated with file descriptor `fd` to blocking by clearing the `O_NONBLOCK` file flag. To clear the flag, use bitwise AND with the complement of the `O_NONBLOCK` flag.

```
#include <fcntl.h>
#include <stdio.h>
#include <unistd.h>

int setblock(int fd) {
   int fdflags;

   if ((fdflags = fcntl(fd, F_GETFL, 0)) == -1)
      return -1;
   fdflags &= ~O_NONBLOCK;
   if (fcntl(fd, F_SETFL, fdflags) == -1)
      return -1;
   return 0;
}
```
———————————————————————————— `setblock.c`

If successful, `setblock` returns 0. If unsuccessful, `setblock` returns −1 and sets `errno`.

∎ Example 4.39

The following function assumes that `fd1` and `fd2` are open for reading in non-blocking mode. If input is available from either one, the function calls `docommand` with the data read. Otherwise, the code calls `dosomething`. This implementation gives priority to `fd1` and always handles input from this file descriptor before handling `fd2`.

```
#include <errno.h>
#include <unistd.h>
#include "restart.h"

void docommand(char *, int);
void dosomething(void);

void process_or_do_work(int fd1, int fd2) {
   char buf[1024];
   ssize_t bytesread;

   for ( ; ; ) {
      bytesread = r_read(fd1, buf, sizeof(buf));
```

```
          if ((bytesread == -1) && (errno != EAGAIN))
             return;                                  /* a real error on fd1 */
          else if (bytesread > 0) {
             docommand(buf, bytesread);
             continue;
          }
          bytesread = r_read(fd2, buf, sizeof(buf));
          if ((bytesread == -1) && (errno != EAGATN))
             return;                                  /* a real error on fd2 */
          else if (bytesread > 0)
             docommand(buf, bytesread);
          else
             dosomething();            /* input not available, do something else */
       }
    }
```

_____ **process_or_do_work.c**

4.9 Exercise: Atomic Logging

Sometimes multiple processes need to output to the same log file. Problems can arise if one process loses the CPU while it is outputting to the log file and another process tries to write to the same file. The messages could get interleaved, making the log file unreadable. We use the term *atomic logging* to mean that multiple writes of one process to the same file are not mixed up with the writes of other processes writing to the same file.

This exercise describes a series of experiments to help you understand the issues involved when multiple processes try to write to the same file. We then introduce an atomic logging library and provide a series of examples of how to use the library. Appendix D.1 describes the actual implementation of this library, which is used in several places throughout the book as a tool for debugging programs.

The experiments in this section are based on Program 3.1, which creates a chain of processes. Program 4.19 modifies Program 3.1 so that the original process opens a file before creating the children. Each child writes a message to the file instead of to standard error. Each message is written in two pieces. Since the processes share an entry in the system file table, they share the file offset. Each time a process writes to the file, the file offset is updated.

☐ Exercise 4.40

Run Program 4.19 several times and see if it generates output in the same order each time. Can you tell which parts of the output came from each process?
Answer:
On most systems, the output appears in the same order for most runs and each process generates a single line of output. However, this outcome is not guaranteed by the program. It is possible (but possibly unlikely) for one process to lose the

CPU before both parts of its output are written to the file. In this, case the output is jumbled.

Program 4.19 ———————————————————— **chainopenfork.c**

A program that opens a file before creating a chain of processes.

```c
#include <fcntl.h>
#include <stdio.h>
#include <stdlib.h>
#include <string.h>
#include <unistd.h>
#include <sys/stat.h>

#define BUFSIZE 1024
#define CREATE_FLAGS (O_WRONLY | O_CREAT | O_TRUNC)
#define CREATE_PERMS (S_IRUSR | S_IWUSR| S_IRGRP | S_IROTH)

int main  (int argc, char *argv[]) {
   char buf[BUFSIZE];
   pid_t childpid = 0;
   int fd;
   int i, n;

   if (argc != 3){        /* check for valid number of command-line arguments */
      fprintf (stderr, "Usage: %s processes filename\n", argv[0]);
      return 1;
   }
                                          /* open the log file before the fork */
   fd = open(argv[2], CREATE_FLAGS, CREATE_PERMS);
   if (fd < 0) {
      perror("Failed to open file");
      return 1;
   }
   n = atoi(argv[1]);                            /* create a process chain */
   for (i = 1; i < n; i++)
      if (childpid = fork())
         break;
   if (childpid == -1) {
      perror("Failed to fork");
      return 1;
   }
                                  /* write twice to the common log file */
   sprintf(buf, "i:%d process:%ld ", i, (long)getpid());
   write(fd, buf, strlen(buf));
   sprintf(buf, "parent:%ld child:%ld\n", (long)getppid(), (long)childpid);
   write(fd, buf, strlen(buf));
   return 0;
}
```

Program 4.19 ———————————————————— **chainopenfork.c**

☐ Exercise 4.41

Put sleep(1); after the first write function in Program 4.19 and run it again. Now what happens?

Answer:

Most likely, each process outputs the values of the first two integers and then each process outputs the last two integers.

☐ Exercise 4.42

Copy `chainopenfork.c` to a file called `chainforkopen.c` and move the code to open the file after the loop that forks the children. How does the behavior of `chainforkopen.c` differ from that of `chainopenfork.c`?

Answer:

Each process now has a different system file table entry, and so each process has a different file offset. Because of `O_TRUNC`, each `open` deletes what was previously written to the file. Each process starts writing from the beginning of the file, overwriting what the other processes have written. The last process to write has control of the final file contents.

☐ Exercise 4.43

Run `chainforkopen` several times and see if it generates the same order of the output each time. Which process was executed last? Do you see anything unusual about the contents of the file?

Answer:

The process that outputs last may be different on different systems. If the last process writes fewer bytes than another process, the file contains additional bytes after the line written by the last process.

If independent processes open the same log file, the results might be similar to that of Exercise 4.43. The last process to output overwrites what was previously written. One way to try to solve this problem is to call `lseek` to move to the end of the file before writing.

☐ Exercise 4.44

Copy `chainforkopen.c` to a file called `chainforkopenseek.c`. Add code before each `write` to perform `lseek` to the end of the file. Also, remove the `O_TRUNC` flag from `CREATE_FLAGS`. Run the program several times and observe the behavior. Use a different file name each time.

Answer:

The `lseek` operation works as long as the process does not lose the CPU between `lseek` and `write`. For fast machines, you may have to run the program many times to observe this behavior. You can increase the likelihood of creating mixed-up output, by putting `sleep(1);` between `lseek` and `write`.

If a file is opened with the `O_APPEND` flag, then it automatically does all writes to the end of the file.

☐ **Exercise 4.45**

Copy `chainforkopen.c` to a file called `chainforkappend.c`. Modify the `CREATE_FLAGS` constant by replacing `O_TRUNC` with `O_APPEND`. Run the program several times, possibly inserting `sleep(1)` between the `write` calls. What happens?

Answer:

The `O_APPEND` flag solves the problem of processes overwriting the log entries of other processes, but it does not prevent the individual pieces written by one process from being mixed up with the pieces of another.

☐ **Exercise 4.46**

Copy `chainforkappend.c` to a file called `chainforkonewrite.c`. Combine the pair of `sprintf` calls so that the program uses a single `write` call to output its information. How does the program behave?

Answer:

The output is no longer interleaved.

☐ **Exercise 4.47**

Copy `chainforkonewrite.c` to a file called `chainforkfprintf.c`. Replace `open` with a corresponding `fopen` function. Replace the single `write` with `fprintf`. How does the program behave?

Answer:

The `fprintf` operation causes the output to be written to a buffer in the user area. Eventually, the I/O subsystem calls `write` to output the contents of the buffer. You have no control over when `write` is called except that you can force a `write` operation by calling `fflush`. Process output can be interleaved if the buffer fills in the middle of the `fprintf` operation. Adding `sleep(1);` shouldn't cause the problem to occur more or less often.

4.9.1 An atomic logging library

To make an atomic logger, we have to use a single `write` call to output information that we want to appear together in the log. The file must be opened with the `O_APPEND` flag. Here is the statement about the `O_APPEND` flag from the `write` man page that guarantees that the writing is atomic if we use the `O_APPEND` flag.

> If the `O_APPEND` flag of the file status flags is set, the file offset will be set to the end of the file prior to each write and no intervening file modification operation will occur between changing the file offset and the write operation.

In the examples given here, it is simple to combine everything into a single call to `write`, but later we encounter situations in which it is more difficult. Appendix D.1

contains a complete implementation of a module that can be used with a program in which atomic logging is needed. A program using this module should include Program 4.20, which contains the prototypes for the publicly accessible functions. Note that the interface is simple and the implementation details are completely hidden from the user.

Program 4.20 ———————————————— `atomic_logger.h`

The include file for the atomic logging module.

```
int atomic_log_array(char *s, int len);
int atomic_log_clear();
int atomic_log_close();
int atomic_log_open(char *fn);
int atomic_log_printf(char *fmt, ...);
int atomic_log_send();
int atomic_log_string(char *s);
```

Program 4.20 ———————————————— `atomic_logger.h`

The atomic logger allows you to control how the output of programs that are running on the same machine is interspersed in a log file. To use the logger, first call `atomic_log_open` to create the log file. Call `atomic_log_close` when all logging is completed. The logger stores in a temporary buffer items written with `atomic_log_array`, `atomic_log_string` and `atomic_log_printf`. When the program calls `atomic_log_send`, the logger outputs the entire buffer, using a single `write` call, and frees the temporary buffers. The `atomic_log_clear` operation frees the temporary buffers without actually outputting to the log file. Each function in the atomic logging library returns 0 if successful. If unsuccessful, these functions return −1 and set `errno`.

The atomic logging facility provides three formats for writing to the log. Use `atomic_log_array` to write an array of a known number of bytes. Use `atomic_log_string` to log a string. Alternatively, you can use `atomic_log_printf` with a syntax similar to `fprintf`. Program 4.21 shows a version of the process chain that uses the first two forms for output to the atomic logger.

❏ Exercise 4.48

How would you modify Program 4.21 to use `atomic_log_printf`?

Answer:

Eliminate the `buf` array and replace the four lines of code involving `sprintf`, `atomic_log_array` and `atomic_log_string` with the following.

```
atomic_log_printf("i:%d process:%ld ", i, (long)getpid());
atomic_log_printf("parent:%ld child ID:%ld\n",
                  (long)getppid(), (long)childpid);
```

Alternatively use the following single call.

```
atomic_log_printf("i:%d process:%ld parent:%ld child:%ld\n",
                  i, (long)getpid(), (long)getppid(), (long)childpid);
```

Program 4.21 ───────────────────────── **chainforkopenlog.c**
A program that uses the atomic logging module of Appendix D.1.

```c
#include <stdio.h>
#include <stdlib.h>
#include <string.h>
#include <unistd.h>
#include "atomic_logger.h"

#define BUFSIZE 1024

int main  (int argc, char *argv[]) {
   char buf[BUFSIZE];
   pid_t childpid = 0;
   int i, n;

   if (argc != 3){         /* check for valid number of command-line arguments */
      fprintf (stderr, "Usage: %s processes filename\n", argv[0]);
      return 1;
   }
   n = atoi(argv[1]);                              /* create a process chain */
   for (i = 1; i < n; i++)
      if (childpid = fork())
         break;
   if (childpid == -1) {
      perror("Failed to fork");
      return 1;
   }

   if (atomic_log_open(argv[2]) == -1) {            /* open atomic log file */
      fprintf(stderr, "Failed to open log file");
      return 1;
   }
                                   /* log the output, using two different forms */
   sprintf(buf, "i:%d process:%ld", i, (long)getpid());
   atomic_log_array(buf, strlen(buf));
   sprintf(buf, " parent:%ld child:%ld\n", (long)getppid(), (long)childpid);
   atomic_log_string(buf);
   if (atomic_log_send() == -1) {
      fprintf(stderr, "Failed to send to log file");
      return 1;
   }
   atomic_log_close();
   return 0;
}
```

Program 4.21 ───────────────────────────── **chainforkopenlog.c**

☐ **Exercise 4.49**

Modify Program 4.19 to open an atomic log file after forking the children. (Do
not remove the other open function call.) Repeat Exercises 4.40 through Exercise 4.47 after adding code to output the same information to the atomic logger as
to the original file. Compare the output of the logger with the contents of the file.

◻ **Exercise 4.50**

What happens if Program 4.19 opens the log file before forking the children?
Answer:
Logging should still be atomic. However, if the parent writes information to the
log and doesn't clear it before the fork, the children have a copy of this information
in their logging buffers.

Another logging interface that is useful for debugging concurrent programs is the
remote logging facility described in detail in Appendix D.2. Instead of logging information
being sent to a file, it is sent to another process that has its own environment for displaying
and saving the logged information. The remote logging process has a graphical user
interface that allows the user to display the log. The remote logger does not have a facility
for gathering information from a process to be displayed in a single block in the log file,
but it allows logging from processes on multiple machines.

4.10 Exercise: A `cat` Utility

The `cat` utility has the following POSIX specification[52].

```
NAME
cat - concatenate and print files

SYNOPSIS
cat [-u] [file ...]

DESCRIPTION
        The cat utility shall read files in sequence and shall write
        their contents to the standard output in the same sequence.

OPTIONS
        The cat utility shall conform to the Base Definitions volume
        of IEEE STd 1003.1-2001, Section 12.2, Utility Syntax Guidelines.

        The following option shall be supported:

        -u      Write bytes from the input file to the standard output
                without delay as each is read

OPERANDS
        The following operand shall be supported:

        file    A pathname of an input file. If no file operands are
                specified, the standard input shall be used. If a file
                is '-', the cat utility shall read from the standard
                input at that point in the sequence. The cat utility
                shall not close and reopen standard input when it is
                referenced in this way, but shall accept multiple
                occurrences of '-' as a file operand.
```

STDIN
        The standard input shall be used only if no file operands are
        specified, or if a file operand is '-'. See the INPUT FILES
        section.

INPUT FILES
        The input files can be any file type.

ENVIRONMENT VARIABLES
        (.... a long section omitted here ....)

ASYNCHRONOUS EVENTS
        Default.

STDOUT
        The standard output shall contain the sequence of bytes read from
        the input files. Nothing else shall be written to the standard
        output.

STDERR
        The standard error shall be used only for diagnostic messages.

OUTPUT FILES
        None.

EXTENDED DESCRIPTION
        None.

EXIT STATUS
        The following exit values shall be returned:

        0:       All input files were output successfully.

        >0   An error occurred.

CONSEQUENCES OF ERRORS
        Default.

The actual POSIX description continues with other sections, including APPLICATION
USAGE, EXAMPLES and RATIONALE.
1. Compare the POSIX description of cat with the man page for cat on your system
   and note any differences.
2. Execute the cat command for many examples, including multiple input files and
   files that don't exist. Include a case in which you redirect standard input to a disk
   file and use several '-' files on the command line. Explain what happens.
3. Write your own cat utility to conform to the standard. Try to duplicate the behavior of the actual cat utility.
4. Read the section of the cat man page on ENVIRONMENT VARIABLES.
5. Experiment with the effect of relevant environment variables on the behavior of
   cat.
6. Incorporate the handling of environment variables into your own cat utility.

4.11 Additional Reading

Advanced Programming in the UNIX Environment by Stevens [112] has an extensive discussion of UNIX I/O from a programmer's viewpoint. Many books on Linux or UNIX programming also cover I/O. The *USENIX Conference Proceedings* are a good source of current information on tools and approaches evolving under UNIX.

Chapter 5

Files and Directories

Operating systems organize raw storage devices in file systems so that applications can use high-level operations rather than low-level device calls to access information. UNIX file systems are tree structured, with nodes representing files and arcs representing the *contains* relationship. UNIX directory entries associate filenames with file locations. These entries can either point directly to a structure containing the file location information (hard link) or point indirectly through a symbolic link. Symbolic links are files that associate one filename with another. This chapter also introduces functions for accessing file status information and directories from within programs.

Objectives
- Learn about file systems and directories
- Experiment with directory traversal
- Explore UNIX inode implementation
- Use functions for accessing directories
- Understand hard links and symbolic links

5.1 UNIX File System Navigation

Operating systems organize physical disks into file systems to provide high-level logical access to the actual bytes of a file. A *file system* is a collection of files and attributes such as location and name. Instead of specifying the physical location of a file on disk, an application specifies a filename and an offset. The operating system makes a translation to the location of the physical file through its file systems.

A directory is a file containing *directory entries* that associate a filename with the physical location of a file on disk. When disks were small, a simple table of filenames and their positions was a sufficient representation for the directory. Larger disks require a more flexible organization, and most file systems organize their directories in a tree structure. This representation arises quite naturally when the directories themselves are files.

Figure 5.1 shows a tree-structured organization of a typical file system. The square nodes in this tree are directories, and the / designates the *root directory* of the file system. The root directory is at the top of the file system tree, and everything else is under it.

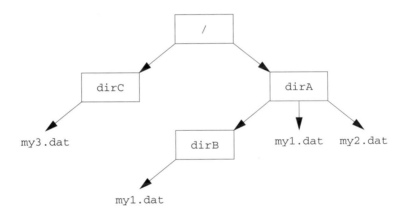

Figure 5.1: Tree structure of a file system.

The directory marked dirA in Figure 5.1 contains the files my1.dat, my2.dat and dirB. The dirB file is called a *subdirectory* of dirA because dirB is a directory contained in dirA of the file system tree. Notice that dirB also contains a file named my1.dat. Clearly, the filename is not enough to uniquely specify a file.

The *absolute* or *fully qualified pathname* specifies all of the nodes in the file system tree on the path from the root to the file itself. The absolute path starts with a slash (/) to designate the root node and then lists the names of the nodes down the path to the file within the file system tree. The successive names are separated by slashes. The file my1.dat in dirA in Figure 5.1 has the fully qualified pathname /dirA/my1.dat, and my1.dat in dirB has the fully qualified pathname /dirA/dirB/my1.dat.

5.1.1 The current working directory

A program does not always have to specify files by fully qualified pathnames. At any time, each process has an associated directory, called the *current working directory*, that it uses for pathname resolution. If a pathname does not start with /, the program prepends the fully qualified path of the current working directory. Hence, pathnames that do not begin with / are sometimes called *relative pathnames* because they are specified relative to the fully qualified pathname of the current directory. A dot (.) specifies the current directory, and a dot-dot (..) specifies the directory above the current directory. The root directory has both dot and dot-dot pointing to itself.

■ **Example 5.1**

After you enter the following command, your shell process has the current working directory /dirA/dirB.

```
cd /dirA/dirB
```

□ **Exercise 5.2**

Suppose the current working directory of a process is the /dirA/dirB directory of Figure 5.1. State three ways by which the process can refer to the file my1.dat in directory dirA. State three ways by which the process can refer to the file my1.dat in directory dirB. What about the file my3.dat in dirC?

Answer:

Since the current working directory is /dirA/dirB, the process can use /dirA/my1.dat, ../my1.dat or even ./../my1.dat for the my1.dat file in dirA. Some of the ways by which the process can refer to the my1.dat file of dirB include my1.dat, /dirA/dirB/my1.dat, ./my1.dat, or ../dirB/my1.dat. The file my3.dat in dirC can be referred to as /dirC/my3.dat or ../../dirC/my3.dat.

The PWD environment variable specifies the current working directory of a process. Do not directly change this variable, but rather use the getcwd function to retrieve the current working directory and use the chdir function to change the current working directory within a process.

The chdir function causes the directory specified by path to become the current working directory for the calling process.

```
SYNOPSIS

   #include <unistd.h>

   int chdir(const char *path);
                                                    POSIX
```

If successful, chdir returns 0. If unsuccessful, chdir returns −1 and sets errno. The following table lists the mandatory errors for chdir.

errno	cause
EACCES	search permission on a path component denied
ELOOP	a loop exists in resolution of path
ENAMETOOLONG	the length of path exceeds PATH_MAX, or
	a pathname component is longer than NAME_MAX
ENOENT	a component of path does not name an existing directory
ENOTDIR	a component of the pathname is not a directory

■ Example 5.3

The following code changes the process current working directory to /tmp.

```
char *directory = "/tmp";

if (chdir(directory) == -1)
    perror("Failed to change current working directory to /tmp");
```

☐ Exercise 5.4

Why do ENOENT and ENOTDIR represent different error conditions for chdir?
Answer:
Some of the components of path may represent symbolic links that have to be followed to get the true components of the pathname. (See Section 5.4 for a discussion of symbolic links.)

The getcwd function returns the pathname of the current working directory. The buf parameter of getcwd represents a user-supplied buffer for holding the pathname of the current working directory. The size parameter specifies the maximum length pathname that buf can accommodate, including the trailing string terminator.

```
SYNOPSIS

   #include <unistd.h>

   char *getcwd(char *buf, size_t size);
                                                              POSIX
```

If successful, getcwd returns a pointer to buf. If unsuccessful, getcwd returns NULL and sets errno. The following table lists the mandatory errors for getcwd.

errno	cause
EINVAL	size is 0
ERANGE	size is greater than 0, but smaller than the pathname + 1.

If buf is not NULL, getcwd copies the name into buf. If buf is NULL, POSIX states that the behavior of getcwd is undefined. In some implementations, getcwd uses malloc to create a buffer to hold the pathname. Do not rely on this behavior.

You should always supply getcwd with a buffer large enough to fit a string containing the pathname. Program 5.1 shows a program that uses PATH_MAX as the buffer size. PATH_MAX is an optional POSIX constant specifying the maximum length of a pathname (including the terminating null byte) for the implementation. The PATH_MAX constant may or may not be defined in limits.h. The optional POSIX constants can be omitted from limits.h if their values are indeterminate but larger than the required POSIX minimum. For PATH_MAX, the _POSIX_PATH_MAX constant specifies that an implementation must accommodate pathname lengths of at least 255. A vendor might allow PATH_MAX to depend on the amount of available memory space on a specific instance of a specific implementation.

Program 5.1 ———————————————————— **getcwdpathmax.c**

A complete program to output the current working directory.

```
#include <limits.h>
#include <stdio.h>
#include <unistd.h>
#ifndef PATH_MAX
#define PATH_MAX 255
#endif

int main(void) {
    char mycwd[PATH_MAX];

    if (getcwd(mycwd, PATH_MAX) == NULL) {
        perror("Failed to get current working directory");
        return 1;
    }
    printf("Current working directory: %s\n", mycwd);
    return 0;
}
```

Program 5.1 ———————————————————— **getcwdpathmax.c**

A more flexible approach uses the pathconf function to determine the real value for the maximum path length at run time. The pathconf function is one of a family of functions that allows a program to determine system and runtime limits in a platform-independent way. For example, Program 2.10 uses the sysconf member of this family to calculate the number of seconds that a program runs. The sysconf function takes a single argument, which is the name of a configurable systemwide limit such as the number of clock ticks per second (_SC_CLK_TCK) or the maximum number of processes allowed per user (_SC_CHILD_MAX).

The pathconf and fpathconf functions report limits associated with a particular file or directory. The fpathconf takes a file descriptor and the limit designator as parameters, so the file must be opened before a call to fpathconf. The pathconf function takes a pathname and a limit designator as parameters, so it can be called without the program actually opening the file. The `sysconf` function returns the current value of a configurable system limit that is not associated with files. Its `name` parameter designates the limit.

```
SYNOPSIS

   #include <unistd.h>

   long fpathconf(int fildes, int name);
   long pathconf(const char *path, int name);
   long sysconf(int name);
                                                                   POSIX
```

If successful, these functions return the value of the limit. If unsuccessful, these functions return −1 and set `errno`. The following table lists the mandatory errors.

errno	cause
EINVAL	name has an invalid value
ELOOP	a loop exists in resolution of `path` (`pathconf`)

Program 5.2 shows a program that avoids the `PATH_MAX` problem by first calling `pathconf` to find the maximum pathname length. Since the program does not know the length of the path until run time, it allocates the buffer for the path dynamically.

Program 5.2 ───────────────────────────── **getcwdpathconf.c**
A program that uses `pathconf` *to output the current working directory*

```c
#include <stdio.h>
#include <stdlib.h>
#include <unistd.h>

int main(void) {
   long maxpath;
   char *mycwdp;

   if ((maxpath = pathconf(".", _PC_PATH_MAX)) == -1) {
      perror("Failed to determine the pathname length");
      return 1;
   }
   if ((mycwdp = (char *) malloc(maxpath)) == NULL) {
      perror("Failed to allocate space for pathname");
      return 1;
   }
   if (getcwd(mycwdp, maxpath) == NULL) {
      perror("Failed to get current working directory");
      return 1;
   }
   printf("Current working directory: %s\n", mycwdp);
   return 0;
}
```

Program 5.2 ───────────────────────────── **getcwdpathconf.c**

5.1.2 Search paths

A user executes a program in a UNIX shell by typing the pathname of the file containing the executable. Most commonly used programs and utilities are not in the user's current working directory (e.g., vi, cc). Imagine how inconvenient it would be if you actually had to know the locations of all system executables to execute them. Fortunately, UNIX has a method of looking for executables in a systematic way. If only a name is given for an executable, the shell searches for the executable in all possible directories listed by the PATH environment variable. PATH contains the fully qualified pathnames of important directories separated by colons.

■ Example 5.5

The following is a typical value of the PATH environment variable.

```
/usr/bin:/etc:/usr/local/bin:/usr/ccs/bin:/home/robbins/bin:.
```

This specification says that when you enter a command your shell should search /usr/bin first. If it does not find the command there, the shell should next examine the /etc directory and so on.

Remember that the shell does not search subdirectories of directories in the PATH unless they are also explicitly specified in the PATH. If in doubt about which version of a particular program you are actually executing, use which to get the fully qualified pathname of the executable. The which command is not part of POSIX, but it is available on most systems. Section 5.5 describes how you can write your own version of which.

It is common for programmers to create a bin directory for executables, making bin a subdirectory of their home directories. The PATH of Example 5.5 contains the /home/robbins/bin directory. The bin directory appears before dot (.), the current directory, in the search path leading to the problem discussed in the next exercise.

❑ Exercise 5.6

A user develops a program called calhit in the subdirectory progs of his or her home directory and puts a copy of the executable in the bin directory of the same account. The user later modifies calhit in the progs directory without copying it to the bin directory. What happens when the programmer tries to test the new version?

Answer:
The result depends on the value of the PATH environment variable. If the user's PATH is set up in the usual way, the shell searches the bin directory first and executes the old version of the program. You can test the new version with ./calhit.

Resist the temptation to put the dot (.) at the beginning of the PATH in spite of the problem mentioned in Exercise 5.6. Such a PATH specification is regarded as a security risk and may lead to strange results when your shell executes local programs instead of the standard system programs of the same name.

5.2 Directory Access

Directories should not be accessed with the ordinary open, close and read functions. Instead, they require specialized functions whose corresponding names end with "dir": opendir, closedir and readdir.

The opendir function provides a handle of type DIR * to a directory stream that is positioned at the first entry in the directory.

SYNOPSIS

```
#include <dirent.h>

DIR *opendir(const char *dirname);
```
                                                                                              POSIX

If successful, opendir returns a pointer to a directory object. If unsuccessful, opendir returns a null pointer and sets errno. The following table lists the mandatory errors for opendir.

errno	cause
EACCES	search permission on a path prefix of dirname or read permission on dirname is denied
ELOOP	a loop exists in resolution of dirname
ENAMETOOLONG	the length of dirname exceeds PATH_MAX, or a pathname component is longer than NAME_MAX
ENOENT	a component of dirname does not name an existing directory
ENOTDIR	a component of dirname is not a directory

The DIR type, which is defined in dirent.h represents a *directory stream*. A directory stream is an ordered sequence of all of the directory entries in a particular directory. *The order of the entries in a directory stream is not necessarily alphabetical by file name.*

The readdir function reads a directory by returning successive entries in a directory stream pointed to by dirp. The readdir returns a pointer to a struct dirent structure containing information about the next directory entry. The readdir moves the stream to the next position after each call.

SYNOPSIS

```
#include <dirent.h>

struct dirent *readdir(DIR *dirp);
```
                                                                                              POSIX

If successful, readdir returns a pointer to a struct dirent structure containing information about the next directory entry. If unsuccessful, readdir returns a NULL pointer and sets errno. The only mandatory error is EOVERFLOW, which indicates that the value in the structure to be returned cannot be represented correctly. The readdir function also returns NULL to indicate the end of the directory, but in this case it does not change errno.

The closedir function closes a directory stream, and the rewinddir function repositions the directory stream at its beginning. Each function has a dirp parameter that corresponds to an open directory stream.

SYNOPSIS

```
#include <dirent.h>

int closedir(DIR *dirp);
void rewinddir(DIR *dirp);
```

POSIX

If successful, the closedir function returns 0. If unsuccessful, it returns −1 and sets errno. The closedir function has no mandatory errors. The rewinddir function does not return a value and has no errors defined.

Program 5.3 displays the filenames contained in the directory whose pathname is passed as a command-line argument.

Program 5.3 ———————————————————— shownames.c

A program to list files in a directory.

```c
#include <dirent.h>
#include <errno.h>
#include <stdio.h>

int main(int argc, char *argv[]) {
   struct dirent *direntp;
   DIR *dirp;

   if (argc != 2) {
      fprintf(stderr, "Usage: %s directory_name\n", argv[0]);
      return 1;
   }

   if ((dirp = opendir(argv[1])) == NULL) {
      perror ("Failed to open directory");
      return 1;
   }

   while ((direntp = readdir(dirp)) != NULL)
      printf("%s\n", direntp->d_name);
   while ((closedir(dirp) == -1) && (errno == EINTR)) ;
   return 0;
}
```

Program 5.3 ———————————————————— shownames.c

☐ Exercise 5.7

Run Program 5.3 for different directories. Compare the output with that from running the `ls` shell command for the same directories. Why are they different?

Answer:

The `ls` command sorts filenames in alphabetical order. The `readdir` function displays filenames in the order in which they occur in the directory file.

Program 5.3 does not allocate a `struct dirent` variable to hold the directory information. Rather, `readdir` returns a pointer to a static `struct dirent` structure. This return structure implies that `readdir` is not thread-safe. POSIX includes `readdir_r` as part of the POSIX:TSF Extension, to provide a thread-safe alternative.

POSIX only requires that the `struct dirent` structure have a `d_name` member, representing a string that is no longer than NAME_MAX. POSIX does not specify where additional information about the file should be stored. Traditionally, UNIX directory entries contain only filenames and inode numbers. The inode number is an index into a table containing the other information about a file. Inodes are discussed in Section 5.3.

5.2.1 Accessing file status information

This section describes three functions for retrieving file status information. The `fstat` function accesses a file with an open file descriptor. The `stat` and `lstat` functions access a file by name.

The `lstat` and `stat` functions each take two parameters. The `path` parameter specifies the name of a file or symbolic link whose status is to be returned. If `path` does not correspond to a symbolic link, both functions return the same results. When `path` is a symbolic link, the `lstat` function returns information about the link whereas the `stat` function returns information about the file referred to by the link. Section 5.4 explains symbolic links. The `buf` parameter points to a user-supplied buffer into which these functions store the information.

```
SYNOPSIS

   #include <sys/stat.h>

   int lstat(const char *restrict path, struct stat *restrict buf);
   int stat(const char *restrict path, struct stat *restrict buf);
                                                                POSIX
```

If successful, these functions return 0. If unsuccessful, they return −1 and set `errno`. *The* `restrict` *modifier on the arguments specifies that* `path` *and* `buf` *are not allowed to overlap.* The following table lists the mandatory errors for these functions.

errno	cause
EACCES	search permission on a `path` component denied
EIO	an error occurred while reading from the file system
ELOOP	a loop exists in resolution of `path`
ENAMETOOLONG	the length of the pathname exceeds PATH_MAX (`lstat`), the length of `path` exceeds PATH_MAX (`stat`), or a pathname component is longer than NAME_MAX
ENOENT	a component of `path` does not name an existing file
ENOTDIR	a component of the path prefix is not a directory
EOVERFLOW	the file size in bytes, the number of blocks allocated to file or the file serial number cannot be represented in the structure pointed to by `buf`

The `struct stat` structure, which is defined in `sys/stat.h`, contains at least the following members.

```
dev_t    st_dev;      /* device ID of device containing file */
ino_t    st_ino;      /* file serial number */
mode_t   st_mode;     /* file mode */
nlink_t  st_nlink;    /* number of hard links */
uid_t    st_uid;      /* user ID of file */
gid_t    st_gid;      /* group ID of file */
off_t    st_size;     /* file size in bytes (regular files) */
                      /* path size (symbolic links) */
time_t   st_atime;    /* time of last access */
time_t   st_mtime;    /* time of last data modification */
time_t   st_ctime;    /* time of last file status change */
```

■ Example 5.8

The following function displays the time that the file `path` was last accessed.

```
#include <stdio.h>
#include <time.h>
#include <sys/stat.h>

void printaccess(char *path) {
   struct stat statbuf;

   if (stat(path, &statbuf) == -1)
      perror("Failed to get file status");
   else
      printf("%s last accessed at %s", path, ctime(&statbuf.st_atime));
}
```

———————————————— **printaccess.c**

◻ **Exercise 5.9**

What is wrong with the following function that attempts to print both the access time and the time of modification of a file? How would you fix it?

```
#include <stdio.h>
#include <time.h>
#include <sys/stat.h>

void printaccessmodbad(char *path) {
   struct stat statbuf;

   if (stat(path, &statbuf) == -1)
      perror("Failed to get file status");
   else
      printf("%s accessed: %s modified: %s", path,
            ctime(&statbuf.st_atime), ctime(&statbuf.st_mtime));
}
```
                                              printaccessmodbad.c

Answer:

The string returned by `ctime` ends with a newline, so the result is displayed on 2 lines. More importantly, `ctime` uses static storage to hold the generated string, so the second call to `ctime` will probably write over the string containing the access time. To solve the problem, save the access time in a buffer before calling `ctime` the second time, as in the following code. An alternative would be to use two separate print statements. After the `strncpy` call, the string is terminated at the position that would have contained the newline.

```
#include <stdio.h>
#include <string.h>
#include <time.h>
#include <sys/stat.h>
#define CTIME_SIZE 26

void printaccessmod(char *path) {
   char atime[CTIME_SIZE];   /* 26 is the size of the ctime string */
   struct stat statbuf;

   if (stat(path, &statbuf) == -1)
      perror("Failed to get file status");
   else {
      strncpy(atime, ctime(&statbuf.st_atime), CTIME_SIZE - 1);
      atime[CTIME_SIZE - 2] = 0;
      printf("%s accessed: %s modified: %s", path, atime,
            ctime(&statbuf.st_mtime));
   }
}
```
                                              printaccessmod.c

The `fstat` function reports status information of a file associated with the open file descriptor `fildes`. The `buf` parameter points to a user-supplied buffer into which `fstat` writes the information.

```
SYNOPSIS

    #include <sys/stat.h>

    int fstat(int fildes, struct stat *buf);
                                                                    POSIX
```

If successful, `fstat` returns 0. If unsuccessful, `fstat` returns −1 and sets `errno`. The following table lists the mandatory errors for `fstat`.

errno	cause
EBADF	`fildes` is not a valid file descriptor
EIO	an I/O error occurred while reading from the file system
EOVERFLOW	the file size in bytes, the number of blocks allocated to file or the file serial number cannot be represented in the structure pointed to by `buf`

5.2.2 Determining the type of a file

The file mode member `st_mode` specifies the access permissions of the file and the type of file. Table 4.1 on page 105 lists the POSIX symbolic names for the access permission bits. POSIX specifies the macros of Table 5.1 for testing the `st_mode` member for the type of file. A *regular file* is a randomly accessible sequence of bytes with no further structure imposed by the system. UNIX stores data and programs as regular files. Directories are files that associate filenames with locations, and *special files* specify devices. *Character special files* represent devices such as terminals; *block special files* represent disk devices. The `ISFIFO` tests for pipes and FIFOs that are used for interprocess communication. Chapter 6 discusses special files, and Chapter 14 discusses interprocess communication based on message queues, semaphores and shared memory.

■ **Example 5.10**

The `isdirectory` function returns true (nonzero) if `path` is a directory, and false (0) otherwise.

```
#include <stdio.h>
#include <time.h>
#include <sys/stat.h>

int isdirectory(char *path) {
   struct stat statbuf;

   if (stat(path, &statbuf) == -1)
      return 0;
   else
      return S_ISDIR(statbuf.st_mode);
}
```

isdirectory.c

macro	tests for
S_ISBLK(*m*)	block special file
S_ISCHR(*m*)	character special file
S_ISDIR(*m*)	directory
S_ISFIFO(*m*)	pipe or FIFO special file
S_ISLNK(*m*)	symbolic link
S_ISREG(*m*)	regular file
S_ISSOCK(*m*)	socket
S_TYPEISMQ(*buf*)	message queue
S_TYPEISSEM(*buf*)	semaphore
S_TYPEISSHM(*buf*)	shared memory object

Table 5.1: POSIX macros for testing for the type of file. Here *m* is of type `mode_t` and the value of *buf* is a pointer to a `struct stat` structure.

5.3 UNIX File System Implementation

Disk formatting divides a physical disk into regions called *partitions*. Each partition can have its own file system associated with it. A particular file system can be mounted at any node in the tree of another file system. The topmost node in a file system is called the *root* of the file system. The *root directory* of a process (denoted by /) is the topmost directory that the process can access. All fully qualified paths in UNIX start from the root directory /.

Figure 5.2 shows a typical root file system tree containing some of the standard UNIX subdirectories. The /dev directory holds specifications for the devices (special files) on the system. The /etc directory holds files containing information regarding the network, accounts and other databases that are specific to the machine. The /home directory is the default directory for user accounts. The /opt directory is a standard location for applications in System V Release 4. Look for include files in the /usr/include directory. The /var directory contains system files that vary and can grow arbitrarily large (e.g., log files, or mail when it arrives but before it has been read). POSIX does not require that a file system have these subdirectories, but many systems organize their directory structure in a similar way.

5.3.1 UNIX file implementation

POSIX does not mandate any particular representation of files on disk, but traditionally UNIX files have been implemented with a modified tree structure, as described in this section. Directory entries contain a filename and a reference to a fixed-length structure

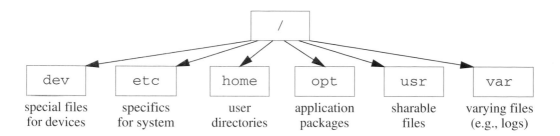

Figure 5.2: Structure of a typical UNIX file system

called an *inode*. The inode contains information about the file size, the file location, the owner of the file, the time of creation, time of last access, time of last modification, permissions and so on.

Figure 5.3 shows the inode structure for a typical file. In addition to descriptive information about the file, the inode contains pointers to the first few data blocks of the file. If the file is large, the indirect pointer is a pointer to a block of pointers that point to additional data blocks. If the file is still larger, the double indirect pointer is a pointer to a block of indirect pointers. If the file is really huge, the triple indirect pointer contains a pointer to a block of double indirect pointers. The word *block* can mean different things (even within UNIX). In this context a block is typically 8K bytes. The number of bytes in a block is always a power of 2.

□ Exercise 5.11

Suppose that an inode is 128 bytes, pointers are 4 bytes long, and the status information takes up 68 bytes. Assume a block size of 8K bytes and block pointers of 32 bits each. How much room is there for pointers in the inode? How big a file can be represented with direct pointers? Indirect? Double indirect? Triple indirect?

Answer:

The single, double, and triple indirect pointers take 4 bytes each, so $128 - 68 - 12 = 48$ bytes are available for 12 direct pointers. The size of the inode and the block size depend on the system. A file as large as $8192 \times 12 = 98,304$ bytes can be represented solely with direct pointers. If the block size is 8K bytes, the single indirect pointer addresses an 8K block that can hold $8192 \div 4 = 2048$ pointers to data blocks. Thus, the single indirect pointer provides the capability of addressing an additional $2048 \times 8192 = 16,777,216$ bytes or 16 megabytes of information. Double indirect addressing provides 2048×2048 pointers with the capability of addressing an additional 32 gigabytes. Triple indirect addressing provides $2048 \times$

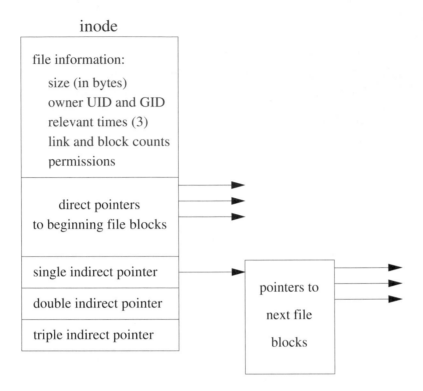

Figure 5.3: Schematic structure of a traditional UNIX file.

2048×2048 pointers with the capability of addressing an additional 64 terabytes. However, since $2048^3 = 2^{33}$, pointers would need to be longer than 4 bytes to fully address this storage.

☐ Exercise 5.12

How large a file can you access using only the single indirect, double indirect, and triple indirect pointers if the block size is 8K bytes and pointers are 64 bits?

Answer:

A block can now hold only 1024 pointers, so the single indirect pointer can address $1024 \times 8192 = 8{,}388{,}608$ bytes. Double indirect addressing provides 1024×1024 pointers with the capability of addressing an additional 8 gigabytes. Triple indirect addressing provides $1024 \times 1024 \times 1024$ pointers with the capability of addressing an additional 8 terabytes.

☐ Exercise 5.13

How big can you make a disk partition if the block size is 8K bytes and pointers are 32 bits? How can bigger disks be handled? What are the tradeoffs?

Answer:

32-bit addresses can access approximately 4 billion blocks (4,294,967,296 to be exact). 8K blocks give $2^{45} \approx 3.5 \times 10^{13}$ bytes. With a block address of fixed size, there is a tradeoff between maximum partition size and block size. Larger blocks mean a larger partition for a fixed address size. The block size usually determines the smallest retrievable unit on disk. Larger blocks can be retrieved relatively more efficiently but can result in greater internal fragmentation because of partially filled blocks.

The tree-structured representation of files is fairly efficient for small files and is also flexible if the size of the file changes. When a file is created, the operating system finds free blocks on the disk in which to place the data. Performance considerations dictate that blocks of the same file should be located close to one another on the disk to reduce the seek time. It takes about twenty times as long to read a 16-megabyte file in which the data blocks are randomly placed than one in which the data blocks are contiguous.

When a system administrator creates a file system on a physical disk partition, the raw bytes are organized into data blocks and inodes. Each physical disk partition has its own pool of inodes that are uniquely numbered. Files created on that partition use inodes from that partition's pool. The relative layout of the disk blocks and inodes has been optimized for performance.

POSIX does not require that a system actually represent its files by using inodes. The `ino_t st_ino` member of the `struct stat` is now called a *file serial number* rather than an *inode number*. POSIX-compliant systems must provide the information corresponding to the mandatory members of the `struct stat` specified on page 155, but POSIX leaves the actual implementation unspecified. In this way, the POSIX standard tries to separate implementation from the interface.

☐ Exercise 5.14

Give some limitations of a file implementation based on inodes.

Answer:

The file must fit entirely in a single disk partition. The partition size and maximum number of files are fixed when the system is set up.

5.3.2 Directory implementation

A *directory* is a file containing a correspondence between filenames and file locations. UNIX has traditionally implemented the location specification as an inode number, but as noted above, POSIX does not require this. The inode itself does not contain the filename. When a program references a file by pathname, the operating system traverses the file system tree to find the filename and inode number in the appropriate directory. Once it has the inode number, the operating system can determine other information about the file by accessing the inode. (For performance reasons, this is not as simple as it seems, because the operating system caches both directory entries and inode entries in main memory.)

A directory implementation that contains only names and inode numbers has the following advantages.

1. Changing the filename requires changing only the directory entry. A file can be moved from one directory to another just by moving the directory entry, as long as the move keeps the file on the same partition or slice. (The mv command uses this technique for moving files to locations within the same file system. Since a directory entry refers to an inode on the same partition as the directory entry itself, mv cannot use this approach to move files between different partitions.)

2. Only one physical copy of the file needs to exist on disk, but the file may have several names or the same name in different directories. Again, all of these references must be on the same physical partition.

3. Directory entries are of variable length because the filename is of variable length. Directory entries are small, since most of the information about each file is kept in its inode. Manipulating small variable-length structures can be done efficiently. The larger inode structures are of fixed length.

5.4 Hard Links and Symbolic Links

UNIX directories have two types of links—links and symbolic links. A link, sometimes called a *hard link*, is a directory entry. Recall that a directory entry associates a filename with a file location. A *symbolic link*, sometimes called a *soft link*, is a file that stores a string used to modify the pathname when it is encountered during pathname resolution. The behavioral differences between hard and soft links in practice is often not intuitively obvious. For simplicity and concreteness, we assume an inode representation of the files. However, the discussion applies to other file implementations.

A directory entry corresponds to a single link, but an inode may be the target of several of these links. Each inode contains the count of the number of links to the inode (i.e., the total number of directory entries that contain the inode number). When a program uses open to create a file, the operating system makes a new directory entry and assigns a free inode to represent the newly created file.

Figure 5.4 shows a directory entry for a file called name1 in the directory /dirA. The file uses inode 12345. The inode has one link, and the first data block is block 23567. Since the file is small, all the file data is contained in this one block, which is represented by the short text in the figure.

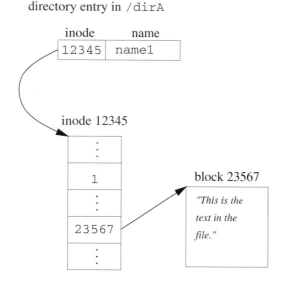

Figure 5.4: Directory entry, inode and data block for a simple file.

5.4.1 Creating or removing a link

You can create additional links to a file with the ln shell command or the link function. The creation of the new link allocates a new directory entry and increments the link count of the corresponding inode. The link uses no other additional disk space.

When you delete a file by executing the rm shell command or by calling the unlink function from a program, the operating system deletes the corresponding directory entry and decrements the link count in the inode. It does not free the inode and the corresponding data blocks unless the operation causes the link count to be decremented to 0.

The link function creates a new directory entry for the existing file specified by path1 in the directory specified by path2.

```
SYNOPSIS

   #include <unistd.h>

   int link(const char *path1, const char *path2);
                                                              POSIX
```

If successful, the link function returns 0. If unsuccessful, link returns −1 and sets errno. The following table lists the mandatory errors for link.

errno	cause
EACCES	search permission on a prefix of `path1` or `path2` denied, or link requires writing in a directory with write permission denied, or process does not have required access permission for file
EEXIST	`path2` resolves to a symbolic link or to an existing file
ELOOP	a loop exists in resolution of `path1` or `path2`
EMLINK	number of links to file specified by `path1` would exceed `LINK_MAX`
ENAMETOOLONG	the length of `path1` or `path2` exceeds `PATH_MAX`, or a pathname component is longer than `NAME_MAX`
ENOENT	a component of either path prefix does not exist, or file named by `path1` does not exist, or `path1` or `path2` points to an empty string
ENOSPC	directory to contain the link cannot be extended
ENOTDIR	a component of either path prefix is not a directory
EPERM	file named by `path1` is a directory and either calling process does not have privileges or implementation does not allow `link` for directories
EROFS	`link` would require writing in a read-only file system
EXDEV	link named by `path2` and file named by `path1` are on different file systems, and implementation does not support links between file systems

■ **Example 5.15**

The following shell command creates an entry called `name2` in `dirB` containing a pointer to the same inode as `/dirA/name1`.

```
ln /dirA/name1 /dirB/name2
```

The result is shown in Figure 5.5.

■ **Example 5.16**

The following code segment performs the same action as the `ln` shell command of Example 5.15.

```
#include <stdio.h>
#include <unistd.h>

if (link("/dirA/name1", "/dirB/name2") == -1)
    perror("Failed to make a new link in /dirB");
```

Figure 5.4 shows a schematic of `/dirA/name1` before the `ln` command of Example 5.15 or the `link` function of Example 5.16 executes. Figure 5.5 shows the result of linking.

The `ln` command (or `link` function) creates a link (directory entry) that refers to the same inode as `dirA/name1`. No additional disk space is required, except possibly if the new directory entry increases the number of data blocks needed to hold the directory information. The inode now has two links.

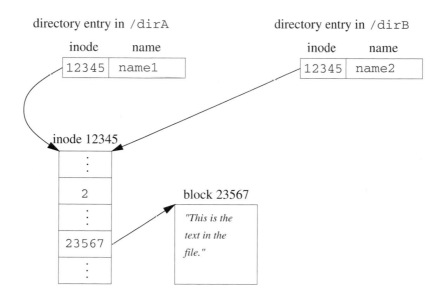

Figure 5.5: Two hard links to the same file shown in Figure 5.4.

The `unlink` function removes the directory entry specified by `path`. If the file's link count is 0 and no process has the file open, the `unlink` frees the space occupied by the file.

```
SYNOPSIS

   #include <unistd.h>

   int unlink(const char *path);
                                                           POSIX
```

If successful, the `unlink` function returns 0. If unsuccessful, `unlink` returns −1 and sets `errno`. The following table lists the mandatory errors for `unlink`.

errno	cause
EACCES	search permission on a component of the path prefix is denied, or write permission is denied for directory containing directory entry to be removed
EBUSY	file named by `path` cannot be unlinked because it is in use and the implementation considers this an error
ELOOP	a loop exists in resolution of `path`
ENAMETOOLONG	the length of `path` exceeds `PATH_MAX`, or a pathname component is longer than `NAME_MAX`
ENOENT	a component of `path` does not name an existing file, or `path` is an empty string
ENOTDIR	a component of the path prefix is not a directory
EPERM	file named by `path` is a directory and either the calling process does not have privileges or implementation does not allow `unlink` for directories
EROFS	`unlink` would require writing in a read-only file system

☐ Exercise 5.17

The following sequence of operations might be performed by a text editor when editing the file /dirA/name1.

> Open the file /dirA/name1.
> Read the entire file into memory.
> Close /dirA/name1.
> Modify the memory image of the file.
> Unlink /dirA/name1.
> Open the file /dirA/name1 (create and write flags).
> Write the contents of memory to the file.
> Close /dirA/name1.

How would Figures 5.4 and 5.5 be modified if you executed this sequence of operations on each configuration?

Answer:

After these operations were applied to Figure 5.4, the new file would have the same name as the old but would have the new contents. It might use a different inode number and block. This is what we would expect. When the text editor applies the same set of operations to the configuration of Figure 5.5, unlinking removes the directory entry for /dirA/name1. The `unlink` reduces the link count but does not delete the file, since the link /dirB/name2 is still pointing to it. When the editor opens the file /dirA/name1 with the create flag set, a new directory entry and new inode are created. We now have /dirA/name1 referring to the new file and /dirB/name2 referring to the old file. Figure 5.6 shows the final result.

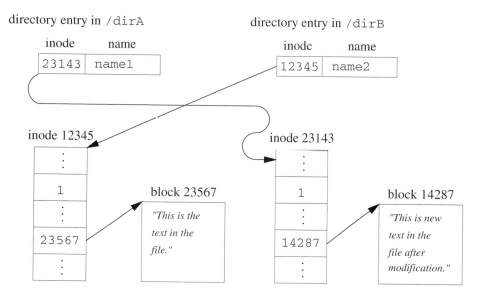

Figure 5.6: Situation after a text editor changes a file. The original file had inode 12345 and two hard links before editing (i.e., the configuration of Figure 5.5).

☐ **Exercise 5.18**

Some editors back up the old file. One possible way of doing this is with the following sequence of operations.

> Open the file /dirA/name1.
> Read the entire file into memory.
> Close /dirA/name1.
> Modify the memory image of the file.
> Rename the file /dirA/name1 /dirA/name1.bak.
> Open the file /dirA/name1 (create and write flags).
> Write the contents of memory to the file.
> Close /dirA/name1.

Describe how this strategy affects each of Figures 5.4 and 5.5.

Answer:

Starting with the configuration of Figure 5.4 produces two distinct files. The file /dirA/name1 has the new contents and uses a new inode. The file /dirA/name1.bak has the old contents and uses the old inode. For the configuration of Figure 5.5, /dirA/name1.bak and /dirB/name2 point to the old contents using the old inode. The second open creates a new inode for dirA/name1, resulting in the configuration of Figure 5.7.

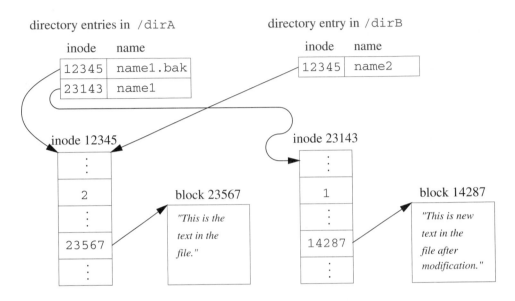

Figure 5.7: Situation after one file is changed with an editor that makes a backup copy.

The behavior illustrated in Exercises 5.17 and 5.18 may be undesirable. An alternative approach would be to have both /dirA/name1 and /dirB/name2 reference the new file. In Exercise 5.22 we explore an alternative sequence of operations that an editor can use.

5.4.2 Creating and removing symbolic links

A *symbolic link* is a file containing the name of another file or directory. A reference to the name of a symbolic link causes the operating system to locate the inode corresponding to that link. The operating system assumes that the data blocks of the corresponding inode contain another pathname. The operating system then locates the directory entry for that pathname and continues to follow the chain until it finally encounters a hard link and a real file. The system gives up after a while if it doesn't find a real file, returning the ELOOP error.

Create a symbolic link by using the ln command with the -s option or by invoking the symlink function. The path1 parameter of symlink contains the string that will be the contents of the link, and path2 gives the pathname of the link. That is, path2 is the newly created link and path1 is what the new link points to.

```
SYNOPSIS

  #include <unistd.h>

  int symlink(const char *path1, const char *path2);
```
POSIX

If successful, `symlink` returns 0. If unsuccessful, `symlink` returns −1 and sets `errno`. The following table lists the mandatory errors for `symlink`.

errno	cause
EACCES	search permission on a component of the path prefix of `path2` is denied, or link requires writing in a directory with write permission denied
EEXIST	`path2` names an existing file or symbolic link
EIO	an I/O error occurred while reading from or writing to the file system
ELOOP	a loop exists in resolution of `path2`
ENAMETOOLONG	the length of `path2` exceeds PATH_MAX, or a pathname component is longer than NAME_MAX or the length `path1` is longer than SYMLINK_MAX
ENOENT	a component of `path2` does not name an existing file, or `path2` is an empty string
ENOSPC	directory to contain the link cannot be extended, or the file system is out of resources
ENOTDIR	a component of the path prefix for `path2` is not a directory
EROFS	the new symbolic link would reside on a read-only file system

■ Example 5.19

Starting with the situation shown in Figure 5.4, the following command creates the symbolic link `/dirB/name2`, as shown in Figure 5.8.

```
ln -s /dirA/name1 /dirB/name2
```

■ Example 5.20

The following code segment performs the same action as the `ln -s` of Example 5.19.

```
if (symlink("/dirA/name1", "/dirB/name2") == -1)
    perror("Failed to create symbolic link in /dirB");
```

Unlike Exercise 5.17, the `ln` command of Example 5.19 and the `symlink` function of Example 5.20 use a new inode, in this case 13579, for the symbolic link. Inodes contain information about the type of file they represent (i.e., ordinary, directory, special,

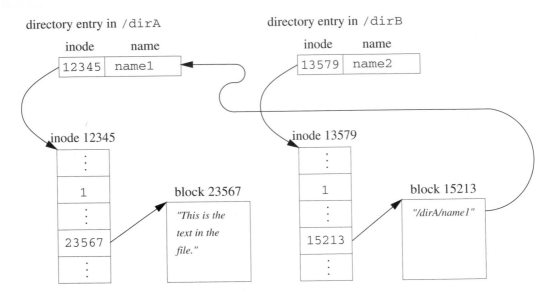

Figure 5.8: Ordinary file with a symbolic link to it.

or symbolic link), so inode 13579 contains information indicating that it is a symbolic link. The symbolic link requires at least one data block. In this case, block 15213 is used. The data block contains the name of the file that /dirB/name2 is linked to, in this case, /dirA/name1. The name may be fully qualified as in this example, or it may be relative to its own directory.

❏ **Exercise 5.21**

Suppose that /dirA/name1 is an ordinary file and /dirB/name2 is a symbolic link to /dirA/name1, as in Figure 5.8. How are the files /dirB/name2 and /dirA/name1 related after the sequence of operations described in Exercise 5.17?

Answer:

/dirA/name1 now refers to a different inode, but /dirB/name2 references the name dirA/name1, so they still refer to the same file, as shown in Figure 5.9. The link count in the inode counts only hard links, not symbolic links. When the editor unlinks /dirA/name1, the operating system deletes the file with inode 12345. If other editors try to edit /dirB/name2 in the interval during which /dirA/name1 is unlinked but not yet created, they get an error.

❏ **Exercise 5.22**

How can the sequence of operations in Exercise 5.17 be modified so that

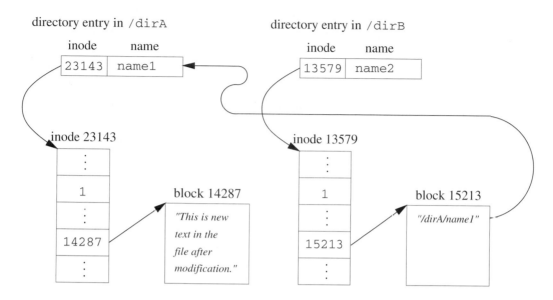

Figure 5.9: Situation after editing a file that has a symbolic link.

`/dirB/name2` references the new file regardless of whether this was a hard link or a symbolic link?

Answer:

The following sequence of operations can be used.

> Open the file `/dirA/name1`.
> Read the entire file into memory.
> Close `/dirA/name1`.
> Modify the memory image of the file.
> Open the file `/dirA/name1` with the `O_WRONLY` and `O_TRUNC` flags.
> Write the contents of memory to the file.
> Close `/dirA/name1`.

When the editor opens the file the second time, the same inode is used but the contents are deleted. The file size starts at 0. The new file will have the same inode as the old file.

◻ **Exercise 5.23**

Exercise 5.22 has a possibly fatal flaw: If the application or operating system crashes between the second open and the subsequent write operation, the file is lost. How can this be prevented?

Answer:
Before opening the file for the second time, write the contents of memory to a temporary file. Remove the temporary file after the close of /dirA/name1 is successful. This approach allows the old version of the file to be retrieved if the application crashes. However, a successful return from close does not mean that the file has actually been written to disk, since the operating system buffers this operation. One possibility is to use a function such as fsync after write. The fsync returns only after the pending operations have been written to the physical medium. The fsync function is part of the POSIX:FSC Extension.

☐ Exercise 5.24

Many programs assume that the header files for the X Window System are in /usr/include/X11, but under Sun's Solaris operating environment these files are in the directory /usr/openwin/share/include/X11. How can a system administrator deal with the inconsistency?

Answer:
There are several ways to address this problem.
1. Copy all these files into /usr/include/X11.
2. Move all the files into /usr/include/X11.
3. Have users modify all programs that contain lines in the following form.

   ```
   #include <X11/xyz.h>
   ```

   Replace these lines with the following.

   ```
   #include "/usr/openwin/share/include/X11/xyz.h"
   ```

4. Have users modify their makefiles so that compilers look for header files in the following directory.

   ```
   /usr/openwin/share/include
   ```

5. Create a symbolic link from /usr/include/X11 to the following directory.

   ```
   /usr/openwin/share/include/X11
   ```

All the alternatives except the last have serious drawbacks. If the header files are copied to the directory /usr/include/X11, then two copies of these files exist. Aside from the additional disk space required, an update might cause these files to be inconsistent. Moving the files (copying them to the directory /usr/include/X11 and then deleting them from /usr/openwin/share/include/X11) may interfere with operating system upgrades. Having users modify all their programs or makefiles is unreasonable. Another alternative not mentioned above is to use an environment variable to modify the search path for header files.

□ **Exercise 5.25**

Because of a large influx of user mail, the root partition of a server becomes full. What can a system administrator do?

Answer:

Pending mail is usually kept in a directory with a name such as /var/mail or /var/spool/mail, which may be part of the root partition. One possibility is to expand the size of the root partition. This expansion usually requires reinstallation of the operating system. Another possibility is to mount an unused partition on var. If a spare partition is not available, the /var/spool/mail directory can be a symbolic link to any directory in a partition that has sufficient space.

□ **Exercise 5.26**

Starting with Figure 5.8, execute the command rm /dirA/name1. What happens to /dirB/name2?

Answer:

This symbolic link still exists, but it is pointing to something that is no longer there. A reference to /dirB/name2 gives an error as if the symbolic link /dirB/name2 does not exist. However, if later a new file named /dirA/name1 is created, the symbolic link then points to that file.

When you reference a file representing a symbolic link by name, does the name refer to the link or to the file that the link references? The answer depends on the function used to reference the file. Some library functions and shell commands automatically follow symbolic links and some do not. For example, the rm command does not follow symbolic links. Applying rm to a symbolic link removes the symbolic link, not what the link references. The ls command does not follow symbolic links by default, but lists properties such as date and size of the link itself. Use the -L option with ls to obtain information about the file that a symbolic link references. Some operations have one version that follows symbolic links (e.g., stat) and another that does not (e.g., lstat). Read the man page to determine a particular function's behavior in traversing symbolic links.

5.5 Exercise: The which Command

The which command is available on many systems. It takes the name of an executable as a command-line argument and displays the fully qualified pathname of the corresponding executable. If the argument to which contains a path specifier (/), which just checks to see if this path corresponds to an executable. If the argument does not contain a path specifier, which uses the PATH environment variable to search directories for the corresponding executable. If which locates the executable, it prints the fully qualified path. Otherwise, which prints an message indicating that it could not find the executable in the path.

Implement a `which` command. If no path-specifier character is given, use `getenv` to get the `PATH` environment variable. Start by creating a fully qualified path, using each component of the `PATH` until an appropriate file is found. Write a `checkexecutable` function with the following prototype.

```
int checkexecutable(char *name);
```

The `checkexecutable` function returns true if the given file is executable by the owner of the current process. Use `geteuid` and `getegid` to find the user ID and group ID of the owner of the process. Use `stat` to see if this user has execute privilege for this file. There are three cases to consider, depending on whether the user is the owner of the file, in the same group as the file or neither.

The `which` command of the `csh` shell also checks to see if an alias is set for the command-line argument and reports that alias instead of searching for an executable. See if you can implement this feature.

5.6 Exercise: Biffing

Some systems have a facility called `biff` that enables mail notification. When a user who is logged in receives mail, `biff` notifies the user in some way (e.g., beeping at the terminal or displaying a message). UNIX folklore has it that `biff`'s original author had a dog named Biff who barked at mail carriers.

Program 5.4 shows the code for a C program called `simplebiff.c` that beeps at the terminal at regular intervals if the user `ostudent` has pending mail. The program beeps by sending a Ctrl-G (ASCII 7) character to standard error. Most terminals handle the receipt of Ctrl-G by producing a short beep. The program continues beeping every 10 seconds, until it is killed or the mail file is removed. This simple version assumes that if the mail file exists, it has mail in it. On some systems the mail file may exist but contain zero bytes when there is no mail. Program 8.10 on page 281 gives a version that does not have this problem.

■ Example 5.27
The following command starts `simplebiff`.

```
simplebiff &
```

The `&` tells the shell to run `simplebiff` in the background so that `ostudent` can do something else.

◻ Exercise 5.28
What happens if you execute the command of Example 5.27 and then log off?

Answer:

The `simplebiff` program continues to run after you log off, since it was started in the background. Execute `ps -a` to determine `simplebiff`'s process ID. Kill the `simplebiff` process by entering the command `kill -KILL pid`. Make sure `simplebiff` is gone by doing another `ps -a`.

Program 5.4 ─────────────────────────────── **simplebiff.c**

A simple program to notify ostudent *of pending mail.*

```c
#include <errno.h>
#include <fcntl.h>
#include <stdio.h>
#include <unistd.h>
#include <sys/stat.h>
#define MAILFILE "/var/mail/ostudent"
#define SLEEPTIME 10

int main(void) {
   int mailfd;

   for( ; ; ) {
      if ((mailfd = open(MAILFILE, O_RDONLY)) != -1) {
         fprintf(stderr, "%s", "\007");
         while ((close(mailfd) == -1) && (errno == EINTR)) ;
      }
      sleep(SLEEPTIME);
   }
}
```

Program 5.4 ─────────────────────────────── **simplebiff.c**

Mail is usually stored in a file in the `/var/mail` or `/var/spool/mail` directory. A file in that directory with the same name as the user's login name contains all unread mail for that user. If `ostudent` has mail, an `open` of `/var/mail/ostudent` succeeds; otherwise, the `open` fails. If the file exists, the user has unread mail and the program beeps. In any case, the program sleeps and then repeats the process indefinitely.

❑ Exercise 5.29

Run Program 5.4 after replacing the user name and mail directory names so that they are appropriate for your system.

Program 5.4 is not very general because the user name, mail directory and sleep time are hardcoded. In addition, the `stat` function provides more information about a file without the overhead of `open`.

❑ Exercise 5.30

Modify Program 5.4 to use `stat` instead of `open`.

◻ **Exercise 5.31**

On some systems, a user's new mail file always exists but has zero bytes if the user has no mail. Modify `simplebiff` to account for this case.

The POSIX-approved way of getting the user name is to call `getuid` to find out the user ID and then call `getpwuid` to retrieve the user's login name. The `getpwuid` function takes the user's numerical ID as a parameter and retrieves a `passwd` structure that has the user's name as a member.

```
SYNOPSIS

   #include <pwd.h>

   struct passwd *getpwuid(uid_t uid);
                                                              POSIX
```

If unsuccessful, `getpwuid` returns a `NULL` pointer and sets `errno`.

The `struct passwd` structure is defined in `pwd.h`. The POSIX base definition specifies that the `struct passwd` structure have at least the following members.

```
char    *pw_name      /* user's login name */
uid_t   pw_uid        /* numerical user ID */
gid_t   pw_gid        /* numerical group ID */
char    *pwd_dir      /* initial working directory */
char    *pw_shell     /* program to use as shell */
```

◻ **Exercise 5.32**

Find out the base directory name of the directory in which unread mail is stored on your system. (The base directory in Program 5.4 is `/var/mail/`.) Construct the pathname of the unread mail by concatenating the base mail directory and the program's user name. Use `getuid` and `getpwuid` in combination to determine the user name at run time.

The directory used for mail varies from system to system, so you must determine the location of the system mail files on your system in order to use `simplebiff`. A better version of the program would allow the user to specify a directory on the command line or to use system-specific information communicated by environment variables if this information is available. The POSIX:Shell and Utilities standard specifies that the `sh` shell use the `MAIL` environment variable to determine the pathname of the user's mail file for the purpose of incoming mail notification. The same standard also specifies that the `MAILCHECK` environment variable be used to specify how often (in seconds) the shell should check for the arrival of new messages for notification. The standard states that the default value of `MAILCHECK` should be 600.

☐ Exercise 5.33

Rewrite Program 5.4 so that it uses the value of MAILCHECK for the sleep time if that environment variable is defined. Otherwise, it should use a default value of 600.

☐ Exercise 5.34

Rewrite your program of Exercise 5.33 so that it uses the value passed on the command line as the pathname for the user's mailbox. If `simplebiff` is called with no command-line arguments, the program should use the value of the MAIL environment variable as the pathname. If MAIL is undefined and there were no command-line arguments, the program should use a default path of `/var/mail/user`. Use the method of Exercise 5.32 to find the value of `user`.

☐ Exercise 5.35

Rewrite Program 5.4 so that it has the following synopsis.

```
simplebiff [-s n]  [-p pathname]
```

The [ ] in the synopsis indicates optional command-line arguments. The first command-line argument specifies a sleep interval. If `-s n` is not provided on the command line and MAILCHECK is not defined, use the value of SLEEPTIME as a default. The `-p pathname` specifies a pathname for the system mail directory. If this option is not specified on the command line, use the MAIL environment variable value as a default value. If MAIL is not defined, use the MAILFILE defined in the program. Read the man page for the `getopt` function and use it to parse the command-line arguments.

5.7 Exercise: News `biff`

The `simplebiff` program informs the user of incoming mail. A user might also want to be informed of changes in other files such as the Internet News files. If a system is a news server, it probably organizes articles as individual files whose pathname contains the newsgroup name.

■ Example 5.36

A system keeps its news files in the directory `/var/spool/news`. Article 1034 in newsgroup `comp.os.unix` is located in the following file.

```
/var/spool/news/comp/os/unix/1034
```

The following exercises develop a facility for biffing when any file in a list of files changes.

1. Write a function called `lastmod` that returns the time at which a file was last modified. The prototype for `lastmod` is as follows.

```
time_t lastmod(char *pathname);
```

Use `stat` to determine the last modification time. The `time_t` is time in seconds since 00:00:00 UTC, January 1, 1970. The `lastmod` function returns −1 if there is an error and sets `errno` to the error number set by `stat`.

2. Write a main program that takes a pathname as a command-line argument and calls `lastmod` to determine the time of last modification of the corresponding file. Use `ctime` to print out the `time_t` value in a readable form. Compare the results with those obtained from `ls -l`.

3. Write a function called `convertnews` that converts a newsgroup name to a fully qualified pathname. The prototype of `convertnews` is as follows.

```
char *convertnews(char *newsgroup);
```

If the environment variable `NEWSDIR` is defined, use it to determine the path. Otherwise, use `/var/spool/news`. (Call `getenv` to determine whether the environment variable is defined.) For example, if the newsgroup is `comp.os.unix` and `NEWSDIR` is not defined, the pathname is the following.

```
/var/spool/news/comp/os/unix
```

The `convertnews` function allocates space to hold the converted string and returns a pointer to that space. (A common error is to return a pointer to an automatic variable defined within `convertnews`.) Do not modify `newsgroup` in `convertnews`. The `convertnews` returns a `NULL` pointer and sets `errno` if there was an error.

4. Write a program that takes a `newsgroup` name and a `sleeptime` value as command-line arguments. Print the time of the last modification of the `newsgroup` and then loop as follows.
   a) Sleep for `sleeptime`.
   b) Test to see whether the `newsgroup` has been modified.
   c) If the `newsgroup` directory has been modified, print a message with the `newsgroup` name and the time of modification.

   Test the program on several newsgroups. Post news to a local newsgroup to verify that the program is working. The `newsgroup` directory can be modified both by news arrival and by expiration. Most systems expire news in the middle of the night.

5. Generalize your `newsbiff` program so that it reads in a list of files to be tracked from a file. Your program should store the files and their last modification times in a list. (For example, you can modify the list object developed in Section 2.9 for this purpose.) Your program should sleep for a specified number of seconds and then update the modification times of the files in the list. If any have changed, print an informative message to standard output.

5.8 Exercise: Traversing Directories

The exercises in this section develop programs to traverse directory trees in depth-first and breadth-first orders. Depth-first searches explore each branch of a tree to its leaves before looking at other branches. Breadth-first searches explore all the nodes at a given level before descending lower in the tree.

■ **Example 5.37**

For the file system tree in Figure 5.1 on page 146, depth-first ordering visits the nodes in the following order.

```
/
   dirC
      my3.dat
   dirA
      dirB
         my1.dat
      my1.dat
      my2.dat
```

The indentation of the filenames in Example 5.37 shows the level in the file system tree. Depth-first search is naturally recursive, as indicated by the following pseudocode.

```
depthfirst(root) {
   for each node at or below root
      visit node;
         if node is a directory
            depthfirst(node);
}
```

■ **Example 5.38**

For the file system tree in Figure 5.1, breadth-first order visits the nodes in the following order.

```
/
/dirC
/dirA
/dirC/my3.dat
/dirA/dirB
/dirA/my1.dat
/dirA/my2.dat
/dirA/dirB/my1.dat
```

Breadth-first search can be implemented with a queue similar to the history queue of Program 2.8 on page 47. As the program encounters each directory node at a particular level, it enqueues the complete pathname for later examination. The following pseudocode assumes the existence of a queue. The `enqueue` operation puts a node at the end of the queue, and the `dequeue` operation removes a node from the front of the queue.

```
breadthfirst(root){
    enqueue(root);
    while (queue is not empty) {
        dequeue(&next);
        for each node directly below next:
            visit the node
            if node is a directory
                enqueue(node)
    }
}
```

☐ Exercise 5.39

The UNIX du shell command is part of the POSIX:UP Extension. The command displays the sizes of the subdirectories of the tree rooted at the directory specified by its command-line argument. If called with no directory, the du utility uses the current working directory. If du is defined on your system, experiment with it. Try to determine which search strategy it uses to traverse the tree.

Develop a program called mydu that uses a depth-first search strategy to display the sizes of the subdirectories in a tree rooted at the specified file.

1. Write a function called depthfirstapply that has the following prototype.

   ```
   int depthfirstapply(char *path, int pathfun(char *path1));
   ```

   The depthfirstapply function traverses the tree, starting at path. It applies the pathfun function to each file that it encounters in the traversal. The depthfirstapply function returns the sum of the positive return values of pathfun, or −1 if it failed to traverse any subdirectory of the directory. An example of a possible pathfun is the sizepathfun function specified in the next part.

2. Write a function called sizepathfun that has the following prototype.

   ```
   int sizepathfun(char *path);
   ```

   The sizepathfun function outputs path along with other information obtained by calling stat for path. The sizepathfun returns the size in blocks of the file given by path or −1 if path does not correspond to an ordinary file.

3. Use depthfirstapply with the pathfun given by sizepathfun to implement the following command.

   ```
   showtreesize pathname
   ```

   The showtreesize command writes pathname followed by its total size to standard output. If pathname is a directory, the total size corresponds to the size of the entire subtree rooted at pathname. If pathname is a special file, print an informative message but no size.

4. Write a command called mydu that is called with a command-line argument rootpath as follows.

```
mydu rootpath
```

The `mydu` program calls a modified `depthfirstapply` with the function `sizepathfun`. It outputs the size of each directory followed by its pathname. The size of the directory does not count the size of subtrees of that directory. The program outputs the total size of the tree at the end and exits.

5. Write `breadthfirstapply` that is similar to `depthfirstapply` but uses a breadth-first search strategy.

5.9 Additional Reading

Advanced Programming in the UNIX Environment by Stevens [112] has a good technical discussion of files and directories. Depth-first and breadth-first search strategies are discussed in standard algorithms books such as *An Introduction to Algorithms* by Cormen, Leiserson and Rivest [25].

Chapter 6

UNIX Special Files

This chapter discusses UNIX special files that represent devices. Two important examples of special files are pipes and FIFOs, inter-process communication mechanisms that allow processes running on the same system to share information and hence cooperate. The chapter introduces the client-server model and also discusses how to handle special files representing devices such as terminals.

Objectives
- Learn about interprocess communication
- Experiment with client-server interactions
- Explore pipes and redirection
- Use device control to set parameters
- Understand how UNIX achieves device independence

6.1 Pipes

The capacity to communicate is essential for processes that cooperate to solve a problem. The simplest UNIX interprocess communication mechanism is the pipe, which is represented by a special file. The `pipe` function creates a communication buffer that the caller can access through the file descriptors `fildes[0]` and `fildes[1]`. The data written to `fildes[1]` can be read from `fildes[0]` on a first-in-first-out basis.

SYNOPSIS

```
#include <unistd.h>

int pipe(int fildes[2]);
```
                                                                                            POSIX

If successful, `pipe` returns 0. If unsuccessful, `pipe` returns −1 and sets `errno`. The following table lists the mandatory errors for `pipe`.

errno	cause
EMFILE	more than `MAX_OPEN-2` file descriptors already in use by this process
ENFILE	number of simultaneously open files in system would exceed system-imposed limit

A pipe has no external or permanent name, so a program can access it only through its two descriptors. For this reason, a pipe can be used only by the process that created it and by descendants that inherit the descriptors on `fork`. The `pipe` function described here creates a traditional unidirectional communication buffer. The POSIX standard does not specify what happens if a process tries to write to `fildes[0]` or read from `fildes[1]`.

When a process calls `read` on a pipe, the `read` returns immediately if the pipe is not empty. If the pipe is empty, the `read` blocks until something is written to the pipe, as long as some process has the pipe open for writing. On the other hand, if no process has the pipe open for writing, a `read` from an empty pipe returns 0, indicating an end-of-file condition. (This description assumes that access to the pipe uses blocking I/O.)

■ Example 6.1

The following code segment creates a pipe.

```
int fd[2];
if (pipe(fd) == -1)
   perror("Failed to create the pipe");
```

If the `pipe` call executes successfully, the process can read from `fd[0]` and write to `fd[1]`.

A single process with a pipe is not very useful. Usually a parent process uses pipes to communicate with its children. Program 6.1 shows a simple program in which the parent creates a pipe before forking a child. The parent then writes a string to the pipe and prints a message to standard error. The child reads a message from the pipe and then prints to standard error. This program does not check for errors on the read or write operations.

Program 6.1 ———————————————————————— **parentwritepipe.c**
A program in which a parent writes a string to a pipe and the child reads the string. The program does not check for I/O errors.

```c
#include <stdio.h>
#include <string.h>
#include <unistd.h>
#include <sys/types.h>
#define BUFSIZE 10

int main(void) {
   char bufin[BUFSIZE] = "empty";
   char bufout[] = "hello";
   int bytesin;
   pid_t childpid;
   int fd[2];

   if (pipe(fd) == -1) {
      perror("Failed to create the pipe");
      return 1;
   }
   bytesin = strlen(bufin);
   childpid = fork();
   if (childpid == -1) {
      perror("Failed to fork");
      return 1;
   }
   if (childpid)                                    /* parent code */
      write(fd[1], bufout, strlen(bufout)+1);
   else                                             /* child code */
      bytesin = read(fd[0], bufin, BUFSIZE);
   fprintf(stderr, "[%ld]:my bufin is {%.*s}, my bufout is {%s}\n",
           (long)getpid(), bytesin, bufin, bufout);
   return 0;
}
```

Program 6.1 ———————————————————————— **parentwritepipe.c**

□ **Exercise 6.2**

Run Program 6.1 and explain the results. Does the child always read the full string?

Answer:
The parent's `bufin` always contains the string `"empty"`. The child's `bufin` most likely contains the string `"hello"`. However, reads from pipes are not atomic. That is, there is no guarantee that a single `read` call actually retrieves everything written by a single `write` call. It is possible (though not likely in this case) that the child's `bufin` could contain something like `"helty"` if `read` retrieves only partial results. If the parent's `write` operation fails, the child's `bufin` contains `"empty"`.

◻ Exercise 6.3

Consider the following code segment from Program 6.1.

```
if (childpid)
    write(fd[1], bufout, strlen(bufout)+1);
else
    bytesin = read(fd[0], bufin, BUFSIZE);
```

What happens if you replace it with the following code?

```
if (childpid)
    copyfile(STDIN_FILENO, fd[1]);
else
    copyfile(fd[0], STDOUT_FILENO);
```

(The `copyfile` function is shown in Program 4.6 on page 100.)

Answer:
The parent process reads from standard input and writes to the pipe, while the child reads from the pipe and echoes to standard output. The parent echoes everything entered at the keyboard as it is typed, and the child writes to the screen as it reads each entered line from the pipe. A difficulty arises, however, when you enter the end-of-file character (usually Ctrl-D) at the terminal. The parent detects the end of the input, displays the message written by its `fprintf`, and exits with no problem, closing its descriptors to the pipe. Unfortunately, the child still has `fd[1]` open, so the `copyfile` function does not detect that input has ended. The child hangs, waiting for input, and does not exit. Since the parent has exited, the prompt appears, but the child process is still running. Unless you execute `ps` you might think that the child terminated also. To fix the problem, replace the substitute code with the following.

```
if (childpid && (close(fd[0]) != -1))
    copyfile(STDIN_FILENO, fd[1]);
else if (close(fd[1]) != -1)
    copyfile(fd[0], STDOUT_FILENO);
```

Program 6.2 shows a modification of Program 3.2 from page 68. The modification demonstrates how to use reading from pipes for synchronization. The parent creates a pipe before creating n-1 children. After creating all its children, the parent writes n characters to the pipe. Each process, including the parent, reads a character from the pipe before proceeding to output its information to standard error. Since the read from the pipe blocks until there is something to read, each child waits until the parent writes to the pipe, thereby providing a synchronization point called a *barrier*. None of the processes can do any writing to standard error until all of the processes have been created. Section 6.8 gives another example of barrier synchronization. Notice that Program 6.2 uses r_write and r_read rather than `write` and `read` to ensure that the parent actually writes everything and that the children actually perform their reads. The children do not synchronize after the barrier.

Program 6.2 ──────────────────────── **synchronizefan.c**

A synchronized process fan. Processes wait until all have been created before echoing their messages to standard error.

```
#include <stdio.h>
#include <stdlib.h>
#include <unistd.h>
#include "restart.h"

int main  (int argc, char *argv[]) {
   char buf[] = "g";
   pid_t childpid = 0;
   int fd[2];
   int i, n;

   if (argc != 2){      /* check for valid number of command-line arguments */
      fprintf (stderr, "Usage: %s processes\n", argv[0]);
      return 1;
   }
   n = atoi(argv[1]);
   if (pipe(fd) == -1) {              /* create pipe for synchronization */
      perror("Failed to create the synchronization pipe");
      return 1;
   }
   for (i = 1; i < n;  i++)                /* parent creates all children */
      if ((childpid = fork()) <= 0)
         break;
   if (childpid > 0) {         /* write synchronization characters to pipe */
      for (i = 0; i < n; i++)
         if (r_write(fd[1], buf, 1) != 1)
            perror("Failed to write synchronization characters");
   }
   if (r_read(fd[0], buf, 1) != 1)                        /* synchronize here */
      perror("Failed to read synchronization characters");
   fprintf(stderr, "i:%d  process ID:%ld  parent ID:%ld  child ID:%ld\n",
           i, (long)getpid(), (long)getppid(), (long)childpid);
   return (childpid == -1);
}
```

Program 6.2 ──────────────────────── **synchronizefan.c**

6.2 Pipelines

Section 4.7 explains how a process can redirect standard input or output to a file. Redirection allows programs that are written as filters to be used very generally. This section describes how to use redirection with pipes to connect processes together. (You may want to review Section 4.7, which explains how a process can redirect standard input or output to a file.)

■ **Example 6.4**

The following commands use the sort filter in conjunction with ls to output a directory listing sorted by size.

```
ls -l > my.file
sort -n +4 < my.file
```

The first option to sort gives the type of sort (n means numeric). The second option instructs the program to find the sort key by skipping four fields.

The first command of Example 6.4 causes the process that runs the ls -l to redirect its standard output to the disk file my.file. Upon completion, my.file contains the unsorted directory listing. At this point, the second command creates a process to run the sort with its standard input redirected from my.file. Since sort is a filter, the sorted listing appears on standard output. Unfortunately, when the pair of commands completes, my.file remains on disk until explicitly deleted.

An alternative approach for outputting a sorted directory listing is to use an interprocess communication (IPC) mechanism such as a pipe to send information directly from the ls process to the sort process.

■ **Example 6.5**

The following alternative to the commands of Example 6.4 produces a sorted directory listing without creating the intermediate file my.file.

```
ls -l | sort -n +4
```

The vertical bar (|) of Example 6.5 represents a pipe. A programmer can build complicated transformations from simple filters by feeding the standard output of one filter into the standard input of the other filter through an intermediate pipe. The pipe acts as a buffer between the processes, allowing them to read and write at different speeds. The blocking nature of read and write effectively synchronize the processes.

The connection between ls and sort in Example 6.5 differs from redirection because no permanent file is created. The standard output of ls is "connected" to the standard input of sort through the intermediate communication buffer. Figure 6.1 shows a schematic of the connection and the corresponding file descriptor tables after the processes representing

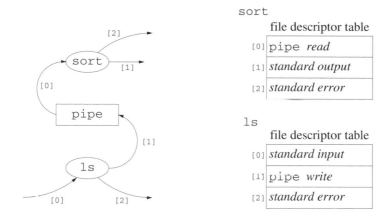

Figure 6.1: Status of the file descriptor table during execution of Example 6.5.

ls and sort establish the connection. The ls process redirects its standard output to the write descriptor of the pipe, and sort redirects its standard input to the read descriptor of the pipe. The sort process reads the data that ls writes on a first-in-first-out basis. The sort process does not have to consume data at the same rate as ls writes it to the pipe.

Program 6.3 shows a program that implements the equivalent of Example 6.5. Figures 6.2 to 6.4 depict the state of the file descriptor table for Program 6.3. In Figure 6.2, the child process inherits a copy of the file descriptor table of the parent. Both processes have read and write descriptors for the pipe. Figure 6.3 shows the file descriptor table after the child redirects its standard output and the parent redirects its standard input, but before either process closes unneeded file descriptors. Figure 6.4 shows the configuration after each process completes the close calls. This is the configuration inherited by execl.

☐ Exercise 6.6

Explain why the only return values in Program 6.3 indicate error conditions. Under what circumstances does this program execute successfully?

Answer:

The program executes successfully when both parent and child successfully run execl on their respective programs and these programs complete successfully. If execution reaches one of the return statements of Program 6.3, at least one of the execl calls failed. Once an execl call completes successfully, the program on which execl was run is responsible for the error handling.

Program 6.3 ─────────────────────────────── `simpleredirect.c`
        A program to execute the equivalent of `ls -l | sort -n +4`.

```c
#include <errno.h>
#include <stdio.h>
#include <unistd.h>
#include <sys/types.h>

int main(void) {
   pid_t childpid;
   int fd[2];

   if ((pipe(fd) == -1) || ((childpid = fork()) == -1)) {
      perror("Failed to setup pipeline");
      return 1;
   }

   if (childpid == 0) {                               /* ls is the child */
      if (dup2(fd[1], STDOUT_FILENO) == -1)
         perror("Failed to redirect stdout of ls");
      else if ((close(fd[0]) == -1) || (close(fd[1]) == -1))
         perror("Failed to close extra pipe descriptors on ls");
      else {
         execl("/bin/ls", "ls", "-l", NULL);
         perror("Failed to exec ls");
      }
      return 1;
   }
   if (dup2(fd[0], STDIN_FILENO) == -1)               /* sort is the parent */
      perror("Failed to redirect stdin of sort");
   else if ((close(fd[0]) == -1) || (close(fd[1]) == -1))
      perror("Failed to close extra pipe file descriptors on sort");
   else {
      execl("/bin/sort", "sort", "-n", "+4", NULL);
      perror("Failed to exec sort");
   }
   return 1;
}
```

Program 6.3 ─────────────────────────────── `simpleredirect.c`

☐ Exercise 6.7

What output would be generated if the file descriptors `fd[0]` and `fd[1]` were not closed before the calls to `execl`?

Answer:

No output would be generated. The `sort` process reads from standard input until an end-of-file occurs. Since it is reading from a pipe, `sort` detects an end-of-file (`read` returns 0) only when the pipe is empty and no processes have the pipe open for writing. As illustrated in Figure 6.4, only the `ls` program (the child) can write to the pipe. Eventually, this program terminates, and `sort` (the parent) detects end-of-file. If Program 6.3 omits the `close` calls, the situation looks like Figure 6.3. When the child terminates, the parent still has file descriptor [4] open for writing to the pipe. The parent blocks indefinitely, waiting for more data.

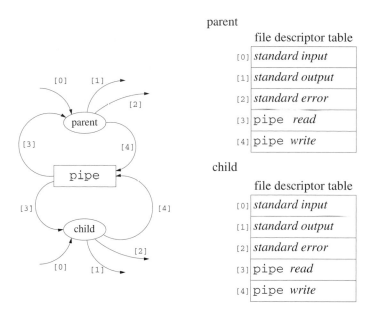

Figure 6.2: Status of the file descriptor table after the fork in Program 6.3.

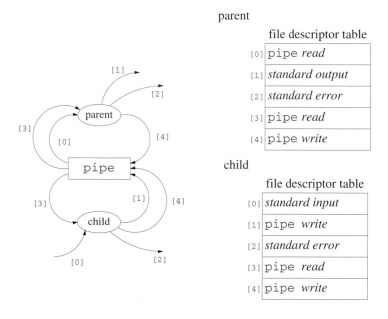

Figure 6.3: Status of the file descriptor table after both `dup2` functions of Program 6.3.

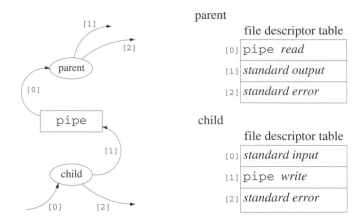

Figure 6.4: Status of the file descriptor table after all `close` calls of Program 6.3.

6.3 FIFOs

Pipes are temporary in the sense that they disappear when no process has them open. POSIX represents *FIFOs* or *named pipes* by special files that persist even after all processes have closed them. A FIFO has a name and permissions just like an ordinary file and appears in the directory listing given by `ls`. Any process with the appropriate permissions can access a FIFO. Create a FIFO by executing the `mkfifo` command from a shell or by calling the `mkfifo` function from a program.

The `mkfifo` function creates a new FIFO special file corresponding to the pathname specified by `path`. The `mode` argument specifies the permissions for the newly created FIFO.

```
SYNOPSIS

   #include <sys/stat.h>

   int mkfifo(const char *path, mode_t mode);
                                                          POSIX
```

If successful, `mkfifo` returns 0. If unsuccessful, `mkfifo` returns −1 and sets `errno`. A return value of −1 means that the FIFO was not created. The following table lists the mandatory errors for `mkfifo`.

errno	cause
EACCES	search permission on a component of path prefix denied, or write permission on parent directory of FIFO denied
EEXIST	named file already exists
ELOOP	a loop exists in resolution of path
ENAMETOOLONG	length of path exceeds PATH_MAX, or a pathname component is longer than NAME_MAX
ENOENT	component of path prefix specified by path does not name existing file, or path is an empty string
ENOSPC	directory to contain new file cannot be extended, or the file system is out of resources
ENOTDIR	component of path prefix is not a directory
EROFS	the named file would reside on a read-only file system

Unlike many other I/O functions, mkfifo does not set errno to EINTR.

■ Example 6.8

The following code segment creates a FIFO, myfifo, in the current working directory. This FIFO can be read by everybody but is writable only by the owner.

```
#define FIFO_PERMS   (S_IRUSR | S_IWUSR | S_IRGRP | S_IROTH)

if (mkfifo("myfifo", FIFO_PERMS) == -1)
   perror("Failed to create myfifo");
```

Remove a FIFO the same way you remove a file. Either execute the rm command from a shell or call unlink from a program. Example 6.9 shows a code segment that removes the FIFO that Example 6.8 created. The code assumes that the current working directory of the calling program contains myfifo.

■ Example 6.9

The following code segment removes myfifo from the current working directory.

```
if (unlink("myfifo") == -1)
   perror("Failed to remove myfifo");
```

Program 6.4 creates a named pipe from a path specified on the command line. It then forks a child. The child process writes to the named pipe, and the parent reads what the child has written. Program 6.4 includes error checking, identifying each message with the process ID. This identification of messages is important because the parent and child share standard error.

Program 6.4 ───────────────────────────── **parentchildfifo.c**
The parent reads what its child has written to a named pipe.

```c
#include <errno.h>
#include <fcntl.h>
#include <stdio.h>
#include <string.h>
#include <unistd.h>
#include <sys/stat.h>
#include <sys/wait.h>
#define BUFSIZE 256
#define FIFO_PERM  (S_IRUSR | S_IWUSR)

int dofifochild(const char *fifoname, const char *idstring);
int dofifoparent(const char *fifoname);

int main (int argc, char *argv[]) {
   pid_t childpid;

   if (argc != 2) {                              /* command line has pipe name */
      fprintf(stderr, "Usage: %s pipename\n", argv[0]);
      return 1;
   }
   if (mkfifo(argv[1], FIFO_PERM) == -1) {           /* create a named pipe */
      if (errno != EEXIST) {
         fprintf(stderr, "[%ld]:failed to create named pipe %s: %s\n",
               (long)getpid(), argv[1], strerror(errno));
         return 1;
      }
   }
   if ((childpid = fork()) == -1){
      perror("Failed to fork");
      return 1;
   }
   if (childpid == 0)                                    /* The child writes */
      return dofifochild(argv[1], "this was written by the child");
   else
      return dofifoparent(argv[1]);
}
```

Program 6.4 ─────────────────────────── **parentchildfifo.c**

The `dofifochild` function of Program 6.5 shows the actions taken by the child to write to the pipe. Notice that Program 6.5 uses `snprintf` rather than `sprintf` to construct the message. The first three parameters to `snprintf` are the buffer address, the buffer size and the format string. The `snprintf` does not write beyond the specified size and always inserts a null character to terminate what it has inserted. Program 6.5 also uses `r_write` instead of `write` to make sure that the child writes the entire message.

┌ **Program 6.5** ─────────────────────── `dofifochild.c` ┐
The child writes to the pipe and returns.

```
#include <errno.h>
#include <fcntl.h>
#include <stdio.h>
#include <string.h>
#include <unistd.h>
#include <sys/stat.h>
#include "restart.h"
#define BUFSIZE 256

int dofifochild(const char *fifoname, const char *idstring) {
   char buf[BUFSIZE];
   int fd;
   int rval;
   ssize_t strsize;

   fprintf(stderr, "[%ld]:(child) about to open FIFO %s...\n",
           (long)getpid(), fifoname);
   while (((fd = open(fifoname, O_WRONLY)) == -1) && (errno == EINTR)) ;
   if (fd == -1) {
      fprintf(stderr, "[%ld]:failed to open named pipe %s for write: %s\n",
              (long)getpid(), fifoname, strerror(errno));
      return 1;
   }
   rval = snprintf(buf, BUFSIZE, "[%ld]:%s\n", (long)getpid(), idstring);
   if (rval < 0) {
      fprintf(stderr, "[%ld]:failed to make the string:\n", (long)getpid());
      return 1;
   }
   strsize = strlen(buf) + 1;
   fprintf(stderr, "[%ld]:about to write...\n", (long)getpid());
   rval = r_write(fd, buf, strsize);
   if (rval != strsize) {
      fprintf(stderr, "[%ld]:failed to write to pipe: %s\n",
              (long)getpid(), strerror(errno));
      return 1;
   }
   fprintf(stderr, "[%ld]:finishing...\n", (long)getpid());
   return 0;
}
```

└ **Program 6.5** ─────────────────────── `dofifochild.c` ┘

The `dofifoparent` function of Program 6.6 shows the actions taken by the parent to read from the pipe.

❑ Exercise 6.10

What happens to the named pipe after the processes of Program 6.4 exit?

Answer:

Since neither process called `unlink` for the FIFO, it still exists and appears in the directory listing of its path.

Program 6.6 ———————————————————————— `dofifoparent.c`

The parent reads what was written to a named pipe.

```c
#include <errno.h>
#include <fcntl.h>
#include <stdio.h>
#include <string.h>
#include <unistd.h>
#include <sys/stat.h>
#include "restart.h"
#define BUFSIZE 256
#define FIFO_MODES O_RDONLY

int dofifoparent(const char *fifoname) {
   char buf[BUFSIZE];
   int fd;
   int rval;

   fprintf(stderr, "[%ld]:(parent) about to open FIFO %s...\n",
                       (long)getpid(), fifoname);
   while ((((fd = open(fifoname, FIFO_MODES)) == -1) && (errno == EINTR))  ;
   if (fd == -1) {
      fprintf(stderr, "[%ld]:failed to open named pipe %s for read: %s\n",
              (long)getpid(), fifoname, strerror(errno));
      return 1;
   }
   fprintf(stderr, "[%ld]:about to read...\n", (long)getpid());
   rval = r_read(fd, buf, BUFSIZE);
   if (rval == -1) {
      fprintf(stderr, "[%ld]:failed to read from pipe: %s\n",
              (long)getpid(), strerror(errno));
      return 1;
   }
   fprintf(stderr, "[%ld]:read %.*s\n", (long)getpid(), rval, buf);
   return 0;
}
```

Program 6.6 ———————————————————————— `dofifoparent.c`

6.4 Pipes and the Client-Server Model

The client-server model is a standard pattern for process interaction. One process, designated the *client*, requests a service from another process, called the *server*. The chapters
in Part 4 of the book develop and analyze applications that are based on the client-server
model with network communication. This section introduces client-server applications
that use named pipes as the communication vehicle. We look at two types of client-server
communication—*simple-request* and *request-reply*. In simple-request, the client sends
information to the server in a one-way transmission; in request-reply the client sends a
request and the server sends a reply.

Programs 6.7 and 6.8 illustrate how the simple-request protocol can be useful in logging. The client writes logging information to a named pipe rather than to standard error.

A server reads from the named pipe and writes to a file. At first glance, the use of the named pipe appears to have added an extra step with no benefit. However, pipes and FIFOs have a very important property—writes of no more than PIPE_BUF bytes are guaranteed to be atomic. That is, the information is written as a unit with no intervening bytes from other writes. In contrast, an fprintf is not atomic, so pieces of the messages from multiple clients might be interspersed.

The server of Program 6.7 creates the pipe if it does not already exist. The server opens the pipe for both reading and writing, even though it will not write to the pipe. When an attempt is made to open a pipe for reading, open blocks until another process opens the pipe for writing. Because the server opens the pipe for reading and writing, open does not block. The server uses copyfile to read from the pipe and to write to standard output. To write to a file, just redirect standard output when the server is started. Since the server has the pipe open for writing as well as reading, copyfile will never detect an end-of-file. This technique allows the server to keep running even when no clients are currently writing to the pipe. Barring errors, the server runs forever.

Program 6.7 ———————————————————— `pipeserver.c` ┐
   The program reads what is written to a named pipe and writes it to standard output.

```c
#include <errno.h>
#include <fcntl.h>
#include <stdio.h>
#include <stdlib.h>
#include <unistd.h>
#include <sys/stat.h>
#include "restart.h"
#define FIFOARG 1
#define FIFO_PERMS (S_IRWXU | S_IWGRP| S_IWOTH)

int main (int argc, char *argv[]) {
   int requestfd;

   if (argc != 2) {     /* name of server fifo is passed on the command line */
      fprintf(stderr, "Usage: %s fifoname > logfile\n", argv[0]);
      return 1;
   }
                           /* create a named pipe to handle incoming requests */
   if ((mkfifo(argv[FIFOARG], FIFO_PERMS) == -1) && (errno != EEXIST)) {
      perror("Server failed to create a FIFO");
      return 1;
   }
                     /* open a read/write communication endpoint to the pipe */
   if ((requestfd = open(argv[FIFOARG], O_RDWR)) == -1) {
      perror("Server failed to open its FIFO");
      return 1;
   }
   copyfile(requestfd, STDOUT_FILENO);
   return 1;
}
```

Program 6.7 ———————————————————— `pipeserver.c` ┘

The client in Program 6.8 writes a single line to the pipe. The line contains the process ID of the client and the current time. Multiple copies of Program 6.8 can run concurrently. Because of the atomic nature of writes to the pipe, pieces of the messages from different clients are not interleaved.

Program 6.8 ──────────────────────────── **`pipeclient.c`**
The client writes an informative message to a named pipe.

```
#include <errno.h>
#include <fcntl.h>
#include <limits.h>
#include <stdio.h>
#include <stdlib.h>
#include <strings.h>
#include <time.h>
#include <unistd.h>
#include <sys/stat.h>
#include "restart.h"
#define FIFOARG 1

int main (int argc, char *argv[]) {
   time_t curtime;
   int len;
   char requestbuf[PIPE_BUF];
   int requestfd;

   if (argc != 2) {  /* name of server fifo is passed on the command line */
      fprintf(stderr, "Usage: %s fifoname", argv[0]);
      return 1;
   }

   if ((requestfd = open(argv[FIFOARG], O_WRONLY)) == -1) {
       perror("Client failed to open log fifo for writing");
       return 1;
   }

   curtime = time(NULL);
   snprintf(requestbuf, PIPE_BUF, "%d: %s", (int)getpid(), ctime(&curtime));
   len = strlen(requestbuf);
   if (r_write(requestfd, requestbuf, len) != len) {
      perror("Client failed to write");
      return 1;
   }
   r_close(requestfd);
   return 0;
}
```

Program 6.8 ──────────────────────────── **`pipeclient.c`**

☐ **Exercise 6.11**

How would you start Program 6.7 so that it uses the pipe `mypipe` and the log file it creates is called `mylog`? When will the program terminate?

Answer:

```
pipeserver mypipe > mylog
```

The program does not terminate unless it is killed. You can kill it by typing Ctrl-C at the keyboard. No client error can cause the server to terminate.

□ **Exercise 6.12**

Start the `pipeserver` of Program 6.7 and run several copies of the `pipeclient` of Program 6.8 and observe the results.

We now consider a second example of the client-server model with named pipes, a simple time (sequence number) server that illustrates some of the difficulties in using the client-server model with pipes and FIFOs.

The implementation uses two named pipes—a request pipe and a sequence pipe. Clients write a byte to a request pipe (e.g., `'g'`). The server responds by writing a sequence number to the sequence pipe and incrementing the sequence number. Unfortunately, reading from a pipe is not an atomic operation. Since the sequence number is more than one byte, it is possible (though unlikely) that a client may not get all of the bytes of a sequence number in one read. Depending on the interleaving of the client processes, the next client may get part of the previous sequence number. To handle this possibility, a client that does a partial read of the sequence number immediately transmits an error designator (e.g., `'e'`) on the request pipe. When the server encounters the error character, it closes and unlinks the pipes. The other clients then detect an error.

As before, the server opens both pipes for reading and writing. The server terminates only when it receives an `'e'` byte from a client. When that happens, future clients block when they try to open the request pipe for writing. Pending clients receive an error when they try to write to the request pipe since no process has this pipe open. When a process writes to a pipe or FIFO that no process has open for reading, `write` generates a `SIGPIPE` signal. Unless the process has specifically prevented it, the signal causes the process to terminate immediately. Section 8.4 explains how to respond to these types of signals.

Programs 6.9 and 6.10 illustrate the difficulties of implementing a request-reply protocol by using named pipes. When multiple clients make requests, the server replies can be read by any client. This allows a sequence number meant for one process to be read by another process. Second, because reads are not atomic, a partial read by one client causes the next client to receive incorrect results. The solution in Program 6.9 and Program 6.10 is for the client to send an error code, which causes the server to terminate. This strategy may suffice for closely cooperating processes, but it is not applicable in general. A malicious client could cause the protocol to behave incorrectly without detecting an error. In most cases, the client should never be able to cause the server to fail or exit. The exercise of Section 6.10 explores an alternative strategy in which the server creates a separate named pipe for each distinct client. Now each pipe only has a single reader, eliminating the two problems described above.

Program 6.9 ──────────────────────────────────── `seqserverbad.c`

*A sequence server reads a character from the request pipe and transmits a sequence
number to the sequence pipe. (See text for a discussion.)*

```c
#include <errno.h>
#include <fcntl.h>
#include <stdio.h>
#include <stdlib.h>
#include <unistd.h>
#include <sys/stat.h>
#include "restart.h"
#define ERROR_CHAR 'e'
#define OK_CHAR 'g'
#define REQUEST_FIFO 1
#define REQ_PERMS (S_IRUSR | S_IWUSR | S_IWGRP | S_IWOTH)
#define SEQUENCE_FIFO 2
#define SEQ_PERMS (S_IRUSR | S_IWUSR | S_IRGRP| S_IROTH)

int main (int argc, char *argv[]) {
   char buf[1];
   int reqfd, seqfd;
   long seqnum = 1;
   if (argc != 3) {             /* names of fifos passed on the command line */
      fprintf(stderr, "Usage: %s requestfifo sequencefifo\n", argv[0]);
      return 1;
   }
                           /* create a named pipe to handle incoming requests */
   if ((mkfifo(argv[REQUEST_FIFO], REQ_PERMS) == -1) && (errno != EEXIST)) {
      perror("Server failed to create request FIFO");
      return 1;
   }
   if ((mkfifo(argv[SEQUENCE_FIFO], SEQ_PERMS) == -1) && (errno != EEXIST)){
      perror("Server failed to create sequence FIFO");
      if (unlink(argv[REQUEST_FIFO]) == -1)
         perror("Server failed to unlink request FIFO");
      return 1;
   }
   if (((reqfd = open(argv[REQUEST_FIFO], O_RDWR)) == -1) ||
       ((seqfd = open(argv[SEQUENCE_FIFO], O_RDWR)) == -1)) {
      perror("Server failed to open one of the FIFOs");
      return 1;
   }
   for ( ;  ;  ) {
      if (r_read(reqfd, buf, 1) == 1) {
         if ((buf[0] == OK_CHAR) &&
             (r_write(seqfd, &seqnum, sizeof(seqnum)) == sizeof(seqnum)))
            seqnum++;
         else if (buf[0] == ERROR_CHAR)
            break;
      }
   }
   if (unlink(argv[REQUEST_FIFO]) == -1)
      perror("Server failed to unlink request FIFO");
   if (unlink(argv[SEQUENCE_FIFO]) == -1)
      perror("Server failed to unlink sequence FIFO");
   return 0;
}
```

Program 6.9 ──────────────────────────────────── `seqserverbad.c`

The client writes a request to a request pipe and reads the sequence number from the sequence pipe. This client can cause the server to exit.

```c
#include <errno.h>
#include <fcntl.h>
#include <stdio.h>
#include <stdlib.h>
#include <strings.h>
#include <unistd.h>
#include <sys/stat.h>
#include "restart.h"
#define ERROR_CHAR 'e'
#define OK_CHAR 'g'
#define REPEAT_MAX 100
#define REQUEST_FIFO 1
#define SEQUENCE_FIFO 2
#define SLEEP_MAX 5

int main (int argc, char *argv[]) {
   int i;
   char reqbuf[1];
   int reqfd, seqfd;
   long seqnum;

   if (argc != 3) {              /* names of pipes are command-line arguments */
      fprintf(stderr, "Usage: %s requestfifo sequencefifo\n", argv[0]);
      return 1;
   }
   if (((reqfd = open(argv[REQUEST_FIFO], O_WRONLY)) == -1) ||
       ((seqfd = open(argv[SEQUENCE_FIFO], O_RDONLY)) == -1)) {
      perror("Client failed to open a FIFO");
      return 1;
   }
   for (i = 0; i < REPEAT_MAX; i++) {
      reqbuf[0] = OK_CHAR;
      sleep((int)(SLEEP_MAX*drand48()));
      if (r_write(reqfd, reqbuf, 1) == -1) {
         perror("Client failed to write request");
         break;
      }
      if (r_read(seqfd, &seqnum, sizeof(seqnum)) != sizeof(seqnum) ) {
         fprintf(stderr, "Client failed to read full sequence number\n");
         reqbuf[0] = ERROR_CHAR;
         r_write(reqfd, reqbuf, 1);
         break;
      }
      fprintf(stderr, "[%ld]:received sequence number %ld\n",
              (long)getpid(), seqnum);
   }
   return 0;
}
```

The situation with nonatomic reads from pipes can actually be worse than described here. We have assumed that a read becomes nonatomic as follows.

1. The server gets two requests and writes two sequence numbers (4-byte integers) to the pipe.
2. One client calls `read` for the sequence pipe requesting four bytes, but `read` returns only two bytes.
3. The second client calls `read` for the sequence pipe to read the next four bytes. These four bytes consist of the last two bytes from the first sequence number and the first two bytes of the second sequence number.

Under these circumstances the first client detects an error, and the server shuts down. The second client may or may not know an error occurred.

However, another scenario is technically possible, although it is very unlikely. Suppose the server writes two 4-byte integer sequence numbers and the bytes in the pipe are `abcdefgh`. The POSIX standard does not exclude the possibility that the first client will read the bytes `abgh` and the second one will read the bytes `cdef`. In this case, the sequence numbers are incorrect and the error is not detected at all.

☐ Exercise 6.13

Try running one copy of Program 6.9 (`seqserverbad`) and two copies of Program 6.10 (`seqclientbad`). What happens?

Answer:

This should work correctly. The two copies of `seqclientbad` should get disjoint sets of sequence numbers.

☐ Exercise 6.14

Try running two copies of Program 6.9 (`seqserverbad`) and one copy of Program 6.10 (`seqclientbad`). What happens?

Answer:

Either server can respond to a request for a sequence number. It is possible that the client will get the same sequence number twice.

☐ Exercise 6.15

Change the `seqclientbad` to have a SLEEP_MAX of 0 and a REPEAT_MAX of 1,000,000. Comment out the last `fprintf` line. Run two copies of the client with one copy of the server. What happens?

Answer:

It is possible, but unlikely, that the server will terminate because one of the clients received an incorrect number of bytes when requesting the sequence number.

6.5 Terminal Control

Many special files represent devices with characteristics that are platform dependent, making standardization difficult. However, since terminal control was thought to be essential on all systems, the POSIX standards committee decided to include library functions for manipulating special files representing terminals and asynchronous communication ports. This section describes these functions and the way to use them.

The stty command reports or sets terminal I/O characteristics. When executed without any arguments or with the -a or -g options, the stty command outputs information about the current terminal to standard output. The -a produces a longer form of the readable information produced by stty without arguments; the -g option produces the information in a form that can be used by a program. The second form of stty allows operands to change the behavior of the terminal associated with a shell.

SYNOPSIS

```
stty [-a | -g]
stty operands
```

POSIX:Shell and Utilities

□ **Exercise 6.16**

Execute stty, stty -a and stty -g on your system. Try to interpret the results.

Answer:

The stty command outputs the following under Sun Solaris 9.

```
speed 9600 baud; -parity
rows = 34; columns = 80; ypixels = 680; xpixels = 808;
swtch = <undef>;
brkint -inpck -istrip icrnl -ixany imaxbel onlcr tab3
echo echoe echok echoctl echoke iexten
```

The stty -a command on the same system outputs a more complete listing of the terminal settings.

```
speed 9600 baud;
rows = 34; columns = 80; ypixels = 680; xpixels = 808;
csdata ?
eucw 1:0:0:0, scrw 1:0:0:0
intr = ^c; quit = ^\; erase = ^?; kill = ^u;
eof = ^d; eol = <undef>; eol2 = <undef>; swtch = <undef>;
start = ^q; stop = ^s; susp = ^z; dsusp = ^y;
rprnt = ^r; flush = ^o; werase = ^w; lnext = ^v;
-parenb -parodd cs8 -cstopb -hupcl cread -clocal -loblk
-crtscts -crtsxoff -parext -ignbrk brkint ignpar -parmrk
-inpck -istrip -inlcr -igncr icrnl -iuclc ixon -ixany -ixoff
imaxbel isig icanon -xcase echo echoe echok -echonl -noflsh
-tostop echoctl -echoprt echoke -defecho -flusho -pendin iexten
opost -olcuc onlcr -ocrnl -onocr -onlret -ofill -ofdel tab3
```

The `stty -g` command outputs the following on a single line.

```
2506:1805:d00bd:8a3b:3:1c:7f:15:4:0:0:0:11:13:1a:19:12:f:
17:16:0:0:1:1:0:00:0:0:0:0:0:0:0:0:0:0:0:0:0:0:0:0:0:0:
0:0:0:0:0:0:0:0:0:0:0:0:0:0:0:0:0:0:0:0:0
```

The interpretation of the fields closely follows the flags in the `struct termios` structure described below.

The `stty -a` command displays the current terminal settings, and the second form of `stty` allows you to change them. One important operand of `stty` is `sane`. This operand sets all modes to reasonable values and is useful if you terminate a program that has set the modes in an inconvenient way. You can use `stty sane` to recover when, for example, local echo has been turned off and you cannot see what you are typing. Sometimes you will have to terminate the line containing the `stty` command with a Ctrl-J rather than pressing the Return key if Return has been set to send a carriage return rather than a newline.

Programs access terminal characteristics through the `struct termios` structure, which includes at least the following members.

```
tcflag_t      c_iflag;       /* input modes */
tcflag_t      c_oflag;       /* output modes */
tcflag_t      c_cflag;       /* control modes */
tcflag_t      c_lflag;       /* local modes */
cc_t          c_cc[NCCS];    /* control characters */
```

The `c_cc` array of the `struct termios` structure holds the values of the characters that have special meaning to the terminal device drivers, for example, the end of input or program break characters. Table 6.1 on page 206 lists the special characters and their default settings.

The `c_iflag` member of the `struct termios` structure controls the way a terminal handles input; the `c_oflag` controls the way a terminal handles output. The `c_cflag` specifies hardware control information for the terminal, and the `c_lflag` controls the editing functions of the terminal. Table 6.2 on page 210 lists the POSIX values that these flags can take on. You can set an action by performing a bitwise OR of the appropriate `struct termios` field with the corresponding flag, and you can clear it by performing a bitwise AND with the complement of the flag.

■ Example 6.17

The ECHO value of the `c_lflag` field of `struct termios` specifies that characters typed at standard input should be echoed to standard output of the terminal. The following code segment clears the ECHO flag in a `struct termios` structure.

```
struct termio term;
term.c_lflag &= ~ECHO;
```

The `tcgetattr` function retrieves the attributes associated with the terminal referenced by the open file descriptor `fildes`. The attributes are returned in a `struct termios` structure pointed to by `termios_p`. The `tcsetattr` function sets the parameters of the terminal referenced by the open file descriptor `fildes` from the `struct termios` structure pointed to by `termios_p`. The `optional_actions` parameter controls the point at which the changes take effect: `TCSANOW` signifies that changes occur immediately, and `TCSADRAIN` signifies that changes occur after all output to `fildes` is transmitted. If `optional_actions` is `TCSAFLUSH`, the changes occur after all output to `fildes` is transmitted. In this case, all input received but not read is discarded.

```
SYNOPSIS

   #include <termios.h>

   int tcgetattr(int fildes, struct termios *termios_p);
   int tcsetattr(int fildes, int optional_actions,
                 const struct termios *termios_p);
                                                              POSIX
```

These functions return 0 if successful. If unsuccessful, these functions return −1 and set `errno`. The following table lists the mandatory errors for these functions.

errno	cause
EBADF	`fildes` is not a valid file descriptor
EINTR	a signal interrupted `tcsetattr`
EINVAL	`optional_actions` is not a supported value, or attempt to change attribute represented in `struct termios` to an unsupported value
ENOTTY	file associated with `fildes` is not a terminal

Program 6.11 shows a `ttysetchar` function that sets a particular character. The `ttysetchar` function first calls `tcgetattr` to read the current settings of the terminal into a `struct termios` structure. After modifying the desired characters, `ttysetchar` calls `tcsetattr` to change the actual terminal settings. It is possible for `tcsetattr` to be interrupted by a signal while it is waiting for output to drain, so we restart it in this case.

■ Example 6.18

The following code segment calls the `ttysetchar` function of Program 6.11 to set the character that indicates end of terminal input to Ctrl-G. (The usual default is Ctrl-D.)

```
if (ttysetchar(STDIN_FILENO, VEOF, 0x07) == -1)
   perror("Failed to change end-of-file character");
```

canonical mode	noncanonical mode	description	usual default
VEOF		EOF character	Ctrl-D
VEOL		EOL character	none
VERASE		ERASE character	backspace or delete
VINTR	VINTR	INTR character	Ctrl-C
VKILL		KILL character	Ctrl-U
	VMIN	MIN value	1
VQUIT	VQUIT	QUIT character	Ctrl-\
VSUSP	VSUSP	SUSP character	Ctrl-Z
	VTIME	TIME value	0
VSTART	VSTART	START character	Ctrl-Q
VSTOP	VSTOP	STOP character	Ctrl-S

Table 6.1: The POSIX special control characters

Program 6.11 ———————————————————————— **ttysetchar.c**

A function that sets a particular terminal control character to be a particular value.

```c
#include <errno.h>
#include <termios.h>
#include <unistd.h>

int ttysetchar(int fd, int flagname, char c)  {
   int error;
   struct termios term;

   if (tcgetattr(fd, &term) == -1)
      return -1;
   term.c_cc[flagname] = (cc_t)c;
   while (((error = tcsetattr(fd, TCSAFLUSH, &term)) == -1) &&
          (errno == EINTR)) ;
   return error;
}
```

Program 6.11 ———————————————————————— **ttysetchar.c**

Program 6.12 shows a function that uses `tcgetattr` and `tcsetattr` to turn echoing on or off. When echoing is turned off, the characters that you type do not appear on the screen.

❏ **Exercise 6.19**

Why did Program 6.12 use `tcgetattr` to read the existing `struct termios` structure before setting the echo flags?

Answer:

The code shouldn't change any of the other settings, so it reads the existing `struct termios` structure before modifying it.

Program 6.12 ──────────────────────────────────── `setecho.c`

A function to turn terminal echo on or off.

```
#include <errno.h>
#include <termios.h>
#include <unistd.h>
#define ECHOFLAGS (ECHO | ECHOE | ECHOK | ECHONL)

int setecho(int fd, int onflag)  {
    int error;
    struct termios term;

    if (tcgetattr(fd, &term) == -1)
        return -1;
    if (onflag)                                 /* turn echo on */
        term.c_lflag |= ECHOFLAGS;
    else                                        /* turn echo off */
        term.c_lflag &= ~ECHOFLAGS;
    while (((error = tcsetattr(fd, TCSAFLUSH, &term)) == -1) &&
            (errno == EINTR)) ;
    return error;
}
```

Program 6.12 ──────────────────────────────────── `setecho.c`

☐ Exercise 6.20

What happens when you run the following program? Under what circumstances might such behavior be useful?

```
#include <unistd.h>
int setecho(int fd, int onflag);

int main(void) {
    setecho(STDIN_FILENO, 0);
    return 0;
}
```

Answer:

After you run this program, you will not see anything that you type on the computer screen. You can log out or use `stty sane` to set the echo back on. Turning off echoing is used for entering passwords and other secrets.

Program 6.13 shows the `passwordnosigs` function that retrieves the password entered at the controlling terminal of a process. It returns 0 if successful. On failure it returns −1 and sets `errno`. Notice that `passwordnosigs` sets the `errno` based on the first error that occurs. While most functions return immediately after an error, functions that must always restore state have to clean up before they return. The program calls the `setecho` function of Program 6.12 to turn echoing off and on. It must turn the terminal echo back on before returning or the user won't be able to see what is typed.

Program 6.13 ────────────────────────────── **passwordnosigs.c**
A function that prompts for and reads a password, assuming that no signals will occur.

```c
#include <errno.h>
#include <fcntl.h>
#include <stdio.h>
#include <string.h>
#include <termios.h>
#include <unistd.h>
#include "restart.h"

int readline(int fd, char *buf, int nbytes);
int setecho(int fd, int onflag);

int passwordnosigs(char *prompt, char *passbuf, int passmax) {
   int fd;
   int firsterrno = 0;
   int passlen;
   char termbuf[L_ctermid];

   if (ctermid(termbuf) == NULL) {                      /* find the terminal name */
      errno = ENODEV;
      return -1;
   }
   if ((fd = r_open2(termbuf, O_RDWR)) == -1)           /* open the terminal */
      return -1;
   if (setecho(fd, 0) == -1)                            /* turn echo off */
      firsterrno = errno;
   else if (r_write(fd, prompt, strlen(prompt)) == -1)     /* write prompt */
      firsterrno = errno;
   else if ((passlen = readline(fd, passbuf, passmax)) == 0)
      firsterrno = EINVAL;
   else if (passlen == -1)
      firsterrno = errno;
   else
      passbuf[passlen-1] = '\0';                        /* remove newline */
   if ((setecho(fd, 1) == -1) && !firsterrno)  /* always turn echo back on */
      firsterrno =  errno;
   if ((r_write(fd,"\n",1) == -1) && !firsterrno)
      firsterrno = errno;
   if ((r_close(fd) == -1) && !firsterrno)
      firsterrno = errno;
   if (firsterrno)
      errno = firsterrno;
   return firsterrno ? -1 : 0;
}
```

Program 6.13 ────────────────────────────── **passwordnosigs.c**

The passwordnosigs uses readline of Program 4.1 on page 95 to read in a line
from the terminal. We were able to use it here because it was written to use a general file
descriptor rather than just reading from standard input.

The passwordnosigs function uses the controlling terminal as determined by the
ctermid function rather than using standard input. The controlling terminal is usually
something like /dev/tty and often shares the same physical devices as standard input

and standard output, which are usually the keyboard and screen. One of the consequences of using a controlling terminal rather than standard input and standard output is that controlling terminals cannot be redirected from the command line. This is often used for passwords to discourage users from storing passwords in a file.

◻ **Exercise 6.21**

What happens if a signal aborts a program that is executing `passwordnosigs`? This could happen if the user enters Ctrl-C after being prompted for the password.

Answer:

If the signal comes in after `passwordnosigs` turns off echoing, the user won't be able to see subsequent typing at the terminal. If you do this, try typing `stty sane` followed by Return to get the terminal back to echo mode. Chapter 8 addresses this issue more carefully in Program 8.4 on page 266.

Table 6.2 lists the flags for terminal control. Chapter 8 discusses some of the issues related to terminals and signals. The project of Chapter 11 explores many aspects of terminal configuration and the interaction of terminal devices with user processes.

6.5.1 Canonical and noncanonical input processing

A common misconception is that somehow the keyboard and screen are connected, so everything that you type automatically appears on the screen. The keyboard and screen are, in fact, separate devices that communicate with terminal device drivers running on the computer. The device drivers receive bytes from the keyboard, buffering and editing them as specified by the settings for these devices.

The usual method of handling terminal input, *canonical mode*, processes input one line at a time. The special characters of Table 6.1 are used for terminating input and simple editing such as erasing the last character typed. A line is a sequence of bytes delimited by a newline (NL), an end-of-file (EOF) or an end-of-line (EOL).

In canonical mode, `read` requests do not return until the user enters a line delimiter (or the process receives a signal). The ERASE and KILL characters work only on the portion of a line that has not yet been delimited. A `read` request can return only one line, regardless of the number of bytes requested. If the system defines the POSIX constant MAX_CANON for the terminal, input lines cannot be longer than MAX_CANON.

A consequence of canonical mode processing is that input from a terminal behaves differently from input from other devices such as disks. In *noncanonical mode*, input is not assembled into lines. The device driver does not respond to the ERASE and KILL characters. Noncanonical input processing has two controlling parameters—MIN and TIME. The MIN parameter controls the smallest number of bytes that should be gathered before `read` returns. The TIME parameter refers to a timer with a 0.1-second granularity used for timing out bursty transmissions. Table 6.3 summarizes the settings for MIN and TIME.

field	flag	description
c_iflag	BRKINT	signal interrupt on break
	ICRNL	map CR to NL on input
	IGNBRK	ignore break condition
	IGNCR	ignore CR
	IGNPAR	ignore characters with parity errors
	INLCR	map NL to CR on input
	INPCK	enable input parity check
	ISTRIP	strip character
	IXOFF	enable start/stop input control
	IXON	enable start/stop output control
	PARMRK	mark parity errors
c_oflag	OPOST	postprocess output
	OCRNL	map CR to NL on output (POSIX:XSI Extension)
	ONOCR	no CR output at column 0 (POSIX:XSI Extension)
	ONLRET	NL performs CR function (POSIX:XSI Extension)
c_cflag	CSIZE	character size (CS5–CS8 for 5 to 8 bits, respectively)
	CSTOPB	send two stop bits, else one
	CREAD	enable receiver
	PARENB	enable parity
	PARODD	odd parity, else even
	HUPCL	hang up on last close
	CLOCAL	ignore modem status lines
c_lflag	ECHO	enable echo
	ECHOE	echo ERASE as an error-correcting backspace
	ECHOK	enable KILL
	ECHONL	echo a newline
	ICANON	canonical input (erase and kill processing)
	IEXTEN	enable extended (implementation-defined) functions
	ISIG	enable signals
	NOFLSH	disable flush after interrupt, quit, or suspend
	TOSTOP	send SIGTTOU for background output

Table 6.2: The POSIX values of flags for terminal control.

Program 6.14 shows a function that sets the current terminal to be in noncanonical mode with single-character input. After a setnoncanonical call, the terminal device driver delivers each character as typed, treating the ERASE and KILL characters as ordinary characters. The function returns 0 on success. If an error occurs, setnoncanonical returns –1 and sets errno.

☐ Exercise 6.22

How would you set the terminal back to canonical mode after a call to the function setnoncanonical?

case	meaning
MIN > 0, TIME > 0	TIME is an interbyte timer If TIME expires or MIN bytes are received, read is satisfied.
MIN > 0, TIME = 0	read blocks until at least MIN bytes received
MIN = 0, TIME > 0	read is satisfied when a single byte arrives or TIME expires
MIN = 0, TIME = 0	minimum of number of bytes requested or number of bytes available returned

Table 6.3: Parameters for noncanonical mode processing.

Answer:
This may be a problem on some systems. POSIX allows c_cc[MIN] and c_cc[TIME] to be used for VEOF and VEOL in canonical mode. On some systems, a call to setnoncanonical will overwrite these values. Unless these values have been saved, there is no way to restore them to their original values. If you just set the ICANON bit in the c_lflag of the struct termios structure, it may not return the terminal to the previous canonical mode state. Program 6.15 provides a method for handling this.

◻ **Exercise 6.23**

Suppose that standard input has been set to noncanonical mode. Five characters have been typed at the keyboard. You try to read 10 bytes from standard input. What happens in each of the following cases?
  a) MIN = 5 and TIME = 0
  b) MIN = 0 and TIME = 100
  c) MIN = 20 and TIME = 100
  d) MIN = 3 and TIME = 100
  e) MIN = 20 and TIME = 0
  f) MIN = 0 and TIME = 0

Answer:
  a) You receive 5 bytes immediately.
  b) You receive 5 bytes immediately.
  c) You receive 5 bytes after a delay of 10 seconds.
  d) You receive 5 bytes immediately.
  e) You block until at least 5 more characters are entered.
  f) You receive 5 bytes immediately.

Program 6.14 ———————————————————————— **setnoncanonical.c**

A function that sets the terminal associated with the caller to perform single character input (rather than line processing).

```c
#include <errno.h>
#include <fcntl.h>
#include <stdio.h>
#include <termios.h>
#include <unistd.h>
#include "restart.h"

int ttysetchar(int fd, int flagname, char c);

int setnoncanonical(void) {
   int error;
   int fd;
   int firsterrno = 0;
   struct termios term;
   char termbuf[L_ctermid];

   if (ctermid(termbuf) == NULL) {               /* find the terminal name */
      errno = ENODEV;
      return -1;
   }
   if ((fd = r_open2(termbuf, O_RDONLY)) == -1)      /* open the terminal */
      return -1;
   if (tcgetattr(fd, &term) == -1)                    /* get its termios */
      firsterrno = errno;
   else {
      term.c_lflag &= ~ICANON;
      while (((error = tcsetattr(fd, TCSAFLUSH, &term)) == -1) &&
             (errno == EINTR)) ;
      if (error)
         firsterrno = errno;
   }
   if (!firsterrno && (ttysetchar(fd, VMIN, 1) || ttysetchar(fd, VTIME, 0)))
      firsterrno = errno;
   if ((r_close(fd) == -1) && !firsterrno)
      firsterrno = errno;
   if (firsterrno)
      errno = firsterrno;
   return firsterrno ? -1 : 0;
}
```

Program 6.14 ———————————————————————— **setnoncanonical.c**

Program 6.15 shows two functions for saving and restoring the struct termios structure. Each takes a pointer to a struct termios structure as a parameter and returns 0 on success. On error these functions return −1 with errno set. The correct way to temporarily set noncanonical mode is as follows.

1. Call gettermios to save struct termios structure in a local variable.
2. Call setnoncanonical.
3. Do the noncanonical mode processing.
4. Restore the original terminal mode by calling settermios.

Program 6.15 ———————————————————————— **savetermios.c**
Functions for saving and restoring the terminal mode.

```c
#include <errno.h>
#include <fcntl.h>
#include <stdio.h>
#include <termios.h>
#include <unistd.h>
#include "restart.h"

int gettermios(struct termios *termp) {
   int fd;
   int firsterrno = 0;
   char termbuf[L_ctermid];

   if (ctermid(termbuf) == NULL) {                    /* find the terminal name */
      errno = ENODEV;
      return -1;
   }
   if ((fd = r_open2(termbuf, O_RDONLY)) == -1)       /* open the terminal */
      return -1;
   if (tcgetattr(fd, termp) == -1)                     /* get its termios */
      firsterrno = errno;
   if ((r_close(fd) == -1) && !firsterrno)
      firsterrno = errno;
   if (firsterrno) {
      errno = firsterrno;
      return -1;
   }
   return 0;
}

int settermios(struct termios *termp) {
   int error;
   int fd;
   int firsterrno = 0;
   char termbuf[L_ctermid];

   if (ctermid(termbuf) == NULL) {                    /* find the terminal name */
      errno = ENODEV;
      return -1;
   }
   if ((fd = r_open2(termbuf, O_RDONLY)) == -1)       /* open the terminal */
      return -1;
   while (((error = tcsetattr(fd, TCSAFLUSH, termp)) == -1) &&
          (errno == EINTR)) ;
   if (error)
      firsterrno = errno;
   if ((r_close(fd) == -1) && !firsterrno)
      firsterrno = errno;
   if (firsterrno) {
      errno = firsterrno;
      return -1;
   }
   return 0;
}
```

Program 6.15 ———————————————————————— **savetermios.c**

6.6 Audio Device

An audio device (microphone, speaker) is an example of a peripheral device represented by a special file. The device designation for this device on many systems is /dev/audio. The discussion in this section illustrates the nature of special files, but it is specific to Sun systems. The audio device may behave differently on different systems. **Note:** If you logged in from an ASCII terminal or X-terminal, you cannot use the audio device even if the system has one.

■ Example 6.24

The following command plays the audio file sample.au on the speaker of a Sun workstation.

```
cat sample.au > /dev/audio
```

The audio device may support several audio formats, and you may have to set the audio device for the proper format before Example 6.24 works correctly. Audio files typically contain a header giving information about the format of the audio file. Sending the file directly to the audio device, as in this example, may cause the header to be interpreted as audio data. You will probably hear a series of clicks at the beginning of the playback. Many systems have a utility for playing audio. The utility reads the header and uses this information to program the audio device for the correct format. This command utility may be called audioplay or just play.

In this section, we assume that we are using audio files in a fixed format and that the audio device has already been set for that format.

Program 6.16 contains a library of functions for reading and writing from the audio device. None of these library functions pass the file descriptor corresponding to the audio device. Rather, the audio library is treated as an object that calling programs access through the provided interface (open_audio, close_audio, read_audio and write_audio).

The open_audio opens /dev/audio for read or write access, using blocking I/O. If the audio device has already been opened, open hangs until the device is closed. If the audio device had been opened with the O_NONBLOCK flag, open would have returned with an error if the device were busy.

The open_audio function attempts to open both the microphone and the speaker. A process that will only record can call open with O_RDONLY; a process that will only play can call open with O_WRONLY. If it is interrupted by a signal, open_audio restarts open.

The speaker can handle data only at a predetermined rate, so write_audio may not send the entire buffer to the speaker in one write function. Similarly, read_audio reads only the data currently available from the microphone and returns the number of bytes actually read. The get_record_buffer_size function uses ioctl to retrieve the size of the blocks that the audio device driver reads from the audio device.

Program 6.16 ─────────────────────────────────── `audiolib.c`

The audio device object and its basic operations.

```
#include <errno.h>
#include <fcntl.h>
#include <stdio.h>
#include <stropts.h>
#include <unistd.h>
#include <sys/audio.h>
#include "restart.h"
#define AUDIO "/dev/audio"

static int audio_fd = -1;   /* audio device file descriptor */

int open_audio(void) {
   while (((audio_fd = open(AUDIO, O_RDWR)) == -1) && (errno == EINTR)) ;
   if (audio_fd == -1)
      return -1;
   return 0;
}

void close_audio(void) {
   r_close(audio_fd);
   audio_fd = -1;
}

int read_audio(char *buffer, int maxcnt) {
   return r_read(audio_fd, buffer, maxcnt);
}

int write_audio(char *buffer, int maxcnt) {
   return r_write(audio_fd, buffer, maxcnt);
}

int get_record_buffer_size(void) {
   audio_info_t myaudio;
   if (audio_fd == -1)
      return -1;
   if (ioctl(audio_fd, AUDIO_GETINFO, &myaudio) == -1)
      return -1;
   else
      return myaudio.record.buffer_size;
}
```

Program 6.16 ─────────────────────────────────── `audiolib.c`

The `ioctl` function provides a means of obtaining device status information or setting device control options. The `ioctl` function has variable syntax. Its first two parameters are an open file descriptor and an integer specifying the type of request. Different requests may require different additional parameters.

SYNOPSIS

```
  #include <stropts.h>

  int ioctl(int fildes, int request, .... /* arg */);
```

POSIX

If successful, `ioctl` returns a value other than –1 that depends on the `request` value. If unsuccessful, `ioctl` returns –1 and sets `errno`. The mandatory errors depend on the value of `request`. See the man page for `ioctl` for further information.

The `ioctl` function provides a means of obtaining device status information or setting device control options. The Sun Solaris operating environment uses the `AUDIO_GETINFO` request of `ioctl` to retrieve information about the audio device. The `audio_info_t` type defined in `audioio.h` holds configuration information about the audio device.

```
typedef struct audio_info {
    audio_prinfo_t    play;             /* output status information */
    audio_prinfo_t    record;           /* input status information */
    uint_t            monitor_gain;     /* input to output mix */
    uchar_t           output_muted;     /* nonzero if output muted */
    uchar_t _xxx[3];                    /* Reserved for future use */
    uint_t _yyy[3];                     /* Reserved for future use */
} audio_info_t;
```

The `audio_prinfo_t` member of the preceding structure is defined as follows.

```
struct audio_prinfo {
    /* The following values describe the audio data encoding */
    uint_t    sample_rate;  /* samples per second */
    uint_t    channels;     /* number of interleaved channels */
    uint_t    precision;    /* number of bits per sample */
    uint_t    encoding;     /* data encoding method */

    /* The following values control audio device configuration */
    uint_t    gain;         /* volume level */
    uint_t    port;         /* selected I/O port */
    uint_t    avail_ports;  /* available I/O ports */
    uint_t    _xxx[2];      /* reserved for future use */
    uint_t    buffer_size;  /* I/O buffer size */

    /* The following values describe the current device state */
    uint_t    samples;      /* number of samples converted */
    uint_t    eof;          /* end-of-file counter (play only) */
    uchar_t   pause;        /* nonzero if paused, zero to resume */
    uchar_t   error;        /* nonzero if overflow/underflow */
    uchar_t   waiting;      /* nonzero if a process wants access */
    uchar_t   balance;      /* stereo channel balance */
    ushort_t minordev;

    /* The following values are read-only device state flags */
    uchar_t   open;         /* nonzero if open access granted */
    uchar_t   active;       /* nonzero if I/O active */
} audio_prinfo_t;
```

The `buffer_size` member of the `audio_prinfo_t` structure specifies how large a chunk of audio data the device driver accumulates before passing the data to a read request. The `buffer_size` for play specifies how large a chunk the device driver accumulates before sending the data to the speaker. Audio tends to sound better if the program sends and receives chunks that match the corresponding `buffer_size` settings. Use `ioctl` to determine these sizes in an audio application program. The `get_record_buffer_size` function in Program 6.16 returns the appropriate block size to use when reading from the microphone, or −1 if an error occurs.

Program 6.17 reads from the microphone and writes to the speaker. Terminate the program by entering Ctrl-C from the keyboard. It is best to use headphones when trying this program to avoid feedback caused by a microphone and speaker in close proximity. The `audiolib.h` header file contains the following audio function prototypes.

```
int open_audio(void);
void close_audio(void);
int read_audio(char *buffer, int maxcnt);
int write_audio(char *buffer, int length);
```

Program 6.17 ─── **audiocopy.c**

A simple program that reads from the microphone and sends the results to the speaker.

```c
#include <stdio.h>
#include <stdlib.h>
#include "audiolib.h"

#define BUFSIZE 1024
int main (void) {
   char buffer[BUFSIZE];
   int bytesread;

   if (open_audio() == -1) {
      perror("Failed to open audio");
      return 1;
   }
   for( ; ; ) {
      if ((bytesread = read_audio(buffer, BUFSIZE)) == -1) {
         perror("Failed to read microphone");
         break;
      } else if (write_audio(buffer, bytesread) == -1) {
         perror("Failed to write to speaker");
         break;
      }
   }
   close_audio();
   return 1;
}
```

Program 6.17 ─── **audiocopy.c**

The implementation of Program 6.16 opens the audio device for blocking I/O. Nonblocking reads are complicated by the fact that `read` can return −1 either if there is an error or if the audio device is not ready with the data. The latter case has an `errno` value of `EAGAIN` and should not be treated as an error. The primary reason for opening the audio device in nonblocking mode is so that `open` does not hang when the device is already

open. An alternative is to open the audio device in nonblocking mode and then to use
`fcntl` to change the mode to blocking.

■ **Example 6.25**

The following program opens the audio device for nonblocking I/O. It then reads
`BLKSIZE` bytes from the audio device into a buffer. It does nothing with the audio
that is read in other than display the number of bytes read.

```c
#include <errno.h>
#include <fcntl.h>
#include <stdio.h>
#include <stdlib.h>
#include <unistd.h>
#include "restart.h"
#define AUDIO_DEVICE "/dev/audio"
#define BLKSIZE 1024

int main(void) {
   int audiofd;
   char *bp;
   char buffer[BLKSIZE];
   unsigned bytesneeded;
   int bytesread;

   if ((audiofd = open(AUDIO_DEVICE, O_NONBLOCK | O_RDWR)) == -1) {
     perror("Failed to open audio device");
     return 1;
    }

   bp = buffer;
   bytesneeded = BLKSIZE;
   while(bytesneeded != 0) {
      bytesread = r_read(audiofd, bp, bytesneeded);
      if ((bytesread == -1) && (errno != EAGAIN))
         break;
      if (bytesread > 0) {
         bp += bytesread;
         bytesneeded -= bytesread;
      }
   }
   fprintf(stderr, "%d bytes read\n", BLKSIZE - bytesneeded);
   return 0;
}
```

———————————————————————————————— **nonblockingaudio.c**

In testing audio programs, keep in mind that the audio device is closed when the
program exits. If the audio buffer still holds data that has not yet reached the speakers,
that data may be lost. The draining of a device after a `close` is system dependent, so read
the man page before deciding how to handle the situation.

6.7 Exercise: Audio

The exercises in this section assume that the operating system handles the audio device in a way similar to how the Solaris operating environment handles it.

1. Add the following access functions to the audio object of Program 6.16.

    a) The `play_file` function plays an audio file. It has the following prototype.

    ```
    int play_file(char *filename);
    ```

    The `play_file` outputs the audio file specified by `filename` to the audio device, assuming that the speaker has already been opened. If successful, `play_file` returns the total number of bytes output. If unsuccessful, `play_file` returns −1 and sets `errno`.

    b) The `record_file` function saves incoming audio data to a disk file. It has the following prototype.

    ```
    int record_file(char *filename, int seconds);
    ```

    The `record_file` function saves audio information for a time interval of `seconds` in the file given by `filename`, assuming that the microphone has already been opened. If successful, `record_file` returns the total number of bytes recorded. If unsuccessful, `record_file` returns −1 and sets `errno`.

    c) The `get_record_sample_rate` function determines the sampling rate for recording. It has the following prototype.

    ```
    int get_record_sample_rate(void);
    ```

    If successful, `get_record_sample_rate` returns the sampling rate for recording. If unsuccessful, `get_record_sample_rate` returns −1 and sets `errno`.

    d) The `get_play_buffer_size` returns the buffer size that the audio device driver uses to transfer information to the audio output device. It has the following prototype.

    ```
    int get_play_buffer_size(void);
    ```

    If successful, `get_play_buffer_size` returns the buffer size for recording. If unsuccessful, `get_play_buffer_size` returns −1 and sets `errno`.

    e) The `get_play_sample_rate` function determines the sampling rate for playing. It has the following prototype.

    ```
    int get_play_sample_rate(void);
    ```

    If successful, `get_play_sample_rate` returns the sampling

rate used for playing audio files on the speaker. If unsuccessful, `get_play_sample_rate` returns −1 and sets `errno`. A rate of 8000 samples/second is considered voice quality.

f) The `set_play_volume` function changes the volume at which sound plays on the speaker. It has the following prototype.

```
int set_play_volume(double volume);
```

The `set_play_volume` sets the gain on the speaker. The `volume` must be between 0.0 and 1.0. If successful, `set_play_volume` returns 0. If unsuccessful, `set_play_volume` returns −1 and sets `errno`.

g) The `set_record_volume` function changes the volume of incoming sound from the microphone. It has the following prototype.

```
int set_record_volume(double volume);
```

The `set_record_volume` function sets the gain on the microphone. The `volume` value must be between 0.0 and 1.0. If successful, `set_record_volume` returns 0. If unsuccessful, it returns −1 and sets `errno`.

2. Rewrite Program 6.17 to copy from the microphone to the speaker, using the preferred buffer size of each of these devices. Call `get_record_buffer_size` and `get_play_buffer_size` to determine the respective sizes. Do not assume that they are the same in your implementation.

3. Use the `record_file` function to create eight audio files, each of which is ten seconds in duration: `pid1.au`, `pid2.au`, and so on. In the file `pid1.au`, record the following message (in your voice): "I am process 1 sending to standard error." Record similar messages in the remaining files. Play the files back by using the `play_file` function.

4. Be sure to create a header file (say, `audiolib.h`) with the prototypes of the functions in the audio library. Include this header file in any program that calls functions from this library.

5. Record your speaking of the individual numerical digits (from 0 to 9) in ten different files. Write a function called `speak_number` that takes a string representing an integer and speaks the number corresponding to the string by calling `play_file` to play the files for the individual digits. (How does the program sound compared to the computer-generated messages of the phone company?)

6. Replace the `fprintf` statement that outputs the various IDs in Program 3.1 on page 67 with a call to `play_file`. For the process with `i` having value 1, play the file `pid1.au`, and so on. Listen to the results for different numbers of processes when the speaker is opened before the fork loop. What happens when

the speaker is opened after the fork? Be sure to use `snprintf` to construct the filenames from the `i` value. Do not hardcode the filenames into the program.

7. Make a recording of the following statement in file `pid.au`: "My process ID is." Instead of having each process in the previous part play a `pidi.au` file corresponding to its `i` number, use `speak_number` to speak the process ID. Handle the parent and child IDs similarly.

8. Redesign the audio object representation and access functions so that processes have the option of opening separately for read and for write. Replace `audio_fd` with the descriptors `play_fd` and `record_fd`. Change the `open_audio` so that it sets both `play_fd` and `record_fd` to the file descriptor value returned by `open`. Add the following access functions to the audio object of Program 6.16.

    a) The `open_audio_for_record` function opens the audio device for read (`O_RDONLY`). It has the following prototype.

    ```
    int open_audio_for_record(void);
    ```

    The function returns 0 if successful or −1 if an error occurs.

    b) The `open_audio_for_play` function opens the audio device for write (`O_WRONLY`). It has the following prototype.

    ```
    int open_audio_for_play(void);
    ```

    The `open_audio_for_play` function returns 0 if successful or −1 if an error occurs.

6.8 Exercise: Barriers

A *barrier* is a synchronization construct used by cooperating processes to block until all processes reach a particular point. The exercises in this section use a FIFO to implement a barrier. They extend the simple barrier of Program 6.2.

Write a barrier server that takes two command-line arguments: the name of a barrier (`name`) and the size of the barrier (`n`). The size represents the number of processes that need to block at that barrier. The server creates a named pipe, `name.request`, to handle requests for the barrier and a named pipe, `name.release`, for writing the release characters. For example, if the barrier name is `mybarrier`, the server creates pipes called `mybarrier.request` and `mybarrier.release`. The server then does the following in a loop.

1. Open `name.request` for reading.
2. Read exactly `n` characters from `name.request`.
3. Close `name.request`.
4. Open `name.release` for writing.
5. Write exactly `n` characters to `name.release`.
6. Close `name.release`.

Write the following barrier function for use by the clients.

```
int waitatbarrier(char *name);
```

The function blocks at the barrier with the given name. If successful, the `waitatbarrier` function returns 0. If unsuccessful, `waitatbarrier` returns −1 and sets `errno`. The `waitatbarrier` does the following in a loop.

1. Open `name.request` for writing.
2. Write one byte to `name.request`.
3. Close `name.request`.
4. Open `name.release` for reading.
5. Read one byte from `name.release`.
6. Close `name.release`.

Be sure that `waitatbarrier` closes any pipe that it opens, even if an error occurs. If an error occurs on a `read` or `write`, save the value of `errno`, close the pipe, restore `errno` and return −1.

This function works because of the way blocking is done when a pipe is opened. An `open` operation for read will block until at least one process has called open for writing. Similarly, an `open` operation for write will block until at least one process called open for reading. The client will block on the open of the request pipe until the server has opened it. It will then block on the open of the release pipe until the server has read the bytes from all of the other processes and opened the release pipe for writing. A second attempt to use the barrier with the same name will block on the open of the request pipe until all of the processes have passed the first barrier since the server has closed the request pipe.

Test your clients and server by modifying the process chain of Program 3.1 on page 67 or the process fan of Program 3.2 on page 68. Have each one use the same named barrier several times. Each time they wait at the barrier, they should print a message. If the modification is working correctly, all the first messages should be printed before any of the second ones. Are there any circumstances under which reusing a barrier can fail?

Generalize your barrier server to handle many different barriers. You should still have one request pipe. The clients send the name and size of the barrier they are requesting in a single write to the request pipe. The server keeps a dynamic list of the barriers. If a request for a new barrier comes in, the server creates a new release pipe, adds this barrier to its list, and creates a child process to handle the barrier. If a request for an old barrier comes in, it is ignored.

Clients can create as many barriers as they need, but each client now has to know how many other clients there are. Alternatively, the server can be given the number of clients on the command line when it starts up. See if you can devise a mechanism for the server to find out from the clients how many they are. Be careful, this is not easy.

6.9 Exercise: The **stty** Command

Do the following to become more familiar with terminal control.
1. Read the man page on `struct termios`.
2. Execute `stty -a` and try to understand the different fields.
3. Compare the facilities provided by the specific terminal calls to those provided
   by use of `ioctl`. Read the `struct termios` information in Section 7 of the
   man pages for additional information.

Read the man page for `stty` and write your own program modeled after it.

6.10 Exercise: Client-Server Revisited

Section 6.4 developed an implementation of request-reply using named pipes. The implementation was limited because multiple readers do not behave well with pipes. Write
a new version of these programs in which the clients send their process IDs rather than
single characters. To service each request, the server uses a FIFO whose name includes
the process ID of the client. After servicing the request, the server closes the response
FIFO and unlinks it. Be sure that no client can cause this version of the server to exit.

Although the clients are sending multibyte process IDs to the server, the server will
not receive interleaved IDs because writes to the pipe are atomic. Since only one process
is reading from each pipe, reads do not need to be atomic.

If the server is responsible for creating the pipe from the process ID that is sent to it,
the client may try to open the pipe before it exists, generating an error. Have the client
create the reply pipe before sending its ID to the server on the request pipe. After sending
its ID, the client opens the reply pipe for reading and blocks until the server opens it for
writing. After the client receives its reply, it can close and unlink the reply pipe.

Note that both the client and the server need to run in the same directory so that they
can access the same pipes.

6.11 Additional Reading

The *USENIX Conference Proceedings* are a good source of current information on tools
and approaches evolving under UNIX. *Operating Systems Review* is an informal publication of SIGOPS, the Association for Computing Machinery Special Interest Group on
Operating Systems. *Operating Systems Review* sometimes has articles on recent developments in the area of file systems and device management.

Advanced Programming in the UNIX Environment by Stevens [112] contains some
nice case studies on user-level device control, including a program to control a PostScript
printer, a modem dialer, and a pseudo terminal management program. *Understanding the*

LINUX Kernel: From I/O Ports to Process Management by Bovet and Cesati [16] discusses underlying I/O implementation issues in LINUX. *Data Communications Networking Devices* by Held [47] is a general reference on network device management. Finally, *SunOS 5.3 Writing Device Drivers* is a very technical guide to implementing drivers for block-oriented and character-oriented devices under Solaris [119].

Chapter 7

Project: The Token Ring

The projects of this chapter explore pipes, forks and redirection in the context of a ring of processes. Such a ring allows simple and interesting simulations of ring network topologies. The chapter also introduces fundamental ideas of distributed processing, including processor models, pipelining and parallel computation. Distributed algorithms such as leader election illustrate important implementation issues.

Objectives

- Learn about ring-based network architectures
- Experiment with interprocess communication
- Explore distributed algorithms on a ring topology
- Use `fork` and pipes
- Understand implications of inheritance

7.1 Ring Topology

The ring topology is one of the simplest and least expensive configurations for connecting communicating entities. Figure 7.1 illustrates a unidirectional ring structure. Each entity has one connection for input and one connection for output. Information circulates around the ring in a clockwise direction. Rings are attractive because interconnection costs on the ring scale linearly—in fact, only one additional connection is needed for each additional node. The latency increases as the number of nodes increases because the time it takes for a message to circulate is longer. In most hardware implementations, the rate at which nodes can read information from the ring or write information to the ring does not change with increasing ring size, so the bandwidth is independent of the size of the ring. Several network standards, including *token ring* (IEEE 802.5), *token bus* (IEEE 802.4) and *FDDI* (ANSI X3T9.5) are based on ring connectivity.

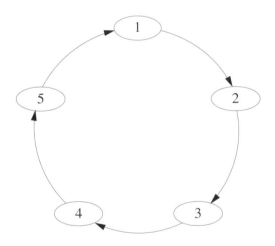

Figure 7.1: Unidirectional ring with five nodes.

This chapter develops several projects based on the ring topology of Figure 7.1. The nodes represent processes and the links represent pipes. Each process is a filter that reads from standard input and writes to standard output. Process n-1 redirects its standard output to the standard input of process n through a pipe. Once the ring structure is set up, the project can be extended to simulate network standards or to implement algorithms for mutual exclusion and leader election based on the ring architecture.

Section 7.2 presents a step-by-step development of a simple ring of processes connected by pipes. Section 7.3 provides several exploratory exercises that build on the basic ring structure. The figures of Section 7.2 trace the code through the creation of two processes on the ring, but the basic ring is too complicated to trace manually much beyond that.

We suggest that before working through Section 7.3, you use the fork-pipe simulator to try some of the examples. The book web page has a link to this simulator, which shows a diagram of the processes and pipes as it traces the code. The simulator also allows experimentation with process chains, fans and trees as well as more complicated structures such as a bidirectional ring. The simulator allows you to experiment with the effects of using different CPU scheduling algorithms, or you can single-step through the code, determining which process runs at each step. The simulator also can produce a log of the output generated and a trace of the instructions executed.

Once you have a thorough understanding of the ring and its behavior, you can go on to the other projects in this chapter. Section 7.4 tests the ring connectivity and operation by having the ring generate a Fibonacci sequence. Section 7.5 and Section 7.6 present two alternative approaches for protecting critical sections on the ring. Once the ring structure is set up, the basic project of Section 7.2 can be extended to simulate network standards or to implement algorithms for mutual exclusion and leader election based on the ring architecture. The remaining sections of the chapter describe extensions exploring different aspects of network communication, distributed processing and parallel algorithms. The extensions described in each of the later sections are independent of those in other sections.

7.2 Ring Formation

This section develops a ring of processes starting with a ring containing a single process. You should review Section 4.6 if you are not clear on file descriptors and redirection.

■ Example 7.1

The following code segment connects the standard output of a process to its standard input through a pipe. We omit the error checking for clarity.

```
int fd[2];

pipe(fd);
dup2(fd[0], STDIN_FILENO);
dup2(fd[1], STDOUT_FILENO);
close(fd[0]);
close(fd[1]);
```

Figures 7.2–7.4 illustrate the status of the process at various stages in the execution of Example 7.1. The figures use [0] to designate standard input and [1] to designate standard output. *Be sure to use* STDIN_FILENO *and* STDOUT_FILENO *when referring to these file descriptors in program code.* The entries of the file descriptor table are pointers to entries in the system file table. For example, `pipe` *write* in entry [4] means "a pointer to the write entry in the system file table for `pipe`," and *standard input* in entry [0] means "a pointer to the entry in the system file table corresponding to the default device for standard input"—usually the keyboard.

Figure 7.2 depicts the file descriptor table after the pipe has been created. File descriptor entries [3] and [4] point to system file table entries that were created by the `pipe` call. The program can now write to the pipe by using a file descriptor value of 4 in a `write` call.

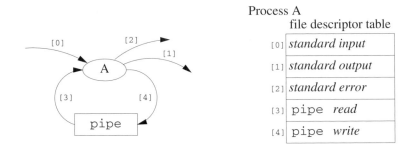

Figure 7.2: Status of the process of Example 7.1 after `pipe(fd)` executes.

Figure 7.3 shows the status of the file descriptor table after the execution of the `dup2` functions. At this point the program can write to the pipe using either 1 or 4 as the file descriptor value. Figure 7.4 shows the configuration after descriptors [3] and [4] are closed.

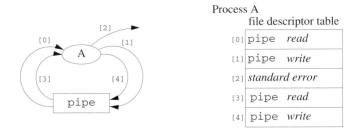

Figure 7.3: Status of the process of Example 7.1 after both `dup2` functions execute.

☐ **Exercise 7.2**

What happens if, after connecting standard output to standard input through a pipe, the process of Example 7.1 executes the following code segment?

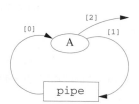

Process A
file descriptor table

[0]	pipe *read*
[1]	pipe *write*
[2]	*standard error*

Figure 7.4: Status of the process at the end of Example 7.1.

```
int i, myint;

for (i = 0; i < 10; i++) {
    write(STDOUT_FILENO, &i, sizeof(i));
    read(STDIN_FILENO, &myint, sizeof(myint));
    fprintf(stderr, "%d\n", myint);
}
```

Answer:

The code segment outputs the integers from 0 to 9 to the screen (assuming that standard error displays on the screen).

◻ **Exercise 7.3**

What happens if you replace the code in Exercise 7.2 by the following code?

```
int i, myint;

for (i = 0; i < 10; i++) {
    read(STDIN_FILENO, &myint, sizeof(myint));
    write(STDOUT_FILENO, &i, sizeof(i));
    fprintf(stderr, "%d\n", myint);
}
```

Answer:

The program hangs on the first `read` because nothing had yet been written to the pipe.

◻ **Exercise 7.4**

What happens if you replace the code in Exercise 7.2 by the following?

```
int i, myint;

for (i = 0; i < 10; i++) {
    printf("%d ", i);
    scanf("%d", &myint);
    fprintf(stderr, "%d\n", myint);
}
```

Answer:

The program may hang on the scanf if the printf buffers its output. Put an fflush(stdout) after the printf to get output.

■ Example 7.5

The following code segment creates a ring of two processes. Again, we omit error checking for clarity.

```
int fd[2];
pid_t haschild;

pipe(fd);                                                  /* pipe a */
dup2(fd[0], STDIN_FILENO);
dup2(fd[1], STDOUT_FILENO);
close(fd[0]);
close(fd[1]);
pipe(fd);                                                  /* pipe b */
haschild = fork();
if (haschild > 0)
    dup2(fd[1], STDOUT_FILENO);        /* parent(A) redirects std output */
else if (!haschild)
    dup2(fd[0], STDIN_FILENO);          /* child(B) redirects std input */
close(fd[0]);
close(fd[1]);
```

The parent process in Example 7.5 redirects standard output to the second pipe. (It was coming from the first pipe.) The child redirects standard input to come from the second pipe instead of the first pipe. Figures 7.5–7.8 illustrate the connection mechanism.

Figure 7.5 shows the file descriptor table after the parent process A creates a second pipe. Figure 7.6 shows the situation after process A forks child process B. At this point, neither of the dup2 functions after the second pipe call has executed.

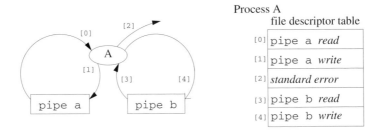

Figure 7.5: Connections to the parent process of Example 7.5 after the second pipe(fd) call executes.

Figure 7.7 shows the situation after the parent and child have each executed their last dup2. Process A has redirected its standard output to write to pipe b, and process B has

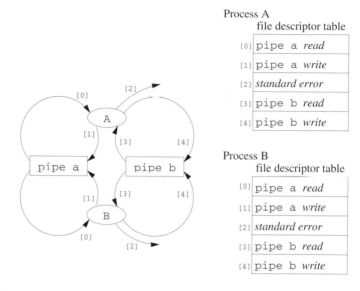

Figure 7.6: Connections of the processes of Example 7.5 after the `fork`. Process A is the parent and process B is the child.

redirected its standard input to read from pipe b. Finally, Figure 7.8 shows the status of the file descriptors after all unneeded descriptors have been closed and a ring of two processes has been formed.

☐ **Exercise 7.6**

What would happen if the code of Exercise 7.2 is inserted after the ring of two processes of Example 7.5?

Answer:

The new code is executed by two processes. Each process writes 10 integers to the pipe and reads the integers written by the other process. The processes cannot get too far out of step, since each process needs to read from the other before writing the next value. You should see two lines of 0 followed by two lines of 1, etc.

The code of Example 7.5 for forming a ring of two processes easily extends to rings of arbitrary size. Program 7.1 sets up a ring of n processes. The value of n is passed on the command line (and converted to the variable `nprocs`). A total of n pipes is needed. Notice, however, that the program needs an array only of size 2 rather than 2n to hold the file descriptors. After the ring of two processes is created, the parent drops out and the child forks again. (Try to write your own code before looking at the ring program.)

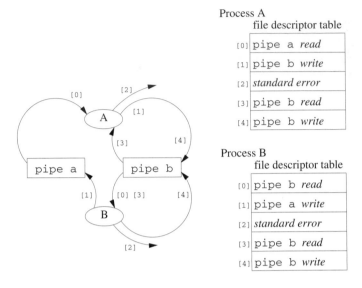

Process A
file descriptor table

[0]	pipe a *read*
[1]	pipe b *write*
[2]	*standard error*
[3]	pipe b *read*
[4]	pipe b *write*

Process B
file descriptor table

[0]	pipe b *read*
[1]	pipe a *write*
[2]	*standard error*
[3]	pipe b *read*
[4]	pipe b *write*

Figure 7.7: Connections of the processes of Example 7.5 after the `if` statement executes. Process A is the parent and process B is the child.

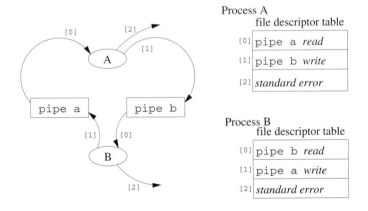

Process A
file descriptor table

[0]	pipe a *read*
[1]	pipe b *write*
[2]	*standard error*

Process B
file descriptor table

[0]	pipe b *read*
[1]	pipe a *write*
[2]	*standard error*

Figure 7.8: Connections of the processes of Example 7.5 after the entire code segment executes. Process A is the parent and process B is the child.

Program 7.1 ——————————————————————— `ring.c`

A program to create a ring of processes.

```c
#include <errno.h>
#include <stdio.h>
#include <stdlib.h>
#include <string.h>
#include <unistd.h>

int main(int argc,  char *argv[ ]) {
    pid_t childpid;              /* indicates process should spawn another   */
    int error;                   /* return value from dup2 call              */
    int fd[2];                   /* file descriptors returned by pipe        */
    int i;                       /* number of this process (starting with 1) */
    int nprocs;                  /* total number of processes in ring        */
            /* check command line for a valid number of processes to generate */
    if ( (argc != 2) || ((nprocs = atoi (argv[1])) <= 0) ) {
        fprintf (stderr, "Usage: %s nprocs\n", argv[0]);
        return 1;
    }
    if (pipe (fd) == -1) {       /* connect std input to std output via a pipe */
        perror("Failed to create starting pipe");
        return 1;
    }
    if ((dup2(fd[0], STDIN_FILENO) == -1) ||
        (dup2(fd[1], STDOUT_FILENO) == -1)) {
        perror("Failed to connect pipe");
        return 1;
    }
    if ((close(fd[0]) == -1) || (close(fd[1]) == -1)) {
        perror("Failed to close extra descriptors");
        return 1;
    }
    for (i = 1; i < nprocs;  i++) {            /* create the remaining processes */
        if (pipe (fd) == -1) {
            fprintf(stderr, "[%ld]:failed to create pipe %d: %s\n",
                    (long)getpid(), i, strerror(errno));
            return 1;
        }
        if ((childpid = fork()) == -1) {
            fprintf(stderr, "[%ld]:failed to create child %d: %s\n",
                    (long)getpid(), i, strerror(errno));
            return 1;
        }
        if (childpid > 0)                /* for parent process, reassign stdout */
            error = dup2(fd[1], STDOUT_FILENO);
        else                             /* for child process, reassign stdin */
            error = dup2(fd[0], STDIN_FILENO);
        if (error == -1) {
            fprintf(stderr, "[%ld]:failed to dup pipes for iteration %d: %s\n",
                    (long)getpid(), i, strerror(errno));
            return 1;
        }
        if ((close(fd[0]) == -1) || (close(fd[1]) == -1)) {
            fprintf(stderr, "[%ld]:failed to close extra descriptors %d: %s\n",
                    (long)getpid(), i, strerror(errno));
            return 1;
        }
        if (childpid)
            break;
    }                                            /* say hello to the world */
    fprintf(stderr, "This is process %d with ID %ld and parent id %ld\n",
            i, (long)getpid(), (long)getppid());
    return 0;
}
```

Program 7.1 ——————————————————————— `ring.c`

7.3 Ring Exploration

The following exercises test and modify Program 7.1. You can try these either by compiling the ring code or by using the fork-pipe simulator. A link to the simulator appears on the book web page. For each modification, make a new copy of the program. Suggested names for the executables are shown in parentheses.

1. Run the program shown in Program 7.1 (`ring`).
2. Create a makefile with descriptions for compiling and linting the program. Use `make` to compile the program. Add targets for additional parts of this project. (Refer to Section A.3 if you are unfamiliar with the `make` utility.)
3. Make any corrections required to eliminate all lint errors and warning messages that reflect problems with the program. (Refer to Section A.4 if you are unfamiliar with the `lint` utility.)
4. Run `ring` for several values of the command-line argument and observe what happens as the number of processes in the ring varies from 1 to 20.
5. Modify the original `ring` program by putting a `wait` call before the final `fprintf` statement (`ring1`). How does this affect the output of the program?
6. Modify the original `ring` program by putting a `wait` call after the final `fprintf` statement (`ring2`). How does this affect the output of the program?
7. Replace the `fprintf` statement in the original `ring` program with calls to `sprintf` and `prtastr` (`ring3`). Write a `prtastr` function with the following prototype.

        void prtastr(const char *s, int fd, int n);

    The `prtastr` function prints the `s` string one character at a time to the file specified by descriptor `fd` using `write`. After outputting each character, `prtastr` calls the following function.

    ```
    void wastesometime(int n) {
       static volatile int dummy = 0;
       int i;

       for (i=0; i < n; i++)
          dummy++;
    }
    ```
    —— **wastesometime.c**

    This just wastes some CPU time. The variable `dummy` is declared to be volatile so that the action of the `for` loop is not optimized away. Use `prtastr` to output the string to standard error. Pass the value of `n` used by `prtastr` as an optional command-line argument to `ring3`. Use 0 as the default value for this parameter. (The single character at a time gives the ring processes more opportunity to interleave their output.) Run the program with a value of `n` that causes a small, but barely noticeable, delay between the output of characters.

8. Compare the results of running the modified `ring3` if you do the following.
   a) Insert `wait` before the call to `prtastr (ring4)`.
   b) Insert `wait` after the call to `prtastr (ring5)`.
9. Modify `ring1` as follows (`ringtopology`).
   a) Before the `wait`, each process allocates an array of `nprocs` elements to hold the IDs of all the processes on the ring. The process puts its own process ID in element zero of the array and sets its variable `next_ID` to its process ID.
   b) Do the following for `k` going from `1` to `nprocs-1`.
      i) Write `next_ID` to standard output.
      ii) Read `next_ID` from standard input.
      iii) Insert `next_ID` into position `k` of the ID array.
   c) Replace the `fprintf` after the `wait` with a loop that outputs the contents of the ID array to standard error in a readable single-line format. This output tests the ring connectivity, since the ID array contains the processes in the order in which they appear upstream from a given process.
10. Modify `ringtopology` by having the child rather than the parent break out of the loop (`ringchildbreak`). We are now creating a process fan instead of a chain. Determine how this affects the topology. Do we still have a ring? If using the simulator, you can just modify `ring` since you do not need to send anything around to ring to determine the topology.
11. Modify `ringtopology` by having neither process break out of the loop (`ringnobreak`). We are now creating a process tree instead of a chain. Determine how this affects the topology. Do we still have a ring? The number of processes is now greater than `nprocs`. How does the number of processes depend on `nprocs`? You will need to adjust the loop that sends the process IDs around the ring.
12. Modify `ring1` to be a bidirectional ring (information can flow in either direction between neighbors on the ring). Standard input and output are used for the flow in one direction. File descriptors 3 and 4 are used for the flow in the other direction. Test the connections by accumulating ID arrays for each direction (`biring`).
13. Modify `ring1` to create a bidirectional torus of processes. Accumulate ID arrays to test connectivity. A torus has a two-dimensional structure. It is like a mesh except that the processes at the ends are connected together. The n^2 processes are arranged in n rings in each dimension (`torus`). Each process has four connections (North, South, East, and West).

Use the ring simulator that is linked on the book web site to explore various aspects of this problem. Modify the ring simulator example to illustrate the effects of items 4 through 6. Make printing nonatomic to illustrate items 7 and 8. Pass data around the ring as in item 9, and construct a bidirectional ring for item 10.

7.4 Simple Communication

Section 7.2 established the connections for a ring of processes. This section develops a simple application in which processes generate a sequence of Fibonacci numbers on the ring. The next number in a Fibonacci sequence is the sum of the previous two numbers in the sequence.

In this project, the processes pass information in character string format. The original parent outputs the string `"1 1"` representing the first two Fibonacci numbers to standard output, sending the string to the next process. The other processes read a string from standard input, decode the string, calculate the next Fibonacci number, and write to standard output a string representing the previous Fibonacci number and the one just calculated. Each process then writes the result of its calculation to standard error and exits. The original parent exits after receiving a string and displaying the numbers received.

Start with the original `ring` function of Program 7.1 and replace the `fprintf` with code to read two integers from standard input in the string format described below, calculate the next integer in a Fibonacci sequence, and write the result to standard output.

1. Each string is the ASCII representation of two integers separated by a single blank.
2. The original parent writes out the string "1 1", representing two ones and then reads a string. Be sure to send the string terminator.
3. All other processes first read a string and then write a string.
4. Fibonacci numbers satisfy the formula $x_{n+1} = x_n + x_{n-1}$. Each process receives two numbers (e.g., a followed by b), calculates c = a + b and writes b followed by c as a null-terminated string. (The b and c values should be written as strings separated by a single blank.)
5. After sending the string to standard output, the process writes a single-line message to standard error in the following form.

   ```
   Process i with PID x and parent PID y received a b and sent b c.
   ```
6. After sending the message to standard error, the process exits.

Try to write the program in such a way that it handles the largest possible number of processes and still calculates the Fibonacci numbers correctly. The execution either runs out of processes or some process generates a numeric overflow when calculating the next number. Attempt to detect this overflow and send the string "0 0".

Notes: The program should be able to calculate Fib(46)=1,836,311,903, using 45 processes or Fib(47)=2,971,215,073, using 46 processes. It may even be able to calculate Fib(78)=8,944,394,323,791,464, using 77 processes. With a little extra work, the program can compute higher values. A possible approach for detecting overflow is to check whether the result is less than the first integer in the string.

This program puts a heavy load on the CPU of a machine. Don't try this project with more than a few processes unless it is running on a dedicated computer. Also, on some systems, a limit on the number of processes for a user may interfere with running the program for a large number of processes.

7.5 Mutual Exclusion with Tokens

All the processes on the ring share the standard error device, and the call to `prtastr` described in Section 7.3 is a critical section for these processes. This section describes a simple token-based strategy for granting exclusive access to a shared device. The token can be a single character that is passed around the ring. When a given process acquires the token (reads the character from standard input), it has exclusive access to the shared device. When that process completes its use of the shared device, it writes the character to standard output so that the next process in the ring can acquire the token. The token algorithm for mutual exclusion is similar to the speaking stick (or a conch [42]) used in some cultures to enforce order at meetings. Only the person who holds the stick can speak.

The acquisition of mutual exclusion starts when the first process writes a token (just a single character) to its standard output. From then on, the processes use the following strategy.

1. Read the token from standard input.
2. Access the shared device.
3. Write the token to standard output.

If a process does not wish to access the shared device, it merely passes the token on.

What happens to the preceding algorithm at the end? After a process has completed writing its messages to standard error, it must continue passing the token until all other processes on the ring are done. One strategy for detecting termination is to replace the character token by an integer. The initial token has a zero value. If a process finishes its critical section but will still access the shared device at a later time, it just passes the token unchanged. When a process no longer needs to access the shared device, it performs the following shutdown procedure.

1. Read the token.
2. Increment the token.
3. Write the token.
4. Repeat until the token has a value equal to the number of processes in the ring.
   a) Read the token.
   b) Write the token.
5. Exit.

The repeat section of the shutdown procedure has the effect of forcing the process to wait until everyone is finished. This strategy requires that the number of processes on the ring be known.

Implement and test mutual exclusion with tokens as follows.

1. Start with version `ring3` of the ring program from Section 7.3.

2. Implement mutual exclusion for standard error by using the integer token method just described but without the shutdown procedure. The critical section should include the call to `prtastr`.

3. Test the program with different values of the command-line arguments. In what order do the messages come out and why?

4. Vary the tests by having each process repeat the critical section a random number of times between 0 and `r`. Pass `r` as a command-line argument. Before each call to `prtastr`, read the token. After calling `prtastr`, write the token. When done with all output, execute a loop that just passes the token. (Hint: Read the man page on `drand48` and its related functions. The `drand48` function generates a pseudorandom double in the range $[0, 1)$. If `drand48` generates a value of x, then `y = (int)(x*n)` is an integer satisfying $0 \le y < n$.) Use the process ID for a seed so that the processes use independent pseudorandom numbers.

5. The messages that each process writes to standard error should include the process ID and the time the operation began. Use the `time` function to obtain a time in seconds. Print the time in a nice format as in Example 5.8. (Page 302 in Chapter 9 has a more detailed description of `time`.)

7.6 Mutual Exclusion by Voting

One problem with the token method is that it generates continuous traffic (a form of busy waiting) even when no process enters its critical section. If all the processes need to enter their critical sections, access is granted by relative position as the token travels around the ring. An alternative approach uses an algorithm of Chang and Roberts for extrema finding [22]. Processes that need to enter their critical sections vote to see which process obtains access. This method generates traffic only when a process requires exclusive access. The approach can be modified to accommodate a variety of priority schemes in the determination of which process goes next.

Each process that is contending for mutual exclusion generates a voting message with a unique two-part ID. The first part of the ID, the sequence number, is based on a priority. The second part of the ID, the process ID, breaks ties if two processes have the same priority. Examples of priority include sequence numbers based on the current clock time or on the number of times that the process has acquired mutual exclusion in the past. In each of these strategies, the lower value corresponds to a higher priority. Use the latter strategy.

To vote, the process writes its ID message on the ring. Each process that is not participating in the vote merely passes the incoming ID messages to the next process on the ring.

When a process that is voting receives an ID message, it bases its actions on the following paradigm.

1. If the incoming message has a higher ID (lower priority) than its own vote, the process throws away the incoming message.
2. If the incoming message has a lower ID (higher priority) than its own vote, the process forwards the message.
3. If the incoming message is its own message, the process has acquired mutual exclusion and can begin the critical section.

Convince yourself that the winner of the vote is the process whose ID message is the lowest for that ballot.

A process relinquishes mutual exclusion by sending a release message around the ring. Once a process detects that the vote has started either because it initiated the request or because it received a message, the process cannot initiate another vote until it detects a release message. Thus, of the processes that decided earliest to participate, the process that received access the fewest times in the past wins the election.

Implement the voting algorithm for exclusive access to standard error. Incorporate random values of the delay value, which is the last parameter of the `prtastr` function defined in Section 7.3. Devise a strategy for graceful exit after all of the processes have completed their output.

7.7 Leader Election on an Anonymous Ring

Specifications of distributed algorithms refer to the entities that execute the algorithm as *processes* or *processors*. Such algorithms often specify an underlying processor model in terms of a finite-state machine. The processor models are classified by how the state transitions are driven (synchrony) and whether the processors are labeled.

In the *synchronous processor model*, the processors proceed in lock step and state transitions are clock-driven. In the *asynchronous processor model*, state transitions are message-driven. The receipt of a message on a communication link triggers a change in processor state. The processor may send messages to its neighbors, perform some computation, or halt as a result of the incoming message. On any given link between processors, the messages arrive in the order they were sent. The messages incur a finite, but unpredictable, transmission delay.

A system of communicating UNIX processes connected by pipes, such as the ring of Program 7.1, is an example of an asynchronous system. A massively parallel SIMD (single-instruction, multiple-data) machine such as the CM-2 is an example of a synchronous system.

A processor model must also specify whether the individual processors are labeled or whether they are indistinguishable. In an *anonymous system*, the processors have no distinguishing characteristic. In general, algorithms involving systems of anonymous processors or processes are more complex than the corresponding algorithms for systems of labeled ones.

The UNIX `fork` function creates a copy of the calling process. If the parent and child were completely identical, `fork` would not accomplish anything beyond the activities of a single process. In fact, UNIX distinguishes the parent and child by their process IDs, and `fork` returns different values to the parent and child so that each is aware of the other's identity. In other words, `fork` breaks the symmetry between parent and child by assigning different process IDs. Systems of UNIX processors are not anonymous because the processes can be labeled by their process IDs.

Symmetry-breaking is a general problem in distributed computing in which identical processes (or processors) must be distinguished to accomplish useful work. Assignment of exclusive access is an example of symmetry-breaking. One possible way of assigning mutual exclusion is to give preference to the process with the largest process ID. Usually, a more equitable method would be better. The voting algorithm of Section 7.6 assigns mutual exclusion to the process that has acquired it the fewest times in the past. The algorithm uses the process ID only in the case of ties.

Leader election is another example of a symmetry-breaking algorithm. Leader-election algorithms are used in some networks to designate a particular processor to partition the network, regenerate tokens, or perform other operations. For example, what happens in a token-ring network if the processor holding the token crashes? When the crashed processor comes back up, it does not have a token and activity on the network comes to a standstill. One of the nonfaulty processors must take the initiative to generate another token. Who should decide which processor is in charge?

There are no deterministic algorithms for electing a leader on an anonymous ring. This section discusses the implementation of a probabilistic leader-election algorithm for an anonymous ring. The algorithm is an asynchronous version of the synchronous algorithm proposed by Itai and Roteh [58]. This is a probabilistic algorithm for leader election on an anonymous synchronous ring of size n. The synchronous version of the algorithm proceeds in phases. Each process keeps track of the number of active processes, m. These are the processes still competing for being chosen as the leader.

1. Phase zero
    a) Set local variable m to n.
    b) Set `active` to TRUE.
2. Phase k
    a) If `active` is TRUE,
        i)   Choose a random number, x, between 1 and m.
        ii) If the number chosen was 1, send a one-bit message around the ring.
    b) Count the number of one-bit messages received in the next n−1 clock pulses as follows.

i) If only one active process chose 1, the election is completed.

ii) If no active processes chose 1, go to the next phase with no change.

iii) If p processes chose 1, set m to p.

iv) If the process is active and it did not choose 1, set its local `active` to `FALSE`.

In summary, on each phase the active processes pick a random number between 1 and the number of active processes. Any process that picks a 1 is active on the next round. If no process picks a 1 on a given round, the active processes try again. The probability of a particular process picking a 1 increases as the number of active processes decreases. On average, the algorithm eliminates processes from contention at a rapid rate. Itai and Roteh showed that the expected number of phases needed to choose a leader on a ring of size n is less than $e \approx 2.718$, independently of n.

Using the ring of Program 7.1, implement a simulation of this leader-election algorithm to estimate the probability distribution $J(n,k)$, which is the probability that it takes k phases to elect a leader on a ring of size n.

The implementation has to address two problems. The first problem is that the algorithm is specified for a synchronous ring, but the implementation is on an asynchronous ring. Asynchronous rings clock on the messages received (i.e., each time a process reads a message, it updates its clock). The processes must read messages at the correct point in the algorithm or they lose synchronization. Inactive processes must still write clock messages.

A second difficulty arises because the theoretical convergence of the algorithm relies on the processes having independent streams of random numbers. In practice, the processes use a pseudorandom-number generator with an appropriate seed. The processes are supposedly identical, but if they start with the same seed, the algorithm will not work. The implementation can cheat by using the process ID to generate a seed, but ultimately it should include a method of generating numbers based on the system clock or other system hardware. (The first few sections of Chapter 10 discuss library functions for accessing the system clock and timers.)

7.8 Token Ring for Communication

This section develops a simulation of communication on a token-ring network. Each process on the ring now represents an Interface Message Processor (IMP) of a node on the network. The IMP handles message passing and network control for the host of the node. Each IMP process creates a pair of pipes to communicate with its host process, as shown in Figure 7.9. The host is represented by a child process forked from the IMP.

Each IMP waits for messages from its host and from the ring. For simplicity, a message consists of five integers—a message type, the ID of the source IMP, the ID of the destination IMP, a status, and a message number. The possible message types are defined by the enumerated type `msg_type_t`.

```
typedef enum msg_type{TOKEN, HOST2HOST, IMP2HOST, HOST2IMP, IMP2IMP} msg_type_t;
```

The IMP must read a `TOKEN` message from the ring before it writes any message it originates to the ring. When it receives an acknowledgment of its message, it writes a new `TOKEN` message on the ring. The acknowledgments are indicated in the status member that is of type `msg_status_t` defined by the following.

```
typedef enum msg_status{NONE, NEW, ACK} msg_status_t;
```

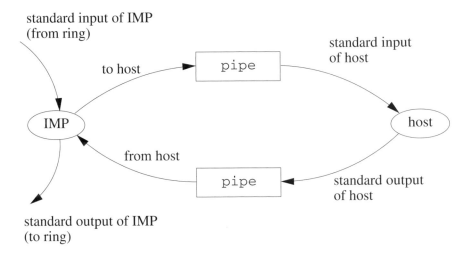

Figure 7.9: IMP-host structure.

The IMP waits for a message from either its host or the ring. When an IMP detects that the host wants to send a message, it reads the message into a temporary buffer and sets the `got_msg` flag. Once the `got_msg` flag is set, the IMP cannot read any additional messages from the host until the `got_msg` flag is clear.

When the IMP detects a message from the network, its actions depend on the type of message. If the IMP reads a `TOKEN` message and it has a host message to forward (`got_msg` is set), the IMP writes the host message to the network. If the IMP has no message to send (`got_msg` is clear), it writes the `TOKEN` message on the network.

If the IMP reads a message other than a `TOKEN` message from the ring, its actions depend on the source and destination IDs in the message.

1. If the source ID of the message matches the IMP's ID, the message was its own.
    The IMP prints a message to standard error reporting whether the message was

received by the destination. In any case, the IMP writes a TOKEN message to the ring and clears got_msg.

2. If the destination ID of the message matches the IMP's ID, the message is for the IMP or the IMP's host. The IMP prints a status message to standard error reporting the type of message. The IMP changes the status of the message to ACK and writes the message to the ring. If the message is for the host, also send the message to the host through the pipe.

3. Otherwise, the IMP writes the message to the ring unchanged.

The actual IEEE 802.5 token-ring protocol is more complicated than this. Instead of fixed-length messages, the IMPs use a token-holding timer set to a prespecified value when transmission starts. An IMP can transmit until the timer expires, so messages can be quite long. There can also be a priority scheme [111]. In the actual token-ring protocol, one IMP is designated as the active monitor for the ring. It periodically issues control frames to tell the other stations that the active monitor is present. The active monitor detects whether a token has been lost and is responsible for regenerating tokens. All the stations periodically send standby-monitor-present control frames downstream to detect breaks in the ring.

Start with Program 7.1. Modify it so that after the ring is created, each IMP process creates two pipes and a child host process, as shown in Figure 7.9. Redirect standard output and standard input of the child host as shown in Figure 7.9, and have the child execute the hostgen program with the appropriate command-line arguments. The IMP enters an infinite loop to monitor its possible inputs, using select. When input is available, the IMP performs the simple token-ring protocol described above.

Write and test a separate program, hostgen, that takes two command-line arguments: an integer process number n and an integer sleep time s. The hostgen program monitors standard input and logs any input it receives to standard error. Use the read_timed of Program 4.16 on page 115 with a random timeout between 0 and s seconds. If a timeout occurs, write a random integer between 0 and n to standard output. Test the hostgen program separately.

7.9 Pipelined Preprocessor

The C preprocessor, cpp, preprocesses C source code so that the C compiler itself does not have to worry about certain things. For example, say a C program has a line such as the following.

```
#define BUFSIZE 250
```

In this case, cpp replaces all instances of the token BUFSIZE by 250. The C preprocessor deals with tokens, so it does not replace an occurrence of BUFSIZE1 with 2501. This behavior is clearly needed for C source code. It should not be possible to get cpp into a loop with something like the following.

```
#define BUFSIZE (BUFSIZE + 1)
```

Various versions of cpp handle this difficulty in different ways.

In other situations, the program may not be dealing with tokens and might replace any occurrence of a string, even if that string is part of a token or consists of several tokens. One method of handling the loops that may be generated by recursion is not to perform any additional test on a string that has already been replaced. This method fails on something as simple as the following statements.

```
#define BUFSIZE 250
#define BIGGERBUFSIZE (BUFSIZE + 1)
```

Another way to handle this situation is to make several passes through the input file, one for each #define and to make the replacements sequentially. The processing can be done more efficiently (and possibly in parallel) with a pipeline. Figure 7.10 shows a four-stage pipeline. Each stage in the pipeline applies a transformation to its input and then outputs the result for input to the next stage. A pipeline resembles an assembly line in manufacturing.

Figure 7.10: Four-stage pipeline.

This section develops a pipeline of preprocessors based on the ring of Program 7.1. To simplify the programming, the preprocessors just convert single characters to strings of characters.

1. Write a processchar function that has the following prototype.

   ```
   int processchar(int fdin, int fdout, char inchar, char *outstr);
   ```

   The processchar function reads from file descriptor fdin until end-of-file and writes to file descriptor fdout, translating any occurrence of the character inchar into the string outstr. If successful, processchar returns 0. If unsuccessful, processchar returns –1 and sets errno. Write a driver to test this function before using it with the ring.

2. Modify Program 7.1 so that it now takes four command-line arguments (ringpp). Run the program by executing the following command.

   ```
   ringpp n conf.in file.in file.out
   ```

The value of the command-line argument n specifies the number of stages in the pipeline. It corresponds to nprocs-2 in Program 7.1. The original parent is responsible for generating pipeline input by reading file.in, and the last child is responsible for removing output from the pipeline and writing it to file.out. Before ringpp creates the ring, the original parent opens the file conf.in, reads in n lines, each containing a character and a string. It stores this information in an array. The ringpp program reads the conf.in file before any forking, so the information in the array is available to all children.

3. The original parent is responsible for copying the contents of the file.in input file to its standard output. When it encounters end-of-file on file.in, the process exits. The original parent generates the input for the pipeline and does not perform any pipeline processing.

4. The last child is responsible for removing output from the pipeline. The process copies data from its standard input to file.out, but it does not perform any pipeline processing. The process exits when it encounters an end-of-file on its standard input.

5. For i between 2 and n+1, child process i uses the information in the (i-1)-th entry of the translation array to translate a character to a string. Each child process acts like a filter, reading the input from standard input, making the substitution and writing the result to standard output. Call the processchar function to process the input. When processchar encounters an end-of-file on input, each process closes its standard input and standard output, then exits.

6. After making sure that the program is working correctly, try it with a big file (many megabytes) and a moderate number (10 to 20) of processes.

7. If possible, try the program on a multiprocessor machine to measure the speedup. (See Section 7.10 for a definition of speedup.)

Each stage of the pipeline reads from its standard input and writes to its standard output. You can generalize the problem by having each stage run execvp on an arbitrary process instead of calling the same function. The conf.in file could contain the command lines to execvp instead of the table of string replacements specific to this problem.

It is also possible to have the original parent handle both the generation of pipeline input and the removal of its output. In this case, the parent opens file.in and file.out after forking its child. The process must now handle input from two sources: file.in and its standard input. It is possible to use select to handle this, but the problem is more complicated than might first appear. The process must also monitor its standard output with select because a pipe can fill up and block additional writes. If the process blocks while writing to standard output, it is not able to remove output from the final stage of the pipeline. The pipeline might deadlock in this case. The original parent is a perfect candidate for threading. Threads are discussed in Chapters 12 and 13.

7.10 Parallel Ring Algorithms

Parallel processing refers to the partitioning of a problem so that pieces of the problem can be solved in parallel, thereby reducing the overall execution time. One measure of the effectiveness of the partitioning is the speedup, $S(n)$, which is defined as follows.

$$S(n) = \frac{\text{execution time with one processor}}{\text{execution time with } n \text{ processors}}$$

Ideally, the execution time is inversely proportional to the number of processors, implying that the speedup $S(n)$ is just n. Unfortunately, linear speedup is a rare achievement in practical settings for a number of reasons. There is always a portion of the work that cannot be done in parallel, and the parallel version of the algorithm incurs overhead when the processors synchronize or communicate to exchange information.

The problems that are most amenable to parallelization have a regular structure and involve exchange of information following well-defined patterns. This section looks at two parallel algorithms for the ring: image filtering and matrix multiplication. The image filtering belongs to a class of problems in which each processor performs its calculation independently or by exchanging information with its two neighbors. In matrix multiplication, a processor must obtain information from all the other processors to complete the calculation. However, the information can be propagated by a simple shift. Other parallel algorithms can also be adapted for efficient execution on the ring, but the communication patterns are more complicated than those of the examples done here.

7.10.1 Image filtering

A filter is a transformation applied to an image. Filtering may remove noise, enhance detail or blur image features, depending on the type of transformation. This discussion considers a greyscale digital image represented by an $n \times n$ array of bytes. Common *spatial filters* replace each pixel value in such an image by a function of the original pixel and its neighbors. The filter algorithm uses a mask to specify the neighborhood that contributes to the calculation. Figure 7.11 shows a 3×3 mask of nearest neighbors. This particular mask represents a *linear filter* because the function is a weighted sum of the pixels in the mask. In contrast, a nonlinear filter cannot be written as a linear combination of pixels under the mask. Taking the median of the neighboring pixels is an example of a nonlinear filter.

The values in the mask are the weights applied to each pixel in the sum when the mask is centered on the pixel being transformed. In Figure 7.11, all weights are $1/9$. If $a_{i,j}$ is the pixel at position (i, j) of the original image and $b_{i,j}$ is the pixel at the corresponding position in the filtered image, the mask in Figure 7.11 represents the pixel transformation

$$b_{i,j} = \frac{1}{9} \left[a_{i-1,j-1} + a_{i,j-1} + a_{i+1,j-1} + a_{i-1,j} + a_{i,j} + a_{i+1,j} + a_{i-1,j+1} + a_{i,j+1} + a_{i+1,j+1} \right]$$

$$\frac{1}{9} \times \begin{array}{|c|c|c|} \hline 1 & 1 & 1 \\ \hline 1 & 1 & 1 \\ \hline 1 & 1 & 1 \\ \hline \end{array}$$

Figure 7.11: Mask for applying a smoothing filter to an image.

This transformation blurs sharp edges and eliminates contrast in an image. In filtering terminology, the mask represents a low-pass filter because it keeps slowly varying (low-frequency) components and eliminates high-frequency components. The mask in Figure 7.12 is a high-pass filter that enhances edges and darkens the background.

$$\frac{1}{9} \times \begin{array}{|c|c|c|} \hline -1 & -1 & -1 \\ \hline -1 & 8 & -1 \\ \hline -1 & -1 & -1 \\ \hline \end{array}$$

Figure 7.12: Mask for applying a difference filter to an image.

Filtering algorithms on the ring

The ring of processes is a natural architecture for parallelizing the types of filters described by masks such as those of Figures 7.11 and 7.12. Suppose a ring of n processes is to filter an n×n image. Each process can be responsible for computing the filter for one row or one column of the image. Since ISO C stores arrays in row-major format (i.e., the elements of a two-dimensional array are stored linearly in memory by first storing all elements of row zero followed by all elements of row one, and so on), it is more convenient to have each process handle one row.

   To perform the filtering operation in process p, do the following.

1. Obtain rows p-1, p, and p+1 of the original image. Represent the pixel values of three rows of the original image by the following array.

    ```
    unsigned char a[3][n+2];
    ```

    Put the image pixels of row p-1 in a[0][1], ..., a[0][n]. Set a[0][0] and a[0][n+1] to 0 to compute the result for border pixels without worrying about array bounds. Handle rows p and p+1 similarly. If p is 1, set a[0][0],

..., a[0][n+1] to 0 corresponding to the row above the image. If p is n, set
a[2][0], ..., a[2][n+1] to 0 corresponding to the row of pixels below the
bottom of the image.

2. Compute the new values for the pixels in row p and store the new values in an
array.

```
unsigned char b[n+2];
```

To compute the value of b[i], use the following program segment.

```
int sum;
int i;
int j;
int m;

sum = 0;
for (j = 0; j < 3; j++)
   for (m = i - 1; m < i + 2; m++)
      sum += a[j][m];
b[i] = (unsigned char) (sum/9);
```

The value of b[i] is the pixel value $b_{p,i}$ in the new image.

3. Insert b in row p of the new image.

The preceding description is purposely vague about where the original image comes
from and where it goes. This I/O is the heart of the problem. The simplest approach is
to have each process read the part of the input image it needs from a file and write the
resulting row to another file. In this approach, the processes are completely independent
of each other. Assume that the original image is stored as a binary file of bytes in row-
major order. Use lseek to position the file offset at the appropriate place in the file, and
use read to input the three needed rows. After computing the new image, use lseek and
write to write the row in the appropriate place in the image. Be sure to open the input and
output image files after the fork so that each process on the ring has its own file offsets.

A bidirectional ring

An alternative approach uses nearest-neighbor communication. Process p on the ring reads
in only row p. It then writes row p to its neighbors on either side and reads rows p-1 and
p+1 from its neighbors. This exchange of information requires the ring to be bidirectional,
that is, a process node can read or write from the links in each direction. (Alternatively,
replace each link in the ring by two unidirectional links, one in each direction.) It is
probably overkill to implement the linear filter with nearest-neighbor communication, but
several related problems require it.

For example, the explicit method of solving the heat equation on an n × n grid uses a
nearest-neighbor update of the form

$$b_{i,j} = a_{i,j} + D\left[a_{i-1,j} + a_{i+1,j} + a_{i,j-1} + a_{i,j+1}\right]$$

The constant D is related to the rate that heat diffuses on the grid. The array $b_{i,j}$ is the new heat distribution on the grid after one unit of time has lapsed. It becomes the initial array $a_{i,j}$ for the next time step. Clearly, the program should not write the grid to disk between each time step, so here a nearest-neighbor exchange is needed.

Block computation

Another important issue in parallel processing is the granularity of the problem and how it maps to the number of processes. The ring is typically under 100 processes, while the images of interest may be 1024×1024 pixels. In this case, each process computes the filter for a block of rows.

Suppose the ring has m processes and the image has n×n pixels, where n = qm+r. The first r processes are responsible for q+1 rows, and the remaining processes are responsible for q rows. Each process computes from q and r the range of rows that it is responsible for. Pass m and n as command-line arguments to the original process in the ring.

7.10.2 Matrix multiplication

Another problem that lends itself to parallel execution on a ring is matrix multiplication. To multiply two n×n matrices, A and B, form a third matrix C that has an entry in position (i, j) given by the following.

$$c_{i,j} = \sum_{k=1}^{n} a_{i,k} b_{k,j}$$

In other words, element (i, j) of the result is the product of row i of the first matrix with column j of the second matrix. Start by assuming that there are n processes on the ring. Each input array is stored as a binary file in row-major form. The elements of the array are of type int.

One approach to matrix multiplication is for process p to read row p of the input file for matrix A and column p of the input file for matrix B. Process p accumulates row p of matrix C. It multiplies row p of A by column p of B and sets c[p,p] to the resulting value. It then writes column p of matrix B to the ring and reads column p-1 from its neighbor. Process p then computes element c[p,p-1], and so on.

The row-column is very efficient once the processes have read the columns of B, but since B is stored in row-major form, the file accesses are inefficient if the process is accessing a column of B, since the read must seek for each element. In addition it is likely that matrix multiplication is an intermediate step in a larger calculation that might have the A and B distributed to processes in row-major form. The following algorithm performs matrix multiplication when process p starts with row p of A and row p of B.

Process p is going to compute row p of the result. On each iteration, a row of B contributes one term to the sum needed to calculate each element of row p of the product matrix. Each process eventually needs all the entries of B, and it receives the rows of B one at a time from its neighbors. Use the following arrays.

```
int a[n+1];      /* holds the pth row of A */
int b[n+1];      /* starts with the pth row of B */
int c[n+1];      /* holds the pth row of C */
```

Initialize the elements of a[] and b[] from their respective files. Initialize c[], using

```
for (k = 1; k < n+1; k++)
   c[k] = a[p] * b[k];
```

In process p, this approach accounts for the contribution of row p of B to row p of the output C. In other words, `c[p,k] = a[p,p]*b[p,k]`. Process p does the following.

```
m = p;
write(STDOUT_FILENO, &b[1], n*sizeof(int));
read(STDIN_FILENO, &b[1], n*sizeof(int));
for (k = 1; k < n+1; k++) {
   if (m-- == 0)
      m = n;
   c[k]  += a[m]*b[k];
}
```

The `read` function fills the b[] array with the values of the row of B held initially by the process immediately before it on the ring. One execution of the `for` loop adds the contribution of row p-1 of B to row p of the result corresponding to `c[p,k] = c[p,k] + a[p,p-1]* b[p-1,k]`. Execute this code n-1 times to multiply the entire array. Write the resulting c[] as row p of the output file. **Note:** The proposed strategy may cause a deadlock if n is so large that the write exceeds the size of PIPE_BUF. A more robust strategy might use `select` to process the reading and writing simultaneously.

7.11 Flexible Ring

A flexible ring is a ring in which nodes can be added and deleted. The flexibility is useful for fault recovery and for network maintenance.

1. Modify `ring` of Program 7.1 to use named pipes or FIFOs instead of unnamed pipes. Devise an appropriate naming scheme for the pipes.
2. Devise and implement a scheme for adding a node after node i in the ring. Pass i on the command line.
3. Devise and implement a scheme for deleting a node i in the ring. Pass i on the command line.

After testing the strategies for inserting and deleting nodes, convert the token-ring implementation of Section 7.8 to one using named pipes. Develop a protocol so that any node can initiate a request to add or delete a node. Implement the protocol.

This project leaves most of the specification open. Figure out what it means to insert or delete a node.

7.12 Additional Reading

Early versions of the ring project described in this chapter can be found in [95]. A simulator that explores the interaction between pipes and forks is discussed in [97]. This simulator can be run either locally or from the Web and is available on the book web site. *Local and Metropolitan Area Networks*, 6th ed. by Stallings [111] has a good discussion of the token ring, token bus and FDDI network standards. Each of these networks is based on a ring architecture. Stallings also discusses the election methods used by these architectures for token regeneration and reconfiguration. The paper "A resilient mutual exclusion algorithm for computer networks" by Nishio et al. [88] analyzes the general problem of regenerating lost tokens in computer networks.

The theoretical literature on distributed algorithms for rings is large. The algorithms of Section 7.6 are based on a paper by Chang and Roberts [22], and the algorithms of Section 7.7 are discussed in Itai and Roteh [58]. A nice theoretical article on anonymous rings is "Computing on an anonymous ring" by Attiya et al. [7]. *Introduction to Parallel Computing: Design and Analysis of Algorithms* by Kumar et al. [67] presents a good overview of parallel algorithms and a discussion of how to map these algorithms onto particular machine architectures.

Part II

Asynchronous Events

Chapter 8

Signals

Few people appreciate the insidious nature of asynchronous events until they encounter a problem that is difficult to reproduce. This chapter discusses signals and their effect on processes, emphasizing the concurrent aspects of signal handling. The chapter begins by defining basic signal concepts such as generation and delivery as well as explaining the difference between ignoring a signal and blocking a signal. Sample programs demonstrate how to use signals for notification and how to suspend a process while waiting for a signal. The chapter also covers error handling, signal safety and asynchronous I/O.

Objectives
- Learn the fundamentals of signal handling
- Experiment with signals for control
- Explore the POSIX signal facilities
- Use signal masks and handlers
- Understand async-signal safety

8.1 Basic Signal Concepts

A *signal* is a software notification to a process of an event. A signal is *generated* when the event that causes the signal occurs. A signal is *delivered* when the process takes action based on that signal. The *lifetime* of a signal is the interval between its generation and its delivery. A signal that has been generated but not yet delivered is said to be *pending*. There may be considerable time between signal generation and signal delivery. The process must be running on a processor at the time of signal delivery.

A process *catches* a signal if it executes a *signal handler* when the signal is delivered. A program installs a *signal handler* by calling `sigaction` with the name of a user-written function. The `sigaction` function may also be called with `SIG_DFL` or `SIG_IGN` instead of a handler. The `SIG_DFL` means take the default action, and `SIG_IGN` means ignore the signal. Neither of these actions is considered to be "catching" the signal. If the process is set to *ignore* a signal, that signal is thrown away when delivered and has no effect on the process.

The action taken when a signal is generated depends on the current signal handler for that signal and on the *process signal mask*. The signal mask contains a list of currently *blocked signals*. It is easy to confuse blocking a signal with ignoring a signal. Blocked signals are not thrown away as ignored signals are. If a pending signal is blocked, it is delivered when the process unblocks that signal. A program blocks a signal by changing its process signal mask, using `sigprocmask`. A program ignores a signal by setting the signal handler to `SIG_IGN`, using `sigaction`.

This chapter discusses many aspects of POSIX signals. Section 8.2 introduces signals and presents examples of how to generate them. Section 8.3 discusses the signal mask and the blocking of signals, and Section 8.4 covers the catching and ignoring of signals. Section 8.5 shows how a process should wait for the delivery of a signal. The remaining sections of the chapter cover more advanced signal handling topics. Section 8.6 discusses interactions between library functions and signal handling, Section 8.7 covers `siglongjmp`, and Section 8.8 introduces POSIX asynchronous I/O. Other aspects of signals are covered in other chapters. Section 9.4 covers POSIX realtime signals, and Section 13.5 covers the use of signals with threads.

8.2 Generating Signals

Every signal has a symbolic name starting with `SIG`. The signal names are defined in `signal.h`, which must be included by any C program that uses signals. The names of the signals represent small integers greater than 0. Table 8.1 describes the required POSIX signals and lists their default actions. Two signals, `SIGUSR1` and `SIGUSR2`, are available for users and do not have a preassigned use. Some signals such as `SIGFPE` or `SIGSEGV` are generated when certain errors occur; other signals are generated by specific calls such as `alarm`.

signal	description	default action
SIGABRT	process abort	implementation dependent
SIGALRM	alarm clock	abnormal termination
SIGBUS	access undefined part of memory object	implementation dependent
SIGCHLD	child terminated, stopped or continued	ignore
SIGCONT	execution continued if stopped	continue
SIGFPE	error in arithmetic operation as in division by zero	implementation dependent
SIGHUP	hang-up (death) on controlling terminal (process)	abnormal termination
SIGILL	invalid hardware instruction	implementation dependent
SIGINT	interactive attention signal (usually Ctrl-C)	abnormal termination
SIGKILL	terminated (cannot be caught or ignored)	abnormal termination
SIGPIPE	write on a pipe with no readers	abnormal termination
SIGQUIT	interactive termination: core dump (usually Ctrl-|)	implementation dependent
SIGSEGV	invalid memory reference	implementation dependent
SIGSTOP	execution stopped (cannot be caught or ignored)	stop
SIGTERM	termination	abnormal termination
SIGTSTP	terminal stop	stop
SIGTTIN	background process attempting to read	stop
SIGTTOU	background process attempting to write	stop
SIGURG	high bandwidth data available at a socket	ignore
SIGUSR1	user-defined signal 1	abnormal termination
SIGUSR2	user-defined signal 2	abnormal termination

Table 8.1: The POSIX required signals.

Generate signals from the shell with the `kill` command. The name `kill` derives from the fact that, historically, many signals have the default action of terminating the process. The `signal_name` parameter is a symbolic name for the signal formed by omitting the leading `SIG` from the corresponding symbolic signal name.

```
SYNOPSIS

    kill -s signal_name pid...
    kill -l [exit_status]
    kill [-signal_name] pid...
    kill [-signal_number] pid...
                                              POSIX:Shell and Utilities
```

The last two lines of the synopsis list the traditional forms of the `kill` command. Despite the fact that these two forms do not follow the POSIX guidelines for command-line arguments, they continue to be included in the POSIX standard because of their widespread use. The last form of `kill` supports only the `signal_number` values of 0 for signal 0, 1 for signal SIGHUP, 2 for signal SIGINT, 3 for signal SIGQUIT, 6 for signal SIGABRT, 9 for signal SIGKILL, 14 for signal SIGALRM and 15 for signal SIGTERM.

■ **Example 8.1**

The following command is the traditional way to send signal number 9 (SIGKILL) to process 3423.

```
kill -9 3423
```

■ **Example 8.2**

The following command sends the SIGUSR1 signal to process 3423.

```
kill -s USR1 3423
```

■ **Example 8.3**

The kill -l command gives a list of the available symbolic signal names. A system running Sun Solaris produced the following sample output.

```
% kill -l
HUP INT QUIT ILL TRAP ABRT EMT FPE
KILL BUS SEGV SYS PIPE ALRM TERM USR1
USR2 CLD PWR WINCH URG POLL STOP TSTP
CONT TTIN TTOU VTALRM PROF XCPU XFSZ WAITING
LWP FREEZE THAW CANCEL LOST XRES RTMIN RTMIN+1
RTMIN+2 RTMIN+3 RTMAX-3 RTMAX-2 RTMAX-1 RTMAX
```

Call the kill function in a program to send a signal to a process. The kill function takes a process ID and a signal number as parameters. If the pid parameter is greater than zero, kill sends the signal to the process with that ID. If pid is 0, kill sends the signal to members of the caller's process group. If the pid parameter is −1, kill sends the signal to all processes for which it has permission to send. If the pid parameter is another negative value, kill sends the signal to the process group with group ID equal to |pid|. Section 11.5 discusses process groups.

SYNOPSIS

```
#include <signal.h>

int kill(pid_t pid, int sig);
```

                                                         POSIX:CX

If successful, kill returns 0. If unsuccessful, kill returns −1 and sets errno. The following table lists the mandatory errors for kill.

errno	cause
EINVAL	sig is an invalid or unsupported signal
EPERM	caller does not have the appropriate privileges
ESRCH	no process or process group corresponds to pid

A user may send a signal only to processes that he or she owns. For most signals, `kill` determines permissions by comparing the user IDs of caller and target. `SIGCONT` is an exception. For `SIGCONT`, user IDs are not checked if `kill` is sent to a process that is in the same session. Section 11.5 discusses sessions. For security purposes, a system may exclude an unspecified set of processes from receiving the signal.

■ Example 8.4

The following code segment sends `SIGUSR1` to process `3423`.

```
if (kill(3423, SIGUSR1) == -1)
    perror("Failed to send the SIGUSR1 signal");
```

Normally, programs do not hardcode specific process IDs such as `3423` in the `kill` function call. The usual way to find out relevant process IDs is with `getpid`, `getppid`, `getgpid` or by saving the return value from `fork`.

■ Example 8.5

This scenario sounds grim, but a child process can kill its parent by executing the following code segment.

```
if (kill(getppid(), SIGTERM) == -1)
    perror ("Failed to kill parent");
```

A process can send a signal to itself with the `raise` function. The `raise` function takes just one parameter, a signal number.

```
SYNOPSIS

  #include <signal.h>

  int raise(int sig);

                                          POSIX:CX
```

If successful, `raise` returns 0. If unsuccessful, `raise` returns a nonzero error value and sets `errno`. The `raise` function sets `errno` to `EINVAL` if `sig` is invalid.

■ Example 8.6

The following statement causes a process to send the `SIGUSR1` signal to itself.

```
if (raise(SIGUSR1) != 0)
    perror("Failed to raise SIGUSR1");
```

A key press causes a hardware interrupt that is handled by the device driver for the keyboard. This device driver and its associated modules may perform buffering and editing of the keyboard input. Two special characters, the `INTR` and `QUIT` characters, cause the device driver to send a signal to the foreground process group. A user can send the `SIGINT` signal to the foreground process group by entering the `INTR` character. This user-settable character is often Ctrl-C. The user-settable `QUIT` character sends the `SIGQUIT` signal.

■ **Example 8.7**

The `stty -a` command reports on the characteristics of the device associated with standard input, including the settings of the signal-generating characters. A system running Sun Solaris produced the following output.

```
% stty -a
speed 9600 baud;
rows = 57; columns = 103; ypixels = 0; xpixels = 0;
eucw 1:0:0:0, scrw 1:0:0:0
intr = ^c; quit = ^|; erase = ^?; kill = ^u;
eof = ^d; eol = <undef>; eol2 = <undef>; swtch = <undef>;
start = ^q; stop = ^s; susp - ^z; dsusp - ^y;
rprnt = ^r; flush = ^o; werase = ^w; lnext = ^v;
-parenb -parodd cs8 -cstopb hupcl cread -clocal -loblk -crtscts
-parext -ignbrk brkint ignpar -parmrk -inpck -istrip -inlcr -igncr
icrnl -iuclc ixon -ixany -ixoff imaxbel
isig icanon -xcase echo echoe echok -echonl -noflsh
-tostop echoctl -echoprt echoke -defecho -flusho -pendin iexten
opost -olcuc onlcr -ocrnl -onocr -onlret -ofill -ofdel
```

The terminal in Example 8.7 interprets Ctrl-C as the `INTR` character. The `QUIT` character (Ctrl-| above) generates `SIGQUIT`. The `SUSP` character (Ctrl-Z above) generates `SIGSTOP`, and the `DSUSP` character (Ctrl-Y above) generates `SIGCONT`.

The `alarm` function causes a `SIGALRM` signal to be sent to the calling process after a specified number of real seconds has elapsed. Requests to `alarm` are not stacked, so a call to `alarm` before the previous timer expires causes the alarm to be reset to the new value. Call `alarm` with a zero value for `seconds` to cancel a previous alarm request.

SYNOPSIS

```
#include <unistd.h>

unsigned alarm(unsigned seconds);
```
                                                                                              POSIX

The `alarm` function returns the number of seconds remaining on the alarm before the call reset the value, or 0 if no previous alarm was set. The `alarm` function never reports an error.

■ **Example 8.8**

Since the default action for `SIGALRM` is to terminate the process, the following program runs for approximately ten seconds of wall-clock time.

```
#include <unistd.h>

int main(void) {
   alarm(10);
   for ( ; ; ) ;
}
```
                                                                              simplealarm.c

8.3 Manipulating Signal Masks and Signal Sets

A process can temporarily prevent a signal from being delivered by blocking it. Blocked signals do not affect the behavior of the process until they are delivered. The process *signal mask* gives the set of signals that are currently blocked. The signal mask is of type `sigset_t`.

Blocking a signal is different from ignoring a signal. When a process blocks a signal, the operating system does not deliver the signal until the process unblocks the signal. A process blocks a signal by modifying its signal mask with `sigprocmask`. When a process ignores a signal, the signal is delivered and the process handles it by throwing it away. The process sets a signal to be ignored by calling `sigaction` with a handler of `SIG_IGN`, as described in Section 8.4.

Specify operations (such as blocking or unblocking) on groups of signals by using signal sets of type `sigset_t`. Signal sets are manipulated by the five functions listed in the following synopsis box. The first parameter for each function is a pointer to a `sigset_t`. The `sigaddset` adds `signo` to the signal set, and the `sigdelset` removes `signo` from the signal set. The `sigemptyset` function initializes a `sigset_t` to contain no signals; `sigfillset` initializes a `sigset_t` to contain all signals. Initialize a signal set by calling either `sigemptyset` or `sigfillset` before using it. The `sigismember` reports whether `signo` is in a `sigset_t`.

```
SYNOPSIS

   #include <signal.h>

   int sigaddset(sigset_t *set, int signo);
   int sigdelset(sigset_t *set, int signo);
   int sigemptyset(sigset_t *set);
   int sigfillset(sigset_t *set);
   int sigismember(const sigset_t *set, int signo);
                                                              POSIX:CX
```

The `sigismember` function returns 1 if `signo` is in `*set` and 0 if `signo` is not in `*set`. If successful, the other functions return 0. If unsuccessful, these other functions return −1 and set `errno`. POSIX does not define any mandatory errors for these functions.

■ Example 8.9

The following code segment initializes signal set `twosigs` to contain exactly the two signals `SIGINT` and `SIGQUIT`.

```
if ((sigemptyset(&twosigs) == -1) ||
    (sigaddset(&twosigs, SIGINT) == -1)   ||
    (sigaddset(&twosigs, SIGQUIT) == -1))
   perror("Failed to set up signal mask");
```

A process can examine or modify its process signal mask with the `sigprocmask` function. The `how` parameter is an integer specifying the manner in which the signal mask is to be modified. The `set` parameter is a pointer to a signal set to be used in the modification. If `set` is `NULL`, no modification is made. If `oset` is not `NULL`, the `sigprocmask` returns in `*oset` the signal set before the modification.

```
SYNOPSIS

   #include <signal.h>

   int sigprocmask(int how, const sigset_t *restrict set,
                   sigset_t *restrict oset);
                                                              POSIX:CX
```

If successful, `sigprocmask` returns 0. If unsuccessful, `sigprocmask` returns −1 and sets errno. The `sigprocmask` function sets `errno` to `EINVAL` if `how` is invalid. The `sigprocmask` function should only be used by a process with a single thread. When multiple threads exist, the `pthread_sigmask` function (page 474) should be used.

The `how` parameter, which specifies the manner in which the signal mask is to be modified, can take on one of the following three values.

SIG_BLOCK:	add a collection of signals to those currently blocked
SIG_UNBLOCK:	delete a collection of signals from those currently blocked
SIG_SETMASK:	set the collection of signals being blocked to the specified set

Keep in mind that some signals, such as `SIGSTOP` and `SIGKILL`, cannot be blocked. If an attempt is made to block these signals, the system ignores the request without reporting an error.

■ Example 8.10

The following code segment adds `SIGINT` to the set of signals that the process has blocked.

```
sigset_t newsigset;

if ((sigemptyset(&newsigset) == -1) ||
    (sigaddset(&newsigset, SIGINT) == -1))
  perror("Failed to initialize the signal set");
else if (sigprocmask(SIG_BLOCK, &newsigset, NULL) == -1)
  perror("Failed to block SIGINT");
```

If `SIGINT` is already blocked, the call to `sigprocmask` has no effect.

Program 8.1 displays a message, blocks the `SIGINT` signal while doing some useless work, unblocks the signal, and does more useless work. The program repeats this sequence continually in a loop.

If a user enters Ctrl-C while `SIGINT` is blocked, Program 8.1 finishes the calculation and prints a message before terminating. If a user types Ctrl-C while `SIGINT` is unblocked, the program terminates immediately.

Program 8.1 ———————————————————————— `blocktest.c`

A program that blocks and unblocks `SIGINT`*.*

```c
#include <math.h>
#include <signal.h>
#include <stdio.h>
#include <stdlib.h>
#include <unistd.h>

int main(int argc,  char *argv[]) {
   int i;
   sigset_t intmask;
   int repeatfactor;
   double y = 0.0;

   if (argc != 2) {
      fprintf(stderr, "Usage: %s repeatfactor\n", argv[0]);
      return 1;
   }
   repeatfactor = atoi(argv[1]);
   if ((sigemptyset(&intmask) == -1) || (sigaddset(&intmask, SIGINT) == -1)){
      perror("Failed to initialize the signal mask");
      return 1;
   }
   for ( ; ; ) {
      if (sigprocmask(SIG_BLOCK, &intmask, NULL) == -1)
         break;
      fprintf(stderr, "SIGINT signal blocked\n");
      for (i = 0; i < repeatfactor; i++)
         y += sin((double)i);
      fprintf(stderr, "Blocked calculation is finished, y = %f\n", y);
      if (sigprocmask(SIG_UNBLOCK, &intmask, NULL) == -1)
         break;
      fprintf(stderr, "SIGINT signal unblocked\n");
      for (i = 0; i < repeatfactor; i++)
         y += sin((double)i);
      fprintf(stderr, "Unblocked calculation is finished, y=%f\n", y);
   }
   perror("Failed to change signal mask");
   return 1;
}
```

Program 8.1 ———————————————————————— `blocktest.c`

The function `makepair` of Program 8.2 takes two pathnames as parameters and creates two named pipes with these names. If successful, `makepair` returns 0. If unsuccessful, `makepair` returns −1 and sets `errno`. The function blocks all signals during the creation of the two pipes to be sure that it can deallocate both pipes if there is an error. The function restores the original signal mask before the return. The `if` statement relies on the conditional left-to-right evaluation of `&&` and `||`.

❏ Exercise 8.11

Is it possible that after a call to `makepair`, `pipe1` exists but `pipe2` does not?

Answer:

Yes. This could happen if `pipe1` already exists but `pipe2` does not and the user does not have write permission to the directory. It could also happen if the `SIGKILL` signal is delivered between the two calls to `mkfifo`.

Program 8.2 ──────────────────────────────────── `makepair.c`

A function that blocks signals while creating two pipes. (See Exercise 8.11 and Exercise 8.12 for a discussion of some flaws.)

```c
#include <errno.h>
#include <signal.h>
#include <unistd.h>
#include <sys/stat.h>
#define R_MODE (S_IRUSR | S_IRGRP | S_IROTH)
#define W_MODE (S_IWUSR | S_IWGRP | S_IWOTH)
#define RW_MODE (R_MODE | W_MODE)

int makepair(char *pipe1, char *pipe2) {
   sigset_t blockmask;
   sigset_t oldmask;
   int returncode = 0;

   if (sigfillset(&blockmask) == -1)
      return -1;
   if (sigprocmask(SIG_SETMASK, &blockmask, &oldmask) == -1)
      return -1;
   if (((mkfifo(pipe1, RW_MODE) == -1) && (errno != EEXIST)) ||
       ((mkfifo(pipe2, RW_MODE) == -1) && (errno != EEXIST))) {
      returncode = errno;
      unlink(pipe1);
      unlink(pipe2);
   }
   if ((sigprocmask(SIG_SETMASK, &oldmask, NULL) == -1) && !returncode)
      returncode = errno;
   if (returncode) {
      errno = returncode;
      return -1;
   }
   return 0;
}
```

Program 8.2 ──────────────────────────────────── `makepair.c`

☐ Exercise 8.12

Does a `makepair` return value of 0 guarantee that FIFOs corresponding to `pipe1` and `pipe2` are available on return?

Answer:

If one of the files already exists, `mkfifo` returns −1 and sets `errno` to `EEXIST`. The `makepair` function assumes that the FIFO exists without checking whether the file was a FIFO or an ordinary file. Thus, it is possible for `makepair` to indicate success even if this previously existing file is not a FIFO.

In Program 8.3, the parent blocks all signals before forking a child process to execute an `ls` command. Processes inherit the signal mask after both `fork` and `exec`, so the `ls` command executes with signals blocked. The child created by `fork` in Program 8.3 has a copy of the original signal mask saved in `oldmask`. An exec command overwrites all program variables, so an executed process cannot restore the original mask once `exec` takes place. The parent restores the original signal mask and then waits for the child.

Program 8.3 ———————————————————————— **blockchild.c**

A program that blocks signals before calling `fork` *and* `execl`*.*

```c
#include <errno.h>
#include <stdio.h>
#include <signal.h>
#include <unistd.h>
#include <sys/types.h>
#include <sys/wait.h>
#include "restart.h"

int main(void) {
    pid_t child;
    sigset_t mask, omask;

    if ((sigfillset(&mask) == -1) ||
         (sigprocmask(SIG_SETMASK, &mask, &omask) == -1)) {
       perror("Failed to block the signals");
       return 1;
    }
    if ((child = fork()) == -1) {
       perror("Failed to fork child");
       return 1;
    }
    if (child == 0) {                                    /* child code */
       execl("/bin/ls", "ls", "-l", NULL);
       perror("Child failed to exec");
       return 1;
    }
    if (sigprocmask(SIG_SETMASK, &omask, NULL) == -1){ /* parent code */
       perror("Parent failed to restore signal mask");
       return 1;
    }
  if (r_wait(NULL) == -1) {
    perror("Parent failed to wait for child");
    return 1;
  }
    return 0;
}
```

Program 8.3 ——————————————————————— **blockchild.c**

☐ Exercise 8.13

Run Program 8.3 from a working directory with a large number of files. Experiment with entering Ctrl-C at various points during the execution and explain what happens.

Answer:

The `main` program can be interrupted while the listing is being displayed, and the prompt will appear in the middle of the listing. The execution of `ls` will not be interrupted by the signal.

A function that retrieves a user password.

```c
#include <errno.h>
#include <fcntl.h>
#include <signal.h>
#include <stdio.h>
#include <string.h>
#include <termios.h>
#include <unistd.h>
#include "restart.h"

int setecho(int fd, int onflag);

int password(const char *prompt, char *passbuf, int passmax) {
    int fd;
    int firsterrno = 0;
    sigset_t signew, sigold;
    char termbuf[L_ctermid];

    if (ctermid(termbuf) == NULL) {                        /* find the terminal name */
       errno = ENODEV;
       return -1;
    }
    if ((fd = open(termbuf, O_RDONLY)) == -1)  /* open descriptor to terminal */
       return -1;
    if ((sigemptyset(&signew) == -1) ||   /* block SIGINT, SIGQUIT and SIGTSTP */
        (sigaddset(&signew, SIGINT) == -1) ||
        (sigaddset(&signew, SIGQUIT) == -1) ||
        (sigaddset(&signew, SIGTSTP) == -1) ||
        (sigprocmask(SIG_BLOCK, &signew, &sigold) == -1) ||
        (setecho(fd, 0) == -1)) {                          /* set terminal echo off */
         firsterrno = errno;
       sigprocmask(SIG_SETMASK, &sigold, NULL);
       r_close(fd);
       errno = firsterrno;
       return -1;
    }
    if ((r_write(STDOUT_FILENO, (char *)prompt, strlen(prompt)) == -1) ||
        (readline(fd, passbuf, passmax) == -1))            /* read password */
         firsterrno = errno;
    else
       passbuf[strlen(passbuf) - 1] = 0;                   /* remove newline */
    if ((setecho(fd, 1) == -1) && !firsterrno)             /* turn echo back on */
       firsterrno = errno;
    if ((sigprocmask(SIG_SETMASK, &sigold, NULL) == -1) && !firsterrno )
       firsterrno = errno;
    if ((r_close(fd) == -1) && !firsterrno)   /* close descriptor to terminal */
       firsterrno = errno;
    return firsterrno ? errno = firsterrno, -1: 0;
}
```

Program 8.4 shows an improvement on the `passwordnosigs` function of Program 6.13 on page 208. The `password` function blocks `SIGINT`, `SIGQUIT` and `SIGTSTP` while terminal echo is set off, preventing the terminal from being placed in an unusable state if one of these signals is delivered to the process while this function is executing.

8.4 Catching and Ignoring Signals—`sigaction`

The `sigaction` function allows the caller to examine or specify the action associated with a specific signal. The `sig` parameter of `sigaction` specifies the signal number for the action. The `act` parameter is a pointer to a `struct sigaction` structure that specifies the action to be taken. The `oact` parameter is a pointer to a `struct sigaction` structure that receives the previous action associated with the signal. If `act` is `NULL`, the call to `sigaction` does not change the action associated with the signal. If `oact` is `NULL`, the call to `sigaction` does not return the previous action associated with the signal.

```
SYNOPSIS

   #include <signal.h>

   int sigaction(int sig, const struct sigaction *restrict act,
                 struct sigaction *restrict oact);
                                                              POSIX:CX
```

If successful, `sigaction` returns 0. If unsuccessful, `sigaction` returns −1 and sets `errno`. The following table lists the mandatory errors for `sigaction`.

errno	cause
EINVAL	`sig` is an invalid signal number, or
	attempt to catch a signal that cannot be caught, or
	attempt to ignore a signal that cannot be ignored
ENOTSUP	SA_SIGINFO bit of the sa_flags is set and the
	implementation does not support POSIX:RTS or POSIX:XSI

The `struct sigaction` structure must have at least the following members.

```
struct sigaction {
   void (*sa_handler)(int);  /* SIG_DFL, SIG_IGN or pointer to function */
   sigset_t sa_mask;         /* additional signals to be blocked
                                during execution of handler */
   int sa_flags;             /* special flags and options */
   void(*sa_sigaction) (int, siginfo_t *, void *); /* realtime handler */
};
```

The storage for `sa_handler` and `sa_sigaction` may overlap, and an application should use only one of these members to specify the action. If the `SA_SIGINFO` flag of the sa_flags field is cleared, the sa_handler specifies the action to be taken for the specified signal. If the SA_SIGINFO flag of the sa_flags field is set and the implementation supports either the POSIX:RTS or the POSIX:XSI Extension, the sa_sigaction field specifies a signal-catching function.

■ **Example 8.14**

The following code segment sets the signal handler for SIGINT to mysighand.

```
struct sigaction newact;

newact.sa_handler = mysighand;   /* set the new handler */
newact.sa_flags = 0;             /* no special options */
if ((sigemptyset(&newact.sa_mask) == -1) ||
    (sigaction(SIGINT, &newact, NULL) == -1))
    perror("Failed to install SIGINT signal handler");
```

In the POSIX base standard, a signal handler is an ordinary function that returns void and has one integer parameter. When the operating system delivers the signal, it sets this parameter to the number of the signal that was delivered. Most signal handlers ignore this value, but it is possible to have a single signal handler for many signals. The usefulness of signal handlers is limited by the inability to pass values to them. This capability has been added to the POSIX:RTS and POSIX:XSI Extensions, which can use the alternative sa_sigaction field of the struct sigaction structure to specify a handler. This section describes using the sa_handler field of sigaction to set up the handler; Section 9.4 describes using the sa_sigaction field for the handler.

Two special values of the sa_handler member of struct sigaction are SIG_DFL and SIG_IGN. The SIG_DFL value specifies that sigaction should restore the default action for the signal. The SIG_IGN value specifies that the process should handle the signal by ignoring it (throwing it away).

■ **Example 8.15**

The following code segment causes the process to ignore SIGINT if the default action is in effect for this signal.

```
struct sigaction act;

if (sigaction(SIGINT, NULL, &act) == -1)  /* Find current SIGINT handler */
    perror("Failed to get old handler for SIGINT");
else if (act.sa_handler == SIG_DFL) {     /* if SIGINT handler is default */
    act.sa_handler = SIG_IGN;             /* set new SIGINT handler to ignore */
    if (sigaction(SIGINT, &act, NULL) == -1)
        perror("Failed to ignore SIGINT");
}
```

■ **Example 8.16**

The following code segment sets up a signal handler that catches the SIGINT signal generated by Ctrl-C.

```
void catchctrlc(int signo) {
   char handmsg[] = "I found Ctrl-C\n";
   int msglen = sizeof(handmsg);

   write(STDERR_FILENO, handmsg, msglen);
}
...
struct sigaction act;
act.sa_handler = catchctrlc;
act.sa_flags = 0;
if ((sigemptyset(&act.sa_mask) == -1) ||
    (sigaction(SIGINT, &act, NULL) == -1))
   perror("Failed to set SIGINT to handle Ctrl-C");
```

☐ **Exercise 8.17**

Why didn't Example 8.16 use `fprintf` or `strlen` in the signal handler?

Answer:

POSIX guarantees that `write` is async-signal safe, meaning that it can be called safely from inside a signal handler. There are no similar guarantees for `fprintf` or `strlen`, but they may be async-signal safe in some implementations. Table 8.2 on page 285 lists the functions that POSIX guarantees are async-signal safe.

■ **Example 8.18**

The following code segment sets the action of `SIGINT` to the default.

```
struct sigaction newact;

newact.sa_handler = SIG_DFL;    /* new handler set to default */
newact.sa_flags = 0;            /* no special options */
if ((sigemptyset(&newact.sa_mask) == -1) ||
    (sigaction(SIGINT, &newact, NULL) == -1))
   perror("Failed to set SIGINT to the default action");
```

■ **Example 8.19**

The following function takes a signal number parameter and returns 1 if that signal is ignored and 0 otherwise.

```
#include <signal.h>
#include <stdio.h>

int testignored(int signo) {
   struct sigaction act;
   if ((sigaction(signo, NULL, &act) == -1) || (act.sa_handler != SIG_IGN))
      return 0;
   return 1;
}
```

─── **`testignored.c`**

Program 8.5 estimates the average value of sin(x) on the interval from 0 to 1 by computing the average of the sine of randomly picked values. The `main` program loop chooses a random value, x, between 0 and 1, adds sin(x) to a running sum, increments the count of the values, and prints the current count and average. The program illustrates the use of a signal handler to gracefully terminate a program. When the user enters Ctrl-C at standard input, the signal handler sets doneflag to signify that the program should terminate. On each iteration of the computation loop, the program tests doneflag to see whether it should drop out of the loop and print a final message.

Program 8.5 ──────────────────────────── **signalterminate.c**

A program that terminates gracefully when it receives a Ctrl-C.

```c
#include <math.h>
#include <signal.h>
#include <stdio.h>
#include <stdlib.h>

static volatile sig_atomic_t doneflag = 0;

/* ARGSUSED */
static void setdoneflag(int signo) {
   doneflag = 1;
}

int main (void) {
   struct sigaction act;
   int count = 0;
   double sum = 0;
   double x;

   act.sa_handler = setdoneflag;                 /* set up signal handler */
   act.sa_flags = 0;
   if ((sigemptyset(&act.sa_mask) == -1) ||
       (sigaction(SIGINT, &act, NULL) == -1)) {
      perror("Failed to set SIGINT handler");
      return 1;
   }

   while (!doneflag) {
      x = (rand() + 0.5)/(RAND_MAX + 1.0);
      sum += sin(x);
      count++;
      printf("Count is %d and average is %f\n", count, sum/count);
   }

   printf("Program terminating ...\n");
   if (count == 0)
      printf("No values calculated yet\n");
   else
      printf("Count is %d and average is %f\n", count, sum/count);
   return 0;
}
```

Program 8.5 ──────────────────────────── **signalterminate.c**

Code that accesses doneflag is a critical section because the signal handler can modify this variable while the main program examines it. (See Chapter 14 for a discussion of critical sections and atomic operations.) We handle the problem here by declaring doneflag to be sig_atomic_t, an integral type that is small enough to be accessed atomically. The volatile qualifier on doneflag informs the compiler that the variable may be changed asynchronously to program execution. Otherwise, the compiler might assume that doneflag is not modified in the while loop and generate code that only tests the condition on the first iteration of the loop.

☐ Exercise 8.20

Why is it okay to use perror and printf in Program 8.5 even though these functions are not "signal safe"?

Answer:

Signal safety is a problem when both the signal handler and the main program use these functions. In this case, only the main program uses these functions.

When both a signal handler and the main program need to access data that is larger than sig_atomic_t, care must be taken so that the data is not modified in one part of the program while being read in another. Program 8.6 also calculates the average value of sin(x) over the interval from 0 to 1, but it does not print the result on each iteration. Instead, the main program loop generates a string containing the results every 10,000th iteration. A signal handler for SIGUSR1 outputs the string when the user sends SIGUSR1 to the process.

┌ **Program 8.6** ─────────────────────────────── **averagesin.c** ┐
  A program to estimate the average values of sin(x) over the interval from 0 to 1.

```
#include <errno.h>
#include <limits.h>
#include <math.h>
#include <signal.h>
#include <stdio.h>
#include <stdlib.h>
#include <string.h>
#include <unistd.h>
#define BUFSIZE 100

static char buf[BUFSIZE];
static int buflen = 0;

/* ARGSUSED */
static void handler(int signo) {               /* handler outputs result string */
   int savederrno;

   savederrno = errno;
   write(STDOUT_FILENO, buf, buflen);
   errno = savederrno;
}
```

```c
static void results(int count, double sum) {        /* set up result string */
    double average;
    double calculated;
    double err;
    double errpercent;
    sigset_t oset;
    sigset_t sigset;

    if ((sigemptyset(&sigset) == -1) ||
         (sigaddset(&sigset, SIGUSR1) == -1) ||
         (sigprocmask(SIG_BLOCK, &sigset, &oset) == -1) )
       perror("Failed to block signal in results");
    if (count == 0)
       snprintf(buf, BUFSIZE, "No values calculated yet\n");
    else {
       calculated = 1.0 - cos(1.0);
       average = sum/count;
       err = average - calculated;
       errpercent = 100.0*err/calculated;
       snprintf(buf, BUFSIZE,
                "Count = %d, sum = %f, average = %f, error = %f or %f%%\n",
                count, sum, average, err, errpercent);
    }
    buflen = strlen(buf);
    if (sigprocmask(SIG_SETMASK, &oset, NULL) == -1)
       perror("Failed to unblock signal in results");
}

int main(void) {
    int count = 0;
    double sum = 0;
    double x;
    struct sigaction act;

    act.sa_handler = handler;
    act.sa_flags = 0;
    if ((sigemptyset(&act.sa_mask) == -1) ||
         (sigaction(SIGUSR1, &act, NULL) == -1) ) {
       perror("Failed to set SIGUSR1 signal handler");
       return 1;
    }
    fprintf(stderr, "Process %ld starting calculation\n", (long)getpid());
    for ( ; ; ) {
       if ((count % 10000) == 0)
          results(count, sum);
       x = (rand() + 0.5)/(RAND_MAX + 1.0);
       sum += sin(x);
       count++;
       if (count == INT_MAX)
          break;
    }
    results(count, sum);
    handler(0);          /* call handler directly to write out the results */
    return 0;
}
```

Program 8.6 ———————————————————————————————— **averagesin.c**

The signal handler uses `write` instead of `printf`, since `printf` may not be safe to use in a signal handler. The handler avoids `strlen` for the same reason. The string and its length are global variables accessible to both the `main` program and the signal handler. Modifying the string in the `main` program and writing the string to standard output in the signal handler are critical sections for this program. The `main` program protects its critical section by having `results` block the signal while modifying the string and its length. Notice also that `handler` saves and restores `errno`, since `write` may change it.

Legacy programs sometimes use `signal` instead of `sigaction` to specify signal handlers. Although `signal` is part of ISO C, it is unreliable even when used in a program with a single thread. *Always use `sigaction` to set up your handlers.*

8.5 Waiting for Signals—`pause`, `sigsuspend` and `sigwait`

Signals provide a method for waiting for an event without *busy waiting*. Busy waiting means continually using CPU cycles to test for the occurrence of an event. Typically, a program does this testing by checking the value of a variable in a loop. A more efficient approach is to suspend the process until the waited-for event occurs; that way, other processes can use the CPU productively. The POSIX `pause`, `sigsuspend` and `sigwait` functions provide three mechanisms for suspending a process until a signal occurs.

8.5.1 The `pause` function

The `pause` function suspends the calling thread until the delivery of a signal whose action is either to execute a user-defined handler or to terminate the process. If the action is to terminate, `pause` does not return. If a signal is caught by the process, `pause` returns after the signal handler returns.

```
SYNOPSIS

   #include <unistd.h>

   int pause(void);

                                                    POSIX
```

The `pause` function always returns –1. If interrupted by a signal, `pause` sets `errno` to `EINTR`.

To wait for a particular signal by using `pause`, you must determine which signal caused `pause` to return. This information is not directly available, so the signal handler must set a flag for the program to check after `pause` returns.

◻ Exercise 8.21

The following code segment uses `pause` to cause a process to wait for a particular signal by having the signal handler set the `sigreceived` variable to 1. What happens if a signal is delivered between the test of `sigreceived` and `pause`?

```
static volatile sig_atomic_t sigreceived = 0;

while(sigreceived == 0)
    pause();
```

Answer:
The previously delivered signal does not affect `pause`. The `pause` function does not return until some other signal or another occurrence of the same signal is delivered to the process. A workable solution must test the value of `sigreceived` while the signal is blocked.

☐ Exercise 8.22

What is wrong with the following attempt to prevent a signal from being delivered between the test of `sigreceived` and the execution of `pause` in Exercise 8.21?

```
static volatile sig_atomic_t sigreceived = 0;

int signum;
sigset_t sigset;

sigemptyset(&sigset);
sigaddset(&sigset, signum);
sigprocmask(SIG_BLOCK, &sigset, NULL);
while(sigreceived == 0)
    pause();
```

Answer:
Unfortunately, the code segment executes `pause` while the signal is blocked. As a result, the program never receives the signal and `pause` never returns. If the program unblocks the signal before executing `pause`, it might receive the signal between the unblocking and the execution of `pause`. This event is actually more likely than it seems. If a signal is generated while the process has the signal blocked, the process receives the signal right after unblocking it.

8.5.2 The `sigsuspend` function

The delivery of a signal before `pause` was one of the major problems with the original UNIX signals, and there was no simple, reliable way to get around the problem. The program must do two operations "at once"—unblock the signal and start `pause`. Another way of saying this is that the two operations together should be atomic (i.e., the program cannot be logically interrupted between execution of the two operations). The `sigsuspend` function provides a method of achieving this.

The `sigsuspend` function sets the signal mask to the one pointed to by `sigmask` and suspends the process until a signal is caught by the process. The `sigsuspend` function returns when the signal handler of the caught signal returns. The `sigmask` parameter can be used to unblock the signal the program is looking for. When `sigsuspend` returns, the signal mask is reset to the value it had before the `sigsuspend` function was called.

```
SYNOPSIS

  #include <signal.h>

  int sigsuspend(const sigset_t *sigmask);

                                                           POSIX:CX
```

The `sigsuspend` function always returns −1 and sets `errno`. If interrupted by a signal, `sigsuspend` sets `errno` to `EINTR`.

☐ Exercise 8.23

What is wrong with the following code that uses `sigsuspend` to wait for a signal?

```
sigfillset(&sigmost);
sigdelset(&sigmost, signum);
sigsuspend(&sigmost);
```

Answer:

The `sigmost` signal set contains all signals except the one to wait for. When the process suspends, only the signal `signum` is unblocked and so it seems that only this signal can cause `sigsuspend` to return. However, the code segment has the same problem that the solution using `pause` had. If the signal is delivered before the start of the code segment, the process still suspends itself and deadlocks if another `signum` signal is not generated.

■ Example 8.24

The following code segment shows a correct way to wait for a single signal. Assume that a signal handler has been set up for the `signum` signal and that the signal handler sets `sigreceived` to 1.

```
1   static volatile sig_atomic_t sigreceived = 0;
2
3   sigset_t maskall, maskmost, maskold;
4   int signum = SIGUSR1;
5
6   sigfillset(&maskall);
7   sigfillset(&maskmost);
8   sigdelset(&maskmost, signum);
9   sigprocmask(SIG_SETMASK, &maskall, &maskold);
10  if (sigreceived == 0)
11      sigsuspend(&maskmost);
12  sigprocmask(SIG_SETMASK, &maskold, NULL);
```

The code omits error checking for clarity.

Example 8.24 uses three signal sets to control the blocking and unblocking of signals at the appropriate time. Lines 6 through 8 set `maskall` to contain all signals and `maskmost` to contain all signals but `signum`. Line 9 blocks all signals. Line 10 tests `sigreceived`, and line 11 suspends the process if the signal has not yet been received. Note that no signals can be caught between the testing and the suspending, since the signal is blocked at this point. The process signal mask has the value `maskmost` while the process is suspended, so only `signum` is not blocked. When `sigsuspend` returns, the signal must have been received.

■ **Example 8.25**

The following code segment shows a modification of Example 8.24 that allows other signals to be handled while the process is waiting for `signum`.

```
1   static volatile sig_atomic_t sigreceived = 0;
2
3   sigset_t maskblocked, maskold, maskunblocked;
4   int signum = SIGUSR1;
5
6   sigprocmask(SIG_SETMASK, NULL, &maskblocked);
7   sigprocmask(SIG_SETMASK, NULL, &maskunblocked);
8   sigaddset(&maskblocked, signum);
9   sigdelset(&maskunblocked, signum);
10  sigprocmask(SIG_BLOCK, &maskblocked, &maskold);
11  while(sigreceived == 0)
12      sigsuspend(&maskunblocked);
13  sigprocmask(SIG_SETMASK, &maskold, NULL);
```

The code omits error checking for clarity.

Instead of blocking all signals and then unblocking only `signum`, Example 8.25 does not change the other signals in the signal mask. As before, the `sigreceived` variable declared in line 1 is declared outside any block and has static storage class. The code assumes that `sigreceived` is modified only in the signal handler for `signum` and that signal handler sets the value to 1. Thus, only the delivery of `signum` can make this variable nonzero. The rest of the code starting with line 3 is assumed to be inside some function.

The three signal sets declared in line 3 are initialized to contain the currently blocked signals in lines 6, 7 and 10. Line 8 adds the signal `signum` to the set `maskblocked` if it was not already blocked, and line 9 removes `signum` from `maskunblocked` if it was not already unblocked. The consequence of these two lines is that `maskblocked` contains exactly those signals that were blocked at the start of the code segment, except that `signum` is guaranteed to be in this set. Similarly, `maskunblocked` contains exactly those signals that were blocked at the start of the code segment, except that `signum` is guaranteed not to be in this set.

Line 10 guarantees that the `signum` signal is blocked while the value of `sigreceived` is being tested. No other signals are affected. The code ensures that `sigreceived` does not change between its testing in line 11 and the suspending of the process in line 12. Using `maskunblocked` in line 12 guarantees that the signal will not be blocked while the process is suspended, allowing a generated signal to be delivered and to cause `sigsuspend` to return. When `sigsuspend` does return, the `while` in line 11 executes again and tests `sigreceived` to see if the correct signal came in. Signals other than `signum` may have been unblocked before entry to the code segment and delivery of these signals causes `sigsuspend` to return. The code tests `sigreceived` each time and suspends the process again until the right signal is delivered. When the `while` condition is false, the signal has been received and line 13 executes, restoring the signal mask to its original state.

■ **Example 8.26**

The following code segment shows a shorter, but equivalent, version of the code in Example 8.25.

```
1   static volatile sig_atomic_t sigreceived = 0;
2
3   sigset_t masknew, maskold;
4   int signum = SIGUSR1;
5
6   sigprocmask(SIG_SETMASK, NULL, &masknew);
7   sigaddset(&masknew, signum);
8   sigprocmask(SIG_SETMASK, &masknew, &maskold);
9   sigdelset(&masknew, signum);
10  while(sigreceived == 0)
11      sigsuspend(&masknew);
12  sigprocmask(SIG_SETMASK, &maskold, NULL);
```

This code omits error checking for clarity.

Lines 6 and 7 set `masknew` to contain the original signal mask plus `signum`. Line 8 modifies the signal mask to block `signum`. Line 9 modifies `masknew` again so that now it does not contain `signum`. This operation does not change the process signal mask or the signals that are currently blocked. The signal `signum` is still blocked when line 10 tests `sigreceived`, but it is unblocked when line 11 suspends the process because of the change made to `masknew` on line 9.

The code segment in Example 8.26 assumes that `sigreceived` is initially 0 and that the handler for `signum` sets `sigreceived` to 1. It is important that the signal be blocked when the `while` is testing `sigreceived`. Otherwise, the signal can be delivered between the test of `sigreceived` and the call to `sigsuspend`. In this case, the process blocks until another signal causes the `sigsuspend` to return.

❑ **Exercise 8.27**

Suppose the `sigsuspend` in Example 8.26 returns because of a different signal. Is the `signum` signal blocked when the `while` tests `sigreceived` again?
Answer:
Yes, when `sigsuspend` returns, the signal mask has been restored to the state it had before the call to `sigsuspend`. The call to `sigprocmask` before the `while` guarantees that this signal is blocked.

Program 8.7 ─────────────────────────────── `simplesuspend.c`
An object that allows a program to safely block on a specific signal.

```c
#include <errno.h>
#include <signal.h>
#include <unistd.h>

static int isinitialized = 0;
static struct sigaction oact;
static int signum = 0;
static volatile sig_atomic_t sigreceived = 0;

/* ARGSUSED */
static void catcher (int signo) {
    sigreceived = 1;
}

int initsuspend (int signo) {          /* set up the handler for the pause */
   struct sigaction act;
   if (isinitialized)
      return 0;
   act.sa_handler = catcher;
   act.sa_flags = 0;
   if ((sigfillset(&act.sa_mask) == -1) ||
       (sigaction(signo, &act, &oact) == -1))
      return -1;
   signum = signo;
   isinitialized = 1;
   return 0;
}

int restore(void) {
   if (!isinitialized)
      return 0;
   if (sigaction(signum, &oact, NULL) == -1)
      return -1;
   isinitialized = 0;
   return 0;
}

int simplesuspend(void) {
   sigset_t maskblocked, maskold, maskunblocked;
   if (!isinitialized) {
      errno = EINVAL;
      return -1;
   }
   if ((sigprocmask(SIG_SETMASK, NULL, &maskblocked) == -1) ||
       (sigaddset(&maskblocked, signum) == -1) ||
       (sigprocmask(SIG_SETMASK, NULL, &maskunblocked) == -1) ||
       (sigdelset(&maskunblocked, signum) == -1) ||
       (sigprocmask(SIG_SETMASK, &maskblocked, &maskold) == -1))
      return -1;
   while(sigreceived == 0)
      sigsuspend(&maskunblocked);
   sigreceived = 0;
   return sigprocmask(SIG_SETMASK, &maskold, NULL);
}
```

Program 8.7 ─────────────────────────────── `simplesuspend.c`

Program 8.7 shows an object implementation of functions to block on a specified signal. Before calling `simplesuspend`, the program calls `initsuspend` to set up the handler for the signal to pause on. The program calls `restore` to reset signal handling to the prior state.

Program 8.8 uses the functions of Program 8.7 to wait for SIGUSR1.

Program 8.8 ———————————————— `simplesuspendtest.c`

A program that waits for SIGUSR1.

```
#include <signal.h>
#include <stdio.h>
#include <unistd.h>

int initsuspend(int signo);
int restore(void);
int simplesuspend(void);

int main(void) {
   fprintf(stderr, "This is process %ld\n", (long)getpid());
   for ( ; ; ) {
      if (initsuspend(SIGUSR1)) {
         perror("Failed to setup handler for SIGUSR1");
         return 1;
      }
      fprintf(stderr, "Waiting for signal\n");
      if (simplesuspend()) {
         perror("Failed to suspend for signal");
         return 1;
      }
      fprintf(stderr, "Got signal\n");
      if (restore()) {
         perror("Failed to restore original handler");
         return 1;
      }
   }
   return 1;
}
```

Program 8.8 ———————————————— `simplesuspendtest.c`

Program 8.9, which is based on the strategy of Example 8.25, uses two signals to control the setting or clearing of a flag. To use the service, a program calls `initnotify` with the two signals that are to be used for control. The `signo1` signal handler sets the `notifyflag`; the `signo2` signal handler clears the `notifyflag`. After the initialization, the program can call `waitnotifyon` to suspend until the notification is turned on by the delivery of a `signo1` signal.

An object that provides two-signal control for turning on or off a service.

```c
#include <errno.h>
#include <signal.h>
#include <stdio.h>

static volatile sig_atomic_t notifyflag = 1;
static int signal1 = 0;
static int signal2 = 0;

/* ARGSUSED */
static void turnon(int s) {
   notifyflag = 1;
}

/* ARGSUSED */
static void turnoff(int s) {
   notifyflag = 0;
}

/* -------------------------Public functions -------------------------*/
int initnotify(int signo1, int signo2) {        /* set up for the notify */
   struct sigaction newact;

   signal1 = signo1;
   signal2 = signo2;
   newact.sa_handler = turnon;                   /* set up signal handlers */
   newact.sa_flags = 0;
   if ((sigemptyset(&newact.sa_mask) == -1) ||
       (sigaddset(&newact.sa_mask, signo1) == -1) ||
       (sigaddset(&newact.sa_mask, signo2) == -1) ||
       (sigaction(signo1, &newact, NULL) == -1))
      return -1;
    newact.sa_handler = turnoff;
    if (sigaction(signo2, &newact, NULL) == -1)
       return -1;
    return 0;
}

int waitnotifyon(void) {             /* Suspend until notifyflag is nonzero */
   sigset_t maskblocked, maskold, maskunblocked;

   if ((sigprocmask(SIG_SETMASK, NULL, &maskblocked) == -1) ||
       (sigprocmask(SIG_SETMASK, NULL, &maskunblocked) == -1) ||
       (sigaddset(&maskblocked, signal1) == -1) ||
       (sigaddset(&maskblocked, signal2) == -1) ||
       (sigdelset(&maskunblocked, signal1) == -1) ||
       (sigdelset(&maskunblocked, signal2) == -1) ||
       (sigprocmask(SIG_BLOCK, &maskblocked, &maskold) == -1))
      return -1;
   while (notifyflag == 0)
      sigsuspend(&maskunblocked);
   if (sigprocmask(SIG_SETMASK, &maskold, NULL) == -1)
      return -1;
   return 0;
}
```

Section 5.6 presented a simplebiff program to notify a user when mail is present. Program 8.10 shows a more sophisticated version that uses stat to determine when the size of the mail file increases. The program outputs the bell character to inform the user that new mail has arrived. This program uses the service of Program 8.9 to turn mail notification on or off without killing the process. The user sends a SIGUSR1 signal to turn on mail notification and a SIGUSR2 signal to turn off mail notification.

Program 8.10 ────────────────────────────── **biff.c**

A biff program that uses the notifyonoff *service.*

```
#include <errno.h>
#include <limits.h>
#include <pwd.h>
#include <signal.h>
#include <stdio.h>
#include <stdlib.h>
#include <string.h>
#include <unistd.h>
#include <sys/stat.h>
#include "notifyonoff.h"
#define MAILDIR "/var/mail/"

static int checkmail(char *filename) {                /* is there new mail ? */
   struct stat buf;
   int error = 0;
   static long newsize = 0;
   static long oldsize = 0;

   error = stat(filename, &buf);                      /* check the file status */
   if ((error == -1) && (errno != ENOENT))
      return -1;                          /* real error indicated by -1 return */
   if (!error)
      newsize = (long)buf.st_size;
   else
      newsize = 0;
   if (newsize > oldsize)
      error = 1;                                 /* return 1 to indicate new mail */
   else
      error = 0;                          /* return 0 to indicate no new mail */
   oldsize = newsize;
   return error;
}

int main(int argc, char *argv[]) {
   int check;
   char mailfile[PATH_MAX];
   struct passwd *pw;
   int sleeptime;

   if (argc != 2) {
      fprintf(stderr, "Usage: %s sleeptime\n", argv[0]);
      return 1;
   }
   sleeptime = atoi(argv[1]);
   if ((pw = getpwuid(getuid())) == NULL) {
```

```
            perror("Failed to determine login name");
            return 1;
        }
        if (initnotify(SIGUSR1, SIGUSR2) == -1) {
            perror("Failed to set up turning on/off notification");
            return 1;
        }
        snprintf(mailfile, PATH_MAX,"%s%s",MAILDIR,pw->pw_name);

        for( ; ; ) {
            waitnotifyon();
            sleep(sleeptime);
            if ((check = checkmail(mailfile)) == -1) {
                perror("Failed to check mail file");
                break;
            }
            if (check)
                fprintf(stderr, "\007");
        }
        return 1;
    }
```

Program 8.10 ── `biff.c`

8.5.3 The `sigwait` function

The `sigwait` function blocks until any of the signals specified by `*sigmask` is pending
and then removes that signal from the set of pending signals and unblocks. When `sigwait`
returns, the number of the signal that was removed from the pending signals is stored in
the location pointed to by `signo`.

```
SYNOPSIS

   #include <signal.h>

   int sigwait(const sigset_t *restrict sigmask,
               int *restrict signo);
                                                        POSIX:CX
```

If successful, `sigwait` returns 0. If unsuccessful, `sigwait` returns −1 and sets `errno`.
No mandatory errors are defined for `sigwait`.

   Note the differences between `sigwait` and `sigsuspend`. Both functions have a first
parameter that is a pointer to a signal set (`sigset_t *`). For `sigsuspend`, this set holds
the new signal mask and so the signals that are *not in* the set are the ones that can cause
`sigsuspend` to return. For `sigwait`, this parameter holds the set of signals to be waited
for, so the signals *in* the set are the ones that can cause the `sigwait` to return. Unlike
`sigsuspend`, `sigwait` does not change the process signal mask. The signals in `sigmask`
should be blocked before `sigwait` is called.

Program 8.11 uses `sigwait` to count the number of times the `SIGUSR1` signal is delivered to the process. Notice that no signal handler is necessary, since the signal is always blocked.

┌─ **Program 8.11** ──────────────────────── **countsignals.c** ─
│ *A program that counts the number of* `SIGUSR1` *signals sent to it.*
│
```
#include <signal.h>
#include <stdio.h>
#include <unistd.h>

int main(void) {
   int signalcount = 0;
   int signo;
   int signum = SIGUSR1;
   sigset_t sigset;

   if ((sigemptyset(&sigset) == -1) ||
       (sigaddset(&sigset, signum) == -1) ||
       (sigprocmask(SIG_BLOCK, &sigset, NULL) == -1))
      perror("Failed to block signals before sigwait");
   fprintf(stderr, "This process has ID %ld\n", (long)getpid());
   for ( ; ; ) {
      if (sigwait(&sigset, &signo) == -1) {
         perror("Failed to wait using sigwait");
         return 1;
      }
      signalcount++;
      fprintf(stderr, "Number of signals so far: %d\n", signalcount);
   }
}
```
└─ **Program 8.11** ──────────────────────── **countsignals.c** ─

8.6 Handling Signals: Errors and Async-signal Safety

Be aware of three difficulties that can occur when signals interact with function calls. The first concerns whether POSIX functions that are interrupted by signals should be restarted. Another problem occurs when signal handlers call nonreentrant functions. A third problem involves the handling of errors that use `errno`.

What happens when a process catches a signal while it is executing a library function? The answer depends on the type of call. Terminal I/O can block the process for an undetermined length of time. There is no limit on how long it takes to get a key value from a keyboard or to read from a pipe. Function calls that perform such operations are sometimes characterized as "slow." Other operations, such as disk I/O, can block for short periods of time. Still others, such as `getpid`, do not block at all. Neither of these last types is considered to be "slow."

The slow POSIX calls are the ones that are interrupted by signals. They return when a signal is caught and the signal handler returns. The interrupted function returns −1 with `errno` set to `EINTR`. Look in the ERRORS section of the man page to see if a given function can be interrupted by a signal. If a function sets `errno` and one of the possible values is `EINTR`, the function can be interrupted. The program must handle this error explicitly and restart the system call if desired. It is not always possible to logically determine which functions fit into this category, so be sure to check the man page.

It was originally thought that the operating system needs to interrupt slow calls to allow the user the option of canceling a blocked call. This traditional treatment of handling blocked functions has been found to add unneeded complexity to many programs. The POSIX committee decided that new functions (such as those in the POSIX threads extension) would never set `errno` to `EINTR`. However, the behavior of traditional functions such as `read` and `write` was not changed. Appendix B gives a restart library of wrappers that restart common interruptible functions such as `read` and `write`.

Recall that a function is *async-signal safe* if it can be safely called from within a signal handler. Many POSIX library functions are not async-signal safe because they use static data structures, call `malloc` or `free`, or use global data structures in a nonreentrant way. Consequently, a single process might not correctly execute concurrent calls to these functions.

Normally this is not a problem, but signals add concurrency to a program. Since signals occur asynchronously, a process may catch a signal while it is executing a library function. (For example, suppose the program interrupts a `strtok` call and executes another `strtok` in the signal handler. What happens when the first call resumes?) *You must therefore be careful when calling library functions from inside signal handlers.* Table 8.2 lists the functions that POSIX guarantees are safe to call from a signal handler. Notice that functions such as `fprintf` from the C standard I/O library are not on the list.

Signal handlers can be entered asynchronously, that is, at any time. Care must be taken so that they do not interfere with error handling in the rest of the program. Suppose a function reports an error by returning −1 and setting `errno`. What happens if a signal is caught before the error message is printed? If the signal handler calls a function that changes `errno`, an incorrect error might be reported. As a general rule, signal handlers should save and restore `errno` if they call functions that might change `errno`.

■ **Example 8.28**

The following function can be used as a signal handler. The `myhandler` saves the value of `errno` on entry and restores it on return.

```
void myhandler(int signo) {
    int esaved;
    esaved = errno;
    write(STDOUT_FILENO, "Got a signal\n", 13);
    errno = esaved;
}
```

_Exit	getpid	sigaddset
_exit	getppid	sigdelset
accept	getsockname	sigemptyset
access	getsockopt	sigfillset
aio_error	getuid	sigismember
aio_return	kill	signal
aio_suspend	link	sigpause
alarm	listen	sigpending
bind	lseek	sigprocmask
cfgetispeed	lstat	sigqueue
cfgetospeed	mkdir	sigset
cfsetispeed	mkfifo	sigsuspend
cfsetospeed	open	sleep
chdir	pathconf	socket
chmod	pause	socketpair
chown	pipe	stat
clock_gettime	poll	symlink
close	posix_trace_event	sysconf
connect	pselect	tcdrain
creat	raise	tcflow
dup	read	tcflush
dup2	readlink	tcgetattr
execle	recv	tcgetpgrp
execve	recvfrom	tcsendbreak
fchmod	recvmsg	tcsetattr
fchown	rename	tcsetpgrp
fcntl	rmdir	time
fdatasync	select	timer_getoverrun
fork	sem_post	timer_gettime
fpathconf	send	timer_settime
fstat	sendmsg	times
fsync	sendto	umask
ftruncate	setgid	uname
getegid	setpgid	unlink
geteuid	setsid	utime
getgid	setsockopt	wait
getgroups	setuid	waitpid
getpeername	shutdown	write
getpgrp	sigaction	

Table 8.2: Functions that POSIX guarantees to be async-signal safe.

Signal handling is complicated, but here are a few useful rules.

- When in doubt, explicitly restart library calls within a program or use the restart library of Appendix B.
- Check each library function used in a signal handler to make sure that it is on the list of *async-signal safe* functions.
- Carefully analyze the potential interactions between a signal handler that changes an external variable and other program code that accesses the variable. Block signals to prevent unwanted interactions.
- Save and restore `errno` when appropriate.

8.7 Program Control with `siglongjmp` and `sigsetjmp`

Programs sometimes use signals to handle errors that are not fatal but that can occur in many places in a program. For example, a user might want to avoid terminating a program while aborting a long calculation or an I/O operation that has blocked for a long time. The program's response to Ctrl-C should be to start over at the beginning (or at some other specified location). A similar situation occurs when the program has nested prompts or menus and should start over when a user misenters a response. Object-oriented languages often handle these situations by throwing exceptions that are caught elsewhere. C programs can use signals indirectly or directly to handle this type of problem.

In the indirect approach, the signal handler for SIGINT sets a flag in response to Ctrl-C. The program tests the flag in strategic places and returns to the desired termination point if the flag is set. The indirect approach is complicated, since the program might have to return through several layers of functions. At each return layer, the program tests the flag for this special case.

In the direct approach, the signal handler jumps directly back to the desired termination point. The jump requires unraveling the program stack. A pair of functions, `sigsetjmp` and `siglongjmp`, provides this capability. The `sigsetjmp` function is analogous to a statement label, and `siglongjmp` function is analogous to a `goto` statement. The main difference is that the `sigsetjmp` and `siglongjmp` pair cleans up the stack and signal states as well as doing the jump.

Call the `sigsetjmp` at the point the program is to return to. The `sigsetjmp` provides a marker in the program similar to a statement label. The caller must provide a buffer, `env`, of type `sigjmp_buf` that `sigsetjmp` initializes to the collection of information needed for a jump back to that marker. If `savemask` is nonzero, the current state of the signal mask is saved in the `env` buffer. When the program calls `sigsetjmp` directly, it returns 0. To jump back to the `sigsetjmp` point from a signal handler, execute `siglongjmp` with the same `sigjmp_buf` variable. The call makes it appear that the program is returning from `sigsetjmp` with a return value of `val`.

SYNOPSIS

```
#include <setjmp.h>

void siglongjmp(sigjmp_buf env, int val);
int sigsetjmp(sigjmp_buf env, int savemask);
```

POSIX:CX

No errors are defined for `siglongjmp`. The `sigsetjmp` returns 0 when invoked directly and the `val` parameter value when invoked by calling `siglongjmp`.

The C standard library provides functions `setjmp` and `longjmp` for the types of jumps referred to above, but the action of these functions on the signal mask is system dependent. The `sigsetjmp` function allows the program to specify whether the signal mask should be reset when a signal handler calls this function. The `siglongjmp` function causes the signal mask to be restored if and only if the value of `savemask` is nonzero. The `val` parameter of `siglongjmp` specifies the value that is to be returned at the point set by `sigsetjmp`.

Program 8.12 ── **sigjmp.c**

Code to set up a signal handler that returns to the main loop when Ctrl-C is typed.

```c
#include <setjmp.h>
#include <signal.h>
#include <stdio.h>
#include <unistd.h>

static sigjmp_buf jmpbuf;
static volatile sig_atomic_t jumpok = 0;

/* ARGSUSED */
static void chandler(int signo) {
   if (jumpok == 0) return;
   siglongjmp(jmpbuf, 1);
}

int main(void)  {
   struct sigaction act;

   act.sa_flags = 0;
   act.sa_handler = chandler;
   if ((sigemptyset(&act.sa_mask) == -1) ||
       (sigaction(SIGINT, &act, NULL) == -1)) {
     perror("Failed to set up SIGINT handler");
     return 1;
   }
                                            /* stuff goes here */
   fprintf(stderr, "This is process %ld\n", (long)getpid());
   if (sigsetjmp(jmpbuf, 1))
      fprintf(stderr, "Returned to main loop due to ^c\n");
   jumpok = 1;
   for ( ; ; )
      ;                                     /* main loop goes here */
}
```

Program 8.12 ── **sigjmp.c**

Program 8.12 shows how to set up a SIGINT handler that causes the program to return to the main loop when Ctrl-C is typed. It is important to execute sigsetjmp before calling siglongjmp in order to establish a point of return. The call to sigaction should appear before the sigsetjmp so that it is called only once. To prevent the signal handler from calling siglongjmp before the program executes sigsetjmp, Program 8.12 uses the flag jumpok. The signal handler tests this flag before calling siglongjmp.

8.8 Programming with Asynchronous I/O

Normally, when performing a read or write, a process blocks until the I/O completes. Some types of performance-critical applications would rather initiate the request and continue executing, allowing the I/O operation to be processed *asynchronously* with program execution. The older method of asynchronous I/O uses either SIGPOLL or SIGIO to notify a process when I/O is available. The mechanism for using these signals is set up with ioctl. This section discusses the newer version which is part of the POSIX:AIO Asynchronous I/O Extension that was introduced with the POSIX:RTS Realtime Extension.

The POSIX:AIO Extension bases its definition of asynchronous I/O on four main functions. The aio_read function allows a process to queue a request for reading on an open file descriptor. The aio_write function queues requests for writing. The aio_return function returns the status of an asynchronous I/O operation after it completes, and the aio_error function returns the error status. A fifth function, aio_cancel, allows cancellation of asynchronous I/O operations that are already in progress.

The aio_read and aio_write functions take a single parameter, aiocbp, which is a pointer to an asynchronous I/O control block. The aio_read function reads aiocbp->aio_bytes from the file associated with aiocbp->aio_fildes into the buffer specified by aiocbp->aio_buf. The function returns when the request is queued. The aio_write function behaves similarly.

SYNOPSIS

```
#include <aio.h>

int aio_read(struct aiocb *aiocbp);
int aio_write(struct aiocb *aiocbp);
```
POSIX:AIO

If the request was successfully queued, aio_read and aio_write return 0. If unsuccessful, these functions return −1 and set errno. The following table lists the mandatory errors for these functions that are specific to asynchronous I/O.

errno	cause
EAGAIN	system did not have the resources to queue request (*B*)
EBADF	`aiocbp->aio_fildes` invalid (*BA*)
EFBIG	`aiocbp->aio_offset` exceeds maximum (`aio_write`) (*BA*)
ECANCELED	request canceled because of explicit `aio_cancel` (*A*)
EINVAL	invalid member of `aiocbp` (*BA*)
EOVERFLOW	`aiocbp->aio_offset` exceeds maximum (`aio_read`) (*BA*)

Errors that occur before the return of `aio_read` or `aio_write` have a *B* tag. These are values that `errno` can have if the call returns −1. The errors that may occur after the return have an *A* tag. These errors are returned by a subsequent call to `aio_error`. The `aio_read` and `aio_write` functions also have the mandatory errors of their respective `read` and `write` counterparts.

The `struct aiocb` structure has at least the following members.

```
int             aio_fildes;    /* file descriptor */
volatile void   *aio_buf;      /* buffer location */
size_t          aio_nbytes;    /* length of transfer */
off_t           aio_offset;    /* file offset */
int             aio_reqprio;   /* request priority offset */
struct sigevent aio_sigevent;  /* signal number and value */
int             aio_lio_opcode; /* listio operation */
```

The first three members of this structure are similar to the parameters in an ordinary `read` or `write` function. The `aio_offset` specifies the starting position in the file for the I/O. If the implementation supports user scheduling (`_POSIX_PRIORITIZED_IO` and `_POSIX_PRIORITY_SCHEDULING` are defined), `aio_reqprio` lowers the priority of the request. The `aio_sigevent` field specifies how the calling process is notified of the completion. If `aio_sigevent.sigev_notify` has the value `SIGEV_NONE`, the operating system does not generate a signal when the I/O completes. If `aio_sigevent.sigev_notify` is `SIGEV_SIGNAL`, the operating system generates the signal specified in `aio_sigevent.sigev_signo`. The `aio_lio_opcode` function is used by the `lio_listio` function (not discussed here) to submit multiple I/O requests.

The `aio_error` and `aio_return` functions return the status of the I/O operation designated by `aiocbp`. Monitor the progress of the asynchronous I/O operation with `aio_error`. When the operation completes, call `aio_return` to retrieve the number of bytes read or written.

SYNOPSIS

```
#include <aio.h>

ssize_t aio_return(struct aiocb *aiocbp);
int aio_error(const struct aiocb *aiocbp);
```

                                                                    POSIX:AIO

The `aio_error` function returns 0 when the I/O operation has completed successfully or `EINPROGRESS` if the I/O operation is still executing. If the operation fails, `aio_error` returns the error code associated with the failure. This error status corresponds to the value of `errno` that would have been set by the corresponding `read` or `write` function. The `aio_return` function returns the status of a completed underlying I/O operation. If the operation was successful, the return value is the number of bytes read or written. Once `aio_return` has been called, neither `aio_return` nor `aio_error` should be called for the same `struct aiocb` until another asynchronous operation is started with this buffer. The results of `aio_return` are undefined if the asynchronous I/O has not yet completed.

POSIX asynchronous I/O can be used either with or without signals, depending on the setting of the `sigev_notify` field of the `struct aiocb`. Programs 8.13 and 8.14 illustrate how to do asynchronous I/O with signals. The general idea is to set up a signal handler that does all the work after the initial I/O operation is started.

Program 8.13 is a program for copying one file to another. The reading from the first file is done with asynchronous I/O, and the writing to the second file is done with ordinary I/O. This approach is appropriate if the input is from a pipe or a network connection that might block for long periods of time and if the output is to an ordinary file. Program 8.13 takes two filenames as command-line arguments and opens the first for reading and the second for writing. The program then calls the `initsignal` function to set up a signal handler and `initread` to start the first read. The signal is set up as a realtime signal as described in Section 9.4. The `main` program's loop calls `dowork` and checks to see if the asynchronous copy has completed with a call to `getdone`. When the copying is done, the program displays the number of bytes copied or an error message.

Program 8.14 contains the signal handler for the asynchronous I/O as well as initialization routines. The `initread` function sets up a `struct aiocb` structure for reading asynchronously and saves the output file descriptor in a global variable. It initializes three additional global variables and starts the first read with a call to `readstart`.

Program 8.14 keeps track of the first error that occurs in `globalerror` and the total number of bytes transferred in `totalbytes`. A `doneflag` has type `sig_atomic_t` so that it can be accessed atomically. This is necessary since it is modified asynchronously by the signal handler and can be read from the `main` program with a call to `getdone`. The variables `globalerror` and `totalbytes` are only available after the I/O is complete, so they are never accessed concurrently by the signal handler and the `main` program.

The signal handler in Program 8.14 uses the `struct aiocb` that is stored in the global variable `aiocb`. The signal handler starts by saving `errno` so that it can be restored when the handler returns. If the handler detects an error, it calls `seterror` to store `errno` in the variable `globalerror`, provided that this was the first error detected. The signal handler sets the `doneflag` if an error occurs or end-of-file is detected. Otherwise, the signal handler does a write to the output file descriptor and starts the next read. Since `aio_read` is not async-signal safe, `initread` blocks all signals before calling `readstart`.

A `main` *program that uses asynchronous I/O with signals to copy a file while doing other work.*

```c
#include <errno.h>
#include <fcntl.h>
#include <signal.h>
#include <stdio.h>
#include <string.h>
#include <unistd.h>
#include <sys/stat.h>
#include "asyncmonitorsignal.h"
#define BLKSIZE 1024
#define MODE (S_IRUSR | S_IWUSR | S_IRGRP | S_IROTH)

void dowork(void);

int main(int argc, char *argv[]) {
    char buf[BLKSIZE];
    int done = 0;
    int error;
    int fd1;
    int fd2;
                                        /* open the file descriptors for I/O */
    if (argc != 3) {
        fprintf(stderr, "Usage: %s filename1 filename2\n", argv[0]);
        return 1;
    }
    if ((fd1 = open(argv[1], O_RDONLY)) == -1) {
        fprintf(stderr, "Failed to open %s:%s\n", argv[1], strerror(errno));
        return 1;
    }
    if ((fd2 = open(argv[2], O_WRONLY | O_CREAT | O_TRUNC, MODE)) == -1) {
        fprintf(stderr, "Failed to open %s: %s\n", argv[2], strerror(errno));
        return 1;
    }
    if (initsignal(SIGRTMAX) == -1) {
        perror("Failed to initialize signal");
        return 1;
    }
    if (initread(fd1, fd2, SIGRTMAX, buf, BLKSIZE) == -1) {
        perror("Failed to initate the first read");
        return 1;
    }
    for ( ; ; ) {
        dowork();
        if (!done)
            if (done = getdone())
                if (error = geterror())
                    fprintf(stderr, "Failed to copy file:%s\n", strerror(error));
                else
                    fprintf(stderr, "Copy successful, %d bytes\n", getbytes());
    }
}
```

Program 8.14 ————————————————— `asyncmonitorsignal.c`
           Utility functions for handling asynchronous I/O with signals.

```c
#include <aio.h>
#include <errno.h>
#include <signal.h>
#include "restart.h"

static struct aiocb aiocb;
static sig_atomic_t doneflag;
static int fdout, globalerror, totalbytes;
static int readstart();
static void seterror(int error);

/* ARGSUSED */
static void aiohandler(int signo, siginfo_t *info, void *context) {
   int  myerrno, mystatus, serrno;
   serrno = errno;
   myerrno = aio_error(&aiocb);
   if (myerrno == EINPROGRESS) {
      errno = serrno;
      return;
   }
   if (myerrno) {
      seterror(myerrno);
      errno = serrno;
      return;
   }
   mystatus = aio_return(&aiocb);
   totalbytes += mystatus;
   aiocb.aio_offset += mystatus;
   if (mystatus == 0)
      doneflag = 1;
   else if (r_write(fdout, (char *)aiocb.aio_buf, mystatus) == -1)
      seterror(errno);
   else if (readstart() == -1)
      seterror(errno);
   errno = serrno;
}

static int readstart() {                         /* start an asynchronous read */
   int error;
   if (error = aio_read(&aiocb))
      seterror(errno);
   return error;
}

static void seterror(int error) {               /* update globalerror if zero */
   if (!globalerror)
      globalerror = error;
   doneflag = 1;
}

/* -------------------------Public Functions -------------------------- */
int getbytes() {
   if (doneflag)
      return totalbytes;
   errno = EINVAL;
   return -1;
}
```

```
int getdone() {                                        /* check for done */
   return doneflag;
}

int geterror() {             /* return the globalerror value if doneflag */
   if (doneflag)
      return globalerror;
   errno = EINVAL;
   return errno;
}

int initread(int fdread, int fdwrite, int signo, char *buf, int bufsize) {
   int error;
   sigset_t oldset, fullset;

   if ((sigfillset(&fullset) == -1) ||
       (sigprocmask(SIG_SETMASK, &fullset, &oldset) == -1)) {
      seterror(errno);
      return -1;
   }
   aiocb.aio_fildes = fdread;                          /* set up structure */
   aiocb.aio_offset = 0;
   aiocb.aio_buf = (void *)buf;
   aiocb.aio_nbytes = bufsize;
   aiocb.aio_sigevent.sigev_notify = SIGEV_SIGNAL;
   aiocb.aio_sigevent.sigev_signo = signo;
   aiocb.aio_sigevent.sigev_value.sival_ptr = &aiocb;
   fdout = fdwrite;
   doneflag = 0;
   globalerror = 0;
   totalbytes = 0;
   error = readstart();                               /* start first read */
   if (sigprocmask(SIG_SETMASK, &oldset, NULL) == -1) {
      seterror(errno);
      return -1;
   }
   return error;
}

int initsignal(int signo) {      /* set up the handler for the async I/O */
   struct sigaction newact;

   newact.sa_sigaction = aiohandler;
   newact.sa_flags = SA_SIGINFO;
   if ((sigemptyset(&newact.sa_mask) == -1) ||
       (sigaction(signo, &newact, NULL) == -1))
      return -1;
   return 0;
}

int suspenduntilmaybeready() {           /* return 1 if done, 0 otherwise */
   const struct aiocb *aiocblist;
   aiocblist = &aiocb;
   aio_suspend(&aiocblist, 1, NULL);
   return doneflag;
}
```

Program 8.14 ─────────────────────────────── **asyncmonitorsignal.c**

The `r_write` function from the restart library in Appendix B guarantees that all the bytes requested are written if possible. Program 8.14 also contains the `suspenduntilmaybeready` function, which is not used in Program 8.13 but will be described later.

The signal handler does not output any error messages. Output from an asynchronous signal handler can interfere with I/O operations in the `main` program, and the standard library routines such as `fprintf` and `perror` may not be safe to use in signal handlers. Instead, the signal handler just keeps track of the `errno` value of the first error that occurred. The `main` program can then print an error message, using `strerror`.

■ Example 8.29

The following command line calls Program 8.13 to copy from `pipe1` to `pipe2`.

```
asyncsignalmain pipe1 pipe2
```

Asynchronous I/O can be used without signals if the application has to do other work that can be broken into small pieces. After each piece of work, the program calls `aio_error` to see if the I/O operation has completed and handles the result if it has. This procedure is called *polling*.

Program 8.15 shows a `main` program that takes a number of filenames as parameters. The program reads each file, using asynchronous I/O, and calls `processbuffer` to process each input. While this is going on, the program calls `dowork` in a loop.

Program 8.15 uses utility functions from Program 8.16. The `main` program starts by opening each file and calling `initaio` to set up the appropriate information for each descriptor as an entry in the static array defined in Program 8.16. Each element of the array contains a `struct aiocb` structure for holding I/O and control information. Next, the first read for each file is started with a call to `readstart`. The program does not use signal handlers. The `main` program executes a loop in which it calls `readcheck` to check the status of each operation after each piece of `dowork`. If a read has completed, the `main` program calls `processbuffer` to handle the bytes read and starts a new asynchronous read operation. The `main` program keeps track of which file reads have completed (either successfully or due to an error) in an array called `done`.

Program 8.15 ──────────────────────────────── `asyncpollmain.c`

A `main` *program that uses polling with asynchronous I/O to process input from multiple file descriptors while doing other work.*

```
#include <errno.h>
#include <fcntl.h>
#include <stdio.h>
#include <string.h>
#include "asyncmonitorpoll.h"

void dowork(void);
void processbuffer(int which, char *buf, int bufsize);
```

```c
int main(int argc, char *argv[]) {
    char *buf;
    int done[NUMOPS];
    int fd[NUMOPS];
    int i;
    int numbytes, numfiles;

    if (argc < 2) {
        fprintf(stderr, "Usage: %s filename1 filename2 ...\n", argv[0]);
        return 1;
    } else if (argc > NUMOPS + 1) {
        fprintf(stderr, "%s: only supports %d simultaneous operations\n",
                argv[0],  NUMOPS);
        return 1;
    }
    numfiles = argc - 1;

    for (i = 0; i < numfiles; i++)  {            /* set up the I/O operations */
        done[i] = 0;
        if ((fd[i] = open(argv[i+1], O_RDONLY)) == -1) {
            fprintf(stderr, "Failed to open %s:%s\n", argv[i+1], strerror(errno));
            return 1;
        }
        if (initaio(fd[i], i) == -1) {
            fprintf(stderr, "Failed to setup I/O op %d:%s\n", i, strerror(errno));
            return 1;
        }
        if (readstart(i) == -1) {
            fprintf(stderr, "Failed to start read %d:%s\n", i, strerror(errno));
            return 1;
        }
    }
    for (  ;  ;  ) {                                        /* loop and poll */
        dowork();
        for (i = 0; i < numfiles; i++) {
            if (done[i])
                continue;
            numbytes = readcheck(i, &buf);
            if ((numbytes == -1) && (errno == EINPROGRESS))
                continue;
            if (numbytes <= 0) {
                if (numbytes == 0)
                    fprintf(stderr, "End of file on %d\n", i);
                else
                    fprintf(stderr, "Failed to read %d:%s\n", i, strerror(errno));
                done[i] = 1;
                continue;
            }
            processbuffer(i, buf, numbytes);
            reinit(i);
            if (readstart(i) == -1) {
                fprintf(stderr, "Failed to start read %d:%s\n", i, strerror(errno));
                done[i] = 1;
            }
        }
    }
}
```

Program 8.15 ———————————————————————————— `asyncpollmain.c`

Program 8.16 ———————————————————— `asyncmonitorpoll.c`

Utility functions for handling asynchronous I/O with polling.

```c
#include <aio.h>
#include <errno.h>
#include <stdio.h>
#include <unistd.h>
#include "asyncmonitorpoll.h"
#define BLKSIZE 1024                            /* size of blocks to be read */

typedef struct {
   char buf[BLKSIZE];
   ssize_t bytes;
   struct aiocb control;
   int doneflag;
   int startedflag;
} aio_t;

static aio_t iops[NUMOPS];                          /* information for the op */

/* ------------------------ Public Functions ------------------------- */
int initaio(int fd, int handle)        {           /* set up control structure */
   if (handle >= NUMOPS) {
      errno = EINVAL;
      return -1;
   }
   iops[handle].control.aio_fildes = fd;               /* I/O operation on fd */
   iops[handle].control.aio_offset = 0;
   iops[handle].control.aio_buf = (void *)iops[handle].buf;
   iops[handle].control.aio_nbytes = BLKSIZE;
   iops[handle].control.aio_sigevent.sigev_notify = SIGEV_NONE;
   iops[handle].doneflag = 0;
   iops[handle].startedflag = 0;
   iops[handle].bytes = 0;
   return 0;
}

/* return -1 if not done or error
            errno = EINPROGRESS if not done
   otherwise, return number of bytes read with *buf pointing to buffer
*/
int readcheck(int handle, char **bufp) {    /* see if read for handle is done */
   int error;
   ssize_t numbytes;
   struct aiocb *thisp;

   thisp = &(iops[handle].control);                /* get a pointer to the aiocp */
   if (iops[handle].doneflag) {         /* done already, don't call aio_return */
      numbytes = iops[handle].bytes;
      *bufp = (char *)iops[handle].control.aio_buf; /* set pointer to buffer */
      return numbytes;
   }
   error = aio_error(thisp);
   if (error) {
      errno = error;
      return -1;
   }
```

```
      numbytes = aio_return(thisp);
      iops[handle].bytes = numbytes;
      *bufp = (char *)iops[handle].control.aio_buf;    /* set pointer to buffer */
      iops[handle].doneflag = 1;
      return numbytes;
   }

int readstart(int handle) {    /* start read for I/O corresponding to handle */
   int error;
   struct aiocb *thisp;

   thisp = &(iops[handle].control);                  /* get a pointer to the aiocp */
   if (iops[handle].startedflag) {                          /* already started */
      errno = EINVAL;
      return -1;
   }
   if ((error = aio_read(thisp)) == -1) {
      errno = error;
      return -1;
   }
   iops[handle].startedflag = 1;
   return 0;
}

void reinit(int handle) {   /* must be called before doing another readstart */
   iops[handle].doneflag = 0;
   iops[handle].startedflag = 0;
   iops[handle].bytes = 0;
}
```

Program 8.16 ────────────────────────────────── **asyncmonitorpoll.c**

■ **Example 8.30**

The following command line calls Program 8.15 for inputs `pipe1`, `pipe2` and `pipe3`.

```
asyncpollmain pipe1 pipe2 pipe3
```

What if a program starts asynchronous I/O operations as in Program 8.13 and runs out of other work to do? Here are several options for avoiding busy waiting.

1. Switch to using standard blocking I/O with `select`.
2. Use signals as in Program 8.13, or use `pause` or `sigsuspend` in a loop. Do not use `sigwait`, since this function requires the signals to be blocked.
3. Switch to using signals as in Program 8.15 by blocking the signal and calling `sigwait` in a loop.
4. Use `aio_suspend`.

The `aio_suspend` function takes three parameters, an array of pointers to `struct aiocb` structures, the number of these structures and a timeout specification. If the timeout specification is not `NULL`, `aio_suspend` may return after the specified time. Otherwise, it returns when at least one of the I/O operations has completed and `aio_error` no longer returns `EINPROGRESS`. Any of the entries in the array may be `NULL`, in which case they are ignored.

```
SYNOPSIS

  #include <aio.h>

  int aio_suspend(const struct aiocb * const list[], int nent,
                  const struct timespec *timeout);
                                                            POSIX:AIO
```

If successful, `aio_suspend` returns 0. If unsuccessful, `aio_suspend` returns −1 and sets errno. The following table lists the mandatory errors for `aio_suspend`.

errno	cause
EAGAIN	timeout occurred before asynchronous I/O completed
EINTR	a signal interrupted `aio_suspend`

Program 8.14 has a `suspenduntilmaybeready` function that uses `aio_suspend` to suspend the calling process until the asynchronous I/O operation is ready. It can be called from the `main` program of Program 8.13 in place of `dowork` when there is no other work to be done. In this case, there is only one asynchronous I/O operation and the function returns 1 if it has completed, and 0 otherwise.

The `aio_cancel` function attempts to cancel one or more asynchronous I/O requests on the file descriptor `fildes`. The `aiocbp` parameter points to the control block for the request to be canceled. If `aiocbp` is `NULL`, the `aio_cancel` function attempts to cancel all pending requests on `fildes`.

```
SYNOPSIS

  #include <aio.h>

  int aio_cancel(int fildes, struct aioch *aiocbp);
                                                            POSIX:AIO
```

The `aio_cancel` function returns `AIO_CANCELED` if the requested operations were successfully canceled or `AIO_NOTCANCELED` if at least one of the requested operations could not be canceled because it was in progress. It returns `AIO_ALLDONE` if all the operations have already completed. Otherwise, the `aio_cancel` function returns −1 and sets errno. The `aio_cancel` function sets errno to `EBADF` if the `fildes` parameter does not correspond to a valid file descriptor.

☐ Exercise 8.31

How would you modify Programs 8.15 and 8.16 so that a `SIGUSR1` signal cancels all the asynchronous I/O operations without affecting the rest of the program?

Answer:

Set up a signal handler for `SIGUSR1` in `asyncmonitorpoll` that cancels all pending operations using `aio_cancel`. Also set a flag signifying that all I/O has been canceled. The `readcheck` function checks this flag. If the flag is set, `readcheck` returns −1 with `errno` set to `ECANCELED`.

8.9 Exercise: Dumping Statistics

The `atexit` function `showtimes` of Program 2.10 on page 53 can almost work as a signal handler to report the amount of CPU time used. It needs an unused parameter for the signal number, and the functions used in `showtimes` must be async-signal safe. Implement a signal handler for `SIGUSR1` that outputs this information to standard error. The program probably produces correct output most of the time, even though it calls functions such as `perror` and `fprintf` that are not async-signal safe.

Read your system documentation and try to find out if these functions are async-signal safe on your system. This information may be difficult to find. If you are using unsafe functions, try to make your program fail. This may not be easy to do, as it may happen very rarely. In any case, write a version that uses only those functions that POSIX requires to be async-signal safe as listed in Table 8.2 on page 285. You can avoid using `perror` by producing your own error messages. You will need to write your own functions for converting a double value to a string. Section 13.7 gives a signal-safe implementation of `perror` that uses mutex locks from the POSIX:THR Threads Extension.

8.10 Exercise: Spooling a Slow Device

This exercise uses asynchronous I/O to overlap the handling of I/O from a slow device with other program calculations. Examples include printing or performing a file transfer over a slow modem. Another example is a program that plays an audio file in the background while doing something else. In these examples, a program reads from a disk file and writes to a slow device.

Write a program that uses `aio_read` and `aio_write` to transfer data to a slow device. The source of information is a disk file. Model your program after Programs 8.13 and 8.14. Pass the name of the input and output files as command-line arguments.

The `main` program still initiates the first read. However, now the signal handler initiates an `aio_write` if the asynchronous read completes. Similarly, when the asynchronous write completes, the signal handler initiates another `aio_read`.

Begin testing with two named pipes for the input and the output. Then, use a disk file for the output. Redirect the output from the pipe to a file and use `diff` to check that they are the same. If a workstation with a supported audio device is available, use an audio file on disk as input and `"/dev/audio"` as the output device.

Keep statistics on the number of bytes transferred and the number of write operations needed. Add a signal handler that outputs this information when the program receives a `SIGUSR1` signal. The statistics can be kept in global variables. Block signals when necessary to prevent different signal handlers from accessing these shared variables concurrently.

This program is particularly interesting when the output goes to the audio device. It is possible to tell when the program is computing by the gaps that occur in the audio output. Estimate the percentage of time spent handling I/O as compared with calculation time.

8.11 Additional Reading

Advanced Programming in the UNIX Environment by Stevens [112] has a good historical overview of signals. *Beginning Linux Programming*, 2nd ed. by Stones and Matthew discusses signals in Linux [117]. The article "Specialization tools and techniques for systematic optimization of system software" by McNamee et al. [80] introduces a toolkit for writing efficient system code and uses signal handling as a principal case study for the toolkit.

Chapter 9

Times and Timers

Operating systems use timers for purposes such as process scheduling, timeouts for network protocols, and periodic updates of system statistics. Applications access system time and timer functions to measure performance or to identify the time when events occur. Applications also use timers to implement protocols and to control interaction with users such as that needed for rate-limited presentations. This chapter discusses representations of time in the POSIX base standard as well as interval timers in the POSIX:XSI Extension and POSIX:TMR Extension. The chapter also explores concepts such as timer drift and timer overrun and demonstrates how to use POSIX realtime signals with timers.

Objectives
- Learn how time is represented
- Experiment with interval timers
- Explore interactions of timers and signals
- Use timers to assess performance
- Understand POSIX realtime signals

9.1 POSIX Times

POSIX specifies that systems should keep time in terms of seconds since the Epoch and that each day be accounted for by exactly 86,400 seconds. The *Epoch* is defined as 00:00 (midnight), January 1, 1970, Coordinated Universal Time (also called UTC, Greenwich Mean Time or GMT). POSIX does not specify how an implementation should align its system time with the actual time and date.

Most operations need to be measured with timers with greater than one-second resolution. Two POSIX extensions, the POSIX:XSI Extension and the POSIX:TMR Extension, define time resolutions of microseconds and nanoseconds, respectively.

9.1.1 Expressing time in seconds since the Epoch

The POSIX base standard supports only a time resolution of seconds and expresses time since the Epoch using a `time_t` type, which is usually implemented as a `long`. A program can access the system time (expressed in seconds since the Epoch) by calling the `time` function. If `tloc` is not `NULL`, the `time` function also stores the time in `*tloc`.

```
SYNOPSIS

   #include <time.h>

   time_t time(time_t *tloc);
                                                                POSIX:CX
```

If successful, `time` returns the number of seconds since the Epoch. If unsuccessful, `time` returns `(time_t)−1`. POSIX does not define any mandatory errors for `time`.

☐ Exercise 9.1

The `time_t` type is usually implemented as a `long`. If a `long` is 32 bits, at approximately what date would `time_t` overflow? (Remember that one bit is used for the sign.) What date would cause an overflow if an `unsigned long` were used? What date would cause an overflow if a 64-bit data type were used?

Answer:

For a 32-bit `long`, time would overflow in approximately 68 years from January 1, 1970, so the system would not have a "Y2K" problem until the year 2038. For a `time_t` value that is an `unsigned long`, the overflow would occur in the year 2106, but this would not allow `time` to return an error. For a 64-bit data type, the overflow would not occur for another 292 billion years, long after the sun has died!

The `difftime` function computes the difference between two calendar times of type `time_t`, making it convenient for calculations involving time. The `difftime` function has two `time_t` parameters and returns a `double` containing the first parameter minus the second.

```
SYNOPSIS

  #include <time.h>

  double difftime(time_t time1, time_t time0);
                                                          POSIX:CX
```

No errors are defined for `difftime`.

■ Example 9.2

The following program calculates the wall-clock time that it takes to execute `function_to_time`.

```c
#include <stdio.h>
#include <time.h>
void function_to_time(void);

int main(void) {
   time_t tstart;

   tstart = time(NULL);
   function_to_time();
   printf("function_to_time took %f seconds of elapsed time\n",
           difftime(time(NULL), tstart));
   return 0;
}
```
————————————————————————————————————— **simpletiming.c**

Example 9.2 uses a time resolution of one second, which may not be accurate enough unless `function_to_time` involves substantial computation or waiting. Also, the `time` function measures wall-clock or elapsed time, which may not meaningfully reflect the amount of CPU time used. Section 9.1.5 presents alternative methods of timing code.

9.1.2 Displaying date and time

The `time_t` type is convenient for calculations requiring the difference between times, but it is cumbersome for printing dates. Also, a program should adjust dates and times to account for factors such as time zone, daylight-saving time and leap seconds.

The `localtime` function takes a parameter specifying the seconds since the Epoch and returns a structure with the components of the time (such as day, month and year) adjusted for local requirements. The `asctime` function converts the structure returned by `localtime` to a string. The `ctime` function is equivalent to `asctime(localtime(clock))`. The `gmtime` function takes a parameter representing seconds since the Epoch and returns a structure with the components of time expressed as Coordinated Universal Time (UTC).

```
SYNOPSIS

  #include <time.h>

  char *asctime(const struct tm *timeptr);
  char *ctime(const time_t *clock);
  struct tm *gmtime(const time_t *timer);
  struct tm *localtime(const time_t *timer);
                                                        POSIX:CX
```

No errors are defined for these functions.

The ctime function takes one parameter, a pointer to a variable of type time_t, and returns a pointer to a 26-character English-language string. The ctime function takes into account both the time zone and daylight saving time. Each of the fields in the string has a constant width. The string might be stored as follows.

```
Sun Oct 06 02:21:35 1986\n\0
```

■ Example 9.3

The following program prints the date and time. The printf format did not include '\n' because ctime returns a string that ends in a newline.

```
#include <stdio.h>
#include <time.h>

int main(void) {
   time_t tcurrent;

   tcurrent = time(NULL);
   printf("The current time is %s", ctime(&tcurrent));
   return 0;
}
```
———————————————————————————————— `timeprint.c`

□ Exercise 9.4

What is wrong with the following program that prints the time before and after the function function_to_time executes?

```
#include <stdio.h>
#include <time.h>

void function_to_time(void);

int main(void) {
   time_t tend, tstart;

   tstart = time(NULL);
   function_to_time();
   tend = time(NULL);
   printf("The time before was %sThe time after  was %s",
          ctime(&tstart), ctime(&tend));
   return 0;
}
```
———————————————————————————————— `badtiming.c`

Answer:

The ctime function uses static storage to hold the time string. Both calls to ctime store the string in the same place, so the second call may overwrite the first value before it is used. Most likely, both times will be printed as the same value.

The gmtime and localtime functions break the time into separate fields to make it easy for programs to output components of the date or time. ISO C defines the struct tm structure to have the following members.

```
int tm_sec;         /* seconds after the minute [0,60] */
int tm_min;         /* minutes after the hour [0,59] */
int tm_hour;        /* hours since midnight [0,23] */
int tm_mday;        /* day of the month [1,31] */
int tm_mon;         /* months since January [0,11] */
int tm_year;        /* years since 1900 */
int tm_wday;        /* days since Sunday [0,6] */
int tm_yday;        /* days since January 1 [0,365] */
int tm_isdst;       /* flag indicating daylight-saving time */
```

■ Example 9.5

The following code segment prints the number of days since the beginning of the year.

```
struct tm *tcurrent;

tcurrent = localtime(time(NULL));
printf("%d days have elapsed since Jan 1\n", tcurrent->tm_yday);
```

Unfortunately, the asctime, ctime and localtime are not thread-safe. The POSIX:TSF Thread Safe Extension specifies thread-safe alternatives that have a caller-supplied buffer as an additional parameter.

```
SYNOPSIS

   #include <time.h>

   char *asctime_r(const struct tm *restrict timeptr, char *restrict buf);
   char *ctime_r(const time_t *clock, char *buf);
   struct tm *gmtime_r(const time_t *restrict timer,
                       struct tm *restrict result);
   struct tm *localtime_r(const time_t *restrict timer,
                       struct tm *restrict result);
                                                             POSIX:TSF
```

If successful, these functions return a pointer to the parameter holding the result. For asctime_r and ctime_r, the result is in buf. For gmtime_r and localtime_r, the result is in result. If unsuccessful, these functions return a NULL pointer.

■ Example 9.6

The following code segment prints the number of days since the beginning of the year, using the thread-safe localtime_r function.

```
struct tm tbuffer;

if (localtime_r(time(NULL), &tbuffer) != NULL)
    printf("%d days have elapsed since Jan 1\n", tbuffer.tm_yday);
```

9.1.3 Using `struct timeval` to express time

A time scale of seconds is too coarse for timing programs or controlling program events. The POSIX:XSI Extension uses the `struct timeval` structure to express time on a finer scale. The `struct timeval` structure includes the following members.

```
time_t    tv_sec;    /* seconds since the Epoch */
time_t    tv_usec;   /* and microseconds */
```

Certain POSIX functions that support a timeout option (e.g., `select`) specify the timeout values by using variables of type `struct timeval`. In this case, the structure holds the length of the interval in seconds and microseconds.

The `gettimeofday` function retrieves the system time in seconds and microseconds since the Epoch. The `struct timeval` structure pointed to by `tp` receives the retrieved time. The `tzp` pointer must be `NULL` and is included for historical reasons.

SYNOPSIS

```
#include <sys/time.h>

int gettimeofday(struct timeval *restrict tp, void *restrict tzp);
```

POSIX:XSI

The `gettimeofday` function returns 0. No values are reserved to indicate an error. However, many systems have implemented `gettimeofday` so that it returns −1 and sets `errno` if unsuccessful. Our programs check to make sure `gettimeofday` returns 0.

Program 9.1 shows how to measure the running time of `function_to_time` by using `gettimeofday`. The `gettimeofdaytiming` program reads the time before and after calling `function_to_time` and prints the time difference as a number of microseconds.

☐ Exercise 9.7

What is the maximum duration that can be timed by the method of Program 9.1? How could you extend this?

Answer:

If a `long` is 32 bits, the maximum duration is $2^{31} - 1$ microseconds, or approximately 35 minutes. You could extend this by using a `long long` (usually 64 bits) for `timedif`. Changes must be made in the declaration of `timedif`, the definition of `MILLION` (`1000000LL`) and the format specifier (`lld`).

Program 9.1 ──────────────────────── `gettimeofdaytiming.c`

A program that measures the running time of a function by using `gettimeofday`*.*

```c
#include <stdio.h>
#include <sys/time.h>
#define MILLION 1000000L

void function_to_time(void);

int main(void) {
   long timedif;
   struct timeval tpend;
   struct timeval tpstart;

   if (gettimeofday(&tpstart, NULL)) {
      fprintf(stderr, "Failed to get start time\n");
      return 1;
   }
   function_to_time();                           /* timed code goes here */
   if (gettimeofday(&tpend, NULL)) {
      fprintf(stderr, "Failed to get end time\n");
      return 1;
   }
   timedif = MILLION*(tpend.tv_sec - tpstart.tv_sec) +
                     tpend.tv_usec - tpstart.tv_usec;
   printf("The function_to_time took %ld microseconds\n", timedif);
   return 0;
}
```

Program 9.1 ──────────────────────── `gettimeofdaytiming.c`

The `gettimeofdaytest` program shown in Program 9.2 tests `gettimeofday` resolution by calling `gettimeofday` in a loop until it produces 20 differences. Program 9.2 displays the differences along with the average difference and the number of calls made to `gettimeofday`. On most systems, the resolution will be a small number of microseconds. If the number of calls to `gettimeofday` is not much more than 21, then the limiting factor on the resolution is the time it takes to execute `gettimeofday`. On most modern systems, many consecutive calls to `gettimeofday` will return the same value. Often, one of the values displayed will be much greater than the others. This can happen if a context switch occurs while the timing loop is executing.

9.1.4 Using realtime clocks

A *clock* is a counter that increments at fixed intervals called the *clock resolution*. The POSIX:TMR Timers Extension contains clocks that are represented by variables of type `clockid_t`. POSIX clocks may be systemwide or only visible within a process. All implementations must support a systemwide clock with a `clockid_t` value of `CLOCK_REALTIME` corresponding to the system realtime clock. Only privileged users may set this clock, but any user can read it.

A program to test the resolution of gettimeofday.

```c
#include <stdio.h>
#include <sys/time.h>
#define MILLION 1000000L
#define NUMDIF 20

int main(void) {
   int i;
   int numcalls = 1;
   int numdone = 0;
   long sum = 0;
   long timedif[NUMDIF];
   struct timeval tlast;
   struct timeval tthis;

   if (gettimeofday(&tlast, NULL)) {
      fprintf(stderr, "Failed to get first gettimeofday.\n");
      return 1;
   }
   while (numdone < NUMDIF) {
      numcalls++;
      if (gettimeofday(&tthis, NULL)) {
         fprintf(stderr, "Failed to get a later gettimeofday.\n");
         return 1;
      }
      timedif[numdone] =  MILLION*(tthis.tv_sec - tlast.tv_sec) +
                     tthis.tv_usec - tlast.tv_usec;
      if (timedif[numdone] != 0) {
         numdone++;
         tlast = tthis;
      }
   }
   printf("Found %d differences in gettimeofday:\n", NUMDIF);
   printf("%d calls to gettimeofday were required\n", numcalls);
   for (i = 0; i < NUMDIF; i++) {
      printf("%2d: %10ld microseconds\n", i, timedif[i]);
      sum += timedif[i];
   }
   printf("The average nonzero difference is %f\n", sum/(double)NUMDIF);
   return 0;
}
```

The struct timespec structure specifies time for both POSIX:TMR clocks and timers, as well as the timeout values for the POSIX thread functions that support timeouts. The struct timespec structure has at least the following members.

```c
time_t  tv_sec;  /* seconds */
long    tv_nsec; /* nanoseconds */
```

POSIX provides functions to set the clock time (clock_settime), to retrieve the clock time (clock_gettime), and to determine the clock resolution (clock_getres).

Each of these functions takes two parameters: a clockid_t used to identify the particular clock and a pointer to a struct timespec structure.

```
SYNOPSIS

   #include <time.h>

   int clock_getres(clockid_t clock_id, struct timespec *res);
   int clock_gettime(clockid_t clock_id, struct timespec *tp);
   int clock_settime(clockid_t clock_id, const struct timespec *tp);
                                                           POSIX:TMR
```

If successful, these functions return 0. If unsuccessful, these functions return −1 and set errno. All three functions set errno to EINVAL if clockid_t does not specify a known clock. The clock_settime also sets errno to EINVAL if tp is out of the range of clock_id or if tp->tv_nsec is not in the range $[0, 10^9)$.

■ Example 9.8

The following program measures the running time of function_to_time by using the POSIX:TMR clocks.

```c
#include <stdio.h>
#include <time.h>
#define MILLION 1000000L

void function_to_time(void);

int main (void) {
   long timedif;
   struct timespec tpend, tpstart;

   if (clock_gettime(CLOCK_REALTIME, &tpstart) == -1) {
      perror("Failed to get starting time");
      return 1;
   }
   function_to_time();                        /* timed code goes here */
   if (clock_gettime(CLOCK_REALTIME, &tpend) == -1) {
      perror("Failed to get ending time");
      return 1;
   }
   timedif = MILLION*(tpend.tv_sec - tpstart.tv_sec) +
             (tpend.tv_nsec - tpstart.tv_nsec)/1000;
   printf("The function_to_time took %ld microseconds\n", timedif);
   return 0;
}
```
_____ **clockrealtimetiming.c**

The CLOCK_REALTIME typically has a higher resolution than gettimeofday. Program 9.3, which is similar to Program 9.2, tests the resolution of CLOCK_REALTIME by measuring the average of 20 changes in the clock reading. The program also calls clock_getres to display the nominal resolution in nanoseconds for setting the clock and for timer interrupts (Section 9.5). This nominal resolution is typically large, on the order of milliseconds, and is unrelated to the resolution of clock_gettime for timing. The resolution of clock_gettime is typically better than one microsecond.

Program 9.3 ─────────────────────────── **clockrealtimetest.c**

A program to test the resolution of CLOCK_REALTIME.

```c
#include <stdio.h>
#include <time.h>
#define BILLION 1000000000L
#define NUMDIF 20

int main(void) {
   int i;
   int numcalls = 1;
   int numdone = 0;
   long sum = 0;
   long timedif[NUMDIF];
   struct timespec tlast;
   struct timespec tthis;

   if (clock_getres(CLOCK_REALTIME, &tlast))
      perror("Failed to get clock resolution");
   else if (tlast.tv_sec != 0)
      printf("Clock resolution no better than one second\n");
   else
      printf("Clock resolution: %ld nanoseconds\n", (long)tlast.tv_nsec);
   if (clock_gettime(CLOCK_REALTIME, &tlast)) {
      perror("Failed to get first time");
      return 1;
   }
   while (numdone < NUMDIF) {
      numcalls++;
      if (clock_gettime(CLOCK_REALTIME, &tthis)) {
         perror("Failed to get a later time");
         return 1;
      }
      timedif[numdone] =  BILLION*(tthis.tv_sec - tlast.tv_sec) +
                     tthis.tv_nsec - tlast.tv_nsec;
      if (timedif[numdone] != 0) {
         numdone++;
         tlast = tthis;
      }
   }
   printf("Found %d differences in CLOCK_REALTIME:\n", NUMDIF);
   printf("%d calls to CLOCK_REALTIME were required\n", numcalls);
   for (i = 0; i < NUMDIF; i++) {
      printf("%2d: %10ld nanoseconds\n", i, timedif[i]);
      sum += timedif[i];
   }
   printf("The average nonzero difference is %f\n", sum/(double)NUMDIF);
   return 0;
}
```

Program 9.3 ─────────────────────────── **clockrealtimetest.c**

9.1.5 Contrasting elapsed time to processor time

The `time` function measures *real time*, sometimes called elapsed time or wall-clock time. In a multiprogramming environment many processes share the CPU, so real time is not an accurate measure of execution time. The *virtual time* for a process is the amount of time that the process spends in the *running* state. Execution times are usually expressed in terms of virtual time rather than wall-clock time.

The `times` function fills the `struct tms` structure pointed to by its `buffer` parameter with time-accounting information.

SYNOPSIS

```
#include <sys/times.h>

clock_t times(struct tms *buffer);
```
                                                                    POSIX

If successful, `times` returns the elapsed real time, in clock ticks, since an arbitrary point in the past such as system or process startup time. The return value may overflow its possible range. If `times` fails, it returns `(clock_t)-1` and sets `errno`.

The `struct tms` structure contains at least the following members.

```
clock_t    tms_utime;  /* user CPU time of process */
clock_t    tms_stime;  /* system CPU time on behalf of process */
clock_t    tms_cutime  /* user CPU time of process and terminated children */
clock_t    tms_cstime; /* system CPU time of process and terminated children */
```

Program 9.4 estimates the total of the amount of CPU time used by `function_to_time` as well as the fraction of the total CPU time used. It displays the total time in units of seconds expressed as a `double`. The resolution of the calculation is in clock ticks. A typical value for the number of ticks per second is 100. This number is suitable for accounting but does not have enough resolution for performance measurements of short events. If `function_to_time` takes only a few clock ticks to execute, you can obtain better resolution by calling it in a loop several times and dividing the resulting time by the number of iterations of the loop.

Program 9.4 calls `sysconf` as introduced in `showtimes` (Program 2.10 on page 53) to determine the number of clock ticks in a second. The calculation does not include any CPU time used by children of the process, but it does include both the user time and the system time used on behalf of the process. The fraction of the total CPU time may be inaccurate if a context switch occurs during the execution of the function.

Program 9.5, which is similar to the `time` shell command, prints the number of clock ticks and seconds used to execute an arbitrary program. The `timechild` function passes its own command-line argument array to `execv` in the same way as does Program 3.5 on page 81 and calculates the child's time by subtracting the process time from the total time. Since the process has only one child, what is left is the child's time.

Program 9.4 ———————————————————————— **cpufraction.c**

A program that calculates the CPU time in seconds for function_to_time *and its fraction of total.*

```
#include <stdio.h>
#include <stdlib.h>
#include <unistd.h>
#include <sys/times.h>

void function_to_time(void);

int main(void) {
   double clockticks, cticks;
   clock_t tcend, tcstart;
   struct tms tmend, tmstart;

   if ((clockticks = (double) sysconf(_SC_CLK_TCK)) == -1) {
      perror("Failed to determine clock ticks per second");
      return 1;
   }
   printf("The number of ticks per second is %f\n", clockticks);
   if (clockticks == 0) {
      fprintf(stderr, "The number of ticks per second is invalid\n");
      return 1;
   }
   if ((tcstart = times(&tmstart)) == -1) {
      perror("Failed to get start time");
      return 1;
   }
   function_to_time();
   if ((tcend = times(&tmend)) == -1) {
      perror("Failed to get end times");
      return 1;
   }
   cticks = tmend.tms_utime + tmend.tms_stime
            - tmstart.tms_utime - tmstart.tms_stime;
   printf("Total CPU time for operation is %f seconds\n", cticks/clockticks);
   if ((tcend <= tcstart) || (tcend < 0) || (tcstart < 0)) {
      fprintf(stderr, "Tick time wrapped, couldn't calculate fraction\n");
      return 1;
   }
   printf("Fraction of CPU time used is %f\n", cticks/(tcend - tcstart));
   return 0;
}
```

Program 9.4 ———————————————————————— **cpufraction.c**

■ **Example 9.9**

   The following command line uses timechild of Program 9.5 to time the execution of Program 9.4.

```
timechild cpufraction
```

Program 9.5 ─── **timechild.c**

A program that executes its command-line argument array as a child process and
returns the amount of time taken to execute the child.

```c
#include <errno.h>
#include <stdio.h>
#include <unistd.h>
#include <sys/times.h>
#include <sys/types.h>
#include <sys/wait.h>
#include "restart.h"

int main(int argc, char *argv[]) {
   pid_t child;
   double clockticks;
   double cticks;
   struct tms tmend;

   if (argc < 2){   /* check for valid number of command-line arguments */
      fprintf (stderr, "Usage: %s command\n", argv[0]);
      return 1;
   }
   if ((child = fork()) == -1) {
      perror("Failed to fork");
      return 1;
   }
   if (child == 0) {                                    /* child code */
      execvp(argv[1], &argv[1]);
      perror("Child failed to execvp the command");
      return 1;
   }
   if (r_wait(NULL) == -1) {                        /* parent code */
      perror("Failed to wait for child");
      return 1;
   }
   if (times(&tmend) == (clock_t)-1) {
      perror("Failed to get end time");
      return 1;
   }
   if ((clockticks = (double) sysconf(_SC_CLK_TCK)) == -1) {
      perror("Failed to determine clock ticks per second");
      return 1;
   }
   if (clockticks == 0) {
      fprintf(stderr, "Invalid number of ticks per second\n");
      return 1;
   }

   cticks = tmend.tms_cutime + tmend.tms_cstime
          - tmend.tms_utime - tmend.tms_stime;
   printf("%s used %ld clock ticks or %f seconds\n", argv[1],
          (long)cticks, cticks/clockticks);
   return 0;
}
```

Program 9.5 ─── **timechild.c**

9.2 Sleep Functions

A process that voluntarily blocks for a specified time is said to *sleep*. The sleep function causes the calling thread to be suspended either until the specified number of seconds has elapsed or until the calling thread catches a signal.

```
SYNOPSIS

   #include <unistd.h>

   unsigned sleep(unsigned seconds);

                                                                        POSIX
```

The sleep function returns 0 if the requested time has elapsed or the amount of unslept time if interrupted. The sleep function interacts with SIGALRM, so avoid using them concurrently in the same process.

■ **Example 9.10**

The following program beeps every n seconds, where n is passed as a command-line argument.

```c
#include <stdio.h>
#include <stdlib.h>
#include <unistd.h>

int main(int argc, char *argv[]) {
   int sleeptime;

   if (argc != 2) {
      fprintf(stderr, "Usage:%s n\n", argv[0]);
      return 1;
   }
   sleeptime = atoi(argv[1]);
   fprintf(stderr, "Sleep time is %d\n", sleeptime);
   for ( ; ; ) {
      sleep(sleeptime);
      printf("\007");
      fflush(stdout);
   }
}
```
                                                                    beeper.c

The nanosleep function causes the calling thread to suspend execution until the time interval specified by rqtp has elapsed or until the thread receives a signal. If nanosleep is interrupted by a signal and rmtp is not NULL, the location pointed to by rmtp contains the time remaining, allowing nanosleep to be restarted. The system clock CLOCK_REALTIME determines the resolution of rqtp.

SYNOPSIS

```
#include <time.h>

int nanosleep(const struct timespec *rqtp, struct timespec *rmtp);
```
                                                                    POSIX:TMR

If successful, `nanosleep` returns 0. If unsuccessful, `nanosleep` returns −1 and sets `errno`. The following table lists the mandatory errors for `nanosleep`.

errno	cause
EINTR	`nanosleep` interrupted by a signal
EINVAL	`rqtp` specifies a nanosecond value that is not in $[0, 10^9)$

The data structures used by `nanosleep` allow for nanosecond resolution, but the resolution of `CLOCK_REALTIME` is typically much larger, on the order of 10 ms. The `nanosleep` function is meant to replace `usleep`, which is now considered obsolete. The main advantage of `nanosleep` over `usleep` is that `nanosleep`, unlike `sleep` or `usleep`, does not affect the use of any signals, including `SIGALRM`.

Program 9.6 tests the resolution of the `nanosleep` function. It executes 100 calls to `nanosleep` with a sleep time of 1000 nanoseconds. If `nanosleep` had a true resolution of 1 ns, this would complete in 100 μsec. The program takes about one second to complete on a system with a 10 ms resolution.

9.3 POSIX:XSI Interval Timers

A timer generates a notification after a specified amount of time has elapsed. In contrast to a clock, which increments to track the passage of time, a timer usually decrements its value and generates a signal when the value becomes zero. A computer system typically has a small number of hardware interval timers, and the operating system implements multiple software timers by using these hardware timers.

Operating systems use interval timers in many ways. An interval timer can cause a periodic interrupt, triggering the operating system to increment a counter. This counter can keep the time since the operating system was booted. UNIX systems traditionally keep the time of day as the number of seconds since January 1, 1970. If an underlying interval timer generates an interrupt after 100 microseconds and is restarted each time it expires, the timer interrupt service routine can keep a local counter to measure the number of seconds since January 1, 1970, by incrementing this local counter after each 10,000 expirations of the interval timer.

Program 9.6 ──────────────────────────────────── `nanotest.c`

A function that tests the resolution of `nanosleep`.

```c
#include <stdio.h>
#include <stdlib.h>
#include <unistd.h>
#include <sys/time.h>
#define COUNT 100
#define D_BILLION 1000000000.0
#define D_MILLION 1000000.0
#define MILLION 1000000L
#define NANOSECONDS 1000

int main(void) {
   int i;
   struct timespec slptm;
   long tdif;
   struct timeval tend, tstart;

   slptm.tv_sec = 0;
   slptm.tv_nsec = NANOSECONDS;
   if (gettimeofday(&tstart, NULL) == -1) {
      fprintf(stderr, "Failed to get start time\n");
      return 1;
   }
   for (i = 0; i < COUNT; i++)
      if (nanosleep(&slptm, NULL) == -1) {
         perror("Failed to nanosleep");
         return 1;
      }
   if (gettimeofday(&tend, NULL) == -1) {
      fprintf(stderr, "Failed to get end time\n");
      return 1;
   }
   tdif = MILLION*(tend.tv_sec - tstart.tv_sec) +
               tend.tv_usec - tstart.tv_usec;
   printf("%d nanosleeps of %d nanoseconds\n", COUNT, NANOSECONDS);
   printf("Should take   %11d microseconds or %f seconds\n",
          NANOSECONDS*COUNT/1000, NANOSECONDS*COUNT/D_BILLION);
   printf("Actually took %11ld microseconds or %f seconds\n", tdif,
          tdif/D_MILLION);
   printf("Number of seconds per nanosleep was       %f\n",
          (tdif/(double)COUNT)/MILLION);
   printf("Number of seconds per nanosleep should be %f\n",
          NANOSECONDS/D_BILLION);
   return 0;
}
```

Program 9.6 ──────────────────────────────────── `nanotest.c`

Time-sharing operating systems can also use interval timers for process scheduling. When the operating system schedules a process, it starts an interval timer for a time interval called the *scheduling quantum*. If this timer expires and the process is still executing, the scheduler moves the process to a ready queue so that another process can execute. Multiprocessor systems need one of these interval timers for each processor.

Most scheduling algorithms have a mechanism for raising the priority of processes that have been waiting a long time to execute. The scheduler might use an interval timer for priority management. Every time the timer expires, the scheduler raises the priority of the processes that have not executed.

The interval timers of the POSIX:XSI Extension use a `struct itimerval` structure that contains the following members.

```
struct timeval it_value;    /* time until next expiration */
struct timeval it_interval; /* value to reload into the timer */
```

Here `it_value` holds the time remaining before the timer expires, and `it_interval` holds the time interval to be used for resetting the timer after it expires. Recall that a `struct timeval` structure has fields for seconds and microseconds.

A conforming POSIX:XSI implementation must provide each process with the following three user interval timers.

ITIMER_REAL: decrements in real time and generates a SIGALRM signal when it expires.

ITIMER_VIRTUAL: decrements in virtual time (time used by the process) and generates a SIGVTALRM signal when it expires.

ITIMER_PROF: decrements in virtual time and system time for the process and generates a SIGPROF signal when it expires.

POSIX provides the `getitimer` function for retrieving the current time interval and the `setitimer` function for starting and stopping a user interval timer. The `which` parameter specifies the timer (i.e., ITIMER_REAL, ITIMER_VIRTUAL or ITIMER_PROF). The `getitimer` function stores the current value of the time for timer `which` in the location pointed to by `value`. The `setitimer` function sets the timer specified by `which` to the value pointed to by `value`. If `ovalue` is not NULL, `setitimer` places the previous value of the timer in the location pointed to by `ovalue`. If the timer was running, the `it_value` member of `*ovalue` is nonzero and contains the time remaining before the timer would have expired.

```
SYNOPSIS

   #include <sys/time.h>

   int getitimer(int which, struct itimerval *value);
   int setitimer(int which, const struct itimerval *restrict value,
                            struct itimerval *restrict ovalue);
                                                           POSIX:XSI
```

If successful, these functions return 0. If unsuccessful, they return −1 and set `errno`. The `setitimer` function sets `errno` to EINVAL if the number of microseconds in `value` is not in the range $[0, 10^6)$.

If the `it_interval` member of `*value` is not 0, the timer restarts with this value when it expires. If the `it_interval` of `*value` is 0, the timer does not restart after it expires. If the `it_value` of `*value` is 0, `setitimer` stops the timer if it is running.

Program 9.7 uses an `ITIMER_PROF` timer to print out an asterisk for each two seconds of CPU time used. The program first calls `setupinterrupt` to install `myhandler` as the signal handler for `SIGPROF`. Then, the program calls `setupitimer` to set up a periodic timer, using `ITIMER_PROF`, that expires every 2 seconds. The `ITIMER_PROF` timer generates a `SIGPROF` signal after every two seconds of CPU time used by the process. The process catches the `SIGPROF` signal and handles it with `myhandler`. This handler function outputs an asterisk to standard error.

Program 9.7 ———————————————————— **periodicasterisk.c**

A program that prints an asterisk for each two seconds of CPU time used.

```c
#include <errno.h>
#include <signal.h>
#include <stdio.h>
#include <unistd.h>
#include <sys/time.h>

/* ARGSUSED */
static void myhandler(int s) {
   char aster = '*';
   int errsave;
   errsave = errno;
   write(STDERR_FILENO, &aster, 1);
   errno = errsave;
}

static int setupinterrupt(void) {              /* set up myhandler for  SIGPROF */
   struct sigaction act;
   act.sa_handler = myhandler;
   act.sa_flags = 0;
   return (sigemptyset(&act.sa_mask) || sigaction(SIGPROF, &act, NULL));
}

static int setupitimer(void) {     /* set ITIMER_PROF for 2-second intervals */
   struct itimerval value;
   value.it_interval.tv_sec = 2;
   value.it_interval.tv_usec = 0;
   value.it_value = value.it_interval;
   return (setitimer(ITIMER_PROF, &value, NULL));
}

int main(void) {
   if (setupinterrupt() == -1) {
      perror("Failed to set up handler for SIGPROF");
      return 1;
   }
   if (setupitimer() == -1) {
      perror("Failed to set up the ITIMER_PROF interval timer");
      return 1;
   }
   for ( ; ; );                         /* execute rest of main program here */
}
```

Program 9.7 ———————————————————————— **periodicasterisk.c**

☐ Exercise 9.11

Write a program that sets ITIMER_REAL to expire in two seconds and then sleeps for ten seconds. How long does it take for the program to terminate? Why?

Answer:

POSIX states that the interaction between setitimer and any of alarm, sleep or usleep is unspecified, so we can't predict how long it will take. Avoid this combination in your programs by using nanosleep instead of sleep.

☐ Exercise 9.12

What is wrong with the following code, which should print out the number of seconds remaining on the ITIMER_VIRTUAL interval timer?

```
struct itimerval *value;

getitimer(ITIMER_VIRTUAL, value);
fprintf(stderr, "Time left is %ld seconds\n", value->it_value.tv_sec);
```

Answer:

Although the variable value is declared as a pointer to a struct itimerval structure, it does not point to anything. That is, there is no declaration of an actual struct itimerval structure that value represents.

Program 9.8 uses the interval timer ITIMER_VIRTUAL to measure the execution time of function_to_time. This example, unlike Program 9.1, uses virtual time. Remember that the value returned by getitimer is the time remaining, so the quantity is decreasing.

☐ Exercise 9.13

How can you modify Program 9.8 to compensate for the overhead of calling setitimer and getitimer?

Answer:

Call the setitimer and getitimer pair with no intervening statements and use the time difference as an estimate of the timing overhead.

☐ Exercise 9.14

What happens if we replace the final return in Program 9.8 with the infinite loop for(; ;);?

Answer:

After using one million seconds of virtual time, the program receives a SIGVTALRM signal and terminates. One million seconds is approximately 12 days.

delivered if the signal is unblocked. Additional instances may be lost. For applications in which it is important to receive every signal, use the POSIX:RTS signal queuing facility. The `sigqueue` function is an extension to `kill` that permits signals to be queued. Multiple instances of a signal generated with the `kill` function may not be queued, even if instances of the same signal generated by `sigqueue` are.

The `sigqueue` function sends signal `signo` with value `value` to the process with ID `pid`. If `signo` is zero, error checking is performed, but no signal is sent. If `SA_SIGINFO` in the `sa_flags` field of the `struct sigaction` structure was set when the handler for `signo` was installed, the signal is queued and sent to the receiving process. If `SA_SIGINFO` was not set for `signo`, the signal is sent at least once but might not be queued.

SYNOPSIS

```
#include <signal.h>

int sigqueue(pid_t pid, int signo, const union sigval value);
```
                                                                           POSIX:RTS

If successful, `sigqueue` returns 0. If unsuccessful, `sigqueue` returns −1 and sets `errno`. The following table lists the mandatory errors for `sigqueue`.

errno	cause
EAGAIN	system does not have resources to queue this signal
EINVAL	`signo` is an invalid or unsupported signal
EPERM	caller does not have the appropriate privileges
ESRCH	no process corresponds to `pid`

■ Example 9.15

The following code segment checks to see whether process ID `mypid` corresponds to a valid process.

```
pid_t mypid;
union sigval qval;

if ((sigqueue(mypid, 0, qval) == -1) && (errno == ESRCH))
    fprintf(stderr, "%ld is not a valid process ID\n", (long)mypid);
```

Program 9.9 shows a program that sends queued signals to a process. The program behaves like the `kill` command, but it calls `sigqueue` instead of `kill`. The process ID, the signal number and the signal value are command-line arguments.

The `union sigval` union can hold either a pointer or an integer. When the signal is generated from the same process by `sigqueue`, a timer, asynchronous I/O or a message queue, the pointer can pass an arbitrary amount of information to the signal handler. It does not make sense to use `sigqueue` to send a pointer from another process unless the address space of the sending process is accessible to the receiver.

┌─ **Program 9.9** ─────────────────────────────── **sendsigqueue.c** ─
A program that sends a queued signal to a process.

```
#include <signal.h>
#include <stdio.h>
#include <stdlib.h>

int main(int argc, char *argv[]) {
   int pid;
   int signo;
   int sval;
   union sigval value;

   if (argc != 4) {
      fprintf(stderr, "Usage: %s pid signal value\n", argv[0]);
      return 1;
   }
   pid = atoi(argv[1]);
   signo = atoi(argv[2]);
   sval = atoi(argv[3]);
   fprintf(stderr, "Sending signal %d with value %d to process %d\n",
                   signo, sval, pid);
   value.sival_int = sval;
   if (sigqueue(pid, signo, value) == -1) {
      perror("Failed to send the signal");
      return 1;
   }
   return 0;
}
```
└─ **Program 9.9** ─────────────────────────────── **sendsigqueue.c** ─

Program 9.10 prints its process ID, sets up a signal handler for SIGUSR1, and suspends itself until a signal arrives. The signal handler just displays the values it receives from its parameters. Notice that the signal handler uses `fprintf`, which is not async-signal safe. This risky use works only because the `main` program does not use `fprintf` after it sets up the handler. The signal handler blocks other SIGUSR1 signals. Any other signal causes the process to terminate. You can use Program 9.9 in conjunction with Program 9.10 to experiment with POSIX realtime signals.

The `asyncmonitorsignal.c` module of Program 8.14 on page 292 showed how to use a realtime signal with asynchronous I/O. The read is started by `initread`. Three fields of the `aio_sigevent` structure are used to set up the signal. The `sigev_notify` field is set to SIGEV_SIGNAL, and the signal number is set in the `sigev_signo` field. Setting the `sigev_value.sival_ptr` field to `&aiocb` makes this pointer available to the signal handler in the `si_value.sival_ptr` field of the handler's second parameter. In Program 8.14, `aiocb` was a global variable, so it was accessed directly. Instead, `aiocb` could have been local to `initread` with a static storage class.

┌─ **Program 9.10** ──────────────────────────── `sigqueuehandler.c` ┐

A program that receives `SIGUSR1` *signals and displays their values. See the text for comments about using* `fprintf` *in the signal handler.*

```
#include <signal.h>
#include <stdio.h>
#include <unistd.h>

static void my_handler(int signo, siginfo_t* info, void *context) {
   char *code = NULL;

   switch(info->si_code) {
      case SI_USER:     code = "USER"; break;
      case SI_QUEUE:    code = "QUEUE"; break;
      case SI_TIMER:    code = "TIMER"; break;
      case SI_ASYNCIO:  code = "ASYNCIO"; break;
      case SI_MESGQ:    code = "MESGQ"; break;
      default:          code = "Unknown";
   }
   fprintf(stderr, "Signal handler entered for signal number %d\n", signo);
   fprintf(stderr, "Signal=%3d, si_signo=%3d, si_code=%d(%s), si_value=%d\n",
           signo, info->si_signo, info->si_code, code, info->si_value.sival_int);
}

int main(void) {
   struct sigaction act;

   fprintf(stderr, "Process ID is %ld\n", (long)getpid());
   fprintf(stderr, "Setting up signal SIGUSR1 = %d ready\n", SIGUSR1);

   act.sa_flags = SA_SIGINFO;
   act.sa_sigaction = my_handler;
   if ((sigemptyset(&act.sa_mask) == -1) ||
       (sigaction(SIGUSR1, &act, NULL) == -1)) {
      perror("Failed to set up SIGUSR1 signal");
      return 1;
   }
   /* no fprintf calls from here on */
   for( ; ; )
      pause();
}
```

└─ **Program 9.10** ──────────────────────────── `sigqueuehandler.c` ┘

9.5 POSIX:TMR Interval Timers

The interval timer facility of the POSIX:XSI Extension gives each process a small fixed number of timers, one of each of the types `ITIMER_REAL`, `ITIMER_VIRTUAL`, `ITIMER_PROF` and so on. The POSIX:TMR Extension takes an alternative approach in which there are a small number of clocks, such as `CLOCK_REALTIME`, and a process can create many independent timers for each clock.

POSIX:TMR timers are based on the `struct itimerspec` structure, which has the following members.

```
struct timespec  it_interval;  /* timer period */
struct timespec  it_value;     /* timer expiration */
```

As with POSIX:XSI timers, the `it_interval` is the time used for resetting the timer after it expires. The `it_value` member holds the time remaining before expiration. The `struct timespec` structure has the potential of offering better resolution than `struct timeval` since its fields measure seconds and nanoseconds rather than seconds and microseconds.

A process can create specific timers by calling `timer_create`. The timers are per-process timers that are not inherited on `fork`. The `clock_id` parameter of `timer_create` specifies which clock the timer is based on, and `*timerid` holds the ID of the created timer. The `evp` parameter specifies the asynchronous notification to occur when the timer expires. The `timer_create` function creates the timer and puts its ID in the location pointed to by `timerid`.

```
SYNOPSIS

  #include <signal.h>
  #include <time.h>

  int timer_create(clockid_t clock_id, struct sigevent *restrict evp,
                  timer_t *restrict timerid);

  struct sigevent {
        int             sigev_notify    /* notification type */
        int             sigev_signo;    /* signal number */
        union sigval    sigev_value;    /* signal value */
  };

  union sigval {
        int             sival_int;      /* integer value */
        void            *sival_ptr;     /* pointer value */
  };
                                                         POSIX:TMR
```

If successful, `timer_create` returns 0. If unsuccessful, `timer_create` returns −1 and sets `errno`. The following table lists the mandatory errors for `timer_create`.

errno	cause
EAGAIN	system does not have resources to honor request, or
	calling process already has maximum number of timers allowed
EINVAL	specified clock ID is not defined

The members of the `struct sigevent` structure shown in the synopsis are required by the POSIX:TMR Extension. The standard does not prohibit an implementation from including additional members.

■ **Example 9.16**

The following code segment creates a POSIX:TMR timer based on the
CLOCK_REALTIME.

```
timer_t timerid;

if (timer_create(CLOCK_REALTIME, NULL, &timerid) == -1)
    perror("Failed to create a new timer");
```

The *evp parameter of timer_create specifies which signal should be sent to
the process when the timer expires. If evp is NULL, the timer generates the default
signal when it expires. For CLOCK_REALTIME, the default signal is SIGALRM. For the
timer expiration to generate a signal other than the default signal, the program must set
evp->sigev_signo to the desired signal number. The evp->sigev_notify member
of the struct sigevent structure specifies the action to be taken when the timer expires. Normally, this member is SIGEV_SIGNAL, which specifies that the timer expiration
generates a signal. The program can prevent the timer expiration from generating a signal
by setting the evp->sigev_notify member to SIGEV_NONE.

The timer_delete function deletes the POSIX:TMR timer with ID timerid.

SYNOPSIS

```
#include <time.h>

int timer_delete(timer_t timerid);
```

                                                                              POSIX:TMR

If successful, timer_delete returns 0. If unsuccessful, timer_delete returns −1 and
sets errno. The timer_delete function sets errno to EINVAL if timerid does not
correspond to a valid timer.

□ **Exercise 9.17**

What happens if a program calls timer_delete when there are pending signals
for timerid?
Answer:
POSIX does not specify what happens to pending signals. You should not make
any assumptions about their disposition when calling timer_delete.

If several timers generate the same signal, the handler can use evp->sigev_value
to distinguish which timer generated the signal. To do this, the program must use the
SA_SIGINFO flag in the sa_flags member of struct sigaction when it installs the
handler for the signal. (See Program 9.13 for an example of how to do this.)

The following three functions manipulate the per-process POSIX:TMR timers. The
timer_settime function starts or stops a timer that was created by timer_create.
The flags parameter specifies whether the timer uses relative or absolute time. Relative
time is similar to the scheme used by POSIX:XSI timers, whereas absolute time allows

for greater accuracy and control of timer drift. Absolute time is further discussed in Section 9.6. The `timer_settime` function sets the timer specified by `timerid` to the value pointed to by `value`. If `ovalue` is not `NULL`, `timer_settime` places the previous value of the timer in the location pointed to by `ovalue`. If the timer was running, the `it_value` member of `*ovalue` is nonzero and contains the time remaining before the timer would have expired. Use `timer_gettime` like `getitimer` to get the time remaining on an active timer.

It is possible for a timer to expire while a signal is still pending from a previous expiration of the same timer. In this case, one of the signals generated may be lost. This is called *timer overrun*. A program can determine the number of such overruns for a particular timer by calling `timer_getoverrun`. Timer overruns occur only for signals generated by the same timer. Signals generated by multiple timers, even timers using the same clock and signal, are queued and not lost.

```
SYNOPSIS

   #include <time.h>

   int timer_getoverrun(timer_t timerid);
   int timer_gettime(timer_t timerid, struct itimerspec *value);
   int timer_settime(timer_t timerid, int flags,
       const struct itimerspec *value, struct itimerspec *ovalue);
                                                          POSIX:TMR
```

If successful, the `timer_settime` and `timer_gettime` functions return 0, and the `timer_getoverrun` function returns the number of timer overruns. If unsuccessful, all three functions return −1 and set `errno`. All three functions set `errno` to `EINVAL` when `timerid` does not correspond to a valid POSIX:TMR timer. The `timer_settime` function also sets `errno` to `EINVAL` when the nanosecond field of `value` is not in the range $[0, 10^9)$.

Program 9.11 shows how to create a timer that generates periodic interrupts. It generates a `SIGALRM` interrupt every two seconds of real time.

❑ Exercise 9.18

Why didn't we use `strlen` in Program 9.11 to find the length of the message?
Answer:
The `strlen` function is not guaranteed to be async-signal safe.

❑ Exercise 9.19

Program 9.11 uses `pause` in an infinite loop at the end of the program but Program 9.7 does not. What would happen if we used `pause` in Program 9.7?
Answer:
Nothing! There is no output. Program 9.7 measures virtual time and the process is not using any virtual time when it is suspended. Program 9.11 uses real time.

Program 9.11 ———————————————————— `periodicmessage.c`

A program that displays a message every two seconds.

```c
#include <errno.h>
#include <signal.h>
#include <stdio.h>
#include <time.h>
#include <unistd.h>
#define BILLION 1000000000L
#define TIMER_MSG "Received Timer Interrupt\n"

/* ARGSUSED */
static void interrupt(int signo, siginfo_t *info, void *context) {
   int errsave;

   errsave = errno;
   write(STDOUT_FILENO, TIMER_MSG, sizeof(TIMER_MSG) - 1);
   errno = errsave;
}

static int setinterrupt() {
   struct sigaction act;

   act.sa_flags = SA_SIGINFO;
   act.sa_sigaction = interrupt;
   if ((sigemptyset(&act.sa_mask) == -1) ||
       (sigaction(SIGALRM, &act, NULL) == -1))
      return -1;
   return 0;
}

static int setperiodic(double sec) {
   timer_t timerid;
   struct itimerspec value;

   if (timer_create(CLOCK_REALTIME, NULL, &timerid) == -1)
      return -1;
   value.it_interval.tv_sec = (long)sec;
   value.it_interval.tv_nsec = (sec - value.it_interval.tv_sec)*BILLION;
   if (value.it_interval.tv_nsec >= BILLION) {
      value.it_interval.tv_sec++;
      value.it_interval.tv_nsec -= BILLION;
   }
   value.it_value = value.it_interval;
   return timer_settime(timerid, 0, &value, NULL);
}

int main(void) {
   if (setinterrupt() == -1) {
      perror("Failed to setup SIGALRM handler");
      return 1;
   }
   if (setperiodic(2.0) == -1) {
      perror("Failed to setup periodic interrupt");
      return 1;
   }
   for ( ; ; )
      pause();
}
```

Program 9.11 ———————————————————— `periodicmessage.c`

Program 9.12 creates a POSIX:TMR timer to measure the running time of `function_to_time`. The program is similar to Program 9.8, but it uses real time rather than virtual time.

Program 9.12 ———————————————————————— `tmrtimer.c`

A program that uses a POSIX:TMR timer to measure the running time of a function.

```c
#include <stdio.h>
#include <time.h>
#define MILLION 1000000L
#define THOUSAND 1000

void function_to_time(void);

int main(void) {
   long diftime;
   struct itimerspec nvalue, ovalue;
   timer_t timeid;

   if (timer_create(CLOCK_REALTIME, NULL, &timeid) == -1) {
      perror("Failed to create a timer based on CLOCK_REALTIME");
      return 1;
   }
   ovalue.it_interval.tv_sec = 0;
   ovalue.it_interval.tv_nsec = 0;
   ovalue.it_value.tv_sec = MILLION;                /* a large number */
   ovalue.it_value.tv_nsec = 0;
   if (timer_settime(timeid, 0, &ovalue, NULL) == -1) {
      perror("Failed to set interval timer");
      return 1;
   }
   function_to_time();                          /* timed code goes here */
   if (timer_gettime(timeid, &nvalue) == -1) {
      perror("Failed to get interval timer value");
      return 1;
   }
   diftime = MILLION*(ovalue.it_value.tv_sec - nvalue.it_value.tv_sec) +
      (ovalue.it_value.tv_nsec - nvalue.it_value.tv_nsec)/THOUSAND;
   printf("The function_to_time took %ld microseconds or %f seconds.\n",
          diftime, diftime/(double)MILLION);
   return 0;
}
```

Program 9.12 ———————————————————————— `tmrtimer.c`

9.6 Timer Drift, Overruns and Absolute Time

One of the problems associated with POSIX:TMR timers and POSIX:XSI timers, as described so far, is the way they are set according to relative time. Suppose you set a periodic interrupt with an interval of 2 seconds, as in Program 9.7 or Program 9.11. When the timer expires, the system automatically restarts the timer for another 2-second interval. Let's say the latency between when the timer was due to expire and when the timer was reset is 5 μsec. The actual period of the timer is 2.000005 seconds. After 1000 interrupts the timer will be off by 5 ms. This inaccuracy is called *timer drift*.

The problem can be even more severe when the timer is restarted from the timer signal handler rather than from the `it_interval` field of `struct itimerval` or `struct itimerspec`. In this case, the latency depends on the scheduling of the processes and the timer resolution. A typical timer resolution is 10 ms. With a latency of 10 ms, the timer drift will be 10 seconds after 1000 iterations.

❑ Exercise 9.20

Consider an extreme case of a repeating timer with period of 22 ms when the timer has a resolution of 10 ms. Estimate the timer drift for 10 expirations of the timer.

Answer:

If you set the time until expiration to be 22 ms, this value will be rounded up to the clock resolution to give 30 ms, giving a drift of 8 ms every 30 ms. These results are summarized in the following table. The drift grows by 8 ms on each expiration.

expiration number			1	2	3	4	5	6	7	8	9	10
time	0	30	60	90	120	150	180	210	240	270	300
drift	0	8	16	24	32	40	48	56	64	72	80
desired expiration	22	44	66	88	110	132	154	176	198	220	242
timer set for	22	22	22	22	22	22	22	22	22	22	22
rounded to resolution	30	30	30	30	30	30	30	30	30	30	30

One way to handle the drift problem is keep track of when the timer should actually expire and adjust the value for setting the timer each time. This method uses *absolute time* for setting the timer rather than *relative time*.

❑ Exercise 9.21

For the specific case described by Exercise 9.20, devise a procedure for setting the timers according to absolute time. What is the timer drift for 10 iterations? Work out a chart similar to the one of Exercise 9.20.

Answer:

1. Before starting the timer for the first time, determine the current time, add 22 ms to this and save the value as T. This is the desired expiration time.
2. Set the timer to expire in 22 ms.
3. In the signal handler, determine the current time, t. Set the timer to expire in time (T - t + 22 ms). Add 22 ms to T so that T represents the next desired expiration time.

If the timer resolution is 30 ms, then the time at the beginning of step 3 is approximately t = T + 30 ms, and the timer is set to expire in 12 ms. No matter how long the program runs, the total timer drift will be less than 10 ms.

expiration number		1	2	3	4	5	6	7	8	9	10
time	0	30	50	70	90	110	140	160	180	200	220
drift	0	8	6	4	2	0	8	6	4	2	0
desired expiration	22	44	66	88	10	132	154	176	198	220	242
timer set for	22	14	16	18	20	22	14	16	18	20	22
rounded to resolution	30	20	20	20	20	30	20	20	20	20	30

The procedure of Exercise 9.21 assumes that the value (T - t + 22 ms) is never negative. You cannot set a timer to expire in the past. A negative value means that a timer expiration has been missed completely. This is called a *timer overrun*. A timer overrun also occurs when the timer is set to automatically restart and a new signal is generated before the previous one has been handled by the process.

The POSIX:TMR timers can make it easier to use absolute time, and they can keep track of timer overruns. POSIX:TMR does not queue signals generated by the same timer. The `timer_getoverrun` function can be called from within the timer signal handler to obtain the number of missed signals. The `flags` parameter of `timer_settime` can be set to `TIMER_ABSOLUTE` to signify that the time given in the `it_value` member of the `*value` parameter represents the real time rather than a time interval. The time is related to the clock from which the timer was generated.

◻ **Exercise 9.22**

Outline the procedure for using POSIX:TMR timers with absolute time to solve the problem of Exercise 9.21.

Answer:

The procedure for using absolute time with POSIX:TMR timers is as follows.

1. Before starting the first timer for the first time, determine the current time by using `clock_gettime` and add 22 ms to this. Save this value as T.
2. Set the timer to expire at time T. Use the `TIMER_ABSOLUTE` flag.
3. In the timer signal handler, add 22 ms to T and set the timer to expire at time T.

The `abstime` program of Program 9.13 demonstrates various scenarios for using the POSIX:TMR timer facility. Program 9.13 has three modes of operation: absolute time, relative time and automatic periodic reset. Use the `abstime` program as follows.

```
abstime -a | -r | -p [inctime [numtimes [spintime]]]
```

The first command-line argument must be `-a`, `-r` or `-p` specifying absolute time, relative time or automatic periodic reset. The optional additional arguments (`inctime`, `numtimes` and `spintime`) control the sequence in which timer expirations occur. The program generates `numtimes` SIGALARM signals that are `inctime` seconds apart. The signal handler wastes `spintime` seconds before handling the timer expiration.

The `abstime` program uses a POSIX:TMR timer that is created with `timer_create` and started with `timer_settime`. For absolute times, the `abstime` program sets the `TIMER_ABSTIME` flag in `timer_settime` and sets the `it_value` member of `value` field to the current absolute time (time since January 1, 1970) plus the `inctime` value. When the timer expires, `abstime` calculates a new absolute expiration time by adding `inctime` to the previous expiration time. If relative time is set, the program sets `it_value` to the value specified by `inctime`. When the timer expires, the handler uses `inctime` to restart the timer. For periodic time, `abstime` sets relative time and automatically restarts the timer so that the handler does not have to restart it. The program calculates the time it should take to finish `numtimes` timer expirations and compares the calculated value with the actual time taken.

Program 9.14 is a header file that defines a data type and the prototypes of the functions in Program 9.15 that are used in the `main` program of Program 9.13. You must link these files with Program 9.13 to run the `abstime` program.

■ Example 9.23

The following command uses `abstime` with absolute time. It simulates a signal handler that takes 5 milliseconds to execute and does 1000 iterations with a time interval of 22 milliseconds. If the timing were exact, the 5 milliseconds of spin time would not affect the total running time, which should be 22 seconds.

```
abstime -a 0.022 1000 0.005
```

□ Exercise 9.24

The command of Example 9.23 uses absolute time. Are there differences in output when it is run with relative time instead?

Answer:

For an execution of

```
abstime -a 0.022 1000 0.005
```

the output might be the following.

```
pid = 12374
Clock resolution is 10000.000 microseconds or 0.010000 sec.
Using absolute time
Interrupts: 1000 at 0.022000 seconds, spinning 0.005000
Total time: 22.0090370, calculated: 22.0000000, error = 0.0090370
```

For an execution of

```
abstime -r 0.022 1000 0.005
```

the output might be the following.

```
pid = 12376
Clock resolution is 10000.000 microseconds or 0.010000 sec.
Using relative time
Interrupts: 1000 at 0.022000 seconds, spinning 0.005000
Total time: 30.6357934, calculated: 22.0000000, error = 8.6357934
```

When absolute timers are used, the error is much less than 1 percent, while relative timers show the expected drift corresponding to the amount of processing time and timer resolution.

The resolution of the clock is displayed by means of a call to `clock_getres`. A typical value for this might be anywhere from 1000 nanoseconds to 20 milliseconds. The 20 milliseconds (20,000,000 nanoseconds or 50 Hertz) is the lowest resolution allowed by the POSIX:TMR Extension. One microsecond (1000 nanoseconds) is the time it takes to execute a few hundred instructions on most fast machines. Just because a system has a clock resolution of 1 microsecond does not imply that a program can use timers with anything near this resolution. A context switch is often needed before the signal handler can be entered and, as Table 1.1 on page 5 points out, a context switch can take considerably longer than this.

■ Example 9.25

The following command uses Program 9.13 to estimate the effective resolution of the hardware timer on a machine by calling `abstime` with an `inctime` of 0, default `numtimes` of 1 and default `spintime` of 0. The `abstime` program displays the clock resolution and starts one absolute time clock interrupt to expire at the current time. The timer expires immediately.

```
abstime -a 0
```

■ Example 9.26

The following command uses Program 9.13 to determine the maximum number of timer signals that can be handled per second by starting 1000 timer interrupts with an `inctime` of 0. These should all expire immediately. The `abstime` program then displays the minimum time for 1000 interrupts.

```
abstime -a 0.0 1000 0.0
```

Program 9.13 illustrates some other useful tips in using POSIX:TMR timers. Information about the timer that generated the signal is available in the signal handler. When a timer is created, an integer or a pointer can be stored in the `sigev_value` member of the `struct sigevent` structure. If the signal handler is to restart that timer or if multiple timers are to share a signal handler, the signal handler must have access to the timer ID of the timer that generated the signal. If the signal handler was set up with the `SA_SIGINFO` flag, it can access the value that `timer_create` stored in `sigev_value` through its second parameter. The `timer_create` cannot directly store the timer ID in its `sigev_value` because the ID is not known until after the timer has been created. It therefore stores a pointer to the timer ID in the `sival_ptr` member of `union sigval`.

Program 9.13 ——————————————————————————— `abstime.c`

The `abstime` *program illustrates POSIX:TMR timers with absolute time. Program 9.14 and Program 9.15 are called.*

```c
#include <signal.h>
#include <stdio.h>
#include <stdlib.h>
#include <string.h>
#include <time.h>
#include <unistd.h>
#include "abstime.h"
#define INCTIME 0.01
#define NUMTIMES 1
#define SPINTIME 0.0

int main(int argc, char *argv[]) {
    struct sigaction act;
    struct timespec clockres, currenttime;
    timer_data data;
    struct sigevent evp;
    sigset_t sigset;
    double tcalc, tend, tstart, ttotal;

    data.exitflag = 0;
    data.inctime = INCTIME;
    data.numtimes = NUMTIMES;
    data.spintime = SPINTIME;
    data.type = -1;
    if (argc > 1) {
        if (!strcmp(argv[1], "-r"))
           data.type = TYPE_RELATIVE;
        else if (!strcmp(argv[1], "-a"))
            data.type = TYPE_ABSOLUTE;
        else if (!strcmp(argv[1], "-p"))
            data.type = TYPE_PERIODIC;
    }
    if ( (argc < 2) || (argc > 5) || (data.type < 0) ){
        fprintf(stderr,
            "Usage:  %s -r | -a | -p [inctime [numtimes [spintime]]]\n",
            argv[0]);
        return 1;
    }
    if (argc > 2)
        data.inctime = atof(argv[2]);
    if (argc > 3)
        data.numtimes = atoi(argv[3]);
    if (argc > 4)
        data.spintime = atof(argv[4]);
    fprintf(stderr, "pid = %ld\n", (long)getpid());

    act.sa_flags = SA_SIGINFO;
    act.sa_sigaction = timehandler;
    if ((sigemptyset(&act.sa_mask) == -1) ||
        (sigaction(SIGALRM, &act, NULL)) == -1) {
      perror("Failed to set handler for SIGALRM");
      return 1;
    }
    evp.sigev_notify = SIGEV_SIGNAL;
    evp.sigev_signo = SIGALRM;
```

```
      evp.sigev_value.sival_ptr = &data;
      if (timer_create(CLOCK_REALTIME, &evp, &data.timid) < 0) {
         perror("Failed to create a timer");
         return 1;
      }
      if (clock_getres(CLOCK_REALTIME, &clockres) == -1)
         perror("Failed to get clock resolution");
      else
         fprintf(stderr, "Clock resolution is %0.3f microseconds or %0.6f sec.\n",
            D_MILLION*time_to_double(clockres), time_to_double(clockres));
      data.tvalue.it_interval.tv_sec = 0;
      data.tvalue.it_interval.tv_nsec = 0;
      data.tvalue.it_value = double_to_time(data.inctime);
      data.flags = 0;
      if (clock_gettime(CLOCK_REALTIME, &currenttime) == -1) {
         perror("Failed to get current time");
         return 1;
      }
      tstart = time_to_double(currenttime);
      if (data.type == TYPE_ABSOLUTE) {
         data.tvalue.it_value.tv_nsec += currenttime.tv_nsec;
         data.tvalue.it_value.tv_sec += currenttime.tv_sec;
         if (data.tvalue.it_value.tv_nsec >= BILLION) {
            data.tvalue.it_value.tv_nsec -=  BILLION;
            data.tvalue.it_value.tv_sec++;
         }
         data.flags = TIMER_ABSTIME;
         fprintf(stderr,"Using absolute time\n");
      }
      else if (data.type == TYPE_RELATIVE)
         fprintf(stderr,"Using relative time\n");
      else if (data.type == TYPE_PERIODIC) {
         data.tvalue.it_interval = data.tvalue.it_value;
         fprintf(stderr,"Using periodic time\n");
      }
      fprintf(stderr, "Interrupts: %d at %.6f seconds, spinning %.6f\n",
            data.numtimes, data.inctime, data.spintime);
      if (timer_settime(data.timid, data.flags, &data.tvalue, NULL) == -1){
         perror("Failed to start timer");
         return 1;
      }
      if (sigemptyset(&sigset) == -1) {
         perror("Failed to set up suspend mask");
         return 1;
      }
      while (!data.exitflag)
         sigsuspend(&sigset);
      if (clock_gettime(CLOCK_REALTIME, &currenttime) == -1) {
         perror("Failed to get expiration time");
         return 1;
      }
      tend = time_to_double(currenttime);
      ttotal=tend - tstart;
      tcalc = data.numtimes*data.inctime;
      fprintf(stderr, "Total time: %1.7f, calculated: %1.7f, error = %1.7f\n",
          ttotal, tcalc, ttotal - tcalc);
      return 0;
}
```

Program 9.13 ─── **abstime.c**

The `abstime.h` *include file contains constants, type definitions, and prototypes used*
by abstime *and* abstimelib.

```
#define BILLION  1000000000L
#define D_BILLION 1000000000.0
#define D_MILLION 1000000.0
#define TYPE_ABSOLUTE 0
#define TYPE_RELATIVE 1
#define TYPE_PERIODIC 2

typedef struct {
   timer_t timid;
   int type;
   int flags;
   int numtimes;
   int exitflag;
   double inctime;
   double spintime;
   struct itimerspec tvalue;
} timer_data;

struct timespec double_to_time(double tm);
double time_to_double(struct timespec t);
void timehandler(int signo, siginfo_t* info, void *context);
```

The `abstimelib` *module contains the signal handler and utility routines used by*
abstime.

```
#include <signal.h>
#include <stdio.h>
#include <stdlib.h>
#include <string.h>
#include <time.h>
#include <unistd.h>
#include "abstime.h"

static struct timespec add_to_time(struct timespec t, double tm) {
   struct timespec t1;

   t1 = double_to_time(tm);
   t1.tv_sec = t1.tv_sec + t.tv_sec;
   t1.tv_nsec = t1.tv_nsec + t.tv_nsec;
   while (t1.tv_nsec >= BILLION) {
      t1.tv_nsec = t1.tv_nsec - BILLION;
      t1.tv_sec++;
   }
   return t1;
}

static int spinit (double stime) {    /* loops for stime seconds and returns */
   struct timespec tcurrent;
   double tend, tnow;
```

```
   if (stime == 0.0)
      return 0;
   if (clock_gettime(CLOCK_REALTIME, &tcurrent) == -1)
      return -1;
   tnow = time_to_double(tcurrent);
   tend = tnow + stime;
   while (tnow < tend) {
      if (clock_gettime(CLOCK_REALTIME, &tcurrent)  == -1)
         return -1;
      tnow = time_to_double(tcurrent);
   }
   return 0;
}

/* ----------------------- Public functions -----------------------  */

double time_to_double(struct timespec t) {
   return t.tv_sec + t.tv_nsec/D_BILLION;
}

struct timespec double_to_time(double tm) {
   struct timespec t;

   t.tv_sec = (long)tm;
   t.tv_nsec = (tm - t.tv_sec)*BILLION;
   if (t.tv_nsec == BILLION) {
      t.tv_sec++;
      t.tv_nsec = 0;
   }
   return t;
}

void timehandler(int signo, siginfo_t* info, void *context) {
   timer_data *datap;
   static int timesentered = 0;

   timesentered++;
   datap = (timer_data *)(info->si_value.sival_ptr);
   if (timesentered >=  datap->numtimes) {
      datap->exitflag = 1;
      return;
   }
   if (spinit(datap->spintime) == -1) {
      write(STDERR_FILENO, "Spin failed in handler\n", 23);
      datap->exitflag = 1;
   }
   if (datap->type == TYPE_PERIODIC)
      return;
   if (datap->type == TYPE_ABSOLUTE)
      datap->tvalue.it_value =
         add_to_time(datap->tvalue.it_value, datap->inctime);
   if (timer_settime(datap->timid, datap->flags, &datap->tvalue, NULL) == -1) {
      write(STDERR_FILENO, "Could not start timer in handler\n",33);
      datap->exitflag = 1;
   }
}
```

Program 9.15 ─────────────────────────────── **abstimelib.c**

Program 9.16 ━━━━━━━━━━━━━━━━━━━━━━━━━━━━━━━ **timesignals.c** ⌐

A program that calculates the time to receive 1000 SIGALRM *signals.*

```c
#include <signal.h>
#include <stdio.h>
#include <string.h>
#include <unistd.h>
#include <sys/time.h>
#define COUNT 1000
#define MILLION 1000000L

static int count = 0;

/* ARGSUSED */
static void handler(int signo, siginfo_t *info, void *context) {
   count++;
}

int main(void) {
   struct sigaction act;
   sigset_t sigblocked, sigunblocked;
   long tdif;
   struct timeval tend, tstart;

   act.sa_flags = SA_SIGINFO;
   act.sa_sigaction = handler;
   if ((sigemptyset(&act.sa_mask) == -1) ||
       (sigaction(SIGALRM, &act, NULL) == -1)) {
     perror("Failed to set up handler for SIGALRM");
     return 1;
   }
   if ((sigemptyset(&sigblocked) == -1) ||
       (sigemptyset(&sigunblocked) == -1) ||
       (sigaddset(&sigblocked, SIGALRM) == -1) ||
       (sigprocmask(SIG_BLOCK, &sigblocked, NULL) == -1)) {
     perror("Failed to block signal");
     return 1;
   }
   printf("Process %ld waiting for first SIGALRM (%d) signal\n",
          (long)getpid(), SIGALRM);
   sigsuspend(&sigunblocked);
   if (gettimeofday(&tstart, NULL) == -1) {
     perror("Failed to get start time");
     return 1;
   }
   while (count <= COUNT)
     sigsuspend(&sigunblocked);
   if (gettimeofday(&tend, NULL) == -1) {
     perror("Failed to get end time");
     return 1;
   }
   tdif = MILLION*(tend.tv_sec - tstart.tv_sec) +
                  tend.tv_usec - tstart.tv_usec;
   printf("Got %d signals in %ld microseconds\n", count-1, tdif);
   return 0;
}
```

└ **Program 9.16** ━━━━━━━━━━━━━━━━━━━━━━━━━━━━ **timesignals.c** ⌐

Although the timer resolution might be as large as 10 ms, signals may be processed at a much higher rate than timer signals can be generated. Program 9.16 waits for SIGALRM signals and calculates the time to receive 1000 signals after the first one arrives. You can use Program 9.17 to send signals to a process. It takes two command-line arguments: a process ID and a signal number. It sends the signals as fast as it can until the process dies. A reasonably fast machine should be able to handle several thousand signals per second.

Program 9.17 ———————————————————————— **multikill.c**

The multikill *program continually sends signals to another process until the process dies.*

```
#include <signal.h>
#include <stdio.h>
#include <stdlib.h>

int main(int argc, char *argv[]) {
   int pid;
   int sig;
   if (argc != 3) {
       fprintf(stderr, "Usage: %s pid signal\n", argv[0]);
       return 1;
   }
   pid = atoi(argv[1]);
   sig = atoi(argv[2]);
   while (kill(pid, sig) == 0) ;
   return 0;
}
```

Program 9.17 ———————————————————————— **multikill.c**

9.7 Additional Reading

Realtime issues promise to become more important in the future. The book *POSIX.4: Programming for the Real World* by Gallmeister [39] provides a general introduction to realtime programming under the POSIX standard. POSIX.4 was the name of the standard before it was approved. It is now an extension of the POSIX standard referred to as POSIX:RTS. The POSIX:TMR Extension is one of the required components for systems supporting POSIX:RTS.

Chapter 10

Project: Virtual Timers

Many systems create multiple "virtual" timers from a single hardware timer. This chapter develops application-level virtual timers based on a single operating system timer. The project explores timers, signals and the testing of asynchronous programs with timed input. Special care must be taken in blocking and unblocking the signals at the right times. The project emphasizes careful, modular design by specifying a well-defined interface between the user-implemented virtual timers and the underlying timer facility.

Objectives
- Learn about testing and timing
- Experiment with POSIX interval timers
- Explore implications of asynchronous operation
- Use POSIX realtime signals
- Understand timer implementation

10.1 Project Overview

This chapter's project develops an implementation of multiple timers in terms of a single operating system timer. The project consists of five semi-independent modules. Three of these are created as objects with internal static data; the other two are standalone programs designed for driving the timers and for debugging output. Figure 10.1 shows the five modules and their relationships. A dashed arrow indicates communication through a pipe. A solid arrow signifies that a function in the source module calls a function in the target module.

Standard output of the `testtime` program is fed into standard input of the `timermain` program. The `timermain` program calls only functions in `virtualtimers`. The `virtualtimers` object calls functions in `hardwaretimer` and `show`. The `show` object, which is only for debugging, calls functions in `virtualtimers`.

The project design has two layers—a "hardware" level (`hardwaretimer`) and a virtual timer level (`virtualtimers`). The `hardwaretimer` layer encapsulates a single operating system timer that generates a signal when it expires. The underlying timer object can be either a POSIX:XSI timer or a POSIX:TMR timer. While not truly a hardware timer, it is treated as such. The object provides interface functions that hide the underlying timer from outside users. In theory, if the program has access to a real hardware timer, the underlying object can be this timer and the interface remains the same. The interface functions manipulate a single timer that generates a signal when it expires.

The `virtualtimers` object provides the core facilities for creating and manipulating multiple, low-overhead, application-level software timers. The `virtualtimers` object calls functions in the `hardwaretimer` to implement these software timers. The `virtualtimers` object also calls functions in the `show` object for logging and debugging.

The `show` object contains functions to display a running log of the timer operations during debugging. The `show` object calls functions from `virtualtimers` to obtain status information about the timers.

Each of the objects has a header file with the same name and a `.h` extension that contains prototypes for the functions accessible from outside the module. Any program that calls functions from one of these modules should include its corresponding `.h` file.

Two main programs are used for testing the timer objects. The first one, `timermain`, receives input from standard input and calls functions in the `virtualtimers` object. The `timermain` program might, for example, start a timer to expire after a given interval when it receives appropriate input. The `timermain` program calls only functions in the `virtualtimers` object.

It is critical to the debugging process that experiments producing incorrect results be precisely repeatable. Then, when a bug is detected, the programmer can fix the code and repeat the same experiment with the modified code. Experiments that rely on the timing of keyboard input are almost impossible to repeat. To solve this problem, the `testtime`

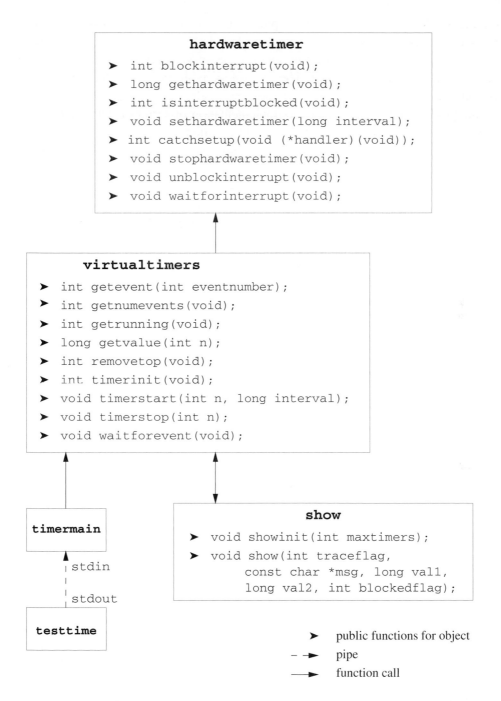

Figure 10.1: The five timer modules to be created in this project.

program supplies input data through a pipe to `timermain` at precisely timed intervals. The `testtime` program reads lines from standard input and interprets the first integer on the line as a delay time. After waiting for this amount of time, `testtime` sends the rest of the input line to standard output. The `testtime` program then reads its next input line and continues.

This project chapter describes the implementation of virtual timers in stages. Section 10.2 introduces the data structures and gives examples of setting a single timer. Section 10.3 introduces the three objects and specifies how to handle the setting of a single timer with POSIX:XSI timers. Section 10.4 handles multiple active timers. Section 10.5 discusses some of the race conditions that can occur with multiple timers and ways to avoid them, and Section 10.6 discusses advanced timer issues in terms of POSIX:TMR timers. Section 10.7 introduces a simple timer application.

10.2 Simple Timers

Operating systems often implement multiple software timers that are based on a single hardware timer. A software timer can be represented by a timer number and an indication of when the timer expires. The implementation depends on the type of hardware timer available.

Suppose the hardware timer generates interrupts at regular short intervals called the *clock tick time*. The timer interrupt service routine monitors the time remaining on each timer (in terms of clock ticks) and decrements this time for each tick of the clock. When a timer decrements to 0, the program takes the appropriate action. This approach is inefficient if the number of timers is large or if the clock tick time is short.

Alternatively, a program can keep the timer information in a list sorted by expiration time. Each entry contains a timer number and an expiration time. The first entry in the list contains the first timer to expire and the time until expiration (in clock ticks). The second entry contains the next timer to expire and the expiration time relative to the time the first timer expires, and so on. With this representation, the interrupt service routine decrements only one counter on each clock tick, but the program incurs additional overhead when starting a timer. The program must insert the new timer in a sorted list and update the time of the timer that expires immediately after the new one.

☐ Exercise 10.1

For each of the two implementation approaches described above, what is the time complexity of the interrupt handler and the start timer function in terms of the number of timers?

Answer:

Suppose there are n timers. For the first method, the interrupt handler is O(n) since all timer values must be decremented. The start timer function is O(1) since a timer can be started independently of the other timers. For the second method, the interrupt handler is usually O(1) since only the first timer value must be decremented. However, when the decrement causes the first timer to expire, the next entry has to be examined to make sure it did not expire at the same time. This algorithm can degenerate to O(n) in the worst case, but in practice the worst case is unlikely. The start timer function is O(n) to insert the timer in a sorted array but can take less than O(n) if the timer data is represented by a more complex data structure such as a heap.

If the system has a hardware interval timer instead of a simple clock, a program can set the interval timer to expire at a time corresponding to the software timer with the earliest expiration. There is no overhead unless a timer expires, one is started, or one is stopped. Interval timers are efficient when the timer intervals are long.

◻ **Exercise 10.2**

Analyze the interrupt handler and the start timer function for an interval timer.
Answer:
The interrupt handler is the same order as the clock tick timer above. The complexity of starting the timer depends on how the timers are stored. If the timers are kept in a sorted array, the start timer function is O(n).

The first version of the project uses an interval timer to implement multiple timers, replacing the hardware timer by a POSIX:XSI `ITIMER_REAL` timer. When `ITIMER_REAL` expires, it generates a `SIGALRM` signal. The `SIGALRM` signal handler puts an entry in an event list sorted by order of occurrence. Each entry just contains a timer number giving a timer that expired.

Figure 10.2 shows a simple implementation of five software timers represented by the `timers` data structure. The individual timers (designated by [0] through [4]) are represented by `long` entries in the array `active`. An array entry of −1 represents a timer that is not active. The `events` array keeps a list of timers that have expired, and `numevents` holds the number of unhandled events. The `running` variable, which holds the timer number of the currently running timer, will be needed for later parts of the project.

Start a timer by specifying a timer number and an interval in microseconds. Figure 10.3 shows the data structure after timer [2] is started for five seconds (5,000,000 microseconds). No timers have expired, so the event list is still empty.

Just writing the information into the `active` array in Figure 10.2 is not enough to implement a timer. The program must set the `ITIMER_REAL` timer for 5,000,000 microseconds. On delivery of a `SIGALRM` signal, the program must clear the `active` array entry and insert an entry in the `events` array. Figure 10.4 shows the `timers` data structure after `ITIMER_REAL` expires.

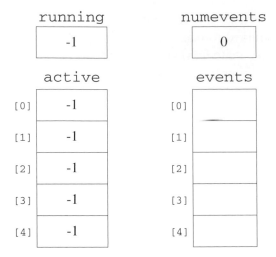

Figure 10.2: The `timers` data structure with no timers active.

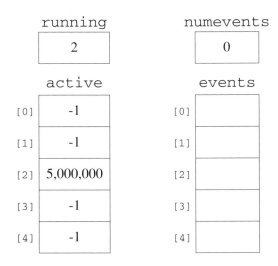

Figure 10.3: The `timers` data structure after timer `[2]` has been set for five seconds.

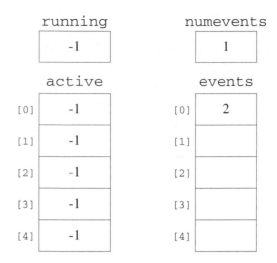

Figure 10.4: The `timers` data structure after timer `[2]` expires.

10.3 Setting One of Five Single Timers

This section describes an implementation for setting one of five possible software timers, using the underlying process interval timer `ITIMER_REAL`. The main program takes the timer number and the timer interval (in microseconds) as command-line arguments and calls the `timerstart` function. The main program then waits for the timer to expire, prints out a message that the timer has expired, and exits.

10.3.1 The `virtualtimers` object

Implement the software timers in an object called `virtualtimers`. Use a static variable called `timers` of type `timerdata_t` to hold the internal timer data for the object as shown below.

```
#define MAXTIMERS 5
typedef struct timerdata_t {
   long active[MAXTIMERS];
   int events[MAXTIMERS];
   int numevents;
   int running;
} timerdata_t;
```

The members of `timerdata_t` have the following meanings.

> `active` is an array with an entry for each timer. Each entry holds the expiration time (in μsec) relative to the starting time of the

running timer. A negative value signifies that the timer is not active. (In this part only one timer is ever active.)

events   is an array with an entry for each timer that has expired and has not yet been removed. The entries contain timer numbers and appear in increasing order of expiration time. (There is at most one timer on the list for the program of this section.)

numevents   is the number of entries in the events array.

running   is the number of the timer that is running or –1 if none are active. The running timer is the one that is next to expire. It is the one whose expiration time causes the one real timer (set with sethardwaretimer) to generate a signal.

The integer representation of the time intervals simplifies the code but limits the length of the intervals to about 2000 seconds (a little more than half an hour) for 32-bit integers. This should be more than enough time for testing the algorithms of the project.

Place the timers data structure in virtualtimers.c along with the following functions that are callable from outside the object.

int getevent(int eventnumber);

Return the timer number associated with a particular entry in the events array. The eventnumber parameter specifies the position in the events array, which is indexed from 0. The getevent functions returns –1 if eventnumber is negative or greater than or equal to numevents.

int getnumevents(void);

Return the value of numevents.

int getrunning(void);

Return the timer number of the running timer or –1 if there is no running timer.

long getvalue(int n);

Return the current value of a timer n from the active array or –1 if the timer is not active or the timer number is invalid.

int removetop(void);

Remove the top event from events and return the event's timer number or –1 if events is empty. This function is needed later when multiple timers are handled.

int timerinit(void);

Initialize the timers data structure as shown in Figure 10.2. The function also calls catchsetup of the hardwaretimer object and showinit of the show object. If successful, timerinit returns 0. If unsuccessful, timerinit returns –1 and sets errno.

```
void timerstart(int n, long interval);
```
Start timer n with the time interval given in microseconds. For this part, assume that no timers are active. The `interval` is the number of microseconds in the future after which the timer should expire. To start timer n, do the following.
1. Remove timer n from the event list if it is there.
2. Set `running` to timer n.
3. Set `active[n]` to the appropriate time value.
4. Start the interval timer by calling the `sethardwaretimer` function in the `hardwaretimer` object.

```
void timerstop(int n);
```
Stop timer n if it is active and remove the timer from `events` if it is there. This function is needed later when multiple timers are handled.

```
void waitforevent(void);
```
Wait until there is an event in `events` and then return without changing `events`. Do not use busy waiting, but instead, call `waitforinterrupt` from the `hardwaretimer` module.

The `virtualtimers` object also contains the private `timerhandler` function, which it passes to the hardware timer module by calling `catchsetup` in `timerinit`.

```
static void timerhandler(void);
```
Handle the timer signal. This function is called by the actual signal handler in `hardwaretimer` to maintain the `timers` structure when the real hardware timer expires. Do the following steps in `timerhandler`.
1. Add the `running` timer to the end of `events`.
2. Make the `running` timer inactive.
3. Update the `timers` data structure.
4. Reset the interval timer if there is an active timer. (There will not be one in the single-timer case.)

Since the `hardwaretimer` object handles the signals, it must contain the actual signal handler. The prototype of the signal handler may depend on the implementation and should not be part of the `virtualtimers` object. Since the timers must be manipulated when the signal is caught, this work should be done in the `virtualtimers` object. The real signal handler calls `timerhandler` to do this. Since `timerhandler` has internal linkage, the `timerinit` function passes a reference to it when calling `catchsetup` in the `hardwaretimer` object. The `timerhandler` is an example of a *callback*. Callbacks are frequently used by applications to request that a service call one of the application's functions when some event occurs.

10.3.2 The `hardwaretimer` object

The `hardwaretimer` object contains code to handle a single "hardware" timer. The functions that are accessible from outside the object are as follows.

`int blockinterrupt(void);`

> Block the `SIGALRM` signal. The `blockinterrupt` function returns 1 if the signal was already blocked and 0 otherwise.

`int catchsetup(void (*handler)(void));`

> Set up a signal handler to catch the `SIGALRM` signal by calling `sigaction`. If successful, `catchsetup` returns 0. If unsuccessful, `catchsetup` returns −1 and sets `errno`. The `handler` parameter is the name of the function that does the work of handling the signal. The actual signal handler in `hardwaretimer` just calls the `handler` function. The `virtualtimers` object calls the function `catchsetup` to set up signal handling.

`long gethardwaretimer(void);`

> Return the time remaining on the hardware timer if it is running or 0 if it is not running. If unsuccessful, `gethardwaretimer` returns −1 and sets `errno`. Use `getitimer` to implement this function.

`int isinterruptblocked(void);`

> Return 1 if the `SIGALRM` signal is blocked and 0 otherwise.

`void sethardwaretimer(long interval);`

> Start the `ITIMER_REAL` timer running with the given interval in microseconds. Call `sethardwaretimer` only when the timer interrupt is blocked or the interval timer is stopped. The `interval` parameter specifies the interval for setting the timer in microseconds. Use `setitimer` to implement this function.

`void stophardwaretimer(void);`

> Stop the hardware timer if it is running. This function is harder to implement than it might seem. We discuss this later since it is not needed in this section.

`void unblockinterrupt(void);`

> Unblock the `SIGALRM` signal.

`void waitforinterrupt(void);`

> Call `sigsuspend` to wait until a signal is caught. The `waitforinterrupt` function does not guarantee that the signal was from a timer expiration. This function is normally entered with the timer signal blocked. The signal set used by `sigsuspend` must not unblock any signals that were already blocked, other than the one being used for the timers. If the main program has blocked `SIGINT`, the program should not terminate if Ctrl-C is entered.

Some of these functions are not needed until a later part of this project. The interface to the hardware timer is isolated in this file, so using POSIX:TMR timers or a different underlying timer than `ITIMER_REAL` only requires changing these functions. Define a header file called `hardwaretimer.h` that has the prototypes of the functions in the `hardwaretimer` object.

10.3.3 Main program implementation

Write a main program called `timermain` that initializes everything by calling `timerinit` and then loops, reading from standard input until an error or end-of-file occurs. Specifically, `timermain` does the following tasks in the loop.

1. Read a pair of integers (a timer number and an interval in microseconds) from standard input.
2. Call `timerstart` with these values.
3. Call `waitforevent`.
4. Print the return value of `waitforevent` to standard output.

Use `scanf` to read in the values from standard input.

10.3.4 Instrumentation of the timer code with `show`

Code with signal handlers and timers is hard to test because of the unpredictable nature of the events that drive the program. A particular timing of events that causes an error might occur rarely and not be easily reproducible. Furthermore, the behavior of the program depends not only on the input values but also on the rate at which input data is generated.

This section describes how to instrument the code with calls to a `show` function as a preliminary step in testing. This instrumentation is critical for debugging the later parts of the project. Two versions of the `show` function are presented here: one outputs to standard output and the other uses remote logging. This subsection explains what `show` does and how to use it in the program.

The prototype for `show` is as follows.

```
void show(int traceflag, const char *msg, long val1, long val2,
          int blockedflag);
```

If the `traceflag` is 0, `show` does nothing, allowing you to easily remove the debugging output. If `traceflag` is 1, the `show` function displays the message in the second parameter and the status of the timer data structure. The `show` function displays the `val1` and `val2` parameters if they are nonnegative. Usually, these parameters will represent a timer number and an interval in microseconds, but sometimes they will represent two timers. The `blockedflag` is 1 if the timer signal is supposed to be blocked when the call is made and 0 if the timer signal should not be blocked. It will be important to keep track of the blocking and unblocking of the signal in the complete timer implementation.

The `virtualtimers` file should have a `traceflag` global variable initialized to 1. Insert a call to `showinit` in the `timerinit` function of the `virtualtimers` module.

Insert calls to show liberally throughout the virtualtimers module. For example, the first line of timerstart could be the following.

```
show(traceflag, "Timer Start Enter", n, interval, 0);
```

A call to start timer [3] for 1,000,000 microseconds might then produce the following output.

```
****  4.0067: Timer Start Enter 3 1000000 U(2,5.000) A:(2,5.000) (4,9.010)  (1E 4)
```

The fields are as follows.

- 4.0067 is the time in seconds since showinit was called.
- The message states where the show function was called.
- 3 is the timer being started.
- 1000000 is the duration of the timer interval.
- U indicates that the call was made with the interrupt unblocked.
- (2,5.000) gives the currently running timer and its interval in seconds.
- A:(2,5.000) (4,9.010) shows two active timers and their corresponding intervals.
- (1E 4) indicates one event for timer [4].

Program 10.1 can be used with this project to display messages similar to the one above.

Program 10.1 ──────────────────────────── **show.c**

A version of show *that prints to standard output.*

```c
#include <stdio.h>
#include <stdlib.h>
#include <string.h>
#include <sys/time.h>
#include "hardwaretimer.h"
#include "show.h"
#include "virtualtimers.h"
#define MILLION 1000000L

static double initialtod = 0.0;
static int maxtimers;
static double gettime(void);
static double timetodouble(long interval);

static double getrelativetime(void) {    /* seconds since showinit was called */
   return gettime() - initialtod;
}

static double gettime(void) {    /* seconds since January 1, 1970 as a double */
   double thistime = 0.0;
   struct timeval tval;

   if (gettimeofday(&tval, NULL))
      fprintf(stderr, "Failed to get time of day\n");
```

```
      else
          thistime = tval.tv_sec + (double)tval.tv_usec/MILLION;
      return thistime;
  }

  static void showtimerdata(void) {        /* display the timers data structure */
      int i;

      printf("(%d,%.3f) A:", getrunning(),
          timetodouble(getvalue(getrunning())));
      for (i = 0; i < maxtimers; i++)
          if (getvalue(i) >= 0)
              printf("(%d,%.3f) ", i, timetodouble(getvalue(i)));
      printf(" (%dE", getnumberevents());
      for (i = 0; i < getnumberevents(); i++)
          printf(" %d", getevent(i));
      printf(")\n");
  }

  static double timetodouble(long interval) {        /* microseconds to seconds */
      return (double)interval/MILLION;
  }

  /* -----------------------Public Functions --------------------------------- */
  void show(int traceflag, const char *msg, long val1, long val2,
              int blockedflag) {    /* displays timers with message for evtype */
      int wasblockedflag;

      if (!traceflag)
          return;
      wasblockedflag = blockinterrupt();
      printf("**** %8.4f: ", getrelativetime());
      printf("%s ",msg);
      if (val1 >= 0)
          printf("%ld ", val1);
      if (val2 >= 0)
          printf("%ld ", val2);
      if (blockedflag)
          printf("B");
      else
          printf("U");
      if (blockedflag != wasblockedflag)
          printf("***");
      showtimerdata();
      fflush(stdout);
      if (!wasblockedflag)
          unblockinterrupt();
  }

  void showinit(int maxt) {        /* set initialtod to seconds since Jan 1, 1970 */
      initialtod = gettime();
      maxtimers = maxt;
  }
```

Program 10.1 ——————————————————————————————————— **show.c**

Put the code of Program 10.1 in a separate file. Instrument the timer functions so that each time something of interest occurs, the program calls `show` with the appropriate parameters. For this part, just insert the following four lines.

- In the first line of `timerhandler` insert the following.

  ```
  show(traceflag, "Timer Handler Enter", timers.running, -1, 1);
  ```

- Before returning from `timerhandler` insert the following.

  ```
  show(traceflag, "Timer Handler Exit", timers.running, -1, 1);
  ```

- Before the first line of `timerstart` insert the following.

  ```
  show(traceflag, "Timer Start Enter", n, interval, 0);
  ```

- Before returning from `timerstart` insert the following.

  ```
  show(traceflag, "Timer Start Exit", n, interval, 0);
  ```

Test the program with a variety of appropriate inputs and observe the output of `show`. Remember that `printf` is not async-signal safe. The calls to `show` in `timerhandler` cause a problem if `timermain` also uses the standard I/O library without blocking the signals during the calls. The `show` function blocks the timer interrupt before producing any output to avoid this problem as well as to protect the shared `timers` data structure.

Program 10.2 gives an alternative implementation of `show` that uses the remote logging facility described in Appendix D.2. It avoids a possible buffer overflow by calling `snprintfappend` to add to the message. This function takes parameters similar to those of `snprintf` but appends to a string given by the first parameter. The second parameter is a limit on the total size of the buffer used to hold the string.

In this version, the `showinit` function opens a connection to the remote logger, using the default parameters. Each output message is associated with a generator string indicating the source of the message. The generator is just the timer gotten from the `val1` parameter. The output message has the following fields separated by tabs so they can be displayed in a table.

- The message from the `msg` parameter.
- `val1` (the timer).
- `val2` (a second timer or an interval).
- The letter U if the `blockedflag` parameter is 0 and the letter B otherwise. If this does not correspond to the actual blocked state of the timer signal, this is followed by three asterisks as a warning.
- The number of the currently running timer if any.
- A list of all active timers, each being represented by an ordered pair consisting of the timer number and the remaining time relative to the running timer.
- The number of events followed by the list of events.

Figure 10.9 on page 363 shows sample output from one window of the remote logger.

Program 10.2 ——————————————————————— `showremote.c`

A version of show *that uses a remote logging facility.*

```c
#include <stdarg.h>
#include <stdio.h>
#include <stdlib.h>
#include <string.h>
#include <sys/time.h>
#include "hardwaretimer.h"
#include "rlogging.h"
#include "show.h"
#include "virtualtimers.h"
#define MILLION 1000000L
#define MSGBUFSIZE 256

static double initialtod = 0.0;
static LFILE *lf;
static int maxtimers;
static double gettime(void);
static double timetodouble(long interval);

static void snprintfappend(char *s, size_t n, const char *fmt, ...) {
   va_list ap;
   int sizeleft;

   sizeleft = n - strlen(s) - 1;
   if (sizeleft <= 0)
      return;
   va_start(ap, fmt);
   vsnprintf(s + strlen(s), sizeleft, fmt, ap);
}

static void createlogstring(char *msg, int n) {        /* create string to log */
   int i;

   if (getrunning() >= 0)
      snprintfappend(msg, n, "\t%d\t", getrunning());
   else
      snprintfappend(msg, n, "\t\t");
   for (i = 0; i < maxtimers; i++)
      if (getvalue(i) >= 0)
         snprintfappend(msg, n, "(%d,%.3f) ",
                 i, timetodouble(getvalue(i)));
   snprintfappend(msg, n, "\t (%dE", getnumberevents());
   for (i = 0; i < getnumberevents(); i++)
      snprintfappend(msg, n, " %d", getevent(i));
   snprintfappend(msg, n, ")\n");
}

static double getrelativetime(void) {    /* seconds since showinit was called */
   return gettime() - initialtod;
}

static double gettime(void) {    /* seconds since January 1, 1970 as a double */
   double thistime = 0.0;
   struct timeval tval;

   if (gettimeofday(&tval, NULL))
```

```c
            fprintf(stderr, "Warning, cannot get time of day\n");
        else
            thistime = tval.tv_sec + (double)tval.tv_usec/MILLION;
        return thistime;
    }

    static double timetodouble(long interval) {        /* microseconds to seconds */
        return (double)interval/MILLION;
    }

    /* -----------------------Public Functions --------------------------------- */
    void showinit(int maxt) {        /* set initialtod to seconds since Jan 1, 1970 */
        initialtod = gettime();
        maxtimers = maxt;
        lf = lopen(NULL, 0);
        if (lf == NULL)
            fprintf(stderr,"Cannot open remote logger\n");
        else
            lsendtime(lf);
    }

    void show(int traceflag, const char *msg, long val1, long val2,
                int blockedflag) {        /* log timers with message for evtype */
        char genbuf[20];
        char msgbuf[MSGBUFSIZE];
        int wasblockedflag;

        if (!traceflag)
            return;
        wasblockedflag = blockinterrupt();
        if (val1 < 0)
            genbuf[0] = 0;
        else
            sprintf(genbuf, "Timer %ld", val1);
        snprintf(msgbuf, MSGBUFSIZE, "%8.4f: ", getrelativetime());
        snprintfappend(msgbuf, MSGBUFSIZE, "%s", msg);
        if (val1 >= 0)
            snprintfappend(msgbuf, MSGBUFSIZE, "\t%ld", val1);
        else
            snprintfappend(msgbuf, MSGBUFSIZE, "%s", "\t");
        if (val2 >= 0)
            snprintfappend(msgbuf, MSGBUFSIZE, "\t%ld", val2);
        else
            snprintfappend(msgbuf, MSGBUFSIZE, "%s", "\t");
        if (blockedflag)
            snprintfappend(msgbuf, MSGBUFSIZE, "%s", "\tB");
        else
            snprintfappend(msgbuf, MSGBUFSIZE, "%s", "\tU");
        if (blockedflag != wasblockedflag)
            snprintfappend(msgbuf, MSGBUFSIZE, "%s", "***");
        createlogstring(msgbuf, MSGBUFSIZE);
        lprintfg(lf, genbuf, msgbuf);
        if (!wasblockedflag)
            unblockinterrupt();
    }
```

Program 10.2 ─── `showremote.c`

10.4 Using Multiple Timers

The potential interactions of multiple timers make their implementation more complex than that of single timers. All the times in the `active` array are specified relative to the start of the underlying `ITIMER_REAL` interval timer. Suppose that a program wants to set timer [4] for seven seconds and that two seconds have elapsed since it set timer [2] for five seconds. Use the following procedure.

1. Find out how much time is left on the real timer.
    (Call `gethardwaretimer`.)
2. Find the start of the real timer relative to the currently `running` timer by subtracting the time left on the real timer from the timer value of the `running` timer. (Use `getrunning`.)
3. Calculate the time of the timer to be set relative to the start time by adding the relative start time from step 2 to the requested time.

Figure 10.3 on page 346 shows the `timers` data structure after a program sets timer 2 for five seconds (5,000,000 microseconds). Suppose that two seconds later the program sets timer [4] for seven seconds (7,000,000 microseconds). Figure 10.5 shows the `timers` data structure after timer [4] is set. The program calls `gethardwaretimer` and finds that there are three seconds left (3,000,000 microseconds) on the interval timer, so two seconds (5,000,000 - 3,000,000 microseconds) have elapsed since it set timer [2]. The program then computes the time for timer [4] relative to the start of the original setting of the real timer as nine seconds (2,000,000 + 7,000,000 microseconds).

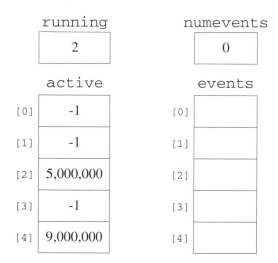

Figure 10.5: The `timers` data structure after timer 4 has been set.

The `running` timer is the same in Figure 10.3 and Figure 10.5 because timer [4] expires after timer [2]. The program did not change the `running` timer designation or reset the timer in this case. Continuing the situation of Figure 10.5, suppose that a program wants to set timer [3] for one second and a call to `gethardwaretimer` shows that the real timer has two seconds left. Timer [3] should expire before the real timer is scheduled to expire, so the program must reset the real timer. Figure 10.6 shows the situation after the program sets timer [3]. The program resets the real timer to expire in one second and adjusts all of the other times in `active`. The new times are relative to the start time of timer [3] rather than to that of timer [2] (three seconds ago), so the program subtracted three seconds from each of the active times.

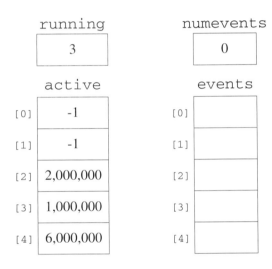

Figure 10.6: The `timers` data structure after timer [3] has been set.

Figure 10.7 shows the situation a little over a second after timer [3] was set. Timer [3] expires and timer [2] becomes the `running` timer. All the times are readjusted to expire relative to timer [2].

Figure 10.8 shows the situation two seconds later. Timer [2] expires and timer [4] becomes the `running` timer.

10.4.1 Setting multiple timers

Modify the `timerstart` function and add a `timerstop` function to handle all of the cases of timers being set while other timers are active. At any moment, each timer is either active or inactive. An active timer cannot appear in `events`, but it is added to `events` when it expires. If any of the timers is active, exactly one of them is *running*.

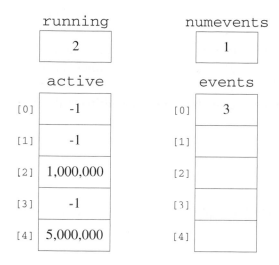

Figure 10.7: The `timers` data structure after timer `[3]` expires.

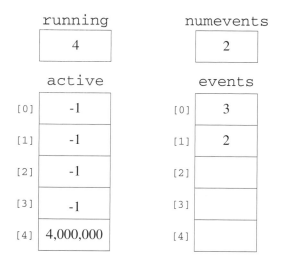

Figure 10.8: The `timers` data structure after timer `[2]` expires.

The `running` timer is the one that is next to expire. Its expiration time has been used in `sethardwaretimer`, so a signal is generated when its time expires.

How starting and stopping should affect `events` is an arbitrary implementation decision. The implementation outlined here removes an event corresponding to the timer to be started or stopped if one is there. This choice ensures that no timer is represented by more than one event in events, so events can be declared to be the same size as active. The bound on events simplifies the implementation.

With multiple timers active, timerhandler must update the timers data structure by subtracting active[running] from all active times. If the time becomes 0, the corresponding timer has expired and that timer number should be placed in events and made inactive. This method handles multiple timers expiring at the same time.

Section 10.3 handled the case of starting a timer when no timer is active. A similar case is the one in which the timer to be started is already active but all other timers are inactive.

Suppose some other timer is the running timer when a timer is started. If the timer to be started expires after the running timer, only one entry in the timers data structure needs to be modified. However, if starting this timer causes it to expire before the currently running timer, the interval timer must be reset. The entries in the active array must also be adjusted relative to the starting time of the new running timer. To make the adjustment, decrement the active times by the time that the currently running timer has been active (runtime). Use gethardwaretimer to find the remaining time on the interval timer and calculate runtime = active[running] - remaining.

When the running timer changes, take the following actions.

1. Remove the new timer from events if it is there.

2. Adjust all active times by runtime.

3. Set a new running timer.

4. Start the interval timer by calling sethardwaretimer.

The case in which the timer to be started is the running timer can be treated either as a special case of the above or as a separate case.

A call to timerstop for a timer that is not active just removes the timer from events. If the timer was active but not running, set it to be inactive. The interesting case is that of stopping the running timer. This case is similar to the case of starting a timer that becomes the running timer because the timers data structure needs to be updated by runtime and a new running timer has to be selected.

In this part, the program should handle all combinations of starting and stopping timers as well as removing events from the event list.   Enhance the timerstart and timerhandler functions appropriately and write the functions removetop and timerstop, which were not needed before. Insert appropriate calls to show.

Modify timermain so that it interprets a negative interval as a command to stop the timer. Instead of waiting for an event in the main loop, remove and display all events without blocking before waiting for additional input.

□ Exercise 10.3

What happens if scanf is used for standard input in this version of timermain?

Answer:
Neither `scanf` or `sscanf` are guaranteed to interact correctly with signals. The
`scanf` function may indicate end-of-file when a signal is caught by the process.
Use the `readline` function from Program 4.1 on page 95. This function detects
end-of-file correctly and is not affected by signals. You can then use `sscanf` to
parse the input line (after blocking the signals).

□ **Exercise 10.4**

Why can the single timer of Section 10.3 use `scanf` without a problem?
Answer:
The program waits for the signal to be caught before calling `scanf`.

10.4.2 Testing with multiple timers

Even code instrumented by `show` is difficult to test systematically, since the action of the
program depends on the speed of the input typing. One approach to this problem is to
use a driver, `testtime`, to generate the input for the program. Program 10.3 shows the
`testtime` program. It must be linked to the `hardwaretimer` object.

As with any filter, `testtime` reads from standard input and writes to standard output.
The input consists of lines containing three integers, n, m and p. The filter reads in these
three integers, waits n microseconds, and then outputs m and p on a single line. If $m < 0$,
`testtime` exits after waiting n microseconds. The `testtime` program ignores any characters on the line after the three integers, so a user can add comments to the end of each
input line.

■ **Example 10.5**

Suppose `testtime` receives the following input.

```
1000000   2   5000000 Timer 2 expires at time 6
2000000   4   7000000 Timer 4 expires at time 10
1000000   3   1000000 Timer 1 preempts 2 to expire at time 5
```

The `testtime` program waits one second and outputs the following line.

```
2 5000000
```

The program then waits two more seconds and outputs the following line.

```
4 7000000
```

The program then waits one second and outputs the following line.

```
3 1000000
```

□ **Exercise 10.6**

Suppose the three lines in Example 10.5 are in the file `timer.input` and you
execute the following command. What happens?

```
testtime < timer.input | timermain
```

Answer:

After getting the third line of the file at time 4 seconds, `timermain` detects end-of-file when `testtime` exits. This occurs before any timers expire. We can fix this problem by adding the following line to `timer.input`.

```
7000000 -1  1000000 Everything done 6 units from now
```

Program 10.3 ── `testtime.c`

The program `testtime`.

```c
#include <stdio.h>
#include <stdlib.h>
#include <sys/time.h>
#include "hardwaretimer.h"

static int timerexpired = 0;

static void myalarm() {
   timerexpired = 1;
}

int main(int argc, char *argv[]) {   /* Test the hardware timer and prototype */
   long interval;
   int n1;
   int n2;

   if (argc != 1) {
      fprintf(stderr, "Usage: %s\n", argv[0]);
      return 1;
   }
   catchinterrupt(myalarm);

   for( ; ; ){
      if (scanf("%ld%d%d%*[^\n]", &interval, &n1, &n2) == EOF)
         break;
      if (interval <= 0)
         break;
      blockinterrupt();
      sethardwaretimer(interval);
      while (!timerexpired)
         waitforinterrupt();
      timerexpired = 0;
      if (n1 < 0)
         break;
      printf("%d %d\n", n1, n2);
      fflush(stdout);
      fprintf(stderr, "%d %d\n", n1, n2);
   }
   return 0;
}
```

Program 10.3 ── `testtime.c`

If the 4-line file described in Example 10.5 and Exercise 10.6 is used as illustrated, the command causes timer [2] to start 1 second after execution begins and to expire five seconds later (at time 6). Two seconds later (at time 3), timer [4] starts and expires in seven seconds (at time 10). One second later (at time 4), timer [3] is set to expire in one second (at time 5). This is exactly the situation illustrated in Figure 10.6 on page 358.

Figure 10.9 displays the output generated for this input by Program 10.1, using an appropriately instrumented implementation of virtualtimers. Figure 10.10 displays the corresponding output generated by Program 10.2.

```
****     0.0001: Initialize U(-1,-0.000) A: (0E)
****     0.9975: Start Enter 2 5000000 U(-1,-0.000) A: (0E)
****     0.9976: None Running 2 5000000 B(-1,-0.000) A: (0E)
****     0.9977: Start Exit 2 5000000 U(2,5.000) A:(2,5.000)   (0E)
****     3.0072: Start Enter 4 7000000 U(2,5.000) A:(2,5.000)   (0E)
****     3.0073: Start Another Running 4 2 B(2,5.000) A:(2,5.000)   (0E)
****     3.0074: Start Running Used 4 2009705 B(2,5.000) A:(2,5.000)   (0E)
****     3.0075: Start Running Expires First 4 B(2,5.000) A:(2,5.000) (4,9.010)   (0E)
****     4.0173: Start Enter 3 1000000 U(2,5.000) A:(2,5.000) (4,9.010)   (0E)
****     4.0174: Start Another Running 3 2 B(2,5.000) A:(2,5.000) (4,9.010)   (0E)
****     4.0175: Start Running Used 3 3019778 B(2,5.000) A:(2,5.000) (4,9.010)   (0E)
****     4.0176: Start This Expires First 3 B(3,1.000) A:(2,1.980) (3,1.000) (4,5.990)   (0E)
****     5.0269: Handler Start 3 1000000 B(3,1.000) A:(2,1.980) (3,1.000) (4,5.990)   (0E)
****     5.0271: Handler Setting Hardware 2 980222 B(2,0.980) A:(2,0.980) (4,4.990)   (1E 3)
****     5.0272: Handler Exit B(2,0.980) A:(2,0.980) (4,4.990)   (1E 3)
****     6.0170: Handler Start 2 980222 B(2,0.980) A:(2,0.980) (4,4.990)   (1E 3)
****     6.0172: Handler Setting Hardware 4 4009705 B(4,4.010) A:(4,4.010)   (2E 3 2)
****     6.0173: Handler Exit B(4,4.010) A:(4,4.010)   (2E 3 2)
****    10.0369: Handler Start 4 4009705 B(4,4.010) A:(4,4.010)   (2E 3 2)
****    10.0371: Handler Setting Hardware 4 B(4,-0.000) A: (3E 3 2 4)
****    10.0372: Handler Exit B(4,-0.000) A: (3E 3 2 4)
```

Figure 10.9: The output generated by Program 10.1.

10.5 A Robust Implementation of Multiple Timers

What happens if a SIGALRM signal is delivered during execution of the timerstart function? Both the timerhandler and the timerstart functions modify the timers data structure, a shared resource. This is the classical critical section problem for shared variables, and care must be taken to ensure that the timers data structure is not corrupted. It is difficult to determine if such a problem exists in the code by testing alone. The events that might cause corruption of the data structure are rare and usually would not show up during testing. If such an event occurred, it would not be easily repeatable and so there might be little information about its cause.

Logging Version 0.12(December 19, 2002) using Jali L158 (December 19, 2002) — Output Frame

Msg	Con	Gen	Time	Output						
1	0			Connection Opened						
2	0	10218	0.000	0.0209: Initialize						
3	0	Timer 2	0.015	0.9937: Start Enter	2	5000000	U	2	(2,5.000)	(0E)
4	0	Timer 2	0.987	0.9958: None Running	2	5000000	B			(0E)
5	0	Timer 2	1.087	0.9959: Start Exit	2	5000000	U	2	(2,5.000)	(0E)
6	0	Timer 4	1.089	0.9959: Start Enter	4	7000000	U	2	(2,5.000)	(0E)
7	0	Timer 4	2.998	3.0035: Start Enter	4	7000000	B	2	(2,5.000)	(0E)
8	0	Timer 4	3.000	3.0036: Start Another Running	4	2	B	2	(2,5.000) (4,9.008)	(0E)
9	0	Timer 4	3.002	3.0037: Start Running Used	4	2007802	B	2	(2,5.000) (4,9.008)	(0E)
10	0	Timer 3	3.011	3.0038: Start Running Expires First	4	1000000	U	2	(2,5.000) (4,9.008)	(0E)
11	0	Timer 3	4.008	4.0135: Start Enter	3	2	B	2	(2,5.000) (4,9.008)	(0E)
12	0	Timer 3	4.014	4.0136: Start Another Running	3	3017733	B	2	(2,5.000) (4,9.008)	(0E)
13	0	Timer 3	4.016	4.0137: Start Running Used	3	1000000	B	3	(2,1.982) (3,1.000) (4,5.990)	(0E)
14	0	Timer 3	4.017	4.0137: Start This Expires First	3	982267	B	3	(2,1.982) (3,1.000) (4,5.990)	(0E)
15	0	Timer 3	5.017	5.0232: Handler Start	2	982267	B	2	(2,0.982) (4,4.990)	(1E 3)
16	0	Timer 2	5.019	5.0233: Handler Setting Hardware	2	5234	B	2	(2,0.982) (4,4.990)	(1E 3)
17	0	10218	5.020	5.0234: Handler Exit	2	6132	B	2	(2,0.982) (4,4.990)	(1E 3)
18	0	Timer 2	6.007	6.0132: Handler Start	4	6133	B	4	(4,4.008)	(2E 3 2)
19	0	Timer 4	6.424	6.0133: Handler Setting Hardware	4	4007802	B	4	(4,4.008)	(2E 3 2)
20	0	10218	6.424	6.0133: Handler Exit	4	4007802	B	4	(4,4.008)	(2E 3 2)
21	0	Timer 4	10.017	10.0232: Handler Start	4		B	4		(3E 3 2 4)
22	0	Timer 4	10.013	10.0233: Handler Setting Hardware	4		B	4		(3E 3 2 4)
23	0	Timer 4	10.013	10.0234: Handler Exit	4		B	4		(3E 3 2 4)
	0	10218	11.024	Connection Closed						

Lines Received: 23

Show Message	Hide
Time Since Start	Always Show Heading	Show Open
Dynamic Tabs	Show Close

Figure 10.10: The output generated by Program 10.2.

A *race condition* occurs when the outcome of a program depends on the exact order in which different threads of execution execute statements. The `timerstart` function is executed by the main thread of execution. That same thread executes `timerhandler`, but the thread that generates the SIGALRM signal determines when the timer expires. You can prevent race conditions of this type by ensuring that the critical sections are executed in a mutually exclusive manner.

You must analyze the problem to determine where the critical sections are. In this case, the analysis is simple since there is only one global variable, the `timers` data structure. Any function that modifies this structure must do so at a time when the SIGALRM signal handler may not be entered. The simplest approach is to block the SIGALRM signal before modifying the `timers` data structure.

Just blocking SIGALRM may not be sufficient. What happens if the interval timer expires during the execution of the `timerstart` function and SIGALRM is blocked? The `timerstart` function might make a new timer the `running` timer and reset the interval timer. Before the `timerstart` function terminates, it unblocks SIGALRM. At this point, the signal is delivered and the handler assumes that the new timer had expired. Although this sequence of events is extremely unlikely, a correctly working program must account for all possibilities. Exercise 10.7 shows another problem.

□ **Exercise 10.7**

Describe a sequence of events in which the `timerstop` function could fail even if it blocked the signal on entry and unblocked it on exit.

Answer:

The `timerstop` function blocks the SIGALRM signal. The timer to be stopped then expires (i.e., the interval timer generates a signal). This signal is not immediately delivered to the process, since the signal is blocked. The `timerstop` function then starts the interval timer corresponding to the next timer to expire. Before it returns, the `timerstop` function unblocks the signal and the signal is delivered. The signal handler behaves as if the `running` timer just expired, when in fact a different timer had expired.

The simplest solution to the problem described in Exercise 10.7 is to modify the `hardwaretimer` module. The `stophardwaretimer` function (which should be called with the SIGALRM signal blocked) should stop the timer and check to see if the SIGALRM signal is pending by using `sigpending`. If it is, the `stophardwaretimer` function removes the signal either by calling `sigwait` or by ignoring it and catching it again. The `sethardwaretimer` function can solve a similar problem by calling `stophardwaretimer`.

☐ **Exercise 10.8**

How would you test to see if you solved this problem correctly?

Answer:

This cannot be done just by simple testing, since the problem occurs only when a timer expires in a narrow window. To test this, you will have to make the `timerstop` take some extra time.

☐ **Exercise 10.9**

What would happen if you put a call to `sleep(10)` in `timerstop` to increase the chance that the error would occur?

Answer:

The `sleep` function might be implemented with `SIGALRM`, so `sleep` should not be called from a program that catches `SIGALRM`. The program has unpredictable results. The `nanosleep` function does not interact with `SIGALRM` and could be used in `timerstop`.

Program 10.4 is a function that can be used to waste a number of microseconds by busy waiting. It calls `gettimeofday` in a loop until the required number of microseconds has passed.

Program 10.4 ─────────────────────────────── **wastetime.c**

A function that does busy waiting for a given number of microseconds.

```c
#include <stdio.h>
#include <sys/time.h>
#define MILLION 1000000L

int wastetime(int maxus) {                 /* waste maxus microseconds of time */
   long timedif;
   struct timeval tp1, tp2;

   if (gettimeofday(&tp1, NULL)) {
      fprintf(stderr, "Failed to get initial time\n");
      return 1;
   }
   timedif = 0;
   while (timedif < maxus) {
      if (gettimeofday(&tp2, NULL)) {
         fprintf(stderr, "Failed to get check time\n");
         return 1;
      }
      timedif = MILLION*(tp2.tv_sec - tp1.tv_sec) +
                  tp2.tv_usec - tp1.tv_usec;
      if (timedif < 0)
         break;
   }
   return 0;
}
```

Program 10.4 ─────────────────────────────── **wastetime.c**

Analyze the `timerstart` and `timerstop` functions and modify the implementation of Section 10.4 so that the timers are handled robustly. Devise a method of testing to verify that the program works correctly. (The test will involve simulating rare events.)

10.6 POSIX:TMR Timer Implementation

POSIX:TMR timers have several advantages over POSIX:XSI timers. A program can create several POSIX:TMR timers for a given clock such as `CLOCK_REALTIME`. The timers have a potentially greater resolution since values are given to the nearest nanosecond rather than the nearest microsecond. The program can specify which signal is delivered for each timer, and the signal handler can determine which timer generated the signal. Also, the signals generated by the timers are queued, and the program can determine when signals have been lost due to overruns.

Several implementations of multiple timers of Section 10.4 with POSIX:TMR timers are possible. The simplest method is to use one timer and make minor changes in the data types to accommodate the higher resolution. Alternatively, a separate POSIX:TMR timer can implement each software timer. Starting and stopping a timer and handling the timer signal are independent of the other timers, so the only shared structure is the event queue. The `virtualtimers` and `hardwaretimer` object might have to be reorganized. There may be a limit to the number of timers that are supported for each process given by the constant `TIMER_MAX`. If the number of timers needed is small, this method would be the easiest to implement. A third approach is to use a single POSIX:TMR timer but modify the method of implementation to make the timing more accurate.

One of the problems with the original timer implementation of this chapter is that there can be a significant amount of timer drift, as discussed in Section 9.6. This drift can be virtually eliminated by the use of absolute time rather than relative time. Instead of storing the times relative to the `running` timer in the active array, store the absolute time of expiration. This approach will probably require 64 bits for each entry, perhaps a `struct timeval` or `struct timespec`. Alternatively, use a `long long` to store the number of microseconds or nanoseconds since the Epoch. This has the advantage of simplifying comparisons of time, but times must be converted to a `struct timespec` or `struct timeval` when timers are set.

10.7 `mycron`, a Small Cron Facility

The cron facility in UNIX allows users to execute commands at specified dates and times. This facility is quite flexible and allows regularly scheduled commands. It is implemented with a `cron` daemon that processes a file containing timing and command information.

Implement a simplified personal cron facility called `mycron`. Write a program that takes one command-line argument. The argument represents a data file containing time intervals and commands. Each line of the data file specifies a command and the frequency at which that command is to be executed. The lines of the data file have the following format.

```
interval command
```

The `interval` argument specifies the number of seconds between execution of instances of the command. The `command` argument is the command to execute with its arguments.

1. Implement the preceding cron facility, assuming that none of the intervals in the cron data file are longer than the maximum interval that the timers can handle (about 30 minutes). Call the executable `mycron`.

2. Handle the case in which the intervals can be arbitrarily large. Assume that the number of seconds in the interval will fit in a `long`. Try to do this without modifying the timer functions.

3. Find a way to adjust the starting times so that if two commands have the same interval, they will not always be executing at the same time.

10.8 Additional Reading

An array representation for timers works well when the number of timers is small. Consider using a priority queue for the timers and a linked list for the events. "Hashed and hierarchical timing wheels: Data structures for efficient implementation of a timer facility" by Varghese and Lauck [128] describes alternative implementations. The POSIX Rationale section on Clocks and Timers [51] provides an excellent discussion of the issues involved in implementing timers at the system level. Aron and Drushel [5] discuss system timer efficiency in "Soft timers: efficient microsecond software timer support for network processing."

Chapter 11

Project: Cracking Shells

By developing a shell from the bottom up, this chapter explores the intricacies of process creation, termination, identification and the correct handling of signals. Example programs handle foreground and background processes, pipelines, process groups, sessions and controlling terminals. The chapter also looks at job control and terminal I/O. The closing project integrates these concepts by incorporating job control into a shell.

Objectives
- Learn how shells work
- Experiment with background processes
- Explore signal handling and job control
- Use redirection and pipelines
- Understand process groups and controlling terminals

11.1 Building a Simple Shell

A *shell* is a process that does command-line interpretation. In other words, a shell reads a command line from standard input and executes the command corresponding to the input line. In the simplest case, the shell reads a command and forks a child to execute the command. The parent then waits for the child to complete before reading in another command. A real shell handles process pipelines and redirection, as well as foreground process groups, background process groups and signals.

This section starts with the simplest of shells. Later sections add features piece by piece. The shells use the `makeargv` function of Program 2.2 on page 37 to parse the command-line arguments. Section 11.2 adds redirection, and Section 11.3 adds pipelines. Section 11.4 explains how a shell handles signals for a foreground process. The programs for each of these phases are given, along with a series of exercises that point out the important issues. Work through these exercises before going on to the main part of the project. The heart of this project is signal handling and job control. Section 11.5 introduces the machinery needed for job control. Section 11.6 describes how background processes are handled without job control, and Section 11.7 introduces job control at the user level. Finally, Section 11.8 specifies the implementation of a complete shell with job control.

Program 11.1 shows Version 1 of `ush` (ultrasimple shell). The shell process forks a child that builds an `argv` type array and calls `execvp` to execute commands entered from standard input.

Program 11.1 ———————————————————————————————— `ush1.c`

Version 1 of `ush` *has no error checking or prompts.*

```c
#include <stdio.h>
#include <string.h>
#include <unistd.h>
#include <sys/wait.h>
#define MAX_BUFFER 256
#define QUIT_STRING "q"

int makeargv(const char *s, const char *delimiters, char ***argvp);

int main (void) {
   char **chargv;
   char inbuf[MAX_BUFFER];

   for( ; ; ) {
      gets(inbuf);
      if (strcmp(inbuf, QUIT_STRING) == 0)
         return 0;
      if ((fork() == 0) && (makeargv(inbuf, " ", &chargv) > 0))
         execvp(chargv[0], chargv);
      wait(NULL);
   }
}
```

Program 11.1 ———————————————————————————————— `ush1.c`

❑ Exercise 11.1

Run Program 11.1 with a variety of commands such as ls, grep and sort. Does ush1 behave as expected?

Answer:

No. Program 11.1 does not display a prompt or expand filenames containing wild-cards such as * and ?. The ush1 shell also does not handle quotation marks in the same way as standard shells do. A normal shell allows quotation marks to guarantee that a particular argument is passed to the exec in its entirety and is not interpreted by the shell as something else. You may also notice that certain commands such as cd do not behave in the expected way.

❑ Exercise 11.2

What happens if Program 11.1 doesn't call wait?

Answer:

If a user enters a command before the previous one completes, the commands execute concurrently.

Another problem is that Version 1 of ush does not trap errors on execvp. This omission has some interesting consequences if you enter an invalid command. When execvp succeeds, control never comes back from the child. However, when it fails, the child falls through and tries to get a command line too!

❑ Exercise 11.3

Run Program 11.1 with several invalid commands. Execute ps and observe the number of shells that are running. Try to quit. What happens?

Answer:

Each time you enter an invalid command, ush1 creates a new process that behaves like an additional shell. You must enter q once for each process.

❑ Exercise 11.4

Only the child parses the command line in Program 11.1. What happens if the parent parses the command line before forking? What are the memory allocation and deallocation issues involved in moving the makeargv call before fork in these programs?

Answer:

When the child exits, all memory allocated by the child is freed. If the parent calls makeargv before fork, the shell has to later free the memory allocated by makeargv.

Version 1 of ush is susceptible to buffer overflows because it uses gets rather than fgets. A long command can exceed the space allocated for input. Program 11.2 shows an improved version of ush that prompts for user input and handles an unsuccessful execvp call. The system-defined constant MAX_CANON replaces the user-defined MAX_BUFFER, and fgets replaces gets.

The shell in Program 11.2 does not exit if there is an error on fork. In general, the shell should be impervious to errors—and bullet-proofing takes a lot of effort. The function executecmd replaces the makeargv and execvp calls. Control should never return from this function.

Program 11.2 ────────────────────────────────── **ush2.c**

Version 2 of ush *handles simple command lines.*

```c
#include <limits.h>
#include <stdio.h>
#include <string.h>
#include <unistd.h>
#include <sys/types.h>
#include <sys/wait.h>
#define PROMPT_STRING "ush2>>"
#define QUIT_STRING "q"

void executecmd(char *incmd);

int main (void) {
   pid_t childpid;
   char inbuf[MAX_CANON];
   int len;

   for( ; ; ) {
      if (fputs(PROMPT_STRING, stdout) == EOF)
         continue;
      if (fgets(inbuf, MAX_CANON, stdin) == NULL)
         continue;
      len = strlen(inbuf);
      if (inbuf[len - 1] == '\n')
         inbuf[len - 1] = 0;
      if (strcmp(inbuf, QUIT_STRING) == 0)
         break;
      if ((childpid = fork()) == -1)
         perror("Failed to fork child");
      else if (childpid == 0) {
         executecmd(inbuf);
         return 1;
      } else
         wait(NULL);
   }
   return 0;
}
```

Program 11.2 ────────────────────────────────── **ush2.c**

Program 11.3 shows a simple version of executecmd for Program 11.2. We will augment this function as we improve the shell. The executecmdsimple.c version simply constructs an argument array and calls execvp.

Program 11.3 ──────────────────────── `executecmdsimple.c`

A simplified version of `executecmd` *for Program 11.2.*

```c
#include <errno.h>
#include <stdio.h>
#include <stdlib.h>
#include <unistd.h>
#define BLANK_STRING " "

int makeargv(const char *s, const char *delimiters, char ***argvp);

void executecmd(char *incmd) {
    char **chargv;
    if (makeargv(incmd, BLANK_STRING, &chargv) <= 0) {
        fprintf(stderr, "Failed to parse command line\n");
        exit(1);
    }
    execvp(chargv[0], chargv);
    perror("Failed to execute command");
    exit(1);
}
```

Program 11.3 ──────────────────────── `executecmdsimple.c`

□ **Exercise 11.5**

Why does Program 11.3 treat a `makeargv` return value of 0 as an error?

Answer:

The `makeargv` returns the number of items in the command argument array. Technically, an empty command is not an error, and a real shell would ignore it without printing a warning message. For more complicated command lines that include redirection and pipelines, an empty command portion is considered to be an error. You may want to consider adding additional checks and not count it as an error in some circumstances.

□ **Exercise 11.6**

Try the `cd` command as input to Program 11.2. What happens? Why? Hint: Read the man page on `cd` for an explanation.

Answer:

The `cd` command changes the user's environment, so it must be internal to the shell. External commands are executed by children of the shell process, and a process cannot change the environment of its parent. Most shells implement `cd` as an internal command or a built-in command.

□ **Exercise 11.7**

What happens when Program 11.2 encounters commands such as `ls -l` and `q` with leading and interspersed extra blanks?

Answer:

Program 11.2 correctly handles commands such as `ls -l` because `makeargv` handles leading and interspersed blanks. The `q` command does not work because this command is handled directly by `ush2`, which has no provision for handling interspersed blanks.

☐ Exercise 11.8

Execute the command `stty -a` under your regular shell and record the current settings of the terminal control characters. The following is a possible example of what might appear.

```
intr = ^c; quit = ^|; erase = ^?; kill = ^u;
eof = ^d; eol = <undef>; eol2 = <undef>; swtch = <undef>;
start = ^q; stop = ^s; susp = ^z; dsusp = ^y;
rprnt = ^r; flush = ^o; werase = ^w; lnext = ^v;
```

Try each of the control characters under `ush2` and under a regular shell and compare the results.

In Exercise 11.8 the `erase` and `werase` continue to work even though there is no explicit code to handle them in `ush2` because `ush2` does not receive characters directly from the keyboard. Instead, the terminal device driver processes input from the keyboard and passes the input through additional modules to the program. As described in Section 6.5.1, terminals can operate in either canonical (line-buffered) or noncanonical mode. Canonical mode is the default.

In canonical mode, the terminal device driver returns one line of input at a time. Thus, a program does not receive any input until the user enters a newline character, even if the program just reads in a single character. The terminal device driver also does some processing of the line while the line is being gathered. If the terminal line driver encounters the `erase` or `werase` characters, it adjusts the input buffer appropriately.

Noncanonical mode allows flexibility in the handling of I/O. For example, an editing application might display the message `"entering cbreak mode"` to report that it is entering noncanonical mode with echo disabled and one-character-at-a-time input. In noncanonical mode, input is made available to the program after a user-specified number of characters have been entered or after a specified time has elapsed. The canonical mode editing features are not available. Programs such as editors usually operate with the terminal in noncanonical mode, whereas user programs generally operate with the terminal in canonical mode.

11.2 Redirection

POSIX handles I/O in a device-independent way through file descriptors. After obtaining an open file descriptor through a call such as `open` or `pipe`, the program can execute read or write, using the handle returned from the call. Redirection allows a program to reassign a handle that has been opened for one file to designate another file. (See Section 4.7 for a review of redirection.)

Most shells allow redirection of standard input, standard output and possibly standard error from the command line. Filters are programs that read from standard input and write to standard output. Redirection on the command line allows filters to operate on other files without recompilation.

■ Example 11.9

The following cat command redirects its standard input to my.input and its standard output to my.output.

```
cat < my.input > my.output
```

Recall that open file descriptors are inherited on exec calls (unless specifically prevented). For shells this means that the child must redirect its I/O before calling execvp. (After the execvp, the process no longer has access to the variables holding the destination descriptors.)

Program 11.4 shows a version of executecmd that redirects standard input and standard output as designated by the input command line incmd. It calls parseandredirectin and parseandredirectout, which are shown in Program 11.5.

Program 11.4 —————————————————— **executecmdredirect.c**

A version of executecmd *that handles redirection.*

```
#include <errno.h>
#include <stdio.h>
#include <unistd.h>

int makeargv(const char *s, const char *delimiters, char ***argvp);
int parseandredirectin(char *s);
int parseandredirectout(char *s);

void executecmd(char *incmd) {
   char **chargv;
   if (parseandredirectout(incmd) == -1)
      perror("Failed to redirect output");
   else if (parseandredirectin(incmd) == -1)
      perror("Failed to redirect input");
   else if (makeargv(incmd, " \t", &chargv) <= 0)
      fprintf(stderr, "Failed to parse command line\n");
   else {
      execvp(chargv[0], chargv);
      perror("Failed to execute command");
   }
   exit(1);
}
```

Program 11.4 —————————————————— **executecmdredirect.c**

The `parseandredirectin` function looks for the standard input redirection symbol $<$. If the symbol is found, the program replaces it with a string terminator. This removes it from the command. The program then uses `strtok` to remove leading and trailing blanks and tabs. What is left is the name of the file to use for redirection. The `parseandredirectout` function works similarly.

Since the version of `executecmd` in Program 11.4 calls `parseandredirectout` before `parseandredirectin`, it assumes that the output redirection appears on the command line after the input redirection.

☐ **Exercise 11.10**

How does Program 11.2 handle the following command? How would you fix it?

```
sort > t.2 < t.1
```

Answer:
After the call to `parseandredirectout`, the $>$ is replaced by a string terminator so the command is just `sort`. The redirection of standard input is ignored. One way to fix this problem is to use `strchr` to find the positions of both redirection symbols before handling redirection. If both symbols are present, the redirection corresponding to the one that appears last should be done first.

Link `ush2` with `executecmdredirect` and `parseandredirect` to obtain a shell that handles simple redirection.

☐ **Exercise 11.11**

How would `ush2` handle redirection from an invalid file?
Answer:
If `parseandredirectin` or `parseandredirectout` fails to open the file, the function returns -1 and `executecmdredirect` does not attempt to execute the command.

11.3 Pipelines

Pipelines, introduced in Section 6.2, connect filters in an assembly line to perform more complicated functions.

■ **Example 11.12**

The following command redirects the output of `ls -l` to the standard input of `sort` and the standard output of `sort` to the file `temp`.

```
ls -l | sort -n +4 > temp
```

The `ls` and the `sort` commands are distinct processes connected in a pipeline. The connection does not imply that the processes share file descriptors, but rather that the shell creates an intervening pipe to act as a buffer between them.

Program 11.5 ——————————————————————— **parseandredirect.c**

Functions to handle redirection of standard input and standard output. These functions must be called in a particular order. The redirection that occurs last must be handled first.

```c
#include <errno.h>
#include <fcntl.h>
#include <string.h>
#include <unistd.h>
#include <sys/stat.h>
#define FFLAG (O_WRONLY | O_CREAT | O_TRUNC)
#define FMODE (S_IRUSR | S_IWUSR)

int parseandredirectin(char *cmd) {     /* redirect standard input if '<' */
   int error;
   int infd;
   char *infile;

   if ((infile = strchr(cmd, '<')) == NULL)
      return 0;
   *infile = 0;                    /* take everything after '<' out of cmd */
   infile = strtok(infile + 1, " \t");
   if (infile == NULL)
      return 0;
   if ((infd = open(infile, O_RDONLY)) == -1)
      return -1;
   if (dup2(infd, STDIN_FILENO) == -1) {
      error = errno;                      /* make sure errno is correct */
      close(infd);
      errno = error;
      return -1;
   }
   return close(infd);
}

int parseandredirectout(char *cmd) {   /* redirect standard output if '>' */
   int error;
   int outfd;
   char *outfile;

   if ((outfile = strchr(cmd, '>')) == NULL)
      return 0;
   *outfile = 0;                   /* take everything after '>' out of cmd */
   outfile = strtok(outfile + 1, " \t");
   if (outfile == NULL)
      return 0;
   if ((outfd = open(outfile, FFLAG, FMODE)) == -1)
      return -1;
   if (dup2(outfd, STDOUT_FILENO) == -1) {
      error = errno;                          /* make sure errno is correct */
      close(outfd);
      errno = error;
      return -1;
   }
   return close(outfd);
}
```

Program 11.5 ——————————————————————— **parseandredirect.c**

Program 11.6 contains a version of `executecmd` that handles a pipeline of arbitrary length. The implementation uses `makeargv` with the pipeline symbol as a delimiter to make an array of commands for the pipeline. For each command (except the last), `executecmd` creates a pipe and a child process. The `executecmd` redirects the standard output of each command, except the last through a pipe, to the standard input of the next one. The parent redirects its standard output to the pipe and executes the command by calling `executeredirect` of Program 11.7. The child redirects its standard input to come from the pipe and goes back to the loop to create a child to handle the next command in the pipeline. For the last command in the list, `executecmd` does not create a child or pipe but directly calls `executeredirect`.

Errors need to be handled very carefully. Program 11.6 creates multiple child processes. This version of `executecmd` never returns. An error in any of the processes results in a call to `perror_exit`, which prints an appropriate message to standard error and exits.

The `executeredirect` function takes three parameters: the command string and two flags. If the first flag is nonzero, `executeredirect` allows standard input to be redirected. If the second flag is nonzero, `executeredirect` allows standard output to be redirected. The pipeline can redirect standard input only for the first command in the pipeline and can redirect standard output only for the last one.

The `executecmd` function only sets the first flag parameter of `executeredirect` for the call with i equals 0. The `executecmd` only sets the second flag after the last loop iteration completes. If the pipeline contains only one command (no pipeline symbol on the command line), `executecmd` does not execute the loop body and calls `executeredirect` with both flags set. In this case, `executeredirect` behaves similarly to the `executecmd` in `executecmdredirect` (Program 11.4).

The first `if` in `executeredirect` handles the case of the output redirection occurring before the input redirection, as discussed in Exercise 11.10.

◻ Exercise 11.13

What would this shell do with the following command.

```
ls -l > temp1 | sort -n +4 > temp
```

Answer:
The redirection of standard output to `temp1` would be ignored. The shell would treat > and `temp1` as names of files to list. Most real shells would detect this as an error.

◻ Exercise 11.14

How are the processes in the following pipeline related when they are executed by `executecmdpipe`?

```
ls -l | sort -n +4 | more
```

Answer:

The first command, `ls -l`, is a child of the shell. The second command, `sort -n +4`, is a child of `ls`. The third command, `more`, is a child of `sort`.

Program 11.6 ———————————————— **executecmdpipe.c**

The `executecmd` function that handles pipelines.

```c
#include <errno.h>
#include <stdio.h>
#include <stdlib.h>
#include <string.h>
#include <unistd.h>

void executeredirect(char *s, int in, int out);
int makeargv(const char *s, const char *delimiters, char ***argvp);

static void perror_exit(char *s) {
   perror(s);
   exit(1);
}

void executecmd(char *cmds) {
   int child;
   int count;
   int fds[2];
   int i;
   char **pipelist;

   count = makeargv(cmds, "|", &pipelist);
   if (count <= 0) {
      fprintf(stderr, "Failed to find any commands\n");
      exit(1);
   }
   for (i = 0; i < count - 1; i++) {              /* handle all but last one */
      if (pipe(fds) == -1)
        perror_exit("Failed to create pipes");
      else if ((child = fork()) == -1)
        perror_exit("Failed to create process to run command");
      else if (child) {                          /* parent code */
        if (dup2(fds[1], STDOUT_FILENO) == -1)
           perror_exit("Failed to connect pipeline");
        if (close(fds[0]) || close(fds[1]))
           perror_exit("Failed to close needed files");
        executeredirect(pipelist[i], i==0, 0);
        exit(1);
      }
      if (dup2(fds[0], STDIN_FILENO) == -1)        /* child code */
        perror_exit("Failed to connect last component");
      if (close(fds[0]) || close(fds[1]))
        perror_exit("Failed to do final close");
   }
   executeredirect(pipelist[i], i==0, 1);          /* handle the last one */
   exit(1);
}
```

Program 11.6 ———————————————— **executecmdpipe.c**

Program 11.7 ─────────────────────────────────────── `executeredirect.c`

A function to handle a single command with possible redirection.

```
#include <errno.h>
#include <stdio.h>
#include <stdlib.h>
#include <string.h>
#include <unistd.h>

int makeargv(const char *s, const char *delimiters, char ***argvp);
int parseandredirectin(char *s);
int parseandredirectout(char *s);

void executeredirect(char *s, int in, int out) {
   char **chargv;
   char *pin;
   char *pout;

   if (in && ((pin = strchr(s, '<')) != NULL) &&
       out && ((pout = strchr(s, '>')) != NULL) && (pin > pout) ) {
      if (parseandredirectin(s) == -1) { /* redirect input is last on line */
         perror("Failed to redirect input");
         return;
      }
      in = 0;
   }
   if (out && (parseandredirectout(s) == -1))
      perror("Failed to redirect output");
   else if (in && (parseandredirectin(s) == -1))
      perror("Failed to redirect input");
   else if (makeargv(s, " \t", &chargv) <= 0)
      fprintf(stderr,"Failed to parse command line\n");
   else {
      execvp(chargv[0], chargv);
      perror("Failed to execute command");
   }
   exit(1);
}
```

Program 11.7 ─────────────────────────────────────── `executeredirect.c`

11.4 Signal Handling in the Foreground

Most shells support job control that allows users to terminate running processes and move processes between the foreground and the background. The ordinary user may not be explicitly aware that signals control these actions.

Suppose a user enters Ctrl-C to terminate a running process. The terminal device driver buffers and interprets characters as they are typed from the keyboard. If the driver encounters the `intr` character (usually Ctrl-C), it sends a `SIGINT` signal. In normal shell operation, Ctrl-C causes the executing command to be terminated but does not cause the shell to exit.

Program 11.8 ——————————————————————— `ush3.c`

A shell that does not exit on SIGINT *or* SIGQUIT.

```c
#include <limits.h>
#include <signal.h>
#include <stdio.h>
#include <string.h>
#include <unistd.h>
#include <sys/types.h>
#include <sys/wait.h>
#define PROMPT_STRING "ush3>>"
#define QUIT_STRING "q"

void executecmd(char *incmd);
int signalsetup(struct sigaction *def, sigset_t *mask, void (*handler)(int));

int main (void) {
   sigset_t blockmask;
   pid_t childpid;
   struct sigaction defaction;
   char inbuf[MAX_CANON];
   int len;

   if (signalsetup(&defaction, &blockmask, SIG_IGN) == -1) {
      perror("Failed to set up shell signal handling");
      return 1;
   }
   if (sigprocmask(SIG_BLOCK, &blockmask, NULL) == -1) {
      perror("Failed to block signals");
      return 1;
   }

   for( ; ; ) {
      if (fputs(PROMPT_STRING, stdout) == EOF)
         continue;
      if (fgets(inbuf, MAX_CANON, stdin) == NULL)
         continue;
      len = strlen(inbuf);
      if (inbuf[len - 1] == '\n')
         inbuf[len - 1] = 0;
      if (strcmp(inbuf, QUIT_STRING) == 0)
         break;
      if ((childpid = fork()) == -1) {
         perror("Failed to fork child to execute command");
      } else if (childpid == 0) {
         if ((sigaction(SIGINT, &defaction, NULL) == -1) ||
             (sigaction(SIGQUIT, &defaction, NULL) == -1) ||
             (sigprocmask(SIG_UNBLOCK, &blockmask, NULL) == -1)) {
            perror("Failed to set signal handling for command ");
            return 1;
         }
         executecmd(inbuf);
         return 1;
      }
      wait(NULL);
   }
   return 0;
}
```

Program 11.8 ——————————————————————— `ush3.c`

If a user enters Ctrl-C with `ush2` in Program 11.2, the shell takes the default action, which is to terminate the shell. The shell should not exit under these circumstances. Program 11.8 shows a modification of `ush2` that ignores `SIGINT` and `SIGQUIT`.

After setting up various signal handling structures by calling `signalsetup`, `ush3` ignores and blocks `SIGINT` and `SIGQUIT`. The `ush3` shell forks a child as before. The key implementation point here is that the child must restore the handlers for `SIGINT` and `SIGQUIT` to their defaults before executing the command. Program 11.9 shows the `signalsetup` function that initializes various signal structures to block `SIGINT` and `SIGQUIT`.

Program 11.9 ─────────────────────────────────────── `signalsetup.c`

A function for setting up signal structures for `ush3`.

```
#include <signal.h>
#include <stdio.h>

int signalsetup(struct sigaction *def, sigset_t *mask, void (*handler)(int)) {
   struct sigaction catch;

   catch.sa_handler = handler;  /* Set up signal structures  */
   def->sa_handler = SIG_DFL;
   catch.sa_flags = 0;
   def->sa_flags = 0;
   if ((sigemptyset(&(def->sa_mask)) == -1) ||
       (sigemptyset(&(catch.sa_mask)) == -1) ||
       (sigaddset(&(catch.sa_mask), SIGINT) == -1) ||
       (sigaddset(&(catch.sa_mask), SIGQUIT) == -1) ||
       (sigaction(SIGINT, &catch, NULL) == -1) ||
       (sigaction(SIGQUIT, &catch, NULL) == -1) ||
       (sigemptyset(mask) == -1) ||
       (sigaddset(mask, SIGINT) == -1) ||
       (sigaddset(mask, SIGQUIT) == -1))
      return -1;
   return 0;
}
```

Program 11.9 ─────────────────────────────────────── `signalsetup.c`

◻ Exercise 11.15

If a user enters Ctrl-C while `ush3` in Program 11.8 is executing `fgets`, nothing appears until the return key is pressed. What happens if the user enters Ctrl-C in the middle of a command line?

Answer:

When the user enters Ctrl-C in the middle of a command line, some systems display the symbols `^C`. All the characters on the line before entry of Ctrl-C are ignored because the terminal driver empties the input buffer when Ctrl-C is entered (canonical input mode). These characters still appear on the current input line because `ush3` does not redisplay the prompt.

☐ Exercise 11.16

The parent process of ush3 ignores and blocks SIGINT and SIGQUIT. The child unblocks these signals after resetting their handlers to the default. Why is this necessary?

Answer:

Suppose the parent does not block SIGINT and the operating system delivers a SIGINT signal before ush3 restores the SIGINT handler to the default. Since the ush3 child ignores SIGINT, the child continues to execute the command after the user enters Ctrl-C.

The ush3 implementation isn't the final answer to correct shell signal handling. In fact, the shell should catch SIGINT rather than ignore it. Also, the parent in ush3 has SIGINT and SIGQUIT blocked at all times. In fact, the parent should have them unblocked and block them only during certain critical time periods. Remember that ignoring is different from blocking. Ignore a signal by setting the signal handler to be SIG_IGN, and block a signal by setting a flag in the signal mask. Blocked signals are not delivered to the process but are held for later delivery.

In ush4, the parent shell and the child command handle the SIGINT in different ways. The parent shell clears the input line and goes back to the prompt, which the shell accomplishes with calls to sigsetjmp and siglongjmp.

The strategy for the child is different. When the child is forked, it inherits the signal mask and has a copy of the signal handler from the parent. The child should not go to the prompt if a signal occurs. Instead, the child should take the default action, which is to exit. To accomplish this, the parent blocks the signal before the fork. The child then installs the default action before unblocking the signal. When the child executes execvp, the default action is automatically installed since execvp restores any signals being caught to have their default actions. The program cannot afford to wait until execvp automatically installs the default action. The reason is that the child needs to unblock the signal before it executes execvp and a signal may come in between unblocking the signal and the execvp.

The parent shell in Program 11.10 uses sigsetjmp, discussed in Section 8.7, to return to the prompt when it receives Ctrl-C. The sigsetjmp function stores the signal mask and current environment in a designated jump buffer. When the signal handler calls siglongjmp with that jump buffer, the environment is restored and control is transferred to the point of the sigsetjmp call. Program 11.10 sets the jumptoprompt point just above the shell prompt. When called directly, sigsetjmp returns 0. When called through siglongjmp, sigsetjmp returns a nonzero value. This distinction allows the shell to output a newline when a signal has occurred. The siglongjmp call pops the stack and restores the register values to those at the point from which the sigsetjmp was originally called.

In the shells discussed in this chapter we do not need to worry about function calls that are interrupted by a signal. No signal handler in any of these shells returns. Instead, the shells call `siglongjmp`, so no function has an opportunity to set `errno` to `EINTR`. Notice also that ush4 executes the command, even if it could not successfully block `SIGINT` and `SIGQUIT`.

─ **Program 11.10** ──────────────────────────────────── **ush4.c** ─
A shell that uses <code>siglongjmp</code> to handle Ctrl-C.

```c
#include <limits.h>
#include <setjmp.h>
#include <signal.h>
#include <stdio.h>
#include <string.h>
#include <unistd.h>
#include <sys/types.h>
#include <sys/wait.h>
#define PROMPT_STRING "ush4>>"
#define QUIT_STRING "q"

void executecmd(char *incmd);
int signalsetup(struct sigaction *def, sigset_t *mask, void (*handler)(int));
static sigjmp_buf jumptoprompt;
static volatile sig_atomic_t okaytojump = 0;

/* ARGSUSED */
static void jumphd(int signalnum) {
   if (!okaytojump) return;
   okaytojump = 0;
   siglongjmp(jumptoprompt, 1);
}

int main (void) {
   sigset_t blockmask;
   pid_t childpid;
   struct sigaction defhandler;
   int len;
   char inbuf[MAX_CANON];

   if (signalsetup(&defhandler, &blockmask, jumphd) == -1) {
      perror("Failed to set up shell signal handling");
      return 1;
   }

   for( ; ; ) {
       if ((sigsetjmp(jumptoprompt, 1)) &&    /* if return from signal, \n */
          (fputs("\n", stdout) == EOF) )
          continue;
      wait(NULL);
      okaytojump = 1;
      if (fputs(PROMPT_STRING, stdout) == EOF)
          continue;
      if (fgets(inbuf, MAX_CANON, stdin) == NULL)
          continue;
```

```
        len = strlen(inbuf);
        if (inbuf[len - 1] == '\n')
            inbuf[len - 1] = 0;
        if (strcmp(inbuf, QUIT_STRING) == 0)
            break;
        if (sigprocmask(SIG_BLOCK, &blockmask, NULL) == -1)
            perror("Failed to block signals");
        if ((childpid = fork()) == -1)
            perror("Failed to fork");
        else if (childpid == 0) {
            if ((sigaction(SIGINT, &defhandler, NULL) == -1) ||
                (sigaction(SIGQUIT, &defhandler, NULL) == -1) ||
                (sigprocmask(SIG_UNBLOCK, &blockmask, NULL) == -1)) {
                perror("Failed to set signal handling for command ");
                return 1;
            }
            executecmd(inbuf);
            return 1;
        }
        if (sigprocmask(SIG_UNBLOCK, &blockmask, NULL) == -1)
            perror("Failed to unblock signals");
    }
    return 0;
}
```

Program 11.10 ———————————————————————— `ush4.c`

Compilers sometimes allocate local variables in registers for efficiency. It is important that variables that should not be changed when `siglongjmp` is executed are not stored in registers. Use the `volatile` qualifier from ISO C to suppress this type of assignment.

Program 11.10 uses the same signal handler for both `SIGINT` and `SIGQUIT`. Therefore, `signalsetup` sets the signals to block both of them when they are caught. It wasn't necessary to block these signals in `ush3`, but it did not hurt to do so. The child of Program 11.10 installs the default action before unblocking the signal after `fork`. The parent shell only blocks `SIGINT` and `SIGQUIT` when it is creating a child to run the command.

☐ Exercise 11.17

Why did we move `wait` in `ush4` from the bottom of the loop to the top of the loop?

Answer:

If `wait` is at the bottom of the loop and you kill a child with Ctrl-C, the shell jumps back to the start of the loop without waiting for the child. When a new command is entered, the shell will wait for the child that was killed instead of waiting for the new command to complete.

☐ Exercise 11.18

Why can't we fix the problem described in Exercise 11.17 by restarting `wait` when `errno` is `EINTR`?

Answer:

When a function like `wait` is interrupted by the signal, it returns only when the signal handler returns. In this case, the signal handler is executing a `siglongjmp`, so `wait` does not return when the signal is caught.

11.5 Process Groups, Sessions and Controlling Terminals

The previous section implemented signal handling for `ush` with simple commands. Signal handling for pipelines and background processes requires additional machinery. Pipelines need process groups, and background processes need sessions and controlling terminals.

11.5.1 Process Groups

A *process group* is a collection of processes established for purposes such as signal delivery. Each process has a *process group ID* that identifies the process group to which it belongs. Both the `kill` command and the `kill` function treat a negative process ID value as a process group ID and send a signal to each member of the corresponding process group.

■ Example 11.19

The following command sends `SIGINT` to the process group `3245`.

```
kill -INT -3245
```

In contrast, the following command sends `SIGINT` just to the process `3245`.

```
kill -INT 3245
```

The *process group leader* is a process whose process ID has the same value as the process group ID. A process group persists as long as any process is in the group. Thus, a process group may not have a leader if the leader dies or joins another group.

A process can change its process group with `setpgid`. The `setpgid` function sets the process group ID of process `pid` to have process group ID `pgid`. It uses the process ID of the calling process if `pid` is 0. If `pgid` is 0, the process specified by `pid` becomes a group leader.

SYNOPSIS

```
#include <unistd.h>

int setpgid(pid_t pid, pid_t pgid);
```

                                                                                    POSIX

The `setpgid` function returns 0 if successful. If unsuccessful, `setpgid` returns −1 and sets `errno`. The following table lists the mandatory errors for `setpgid`.

errno	cause
EACCES	pid corresponds to a child that has already called exec
EINVAL	pgid is negative or has an unsupported value
EPERM	pid is the process ID of a session leader, or
	pid is the process ID of a child process not in the caller's
	session, or pgid does not match pid and there is no process
	with a process ID matching pgid in the caller's session
ESRCH	pid does not match the caller's process ID or
	that of any of its children

When a child is created with fork, it gets a new process ID but it inherits the process group ID of its parent. The parent can use setpgid to change the group ID of a child as long as the child has not yet called exec. A child process can also give itself a new process group ID by setting its process group ID equal to its process ID.

■ **Example 11.20**

The following code segment forks a child that calls executecmd. The child places itself in a new process group.

```
pid = fork();
if ((pid == 0)  && (setpgid(getpid(), getpid()) != -1))) {
   executecmd(cmd);
   return 1;
}
```

Either or both of the calls to getpid could be replaced with 0.

□ **Exercise 11.21**

What can go wrong with the following alternative to the code of Example 11.20?

```
pid = fork();
if ((pid > 0) && (setpgid(pid, pid) == -1)) {
   perror("Failed to set child's process group");
else if (pid == 0) {
    executecmd(cmd);
    return 1;
}
```

Answer:
The alternative code has a race condition. If the child performs execvp in executecmd before the parent calls setpgid, the code fails.

The getpgrp function returns the process group ID of the caller.

```
SYNOPSIS

  #include <unistd.h>

  pid_t getpgrp(void);
                                                              POSIX
```

No errors are defined for `getpgrp`.

The POSIX:XSI Extension also defines a `setpgrp` function that is similar to `setpgid`. However, `setpgrp` allows greater flexibility than is required for job control and may present a security risk.

11.5.2 Sessions

To make signal delivery transparent, POSIX uses sessions and controlling terminals. A *session* is a collection of process groups established for job control purposes. The creator of a session is called the *session leader*. We identify sessions by the process IDs of their leaders. Every process belongs to a session, which it inherits from its parent.

Each session may have a *controlling terminal* associated with it. A shell uses the controlling terminal of its session to interact with the user. A particular controlling terminal is associated with exactly one session. A session may have several process groups, but at any given time only one of these process groups can receive input from and send output to the controlling terminal. The designated process group is called the *foreground process group* or the *foreground job*. The other process groups in the session are called *background process groups* or *background jobs*. The main purpose of job control is to change which process group is in the foreground. The background process groups are not affected by keyboard input from the controlling terminal of the session.

Use the `ctermid` function to obtain the name of the controlling terminal. The `ctermid` function returns a pointer to a string that corresponds to the pathname of the controlling terminal for the current process. This string may be in a statically generated area if s is a `NULL` pointer. If s is not `NULL`, it should point to a character array of at least `L_ctermid` bytes. The `ctermid` function copies a string representing the controlling terminal into that array.

SYNOPSIS

```
#include <stdio.h>

char *ctermid(char *s);
```
                                                                    POSIX:CX

The `ctermid` function returns an empty string if it is unsuccessful.

☐ Exercise 11.22

What happens if you enter Ctrl-C while executing the following command string in `ush4`?

```
ls -l | sort -n +4 | more
```

Answer:

The `SIGINT` signal is delivered to the three child processes executing the three filters as well as to the parent shell process because all of these processes are in the foreground process group. The parent catches SIGINT with jumphd; the three children take the default action and terminate.

Section 3.6 introduced background processes. The & character at the end of the command line designates a command or pipeline to be run as a background process group in most shells.

☐ Exercise 11.23

What happens if you enter Ctrl-C while the following command is executing in the C shell?

```
ls -l | sort -n +4 | more &
```

Answer:

None of the processes in the pipeline receive the SIGINT signal, since the pipeline is in the background and has no connection to the controlling terminal.

A process can create a new session with itself as the leader by calling setsid. The setsid function also creates a new process group with the process group ID equal to the process ID of the caller. The calling process is the only one in the new process group and the new session. The session has no controlling terminal.

```
SYNOPSIS

   #include <unistd.h>

   pid_t setsid(void);
                                                           POSIX
```

If successful, setsid returns the new value of the process group ID. If unsuccessful, setsid returns (pid_t)−1 and sets errno. The setsid function sets errno to EPERM if the caller is already a process group leader.

A process can discover session IDs by calling getsid. The getsid function takes a process group ID parameter, pid, and returns the process group ID of the process that is the session leader of the process specified by pid. If 0, pid specifies the calling process.

```
SYNOPSIS

   #include <unistd.h>

   pid_t getsid(pid_t pid);
                                                        POSIX:XSI
```

If successful, getsid returns a process group ID. If unsuccessful, getsid returns −1 and sets errno. The following table lists the mandatory errors for getsid.

errno	cause
EPERM	process specified by `pid` is not in the same session as the calling process and the implementation does not allow access to the process group ID of that session leader
ESRCH	no process corresponds to `pid`

Figure 11.1 shows a shell with several process groups. Each solid rectangle represents a process with its process ID, process group ID and the session ID. All of the processes have session ID 1357, the process ID and session ID of the shell. The process group ID is the same as the process ID of one of its members, the process group leader.

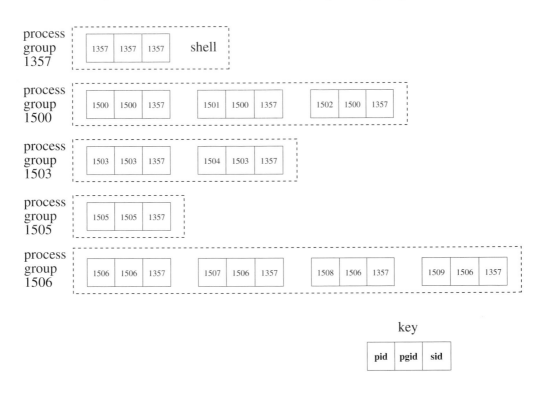

Figure 11.1: Five process groups for session 1357.

■ Example 11.24

The following sequence of commands might give rise to the process group structure of Figure 11.1.

```
ls -l | sort -n +4 | grep testfile > testfile.out &
grep process | sort  > process.out &
du . > du.out &
cat /etc/passwd | grep users | sort | head > users.out &
```

□ **Exercise 11.25**

Write a short program called `showid` that takes one command-line argument. The `showid` program outputs to standard error a single line with its command-line argument, its process ID, parent process ID, process group ID and session ID. After the display, `showid` starts an infinite loop that does nothing. Execute the following commands to verify how your login shell handles process groups and sessions for pipelines.

      `showid 1 | showid 2 | showid 3`

Which process in the pipeline is the process group leader? Is the shell in the same process group as the pipeline? Which processes in the pipeline are children of the shell and which are grandchildren? How does this change if the pipeline is started in the background?

Answer:

The results vary depending on the shell that is used. Some shells make all the processes children of the shell. Others have only the first or last process in the pipeline as a child of the shell and the rest are grandchildren. Either the first or the last process may be the process group leader. If a shell does not support job control, it is possible for the shell to be the process group leader of the pipeline unless the pipeline is started in the background.

Summary:

- The shell is a session leader.
- All processes created by the shell are in this session.
- All processes created on a single command line are in the same process group.
- If the shell supports job control or the command line is started in the background, a new process group is formed for these processes.
- One of the process groups of the shell is the foreground process group and can interact with the controlling terminal.

11.6 Background Processes in `ush`

The main operational properties of a background process are that the shell does not wait for it to complete and that it is not terminated by a `SIGINT` sent from the keyboard. A background process appears to run independently of the terminal. This section explores handling of signals for background processes. A correctly working shell must prevent terminal-generated signals and input from being delivered to a background process and must handle the problem of having a child divorced from its controlling terminal.

    Program 11.11 shows a modification of `ush4` that allows a command to be executed in the background. An ampersand (`&`) at the end of a command line specifies that `ush5` should run the command in the background. The program assumes that there is at most one `&` on

the line and that, if present, it is at the end. The shell determines whether the command
is to be executed in the background before forking the child, since both parent and child
both must know this information. If the command is executed in the background, the child
calls setpgid so that it is no longer in the foreground process group of its session. The
parent shell does not wait for background children.

Program 11.11 ── **ush5.c**

*A shell that attempts to handle background processes by changing their process
groups.*

```c
#include <limits.h>
#include <setjmp.h>
#include <signal.h>
#include <stdio.h>
#include <string.h>
#include <unistd.h>
#include <sys/types.h>
#include <sys/wait.h>
#define BACK_SYMBOL '&'
#define PROMPT_STRING "ush5>>"
#define QUIT_STRING "q"

void executecmd(char *incmd);
int signalsetup(struct sigaction *def, sigset_t *mask, void (*handler)(int));

static sigjmp_buf jumptoprompt;
static volatile sig_atomic_t okaytojump = 0;

/* ARGSUSED */
static void jumphd(int signalnum) {
   if (!okaytojump) return;
   okaytojump = 0;
   siglongjmp(jumptoprompt, 1);
}

int main (void) {
   char *backp;
   sigset_t blockmask;
   pid_t childpid;
   struct sigaction defhandler;
   int inbackground;
   char inbuf[MAX_CANON];
   int len;

   if (signalsetup(&defhandler, &blockmask, jumphd) == -1) {
      perror("Failed to set up shell signal handling");
      return 1;
   }

   for( ; ; ) {
      if ((sigsetjmp(jumptoprompt, 1)) &&    /* if return from signal, \n */
          (fputs("\n", stdout) == EOF) )
         continue;
      okaytojump = 1;
      printf("%d",(int)getpid());
```

```
        if (fputs(PROMPT_STRING, stdout) == EOF)
            continue;
        if (fgets(inbuf, MAX_CANON, stdin) == NULL)
            continue;
        len = strlen(inbuf);
        if (inbuf[len - 1] == '\n')
            inbuf[len - 1] = 0;
        if (strcmp(inbuf, QUIT_STRING) == 0)
            break;
        if ((backp = strchr(inbuf, BACK_SYMBOL)) == NULL)
            inbackground = 0;
        else {
            inbackground = 1;
            *backp = 0;
        }
        if (sigprocmask(SIG_BLOCK, &blockmask, NULL) == -1)
            perror("Failed to block signals");
        if ((childpid = fork()) == -1)
            perror("Failed to fork");
        else if (childpid == 0) {
            if (inbackground && (setpgid(0, 0) == -1))
                return 1;
            if ((sigaction(SIGINT, &defhandler, NULL) == -1) ||
                (sigaction(SIGQUIT, &defhandler, NULL) == -1) ||
                (sigprocmask(SIG_UNBLOCK, &blockmask, NULL) == -1)) {
                perror("Failed to set signal handling for command ");
                return 1;
            }
            executecmd(inbuf);
            return 1;
        }
        if (sigprocmask(SIG_UNBLOCK, &blockmask, NULL) == -1)
            perror("Failed to unblock signals");
        if (!inbackground)     /* only wait for child not in background */
            wait(NULL);
    }
    return 0;
}
```

Program 11.11 ———————————————————————————— `ush5.c`

☐ **Exercise 11.26**

Execute the command `ls &` several times under `ush5`. Then, execute `ps -a` (still under this shell). Observe that the previous `ls` processes still appear as `<defunct>`. Exit from the shell and execute `ps -a` again. Explain the status of these processes before and after the shell exits.

Answer:

Since no process has waited for them, the background processes become zombie processes. They stay in this state until the shell exits. At that time, `init` becomes the parent of these processes, and since `init` periodically waits for its children, the zombies eventually die.

The shell in Program 11.12 fixes the problem of zombie or defunct processes. When a command is to be run in the background, the shell does an extra call to `fork`. The first child exits immediately, leaving the background process as an orphan that can then be adopted by `init`. The shell now waits for all children, including background processes, since the background children exit immediately and the grandchildren are adopted by `init`.

Program 11.12 ───────────────────────────────────── `ush6.c`
                       A shell that cleans up zombie background processes.

```c
#include <errno.h>
#include <limits.h>
#include <setjmp.h>
#include <signal.h>
#include <stdio.h>
#include <string.h>
#include <unistd.h>
#include <sys/types.h>
#include <sys/wait.h>
#define BACK_SYMBOL '&'
#define PROMPT_STRING ">>"
#define QUIT_STRING "q"

void executecmd(char *incmd);
int signalsetup(struct sigaction *def, struct sigaction *catch,
                sigset_t *mask, void (*handler)(int));

static sigjmp_buf jumptoprompt;
static volatile sig_atomic_t okaytojump = 0;

/* ARGSUSED */
static void jumphd(int signalnum) {
   if (!okaytojump) return;
   okaytojump = 0;
   siglongjmp(jumptoprompt, 1);
}

int main (void) {
   char *backp;
   sigset_t blockmask;
   pid_t childpid;
   struct sigaction defhandler, handler;
   int inbackground;
   char inbuf[MAX_CANON+1];

   if (signalsetup(&defhandler, &handler, &blockmask, jumphd) == -1) {
      perror("Failed to set up shell signal handling");
      return 1;
   }

   for( ; ; ) {
      if ((sigsetjmp(jumptoprompt, 1)) &&    /* if return from signal, \n */
          (fputs("\n", stdout) == EOF) )
         continue;
      if (fputs(PROMPT_STRING, stdout) == EOF)
         continue;
```

```
      if (fgets(inbuf, MAX_CANON, stdin) == NULL)
         continue;
      if (*(inbuf + strlen(inbuf) - 1) == '\n')
         *(inbuf + strlen(inbuf) - 1) = 0;
      if (strcmp(inbuf, QUIT_STRING) == 0)
         break;
      if ((backp = strchr(inbuf, BACK_SYMBOL)) == NULL)
         inbackground = 0;
      else {
         inbackground = 1;
         *backp = 0;
      if (sigprocmask(SIG_BLOCK, &blockmask, NULL) == -1)
         perror("Failed to block signals");
      if ((childpid = fork()) == -1) {
         perror("Failed to fork child to execute command");
         return 1;
      } else if (childpid == 0) {
         if (inbackground && (fork() != 0) && (setpgid(0, 0) == -1))
            return 1;
         if ((sigaction(SIGINT, &defhandler, NULL) == -1) ||
             (sigaction(SIGQUIT, &defhandler, NULL) == -1) ||
             (sigprocmask(SIG_UNBLOCK, &blockmask, NULL) == -1)) {
            perror("Failed to set signal handling for command ");
            return 1;
         }
         executecmd(inbuf);
         perror("Failed to execute command");
         return 1;
      }
      if (sigprocmask(SIG_UNBLOCK, &blockmask, NULL) == -1)
         perror("Failed to unblock signals");
      wait(NULL);
   }
   return 0;
}
```

Program 11.12 ─── **ush6.c**

☐ **Exercise 11.27**

Execute a long-running background process such as `rusers &` under the shell given in Program 11.12. What happens when you enter Ctrl-C?

Answer:

The background process is not interrupted because it is not part of the foreground process group. The parent shell catches `SIGINT` and jumps back to the `main` prompt.

☐ **Exercise 11.28**

Use the `showid` function from Exercise 11.25 to determine which of three processes in a pipeline becomes the process group leader and which are children of the shell in `ush6`. Do this for pipelines started both in the foreground and background.

Answer:

If the parent starts the pipeline in the foreground, all the processes have the same process group as the shell and the shell is the process group leader. The first process in the pipeline is a child of the shell and the others are grandchildren. If the shell starts the pipeline in the background, the first process in the pipeline is the process group leader. Its parent will eventually be `init`. The other processes are children or grandchildren of the first process in the pipeline.

The zombie child problem is more complicated if the shell does job control. In this case, the shell must be able to detect whether the background process is stopped because of a signal (e.g., `SIGSTOP`). The `waitpid` function has an option for detecting children stopped by signals, but not for detecting grandchildren. The background process of Program 11.12 is a grandchild because of the extra `fork` call, so ush6 cannot detect it.

Program 11.13 shows a direct approach, using `waitpid`, for handling zombies. To detect whether background processes are stopped for a signal, ush7 uses `waitpid` with the `WNOHANG` for background processes rather than forking an extra child. The –1 for the first argument to `waitpid` means to wait for any process. If the command is not a background command, ush7 explicitly waits for the corresponding child to complete.

Program 11.13 ─────────────────────────────── `ush7.c`

A shell that handles zombie background processes by using `waitpid`.

```
#include <limits.h>
#include <setjmp.h>
#include <signal.h>
#include <stdio.h>
#include <string.h>
#include <unistd.h>
#include <sys/types.h>
#include <sys/wait.h>
#define BACK_SYMBOL '&'
#define PROMPT_STRING "ush7>>"
#define QUIT_STRING "q"

void executecmd(char *incmd);
int signalsetup(struct sigaction *def, sigset_t *mask, void (*handler)(int));
static sigjmp_buf jumptoprompt;
static volatile sig_atomic_t okaytojump = 0;

/* ARGSUSED */
static void jumphd(int signalnum) {
   if (!okaytojump) return;
   okaytojump = 0;
   siglongjmp(jumptoprompt, 1);
}

int main (void) {
   char *backp;
   sigset_t blockmask;
   pid_t childpid;
```

```
      struct sigaction defhandler;
      int inbackground;
      char inbuf[MAX_CANON];
      int len;

      if (signalsetup(&defhandler, &blockmask, jumphd) == -1) {
         perror("Failed to set up shell signal handling");
         return 1;
      }

      for( ; ; ) {
         if ((sigsetjmp(jumptoprompt, 1)) &&    /* if return from signal, newline */
             (fputs("\n", stdout) == EOF) )
            continue;
         okaytojump = 1;
         printf("%d",(int)getpid());
         if (fputs(PROMPT_STRING, stdout) == EOF)
            continue;
         if (fgets(inbuf, MAX_CANON, stdin) == NULL)
            continue;
         len = strlen(inbuf);
         if (inbuf[len - 1] == '\n')
            inbuf[len - 1] = 0;
         if (strcmp(inbuf, QUIT_STRING) == 0)
            break;
         if ((backp = strchr(inbuf, BACK_SYMBOL)) == NULL)
            inbackground = 0;
         else {
            inbackground = 1;
            *backp = 0;
         }
         if (sigprocmask(SIG_BLOCK, &blockmask, NULL) == -1)
            perror("Failed to block signals");
         if ((childpid = fork()) == -1)
            perror("Failed to fork");
         else if (childpid == 0) {
            if (inbackground && (setpgid(0, 0) == -1))
               return 1;
            if ((sigaction(SIGINT, &defhandler, NULL) == -1) ||
                (sigaction(SIGQUIT, &defhandler, NULL) == -1) ||
                (sigprocmask(SIG_UNBLOCK, &blockmask, NULL) == -1)) {
               perror("Failed to set signal handling for command ");
               return 1;
            }
            executecmd(inbuf);
            return 1;
         }
         if (sigprocmask(SIG_UNBLOCK, &blockmask, NULL) == -1)
            perror("Failed to unblock signals");
         if (!inbackground)            /* wait explicitly for the foreground process */
            waitpid(childpid, NULL, 0);
         while (waitpid(-1, NULL, WNOHANG) > 0);    /* wait for background procs */
      }
      return 0;
}
```

Program 11.13 ———————————————————————————— **ush7.c**

☐ **Exercise 11.29**

Repeat Exercise 11.28 for Program 11.13.

Answer:

The results are the same as for Exercise 11.28 except that when started in the background, the first process in the pipeline is a child of the shell.

☐ **Exercise 11.30**

Compare the behavior of ush6 and ush7 under the following scenario. Start a foreground process that ignores SIGINT. While that process is executing, enter Ctrl-C.

Answer:

The shell of ush6 jumps back to the main loop before waiting for the process. If this shell executes another long-running command and the first command terminates, the shell waits for the wrong command and returns to the prompt before the second command completes. This difficulty does not arise in ush7 since the ush7 shell waits for a specific foreground process.

11.7 Job Control

A shell is said to have *job control* if it allows a user to move the foreground process group into the background and to move a process group from the background to the foreground. Job control involves changing the foreground process group of a controlling terminal.

The tcgetpgrp function returns the process group ID of the foreground process group of a particular controlling terminal. To obtain an open file descriptor for the controlling terminal, open the pathname obtained from the ctermid function described in Section 11.5.

```
SYNOPSIS

   #include <unistd.h>

   pid_t tcgetpgrp(int fildes);
                                                              POSIX
```

If successful, the tcgetpgrp function returns the process group ID of the foreground process group associated with the terminal. If the terminal has no foreground process group, tcgetpgrp returns a value greater than 1 that doesn't match any existing process group ID. If unsuccessful, the tcgetpgrp function returns −1 and sets errno. The following table lists the mandatory errors for tcgetpgrp.

errno	cause
EBADF	fildes is invalid
ENOTTY	caller does not have a controlling terminal, or fildes does not correspond to a controlling terminal

The `tcsetpgrp` function sets the foreground process group of the controlling terminal associated with `fildes` to `pgid_id`. If a background process calls `tcsetpgrp` on a `fildes` associated with its controlling terminal, its process group receives a `SIGTTOU` signal, provided that this process is not blocking or ignoring `SIGTTOU`.

SYNOPSIS

```
#include <unistd.h>

int tcsetpgrp(int fildes, pid_t pgid_id);
```

POSIX

If successful, `tcsetpgrp` returns 0. If unsuccessful, `tcsetpgrp` returns –1 and sets `errno`. The following table lists the mandatory errors for `tcsetpgrp`.

`errno`	cause
EBADF	`fildes` is invalid
EINVAL	implementation does not support the value of `pgid_id`
ENOTTY	caller does not have a controlling terminal, or
	`fildes` does not correspond to a controlling terminal, or
	controlling terminal is no longer associated with the
	session of the caller
EPERM	value of `pgid_id` is supported but does not match the
	process group ID of any process in the session of the caller

In addition to running processes in the foreground and background, job control allows users to selectively stop processes and resume their execution later. For example, you may want to run a long job in the background but periodically halt it to examine its status or provide input. The C shell and the KornShell allow job control, as do most shells under Linux, but the Bourne shell does not. This section describes job control in the C shell. The Linux shells and the KornShell are almost identical with respect to job control.

A job consists of the processes needed to run a single command line. When a shell starts a job in the background, it assigns a job number and displays the job number and process IDs of the processes in the job. If a pipeline is started in the background, all processes in the pipeline have the same job number. The job number is typically a small integer. If there are no other jobs in the background, the shell assigns the command job number 1. Generally, shells assign a background job a number that is one greater than the current largest background job number.

The `jobs` command displays the jobs running under a shell.

■ Example 11.31

The following commands illustrate job control for the C shell. The shell displays the prompt `ospmt%`. The commands appear after this prompt. The shell produces the other messages shown.

```
ospmt% du . | sort -n > duout &
[1] 23145 23146
ospmt% grep mybook *.tex > mybook.out &
[2] 23147
ospmt% rusers | grep myboss > myboss.out &
[3] 23148 23149
ospmt% jobs
[1]   + Running          du . | sort -n > duout
[2]   - Running          grep mybook *.tex > mybook.out
[3]     Running          rusers | grep myboss > myboss.out
```

The `jobs` command shows three running background jobs. The job number is at the start of the line in square brackets. If the second job finishes first, the shell displays the following line when the user presses the return.

```
[2]     Done               grep mybook *.tex > mybook.out
```

If at that time the user executes another `jobs` command, the following output appears.

```
[1]   + Running          du . | sort -n > duout
[3]   - Running          rusers | grep myboss > myboss.out
```

You may refer to job n by `%n` in various shell commands. Example 11.31 shows a + after the job number of job `[1]`, meaning that it is the *current job* and is the default for the `fg` and `bg` commands. The - represents the previous job.

■ Example 11.32

The following command kills job 2 without referring to process IDs.

```
kill -KILL %2
```

A background job can be either running or stopped. To stop a running job, use the `stop` command. The stopped job becomes the current job and is suspended.

■ Example 11.33

The following command stops job two.

```
stop %2
```

To start a stopped job running in the background, use the `bg` command. In this case, `bg` or `bg %` or `bg %2` all work, since job 2 is the current job.

Use the `fg` command to move a background job (either running or stopped) into the foreground, and the `SIGSTOP` character (typically Ctrl-Z) to move the foreground job into the background in the stopped state. The combination Ctrl-Z and `bg` makes the foreground job a running background job.

Since `fg`, `bg` and `jobs` are built into the shell, these commands may not have their own man pages. To get information on these commands in the C shell, execute `man csh`.

☐ **Exercise 11.34**

Experiment with job control (assuming that it is available). Move processes in and out of the foreground.

A shell that supports job control must keep track of all foreground and background process groups in its session. When the terminal generates a SIGSTOP interrupt (usually in response to Ctrl-Z), the foreground process group is placed in the stopped state. How should the shell get back in control? Fortunately, waitpid blocks the parent shell until the state of one of its children changes. Thus, an appropriate call to waitpid by the parent shell allows the shell to regain control after the foreground process group is suspended. The shell can start a suspended process group by sending it the SIGCONT signal. If the shell wants to restart that group in the foreground, it must use tcsetpgrp to tell the controlling terminal what the foreground process group is. Since a given process or process group can run in the foreground or the background at different times during its execution, each child command must start a new process group regardless of whether it is started in the background or foreground.

One job control problem not yet addressed in this discussion is how a process obtains input from standard input. If the process is in the foreground, there is no problem. If there is no job control and the process is started in the background, its standard input is redirected to /dev/null to prevent it from grabbing characters from the foreground process. This simple redirection does not work with job control. Once a process redirects standard input, it cannot use standard input to read from the original controlling terminal when brought to the foreground. The solution specified by POSIX is for the kernel to generate a SIGTTIN signal when a background process attempts to read from the controlling terminal. The default action for SIGTTIN stops the job. The shell detects a change in the status of the child when it executes waitpid and then displays a message. The user can then choose to move the process to the foreground so it can receive input.

Background jobs can write to standard error. If a background process attempts to write to standard output while standard output is still directed to the controlling terminal, the terminal device driver generates a SIGTTOU for the process. In this case, the c_lflag member of the struct termios structure for the terminal has the TOSTOP flag set. A user then has the option of moving the job to the foreground so that it can send output to the controlling terminal. If the process has redirected standard input and standard output, it does I/O from the redirected sources.

☐ **Exercise 11.35**

Write a simple program that writes to standard output. Start the program in the background under your regular shell and see if it can write to standard output without generating a SIGTTOU signal.

11.8 Job Control for `ush`

This section describes an implementation of job control for `ush`. Start by testing `ush7` in the following cases to make sure that it correctly handles the `SIGINT` and `SIGQUIT`.

1. Simple commands.
2. Incorrect commands.
3. Commands with standard input and output redirected.
4. Pipelines.
5. Background processes.
6. All of the above interrupted by Ctrl-C.

11.8.1 A job list object

To do job control, `ush` must keep track of its children. Use a list object similar to the one used in Program 2.9 to keep a program history. The nodes in the list should have the following structure.

```
typedef enum jstatus
        {FOREGROUND, BACKGROUND, STOPPED, DONE, TERMINATED}
    job_status_t;

typedef struct job_struct {
    char *cmdstring;
    pid_t pgid;
    int job;
    job_status_t jobstat;
    struct job_struct *next;
} joblist_t;

static joblist_t *jobhead = NULL;
static joblist_t *jobtail = NULL;
```

Place the list structure in a separate file along with the following functions to manipulate the job list.

`int add(pid_t pgid, char *cmd, job_status_t status);`
> Add the specified job to the list. The `pgid` is the process group ID, and `cmd` is the command string for the job. The `status` value can be either `FOREGROUND` or `BACKGROUND`. If successful, `add` returns the job number. If unsuccessful, `add` returns −1 and sets `errno`. It uses `getlargest` to determine the largest job number and uses a job number that is one greater than this.

`int delete(int job);`
> Remove the node corresponding to the specified job from the list. If successful, `delete` returns the job number. If unsuccessful, `delete` returns −1 and sets `errno`. Be sure to free all space associated with the deleted node.

`showjobs(void);`

> Output a list of jobs and each one's status. Use the following format.
>
> ```
> [job]     status         pgid        cmd
> ```

`int setstatus(int job, job_status_t status);`

> Set the status value of the node of the corresponding job. If successful, `setstatus` returns 0. If unsuccessful, `setstatus` returns −1 and sets `errno`.

`int getstatus(int job, job_status_t *pstatus);`

> Return the status value associated with the specified job in `*pstatus`. If successful, `getstatus` returns 0. If unsuccessful, `getstatus` returns −1 and sets `errno`.

`pid_t getprocess(int job);`

> Return the process group ID of the specified job. If `job` doesn't exist, `getprocess` returns 0.

`int getlargest(void);`

> Scan the job list for the largest job number currently in the list. The `getlargest` function returns the largest job number if any nodes are on the list or 0 if the list is empty.

Write a driver program to thoroughly test the list functions independently of `ush`.

11.8.2 The job list in `ush`

After the job list functions are working, add the job list object to `ush` as follows.

1. Each time `ush` forks a child to run a background process, it adds a node to the job list. It sets the `pgid` member of the `joblist_t` node to the value returned from `fork`. The process status is BACKGROUND.

2. If the command is executed in the background, `ush` outputs a message of the following form.

   ```
   [job]     pid1  pid2  ....
   ```

   `job` is the job number and `pid1`, `pid2` and so on are the process IDs of the children in the process group for the command. The parent `ush` knows only the process ID of the initial child, so the child that calls `executecmd` must produce this message.

3. The `ush` calls `showjobs` when a user enters the `jobs` command.

4. Replace the `waitpid` call in `ush` with a more sophisticated strategy by using `waitpid` in a loop with the WUNTRACED option. The WUNTRACED option specifies that `waitpid` should report the status of any stopped child whose status has not yet been reported. This report is necessary for implementing job control in the next stage.

Test ush with the job list. Do not add job control in this step. Execute the jobs command frequently to see the status of the background processes. Carefully experiment with an existing shell that has job control. Make sure that ush handles background and foreground processes similarly.

11.8.3 Job control in ush

Incorporate job control into ush by adding the following commands to ush in addition to the jobs command of the previous section.

stop	stop the current job
bg	start the current job running in the background
bg %n	start job n running in the background
fg %n	start job n running in the foreground
mykill -NUM %n	send the signal SIGNUM to job n

Some of these commands refer to the current job. When there are several jobs, one is *the current job*. The current job starts out as the first background job to be started. A user can make another job the current job by bringing it to the foreground with fg.

The ush shell now must handle SIGCONT, SIGTSTP, SIGTTIN and SIGTTOU in addition to SIGINT and SIGQUIT. When ush detects that a child has stopped because of a SIGTTIN or a SIGTTOU, it writes an informative message to standard error to notify the user that the child is waiting for input or output, respectively. The user can move that job to the foreground to read from or write to the controlling terminal.

Test the program thoroughly. Pay particular attention to how your regular shell does job control and adjust ush to look as similar as possible.

11.8.4 Process behavior in waiting for a pipeline

What happens when a shell starts a pipeline in the foreground and one of the processes in the pipeline terminates? The result depends on which process in the pipeline is the child of the shell.

☐ Exercise 11.36

Make a new version of showid from Exercise 11.28 on page 395 that sleeps for one minute after displaying the IDs. Call the new program showidsleep. Run ush7 with each of the following command lines. What happens?

```
showidsleep first | showid second
showid first | showidsleep second
```

Answer:
For the first command line, the shell displays the prompt after one minute since the first command in the pipeline is the child of the shell. For the second command

line, the shell displays the prompt immediately since it waits only for the first command in the pipeline. This is probably not the desired behavior. Typically, a pipeline consists of a sequence of filters, and the last one in the sequence is the last to finish.

☐ Exercise 11.37

How would you solve the problem described in Exercise 11.36?

Answer:

One solution would be to rewrite `executecmdpipe` so that the last command of the pipeline was executed by the first process created. A better solution would be to have all of the processes in the pipeline be children of the shell and have the shell wait for all of them.

11.9 Additional Reading

Books on C shell programming include *UNIX Shell Programming* by Arthur [6], *UNIX Shell Programming, Revised Edition* by Kochan and Wood [64] and *Portable Shell Programming* by Blinn [13]. *Learning the Korn Shell, 2nd ed.* by Rosenblatt [101] is a clear reference on the KornShell. Another book on the KornShell is *The New KornShell Command and Programming Language*, 2nd ed. by Bolsky and Korn [15]. *Using csh and tsch* by DuBois [33] is another general shell reference. *Linux Application Development* by Johnson and Troan [60] develops a shell called `ladsh` over several chapters to illustrate application programming concepts.

Part III

Concurrency

Chapter 12

POSIX Threads

One method of achieving parallelism is for multiple processes to cooperate and synchronize through shared memory or message passing. An alternative approach uses multiple threads of execution in a single address space. This chapter explains how threads are created, managed and used to solve simple problems. The chapter then presents an overview of basic thread management under the POSIX standard. The chapter discusses different thread models and explains how these models are accommodated under the standard.

Objectives

- Learn basic thread concepts
- Experiment with POSIX thread calls
- Explore threaded application design
- Use threads in unsynchronized applications
- Understand thread-safety and error handling

12.1 A Motivating Problem: Monitoring File Descriptors

A blocking read operation causes the calling process to block until input becomes available. Such blocking creates difficulties when a process expects input from more than one source, since the process has no way of knowing which file descriptor will produce the next input. The multiple file descriptor problem commonly appears in client-server programming because the server expects input from multiple clients. Six general approaches to monitoring multiple file descriptors for input under POSIX are as follows.

1. A separate process monitors each file descriptor (Program 4.11)
2. `select` (Program 4.12 and Program 4.14)
3. `poll` (Program 4.17)
4. Nonblocking I/O with polling (Example 4.39)
5. POSIX asynchronous I/O (Program 8.14 and Program 8.16)
6. A separate thread monitors each file descriptor (Section 12.2)

In the separate process approach, the original process forks a child process to handle each file descriptor. This approach works for descriptors representing independent I/O streams, since once forked, the children don't share any variables. If processing of the descriptors is not independent, the children may use shared memory or message passing to exchange information.

Approaches two and three use blocking calls (`select` or `poll`) to explicitly wait for I/O on the descriptors. Once the blocking call returns, the calling program handles each ready file descriptor in turn. The code can be complicated when some of the file descriptors close while others remain open (e.g., Program 4.17). Furthermore, the program can do no useful processing while blocked.

The nonblocking strategy of the fourth approach works well when the program has "useful work" that it can perform between its intermittent checks to see if I/O is available. Unfortunately, most problems are difficult to structure in this way, and the strategy sometimes forces hard-coding of the timing for the I/O check relative to useful work. If the platform changes, the choice may no longer be appropriate. Without very careful programming and a very specific program structure, the nonblocking I/O strategy can lead to busy waiting and inefficient use of processor resources.

POSIX asynchronous I/O can be used with or without signal notification to overlap processing with monitoring of file descriptors. Without signal notification, asynchronous I/O relies on polling as in approach 4. With signal notification, the program does its useful work until it receives a signal advising that the I/O may be ready. The operating system transfers control to a handler to process the I/O. This method requires that the handler use only async-signal-safe functions. The signal handler must synchronize with the rest of the program to access the data, opening the potential for deadlocks and race conditions. Although asynchronous I/O can be tuned very efficiently, the approach is error-prone and difficult to implement.

The final approach uses a separate thread to handle each descriptor, in effect reducing the problem to one of processing a single file descriptor. The threaded code is simpler than the other implementations, and a program can overlap processing with waiting for input in a transparent way.

Threading is not as widely used as it might be because, until recently, threaded programs were not portable. Each vendor provided a proprietary thread library with different calls. The POSIX standard addresses the portability issue with POSIX threads, described in the POSIX:THR Threads Extension. Table E.1 on page 860 lists several additional extensions that relate to the more esoteric aspects of POSIX thread management. Section 12.2 introduces POSIX threads by solving the multiple file descriptor problem. Do not focus on the details of the calls when you first read this section. The remainder of this chapter discusses basic POSIX thread management and use of the library. Chapter 13 explains synchronization and signal handling with POSIX threads. Chapters 14 and 15 discuss the use of semaphores for synchronization. Semaphores are part of the POSIX:SEM Extension and the POSIX:XSI Extension and can be used with threads. Chapters 16 and 17 discuss projects that use threads and synchronization.

12.2 Use of Threads to Monitor Multiple File Descriptors

Multiple threads can simplify the problem of monitoring multiple file descriptors because a dedicated thread with relatively simple logic can handle each file descriptor. Threads also make the overlap of I/O and processing transparent to the programmer.

We begin by comparing the execution of a function by a separate thread to the execution of an ordinary function call within the same thread of execution. Figure 12.1 illustrates a call to the `processfd` function within the same thread of execution. The calling mechanism creates an activation record (usually on the stack) that contains the return address. The thread of execution jumps to `processfd` when the calling mechanism writes the starting address of `processfd` in the processor's program counter. The thread uses the newly created activation record as the environment for execution, creating automatic variables on the stack as part of the record. The thread of execution continues in `processfd` until reaching a `return` statement (or the end of the function). The `return` statement copies the return address that is stored in the activation record into the processor program counter, causing the thread of execution to jump back to the calling program.

Figure 12.2 illustrates the creation of a separate thread to execute the `processfd` function. The `pthread_create` call creates a new "schedulable entity" with its own value of the program counter, its own stack and its own scheduling parameters. The "schedulable entity" (i.e., thread) executes an independent stream of instructions, never returning to the point of the call. The calling program continues to execute concurrently. In contrast, when `processfd` is called as an ordinary function, the caller's thread of

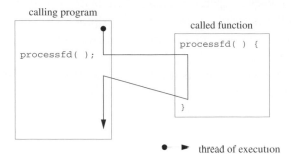

Figure 12.1: Program that makes an ordinary call to processfd has a single thread of execution.

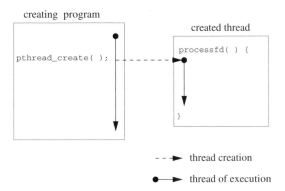

Figure 12.2: Program that creates a new thread to execute processfd has two threads of execution.

execution moves through the function code and returns to the point of the call, generating a single thread of execution rather than two separate ones.

We now turn to the specific problem of handling multiple file descriptors. The processfd function of Program 12.1 monitors a single file descriptor by calling a blocking read. The function returns when it encounters end-of-file or detects an error. The caller passes the file descriptor as a pointer to void, so processfd can be called either as an ordinary function or as a thread.

The processfd function uses the r_read function of Program 4.3 instead of read to restart reading if the thread is interrupted by a signal. However, we recommend a dedicated thread for signal handling, as explained in Section 13.5. In this case, the thread that executes processfd would have all signals blocked and could call read.

Program 12.1 ——————————————————————————————— `processfd.c`

The `processfd` *function monitors a single file descriptor for input.*

```
#include <stdio.h>
#include "restart.h"
#define BUFSIZE 1024

void docommand(char *cmd, int cmdsize);

void *processfd(void *arg) { /* process commands read from file descriptor */
   char buf[BUFSIZE];
   int fd;
   ssize_t nbytes;

   fd = *((int *)(arg));
   for ( ; ; )  {
      if ((nbytes = r_read(fd, buf, BUFSIZE)) <= 0)
         break;
      docommand(buf, nbytes);
   }
   return NULL;
}
```

Program 12.1 ————————————————————————————— `processfd.c`

■ **Example 12.1**

The following code segment calls `processfd` as an ordinary function. The code
assumes that `fd` is open for reading and passes it by reference to `processfd`.

```
void *processfd(void *);
int fd;

processfd(&fd);
```

■ **Example 12.2**

The following code segment creates a new thread to run `processfd` for the open
file descriptor `fd`.

```
void *processfd(void *arg);

int error;
int fd;
pthread_t tid;

if (error = pthread_create(&tid, NULL, processfd, &fd))
   fprintf(stderr, "Failed to create thread: %s\n", strerror(error));
```

The code of Example 12.1 has a single thread of execution, as illustrated in Figure 12.1. The thread of execution for the calling program traverses the statements in the
function and then resumes execution at the statement after the call. Since `processfd` uses
blocking I/O, the program blocks on `r_read` until input becomes available on the file descriptor. Remember that the thread of execution is really the sequence of statements that

the thread executes. The sequence contains no timing information, so the fact that execution blocks on a `read` call is not directly visible to the caller. The code in Example 12.2 has two threads of execution. A separate thread executes `processfd`, as illustrated in Figure 12.2.

The function `monitorfd` of Program 12.2 uses threads to monitor an array of file descriptors. Compare this implementation with those of Program 4.14 and Program 4.17. The threaded version is considerably simpler and takes advantage of parallelism. If `docommand` causes the calling thread to block for some reason, the thread runtime system schedules another runnable thread. In this way, processing and reading are overlapped in a natural way. In contrast, blocking of `docommand` in the single-threaded implementation causes the entire process to block.

If `monitorfd` fails to create thread `i`, it sets the corresponding thread ID to itself to signify that creation failed. The last loop uses `pthread_join`, described in Section 12.3, to wait until all threads have completed.

Program 12.2 ———————————————————————— **monitorfd.c**

A function to monitor an array of file descriptors, using a separate thread for each descriptor.

```c
#include <pthread.h>
#include <stdio.h>
#include <stdlib.h>
#include <string.h>

void *processfd(void *arg);

void monitorfd(int fd[], int numfds) {          /* create threads to monitor fds */
   int error, i;
   pthread_t *tid;

   if ((tid = (pthread_t *)calloc(numfds, sizeof(pthread_t))) == NULL) {
      perror("Failed to allocate space for thread IDs");
      return;
   }
   for (i = 0; i < numfds; i++)   /* create a thread for each file descriptor */
      if (error = pthread_create(tid + i, NULL, processfd, (fd + i))) {
         fprintf(stderr, "Failed to create thread %d: %s\n",
                       i, strerror(error));
         tid[i] = pthread_self();
      }
   for (i = 0; i < numfds; i++) {
      if (pthread_equal(pthread_self(), tid[i]))
         continue;
      if (error = pthread_join(tid[i], NULL))
         fprintf(stderr, "Failed to join thread %d: %s\n", i, strerror(error));
   }
   free(tid);
   return;
}
```

Program 12.2 ———————————————————————— **monitorfd.c**

12.3 Thread Management

A thread package usually includes functions for thread creation and thread destruction, scheduling, enforcement of mutual exclusion and conditional waiting. A typical thread package also contains a runtime system to manage threads transparently (i.e., the user is not aware of the runtime system). When a thread is created, the runtime system allocates data structures to hold the thread's ID, stack and program counter value. The thread's internal data structure might also contain scheduling and usage information. The threads for a process share the entire address space of that process. They can modify global variables, access open file descriptors, and cooperate or interfere with each other in other ways.

POSIX threads are sometimes called *pthreads* because all the thread functions start with `pthread`. Table 12.1 summarizes the basic POSIX thread management functions introduced in this section. The programs listed in Section 12.1 used `pthread_create` to create threads and `pthread_join` to wait for threads to complete. Other management functions deal with thread termination, signals and comparison of thread IDs. Section 12.6 introduces the functions related to thread attribute objects, and Chapter 13 covers thread synchronization functions.

POSIX function	description
pthread_cancel	terminate another thread
pthread_create	create a thread
pthread_detach	set thread to release resources
pthread_equal	test two thread IDs for equality
pthread_exit	exit a thread without exiting process
pthread_kill	send a signal to a thread
pthread_join	wait for a thread
pthread_self	find out own thread ID

Table 12.1: POSIX thread management functions.

Most POSIX thread functions return 0 if successful and a nonzero error code if unsuccessful. They do not set `errno`, so the caller cannot use `perror` to report errors. Programs can use `strerror` if the issues of thread safety discussed in Section 12.4 are addressed. The POSIX standard specifically states that none of the POSIX thread functions returns `EINTR` and that POSIX thread functions do not have to be restarted if interrupted by a signal.

12.3.1 Referencing threads by ID

POSIX threads are referenced by an ID of type `pthread_t`. A thread can find out its ID by calling `pthread_self`.

```
SYNOPSIS

   #include <pthread.h>

   pthread_t pthread_self(void);
                                                                    POSIX:THR
```

The `pthread_self` function returns the thread ID of the calling thread. No errors are defined for `pthread_self`.

Since `pthread_t` may be a structure, use `pthread_equal` to compare thread IDs for equality. The parameters of `pthread_equal` are the thread IDs to be compared.

```
SYNOPSIS

   #include <pthread.h>

   int pthread_equal(thread_t t1, pthread_t t2);
                                                                    POSIX:THR
```

If `t1` equals `t2`, `pthread_equal` returns a nonzero value. If the thread IDs are not equal, `pthread_equal` returns 0. No errors are defined for `pthread_equal`.

■ **Example 12.3**

In the following code segment, a thread outputs a message if its thread ID is `mytid`.

```
pthread_t mytid;

if (pthread_equal(pthread_self(), mytid))
   printf("My thread ID matches mytid\n");
```

12.3.2 Creating a thread

The `pthread_create` function creates a thread. Unlike some thread facilities, such as those provided by the Java programming language, the POSIX `pthread_create` automatically makes the thread runnable without requiring a separate start operation. The `thread` parameter of `pthread_create` points to the ID of the newly created thread. The `attr` parameter represents an attribute object that encapsulates the attributes of a thread. If `attr` is NULL, the new thread has the default attributes. Section 12.6 discusses the setting of thread attributes. The third parameter, `start_routine`, is the name of a function that the thread calls when it begins execution. The `start_routine` takes a single parameter specified by `arg`, a pointer to `void`. The `start_routine` returns a pointer to `void`, which is treated as an exit status by `pthread_join`.

```
SYNOPSIS

  #include <pthread.h>

  int pthread_create(pthread_t *restrict thread,
                     const pthread_attr_t *restrict attr,
                     void *(*start_routine)(void *), void *restrict arg);
                                                                POSIX:THR
```

If successful, `pthread_create` returns 0. If unsuccessful, `pthread_create` returns a nonzero error code. The following table lists the mandatory errors for `pthread_create`.

error	cause
EAGAIN	system did not have the resources to create the thread, or would exceed system limit on total number of threads in a process
EINVAL	`attr` parameter is invalid
EPERM	caller does not have the appropriate permissions to set scheduling policy or parameters specified by `attr`

Do not let the prototype of `pthread_create` intimidate you—threads are easy to create and use.

■ Example 12.4

The following code segment creates a thread to execute the function `processfd` after opening the `my.dat` file for reading.

```c
void *processfd(void *arg);

int error;
int fd;
pthread_t tid;

if ((fd = open("my.dat", O_RDONLY)) == -1)
   perror("Failed to open my.dat");
else if (error = pthread_create(&tid, NULL, processfd, &fd))
   fprintf(stderr, "Failed to create thread: %s\n", strerror(error));
else
   printf("Thread created\n");
```

12.3.3 Detaching and joining

When a thread exits, it does not release its resources unless it is a detached thread. The `pthread_detach` function sets a thread's internal options to specify that storage for the thread can be reclaimed when the thread exits. Detached threads do not report their status when they exit. Threads that are not detached are joinable and do not release all their resources until another thread calls `pthread_join` for them or the entire process exits.

The `pthread_join` function causes the caller to wait for the specified thread to exit, similar to `waitpid` at the process level. To prevent memory leaks, long-running programs should eventually call either `pthread_detach` or `pthread_join` for every thread.

The `pthread_detach` function has a single parameter, `thread`, the thread ID of the thread to be detached.

SYNOPSIS

```
#include <pthread.h>

int pthread_detach(pthread_t thread);
```

POSIX:THR

If successful, `pthread_detach` returns 0. If unsuccessful, `pthread_detach` returns a nonzero error code. The following table lists the mandatory errors for `pthread_detach`.

error	cause
EINVAL	thread does not correspond to a joinable thread
ESRCH	no thread with ID thread

■ Example 12.5

The following code segment creates and then detaches a thread to execute the function `processfd`.

```
void *processfd(void *arg);

int error;
int fd
pthread_t tid;

if (error = pthread_create(&tid, NULL, processfd, &fd))
    fprintf(stderr, "Failed to create thread: %s\n", strerror(error));
else if (error = pthread_detach(tid))
    fprintf(stderr, "Failed to detach thread: %s\n", strerror(error));
```

■ Example 12.6

When `detachfun` is executed as a thread, it detaches itself.

```
#include <pthread.h>
#include <stdio.h>

void *detachfun(void *arg) {
    int i = *((int *)(arg));
    if (!pthread_detach(pthread_self()))
        return NULL;
    fprintf(stderr, "My argument is %d\n", i);
    return NULL;
}
```

detachfun.c

A nondetached thread's resources are not released until another thread calls `pthread_join` with the ID of the terminating thread as the first parameter. The `pthread_join` function suspends the calling thread until the target thread, specified by the first parameter, terminates. The `value_ptr` parameter provides a location for a pointer to the return status that the target thread passes to `pthread_exit` or `return`. If `value_ptr` is `NULL`, the caller does not retrieve the target thread return status.

SYNOPSIS

```
#include <pthread.h>

int pthread_join(pthread_t thread, void **value_ptr);
```

POSIX:THR

If successful, `pthread_join` returns 0. If unsuccessful, `pthread_join` returns a nonzero error code. The following table lists the mandatory errors for `pthread_join`.

error	cause
EINVAL	thread does not correspond to a joinable thread
ESRCH	no thread with ID thread

■ Example 12.7

The following code illustrates how to retrieve the value passed to `pthread_exit` by a terminating thread.

```
int error;
int *exitcodep;
pthread_t tid;

if (error = pthread_join(tid, &exitcodep))
    fprintf(stderr, "Failed to join thread: %s\n", strerror(error));
else
    fprintf(stderr, "The exit code was %d\n", *exitcodep);
```

□ Exercise 12.8

What happens if a thread executes the following?

```
pthread_join(pthread_self());
```

Answer:

Assuming the thread was joinable (not detached), this statement creates a deadlock. Some implementations detect a deadlock and force `pthread_join` to return with the error `EDEADLK`. However, this detection is not required by the POSIX:THR Extension.

Calling `pthread_join` is not the only way for the main thread to block until the other threads have completed. The main thread can use a semaphore or one of the methods discussed in Section 16.6 to wait for all threads to finish.

12.3.4 Exiting and cancellation

The process can terminate by calling `exit` directly, by executing `return` from `main`, or by having one of the other process threads call `exit`. In any of these cases, all threads terminate. If the main thread has no work to do after creating other threads, it should either block until all threads have completed or call `pthread_exit(NULL)`.

A call to `exit` causes the entire process to terminate; a call to `pthread_exit` causes only the calling thread to terminate. A thread that executes `return` from its top level implicitly calls `pthread_exit` with the return value (a pointer) serving as the parameter to `pthread_exit`. A process will exit with a return status of 0 if its last thread calls `pthread_exit`.

The `value_ptr` value is available to a successful `pthread_join`. However, the `value_ptr` in `pthread_exit` must point to data that exists after the thread exits, so the thread should not use a pointer to automatic local data for `value_ptr`.

```
SYNOPSIS

   #include <pthread.h>

   void pthread_exit(void *value_ptr);
                                                                    POSIX:THR
```

POSIX does not define any errors for `pthread_exit`.

Threads can force other threads to return through the cancellation mechanism. A thread calls `pthread_cancel` to request that another thread be canceled. The target thread's type and cancellability state determine the result. The single parameter of `pthread_cancel` is the thread ID of the target thread to be canceled. The `pthread_cancel` function does not cause the caller to block while the cancellation completes. Rather, `pthread_cancel` returns after making the cancellation request.

```
SYNOPSIS

   #include <pthread.h>

   int pthread_cancel(pthread_t thread);
                                                                    POSIX:THR
```

If successful, `pthread_cancel` returns 0. If unsuccessful, `pthread_cancel` returns a nonzero error code. No mandatory errors are defined for `pthread_cancel`.

What happens when a thread receives a cancellation request depends on its state and type. If a thread has the PTHREAD_CANCEL_ENABLE state, it receives cancellation requests. On the other hand, if the thread has the PTHREAD_CANCEL_DISABLE state, the cancellation requests are held pending. By default, threads have the PTHREAD_CANCEL_ENABLE state.

The pthread_setcancelstate function changes the cancellability state of the calling thread. The pthread_setcancelstate takes two parameters: state, specifying the new state to set; and oldstate, a pointer to an integer for holding the previous state.

```
SYNOPSIS

   #include <pthread.h>

   int pthread_setcancelstate(int state, int *oldstate);
                                                              POSIX:THR
```

If successful, pthread_setcancelstate returns 0. If unsuccessful, it returns a nonzero error code. No mandatory errors are defined for pthread_setcancelstate.

Program 12.3 shows a modification of the processfd function of Program 12.1 that explicitly disables cancellation before it calls docommand, to ensure that the command won't be canceled midstream. The original processfd always returns NULL. The processfdcancel function returns a pointer other than NULL if it cannot change the cancellation state. This function should not return a pointer to an automatic local variable, since local variables are deallocated when the function returns or the thread exits. Program 12.3 uses a parameter passed by the calling thread to return the pointer.

Program 12.3 ──────────────────────── **processfdcancel.c**

This function monitors a file descriptor for input and calls docommand *to process the result. It explicitly disables cancellation before calling* docommand*.*

```c
#include <pthread.h>
#include "restart.h"
#define BUFSIZE 1024

void docommand(char *cmd, int cmdsize);

void *processfdcancel(void *arg) { /* process commands with cancellation */
   char buf[BUFSIZE];
   int fd;
   ssize_t nbytes;
   int newstate, oldstate;

   fd = *((int *)(arg));
   for ( ; ; )  {
      if ((nbytes = r_read(fd, buf, BUFSIZE)) <= 0)
         break;
      if (pthread_setcancelstate(PTHREAD_CANCEL_DISABLE, &oldstate))
         return arg;
      docommand(buf, nbytes);
      if (pthread_setcancelstate(oldstate, &newstate))
         return arg;
   }
   return NULL;
}
```

Program 12.3 ──────────────────────── **processfdcancel.c**

As a general rule, a function that changes its cancellation state or its type should restore the value before returning. A caller cannot make reliable assumptions about the program behavior unless this rule is observed. The `processfdcancel` function saves the old state and restores it rather than just enabling cancellation after calling `docommand`.

Cancellation can cause difficulties if a thread holds resources such as a lock or an open file descriptor that must be released before exiting. A thread maintains a stack of cleanup routines using `pthread_cleanup_push` and `pthread_cleanup_pop`. (We do not discuss these here.) Although a canceled thread can execute a cleanup function before exiting (not discussed here), it is not always feasible to release resources in an exit handler. Also, there may be points in the execution at which an exit would leave the program in an unacceptable state. The cancellation type allows a thread to control the point when it exits in response to a cancellation request. When its cancellation type is `PTHREAD_CANCEL_ASYNCHRONOUS`, the thread can act on the cancellation request at any time. In contrast, a cancellation type of `PTHREAD_CANCEL_DEFERRED` causes the thread to act on cancellation requests only at specified cancellation points. By default, threads have the `PTHREAD_CANCEL_DEFERRED` type.

The `pthread_setcanceltype` function changes the cancellability type of a thread as specified by its `type` parameter. The `oldtype` parameter is a pointer to a location for saving the previous type. A thread can set a cancellation point at a particular place in the code by calling `pthread_testcancel`. Certain blocking functions, such as `read`, are automatically treated as cancellation points. A thread with the `PTHREAD_CANCEL_DEFERRED` type accepts pending cancellation requests when it reaches such a cancellation point.

```
SYNOPSIS

   #include <pthread.h>

   int pthread_setcanceltype(int type, int *oldtype);
   void pthread_testcancel(void);
                                                              POSIX:THR
```

If successful, `pthread_setcanceltype` returns 0. If unsuccessful, it returns a nonzero error code. No mandatory errors are defined for `pthread_setcanceltype`. The `pthread_testcancel` has no return value.

12.3.5 Passing parameters to threads and returning values

The creator of a thread may pass a single parameter to a thread at creation time, using a pointer to `void`. To communicate multiple values, the creator must use a pointer to an array or a structure. Program 12.4 illustrates how to pass a pointer to an array. The `main` program passes an array containing two open file descriptors to a thread that runs `copyfilemalloc`.

Program 12.4 ———————————————————— `callcopymalloc.c`

This program creates a thread to copy a file.

```c
#include <errno.h>
#include <fcntl.h>
#include <pthread.h>
#include <stdio.h>
#include <string.h>
#include <sys/stat.h>
#include <sys/types.h>
#define PERMS (S_IRUSR | S_IWUSR)
#define READ_FLAGS O_RDONLY
#define WRITE_FLAGS (O_WRONLY | O_CREAT | O_TRUNC)

void *copyfilemalloc(void *arg);

int main (int argc, char *argv[]) {          /* copy fromfile to tofile */
   int *bytesptr;
   int error;
   int fds[2];
   pthread_t tid;

   if (argc != 3) {
      fprintf(stderr, "Usage: %s fromfile tofile\n", argv[0]);
      return 1;
   }
   if (((fds[0] = open(argv[1], READ_FLAGS)) == -1) ||
       ((fds[1] = open(argv[2], WRITE_FLAGS, PERMS)) == -1)) {
      perror("Failed to open the files");
      return 1;
   }
   if (error = pthread_create(&tid, NULL, copyfilemalloc, fds)) {
      fprintf(stderr, "Failed to create thread: %s\n", strerror(error));
      return 1;
   }
   if (error = pthread_join(tid, (void **)&bytesptr)) {
      fprintf(stderr, "Failed to join thread: %s\n", strerror(error));
      return 1;
   }
   printf("Number of bytes copied: %d\n", *bytesptr);
   return 0;
}
```

Program 12.4 ———————————————————— `callcopymalloc.c`

Program 12.5 shows an implementation of `copyfilemalloc`, a function that reads from one file and outputs to another file. The `arg` parameter holds a pointer to a pair of open descriptors representing the source and destination files. The variables `bytesp`, `infd` and `outfd` are allocated on `copyfilemalloc`'s local stack and are not directly accessible to other threads.

Program 12.5 also illustrates a strategy for returning values from the thread. The thread allocates memory space for returning the total number of bytes copied since it is not allowed to return a pointer to its local variables. POSIX requires that `malloc` be thread-safe. The `copyfilemalloc` function returns the `bytesp` pointer, which is equivalent to calling `pthread_exit`. It is the responsibility of the calling program (`callcopymalloc`) to free this space when it has finished using it. In this case, the program terminates, so it is not necessary to call `free`.

┌─ **Program 12.5** ───────────────────────────── `copyfilemalloc.c` ─┐

The `copyfilemalloc` *function copies the contents of one file to another by calling the* `copyfile` *function of Program 4.6 on page 100. It returns the number of bytes copied by dynamically allocating space for the return value.*

```
#include <stdlib.h>
#include <unistd.h>
#include "restart.h"

void *copyfilemalloc(void *arg)   { /* copy infd to outfd with return value */
   int *bytesp;
   int infd;
   int outfd;

   infd = *((int *)(arg));
   outfd = *((int *)(arg) + 1);
   if ((bytesp = (int *)malloc(sizeof(int))) == NULL)
      return NULL;
   *bytesp = copyfile(infd, outfd);
   r_close(infd);
   r_close(outfd);
   return bytesp;
}
```

└─ **Program 12.5** ───────────────────────────── `copyfilemalloc.c` ─┘

□ **Exercise 12.9**

What happens if `copyfilemalloc` stores the byte count in a variable with static storage class and returns a pointer to this static variable instead of dynamically allocating space for it?

Answer:

The program still works since only one thread is created. However, in a program with two `copyfilemalloc` threads, both store the byte count in the same place and one overwrites the other's value.

When a thread allocates space for a return value, some other thread is responsible for freeing that space. Whenever possible, a thread should clean up its own mess rather than requiring another thread to do it. It is also inefficient to dynamically allocate space to hold a single integer. An alternative to having the thread allocate space for the return value is for the creating thread to do it and pass a pointer to this space in the argument parameter of the thread. This approach avoids dynamic allocation completely if the space is on the stack of the creating thread.

Program 12.6 creates a `copyfilepass` thread to copy a file. The parameter to the thread is now an array of size 3. The first two entries of the array hold the file descriptors as in Program 12.4. The third array element stores the number of bytes copied. Program 12.6 can retrieve this value either through the array or through the second parameter of `pthread_join`. Alternatively, `callcopypass` could pass an array of size 2, and the thread could store the return value over one of the incoming file descriptors.

Program 12.6 ———————————————————— **callcopypass.c**

A program that creates a thread to copy a file. The parameter of the thread is an array of three integers used for two file descriptors and the number of bytes copied.

```c
#include <errno.h>
#include <fcntl.h>
#include <pthread.h>
#include <stdio.h>
#include <string.h>
#include <sys/stat.h>
#include <sys/types.h>
#define PERMS (S_IRUSR | S_IWUSR)
#define READ_FLAGS O_RDONLY
#define WRITE_FLAGS (O_WRONLY | O_CREAT | O_TRUNC)
void *copyfilepass(void *arg);

int main (int argc, char *argv[]) {
   int *bytesptr;
   int error;
   int targs[3];
   pthread_t tid;

   if (argc != 3) {
      fprintf(stderr, "Usage: %s fromfile tofile\n", argv[0]);
      return 1;
   }

   if (((targs[0] = open(argv[1], READ_FLAGS)) == -1) ||
       ((targs[1] = open(argv[2], WRITE_FLAGS, PERMS)) == -1)) {
      perror("Failed to  open the files");
      return 1;
   }
   if (error = pthread_create(&tid, NULL, copyfilepass, targs)) {
      fprintf(stderr, "Failed to create thread: %s\n", strerror(error));
      return 1;
   }
   if (error = pthread_join(tid, (void **)&bytesptr)) {
      fprintf(stderr, "Failed to join thread: %s\n", strerror(error));
      return 1;
   }
   printf("Number of bytes copied: %d\n", *bytesptr);
   return 0;
}
```

Program 12.6 ———————————————————— **callcopypass.c**

The `copyfilepass` function of Program 12.7 uses an alternative way of accessing the pieces of the argument. Compare this with the method used by the `copyfilemalloc` function of Program 12.5.

Program 12.7 ————————————————————— **`copyfilepass.c`**

A thread that can be used by `callcopypass` *to copy a file.*

```
#include <unistd.h>
#include "restart.h"

void *copyfilepass(void *arg)  {
   int *argint;

   argint = (int *)arg;
   argint[2] = copyfile(argint[0], argint[1]);
   r_close(argint[0]);
   r_close(argint[1]);
   return argint + 2;
}
```

Program 12.7 ————————————————————— **`copyfilepass.c`**

☐ Exercise 12.10

Why have `copyfilepass` return a pointer to the number of bytes copied when `callcopypass` can access this value as `args[2]`?

Answer:

If a thread other than the creating thread joins with `copyfilepass`, it has access to the number of bytes copied through the parameter to `pthread_join`.

Program 12.8 shows a parallel file-copy program that uses the thread in Program 12.7. The `main` program has three command-line arguments: an input file basename, an output file basename and the number of files to copy. The program creates `numcopiers` threads. Thread i copies `infile.i` to `outfile.i`.

☐ Exercise 12.11

What happens in Program 12.8 if a `write` call in `copyfile` of `copyfilepass` fails?

Answer:

The `copyfilepass` returns the number of bytes successfully copied, and the `main` program does not detect an error. You can address the issue by having `copyfilepass` return an error value and pass the number of bytes written in one of the elements of the array used as a parameter for thread creation.

When creating multiple threads, do not reuse the variable holding a thread's parameter until you are sure that the thread has finished accessing the parameter. Because the variable is passed by reference, it is a good practice to use a separate variable for each thread.

Program 12.8 ———————————————————— `copymultiple.c`

A program that creates threads to copy multiple file descriptors.

```c
#include <errno.h>
#include <fcntl.h>
#include <pthread.h>
#include <stdio.h>
#include <stdlib.h>
#include <string.h>
#include <sys/stat.h>
#define MAXNAME 80
#define R_FLAGS O_RDONLY
#define W_FLAGS (O_WRONLY | O_CREAT)
#define W_PERMS (S_IRUSR | S_IWUSR)

typedef struct {
   int args[3];
   pthread_t tid;
} copy_t;

void *copyfilepass(void *arg);

int main(int argc, char *argv[]) {
   int *bytesp;
   copy_t *copies;
   int error;
   char filename[MAXNAME];
   int i;
   int numcopiers;
   int totalbytes = 0;

   if (argc != 4) {
      fprintf(stderr, "Usage: %s infile outfile copies\n", argv[0]);
      return 1;
   }
   numcopiers = atoi(argv[3]);
   if ((copies = (copy_t *)calloc(numcopiers, sizeof(copy_t))) == NULL) {
      perror("Failed to allocate copier space");
      return 1;
   }
            /* open the source and destination files and create the threads */
   for (i = 0; i < numcopiers; i++) {
      copies[i].tid = pthread_self();        /* cannot be value for new thread */
      if (snprintf(filename, MAXNAME, "%s.%d", argv[1], i+1) == MAXNAME) {
         fprintf(stderr, "Input filename %s.%d too long", argv[1], i + 1);
         continue;
      }
      if ((copies[i].args[0] = open(filename, R_FLAGS)) == -1) {
         fprintf(stderr, "Failed to open source file %s: %s\n",
                         filename, strerror(errno));
         continue;
      }
     if (snprintf(filename, MAXNAME, "%s.%d", argv[2], i+1) == MAXNAME) {
         fprintf(stderr, "Output filename %s.%d too long", argv[2], i + 1);
         continue;
      }
```

```
          if ((copies[i].args[1] = open(filename, W_FLAGS, W_PERMS)) == -1) {
             fprintf(stderr, "Failed to open destination file %s: %s\n",
                                filename, strerror(errno));
             continue;
          }
          if (error = pthread_create((&copies[i].tid), NULL,
                                      copyfilepass, copies[i].args)) {
             fprintf(stderr, "Failed to create thread %d: %s\n", i + 1,
                     strerror(error));
             copies[i].tid = pthread_self();    /* cannot be value for new thread */
          }


       }
                     /* wait for the threads to finish and report total bytes */
    for (i = 0; i < numcopiers; i++) {
       if (pthread_equal(copies[i].tid, pthread_self()))            /* not created */
          continue;
       if (error = pthread_join(copies[i].tid, (void**)&bytesp)) {
          fprintf(stderr, "Failed to join thread %d\n", i);
          continue;
       }
       if (bytesp == NULL) {
          fprintf(stderr, "Thread %d failed to return status\n", i);
          continue;
       }
       printf("Thread %d copied %d bytes from %s.%d to %s.%d\n",
              i, *bytesp, argv[1], i + 1, argv[2], i + 1);
       totalbytes += *bytesp;
    }
    printf("Total bytes copied = %d\n", totalbytes);
    return 0;
 }
```

Program 12.8 ————————————————————————————— `copymultiple.c`

Program 12.9 shows a simple example of what can go wrong. The program creates 10 threads that each output the value of their parameter. The `main` program uses the thread creation loop index `i` as the parameter it passes to the threads. Each thread prints the value of the parameter it received. A thread can get an incorrect value if the `main` program changes `i` before the thread has a chance to print it.

☐ Exercise 12.12

Run Program 12.9 and examine the results. What parameter value is reported by each thread?

Answer:

The results vary, depending on how the system schedules threads. One possibility is that `main` completes the loop creating the threads before any thread prints the value of the parameter. In this case, all the threads print the value 10.

Program 12.9 ──────────────── `badparameters.c`
A program that incorrectly passes parameters to multiple threads.

```c
#include <pthread.h>
#include <stdio.h>
#include <string.h>
#define NUMTHREADS 10

static void *printarg(void *arg) {
   fprintf(stderr, "Thread received %d\n", *(int *)arg);
   return NULL;
}

int main (void) {          /* program incorrectly passes parameters to threads */
   int error;
   int i;
   int j;
   pthread_t tid[NUMTHREADS];

   for (i = 0; i < NUMTHREADS; i++)
      if (error = pthread_create(tid + i, NULL, printarg, (void *)&i)) {
         fprintf(stderr, "Failed to create thread: %s\n", strerror(error));
         tid[i] = pthread_self();
      }
   for (j = 0; j < NUMTHREADS; j++)
      if (pthread_equal(pthread_self(), tid[j]))
         continue;
      if (error = pthread_join(tid[j], NULL))
         fprintf(stderr, "Failed to join thread: %s\n", strerror(error));
   printf("All threads done\n");
   return 0;
}
```

Program 12.9 ──────────────── `badparameters.c`

□ **Exercise 12.13**

For each of the following, start with Program 12.9 and make the specified modifications. Predict the output, and then run the program to see if you are correct.
1. Run the original program without any modification.
2. Put a call to `sleep(1);` at the start of `printarg`.
3. Put a call to `sleep(1);` inside the first `for` loop after the call to `pthread_create`.
4. Put a call to `sleep(1);` after the first `for` loop.
5.-8. Repeat each of the items above, using `i` as the loop index rather than `j`.

Answer:

The results may vary if it takes more than a second for the threads to execute. On a fast enough system, the result will be something like the following.
1. Output described in Exercise 12.12.
2. Each thread outputs the value 10, the value of `i` when `main` has finished its loop.

3. Each thread outputs the correct value since it executes before the value of i changes.
4. Same as in Exercise 12.12.
5. All threads output the value 0, the value of i when main waits for the first thread to terminate. The results may vary.
6. Same as 5.
7. Same as 3.
8. Same as 4.

❑ Exercise 12.14

The whichexit function can be executed as a thread.

```
#include <errno.h>
#include <pthread.h>
#include <stdlib.h>
#include <string.h>

void *whichexit(void *arg) {
    int n;
    int np1[1];
    int *np2;
    char s1[10];
    char s2[] = "I am done";
    n = 3;
    np1[0] = n;
    np2 = (int *)malloc(sizeof(int));
    *np2 = n;
    strcpy(s1, "Done");
    return(NULL);
}
```
———————————————————————————————————— **whichexit.c**

Which of the following would be safe replacements for NULL as the parameter to return? Assume no errors occur.

1. n
2. &n
3. (int *)n
4. np1
5. np2
6. s1
7. s2
8. "This works"
9. strerror(EINTR)

Answer:

1. The return value is a pointer, not an integer, so this is invalid.
2. The integer n has automatic storage class, so it is illegal to access it after the function terminates.

3. This is a common way to return an integer from a thread. The integer is cast to a pointer. When another thread calls `pthread_join` for this thread, it casts the pointer back to an integer. While this will probably work in most implementations, it should be avoided. The C standard [56, Section 6.3.2.3] says that an integer may be converted to a pointer or a pointer to an integer, but the result is implementation defined. It does not guarantee that the result of converting an integer to a pointer and back again yields the original integer.

4. The array `np1` has automatic storage class, so it is illegal to access the array after the function terminates.

5. This is safe since the dynamically allocated space will be available until it is freed.

6. The array `s1` has automatic storage class, so it is illegal to access the array after the function terminates.

7. The array `s2` has automatic storage class, so it is illegal to access the array after the function terminates.

8. This is valid in C, since string literals have static storage duration.

9. This is certainly invalid if `strerror` is not thread-safe. Even on a system where `strerror` is thread-safe, the string produced is not guaranteed to be available after the thread terminates.

12.4 Thread Safety

A hidden problem with threads is that they may call library functions that are not thread-safe, possibly producing spurious results. A function is *thread-safe* if multiple threads can execute simultaneous active invocations of the function without interference. POSIX specifies that all the required functions, including the functions from the standard C library, be implemented in a thread-safe manner except for the specific functions listed in Table 12.2. Those functions whose traditional interfaces preclude making them thread-safe must have an alternative thread-safe version designated with an _r suffix.

An important example of a function that does not have to be thread-safe is `strerror`. Although `strerror` is not guaranteed to be thread-safe, many systems have implemented this function in a thread-safe manner. Unfortunately, because `strerror` is listed in Table 12.2, you can not assume that it works correctly if multiple threads call it. We use `strerror` only in the main thread, often to produce error messages for `pthread_create` and `pthread_join`. Section 13.7 gives a thread-safe implementation called `strerror_r`.

Another interaction problem occurs when threads access the same data. The individual copier threads in Program 12.8 work on independent problems and do not interact with

asctime	fcvt	getpwnam	nl_langinfo
basename	ftw	getpwuid	ptsname
catgets	gcvt	getservbyname	putc_unlocked
crypt	getc_unlocked	getservbyport	putchar_unlocked
ctime	getchar_unlocked	getservent	putenv
dbm_clearerr	getdate	getutxent	pututxline
dbm_close	getenv	getutxid	rand
dbm_delete	getgrent	getutxline	readdir
dbm_error	getgrgid	gmtime	setenv
dbm_fetch	getgrnam	hcreate	setgrent
dbm_firstkey	gethostbyaddr	hdestroy	setkey
dbm_nextkey	gethostbyname	hsearch	setpwent
dbm_open	gethostent	inet_ntoa	setutxent
dbm_store	getlogin	l64a	strerror
dirname	getnetbyaddr	lgamma	strtok
dlerror	getnetbyname	lgammaf	ttyname
drand48	getnetent	lgammal	unsetenv
ecvt	getopt	localeconv	wcstombs
encrypt	getprotobyname	localtime	wctomb
endgrent	getprotobynumber	lrand48	
endpwent	getprotoent	mrand48	
endutxent	getpwent	nftw	

Table 12.2: POSIX functions that are not required to be thread-safe.

each other. In more complicated applications, a thread may not exit after completing its assigned task. Instead, a worker thread may request additional tasks or share information. Chapter 13 explains how to control this type of interaction by using synchronization primitives such as mutex locks and condition variables.

In traditional UNIX implementations, errno is a global external variable that is set when system functions produce an error. This implementation does not work for multi-threading (see Section 2.7), and in most thread implementations errno is a macro that returns thread-specific information. In essence, each thread has a private copy of errno. The main thread does not have direct access to errno for a joined thread, so if needed, this information must be returned through the last parameter of pthread_join.

12.5 User Threads versus Kernel Threads

The two traditional models of thread control are *user-level threads* and *kernel-level threads*. User-level threads, shown in Figure 12.3, usually run on top of an existing operating system. These threads are invisible to the kernel and compete among themselves for the resources allocated to their encapsulating process. The threads are scheduled by a thread runtime system that is part of the process code. Programs with user-level threads usually link to a special library in which each library function is enclosed by a *jacket*. The jacket function calls the thread runtime system to do thread management before and possibly after calling the jacketed library function.

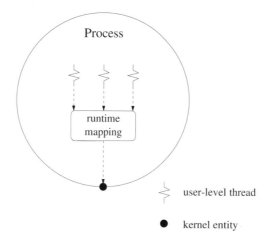

Figure 12.3: User-level threads are not visible outside their encapsulating process.

Functions such as `read` or `sleep` can present a problem for user-level threads because they may cause the process to block. To avoid blocking the entire process on a blocking call, the user-level thread library replaces each potentially blocking call in the jacket by a nonblocking version. The thread runtime system tests to see if the call would cause the thread to block. If the call would not block, the runtime system does the call right away. If the call would block, however, the runtime system places the thread on a list of waiting threads, adds the call to a list of actions to try later, and picks another thread to run. All this control is invisible to the user and to the operating system.

User-level threads have low overhead, but they also have some disadvantages. The user thread model, which assumes that the thread runtime system will eventually regain control, can be thwarted by *CPU-bound threads*. A CPU-bound thread rarely performs library calls and may prevent the thread runtime system from regaining control to schedule other threads. The programmer has to avoid the lockout situation by explicitly forcing CPU-bound threads to yield control at appropriate points. A second problem is that user-level threads can share only processor resources allocated to their encapsulating process. This restriction limits the amount of available parallelism because the threads can run on only one processor at a time. Since one of the prime motivations for using threads is to take advantage of multiprocessor workstations, user-level threads alone are not an acceptable approach.

With kernel-level threads, the kernel is aware of each thread as a schedulable entity and threads compete systemwide for processor resources. Figure 12.4 illustrates the visibility of kernel-level threads. The scheduling of kernel-level threads can be almost as expensive as the scheduling of processes themselves, but kernel-level threads can take advantage of multiple processors. The synchronization and sharing of data for kernel-level threads is less expensive than for full processes, but kernel-level threads are considerably more expensive to manage than user-level threads.

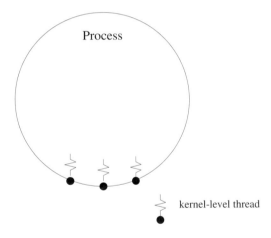

Figure 12.4: Operating system schedules kernel-level threads as though they were individual processes.

Hybrid thread models have advantages of both user-level and kernel-level models by providing two levels of control. Figure 12.5 illustrates a typical hybrid approach. The user writes the program in terms of user-level threads and then specifies how many kernel-schedulable entities are associated with the process. The user-level threads are mapped into the kernel-schedulable entities at runtime to achieve parallelism. The level of control that a user has over the mapping depends on the implementation. In the Sun Solaris thread implementation, for example, the user-level threads are called threads and the kernel-schedulable entities are called *lightweight processes*. The user can specify that a particular

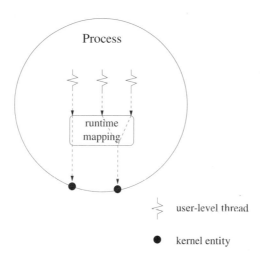

user-level thread

kernel entity

Figure 12.5: Hybrid model has two levels of scheduling, with user-level threads mapped into kernel entities.

thread be run by a dedicated lightweight process or that a particular group of threads be run by a pool of lightweight processes.

The POSIX thread scheduling model is a hybrid model that is flexible enough to support both user-level and kernel-level threads in particular implementations of the standard. The model consists of two levels of scheduling—threads and kernel entities. The threads are analogous to user-level threads. The kernel entities are scheduled by the kernel. The thread library decides how many kernel entities it needs and how they will be mapped.

POSIX introduces the idea of a *thread-scheduling contention scope*, which gives the programmer some control over how kernel entities are mapped to threads.   A thread can have a `contentionscope` attribute of either `PTHREAD_SCOPE_PROCESS` or `PTHREAD_SCOPE_SYSTEM`. Threads with the `PTHREAD_SCOPE_PROCESS` attribute contend for processor resources with the other threads in their process. POSIX does not specify how such a thread contends with threads outside its own process, so `PTHREAD_SCOPE_PROCESS` threads can be strictly user-level threads or they can be mapped to a pool of kernel entities in some more complicated way.

Threads with the `PTHREAD_SCOPE_SYSTEM` attribute contend systemwide for processor resources, much like kernel-level threads. POSIX leaves the mapping between `PTHREAD_SCOPE_SYSTEM` threads and kernel entities up to the implementation, but the obvious mapping is to bind such a thread directly to a kernel entity. A POSIX thread implementation can support `PTHREAD_SCOPE_PROCESS`, `PTHREAD_SCOPE_SYSTEM` or both. You can get the scope with `pthread_attr_getscope` and set the scope with `pthread_attr_setscope`, provided that your POSIX implementation supports both the POSIX:THR Thread Extension and the POSIX:TPS Thread Execution Scheduling Extension.

12.6 Thread Attributes

POSIX takes an object-oriented approach to representation and assignment of properties by encapsulating properties such as stack size and scheduling policy into an object of type `pthread_attr_t`. The attribute object affects a thread only at the time of creation. You first create an attribute object and associate properties, such as stack size and scheduling policy, with the attribute object. You can then create multiple threads with the same properties by passing the same thread attribute object to `pthread_create`. By grouping the properties into a single object, POSIX avoids `pthread_create` calls with a large number of parameters.

Table 12.3 shows the settable properties of thread attributes and their associated functions. Other entities, such as condition variables and mutex locks, have their own attribute object types. Chapter 13 discusses these synchronization mechanisms.

property	function
attribute objects	`pthread_attr_destroy`
	`pthread_attr_init`
state	`pthread_attr_getdetachstate`
	`pthread_attr_setdetachstate`
stack	`pthread_attr_getguardsize`
	`pthread_attr_setguardsize`
	`pthread_attr_getstack`
	`pthread_attr_setstack`
scheduling	`pthread_attr_getinheritsched`
	`pthread_attr_setinheritsched`
	`pthread_attr_getschedparam`
	`pthread_attr_setschedparam`
	`pthread_attr_getschedpolicy`
	`pthread_attr_setschedpolicy`
	`pthread_attr_getscope`
	`pthread_attr_setscope`

Table 12.3: Summary of settable properties for POSIX thread attribute objects.

The `pthread_attr_init` function initializes a thread attribute object with the default values. The `pthread_attr_destroy` function sets the value of the attribute object to be invalid. POSIX does not specify the behavior of the object after it has been destroyed, but the variable can be initialized to a new thread attribute object. Both `pthread_attr_init` and `pthread_attr_destroy` take a single parameter that is a pointer to a `pthread_attr_t` attribute object.

```
SYNOPSIS

   #include <pthread.h>

   int pthread_attr_destroy(pthread_attr_t *attr);
   int pthread_attr_init(pthread_attr_t *attr);
                                                          POSIX:THR
```

If successful, `pthread_attr_destroy` and `pthread_attr_init` return 0. If unsuccessful, these functions return a nonzero error code. The `pthread_attr_init` function sets `errno` to `ENOMEM` if there is not enough memory to create the thread attribute object.

Most of the get/set thread attribute functions have two parameters. The first parameter is a pointer to a thread attribute object. The second parameter is the new value of the attribute for a set operation or a pointer to location to hold the value for a get operation. The `pthread_attr_getstack` and `pthread_attr_setstack` each have one additional parameter.

12.6.1 The thread state

The `pthread_attr_getdetachstate` function examines the state of an attribute object, and the `pthread_attr_setdetachstate` function sets the state of an attribute object. The possible values of the thread state are `PTHREAD_CREATE_JOINABLE` and `PTHREAD_CREATE_DETACHED`. The `attr` parameter is a pointer to the attribute object. The `detachstate` parameter corresponds to the value to be set for `pthread_attr_setdetachstate` and to a pointer to the value to be retrieved for `pthread_attr_getdetachstate`.

```
SYNOPSIS

   #include <pthread.h>

   int pthread_attr_getdetachstate(const pthread_attr_t *attr,
                                   int *detachstate);
   int pthread_attr_setdetachstate(pthread_attr_t *attr, int detachstate);
                                                          POSIX:THR
```

If successful, these functions return 0. If unsuccessful, they return a nonzero error code. The `pthread_attr_setdetachstate` function sets `errno` to `EINVAL` if `detachstate` is invalid.

Detached threads release their resources when they terminate, whereas joinable threads should be waited for with a `pthread_join`. A thread that is detached cannot be waited for with a `pthread_join`. By default, threads are joinable. You can detach a thread by calling the `pthread_detach` function after creating the thread. Alternatively, you can create a thread in the detached state by using an attribute object with thread state `PTHREAD_CREATE_DETACHED`.

■ Example 12.15

The following code segment creates a detached thread to run `processfd`.

```
int error, fd;
pthread_attr_t tattr;
pthread_t tid;

if (error = pthread_attr_init(&tattr))
    fprintf(stderr, "Failed to create attribute object: %s\n",
                     strerror(error));
else if (error = pthread_attr_setdetachstate(&tattr,
                 PTHREAD_CREATE_DETACHED))
    fprintf(stderr, "Failed to set attribute state to detached: %s\n",
            strerror(error));
else if (error = pthread_create(&tid, &tattr, processfd, &fd))
    fprintf(stderr, "Failed to create thread: %s\n", strerror(error));
```

12.6.2 The thread stack

A thread has a stack whose location and size are user-settable, a useful property if the thread stack must be placed in a particular region of memory. To define the placement and size of the stack for a thread, you must first create an attribute object with the specified stack attributes. Then, call `pthread_create` with this attribute object.

The `pthread_attr_getstack` function examines the stack parameters, and the `pthread_attr_setstack` function sets the stack parameters of an attribute object. The `attr` parameter of each function is a pointer to the attribute object. The `pthread_attr_setstack` function takes the stack address and stack size as additional parameters. The `pthread_attr_getstack` takes pointers to these items.

SYNOPSIS

```
#include <pthread.h>

int pthread_attr_getstack(const pthread_attr_t *restrict attr,
        void **restrict stackaddr, size_t *restrict stacksize);
int pthread_attr_setstack(pthread_attr_t *attr,
        void *stackaddr, size_t stacksize);
```
                                                                        POSIX:THR,TSA,TSS

If successful, the `pthread_attr_getstack` and `pthread_attr_setstack` functions return 0. If unsuccessful, these functions return a nonzero error code. The `pthread_attr_setstack` function sets `errno` to `EINVAL` if `stacksize` is out of range.

POSIX also provides functions for examining or setting a guard for stack overflows if the stackaddr has not been set by the user. The pthread_attr_getguardsize function examines the guard parameters, and the pthread_attr_setguardsize function sets the guard parameters for controlling stack overflows in an attribute object. If the guardsize parameter is 0, the stack is unguarded. For a nonzero guardsize, the implementation allocates additional memory of at least guardsize. An overflow into this extra memory causes an error and may generate a SIGSEGV signal for the thread.

```
SYNOPSIS

  #include <pthread.h>

  int pthread_attr_getguardsize(const pthread_attr_t *restrict attr,
                      size_t *restrict guardsize);
  int pthread_attr_setguardsize(pthread_attr_t *attr,
                      size_t guardsize);
                                                        POSIX:THR,XSI
```

If successful, pthread_attr_getguardsize and pthread_attr_setguardsize return 0. If unsuccessful, these functions return a nonzero error code. They return EINVAL if the attr or guardsize parameter is invalid. Guards require the POSIX:THR Extension and the POSIX:XSI Extension.

12.6.3 Thread scheduling

The *contention scope* of an object controls whether the thread competes within the process or at the system level for scheduling resources. The pthread_attr_getscope examines the contention scope, and the pthread_attr_setscope sets the contention scope of an attribute object. The attr parameter is a pointer to the attribute object. The contentionscope parameter corresponds to the value to be set for pthread_attr_setscope and to a pointer to the value to be retrieved for pthread_attr_getscope. The possible values of the contentionscope parameter are PTHREAD_SCOPE_PROCESS and PTHREAD_SCOPE_SYSTEM.

```
SYNOPSIS

  #include <pthread.h>

  int pthread_attr_getscope(const pthread_attr_t *restrict attr,
                      int *restrict contentionscope);
  int pthread_attr_setscope(pthread_attr_t *attr, int contentionscope);
                                                        POSIX:THR,TPS
```

If successful, pthread_attr_getscope and pthread_attr_setscope return 0. If unsuccessful, these functions return a nonzero error code. No mandatory errors are defined for these functions.

■ **Example 12.16**

The following code segment creates a thread that contends for kernel resources.

```
int error;
int fd;
pthread_attr_t tattr;
pthread_t tid;

if (error = pthread_attr_init(&tattr))
    fprintf(stderr, "Failed to create an attribute object:%s\n",
            strerror(error));
else if (error = pthread_attr_setscope(&tattr, PTHREAD_SCOPE_SYSTEM))
    fprintf(stderr, "Failed to set scope to system:%s\n",
            strerror(error));
else if (error = pthread_create(&tid, &tattr, processfd, &fd))
    fprintf(stderr, "Failed to create a thread:%s\n", strerror(error));
```

POSIX allows a thread to inherit a scheduling policy in different ways. The `pthread_attr_getinheritsched` function examines the scheduling inheritance policy, and the `pthread_attr_setinheritsched` function sets the scheduling inheritance policy of an attribute object.

The `attr` parameter is a pointer to the attribute object. The `inheritsched` parameter corresponds to the value to be set for `pthread_attr_setinheritsched` and to a pointer to the value to be retrieved for `pthread_attr_getinheritsched`. The two possible values of `inheritsched` are `PTHREAD_INHERIT_SCHED` and `PTHREAD_EXPLICIT_SCHED`. The value of `inheritsched` determines how the other scheduling attributes of a created thread are to be set. With `PTHREAD_INHERIT_SCHED`, the scheduling attributes are inherited from the creating thread and the other scheduling attributes are ignored. With `PTHREAD_EXPLICIT_SCHED`, the scheduling attributes of this attribute object are used.

SYNOPSIS

```
#include <pthread.h>

int pthread_attr_getinheritsched(const pthread_attr_t *restrict attr,
                       int *restrict inheritsched);
int pthread_attr_setinheritsched(pthread_attr_t *attr,
                       int inheritsched);
```

                                                                    POSIX:THR,TPS

If successful, these functions return 0. If unsuccessful, they return a nonzero error code. No mandatory errors are defined for these functions.

The `pthread_attr_getschedparam` function examines the scheduling parameters, and the `pthread_attr_setschedparam` sets the scheduling parameters of an attribute object. The `attr` parameter is a pointer to the attribute object. The `param` parameter is a pointer to the value to be set for `pthread_attr_setschedparam` and a pointer to the value to be retrieved for `pthread_attr_getschedparam`. Notice that unlike the other `pthread_attr_set` functions, the second parameter is a pointer because it corresponds to a structure rather than an integer. Passing a structure by value is inefficient.

```
SYNOPSIS

  #include <pthread.h>

  int pthread_attr_getschedparam(const pthread_attr_t *restrict attr,
                      struct sched_param *restrict param);
  int pthread_attr_setschedparam(pthread_attr_t *restrict attr,
                      const struct sched_param *restrict param);
                                                         POSIX:THR
```

If successful, these functions return 0. If unsuccessful, they return a nonzero error code. No mandatory errors are defined for these functions.

The scheduling parameters depend on the scheduling policy. They are encapsulated in a `struct sched_param` structure defined in `sched.h`. The `SCHED_FIFO` and `SCHED_RR` scheduling policies require only the `sched_priority` member of `struct sched_param`. The `sched_priority` field holds an `int` priority value, with larger priority values corresponding to higher priorities. Implementations must support at least 32 priorities.

Program 12.10 shows a function that creates a thread attribute object with a specified priority. All the other attributes have their default values. Program 12.10 returns a pointer to the created attribute object or `NULL` if the function failed, in which case it sets `errno`. Program 12.10 illustrates the general strategy for changing parameters—read the existing values first and change only the ones that you need to change.

■ **Example 12.17**

The following code segment creates a `dothis` thread with the default attributes, except that the priority is `HIGHPRIORITY`.

```
#define HIGHPRIORITY 10

int fd;
pthread_attr_t *tattr;
pthread_t tid;
struct sched_param tparam;

if ((tattr = makepriority(HIGHPRIORITY))) {
   perror("Failed to create the attribute object");
else if (error = pthread_create(&tid, tattr, dothis, &fd))
   fprintf(stderr, "Failed to create dothis thread:%s\n", strerror(error));
```

Threads of the same priority compete for processor resources as specified by their scheduling policy. The `sched.h` header file defines `SCHED_FIFO` for first-in-first-out scheduling, `SCHED_RR` for round-robin scheduling and `SCHED_OTHER` for some other policy. One additional scheduling policy, `SCHED_SPORADIC`, is defined for implementations supporting the POSIX:SS Process Sporadic Server Extension and the POSIX:TSP Thread Sporadic Server Extension. Implementations may also define their own policies.

Program 12.10 ───────────────────────────────── `makepriority.c`

A function to create a thread attribute object with the specified priority.

```
#include <errno.h>
#include <pthread.h>
#include <stdlib.h>

pthread_attr_t *makepriority(int priority) {     /* create attribute object */
   pthread_attr_t *attr;
   int error;
   struct sched_param param;

   if ((attr = (pthread_attr_t *)malloc(sizeof(pthread_attr_t))) == NULL)
      return NULL;
   if (!(error = pthread_attr_init(attr)) &&
       !(error = pthread_attr_getschedparam(attr, &param))) {
    param.sched_priority = priority;
    error = pthread_attr_setschedparam(attr, &param);
   }
   if (error) {                         /* if failure, be sure to free memory */
      free(attr);
      errno = error;
      return NULL;
   }
   return attr;
}
```

Program 12.10 ───────────────────────────────── `makepriority.c`

First-in-first-out scheduling policies (e.g., SCHED_FIFO) use a queue for threads in the runnable state at a specified priority. Blocked threads that become runnable are put at the end of the queue corresponding to their priority, whereas running threads that have been preempted are put at the front of their queue.

Round-robin scheduling (e.g., SCHED_RR) behaves similarly to first-in-first-out except that when a running thread has been running for its quantum, it is put at the end of the queue for its priority. The sched_rr_get_interval function returns the quantum.

Sporadic scheduling, which is similar to first-in-first-out, uses two parameters (the replenishment period and the execution capacity) to control the number of threads running at a given priority level. The rules are reasonably complex, but the policy allows a program to more easily regulate the number of threads competing for the processor as a function of available resources.

Preemptive priority policy is the most common implementation of SCHED_OTHER. A POSIX-compliant implementation can support any of these scheduling policies. The actual behavior of the policy in the implementation depends on the scheduling scope and other factors.

The `pthread_attr_getschedpolicy` function gets the scheduling policy, and the `pthread_attr_setschedpolicy` function sets the scheduling policy of an attribute object. The `attr` parameter is a pointer to the attribute object. For the function `pthread_attr_setschedpolicy`, the `policy` parameter is a pointer to the value to be set; for `pthread_attr_getschedpolicy`, it is a pointer to the value to be retrieved. The scheduling policy values are described above.

SYNOPSIS

```
#include <pthread.h>

int pthread_attr_getschedpolicy(const pthread_attr_t *restrict attr,
                                int *restrict policy);
int pthread_attr_setschedpolicy(pthread_attr_t *attr, int policy);
```
                                                                    POSIX:THR

If successful, these functions return 0. If unsuccessful, they return a nonzero error code. No mandatory errors are defined for these functions.

12.7 Exercise: Parallel File Copy

This section develops a parallel file copy as an extension of the copier application of Program 12.8. Be sure to use thread-safe calls in the implementation. The `main` program takes two command-line arguments that are directory names and copies everything from the first directory into the second directory. The copy program preserves subdirectory structure. The same filenames are used for source and destination. Implement the parallel file copy as follows.

1. Write a function called `copydirectory` that has the following prototype.

   ```
   void *copydirectory(void *arg)
   ```

   The `copydirectory` function copies all the files from one directory to another directory. The directory names are passed in `arg` as two consecutive strings (separated by a null character). Assume that both source and destination directories exist when `copydirectory` is called. In this version, only ordinary files are copied and subdirectories are ignored. For each file to be copied, create a thread to run the `copyfilepass` function of Program 12.7. For this version, wait for each thread to complete before creating the next one.

2. Write a `main` program that takes two command-line arguments for the source and destination directories. The `main` program creates a thread to run `copydirectory` and then does a `pthread_join` to wait for the `copydirectory` thread to complete. Use this program to test the first version of `copydirectory`.

3. Modify the `copydirectory` function so that if the destination directory does not exist, `copydirectory` creates the directory. Test the new version.

4. Modify `copydirectory` so that after it creates a thread to copy a file, it continues to create threads to copy the other files. Keep the thread ID and open file descriptors for each `copyfilepass` thread in a linked list with a node structure similar to the following.

```
typedef struct copy_struct {
   char *namestring;
   int sourcefd;
   int destinationfd;
   int bytescopied;
   pthread_t tid;
   struct copy_struct *next;
} copyinfo_t;
copyinfo_t *head = NULL;
copyinfo_t *tail = NULL;
```

After the `copydirectory` function creates threads to copy all the files in the directory, it does a `pthread_join` on each thread in its list and frees the `copyinfo_t` structure.

5. Modify the `copyfilepass` function of Program 12.7 so that its parameter is a pointer to a `copyinfo_t` structure. Test the new version of `copyfilepass` and `copydirectory`.

6. Modify `copydirectory` so that if a file is a directory instead of an ordinary file, `copydirectory` creates a thread to run `copydirectory` instead of `copyfilepass`. Test the new function.

7. Devise a method for performing timings to compare an ordinary copy with the threaded copy.

8. If run on a large directory, the program may attempt to open more file descriptors or more threads than are allowed for a process. Devise a method for handling this situation.

9. See whether there is a difference in running time if the threads have scope `PTHREAD_SCOPE_SYSTEM` instead of `PTHREAD_SCOPE_PROCESS`.

12.8 Additional Reading

A number of books on POSIX thread programming are available. They include *Programming with POSIX(R) Threads* by Butenhof [19], *Pthreads Programming: A POSIX Standard for Better Multiprocessing* by Nichols et al. [87], *Multithreaded Programming with Pthreads* by Lewis and Berg [72] and *Thread Time: The Multithreaded Programming Guide* by Norton and DiPasquale. All these books are based on the original POSIX standard. The book *Distributed Operating Systems* by Tanenbaum [121] presents an understandable general discussion of threads. Approaches to thread scheduling are discussed in [2, 12, 32, 78]. Finally, the POSIX standard [49, 51] is a surprisingly readable account of the conflicting issues and choices involved in implementing a usable threads package.

Chapter 13

Thread Synchronization

POSIX supports mutex locks for short-term locking and condition variables for waiting on events of unbounded duration. Signal handling in threaded programs presents additional complications that can be reduced if signal handlers are replaced with dedicated threads. This chapter illustrates these thread synchronization concepts by implementing controlled access to shared objects, reader-writer synchronization and barriers.

Objectives
- Learn the basics of thread synchronization
- Experiment with mutex locks and condition variables
- Explore classic synchronization problems
- Use threads with signals
- Understand design tradeoffs for synchronization

13.1 POSIX Synchronization Functions

This chapter discusses mutex locks, conditions variables and read-write locks. Table 13.1 summarizes the synchronization functions that are available in the POSIX:THR Extension. Each synchronization mechanism provides an initialization function and a function for destroying the object. The mutex locks and condition variables allow static initialization. All three types of synchronization have associated attribute objects, but we work only with synchronization objects that have the default attributes.

description	POSIX function
mutex locks	`pthread_mutex_destroy`
	`pthread_mutex_init`
	`pthread_mutex_lock`
	`pthread_mutex_trylock`
	`pthread_mutex_unlock`
condition variables	`pthread_cond_broadcast`
	`pthread_cond_destroy`
	`pthread_cond_init`
	`pthread_cond_signal`
	`pthread_cond_timedwait`
	`pthread_cond_wait`
read-write locks	`pthread_rwlock_destroy`
	`pthread_rwlock_init`
	`pthread_rwlock_rdlock`
	`pthread_rwlock_timedrdlock`
	`pthread_rwlock_timedwrlock`
	`pthread_rwlock_tryrdlock`
	`pthread_rwlock_trywrlock`
	`pthread_rwlock_wrlock`

Table 13.1: Synchronization functions for POSIX:THR threads.

13.2 Mutex Locks

A mutex is a special variable that can be either in the *locked* state or the *unlocked* state. If the mutex is locked, it has a distinguished thread that *holds* or *owns* the mutex. If no thread holds the mutex, we say the mutex is *unlocked*, *free* or *available*. The mutex also has a queue for the threads that are waiting to hold the mutex. The order in which the threads in the mutex queue obtain the mutex is determined by the thread-scheduling policy, but POSIX does not require that any particular policy be implemented.

When the mutex is free and a thread attempts to acquire the mutex, that thread obtains the mutex and is not blocked. It is convenient to think of this case as first causing the thread to enter the queue and then automatically removing it from the queue and giving it the mutex.

The *mutex* or *mutex lock* is the simplest and most efficient thread synchronization mechanism. Programs use mutex locks to preserve critical sections and to obtain exclusive access to resources. *A mutex is meant to be held for short periods of time.* Mutex functions are not thread cancellation points and are not interrupted by signals. A thread that waits for a mutex is not logically interruptible except by termination of the process, termination of a thread with `pthread_exit` (from a signal handler), or asynchronous cancellation (which is normally not used).

Mutex locks are ideal for making changes to data structures in which the state of the data structure is temporarily inconsistent, as when updating pointers in a shared linked list. These locks are designed to be held for a short time. *Use condition variables to synchronize on events of indefinite duration such as waiting for input.*

13.2.1 Creating and initializing a mutex

POSIX uses variables of type `pthread_mutex_t` to represent mutex locks. A program must always initialize `pthread_mutex_t` variables before using them for synchronization. For statically allocated `pthread_mutex_t` variables, simply assign `PTHREAD_MUTEX_INITIALIZER` to the variable. For mutex variables that are dynamically allocated or that don't have the default mutex attributes, call `pthread_mutex_init` to perform initialization.

The `mutex` parameter of `pthread_mutex_init` is a pointer to the mutex to be initialized. Pass `NULL` for the `attr` parameter of `pthread_mutex_init` to initialize a mutex with the default attributes. Otherwise, first create and initialize a mutex attribute object in a manner similar to that used for thread attribute objects.

```
SYNOPSIS

   #include <pthread.h>

   int pthread_mutex_init(pthread_mutex_t *restrict mutex,
                       const pthread_mutexattr_t *restrict attr);
   pthread_mutex_t mutex = PTHREAD_MUTEX_INITIALIZER;
                                                          POSIX:THR
```

If successful, `pthread_mutex_init` returns 0. If unsuccessful, `pthread_mutex_init` returns a nonzero error code. The following table lists the mandatory errors for `pthread_mutex_init`.

error	cause
EAGAIN	system lacks nonmemory resources needed to initialize *mutex
ENOMEM	system lacks memory resources needed to initialize *mutex
EPERM	caller does not have appropriate privileges

■ Example 13.1

The following code segment initializes the `mylock` mutex with the default attributes, using the static initializer.

```
pthread_mutex_t mylock = PTHREAD_MUTEX_INITIALIZER;
```

The `mylock` variable must be allocated statically.

Static initializers are usually more efficient than `pthread_mutex_init`, and they are guaranteed to be performed exactly once before any thread begins execution.

■ Example 13.2

The following code segment initializes the `mylock` mutex with the default attributes. The `mylock` variable must be accessible to all the threads that use it.

```
int error;
pthread_mutex_t mylock;

if (error = pthread_mutex_init(&mylock, NULL))
    fprintf(stderr, "Failed to initialize mylock:%s\n", strerror(error));
```

Example 13.2 uses the `strerror` function to output a message associated with `error`. Unfortunately, POSIX does not require `strerror` to be thread-safe (though many implementations have made it thread-safe). If multiple threads don't call `strerror` at the same time, you can still use it in threaded programs. For example, if all functions return error indications and only the main thread prints error messages, the main thread can safely call `strerror`. Section 13.7 gives a thread-safe and signal-safe implementation, `strerror_r`.

□ Exercise 13.3

What happens if a thread tries to initialize a mutex that has already been initialized?

Answer:

POSIX explicitly states that the behavior is not defined, so avoid this situation in your programs.

13.2.2 Destroying a mutex

The `pthread_mutex_destroy` function destroys the mutex referenced by its parameter. The `mutex` parameter is a pointer to the mutex to be destroyed. A `pthread_mutex_t` variable that has been destroyed with `pthread_mutex_destroy` can be reinitialized with `pthread_mutex_init`.

```
SYNOPSIS

   #include <pthread.h>

   int pthread_mutex_destroy(pthread_mutex_t *mutex);

                                                            POSIX:THR
```

If successful, `pthread_mutex_destroy` returns 0. If unsuccessful, it returns a nonzero error code. No mandatory errors are defined for `pthread_mutex_destroy`.

■ Example 13.4

The following code segment destroys a mutex.

```
pthread_mutex_t mylock;

if (error = pthread_mutex_destroy(&mylock))
    fprintf(stderr, "Failed to destroy mylock:%s\n", strerror(error));
```

□ Exercise 13.5

What happens if a thread references a mutex after it has been destroyed? What happens if one thread calls `pthread_mutex_destroy` and another thread has the mutex locked?

Answer:

POSIX explicitly states that the behavior in both situations is not defined.

13.2.3 Locking and unlocking a mutex

POSIX has two functions, `pthread_mutex_lock` and `pthread_mutex_trylock` for acquiring a mutex. The `pthread_mutex_lock` function blocks until the mutex is available, while the `pthread_mutex_trylock` always returns immediately. The `pthread_mutex_unlock` function releases the specified mutex. All three functions take a single parameter, `mutex`, a pointer to a mutex.

```
SYNOPSIS

   #include <pthread.h>

   int pthread_mutex_lock(pthread_mutex_t *mutex);
   int pthread_mutex_trylock(pthread_mutex_t *mutex);
   int pthread_mutex_unlock(pthread_mutex_t *mutex);

                                                            POSIX:THR
```

If successful, these functions return 0. If unsuccessful, these functions return a nonzero error code. The following table lists the mandatory errors for the three functions.

error	cause
EINVAL	mutex has protocol attribute PTHREAD_PRIO_PROTECT and caller's priority is higher than mutex's current priority ceiling (pthread_mutex_lock or pthread_mutex_trylock)
EBUSY	another thread holds the lock (pthread_mutex_trylock)

The PTHREAD_PRIO_PROTECT attribute prevents priority inversions of the sort described in Section 13.8.

■ Example 13.6

The following code segment uses a mutex to protect a critical section.

```
pthread_mutex_t mylock = PTHREAD_MUTEX_INITIALIZER;

pthread_mutex_lock(&mylock);
    /*  critical section */
pthread_mutex_unlock(&mylock);
```

The code omits error checking for clarity.

Locking and unlocking are voluntary in the sense that a program achieves mutual exclusion only when its threads correctly acquire the appropriate mutex before entering their critical sections and release the mutex when finished. Nothing prevents an uncooperative thread from entering its critical section without acquiring the mutex. One way to ensure exclusive access to objects is to permit access only through well-defined functions and to put the locking calls in these functions. The locking mechanism is then transparent to the calling threads.

Program 13.1 shows an example of a thread-safe counter that might be used for reference counts in a threaded program. The locking mechanisms are hidden in the functions, and the calling program does not have to worry about using mutex variables. The count and countlock variables have the static attribute, so these variables can be referenced only from within counter.c. Following the pattern of the POSIX threads library, the functions in Program 13.1 return 0 if successful or a nonzero error code if unsuccessful.

□ Exercise 13.7

What can go wrong in a threaded program if the count variable of Program 13.1 is not protected with mutex locks?

Answer:

Without locking, it is possible to get an incorrect value for count, since incrementing and decrementing a variable are not atomic operations on most machines. (Typically, incrementing consists of three distinct steps: loading a memory location into a CPU register, adding 1 to the register, and storing the value back in memory.) Suppose a thread is in the middle of the increment when the process quantum expires. The thread scheduler may select another thread to run when the process runs again. If the newly selected thread also tries to increment or decrement `count`, the variable's value will be incorrect when the original thread completes its operation.

Program 13.1 ──────────────────────────── `counter.c`

A counter that can be accessed by multiple threads.

```
#include <pthread.h>
static int count = 0;
static pthread_mutex_t  countlock = PTHREAD_MUTEX_INITIALIZER;

int increment(void) {                   /* increment the counter */
   int error;
   if (error = pthread_mutex_lock(&countlock))
      return error;
   count++;
   return pthread_mutex_unlock(&countlock);
}

int decrement(void) {                   /* decrement the counter */
   int error;
   if (error = pthread_mutex_lock(&countlock))
      return error;
   count--;
   return pthread_mutex_unlock(&countlock);
}

int getcount(int *countp) {             /* retrieve the counter */
   int error;
   if (error = pthread_mutex_lock(&countlock))
      return error;
   *countp = count;
   return pthread_mutex_unlock(&countlock);
}
```

Program 13.1 ──────────────────────────── `counter.c`

13.2.4 Protecting unsafe library functions

A mutex can be used to protect an unsafe library function. The `rand` function from the C library takes no parameters and returns a pseudorandom integer in the range 0 to `RAND_MAX`. It is listed in the POSIX standard as being unsafe in multithreaded applications. The `rand` function can be used in a multithreaded environment if it is guaranteed that no two threads are concurrently calling it. Program 13.2 shows an implementation of the function `randsafe` that uses `rand` to produce a single per-process sequence of pseudorandom double values in the range from 0 to 1. Note that `rand` and therefore `randsafe` are not particularly good generators; avoid them in real applications.

Program 13.2 ———————————————— `randsafe.c`

A random number generator protected by a mutex.

```
#include <pthread.h>
#include <stdlib.h>

int randsafe(double *ranp) {
    static pthread_mutex_t lock = PTHREAD_MUTEX_INITIALIZER;
    int error;

    if (error = pthread_mutex_lock(&lock))
        return error;
    *ranp = (rand() + 0.5)/(RAND_MAX + 1.0);
    return pthread_mutex_unlock(&lock);
}
```

Program 13.2 ———————————————— `randsafe.c`

13.2.5 Synchronizing flags and global values

Program 13.3 shows an implementation of a synchronized flag that is initially zero. The `getdone` function returns the value of the synchronized flag, and the `setdone` function changes the value of the synchronized flag to 1.

Program 13.3 ———————————————— `doneflag.c`

A synchronized flag that is 1 if `setdone` has been called at least once.

```
#include <pthread.h>
static int doneflag = 0;
static pthread_mutex_t donelock = PTHREAD_MUTEX_INITIALIZER;

int getdone(int *flag) {                      /* get the flag */
    int error;
    if (error = pthread_mutex_lock(&donelock))
        return error;
    *flag = doneflag;
    return pthread_mutex_unlock(&donelock);
}

int setdone(void) {                           /* set the flag */
    int error;
    if (error = pthread_mutex_lock(&donelock))
        return error;
    doneflag = 1;
    return pthread_mutex_unlock(&donelock);
}
```

Program 13.3 ———————————————— `doneflag.c`

■ Example 13.8

The following code segment uses the synchronized flag of Program 13.3 to decide whether to process another command in a threaded program.

```
void docommand(void);

int error = 0;
int done = 0;

while(!done && !error) {
   docommand();
   error = getdone(&done);
}
```

Program 13.4 shows a synchronized implementation of a global error value. Functions from different files can call `seterror` with return values from various functions. The `seterror` function returns immediately if the `error` parameter is zero, indicating no error. Otherwise, `seterror` acquires the mutex and assigns `error` to `globalerror` if `globalerror` is zero. In this way, `globalerror` holds the error code of the first error that it is assigned. Notice that `seterror` returns the original error unless there was a problem acquiring or releasing the internal mutex. In this case, the global error value may not be meaningful and both `seterror` and `geterror` return the error code from the locking problem.

Program 13.4 ———————————————— **globalerror.c**

A shared global error flag.

```
#include <pthread.h>
static int globalerror = 0;
static pthread_mutex_t errorlock = PTHREAD_MUTEX_INITIALIZER;

int geterror(int *error) {                              /* get the error flag */
   int terror;
   if (terror = pthread_mutex_lock(&errorlock))
      return terror;
   *error = globalerror;
   return pthread_mutex_unlock(&errorlock);
}

int seterror(int error) {          /* globalerror set to error if first error */
   int terror;
   if (!error)              /* it wasn't an error, so don't change globalerror */
      return error;
   if (terror = pthread_mutex_lock(&errorlock))          /* couldn't get lock */
      return terror;
   if (!globalerror)
      globalerror = error;
   terror = pthread_mutex_unlock(&errorlock);
   return terror? terror: error;
}
```

Program 13.4 ———————————————— **globalerror.c**

Program 13.5 shows a synchronized implementation of a shared sum object that uses the global error flag of Program 13.4.

Program 13.5 ——————————————————————— **sharedsum.c**

A shared sum object that uses the global error flag of Program 13.4.

```
#include <pthread.h>
#include "globalerror.h"

static int count = 0;
static double sum = 0.0;
static pthread_mutex_t  sumlock = PTHREAD_MUTEX_INITIALIZER;

int add(double x) {                                        /* add x to sum */
    int error;
    if (error = pthread_mutex_lock(&sumlock))
        return seterror(error);
    sum += x;
    count++;
    error = pthread_mutex_unlock(&sumlock);
    return seterror(error);
}

int getsum(double *sump) {                                 /* return sum */
    int error;
    if (error = pthread_mutex_lock(&sumlock))
        return seterror(error);
    *sump = sum;
    error = pthread_mutex_unlock(&sumlock);
    return seterror(error);
}

int getcountandsum(int *countp, double *sump) {    /* return count and sum */
    int error;
    if (error = pthread_mutex_lock(&sumlock))
        return seterror(error);
    *countp = count;
    *sump = sum;
    error = pthread_mutex_unlock(&sumlock);
    return seterror(error);
}
```

Program 13.5 ——————————————————————— **sharedsum.c**

Because mutex locks must be accessible to all the threads that need to synchronize, they often appear as global variables (internal or external linkage). Although C is not object oriented, an object organization is often useful. Internal linkage should be used for those objects that do not need to be accessed from outside a given file. Programs 13.1 through 13.5 illustrate methods of doing this. We now illustrate how to use these synchronized objects in a program.

Program 13.6 shows a function that can be called as a thread to do a simple calculation. The computethread calculates the sine of a random number between 0 and 1 in a loop, adding the result to the synchronized sum given by Program 13.5. The computethread sleeps for a short time after each calculation, allowing other threads to use the CPU. The computethread thread uses the doneflag of Program 13.3 to terminate when another thread sets the flag.

Program 13.6 ──────────────────────────────── `computethread.c`
A thread that computes sums of random sines.

```c
#include <math.h>
#include <stdlib.h>
#include <time.h>
#include "doneflag.h"
#include "globalerror.h"
#include "randsafe.h"
#include "sharedsum.h"
#define TEN_MILLION 10000000L

/* ARGSUSED */
void *computethread(void *arg1) {                    /* compute a random partial sum */
    int error;
    int localdone = 0;
    struct timespec sleeptime;
    double val;

    sleeptime.tv_sec = 0;
    sleeptime.tv_nsec = TEN_MILLION;                                      /* 10 ms */

    while (!localdone) {
        if (error = randsafe(&val)) /* get a random number between 0.0 and 1.0 */
            break;
        if (error = add(sin(val)))
            break;
        if (error = getdone(&localdone))
            break;
        nanosleep(&sleeptime, NULL);                    /* let other threads in */
    }
    seterror(error);
    return NULL;
}
```

Program 13.6 ──────────────────────────────── `computethread.c`

Program 13.7 is a driver program that creates a number of `computethread` threads and allows them to compute for a given number of seconds before it sets a flag to end the calculations. The `main` program then calls the `showresults` function of Program 13.8 to retrieve the shared sum and number of the summed values. The `showresults` function computes the average from these values. It also calculates the theoretical average value of the sine function over the interval [0,1] and gives the total and percentage error of the average value.

The second command-line argument of `computethreadmain` is the number of seconds to sleep after creating the threads. After sleeping, `computethreadmain` calls `setdone`, causing the threads to terminate. The `computethreadmain` program then uses `pthread_join` to wait for the threads to finish and calls `showresults`. The `showresults` function uses `geterror` to check to see that all threads completed without reporting an error. If all is well, `showresults` displays the results.

Program 13.7 ─────────────────────────── `computethreadmain.c`

A `main` *program that creates a number of* `computethread` *threads and allows them to execute for a given number of seconds.*

```c
#include <math.h>
#include <pthread.h>
#include <stdio.h>
#include <stdlib.h>
#include <string.h>
#include <unistd.h>
#include "computethread.h"
#include "donoflag.h"
#include "globalerror.h"
#include "sharedsum.h"

int showresults(void);

int main(int argc, char *argv[]) {
   int error;
   int i;
   int numthreads;
   int sleeptime;
   pthread_t *tids;

   if (argc != 3) {     /* pass number threads and sleeptime on command line */
      fprintf(stderr, "Usage: %s numthreads sleeptime\n", argv[0]);
      return 1;
   }

   numthreads = atoi(argv[1]);      /* allocate an array for the thread ids */
   sleeptime = atoi(argv[2]);
   if ((tids = (pthread_t *)calloc(numthreads, sizeof(pthread_t))) == NULL) {
      perror("Failed to allocate space for thread IDs");
      return 1;
   }
   for (i = 0; i < numthreads; i++)     /* create numthreads computethreads */
      if (error =  pthread_create(tids + i, NULL, computethread, NULL)) {
         fprintf(stderr, "Failed to start thread %d:%s\n", i, strerror(error));
         return 1;
      }
   sleep(sleeptime);                        /* give them some time to compute */
   if (error = setdone()) {  /* tell the computethreads to quit */
      fprintf(stderr, "Failed to set done:%s\n", strerror(error));
      return 1;
   }
   for (i = 0; i < numthreads; i++)     /* make sure that they are all done */
      if (error = pthread_join(tids[i], NULL)) {
         fprintf(stderr, "Failed to join thread %d:%s\n", i, strerror(error));
         return 1;
      }
   if (showresults())
      return 1;
   return 0;
}
```

Program 13.7 ─────────────────────────── `computethreadmain.c`

A function that displays the results of the computethread *calculations.*

```c
#include <math.h>
#include <stdio.h>
#include <string.h>
#include "globalerror.h"
#include "sharedsum.h"

int showresults(void) {
   double average;
   double calculated;
   int count;
   double err;
   int error;
   int gerror;
   double perr;
   double sum;

   if (((error = getcountandsum(&count, &sum)) != 0) ||
       ((error = geterror(&gerror)) != 0)) {                    /* get results */
      fprintf(stderr, "Failed to get results: %s\n", strerror(error));
      return -1;
   }
   if (gerror) {             /* an error occurred in compute thread computation */
      fprintf(stderr, "Failed to compute sum: %s\n", strerror(gerror));
      return -1;
   }
   if (count == 0)
      printf("No values were summed.\n");
   else {
      calculated = 1.0 - cos(1.0);
      average = sum/count;
      err = average - calculated;
      perr = 100.0*err/calculated;
      printf("The sum is %f and the count is %d\n", sum, count);
      printf("The average is %f and error is %f or %f%%\n", average, err, perr);
   }
   return 0;
}
```

13.2.6 Making data structures thread-safe

Most shared data structures in a threaded program must be protected with synchronization mechanisms to ensure correct results. Program 13.9 illustrates how to use a single mutex to make the list object of Program 2.7 thread-safe. The listlib.c program should be included in the listlib_r.c file. All the functions in listlib.c should be qualified with the static attribute so that they are not accessible outside the file. The list object functions of Program 2.7 return −1 and set errno to report an error. The implementation of Program 13.9 preserves this handling of the errors. Since each thread has its own errno, setting errno in the listlib_r functions is not a problem. The implementation just wraps each function in a pair of mutex calls. Most of the code is for properly handling errors that occur during the mutex calls.

Wrapper functions to make the list object of Program 2.7 thread-safe.

```
#include <errno.h>
#include <pthread.h>
static pthread_mutex_t listlock = PTHREAD_MUTEX_INITIALIZER;

int accessdata_r(void) {   /* return nonnegative traversal key if successful */
   int error;
   int key;
   if (error = pthread_mutex_lock(&listlock)) {        /* no mutex, give up */
      errno = error;
      return  1;
   }
   key = accessdata();
   if (key == -1) {
      error = errno;
      pthread_mutex_unlock(&listlock);
      errno = error;
      return -1;
   }
   if (error = pthread_mutex_unlock(&listlock)) {
      errno = error;
      return -1;
   }
   return key;
}

int adddata_r(data_t data) {        /* allocate a node on list to hold data */
   int error;
   if (error = pthread_mutex_lock(&listlock)) {        /* no mutex, give up */
      errno = error;
      return -1;
   }
   if (adddata(data) == -1) {
      error = errno;
      pthread_mutex_unlock(&listlock);
      errno = error;
      return -1;
   }
   if (error = pthread_mutex_unlock(&listlock)) {
      errno = error;
      return -1;
   }
   return 0;
}

int getdata_r(int key, data_t *datap) {              /* retrieve node by key */
   int error;
   if (error = pthread_mutex_lock(&listlock)) {        /* no mutex, give up */
      errno = error;
      return -1;
   }
   if (getdata(key, datap) == -1) {
      error = errno;
      pthread_mutex_unlock(&listlock);
      errno = error;
      return -1;
   }
```

```
      if (error = pthread_mutex_unlock(&listlock)) {
         errno = error;
         return -1;
      }
      return 0;
}

int freekey_r(int key) {                                    /* free the key */
      int error;
      if (error = pthread_mutex_lock(&listlock)) {       /* no mutex, give up */
         errno = error;
         return -1;
      }
      if (freekey(key) == -1) {
         error = errno;
         pthrcad_mutex_unlock(&listlock);
         errno = error;
         return -1;
      }
      if (error = pthread_mutex_unlock(&listlock)) {
         errno = error;
         return -1;
      }
      return 0;
}
```
Program 13.9 ──────────────────────────────────── `listlib_r.c`

The implementation of Program 13.9 uses a straight locking strategy that allows only one thread at a time to proceed. Section 13.6 revisits this problem with an implementation that allows multiple threads to execute the getdata function at the same time by using reader-writer synchronization.

13.3 At-Most-Once and At-Least-Once-Execution

If a mutex isn't statically initialized, the program must call pthread_mutex_init before using any of the other mutex functions. For programs that have a well-defined initialization phase before they create additional threads, the main thread can perform this initialization. Not all problems fit this structure. Care must be taken to call pthread_mutex_init before any thread accesses a mutex, but having each thread initialize the mutex doesn't work either. The effect of calling pthread_mutex_init for a mutex that has already been initialized is not defined.

The notion of single initialization is so important that POSIX provides the pthread_once function to ensure these semantics. The once_control parameter must be statically initialized with PTHREAD_ONCE_INIT. The init_routine is called the first time pthread_once is called with a given once_control, and init_routine is not called on subsequent calls. When a thread returns from pthread_once without error, the init_routine has been completed by some thread.

```
SYNOPSIS

  #include <pthread.h>

  int pthread_once(pthread_once_t *once_control,
                   void (*init_routine)(void));
  pthread_once_t once_control = PTHREAD_ONCE_INIT;
                                                            POSIX:THR
```

If successful, `pthread_once` returns 0. If unsuccessful, `pthread_once` returns a nonzero error code. No mandatory errors are defined for `pthread_once`.

Program 13.10 uses `pthread_once` to implement an initialization function `printinitmutex`. Notice that `var` isn't protected by a mutex because it will be changed only once by `printinitonce`, and that modification occurs before any caller returns from `printinitonce`.

Program 13.10 ──────────────────────── **printinitonce.c**

A function that uses `pthread_once` *to initialize a variable and print a statement at most once.*

```
#include <pthread.h>
#include <stdio.h>

static pthread_once_t initonce = PTHREAD_ONCE_INIT;
int var;

static void initialization(void) {
   var = 1;
   printf("The variable was initialized to %d\n", var);
}

int printinitonce(void) {          /* call initialization at most once */
   return pthread_once(&initonce, initialization);
}
```

Program 13.10 ──────────────────────── **printinitonce.c**

The `initialization` function of `printinitonce` has no parameters, making it hard to initialize `var` to something other than a fixed value. Program 13.11 shows an alternative implementation of at-most-once initialization that uses a statically initialized mutex. The `printinitmutex` function performs the initialization and printing at most once regardless of how many different variables or values are passed. If successful, `printinitmutex` returns 0. If unsuccessful, `printinitmutex` returns a nonzero error code. The mutex in `printinitmutex` is declared in the function so that it is accessible only inside the function. Giving the mutex static storage class guarantees that the same mutex is used every time the function is called.

Program 13.11 ────────────────────────── **printinitmutex.c**

A function that uses a statically initialized mutex to initialize a variable and print a statement at most once.

```c
#include <pthread.h>
#include <stdio.h>

int printinitmutex(int *var, int value) {
   static int done = 0;
   static pthread_mutex_t lock = PTHREAD_MUTEX_INITIALIZER;
   int error;
   if (error = pthread_mutex_lock(&lock))
      return error;
   if (!done) {
      *var = value;
      printf("The variable was initialized to %d\n", value);
      done = 1;
   }
   return pthread_mutex_unlock(&lock);
}
```

Program 13.11 ────────────────────────── **printinitmutex.c**

■ **Example 13.9**

The following code segment initializes `whichiteration` to the index of the first loop iteration in which `dostuff` returns a nonzero value.

```c
int whichiteration = -1;

void *thisthread(void *) {
   int i;
   for (i = 0; i < 100; i++)
      if (dostuff())
         printinitmutex(&whichiteration, i);
}
```

The `whichiteration` value is changed at most once, even if the program creates several threads running `thisthread`.

The `testandsetonce` function of Program 13.12 atomically sets an internal variable to 1 and returns the previous value of the internal variable in its `ovalue` parameter. The first call to `testandsetonce` initializes `done` to 0, sets `*ovalue` to 0 and sets `done` to 1. Subsequent calls set `*ovalue` to 1. The mutex ensures that no two threads have `ovalue` set to 0. If successful, `testandsetonce` returns 0. If unsuccessful, `testandsetonce` returns a nonzero error code.

□ **Exercise 13.10**

What happens if you remove the `static` qualifier from the `done` and `lock` variables of `testandsetonce` of Program 13.12?

Answer:

The `static` qualifier for variables inside a block ensures that they remain in existence for subsequent executions of the block. Without the `static` qualifier, `done` and `lock` become automatic variables. In this case, each call to `testandsetonce` allocates new variables and each `return` deallocates them. The function no longer works.

Program 13.12 ───────────────────────────── **testandsetonce.c**

A function that uses a mutex to set a variable to 1 at most once.

```c
#include <pthread.h>

int testandsetonce(int *ovalue) {
   static int done = 0;
   static pthread_mutex_t lock = PTHREAD_MUTEX_INITIALIZER;
   int error;
   if (error = pthread_mutex_lock(&lock))
      return error;
   *ovalue = done;
   done = 1;
   return pthread_mutex_unlock(&lock);
}
```

Program 13.12 ───────────────────────────── **testandsetonce.c**

☐ Exercise 13.11

Does `testandsetonce` still work if you move the declarations of `done` and `lock` outside the `testandsetonce` function?

Answer:

Yes, `testandsetonce` still works. However, now `done` and `lock` are accessible to other functions defined in the same file. Keeping them inside the function is safer for enforcing at-most-once semantics.

☐ Exercise 13.12

Does the following use of `testandsetonce` of Program 13.12 ensure that the initialization of `var` and the printing of the message occur at most once?

```c
int error;
int oflag;
int var;

error = testandsetonce(&oflag);
if (!error && !oflag) {
   var = 1;
   printf("The variable has been initialized to 1\n");
}
var++;
```

Answer:

No. Successive calls to testandsetonce of Program 13.12 can return before the variable has been initialized. Consider the following scenario in which var must be initialized before being incremented.

1. Thread A calls testandsetonce.
2. The testandsetonce returns in thread A.
3. Thread A loses the CPU.
4. Thread B calls testandsetonce.
5. The executeonce returns to thread B without printing or initializing var.
6. Thread B assumes that var has been initialized, and it increments the variable.
7. Thread A gets the CPU again and initializes var to 1.

In this case, var should have the value 2 since it was initialized to 1 and incremented once. Unfortunately, it has the value 1.

The strategies discussed in this section guarantee *at-most-once* execution. They do not guarantee that code has been executed at least once. *At-least-once semantics* are important for initialization. For example, suppose that you choose to use pthread_mutex_init rather than the static initializer to initialize a mutex. You need both at-most-once and at-least-once semantics. In other words, you need to perform an operation such as initialization *exactly once*. Sometimes the structure of the program ensures that this is the case—a main thread performs all necessary initialization before creating any threads. In other situations, each thread must call initialization when it starts executing, or each function must call the initialization before accessing the mutex. In these cases, you will need to use at-most-once strategies in conjunction with the calls.

13.4 Condition Variables

Consider the problem of having a thread wait until some arbitrary condition is satisfied. For concreteness, assume that two variables, x and y, are shared by multiple threads. We want a thread to wait until x and y are equal. A typical incorrect busy-waiting solution is

```
while (x != y) ;
```

Having a thread use busy waiting is particularly troublesome. Depending on how the threads are scheduled, the thread doing the busy waiting may prevent other threads from ever using the CPU, in which case x and y never change. Also, access to shared variables should always be protected.

Here is the correct strategy for non-busy waiting for the predicate $x==y$ to become true.

1. Lock a mutex.
2. Test the condition x==y.
3. If true, unlock the mutex and exit the loop.
4. If false, suspend the thread and unlock the mutex.

The mutex must be held until a test determines whether to suspend the thread. Holding the mutex prevents the condition x==y from changing between the test and the suspension of the thread. The mutex needs to be unlocked while the thread is suspended so that other threads can access x and y. The strategy assumes that the code protects all other access to the shared variables x and y with the mutex.

Applications manipulate mutex queues through well-defined system library functions such as pthread_mutex_lock and pthread_mutex_unlock. These functions are not sufficient to implement (in a simple manner) the queue manipulations required here. We need a new data type, one associated with a queue of processes waiting for an arbitrary condition such as x==y to become true. Such a data type is called a *condition variable*.

A classical condition variable is associated with a particular condition. In contrast, POSIX condition variables provide an atomic waiting mechanism but are not associated with particular conditions.

The function pthread_cond_wait takes a condition variable and a mutex as parameters. It atomically suspends the calling thread and unlocks the mutex. It can be thought of as placing the thread in a queue of threads waiting to be notified of a change in a condition. The function returns with the mutex reacquired when the thread receives a notification. The thread must test the condition again before proceeding.

■ Example 13.13

The following code segment illustrates how to wait for the condition x==y, using a POSIX condition variable v and a mutex m.

```
pthread_mutex_lock(&m);
while (x != y)
    pthread_cond_wait(&v, &m);
/* modify x or y if necessary */
pthread_mutex_unlock(&m);
```

When the thread returns from pthread_cond_wait it owns m, so it can safely test the condition again. The code segment omits error checking for clarity.

The function pthread_cond_wait *should be called only by a thread that owns the mutex, and the thread owns the mutex again when the function returns.* The suspended thread has the illusion of uninterrupted mutex ownership because it owns the mutex before the call to pthread_cond_wait and owns the mutex when pthread_cond_wait returns. In reality, the mutex can be acquired by other threads during the suspension.

A thread that modifies x or y can call pthread_cond_signal to notify other threads of the change. The pthread_cond_signal function takes a condition variable as a parameter and attempts to wake up at least one of the threads waiting in the corresponding queue. Since the blocked thread cannot return from `pthread_cond_wait` without owning the mutex, `pthread_cond_signal` has the effect of moving the thread from the condition variable queue to the mutex queue.

■ Example 13.14

The following code might be used by another thread in conjunction with Example 13.13 to notify the waiting thread that it has incremented x.

```
pthread_mutex_lock(&m);
x++;
pthread_cond_signal(&v);
pthread_mutex_unlock(&m);
```

The code segment omits error checking for clarity.

In Example 13.14, the caller holds the mutex while calling `pthread_cond_signal`. POSIX does not require this to be the case, and the caller could have unlocked the mutex before signaling. In programs that have threads of different priorities, holding the mutex while signaling can prevent lower priority threads from acquiring the mutex and executing before a higher-priority thread is awakened.

Several threads may use the same condition variables to wait on different predicates. The waiting threads must verify that the predicate is satisfied when they return from the wait. The threads that modify x or y do not need to know what conditions are being waited for; they just need to know which condition variable is being used.

☐ Exercise 13.15

Compare the use of condition variables with the use of `sigsuspend` as described in Example 8.24 on page 275.

Answer:

The concepts are similar. Example 8.24 blocks the signal and tests the condition. Blocking the signal is analogous to locking the mutex since the signal handler cannot access the global variable `sigreceived` while the signal is blocked. The `sigsuspend` atomically unblocks the signal and suspends the process. When `sigsuspend` returns, the signal is blocked again. With condition variables, the thread locks the mutex to protect its critical section and tests the condition. The `pthread_cond_wait` atomically releases the mutex and suspends the process. When `pthread_cond_wait` returns, the thread owns the mutex again.

13.4.1 Creating and destroying condition variables

POSIX represents condition variables by variables of type `pthread_cond_t`. A program must always initialize `pthread_cond_t` variables before using them. For statically allocated `pthread_cond_t` variables with the default attributes, simply assign

PTHREAD_COND_INITIALIZER to the variable. For variables that are dynamically allocated or don't have the default attributes, call pthread_cond_init to perform initialization. Pass NULL for the attr parameter of pthread_cond_init to initialize a condition variable with the default attributes. Otherwise, first create and initialize a condition variable attribute object in a manner similar to that used for thread attribute objects.

```
SYNOPSIS

    #include <pthread.h>

    int pthread_cond_init(pthread_cond_t *restrict cond,
                          const pthread_condattr_t *restrict attr);
    pthread_cont_t cond = PTHREAD_COND_INITIALIZER;
                                                              POSIX:THR
```

If successful, pthread_cond_init returns 0. If unsuccessful, pthread_cond_init returns a nonzero error code. The following table lists the mandatory errors for pthread_cond_init.

error	cause
EAGAIN	system lacked nonmemory resources needed to initialize *cond
ENOMEM	system lacked memory resources needed to initialize *cond

■ Example 13.16

The following code segment initializes a condition variable.

```
pthread_cond_t barrier;
int error;

if (error = pthread_cond_init(&barrier, NULL));
    fprintf(stderr, "Failed to initialize barrier:%s\n", strerror(error));
```

The code assumes that strerror will not be called by multiple threads. Otherwise, strerror_r of Section 13.7 should be used.

☐ Exercise 13.17

What happens if a thread tries to initialize a condition variable that has already been initialized?
Answer:
The POSIX standard explicitly states that the results are not defined, so you should avoid doing this.

The pthread_cond_destroy function destroys the condition variable referenced by its cond parameter. A pthread_cond_t variable that has been destroyed with pthread_cond_destroy can be reinitialized with pthread_cond_init.

```
SYNOPSIS

  #include <pthread.h>

  int pthread_cond_destroy(pthread_cond_t *cond);
```
POSIX:THR

If successful, `pthread_cond_destroy` returns 0. If unsuccessful, it returns a nonzero error code. No mandatory errors are defined for `pthread_cond_destroy`.

■ Example 13.18

The following code segment destroys the condition variable `tcond`.

```
pthread_cond_t tcond;

if (error = pthread_cond_destroy(&tcond))
    fprintf(stderr, "Failed to destroy tcond:%s\n", strerror(error));
```

□ Exercise 13.19

What happens if a thread references a condition variable that has been destroyed?
Answer:
POSIX explicitly states that the results are not defined. The standard also does not define what happens when a thread attempts to destroy a condition variable on which other threads are blocked.

13.4.2 Waiting and signaling on condition variables

Condition variables derive their name from the fact that they are called in conjunction with testing a predicate or condition. Typically, a thread tests a predicate and calls `pthread_cond_wait` if the test fails. The `pthread_cond_timedwait` function can be used to wait for a limited time. The first parameter of these functions is `cond`, a pointer to the condition variable. The second parameter is `mutex`, a pointer to a mutex that the thread acquired before the call. The wait operation causes the thread to release this mutex when the thread is placed on the condition variable wait queue. The `pthread_cond_timedwait` function has a third parameter, a pointer to the time to return if a condition variable signal does not occur first. Notice that this value represents an absolute time, not a time interval.

```
SYNOPSIS

  #include <pthread.h>

  int pthread_cond_timedwait(pthread_cond_t *restrict cond,
                     pthread_mutex_t *restrict mutex,
                     const struct timespec *restrict abstime);
  int pthread_cond_wait(pthread_cond_t *restrict cond,
                     pthread_mutex_t *restrict mutex);
```
POSIX:THR

If successful, `pthread_cond_timedwait` and `pthread_cond_wait` return 0. If unsuccessful, these functions return nonzero error code. The `pthread_cond_timedwait` function returns `ETIMEDOUT` if the time specified by `abstime` has expired. If a signal is delivered while a thread is waiting for a condition variable, these functions may resume waiting upon return from the signal handler, or they may return 0 because of a spurious wakeup.

■ Example 13.20

The following code segment causes a thread to (nonbusy) wait until `a` is greater than or equal to `b`.

```
pthread_mutex_lock(&mutex);
while (a < b)
    pthread_cond_wait(&cond, &mutex);
pthread_mutex_unlock(&mutex);
```

The code omits error checking for clarity.

The calling thread should obtain a mutex before it tests the predicate or calls `pthread_cond_wait`. The implementation guarantees that `pthread_cond_wait` causes the thread to atomically release the mutex and block.

☐ Exercise 13.21

What happens if one thread executes the code of Example 13.20 by using `mutex` and another thread executes Example 13.20 by using `mutexA`?

Answer:

This is allowed as long as the two threads are not concurrent. The condition variable wait operations `pthread_cond_wait` and `pthread_cond_timedwait` effectively bind the condition variable to the specified mutex and release the binding on return. POSIX does not define what happens if threads use different mutex locks for concurrent wait operations on the same condition variable. The safest way to avoid this situation is to always use the same mutex with a given condition variable.

When another thread changes variables that might make the predicate true, it should awaken one or more threads that are waiting for the predicate to become true. The `pthread_cond_signal` function unblocks at least one of the threads that are blocked on the condition variable pointed to by `cond`. The `pthread_cond_broadcast` function unblocks all threads blocked on the condition variable pointed to by `cond`.

```
SYNOPSIS

   #include <pthread.h>

   int pthread_cond_broadcast(pthread_cond_t *cond);
   int pthread_cond_signal(pthread_cond_t *cond);
                                                        POSIX:THR
```

If successful, `pthread_condition_broadcast` and `pthread_condition_signal` return 0. If unsuccessful, these functions return a nonzero error code.

■ Example 13.22

Suppose `v` is a condition variable and `m` is a mutex. The following is a proper use of the condition variable to access a resource if the predicate defined by `test_condition()` is true. This code omits error checking for clarity.

```
static pthread_mutex_t m = PTHREAD_MUTEX_INITIALIZER;
static pthread_cond_t v = PTHREAD_COND_INITIALIZER;

pthread_mutex_lock(&m);
while (!test_condition())                              /* get resource */
    pthread_cond_wait(&v, &m);
    /*  do critical section, possibly changing test_condition() */
pthread_cond_signal(&v);                     /* inform another thread */
pthread_mutex_unlock(&m);
                                             /* do other stuff */
```

When a thread executes the `pthread_cond_wait` in Example 13.22, it is holding the mutex `m`. It blocks atomically and releases the mutex, permitting another thread to acquire the mutex and modify the variables in the predicate. When a thread returns successfully from a `pthread_cond_wait`, it has acquired the mutex and can retest the predicate without explicitly reacquiring the mutex. Even if the program signals on a particular condition variable only when a certain predicate is true, waiting threads must still retest the predicate. The POSIX standard specifically allows `pthread_cond_wait` to return, even if no thread has called `pthread_cond_signal` or `pthread_cond_broadcast`.

Program 6.2 on page 187 implements a simple barrier by using a pipe. Program 13.13 implements a thread-safe barrier by using condition variables. The `limit` variable specifies how many threads must arrive at the barrier (execute the `waitbarrier`) before the threads are released from the barrier. The `count` variable specifies how many threads are currently waiting at the barrier. Both variables are declared with the `static` attribute to force access through `initbarrier` and `waitbarrier`. If successful, the `initbarrier` and `waitbarrier` functions return 0. If unsuccessful, these functions return a nonzero error code.

Remember that condition variables are not linked to particular predicates and that `pthread_cond_wait` *can return because of spurious wakeups.* Here are some rules for using condition variables.

1. Acquire the mutex before testing the predicate.
2. Retest the predicate after returning from a `pthread_cond_wait`, since the return might have been caused by some unrelated event or by a `pthread_cond_signal` that did not cause the predicate to become true.
3. Acquire the mutex before changing any of the variables appearing in the predicate.

4. Hold the mutex only for a short period of time—usually while testing the predicate or modifying shared variables.

5. Release the mutex either explicitly (with `pthread_mutex_unlock`) or implicitly (with `pthread_cond_wait`).

Program 13.13 ————————————————————————————— **tbarrier.c**

Implementation of a thread-safe barrier.

```c
#include <errno.h>
#include <pthread.h>

static pthread_cond_t bcond = PTHREAD_COND_INITIALIZER;
static pthread_mutex_t bmutex = PTHREAD_MUTEX_INITIALIZER;
static int count = 0;
static int limit = 0;

int initbarrier(int n) {                  /* initialize the barrier to be size n */
   int error;

   if (error = pthread_mutex_lock(&bmutex))        /* couldn't lock, give up */
      return error;
   if (limit != 0) {                    /* barrier can only be initialized once */
      pthread_mutex_unlock(&bmutex);
      return EINVAL;
   }
   limit = n;
   return pthread_mutex_unlock(&bmutex);
}

int waitbarrier(void) {     /* wait at the barrier until all n threads arrive */
   int berror = 0;
   int error;

   if (error = pthread_mutex_lock(&bmutex))        /* couldn't lock, give up */
      return error;
   if (limit <=  0) {                        /* make sure barrier initialized */
      pthread_mutex_unlock(&bmutex);
      return EINVAL;
   }
   count++;
   while ((count < limit) && !berror)
      berror =  pthread_cond_wait(&bcond, &bmutex);
   if (!berror)
      berror = pthread_cond_broadcast(&bcond);            /* wake up everyone */
   error = pthread_mutex_unlock(&bmutex);
   if (berror)
      return berror;
   return error;
}
```

Program 13.13 ————————————————————————————— **tbarrier.c**

13.5 Signal Handling and Threads

All threads in a process share the process signal handlers, but each thread has its own signal mask. The interaction of threads with signals involves several complications because threads can operate asynchronously with signals. Table 13.2 summarizes the three types of signals and their corresponding methods of delivery.

type	delivery action
asynchronous	delivered to some thread that has it unblocked
synchronous	delivered to the thread that caused it
directed	delivered to the identified thread (`pthread_kill`)

Table 13.2: Signal delivery in threads.

Signals such as `SIGFPE` (floating-point exception) are synchronous to the thread that caused them (i.e., they are always generated at the same point in the thread's execution). Other signals are asynchronous because they are not generated at a predictable time nor are they associated with a particular thread. If several threads have an asynchronous signal unblocked, the thread runtime system selects one of them to handle the signal. Signals can also be directed to a particular thread with `pthread_kill`.

13.5.1 Directing a signal to a particular thread

The `pthread_kill` function requests that signal number `sig` be generated and delivered to the thread specified by `thread`.

```
SYNOPSIS

   #include <signal.h>
   #include <pthread.h>

   int pthread_kill(pthread_t thread, int sig);
                                                    POSIX:THR
```

If successful, `pthread_kill` returns 0. If unsuccessful, `pthread_kill` returns a nonzero error code. In the latter case, no signal is sent. The following table lists the mandatory errors for `pthread_kill`.

error	cause
EINVAL	`sig` is an invalid or unsupported signal number
ESRCH	no thread corresponds to specified ID

■ **Example 13.23**

The following code segment causes a thread to kill itself and the entire process.

```
if (pthread_kill(pthread_self(), SIGKILL))
    fprintf(stderr, "Failed to commit suicide\n");
```

Example 13.23 illustrates an important point regarding `pthread_kill`. Although `pthread_kill` delivers the signal to a particular thread, the action of handling it may affect the entire process. A common confusion is to assume that `pthread_kill` always causes process termination, but this is not the case. The `pthread_kill` just causes a signal to be generated for the thread. Example 13.23 causes process termination because the `SIGKILL` signal cannot be caught, blocked or ignored. The same result occurs for any signal whose default action is to terminate the process unless the process ignores, blocks or catches the signal. Table 8.1 lists the POSIX signals with their symbolic names and default actions.

13.5.2 Masking signals for threads

While signal handlers are process-wide, each thread has its own signal mask. A thread can examine or set its signal mask with the `pthread_sigmask` function, which is a generalization of `sigprocmask` to threaded programs. The `sigprocmask` function should not be used when the process has multiple threads, but it can be called by the main thread before additional threads are created. Recall that the signal mask specifies which signals are to be blocked (not delivered). The `how` and `set` parameters specify the way the signal mask is to be modified, as discussed below. If the `oset` parameter is not `NULL`, the `pthread_sigmask` function sets `*oset` to the thread's previous signal mask.

```
SYNOPSIS

   #include <pthread.h>
   #include <signal.h>

   int pthread_sigmask(int how, const sigset_t *restrict set,
                       sigset_t *restrict oset);
                                                          POSIX:THR
```

If successful, `pthread_sigmask` returns 0. If unsuccessful, `pthread_sigmask` returns a nonzero error code. The `pthread_sigmask` function returns `EINVAL` if `how` is not valid.

A `how` value of `SIG_SETMASK` causes the thread's signal mask to be replaced by `set`. That is, the thread now blocks all signals in `set` but does not block any others. A `how` value of `SIG_BLOCK` causes the additional signals in `set` to be blocked by the thread (added to the thread's current signal mask). A `how` value of `SIG_UNBLOCK` causes any of the signals in `set` that are currently being blocked to be removed from the thread's current signal mask (no longer be blocked).

13.5.3 Dedicating threads for signal handling

Signal handlers are process-wide and are installed with calls to `sigaction` as in single-threaded processes. The distinction between process-wide signal handlers and thread-specific signal masks is important in threaded programs.

Recall from Chapter 8 that when a signal is caught, the signal that caused the event is automatically blocked on entry to the signal handler. With a multithreaded application, nothing prevents another signal of the same type from being delivered to another thread that has the signal unblocked. It is possible to have multiple threads executing within the same signal handler.

A recommended strategy for dealing with signals in multithreaded processes is to dedicate particular threads to signal handling. The main thread blocks all signals before creating the threads. The signal mask is inherited from the creating thread, so all threads have the signal blocked. The thread dedicated to handling the signal then executes `sigwait` on that signal. (See Section 8.5.) Alternatively, the thread can use `pthread_sigmask` to unblock the signal. The advantage of using `sigwait` is that the thread is not restricted to async-signal-safe functions.

Program 13.14 is an implementation of a dedicated thread that uses `sigwait` to handle a particular signal. A program calls `signalthreadinit` to block the `signo` signal and to create a dedicated `signalthread` that waits for this signal. When the signal corresponding to `signo` becomes pending, `sigwait` returns and the `signalthread` calls `setdone` of Program 13.3 and returns. You can replace the `setdone` with any thread-safe function. Program 13.14 has some informative messages, which would normally be removed.

Notice that the implementation of `signalthreadinit` uses a thread attribute object to create `signalthread` with higher priority than the default value. The program was tested on a system that used preemptive priority scheduling. When the program executes on this system without first increasing `signalthread`'s priority, it still works correctly, but sometimes the program takes several seconds to react to the signal after it is generated. If a round-robin scheduling policy were available, all the threads could have the same priority.

The dedicated signal-handling thread, `signalthread`, displays its priority to confirm that the priority is set correctly and then calls `sigwait`. No signal handler is needed since `sigwait` removes the signal from those pending. The signal is always blocked, so the default action for `signalnum` is never taken.

Program 13.15 modifies `computethreadmain` of Program 13.7 by using the SIGUSR1 signal to set the done flag for the `computethread` object of Program 13.6. The `main` program no longer sleeps a specified number of seconds before calling `setdone`. Instead, the delivery of a SIGUSR1 signal causes `signalthread` to call `setdone`.

Program 13.14 ———————————————————— `signalthread.c`

A dedicated thread that sets a flag when a signal is received.

```c
#include <errno.h>
#include <pthread.h>
#include <signal.h>
#include <stdio.h>
#include "doneflag.h"
#include "globalerror.h"

static int signalnum = 0;

/* ARGSUSED */
static void *signalthread(void *arg) {     /* dedicated to handling signalnum */
   int error;
   sigset_t intmask;
   struct sched_param param;
   int policy;
   int sig;

   if (error = pthread_getschedparam(pthread_self(), &policy, &param)) {
      seterror(error);
      return NULL;
   }
   fprintf(stderr, "Signal thread entered with policy %d and priority %d\n",
              policy,  param.sched_priority);
   if ((sigemptyset(&intmask) == -1) ||
       (sigaddset(&intmask, signalnum) == -1) ||
       (sigwait(&intmask, &sig) == -1))
      seterror(errno);
   else
      seterror(setdone());
   return NULL;
}

int signalthreadinit(int signo) {
   int error;
   pthread_attr_t highprio;
   struct sched_param param;
   int policy;
   sigset_t set;
   pthread_t sighandid;

   signalnum = signo;                                      /* block the signal */
   if ((sigemptyset(&set) == -1) || (sigaddset(&set, signalnum) == -1) ||
       (sigprocmask(SIG_BLOCK, &set, NULL) == -1))
      return errno;
   if ( (error = pthread_attr_init(&highprio)) ||     /* with higher priority */
        (error = pthread_attr_getschedparam(&highprio, &param)) ||
        (error = pthread_attr_getschedpolicy(&highprio, &policy)) )
      return error;
   if (param.sched_priority < sched_get_priority_max(policy)) {
      param.sched_priority++;
      if (error = pthread_attr_setschedparam(&highprio, &param))
         return error;
   } else
      fprintf(stderr, "Warning, cannot increase priority of signal thread.\n");
   if (error = pthread_create(&sighandid, &highprio, signalthread, NULL))
      return error;
   return 0;
}
```

Program 13.14 ———————————————————— `signalthread.c`

A `main` *program that uses* `signalthread` *with the* `SIGUSR1` *signal to terminate the*
`computethread` *computation of Program 13.6.*

```c
#include <math.h>
#include <pthread.h>
#include <signal.h>
#include <stdio.h>
#include <stdlib.h>
#include <string.h>
#include <unistd.h>
#include "computethread.h"
#include "globalerror.h"
#include "sharedsum.h"
#include "signalthread.h"

int showresults(void);

int main(int argc, char *argv[]) {
   int error;
   int i;
   int numthreads;
   pthread_t *tids;

   if (argc != 2) {                          /* pass number threads on command line */
      fprintf(stderr, "Usage: %s numthreads\n", argv[0]);
      return 1;
   }
   if (error = signalthreadinit(SIGUSR1)) {           /* set up signal thread */
      fprintf(stderr, "Failed to set up signal thread: %s\n", strerror(error));
      return 1;
   }
   numthreads = atoi(argv[1]);
   if ((tids = (pthread_t *)calloc(numthreads, sizeof(pthread_t))) == NULL) {
      perror("Failed to allocate space for thread IDs");
      return 1;
   }
   for (i = 0; i < numthreads; i++)       /* create numthreads computethreads */
      if (error =  pthread_create(tids+ i, NULL, computethread, NULL)) {
         fprintf(stderr, "Failed to start thread %d: %s\n", i,
                 strerror(error));
         return 1;
      }
   fprintf(stderr, "Send SIGUSR1(%d) signal to proc %ld to stop calculation\n",
                 SIGUSR1, (long)getpid());
   for (i = 0; i < numthreads; i++)     /* wait for computethreads to be done */
      if (error = pthread_join(tids[i], NULL)) {
         fprintf(stderr, "Failed to join thread %d: %s\n", i, strerror(error));
         return 1;
      }
   if (showresults())
      return 1;
   return 0;
}
```

The modular design of the `signalthread` object makes the object easy to modify. Chapter 16 uses `signalthread` for some implementations of a bounded buffer.

☐ Exercise 13.24

Run `computethreadsig` of Program 13.15 from one command window. Send the `SIGUSR1` signal from another command window, using the `kill` shell command. What is its effect?

Answer:

The dedicated signal thread calls `setdone` when the signal is pending, and the threads terminate normally.

13.6 Readers and Writers

The reader-writer problem refers to a situation in which a resource allows two types of access (reading and writing). One type of access must be granted exclusively (e.g., writing), but the other type may be shared (e.g., reading). For example, any number of processes can read from the same file without difficulty, but only one process should modify the file at a time.

Two common strategies for handling reader-writer synchronization are called *strong reader synchronization* and *strong writer synchronization*. Strong reader synchronization always gives preference to readers, granting access to readers as long as a writer is not currently writing. Strong writer synchronization always gives preference to writers, delaying readers until all waiting or active writers complete. An airline reservation system would use strong writer preference, since readers need the most up-to-date information. On the other hand, a library reference database might want to give readers preference.

POSIX provides read-write locks that allow multiple readers to acquire a lock, provided that a writer does not hold the lock. POSIX states that it is up to the implementation whether to allow a reader to acquire a lock if writers are blocked on the lock.

POSIX read-write locks are represented by variables of type `pthread_rwlock_t`. Programs must initialize `pthread_rwlock_t` variables before using them for synchronization by calling `pthread_rwlock_init`. The `rwlock` parameter is a pointer to a read-write lock. Pass `NULL` for the `attr` parameter of `pthread_rwlock_init` to initialize a read-write lock with the default attributes. Otherwise, first create and initialize a read-write lock attribute object in a manner similar to that used for thread attribute objects.

SYNOPSIS

```
#include <pthread.h>

int pthread_rwlock_init(pthread_rwlock_t *restrict rwlock,
                const pthread_rwlockattr_t *restrict attr);
```
                                                                POSIX:THR

If successful, `pthread_rwlock_init` returns 0. If unsuccessful, it returns a nonzero error code. The following table lists the mandatory errors for `pthread_rwlock_init`.

error	cause
EAGAIN	system lacked nonmemory resources needed to initialize `*rwlock`
ENOMEM	system lacked memory resources needed to initialize `*rwlock`
EPERM	caller does not have appropriate privileges

❏ Exercise 13.25

What happens when you try to initialize a read-write lock that has already been initialized?

Answer:

POSIX states that the behavior under these circumstances is not defined.

The `pthread_rwlock_destroy` function destroys the read-write lock referenced by its parameter. The `rwlock` parameter is a pointer to a read-write lock. A `pthread_rwlock_t` variable that has been destroyed with `pthread_rwlock_destroy` can be reinitialized with `pthread_rwlock_init`.

```
SYNOPSIS

   #include <pthread.h>

   int pthread_rwlock_destroy(pthread_rwlock_t *rwlock);
                                                              POSIX:THR
```

If successful, `pthread_rwlock_destroy` returns 0. If unsuccessful, it returns a nonzero error code. No mandatory errors are defined for `pthread_rwlock_destroy`.

❏ Exercise 13.26

What happens if you reference a read-write lock that has been destroyed?

Answer:

POSIX states that the behavior under these circumstances is not defined.

The `pthread_rwlock_rdlock` and `pthread_rwlock_tryrdlock` functions allow a thread to acquire a read-write lock for reading. The `pthread_rwlock_wrlock` and `pthread_rwlock_trywrlock` functions allow a thread to acquire a read-write lock for writing. The `pthread_rwlock_rdlock` and `pthread_rwlock_wrlock` functions block until the lock is available, whereas `pthread_rwlock_tryrdlock` and `pthread_rwlock_trywrlock` return immediately. The `pthread_rwlock_unlock` function causes the lock to be released. These functions require that a pointer to the lock be passed as a parameter.

```
SYNOPSIS

  #include <pthread.h>

  int pthread_rwlock_rdlock(pthread_rwlock_t *rwlock);
  int pthread_rwlock_tryrdlock(pthread_rwlock_t *rwlock);
  int pthread_rwlock_wrlock(pthread_rwlock_t *rwlock);
  int pthread_rwlock_trywrlock(pthread_rwlock_t *rwlock);
  int pthread_rwlock_unlock(pthread_rwlock_t *rwlock);

                                                              POSIX:THR
```

If successful, these functions return 0. If unsuccessful, these functions return a nonzero error code. The `pthread_rwlock_tryrdlock` and `pthread_rwlock_trywrlock` functions return EBUSY if the lock could not be acquired because it was already held.

◻ Exercise 13.27

What happens if a thread calls `pthread_rwlock_rdlock` on a lock that it has already acquired with `pthread_rwlock_wrlock`?

Answer:

POSIX states that a deadlock may occur. (Implementations are free to detect a deadlock and return an error, but they are not required to do so.)

◻ Exercise 13.28

What happens if a thread calls `pthread_rwlock_rdlock` on a lock that it has already acquired with `pthread_rwlock_rdlock`?

Answer:

A thread may hold multiple concurrent read locks on the same read-write lock. It should make sure to match the number of unlock calls with the number of lock calls to release the lock.

Program 13.16 uses read-write locks to implement a thread-safe wrapper for the list object of Program 2.7. The `listlib.c` module should be included in this file, and its functions should be qualified with the `static` attribute. Program 13.16 includes an `initialize_r` function to initialize the read-write lock, since no static initialization is available. This function uses `pthread_once` to make sure that the read-write lock is initialized only one time.

◻ Exercise 13.29

Compare Program 13.16 to the thread-safe implementation of Program 13.9 that uses mutex locks. What are the advantages/disadvantages of each?

Answer:

The mutex is a low-overhead synchronization mechanism. Since each of the functions in Program 13.9 holds the `listlock` only for a short period of time, Program 13.9 is relatively efficient. Because read-write locks have some overhead, their advantage comes when the actual read operations take a considerable amount of time (such as incurred by accessing a disk). In such a case, the strictly serial execution order would be inefficient.

Program 13.16 ──────────────────────── `listlibrw_r.c`
The list object of Program 2.7 synchronized with read-write locks.

```c
#include <errno.h>
#include <pthread.h>

static pthread_rwlock_t listlock;
static int lockiniterror = 0;
static pthread_once_t lockisinitialized = PTHREAD_ONCE_INIT;

static void ilock(void) {
    lockiniterror = pthread_rwlock_init(&listlock, NULL);
}

int initialize_r(void) {     /* must be called at least once before using list */
    if (pthread_once(&lockisinitialized, ilock))
        lockiniterror = EINVAL;
    return lockiniterror;
}

int accessdata_r(void) {                 /* get a nonnegative key if successful */
    int error;
    int errorkey = 0;
    int key;
    if (error = pthread_rwlock_wrlock(&listlock)) {  /* no write lock, give up */
        errno = error;
        return -1;
    }
    key = accessdata();
    if (key == -1) {
        errorkey = errno;
        pthread_rwlock_unlock(&listlock);
        errno = errorkey;
        return -1;
    }
    if (error = pthread_rwlock_unlock(&listlock)) {
        errno = error;
        return -1;
    }
    return key;
}

int adddata_r(data_t data) {             /* allocate a node on list to hold data */
    int error;
    if (error = pthread_rwlock_wrlock(&listlock)) { /* no writer lock, give up */
        errno = error;
        return -1;
    }
    if (adddata(data) == -1) {
        error = errno;
        pthread_rwlock_unlock(&listlock);
        errno = error;
        return -1;
```

```
      }
      if (error = pthread_rwlock_unlock(&listlock)) {
         errno = error;
         return -1;
      }
      return 0;
}

int getdata_r(int key, data_t *datap) {               /* retrieve node by key */
      int error;
      if (error = pthread_rwlock_rdlock(&listlock)) { /* no reader lock, give up */
         errno = error;
         return  1;
      }
      if (getdata(key, datap) == -1) {
         error = errno;
         pthread_rwlock_unlock(&listlock);
         errno = error;
         return -1;
      }
      if (error = pthread_rwlock_unlock(&listlock)) {
         errno = error;
         return -1;
      }
      return 0;
}

int freekey_r(int key) {                                        /* free the key */
      int error;
      if (error = pthread_rwlock_wrlock(&listlock)) {
         errno = error;
         return -1;
      }
      if (freekey(key) == -1) {
         error = errno;
         pthread_rwlock_unlock(&listlock);
         errno = error;
         return -1;
      }
      if (error = pthread_rwlock_unlock(&listlock)) {
         errno = error;
         return -1;
      }
      return 0;
}
```

Program 13.16 ───────────────────────────────────── `listlibrw_r.c`

❑ Exercise 13.30

The use of Program 13.16 requires a call to `initialize_r` at least once by some thread before any threads call other functions in this library. How could this be avoided?

Answer:

The function `initialize_r` can be given internal linkage by having the other functions in the library call it before accessing the lock.

13.7 A `strerror_r` Implementation

Unfortunately, POSIX lists `strerror` as one of the few functions that are not thread-safe. Often, this is not a problem since often the main thread is the only thread that prints error messages. If you need to use `strerror` concurrently in a program, you will need to protect it with mutex locks. Neither `perror` nor `strerror` is async-signal safe. One way to solve both the thread-safety and async-signal-safety problems is to encapsulate the synchronization in a wrapper, as shown in Program 13.17.

The `perror_r` and `strerror_r` functions are both thread-safe and async-signal safe. They use a mutex to prevent concurrent acccss to the static buffer used by `strerror`. The `perror` function is also protected by the same mutex to prevent concurrent execution of `strerror` and `perror`. All signals are blocked before the mutex is locked. If this were not done and a signal were caught with the mutex locked, a call to one of these from inside the signal handler would deadlock.

13.8 Deadlocks and Other Pesky Problems

Programs that use synchronization constructs have the potential for deadlocks that may not be detected by implementations of the POSIX base standard. For example, suppose that a thread executes `pthread_mutex_lock` on a mutex that it already holds (from a previously successful `pthread_mutex_lock`). The POSIX base standard states that `pthread_mutex_lock` *may* fail and return `EDEADLK` under such circumstances, but the standard does not *require* the function to do so. POSIX takes the position that implementations of the base standard are not required to sacrifice efficiency to protect programmers from their own bad programming. Several extensions to POSIX allow more extensive error checking and deadlock detection.

Another type of problem arises when a thread that holds a lock encounters an error. You must take care to release the lock before returning from the thread, or other threads might be blocked.

Threads with priorities can also complicate matters. A famous example occurred in the Mars Pathfinder mission. The Pathfinder executed a "flawless" Martian landing on July 4, 1997, and began gathering and transmitting large quantities of scientific data to Earth [34]. A few days after landing, the spacecraft started experiencing total system resets, each of which delayed data collection by a day. Several accounts of the underlying causes and the resolution of the problem have appeared, starting with a keynote address at the IEEE Real-Time Systems Symposium on Dec. 3, 1997, by David Wilner, Chief Technical Officer of Wind River [61].

Async-signal-safe, thread-safe versions of strerror *and* perror.

```c
#include <errno.h>
#include <pthread.h>
#include <signal.h>
#include <stdio.h>
#include <string.h>

static pthread_mutex_t lock = PTHREAD_MUTEX_INITIALIZER;

int strerror_r(int errnum, char *strerrbuf, size_t buflen) {
    char *buf;
    int error1;
    int error2;
    int error3;
    sigset_t maskblock;
    sigset_t maskold;

    if ((sigfillset(&maskblock)== -1) ||
        (sigprocmask(SIG_SETMASK, &maskblock, &maskold) == -1))
        return errno;
    if (error1 = pthread_mutex_lock(&lock)) {
        (void)sigprocmask(SIG_SETMASK, &maskold, NULL);
        return error1;
    }
    buf = strerror(errnum);
    if (strlen(buf) >= buflen)
        error1 = ERANGE;
    else
        (void *)strcpy(strerrbuf, buf);
    error2 = pthread_mutex_unlock(&lock);
    error3 = sigprocmask(SIG_SETMASK, &maskold, NULL);
    return error1 ? error1 : (error2 ? error2 : error3);
}

int perror_r(const char *s) {
    int error1;
    int error2;
    sigset_t maskblock;
    sigset_t maskold;

    if ((sigfillset(&maskblock) == -1) ||
        (sigprocmask(SIG_SETMASK, &maskblock, &maskold) == -1))
        return errno;
    if (error1 = pthread_mutex_lock(&lock)) {
        (void)sigprocmask(SIG_SETMASK, &maskold, NULL);
        return error1;
    }
    perror(s);
    error1 = pthread_mutex_unlock(&lock);
    error2 = sigprocmask(SIG_SETMASK, &maskold, NULL);
    return error1 ? error1 : error2;
}
```

The Mars Pathfinder flaw was found to be a priority inversion on a mutex [105]. A thread whose job was gathering meteorological data ran periodically at low priority. This thread would acquire the mutex for the data bus to publish its data. A periodic high-priority information thread also acquired the mutex, and occasionally it would block, waiting for the low-priority thread to release the mutex. Each of these threads needed the mutex only for a short time, so on the surface there could be no problem. Unfortunately, a long-running, medium-priority communication thread occasionally preempted the low-priority thread while the low-priority thread held the mutex, causing the high-priority thread to be delayed for a long time.

A second aspect of the problem was the system reaction to the error. The system expected the periodic high-priority thread to regularly use the data bus. A watchdog timer thread would notice if the data bus was not being used, assume that a serious problem had occurred, and initiate a system reboot. The high-priority thread should have been blocked only for a short time when the low-priority thread held the mutex. In this case, the high-priority thread was blocked for a long time because the low-priority thread held the mutex and the long-running, medium-priority thread had preempted it.

A third aspect was the test and debugging of the code. The Mars Pathfinder system had debugging code that could be turned on to run real-time diagnostics. The software team used an identical setup in the lab to run in debug mode (since they didn't want to debug on Mars). After 18 hours, the laboratory version reproduced the problem, and the engineers were able to devise a patch. Glenn Reeves [93], leader of the Mars Pathfinder software team, was quoted as saying "We strongly believe in the 'test what you fly and fly what you test' philosophy." The same ideas apply here on Earth too. At a minimum, you should always think about instrumenting code with test and debugging functions that can be turned on or off by conditional compilation. *When possible, allow debugging functions to be turned on dynamically at runtime.*

A final aspect of this story is timing. In some ways, the Mars Pathfinder was a victim of its own success. The software team did extensive testing within the parameters of the mission. They actually saw the system reset problem once or twice during testing, but did not track it down. The reset problem was exacerbated by high data rates that caused the medium-priority communication thread to run longer than expected. Prelaunch testing was limited to "best case" high data rates. In the words of Glenn Reeves, "We did not expect nor test the 'better than we could have ever imagined' case." Threaded programs should never rely on quirks of timing to work—they must work under all possible timings.

13.9 Exercise: Multiple Barriers

Reimplement the barrier of Program 13.13 so that it supports multiple barriers. One possible approach is to use an array or a linked list of barriers. Explore different designs with respect to synchronization. Is it better to use a single `bmutex` lock and `bcond` condition variable to synchronize all the barriers, or should each barrier get its own synchronization? Why?

13.10 Additional Reading

Most operating systems books spend some time on synchronization and use of standard synchronization mechanisms such as mutex locks, condition variables and read-write locks. The review article "Concepts and notations for concurrent programming," by Andrews and Schneider [3] gives an excellent overview of much of the classical work on synchronization. "Interrupts as threads" by Kleiman and Eykholt [63] discusses some interesting aspects of the interaction of threads and interrupts in the kernel. An extensive review of monitors can be found in "Monitor classification," by Buhr et al. [17]. The signal and wait operations of monitors are higher-level implementations of the mutex-conditional variable combination. The *Solaris Multithreaded Programming Guide* [109], while dealing primarily with Solaris threads, contains some interesting examples of synchronization. Finally, the article "Schedule-conscious synchronization" by Kontothanassis et al. [65] discusses implementation of mutex locks, read-write locks and barriers in a multiprocessor environment.

Chapter 14

Critical Sections and Semaphores

Programs that manage shared resources must execute portions of code called critical sections in a mutually exclusive manner. This chapter discusses how critical sections arise and how to protect their execution by means of semaphores. After presenting an overview of the semaphore abstraction, the chapter describes POSIX named and unnamed semaphores. The closing section outlines a license manager project based on semaphores.

Objectives

- Learn about semaphores and their properties
- Experiment with synchronization
- Explore critical section behavior
- Use POSIX named and unnamed semaphores
- Understand semaphore management

14.1 Dealing with Critical Sections

Imagine a computer system in which all users share a single printer and can simultaneously print. How would the output appear? If lines of users' jobs were interspersed, the system would be unusable. Shared devices, such as printers, are called *exclusive resources* because they must be accessed by one process at a time. Processes must execute the code that accesses these shared resources in a *mutually exclusive* manner.

A *critical section* is a code segment that must be executed in a mutually exclusive manner, that is, only one thread of execution can be active in its boundaries. For example, code that modifies a shared variable is considered to be part of a critical section, if other threads of execution might possibly access the shared variable during the modification. The *critical section problem* refers to the problem of executing critical section code in a safe, fair and symmetric manner.

Program 14.1 contains a modification of Program 3.1 on page 67 to generate a process chain. It prints its message one character at a time. The program takes an extra command-line argument giving a delay after each character is output to make it more likely that the process quantum will expire in the output loop. The call to `wait` ensures that the original process does not terminate until all children have completed and prevents the shell prompt from appearing in the middle of the output of one of the children.

☐ **Exercise 14.1**

Explain why the marked section of code in Program 14.1 is a critical section.

Answer:

After falling out of the forking loop, each process outputs an informative message to standard error one character at a time. Since standard error is shared by all processes in the chain, that part of the code is a critical section and should be executed in a mutually exclusive manner. Unfortunately, the critical section of Program 14.1 is not protected, so output from different processes can interleave in a random manner, different for each run.

☐ **Exercise 14.2**

Run Program 14.1 with different values of the delay parameter. What happens?

Answer:

When the delay parameter is near 0, each process usually outputs its entire line without losing the CPU. Longer delays make it more likely that a process will lose the CPU before completing the entire message. For large enough values of the delay, each process outputs only one character before losing the CPU. Depending on the speed of the machine, you might need to use values of the delay in excess of 1 million for this last case.

☐ Exercise 14.3

Program 3.1 on page 67 uses a single `fprintf` to standard error to produce the output. Does this have a critical section?

Answer:

Yes. Although the output is in a single C language statement, the compiled code is a sequence of assembly language instructions and the process can lose the CPU anywhere in this sequence. Although this might be less likely to happen in Program 3.1 than in Program 14.1, it is still possible.

Program 14.1 ───────────────── `chaincritical.c`

A program to generate a chain of processes that write to standard error.

```c
#include <stdio.h>
#include <stdlib.h>
#include <string.h>
#include <unistd.h>
#include <sys/wait.h>
#include "restart.h"
#define BUFSIZE 1024

int main(int argc, char *argv[]) {
   char buffer[BUFSIZE];
   char *c;
   pid_t childpid = 0;
   int delay;
   volatile int dummy = 0;
   int i, n;

   if (argc != 3){   /* check for valid number of command-line arguments */
      fprintf (stderr, "Usage: %s processes delay\n", argv[0]);
      return 1;
   }
   n = atoi(argv[1]);
   delay = atoi(argv[2]);
   for (i = 1; i < n; i++)
      if (childpid = fork())
         break;
   snprintf(buffer, BUFSIZE,
       "i:%d  process ID:%ld  parent ID:%ld  child ID:%ld\n",
       i, (long)getpid(), (long)getppid(), (long)childpid);

   c = buffer;
/******************** start of critical section ********************/
   while (*c != '\0') {
      fputc(*c, stderr);
      c++;
      for (i = 0; i < delay; i++)
         dummy++;
   }
/******************** end of critical section ********************/
   if (r_wait(NULL) == -1)
      return 1;
   return 0;
}
```

Program 14.1 ───────────────── `chaincritical.c`

Each process in Program 14.1 executes the statements in sequential order, but the statements (and hence the output) from the different processes can be arbitrarily interleaved. An analogy to this arbitrary interleaving comes from a deck of cards. Cut a deck of cards. Think of each section of the cut as representing one process. The individual cards in each section represent the statements in the order that the corresponding process executes them. Now shuffle the two sections by interleaving. There are many possibilities for a final ordering, depending on the shuffling mechanics. Similarly, there are many possible interleavings of the statements of two processes because the exact timing of processes relative to each other depends on outside factors (e.g., how many other processes are competing for the CPU or how much time each process spent in previous blocked states waiting for I/O). The challenge for programmers is to develop programs that work for all realizable interleavings of program statements.

Code with synchronized critical sections can be organized into distinct parts. The *entry section* contains code to request permission to modify a shared variable or other resource. You can think of the entry section as the gatekeeper—allowing only one thread of execution to pass through at a time. The *critical section* usually contains code to access a shared resource or to execute code that is nonreentrant. The explicit release of access provided in the *exit section* is necessary so that the gatekeeper knows it can allow the next thread of execution to enter the critical section. After releasing access, a thread may have other code to execute, which we separate into the *remainder section* to indicate that it should not influence decisions by the gatekeeper.

A good solution to the critical section problem requires fairness as well as *exclusive access*. Threads of execution that are trying to enter a critical section should not be *postponed indefinitely*. Threads should also make *progress*. If no thread is currently in the critical section, a waiting thread should be allowed to enter.

Critical sections commonly arise when two processes access a shared resource, such as the example of Program 14.1. Be aware that critical sections can arise in other ways. Code in a signal handler executes asynchronously with the rest of the program, so it can be thought of as logically executing in a separate thread of execution. Variables that are modified in the signal handler and used in the rest of the program must be treated as part of a critical section. In Program 8.6 on page 271, the signal handler and the `results` function compete for access to `buf` and `buflen`. The entry section or gatekeeper is the code in `results` to block `SIGUSR1`; the exit section is the code to unblock `SIGUSR1` and to restore the original signal mask.

Program 2.3 on page 39 illustrates a related problem that can arise with recursive calls to nonreentrant functions such as `strtok`. Although this example is not strictly a critical section problem by the definition given above, it has the same characteristics because the single thread of execution changes its execution environment when a function call pushes a new activation record on the stack.

14.2 Semaphores

In 1965, E. W. Dijkstra [30] proposed the semaphore abstraction for high-level management of mutual exclusion and synchronization. A semaphore is an integer variable with two atomic operations, `wait` and `signal`. Other names for `wait` are `down`, `P` and `lock`. Other names for `signal` are `up`, `V`, `unlock` and `post`.

If `s` is greater than zero, `wait` tests and decrements `s` in an atomic operation. If `s` is equal to zero, the `wait` tests `s` and blocks the caller in an atomic operation.

If threads are blocked on the semaphore, then `s` is equal to zero and `signal` unblocks one of these waiting threads. If no threads are blocked on the semaphore, `signal` increments `s`. In POSIX:SEM terminology, the `wait` and `signal` operations are called *semaphore lock* and *semaphore unlock*, respectively. We can think of a semaphore as an integer value and a list of processes waiting for a `signal` operation.

■ Example 14.4

The following pseudocode shows a blocking implementation of semaphores.

```
void wait(semaphore_t *sp) {
   if (sp->value > 0)
      sp->value--;
   else {
      <Add this process to sp->list>
      <block>
   }
}

void signal(semaphore_t *sp) {
   if (sp->list != NULL)
      <remove a process from sp->list and put in ready state>
   else
      sp->value++;
}
```

The `wait` and `signal` operations must be atomic. An *atomic operation* is an operation that, once started, completes in a logically indivisible way (i.e., without any other related instructions interleaved). In this context, being atomic means that if a process calls `wait`, no other process can change the semaphore until the semaphore is decremented or the calling process is blocked. The signal operation is atomic in a similar way. Semaphore implementations use atomic operations of the underlying operating system to ensure correct execution.

■ Example 14.5

The following pseudocode protects a critical section if the semaphore variable `s` is initially 1.

```
wait(&S);                    /* entry section or gatekeeper */
<critical section>
signal(&S);                              /* exit section */
<remainder section>
```

Processes using semaphores must cooperate to protect a critical section. The code of Example 14.5 works, provided that all processes call `wait(&S)` before entering their critical sections and that they call `signal(&S)` when they leave. If any process fails to call `wait(&S)` because of a mistake or oversight, the processes may not execute the code of the critical section in a mutually exclusive manner. If a process fails to call `signal(&S)` when it finishes its critical section, other cooperative processes are blocked from entering their critical sections.

◻ Exercise 14.6

What happens if `S` is initially 0 in the previous example? What happens if `S` is initially 8? Under what circumstances might initialization to 8 prove useful?

Answer:

If `S` is initially 0, every `wait(&S)` blocks and a deadlock results unless some other process calls `signal` for this semaphore. If `S` is initially 8, at most eight processes execute concurrently in their critical sections. The initialization to 8 might be used when there are eight identical copies of the resource that can be accessed concurrently.

◼ Example 14.7

Suppose process 1 must execute statement a before process 2 executes statement b. The semaphore `sync` enforces the ordering in the following pseudocode, provided that `sync` is initially 0.

```
Process 1 executes:            Process 2 executes:
  a;                             wait(&sync);
  signal(&sync);                 b;
```

Because `sync` is initially 0, process 2 blocks on its `wait` until process 1 calls `signal`.

◻ Exercise 14.8

What happens in the following pseudocode if the semaphores `S` and `Q` are both initially 1? What about other possible initializations?

```
Process 1 executes:            Process 2 executes:
  for( ; ; ) {                   for( ; ; ) {
     wait(&S);                      wait(&Q);
     a;                             b;
     signal(&Q);                    signal(&S);
  }                              }
```

Answer:

Either process might execute its `wait` statement first. The semaphores ensure that a given process is no more than one iteration ahead of the other. If one semaphore

is initially 1 and the other 0, the processes proceed in strict alternation. If both
semaphores are initially 0, a deadlock occurs.

◻ Exercise 14.9

What happens when S is initially 8 and Q is initially 0 in Exercise 14.8? Hint:
Think of S as representing buffer slots and Q as representing items in a buffer.

Answer:

Process 1 is always between zero and eight iterations ahead of process 2. If the
value of S represents empty slots and the value of Q represents items in the slots,
process 1 acquires slots and produces items, and process 2 acquires items and
produces empty slots. This generalization synchronizes access to a buffer with
room for no more than eight items.

◻ Exercise 14.10

What happens in the following pseudocode if semaphores S and Q are both initialized to 1?

```
Process 1 executes:           Process 2 executes:
   for( ; ; ) {                  for( ; ; ) {
      wait(&Q);                     wait(&S);
      wait(&S);                     wait(&Q);
      a;                            b;
      signal(&S);                   signal(&Q);
      signal(&Q);                   signal(&S);
   }                             }
```

Answer:

The result depends on the order in which the processes get the CPU. It should work
most of the time, but if process 1 loses the CPU after executing `wait(&Q)` and
process 2 gets in, both processes block on their second `wait` call and a deadlock
occurs.

A semaphore synchronizes processes by requiring that the value of the semaphore
variable be nonnegative. More general forms of synchronization allow synchronization
on arbitrary conditions and have mechanisms for combining synchronization conditions.
OR synchronization refers to waiting until any condition in a specified set is satisfied.
The use of `select` or `poll` to monitor multiple file descriptors for input is a form of
OR synchronization. *NOT synchronization* refers to waiting until some condition in a set
is not true. NOT synchronization can be used to enforce priority ordering [76]. *AND
synchronization* refers to waiting until all the conditions in a specified set of conditions
are satisfied. AND synchronization can be used for simultaneous control of multiple
resources such as that needed for Exercise 14.10. POSIX:XSI semaphore sets described
in Chapter 15 are capable of providing AND synchronization.

14.3 POSIX:SEM Unnamed Semaphores

A POSIX:SEM semaphore is a variable of type `sem_t` with associated atomic operations for initializing, incrementing and decrementing its value. The POSIX:SEM Semaphore Extension defines two types of semaphores, named and unnamed. An implementation supports POSIX:SEM semaphores if it defines `_POSIX_SEMAPHORES` in `unistd.h`. The difference between unnamed and named semaphores is analogous to the difference between ordinary pipes and named pipes (FIFOs). This section discusses unnamed semaphores. Named semaphores are discussed in Section 14.5.

■ Example 14.11

The following code segment declares a semaphore variable called `sem`.

```
#include <semaphore.h>
sem_t sem;
```

The POSIX:SEM Extension does not specify the underlying type of `sem_t`. One possibility is that `sem_t` acts like a file descriptor and is an offset into a local table. The table values point to entries in a system table. A particular implementation may not use the file descriptor table model but instead may store information about the semaphore with the `sem_t` variable. The semaphore functions take a pointer to the semaphore variable as a parameter, so system implementers are free to use either model. You may not make a copy of a `sem_t` variable and use it in semaphore operations.

POSIX:SEM semaphores must be initialized before they are used. The `sem_init` function initializes the unnamed semaphore referenced by `sem` to `value`. The `value` parameter cannot be negative. Our examples use unnamed semaphores with `pshared` equal to 0, meaning that the semaphore can be used only by threads of the process that initializes the semaphore. If `pshared` is nonzero, any process that can access `sem` can use the semaphore. Be aware that simply forking a child after creating the semaphore does not provide access for the child. The child receives a copy of the semaphore, not the actual semaphore.

SYNOPSIS

```
#include <semaphore.h>

int sem_init(sem_t *sem, int pshared, unsigned value);
```
                                                                   POSIX:SEM

If successful, `sem_init` initializes `sem`. Interestingly, POSIX does not specify the return value on success, but the rationale mentions that `sem_init` may be required to return 0 in a future specification. If unsuccessful, `sem_init` returns –1 and sets `errno`. The following table lists the mandatory errors for `sem_init`.

errno	cause
EINVAL	value is greater than SEM_VALUE_MAX
ENOSPC	initialization resource was exhausted, or number of semaphores exceeds SEM_NSEMS_MAX
EPERM	caller does not have the appropriate privileges

■ Example 14.12

The following code segment initializes an unnamed semaphore to be used by threads of the process.

```
sem_t semA;

if (sem_init(&semA, 0, 1) == -1)
   perror("Failed to initialize semaphore semA");
```

The sem_destroy function destroys a previously initialized unnamed semaphore referenced by the sem parameter.

```
SYNOPSIS

   #include <semaphore.h>

   int sem_destroy(sem_t *sem);
                                                       POSIX:SEM
```

If successful, sem_destroy returns 0. If unsuccessful, sem_destroy returns −1 and sets errno. The sem_destroy function sets errno to EINVAL if *sem is not a valid semaphore.

■ Example 14.13

The following code destroys semA.

```
sem_t semA;

if (sem_destroy(&semA) == -1)
   perror("Failed to destroy semA");
```

❑ Exercise 14.14

What happens if Example 14.13 executes after semA has already been destroyed? What happens if another thread or process is blocked on semA when the sem_destroy function is called?

Answer:

The POSIX standard states that the result of destroying a semaphore that has already been destroyed is undefined. The result of destroying a semaphore on which other threads are blocked is also undefined.

14.4 POSIX:SEM Semaphore Operations

The semaphore operations described in this section apply both to POSIX:SEM unnamed semaphores and to POSIX:SEM named semaphores described in Section 14.5.

The sem_post function implements classic semaphore signaling. If no threads are blocked on sem, then sem_post increments the semaphore value. If at least one thread is blocked on sem, then the semaphore value is zero. In this case, sem_post causes one of the threads blocked on sem to return from its sem_wait function, and the semaphore value remains at zero. The sem_post function is signal-safe and can be called from a signal handler.

```
SYNOPSIS

   #include <semaphore.h>

   int sem_post(sem_t *sem);
                                                                   POSIX:SEM
```

If successful, sem_post returns 0. If unsuccessful, sem_post returns –1 and sets errno. The sem_post operation sets errno to EINVAL if *sem does not correspond to a valid semaphore.

The sem_wait function implements the classic semaphore wait operation. If the semaphore value is 0, the calling thread blocks until it is unblocked by a corresponding call to sem_post or until it is interrupted by a signal. The sem_trywait function is similar to sem_wait except that instead of blocking when attempting to decrement a zero-valued semaphore, it returns –1 and sets errno to EAGAIN.

```
SYNOPSIS

   #include <semaphore.h>

   int sem_trywait(sem_t *sem);
   int sem_wait(sem_t *sem);
                                                                   POSIX:SEM
```

If successful, these functions return 0. If unsuccessful, these functions return –1 and set errno. These functions set errno to EINVAL if *sem does not correspond to a valid semaphore. The sem_trywait sets errno to EAGAIN if it would block on an ordinary sem_wait.

The sem_wait and sem_trywait functions *may* set errno to EINTR if they are interrupted by a signal. Any program that catches signals must take care when using semaphore operations, since the standard allows sem_wait and sem_trywait to return when a signal is caught and the signal handler returns. Program 14.2 restarts the sem_wait if it is interrupted by a signal.

Program 14.2 shows how to implement a shared variable that is protected by semaphores. The `initshared` function initializes the value of the shared variable. It would normally be called only once. The `getshared` function returns the current value of the variable, and the `incshared` function atomically increments the variable. If successful, these functions return 0. If unsuccessful, these functions return −1 and set `errno`. The shared variable (`shared`) is static, so it can be accessed only through the functions of `semshared.c`. Although `shared` is a simple integer in Program 14.2, functions of the same form can be used to implement any type of shared variable or structure.

Program 14.2 ——————————————————— `semshared.c`

A shared variable protected by semaphores.

```
#include <errno.h>
#include <semaphore.h>

static int shared = 0;
static sem_t sharedsem;

int initshared(int val) {
    if (sem_init(&sharedsem, 0, 1) == -1)
        return -1;
    shared = val;
    return 0;
}

int getshared(int *sval) {
    while (sem_wait(&sharedsem) == -1)
        if (errno != EINTR)
            return -1;
    *sval = shared;
    return sem_post(&sharedsem);
}

int incshared() {
    while (sem_wait(&sharedsem) == -1)
        if (errno != EINTR)
            return -1;
    shared++;
    return sem_post(&sharedsem);
}
```

Program 14.2 ——————————————————— `semshared.c`

☐ **Exercise 14.15**

Suppose a variable were to be incremented in the `main` program and also in a signal handler. Explain how Program 14.2 could be used to protect this variable.

Answer:

It could not be used without some additional work. If the signal were caught while a call to one of the functions in Program 14.2 had the semaphore locked, a call to one of these in the signal handler would cause a deadlock. The application should block the signals in the `main` program before calling `getshared` and `incshared`.

Programs 14.3 and 14.4 return to the original critical section problem of Program 14.1. The new version uses threads to illustrate the need to protect the critical section. The function in Program 14.3 is meant to be used as a thread. It outputs a message, one character at a time. To make it more likely to be interrupted in the middle of the message, the thread sleeps for 10 ms after each character is output. Program 14.4 creates a number of `threadout` threads and waits for them to terminate.

Program 14.3 ────────────────────────────── `threadcritical.c`
A thread with an unprotected critical section.

```
#include <pthread.h>
#include <stdio.h>
#include <unistd.h>
#define BUFSIZE 1024
#define TEN_MILLION 10000000L

/* ARGSUSED */
void *threadout(void *args) {
   char buffer[BUFSIZE];
   char *c;
   struct timespec sleeptime;

   sleeptime.tv_sec = 0;
   sleeptime.tv_nsec = TEN_MILLION;
   snprintf(buffer, BUFSIZE, "This is a thread from process %ld\n",
           (long)getpid());
   c = buffer;
   /****************start of critical section ******************/
   while (*c != '\0') {
      fputc(*c, stderr);
      c++;
      nanosleep(&sleeptime, NULL);
   }
   /******************end of critical section ******************/
   return NULL;
}
```

Program 14.3 ────────────────────────────── `threadcritical.c`

☐ **Exercise 14.16**

What would happen if Program 14.4 were run with four threads?

Answer:

Most likely each thread would print the first character of its message, and then each would print the second character of its message, etc. All four messages would appear on one line followed by four newline characters.

☐ **Exercise 14.17**

Why did we use `nanosleep` instead of a busy-waiting loop as in Program 14.1?

Answer:

Some thread-scheduling algorithms allow a busy-waiting thread to exclude other threads of the same process from executing.

□ **Exercise 14.18**

Why didn't we have the thread in Program 14.3 print its thread ID?

Answer:

The thread ID is of type `pthread_t`. Although many systems implement this as an integral type that can be cast to an `int` and printed, the standard does not require that `pthread_t` be of integral type. It may be a structure.

Program 14.4 ──────────────────────────── **maincritical.c**

A `main` program that creates a number of threads.

```c
#include <pthread.h>
#include <stdio.h>
#include <stdlib.h>
#include <string.h>

void *threadout(void *args);

int main(int argc, char *argv[]) {
   int error;
   int i;
   int n;
   pthread_t *tids;

   if (argc != 2){    /* check for valid number of command-line arguments */
      fprintf (stderr, "Usage: %s numthreads\n", argv[0]);
      return 1;
   }
   n = atoi(argv[1]);
   tids = (pthread_t *)calloc(n, sizeof(pthread_t));
   if (tids == NULL) {
      perror("Failed to allocate memory for thread IDs");
      return 1;
   }
   for (i = 0; i < n; i++)
      if (error = pthread_create(tids+i, NULL, threadout, NULL)) {
         fprintf(stderr, "Failed to create thread:%s\n", strerror(error));
         return 1;
      }
   for (i = 0; i < n; i++)
      if (error = pthread_join(tids[i], NULL)) {
         fprintf(stderr, "Failed to join thread:%s\n", strerror(error));
         return 1;
      }
   return 0;
}
```

Program 14.4 ──────────────────────────── **maincritical.c**

Program 14.5 is a version of Program 14.3 that protects its critical section by using a semaphore passed as its parameter. Although the `main` program does not use signals, this program restarts `sem_wait` if interrupted by a signal to demonstrate how to use semaphores with signals. Program 14.6 shows the corresponding `main` program. The `main` program initializes the semaphore to 1 before any of the threads are created.

Program 14.5 ——————————————————— `threadcriticalsem.c`

A thread with a critical section protected by a semaphore passed as its parameter.

```c
#include <errno.h>
#include <pthread.h>
#include <semaphore.h>
#include <stdio.h>
#include <unistd.h>
#define TEN_MILLION 10000000L
#define BUFSIZE 1024

void *threadout(void *args) {
   char buffer[BUFSIZE];
   char *c;
   sem_t *semlockp;
   struct timespec sleeptime;

   semlockp = (sem_t *)args;
   sleeptime.tv_sec = 0;
   sleeptime.tv_nsec = TEN_MILLION;
   snprintf(buffer, BUFSIZE, "This is a thread from process %ld\n",
            (long)getpid());
   c = buffer;
   /***************** entry section *****************************/
   while (sem_wait(semlockp) == -1)         /* Entry section */
      if(errno != EINTR) {
         fprintf(stderr, "Thread failed to lock semaphore\n");
         return NULL;
      }
   /***************** start of critical section *****************/
   while (*c != '\0') {
      fputc(*c, stderr);
      c++;
      nanosleep(&sleeptime, NULL);
   }
   /***************** exit section *****************************/
   if (sem_post(semlockp) == -1)          /* Exit section */
      fprintf(stderr, "Thread failed to unlock semaphore\n");
   /***************** remainder section ************************/
   return NULL;
}
```

Program 14.5 ——————————————————— `threadcriticalsem.c`

◻ Exercise 14.19

What happens if you replace the following line of Program 14.6

```c
    semlock = sem_init(*semlock, 0, 1)
```

with the following?

```c
    semlock = sem_init(*semlock, 0, 0)
```

Answer:
The original `sem_init` sets the initial value of `semlock` to 1, which allows the first process to successfully acquire the semaphore lock when it executes `sem_wait`. The replacement sets the initial value of `semlock` to 0, causing a deadlock. All of the processes block indefinitely on `sem_wait`.

A main *program that creates a semaphore and passes it to a number of threads.*

```c
#include <pthread.h>
#include <semaphore.h>
#include <stdio.h>
#include <stdlib.h>
#include <string.h>

void *threadout(void *args);

int main(int argc, char *argv[]) {
   int error;
   int i;
   int n;
   sem_t semlock;
   pthread_t *tids;

   if (argc != 2){    /* check for valid number of command-line arguments */
      fprintf (stderr, "Usage: %s numthreads\n", argv[0]);
      return 1;
   }
   n = atoi(argv[1]);
   tids = (pthread_t *)calloc(n, sizeof(pthread_t));
   if (tids == NULL) {
      perror("Failed to allocate memory for thread IDs");
      return 1;
   }
   if (sem_init(&semlock, 0, 1) == -1) {
      perror("Failed to initialize semaphore");
      return 1;
   }
   for (i = 0; i < n; i++)
      if (error = pthread_create(tids + i, NULL, threadout, &semlock)) {
         fprintf(stderr, "Failed to create thread:%s\n", strerror(error));
         return 1;
      }
   for (i = 0; i < n; i++)
      if (error = pthread_join(tids[i], NULL)) {
         fprintf(stderr, "Failed to join thread:%s\n", strerror(error));
         return 1;
      }
   return 0;
}
```

Exercise 14.19 illustrates the importance of properly initializing the semaphore value. The sem_getvalue function allows a user to examine the value of either a named or unnamed semaphore. This function sets the integer referenced by sval to the value of the semaphore without affecting the state of the semaphore. Interpretation of sval is a little tricky: It holds the value that the semaphore had at some unspecified time during the call, but not necessarily the value at the time of return. If the semaphore is locked, sem_getvalue either sets sval to zero or to a negative value indicating the number of threads waiting for the semaphore at some unspecified time during the call.

```
SYNOPSIS

    #include <semaphore.h>

    int sem_getvalue(sem_t *restrict sem, int *restrict sval);
                                                                    POSIX:SEM
```

If successful, `sem_getvalue` returns 0. If unsuccessful, `sem_getvalue` returns −1 and
sets `errno`. The `sem_getvalue` function sets `errno` to `EINVAL` if `*sem` does not correspond to a valid semaphore.

14.5 POSIX:SEM Named Semaphores

POSIX:SEM named semaphores can synchronize processes that do not share memory.
Named semaphores have a name, a user ID, a group ID and permissions just as files do.
A semaphore name is a character string that conforms to the construction rules for a pathname. POSIX does not require that the name appear in the filesystem, nor does POSIX
specify the consequences of having two processes refer to the same name unless the name
begins with the slash character. If the name begins with a slash (/), then two processes
(or threads) that open the semaphore with that name refer to the same semaphore. Consequently, always use names beginning with a / for POSIX:SEM named semaphores. Some
operating systems impose other restrictions on semaphore names.

14.5.1 Creating and opening named semaphores

The `sem_open` function establishes the connection between a named semaphore and a
`sem_t` value. The `name` parameter is a string that identifies the semaphore by name. This
name may or may not correspond to an actual object in the file system. The `oflag` parameter determines whether the semaphore is created or just accessed by the function. If the
`O_CREAT` bit of `oflag` is set, the `sem_open` requires two more parameters: a `mode` parameter of type `mode_t` giving the permissions and a `value` parameter of type `unsigned`
giving the initial value of the semaphore. If both the `O_CREAT` and `O_EXCL` bits of `oflag`
are set, the `sem_open` returns an error if the semaphore already exists. If the semaphore
already exists and `O_CREAT` is set but `O_EXCL` is not set, the semaphore ignores `O_CREAT`
and the additional parameters. POSIX:SEM does not provide a way to directly set the
value of a named semaphore once it already exists.

```
SYNOPSIS

    #include <semaphore.h>

    sem_t *sem_open(const char *name, int oflag, ...);
                                                                    POSIX:SEM
```

If successful, the `sem_open` function returns the address of the semaphore. If unsuccessful, `sem_open` returns `SEM_FAILED` and sets `errno`. The following table lists the mandatory errors for `sem_open`.

errno	cause
EACCES	permissions incorrect
EEXIST	O_CREAT and O_EXCL are set and semaphore exists
EINTR	sem_open was interrupted by a signal
EINVAL	name can't be opened as a semaphore, or tried to create semaphore with value greater than SEM VALUE_MAX
EMFILE	too many file descriptors or semaphores in use by process
ENAMETOOLONG	name is longer than PATH_MAX, or it has a component that exceeds NAME_MAX
ENFILE	too many semaphores open on the system
ENOENT	O_CREAT is not set and the semaphore doesn't exist
ENOSPC	not enough space to create the semaphore

Program 14.7 shows a `getnamed` function that creates a named semaphore if it doesn't already exist. The `getnamed` function can be called as an initialization function by multiple processes. The function first tries to create a new named semaphore. If the semaphore already exists, the function then tries to open it without the `O_CREAT` and `O_EXCL` bits of the `oflag` parameter set. If successful, `getnamed` returns 0. If unsuccessful, `getnamed` returns –1 and sets `errno`.

Program 14.7 ———————————————————— `getnamed.c`

A function to access a named semaphore, creating it if it doesn't already exist.

```c
#include <errno.h>
#include <fcntl.h>
#include <semaphore.h>
#include <sys/stat.h>
#define PERMS (mode_t)(S_IRUSR | S_IWUSR | S_IRGRP | S_IROTH)
#define FLAGS (O_CREAT | O_EXCL)

int getnamed(char *name, sem_t **sem, int val) {
   while ((((*sem = sem_open(name, FLAGS , PERMS, val)) == SEM_FAILED) &&
           (errno == EINTR)) ;
   if (*sem != SEM_FAILED)
      return 0;
   if (errno != EEXIST)
      return -1;
   while ((((*sem = sem_open(name, 0)) == SEM_FAILED) && (errno == EINTR)) ;
   if (*sem != SEM_FAILED)
      return 0;
   return -1;
}
```

Program 14.7 ———————————————————— `getnamed.c`

The first parameter of `getnamed` is the name of the semaphore and the last parameter is the value to use for initialization if the semaphore does not already exist. The second parameter is a pointer to a pointer to a semaphore. This double indirection is necessary because `getnamed` needs to change a pointer. Note that if the semaphore already exists, `getnamed` does not initialize the semaphore.

Program 14.8 shows a modification of Program 14.1 that uses named semaphores to protect the critical section. Program 14.8 takes three command-line arguments: the number of processes, the delay and the name of the semaphore to use. Each process calls the `getnamed` function of Program 14.7 to gain access to the semaphore. At most, one of these will create the semaphore. The others will gain access to it.

◻ **Exercise 14.20**

What happens if two copies of `chainnamed`, using the same named semaphore run simultaneously on the same machine?

Answer:

With the named semaphores, each line will be printed without interleaving.

◻ **Exercise 14.21**

What happens if you enter Ctrl-C while `chainnamed` is running and then try to run it again with the same named semaphore?

Answer:

Most likely the signal generated by Ctrl-C will be delivered while the semaphore has value 0. The next time the program is run, all processes will block and no output will result.

14.5.2 Closing and unlinking named semaphores

Like named pipes or FIFOs (Section 6.3), POSIX:SEM named semaphores have permanence beyond the execution of a single program. Individual programs can close named semaphores with the `sem_close` function, but doing so does not cause the semaphore to be removed from the system. The `sem_close` takes a single parameter, `sem`, specifying the semaphore to be closed.

```
SYNOPSIS

   #include <semaphore.h>

   int sem_close(sem_t *sem);

                                                    POSIX:SEM
```

If successful, `sem_close` returns 0. If unsuccessful, `sem_close` returns −1 and sets `errno`. The `sem_close` function sets `errno` to `EINVAL` if `*sem` is not a valid semaphore.

Program 14.8 ——————————————————————— **chainnamed.c**

A process chain with a critical section protected by a POSIX:SEM named semaphore.

```c
#include <errno.h>
#include <semaphore.h>
#include <stdio.h>
#include <stdlib.h>
#include <unistd.h>
#include <sys/wait.h>
#include "restart.h"
#define BUFSIZE 1024
int getnamed(char *name, sem_t **sem, int val);

int main  (int argc, char *argv[]) {
   char buffer[BUFSIZE];
   char *c;
   pid_t childpid = 0;
   int delay;
   volatile int dummy = 0;
   int i, n;
   sem_t *semlockp;

   if (argc != 4){        /* check for valid number of command-line arguments */
      fprintf (stderr, "Usage: %s processes delay semaphorename\n", argv[0]);
      return 1;
   }
   n = atoi(argv[1]);
   delay = atoi(argv[2]);
   for (i = 1; i < n; i++)
      if (childpid = fork())
         break;
   snprintf(buffer, BUFSIZE,
      "i:%d  process ID:%ld  parent ID:%ld  child ID:%ld\n",
       i, (long)getpid(), (long)getppid(), (long)childpid);
   c = buffer;
   if (getnamed(argv[3], &semlockp, 1) == -1) {
      perror("Failed to create named semaphore");
      return 1;
   }
   while (sem_wait(semlockp) == -1)                       /* entry section */
       if (errno != EINTR) {
          perror("Failed to lock semlock");
          return 1;
       }
   while (*c != '\0') {                                   /* critical section */
      fputc(*c, stderr);
      c++;
      for (i = 0; i < delay; i++)
         dummy++;
   }
   if (sem_post(semlockp) == -1) {                        /* exit section */
      perror("Failed to unlock semlock");
      return 1;
   }
   if (r_wait(NULL) == -1)                                /* remainder section */
      return 1;
   return 0;
}
```

Program 14.8 ——————————————————————— **chainnamed.c**

The `sem_unlink` function, which is analogous to the `unlink` function for files or FIFOs, performs the removal of the named semaphore from the system after all processes have closed the named semaphore. A close operation occurs when the process explicitly calls `sem_close`, `_exit`, `exit`, `exec` or executes a return from `main`. The `sem_unlink` function has a single parameter, a pointer to the semaphore that is to be unlinked.

SYNOPSIS

```
#include <semaphore.h>

int sem_unlink(const char *name);
```

POSIX:SEM

If successful, `sem_unlink` returns 0. If unsuccessful, `sem_unlink` returns −1 and sets `errno`. The following table lists the mandatory errors for `sem_unlink`.

errno	cause
EACCES	permissions incorrect
ENAMETOOLONG	name is longer than PATH_MAX, or it has a component that exceeds NAME_MAX
ENOENT	the semaphore doesn't exist

Calls to `sem_open` with the same name refer to a new semaphore after a `sem_unlink`, even if other processes still have the old semaphore open. The `sem_unlink` function always returns immediately, even if other processes have the semaphore open.

❑ Exercise 14.22

What happens if you call `sem_close` for an unnamed semaphore that was initialized by `sem_init` rather than `sem_open`?
Answer:
The POSIX standard states that the result of doing this is not defined.

Program 14.9 shows a function that closes and unlinks a named semaphore. The `destroynamed` calls the `sem_unlink` function, even if the `sem_close` function fails. If successful, `destroynamed` returns 0. If unsuccessful, `destroynamed` returns −1 and sets `errno`.

Remember that POSIX:SEM named semaphores are persistent. If you create one of these semaphores, it stays in the system and retains its value until destroyed, even after the process that created it and all processes that have access to it have terminated. POSIX:SEM does not provide a method for determining which named semaphores exist. They may or may not show up when you display the contents of a directory. They may or may not be destroyed when the system reboots.

Program 14.9 ──────────────────────────── `destroynamed.c`

A function that closes and unlinks a named semaphore.

```
#include <errno.h>
#include <semaphore.h>

int destroynamed(char *name, sem_t *sem) {
    int error = 0;

    if (sem_close(sem) == -1)
       error = errno;
    if ((sem_unlink(name) != -1) && !error)
       return 0;
    if (error)         /* set errno to first error that occurred */
       errno = error;
    return -1;
}
```

Program 14.9 ──────────────────────────── `destroynamed.c`

14.6 Exercise: License Manager

The exercises in this section are along the lines of the `runsim` program developed in the exercises of Section 3.9. In those exercises, `runsim` reads a command from standard input and forks a child that calls `execvp` to execute the command. That `runsim` program takes a single command-line argument specifying the number of child processes allowed to execute simultaneously. It also keeps a count of the children and uses `wait` to block when it reaches the limit.

In these exercises, `runsim` again reads a command from standard input and forks a child. The child in turn forks a grandchild that calls `execvp`. The child waits for the grandchild to complete and then exits. Figure 14.1 shows the structure of `runsim` when three such pairs are executing. This program uses semaphores to control the number of simultaneous executions.

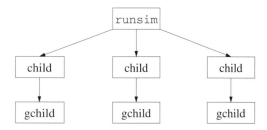

Figure 14.1: The structure of `runsim` when the grandchildren, not the children, call `execvp`.

14.6.1 License object

Implement a `license` object based on a named semaphore generated from the pathname `/tmp.license.uid`, where `uid` is the process user ID. The `license` should have the following public functions.

`int getlicense(void);`
    blocks until a license is available.

`int returnlicense(void);`
    increments the number of available licenses.

`int initlicense(void);`
    performs any needed initialization of the `license` object.

`int addtolicense(int n);`
    adds a certain number of licenses to the number available.

`int removelicenses(int n);`
    decrements the number of licenses by the specified number.

14.6.2 The `runsim` main program

Write a `runsim` program that runs up to n processes at a time. Start the `runsim` program by typing the following command.

```
runsim n
```

Implement `runsim` as follows.

1. Check for the correct number of command-line arguments and output a usage message if incorrect.
2. Perform the following in a loop until end-of-file on standard input.
   a) Read a command from standard input of up to MAX_CANON characters.
   b) Request a license from the `license` object.
   c) Fork a child that calls `docommand` and then exits. Pass the input string to `docommand`.
   d) Check to see if any of the children have finished (`waitpid` with the WNOHANG option).

The `docommand` function has the following prototype.

```
void docommand(char *cline);
```

Implement `docommand` as follows.

1. Fork a child (a grandchild of the original). This grandchild calls `makeargv` on `cline` and calls `execvp` on the resulting argument array.
2. Wait for this child and then return the license to the `license` object.
3. Exit.

Test the program as in Section 3.9. Improve the error messages to make them more readable. Write a test program that takes two command-line arguments: the sleep time and the repeat factor. The test program simply repeats a loop for the specified number of times. In the loop, the test program sleeps and then outputs a message with its process ID to standard error. After completing the specified number of iterations, the program exits. Use `runsim` to run multiple copies of the test program.

Try executing several copies of `runsim` concurrently. Since they all use the same semaphore, the number of grandchildren processes should still be bounded by n.

14.6.3 Extensions to the license manager

Modify the license object so that it supports multiple types of licenses, each type identified by a numerical key. Test the program under conditions similar to those described in the previous section.

14.7 Additional Reading

Most books on operating systems [107, 122] discuss the classical semaphore abstraction. The book *UNIX Systems for Modern Architectures: Symmetric Multiprocessing and Caching for Kernel Programmers* by Schimmel [103] presents an advanced look at how these issues apply to design of multiprocessor kernels.

Chapter 15

POSIX IPC

The classical UNIX interprocess communication (IPC) mechanisms of shared memory, message queues and semaphore sets are standardized in the POSIX:XSI Extension. These mechanisms, which allow unrelated processes to exchange information in a reasonably efficient way, use a key to identify, create or access the corresponding entity. The entities may persist in the system beyond the lifetime of the process that creates them, but conveniently, POSIX:XSI also provides shell commands to list and remove them.

Objectives
- Learn about classical interprocess communication
- Experiment with synchronized shared memory
- Explore semaphore implementations
- Use message queues for interprocess logging
- Understand the consequences of persistence

15.1 POSIX:XSI Interprocess Communication

The POSIX interprocess communication (IPC) is part of the POSIX:XSI Extension and has its origin in UNIX System V interprocess communication. IPC, which includes message queues, semaphore sets and shared memory, provides mechanisms for sharing information among processes on the same system. These three communication mechanisms have a similar structure, and this chapter emphasizes the common elements of their use. Table 15.1 summarizes the POSIX:XSI interprocess communication functions.

mechanism	POSIX function	meaning
message queues	msgctl	control
	msgget	create or access
	msgrcv	receive message
	msgsnd	send message
semaphores	semctl	control
	semget	create or access
	semop	execute operation (wait or post)
shared memory	shmat	attach memory to process
	shmctl	control
	shmdt	detach memory from process
	shmget	create and initialize or access

Table 15.1: POSIX:XSI interprocess communication functions.

15.1.1 Identifying and accessing IPC objects

POSIX:XSI identifies each IPC object by a unique integer that is greater than or equal to zero and is returned from the get function for the object in much the same way as the open function returns an integer representing a file descriptor. For example, msgget returns an integer identifier for message queue objects. Similarly, semget returns an integer identifier for a specified semaphore set, and shmget returns an integer identifier for a shared memory segment. These identifiers are associated with additional data structures that are defined in sys/msg.h, sys/sem.h or sys/shm.h, respectively. The integer identifiers within each IPC object type are unique, but you might well have an integer identifier 1 for two different types of objects, say, a semaphore set and a message queue.

When creating or accessing an IPC object, you must specify a key to designate the particular object to be created or accessed. Pick a key in one of these three ways.

- Let the system pick a key (IPC_PRIVATE).
- Pick a key directly.
- Ask the system to generate a key from a specified path by calling ftok.

The `ftok` function allows independent processes to derive the same key based on a known pathname. The file corresponding to the pathname must exist and be accessible to the processes that want to access an IPC object. The combination of `path` and `id` uniquely identifies the IPC object. The `id` parameter allows several IPC objects of the same type to be keyed from a single pathname.

```
SYNOPSIS

   #include <sys/ipc.h>

   key_t ftok(const char *path, int id);
                                                          POSIX:XSI
```

If successful, `ftok` returns a key. If unsuccessful, `ftok` returns `(key_t)-1` and sets `errno`. The following table lists the mandatory errors for `ftok`.

errno	cause
EACCES	search permission on a `path` component denied
ELOOP	a loop exists in resolution of `path`
ENAMETOOLONG	length of `path` exceeds PATH_MAX, or length of a pathname component exceeds NAME_MAX
ENOENT	a component of `path` is not a file or is empty
ENOTDIR	a component of `path`'s prefix is not a directory

■ Example 15.1

The following code segment derives a key from the filename `/tmp/trouble.c`.

```
if ((thekey = ftok("tmp/trouble.c", 1)) == (key_t)-1))
    perror("Failed to derive key from /tmp/trouble.c");
```

15.1.2 Accessing POSIX:XSI IPC resources from the shell

The POSIX:XSI Extension for shells and utilities defines shell commands for examining and deleting IPC resources, a convenient feature that is missing for the POSIX:SEM semaphores.

The `ipcs` command displays information about POSIX:XSI interprocess communication resources. If you forget which ones you created, you can list them from the shell command line.

```
SYNOPSIS

   ipcs [-qms][-a | -bcopt]
                                            POSIX:XSI,Shell and Utilities
```

If no options are given, `ipcs` outputs, in an abbreviated format, information about message queues, shared memory segments and semaphore sets. You can restrict the display to specific types of IPC resources with the `-q`, `-m` and `-s` options for message queues, shared memory and semaphores, respectively. The `-a` option displays a long format giving all information available. The `-bcopt` options specify which components of the available information to print.

■ Example 15.2

The following command displays all the available information about the semaphores currently allocated on the system.

```
ipcs -s -a
```

You can remove an individual resource by giving either an ID or a key. Use the `ipcrm` command to remove POSIX:XSI interprocess communication resources.

SYNOPSIS

```
ipcrm [-q msgid  |  -Q msgkey | -s semid | -S semkey |
       -m shmid  |  -M shmkey] ....
```

POSIX:XSI,Shell and Utilities

The lower case `-q`, `-s` and `-m` options use the object ID to specify the removal of a message queue, semaphore set or shared memory segment, respectively. The uppercase options use the original creation key.

15.2 POSIX:XSI Semaphore Sets

A POSIX:XSI semaphore consists of an array of *semaphore elements*. The semaphore elements are similar, but not identical, to the classical integer semaphores proposed by Dijsktra, as described in Chapter 14. A process can perform operations on the entire set in a single call. Thus, POSIX:XSI semaphores are capable of AND synchronization, as described in Section 14.2. We refer to POSIX:XSI semaphores as *semaphore sets* to distinguish them from the POSIX:SEM semaphores described in Chapter 14.

Each semaphore element includes at least the following information.

- A nonnegative integer representing the value of the semaphore element (`semval`)
- The process ID of the last process to manipulate the semaphore element (`sempid`)
- The number of processes waiting for the semaphore element value to increase (`semncnt`)
- The number of processes waiting for the semaphore element value to equal 0 (`semzcnt`)

The major data structure for semaphores is `semid_ds`, which is defined in `sys/sem.h` and has the following members.

```
struct ipc_perm sem_perm;   /* operation permission structure */
unsigned short sem_nsems;   /* number of semaphores in the set */
time_t sem_otime;           /* time of last semop */
time_t sem_ctime;           /* time of last semctl */
```

Each semaphore element has two queues associated with it—a queue of processes waiting for the value to equal 0 and a queue of processes waiting for the value to increase. The semaphore element operations allow a process to block until a semaphore element value is 0 or until it increases to a specific value greater than zero.

15.2.1 Semaphore creation

The `semget` function returns the semaphore identifier associated with the `key` parameter. The `semget` function creates the identifier and its associated semaphore set if either the key is `IPC_PRIVATE` or `semflg & IPC_CREAT` is nonzero and no semaphore set or identifier is already associated with `key`. The `nsems` parameter specifies the number of semaphore elements in the set. The individual semaphore elements within a semaphore set are referenced by the integers `0` through `nsems - 1`. Semaphores have permissions specified by the `semflg` argument of `semget`. Set permission values in the same way as described in Section 4.3 for files, and change the permissions by calling `semctl`. Semaphore elements should be initialized with `semctl` before they are used.

SYNOPSIS

```
  #include <sys/sem.h>

  int semget(key_t key, int nsems, int semflg);
```
POSIX:XSI

If successful, `semget` returns a nonnegative integer corresponding to the semaphore identifier. If unsuccessful, the `semget` function returns –1 and sets `errno`. The following table lists the mandatory errors for `semget`.

errno	cause
EACCES	semaphore exists for `key` but permission not granted
EEXIST	semaphore exists for `key` but
	`((semflg & IPC_CREAT) && (semflg & IPC_EXCL)) != 0`
EINVAL	`nsems <= 0` or greater than system limit, or
	`nsems` doesn't agree with semaphore set size
ENOENT	semaphore does not exist for `key` and
	`(semflg & IPC_CREAT) == 0`
ENOSPC	systemwide limit on semaphores would be exceeded

If a process attempts to create a semaphore that already exists, it receives a handle to the existing semaphore unless the `semflg` value includes both `IPC_CREAT` and `IPC_EXCL`. In the latter case, `semget` fails and sets `errno` equal to `EEXIST`.

■ Example 15.3

The following code segment creates a new semaphore set containing three semaphore elements.

```
#define PERMS (S_IRUSR | S_IWUSR)

int semid;
if ((semid = semget(IPC_PRIVATE, 3, PERMS)) == -1)
   perror("Failed to create new private semaphore");
```

This semaphore can only be read or written by the owner.

The `IPC_PRIVATE` key guarantees that `semget` creates a new semaphore. To get a new semaphore set from a made-up key or a key derived from a pathname, the process must specify by using the `IPC_CREAT` flag that it is creating a new semaphore. If both `ICP_CREAT` and `IPC_EXCL` are specified, `semget` returns an error if the semaphore already exists.

■ Example 15.4

The following code segment accesses a semaphore set with a single element identified by the key value `99887`.

```
#define PERMS (S_IRUSR | S_IWUSR | S_IRGRP | S_IWGRP | S_IROTH | S_IWOTH)
#define KEY ((key_t)99887)

int semid;
if ((semid = semget(KEY, 1, PERMS | IPC_CREAT)) == -1)
   perror ("Failed to access semaphore with key 99887");
```

The `IPC_CREAT` flag ensures that if the semaphore set doesn't exist, `semget` creates it. The permissions allow all users to access the semaphore set.

Giving a specific key value allows cooperating processes to agree on a common semaphore set. If the semaphore already exists, `semget` returns a handle to the existing semaphore. If you replace the `semflg` argument of `semget` with `PERMS | IPC_CREAT | IPC_EXCL`, `semget` returns an error when the semaphore already exists.

Program 15.1 demonstrates how to identify a semaphore set by using a key generated from a pathname and an ID, which are passed as command-line arguments. If `semfrompath` executes successfully, the semaphores will exist after the program exits. You will need to call the `ipcrm` command to get rid of them.

Program 15.1 ───────────────────────────── `semfrompath.c`

A program that creates a semaphore from a pathname key.

```c
#include <errno.h>
#include <stdio.h>
#include <stdlib.h>
#include <string.h>
#include <sys/sem.h>
#include <sys/stat.h>
#define PERMS (S_IRUSR | S_IWUSR | S_IRGRP | S_IWGRP | S_IROTH | S_IWOTH)
#define SET_SIZE 2

int main(int argc, char *argv[]) {
   key_t mykey;
   int semid;

   if (argc != 3) {
      fprintf(stderr, "Usage: %s pathname id\n", argv[0]);
      return 1;
   }
   if ((mykey = ftok(argv[1], atoi(argv[2]))) == (key_t)-1) {
      fprintf(stderr, "Failed to derive key from filename %s:%s\n",
              argv[1], strerror(errno));
      return 1;
   }
   if ((semid = semget(mykey, SET_SIZE, PERMS | IPC_CREAT)) == -1) {
      fprintf(stderr, "Failed to create semaphore with key %d:%s\n",
              (int)mykey, strerror(errno));
      return 1;
   }
   printf("semid = %d\n", semid);
   return 0;
}
```

Program 15.1 ───────────────────────────── `semfrompath.c`

15.2.2 Semaphore control

Each element of a semaphore set must be initialized with `semctl` before it is used. The `semctl` function provides control operations in element `semnum` for the semaphore set `semid`. The `cmd` parameter specifies the type of operation. The optional fourth parameter, `arg`, depends on the value of `cmd`.

SYNOPSIS

```c
#include <sys/sem.h>

int semctl(int semid, int semnum, int cmd, ...);
```

POSIX:XSI

If successful, `semctl` returns a nonnegative value whose interpretation depends on `cmd`. The GETVAL, GETPID, GETNCNT and GETZCNT values of `cmd` cause `semctl` to return the value associated with `cmd`. All other values of `cmd` cause `semctl` to return 0 if successful. If unsuccessful, `semctl` returns –1 and sets `errno`. The following table lists the mandatory errors for `semctl`.

errno	cause
EACCES	operation is denied to the caller
EINVAL	value of `semid` or of `cmd` is invalid, or value of `semnum` is negative or too large
EPERM	value of `cmd` is `IPC_RMID` or `IPC_SET` and caller does not have required privileges
ERANGE	`cmd` is `SETVAL` or `SETALL` and value to be set is out of range

Table 15.2 gives the POSIX:XSI values for the `cmd` parameter of `semctl`.

cmd	description
GETALL	return values of the semaphore set in `arg.array`
GETVAL	return value of a specific semaphore element
GETPID	return process ID of last process to manipulate element
GETNCNT	return number of processes waiting for element to increment
GETZCNT	return number of processes waiting for element to become 0
IPC_RMID	remove semaphore set identified by `semid`
IPC_SET	set permissions of the semaphore set from `arg.buf`
IPC_STAT	copy members of `semid_ds` of semaphore set `semid` into `arg.buf`
SETALL	set values of semaphore set from `arg.array`
SETVAL	set value of a specific semaphore element to `arg.val`

Table 15.2: POSIX:XSI values for the `cmd` parameter of `semctl`.

Several of these commands, such as `GETALL` and `SETALL`, require an `arg` parameter to read or store results. The `arg` parameter is of type `union semun`, which must be defined in programs that use it, as follows.

```
union semun {
    int val;
    struct semid_ds *buf;
    unsigned short *array;
} arg;
```

■ Example 15.5

The `initelement` function sets the value of the specified semaphore element to `semvalue`.

```
#include <sys/sem.h>

int initelement(int semid, int semnum, int semvalue) {
    union semun {
        int val;
        struct semid_ds *buf;
        unsigned short *array;
    } arg;
    arg.val = semvalue;
    return semctl(semid, semnum, SETVAL, arg);
}
```

————————————————————————————— **initelement.c**

The `semid` and `semnum` parameters identify the semaphore set and the element within the set whose value is to be set to `semvalue`.

If successful, `initelement` returns 0. If unsuccessful, `initelement` returns −1 with errno set (since `semctl` sets errno).

■ Example 15.6

The `removesem` function deletes the semaphore specified by `semid`.

```
#include <sys/sem.h>

int removesem(int semid) {
    return semctl(semid, 0, IPC_RMID);
}
```

————————————————————————————— **removesem.c**

If successful, `removesem` returns 0. If unsuccessful, `removesem` returns −1 with errno set (since `semctl` sets errno).

15.2.3 POSIX semaphore set operations

The `semop` function atomically performs a user-defined collection of semaphore operations on the semaphore set associated with identifier `semid`. The `sops` parameter points to an array of element operations, and the `nsops` parameter specifies the number of element operations in the `sops` array.

SYNOPSIS

```
#include <sys/sem.h>

int semop(int semid, struct sembuf *sops, size_t nsops);
```

POSIX:XSI

If successful, `semop` returns 0. If unsuccessful, `semop` returns −1 and sets errno. The following table lists the mandatory errors for `semop`.

errno	cause
E2BIG	value of nsops is too big
EACCES	operation is denied to the caller
EAGAIN	operation would block the process but
	(sem_flg & IPC_NOWAIT) != 0
EFBIG	value of sem_num for one of the sops entries is less than 0
	or greater than the number elements in the semaphore set
EIDRM	semaphore identifier semid has been removed from the system
EINTR	semop was interrupted by a signal
EINVAL	value of semid is invalid, or number of individual
	semaphores for a SEM_UNDO has exceeded limit
ENOSPC	limit on processes requesting SEM_UNDO has been exceeded
ERANGE	operation would cause an overflow of a semval or semadj value

The semop function performs all the operations specified in sops array atomically on a single semaphore set. If any of the individual element operations would cause the process to block, the process blocks and none of the operations are performed.

The struct sembuf structure, which specifies a semaphore element operation, includes the following members.

    short sem_num   number of the semaphore element
    short sem_op   particular element operation to be performed
    short sem_flg   flags to specify options for the operation

The sem_op element operations are values specifying the amount by which the semaphore value is to be changed.

- If sem_op is an integer greater than zero, semop adds the value to the corresponding semaphore element value and awakens all processes that are waiting for the element to increase.
- If sem_op is 0 and the semaphore element value is not 0, semop blocks the calling process (waiting for 0) and increments the count of processes waiting for a zero value of that element.
- If sem_op is a negative number, semop adds the sem_op value to the corresponding semaphore element value provided that the result would not be negative. If the operation would make the element value negative, semop blocks the process on the event that the semaphore element value increases. If the resulting value is 0, semop wakes the processes waiting for 0.

The description of semop assumes that sem_flg is 0 for all the element operations. If sem_flg & IPC_NOWAIT is true, the element operation never causes the semop call to block. If a semop returns because it would have blocked on that element operation, it returns –1 with errno set to EAGAIN. If sem_flg & SEM_UNDO is true, the function also modifies the semaphore adjustment value for the process. This adjustment value allows the process to *undo* its effect on the semaphore when it exits. You should read the man page carefully regarding the interaction of semop with various settings of the flags.

☐ **Exercise 15.7**

What is wrong with the following code to declare myopbuf and initialize it so that sem_num is 1, sem_op is 1, and sem_flg is 0?

```
struct sembuf myopbuf = {1, -1, 0};
```

Answer:

The direct assignment assumes that the members of struct sembuf appear in the order sem_num, sem_op and sem_flg. You may see this type of initialization in legacy code and it may work on your system, but try to avoid it. Although the POSIX:XSI Extension specifies that the struct sembuf structure has sem_num, sem_op and sem_flg members, the standard does not specify the order in which these members appear in the definition nor does the standard restrict struct sembuf to contain only these members.

■ **Example 15.8**

The function setsembuf initializes the struct sembuf structure members sem_num, sem_op and sem_flg in an implementation-independent manner.

```
#include <sys/sem.h>

void setsembuf(struct sembuf *s, int num, int op, int flg) {
   s->sem_num = (short)num;
   s->sem_op = (short)op;
   s->sem_flg = (short)flg;
   return;
}
```
── **setsembuf.c**

■ **Example 15.9**

The following code segment atomically increments element zero of semid by 1 and element one of semid by 2, using setsembuf of Example 15.8.

```
struct sembuf myop[2];

setsembuf(myop, 0, 1, 0);
setsembuf(myop + 1, 1, 2, 0);
if (semop(semid, myop, 2) == -1)
   perror("Failed to perform semaphore operation");
```

■ **Example 15.10**

Suppose a two-element semaphore set, S, represents a tape drive system in which Process 1 uses Tape A, Process 2 uses Tape A and B, and Process 3 uses Tape B. The following pseudocode segment defines semaphore operations that allow the processes to access one or both tape drives in a mutually exclusive manner.

```
struct sembuf get_tapes[2];
struct sembuf release_tapes[2];

setsembuf(&(get_tapes[0]), 0, -1, 0);
setsembuf(&(get_tapes[1]), 1, -1, 0);
setsembuf(&(release_tapes[0]), 0, 1, 0);
setsembuf(&(release_tapes[1]), 1, 1, 0);

Process 1:        semop(S, get_tapes, 1);
                  <use tape A>
                  semop(S, release_tapes, 1);

Process 2:        semop(S, get_tapes, 2);
                  <use tapes A and B>
                  semop(S, release_tapes, 2);

Process 3:        semop(S, get_tapes + 1, 1);
                  <use tape B>
                  semop(S, release_tapes + 1, 1);
```

$S[0]$ represents tape A, and $S[1]$ represents tape B. We assume that both elements of S have been initialized to 1.

If semop is interrupted by a signal, it returns -1 and sets errno to EINTR. Program 15.2 shows a function that restarts semop if it is interrupted by a signal.

Program 15.2 ———————————————————————————— **r_semop.c**

A function that restarts semop *after a signal.*

```
#include <errno.h>
#include <sys/sem.h>

int r_semop(int semid, struct sembuf *sops, int nsops) {
   while (semop(semid, sops, nsops) == -1)
      if (errno != EINTR)
         return -1;
   return 0;
}
```

Program 15.2 ———————————————————————————— **r_semop.c**

Program 15.3 modifies Program 14.1 to use POSIX:XSI semaphore sets to protect a critical section. Program 15.3 calls setsembuf (Example 15.8) and removesem (Example 15.6). It restarts semop operations if interrupted by a signal, even though the program does not catch any signals. You should get into the habit of restarting functions that can set errno equal to EINTR.

Once the semaphore of Program 15.3 is created, it persists until it is removed. If a child process generates an error, it just exits. If the parent generates an error, it falls through to the wait call and then removes the semaphore. A program that creates a semaphore for its own use should be sure to remove the semaphore before the program terminates. Be careful to remove the semaphore exactly once.

Program 15.3 ———————————————————— `chainsemset.c`

A modification of Program 14.1 that uses semaphore sets to protect the critical section.

```c
#include <errno.h>
#include <limits.h>
#include <stdio.h>
#include <stdlib.h>
#include <string.h>
#include <unistd.h>
#include <sys/sem.h>
#include <sys/stat.h>
#include <sys/wait.h>
#include "restart.h"
#define BUFSIZE 1024
#define PERMS (S_IRUSR | S_IWUSR)

int initelement(int semid, int semnum, int semvalue);
int r_semop(int semid, struct sembuf *sops, int nsops);
int removesem(int semid);
void setsembuf(struct sembuf *s, int num, int op, int flg);

void printerror(char *msg, int error) {
   fprintf(stderr, "[%ld] %s: %s\n", (long)getpid(), msg, strerror(error));
}

int main (int argc, char *argv[]) {
   char buffer[MAX_CANON];
   char *c;
   pid_t childpid;
   int delay;
   int error;
   int i, j, n;
   int semid;
   struct sembuf semsignal[1];
   struct sembuf semwait[1];

   if ((argc != 3) || ((n = atoi(argv[1])) <= 0) ||
       ((delay = atoi(argv[2])) < 0))   {
      fprintf (stderr, "Usage: %s processes delay\n", argv[0]);
      return 1;
   }
                         /* create a semaphore containing a single element */
   if ((semid = semget(IPC_PRIVATE, 1, PERMS)) == -1) {
      perror("Failed to create a private semaphore");
      return 1;
   }
   setsembuf(semwait, 0, -1, 0);                    /* decrement element 0 */
   setsembuf(semsignal, 0, 1, 0);                   /* increment element 0 */
   if (initelement(semid, 0, 1) == -1) {
      perror("Failed to initialize semaphore element to 1");
      if (removesem(semid) == -1)
         perror("Failed to remove failed semaphore");
      return 1;
   }
   for (i = 1; i < n; i++)
      if (childpid = fork())
         break;
   snprintf(buffer, BUFSIZE, "i:%d PID:%ld  parent PID:%ld  child PID:%ld\n",
            i, (long)getpid(), (long)getppid(), (long)childpid);
   c = buffer;
```

```
/******************** entry section *********************************/
if (((error = r_semop(semid, semwait, 1)) == -1) && (i > 1)) {
   printerror("Child failed to lock semid", error);
   return 1;
}
else if (!error) {
   /**************** start of critical section ********************/
   while (*c != '\0') {
      fputc(*c, stderr);
      c++;
      for (j = 0; j < delay; j++) ;
   }
   /**************** exit section *********************************/
   if ((error = r_semop(semid, semsignal, 1)) == -1)
      printerror("Failed to unlock semid", error);
}
/******************** remainder section ***************************/
if ((r_wait(NULL) == -1) && (errno != ECHILD))
   printerror("Failed to wait", errno);
if ((i == 1) && ((error = removesem(semid)) == -1)) {
   printerror("Failed to clean up", error);
   return 1;
}
return 0;
}
```

Program 15.3 ─────────────────────────────────────── `chainsemset.c`

A program calls `semget` to create or access a semaphore set and calls `semctl` to initialize it. If one process creates and initializes a semaphore and another process calls `semop` between the creation and initialization, the results of the execution are unpredictable. This unpredictability is an example of a *race condition* because the occurrence of the error depends on the precise timing between instructions in different processes. Program 15.3 does not have a race condition because the original parent creates and initializes the semaphore before doing a fork. The program avoids a race condition because only the original process can access the semaphore at the time of creation. One of the major problems with semaphore sets is that the creation and initialization are separate operations and therefore not atomic. Recall that POSIX:SEM named and unnamed semaphores are initialized at the time of creation and do not have this problem.

Program 15.4 can be used to create or access a semaphore set containing a single semaphore element. It takes three parameters, a semaphore key, an initial value and a pointer to a variable of type `sig_atomic_t` that is initialized to 0 and shared among all processes and threads that call this function. If this function is used among threads of a single process, the `sig_atomic_t` variable could be defined outside a block and statically initialized. Using `initsemset` among processes requires shared memory. We use Program 15.4 later in the chapter to protect a shared memory segment. The busywaiting used in `initsemset` is not as inefficient as it may seem, since it is only used when the thread that creates the semaphore set loses the CPU before it can initialize it.

Program 15.4 ──────────────────────────── `initsemset.c`

A function that creates and initializes a semaphore set containing a single semaphore.

```c
#include <errno.h>
#include <signal.h>
#include <stdio.h>
#include <time.h>
#include <sys/sem.h>
#include <sys/stat.h>
#define PERMS (S_IRUSR | S_IWUSR)
#define TEN_MILLION 10000000L
int initelement(int semid, int semnum, int semvalue);

int initsemset(key_t mykey, int value, sig_atomic_t *readyp) {
    int semid;
    struct timespec sleeptime;

    sleeptime.tv_sec = 0;
    sleeptime.tv_nsec = TEN_MILLION;
    semid = semget(mykey, 1, PERMS | IPC_CREAT | IPC_EXCL);
    if ((semid == -1) && (errno != EEXIST))          /* real error, so return */
        return -1;
    if (semid >= 0) {           /* we created the semaphore, so initialize it */
        if (initelement(semid, 0, value) == -1)
            return -1;
        *readyp = 1;
        return semid;
    }
    if ((semid = semget(mykey, 1, PERMS)) == -1)             /* just access it */
        return -1;
    while (*readyp == 0)                              /* wait for initialization */
        nanosleep(&sleeptime, NULL);
    return semid;
}
```

Program 15.4 ──────────────────────────── `initsemset.c`

15.3 POSIX:XSI Shared Memory

Shared memory allows processes to read and write from the same memory segment. The `sys/shm.h` header file defines the data structures for shared memory, including `shmid_ds`, which has the following members.

```c
struct ipc_perm shm_perm; /* operation permission structure */
size_t shm_segsz;         /* size of segment in bytes */
pid_t shm_lpid;           /* process ID of last operation */
pid_t shm_cpid;           /* process ID of creator */
shmatt_t shm_nattch;      /* number of current attaches */
time_t shm_atime;         /* time of last shmat */
time_t shm_dtime;         /* time of last shmdt */
time_t shm_ctime;         /* time of last shctl */
```

The `shmatt_t` data type is an unsigned integer data type used to hold the number of times the memory segment is attached. This type must be at least as large as an `unsigned short`.

15.3.1 Accessing a shared memory segment

The `shmget` function returns an identifier for the shared memory segment associated with the `key` parameter. It creates the segment if either the key is `IPC_PRIVATE` or `shmflg & IPC_CREAT` is nonzero and no shared memory segment or identifier is already associated with `key`. Shared memory segments are initialized to zero.

```
SYNOPSIS

   #include <sys/shm.h>

   int shmget(key_t key, size_t size, int shmflg);
                                                          POSIX:XSI
```

If successful, `shmget` returns a nonnegative integer corresponding to the shared memory segment identifier. If unsuccessful, `shmget` returns −1 and sets `errno`. The following table lists the mandatory errors for `shmget`.

errno	cause
EACCES	shared memory identifier exists for `key` but permissions are not granted
EEXIST	shared memory identifier exists for `key` but `((shmflg & IPC_CREAT) && (shmflg & IPC_EXCL)) != 0`
EINVAL	shared memory segment is to be created but `size` is invalid
EINVAL	no shared memory segment is to be created but `size` is inconsistent with system-imposed limits or with the segment size of `key`
ENOENT	shared memory identifier does not exist for `key` but `(shmflg & IPC_CREAT) == 0`
ENOMEM	not enough memory to create the specified shared memory segment
ENOSPC	systemwide limit on shared memory identifiers would be exceeded

15.3.2 Attaching and detaching a shared memory segment

The `shmat` function attaches the shared memory segment specified by `shmid` to the address space of the calling process and increments the value of `shm_nattch` for `shmid`. The `shmat` function returns a `void *` pointer, so a program can use the return value like an ordinary memory pointer obtained from `malloc`. Use a `shmaddr` value of `NULL`. On some systems it may be necessary to set `shmflg` so that the memory segment is properly aligned.

```
SYNOPSIS

  #include <sys/shm.h>

  void *shmat(int shmid, const void *shmaddr, int shmflg);
                                                      POSIX:XSI
```

If successful, `shmat` returns the starting address of the segment. If unsuccessful, `shmat` returns −1 and sets `errno`. The following table lists the mandatory errors for `shmat`.

errno	cause
EACCES	operation permission denied to caller
EINVAL	value of `shmid` or `shmaddr` is invalid
EMFILE	number of shared memory segments attached to process would exceed limit
ENOMEM	process data space is not large enough to accommodate the shared memory segment

When finished with a shared memory segment, a program calls `shmdt` to detach the shared memory segment and to decrement `shm_nattch`. The `shmaddr` parameter is the starting address of the shared memory segment.

```
SYNOPSIS

  #include <sys/shm.h>

  int shmdt(const void *shmaddr);
                                                      POSIX:XSI
```

If successful, `shmdt` returns 0. If unsuccessful, `shmdt` returns −1 and sets `errno`. The `shmdt` function sets `errno` to `EINVAL` when `shmaddr` does not correspond to the starting address of a shared memory segment.

The last process to detach the segment should deallocate the shared memory segment by calling `shmctl`.

15.3.3 Controlling shared memory

The `shmctl` function provides a variety of control operations on the shared memory segment `shmid` as specified by the `cmd` parameter. The interpretation of the `buf` parameter depends on the value of `cmd`, as described below.

```
SYNOPSIS

  #include <sys/shm.h>

  int shmctl(int shmid, int cmd, struct shmid_ds *buf);
                                                      POSIX:XSI
```

If successful, `shmctl` returns 0. If unsuccessful, `shmctl` returns −1 and sets `errno`. The following table lists the mandatory errors for `shmctl`.

errno	cause
EACCES	cmd is IPC_STAT and caller does not have read permission
EINVAL	value of shmid or cmd is invalid
EPERM	cmd is IPC_RMID or IPC_SET and caller does not have correct permissions

Table 15.3 gives the POSIX:XSI values of cmd for shmctl.

cmd	description
IPC_RMID	remove shared memory segment shmid and destroy corresponding shmid_ds
IPC_SET	set values of fields for shared memory segment shmid from values found in buf
IPC_STAT	copy current values for shared memory segment shmid into buf

Table 15.3: POSIX:XSI values of cmd for shmctl.

■ **Example 15.11**

The `detachandremove` function detaches the shared memory segment `shmaddr` and then removes the shared memory segment specified by `semid`.

```
#include <stdio.h>
#include <errno.h>
#include <sys/shm.h>

int detachandremove(int shmid, void *shmaddr) {
   int error = 0;

   if (shmdt(shmaddr) == -1)
      error = errno;
   if ((shmctl(shmid, IPC_RMID, NULL) == -1) && !error)
      error = errno;
   if (!error)
      return 0;
   errno = error;
   return -1;
}
```
── **detachandremove.c**

15.3.4 Shared memory examples

Program 4.11 on page 108 monitors two file descriptors by using a parent and a child. Each process echoes the contents of the files to standard output and then writes to standard error the total number of bytes received. There is no simple way for this program to report the total number of bytes received by the two processes without using a communication mechanism such as a pipe.

Program 15.5 modifies Program 4.11 so that the parent and child share a small memory segment. The child stores its byte count in the shared memory. The parent waits for the child to finish and then outputs the number of bytes received by each process along with the sum of these values. The parent creates the shared memory segment by using the key IPC_PRIVATE, which allows the memory to be shared among its children. The synchronization of the shared memory is provided by the wait function. The parent does not access the shared memory until it has detected the termination of the child. Program 15.5 calls detachandremove of Example 15.11 when it must both detach and remove the shared memory segment.

Program 15.5 —————————————————— **monitorshared.c**

A program to monitor two file descriptors and keep information in shared memory. The parent waits for the child, to ensure mutual exclusion.

```c
#include <errno.h>
#include <fcntl.h>
#include <stdio.h>
#include <string.h>
#include <unistd.h>
#include <sys/shm.h>
#include <sys/stat.h>
#include <sys/wait.h>
#include "restart.h"
#define PERM (S_IRUSR | S_IWUSR)

int detachandremove(int shmid, void *shmaddr);

int main(int argc, char *argv[]) {
   int bytesread;
   int childpid;
   int fd, fd1, fd2;
   int id;
   int *sharedtotal;
   int totalbytes = 0;

   if (argc != 3) {
      fprintf(stderr, "Usage: %s file1 file2\n", argv[0]);
      return 1;
   }
   if (((fd1 = open(argv[1], O_RDONLY)) == -1) ||
       ((fd2 = open(argv[2], O_RDONLY)) == -1)) {
      perror("Failed to open file");
      return 1;
   }
   if ((id = shmget(IPC_PRIVATE, sizeof(int), PERM)) == -1) {
      perror("Failed to create shared memory segment");
      return 1;
   }
```

```
    if ((sharedtotal = (int *)shmat(id, NULL, 0)) == (void *)-1) {
        perror("Failed to attach shared memory segment");
        if (shmctl(id, IPC_RMID, NULL) == -1)
            perror("Failed to  remove memory segment");
        return 1;
    }
    if ((childpid = fork()) == -1) {
        perror("Failed to create child process");
        if (detachandremove(id, sharedtotal) == -1)
            perror("Failed to destroy shared memory segment");
        return 1;
    }
    if (childpid > 0)                                    /* parent code */
        fd = fd1;
    else
        fd = fd2;
    while ((bytesread = readwrite(fd, STDOUT_FILENO)) > 0)
        totalbytes += bytesread;
    if (childpid == 0) {                                  /* child code */
        *sharedtotal = totalbytes;
        return 0;
    }
    if (r_wait(NULL) == -1)
        perror("Failed to wait for child");
    else {
        fprintf(stderr, "Bytes copied: %8d by parent\n", totalbytes);
        fprintf(stderr, "              %8d by child\n", *sharedtotal);
        fprintf(stderr, "              %8d total\n", totalbytes + *sharedtotal);
    }
    if (detachandremove(id, sharedtotal) == -1) {
        perror("Failed to destroy shared memory segment");
        return 1;
    }
    return 0;
}
```

Program 15.5 ─────────────────────────────────── **monitorshared.c**

Using shared memory between processes that do not have a common ancestor requires the processes to agree on a key, either directly or with `ftok` and a pathname.

Program 13.5 on page 456 used mutex locks to keep a sum and count for threads of a given process. This was particularly simple because the threads automatically share the mutex and the mutex could be initialized statically. Implementing synchronized shared memory for independent processes is more difficult because you must set up the sharing of the synchronization mechanism as well as the memory for the sum and the count.

Program 15.6 uses a semaphore and a small shared memory segment to keep a sum and count. Each process must first call the `initshared` function with an agreed-on key. This function first tries to create a shared memory segment with the given key. If successful, `initshared` initializes the sum and count. Otherwise, `initshared` just accesses the shared memory segment. In either case, `initshared` calls `initsemset` with the `ready` flag in shared memory to access a semaphore set containing a single semaphore initialized to 1. This semaphore element protects the shared memory segment. The add and getcountandsum functions behave as in Program 13.5, this time using the semaphore, rather than a mutex, for protection.

Program 15.6 ————————————————— `sharedmemsum.c`

A function that keeps a synchronized sum and count in shared memory.

```
#include <errno.h>
#include <signal.h>
#include <stdio.h>
#include <sys/sem.h>
#include <sys/shm.h>
#include <sys/stat.h>
#define PERM (S_IRUSR | S_IWUSR)

int initsemset(key_t mykey, int value, sig_atomic_t *readyp);
void setsembuf(struct sembuf *s, int num, int op, int flg);

typedef struct {
   int count;
   double sum;
   sig_atomic_t ready;
} shared_sum_t;

static int semid;
static struct sembuf semlock;
static struct sembuf semunlock;
static shared_sum_t *sharedsum;

int initshared(int key) {                /* initialize shared memory segment */
   int shid;

   setsembuf(&semlock, 0, -1, 0);           /* setting for locking semaphore */
   setsembuf(&semunlock, 0, 1, 0);        /* setting for unlocking semaphore */
                        /* get attached memory, creating it if necessary */
   shid = shmget(key, sizeof(shared_sum_t), PERM | IPC_CREAT | IPC_EXCL);
   if ((shid == -1) && (errno != EEXIST))                     /* real error */
      return -1;
   if (shid == -1) {                /* already created, access and attach it */
      if (((shid = shmget(key, sizeof(shared_sum_t), PERM)) == -1) ||
          ((sharedsum = (shared_sum_t *)shmat(shid, NULL, 0)) == (void *)-1) )
         return -1;
   }
   else {    /* successfully created, must attach and initialize variables */
      sharedsum = (shared_sum_t *)shmat(shid, NULL, 0);
      if (sharedsum == (void *)-1)
         return -1;
      sharedsum -> count = 0;
      sharedsum -> sum = 0.0;
   }
   semid = initsemset(key, 1, &sharedsum->ready);
   if (semid == -1)
      return -1;
   return 0;
}
```

```
int add(double x) {                                        /* add x to sum */
    if (semop(semid, &semlock, 1) == -1)
        return -1;
    sharedsum -> sum += x;
    sharedsum -> count++;
    if (semop(semid, &semunlock, 1) == -1)
        return -1;
    return 0;
}

int getcountandsum(int *countp, double *sum) {    /* return sum and count */
    if (semop(semid, &semlock, 1) == -1)
        return -1;
    *countp = sharedsum -> count;
    *sum = sharedsum -> sum;
    if (semop(semid, &semunlock, 1) == -1)
        return -1;
    return 0;
}
```

Program 15.6 ───────────────────────────────────── **sharedmemsum.c**

Each process must call `initshared` at least once before calling `add` or
`getcountandsum`. A process may call `initshared` more than once, but one thread
of the process should not call `initshared` while another thread of the same process is
calling `add` or `getcountandsum`.

☐ Exercise 15.12

In Program 15.6, the three fields of the shared memory segment are treated differently. The `sum` and `count` are explicitly initialized to 0 whereas the function
relies on the fact that `ready` is initialized to 0 when the shared memory segment
is created. Why is it done this way?

Answer:

All three fields are initialized to 0 when the shared memory segment is created, so
in this case the explicit initialization is not necessary. The program relies on the
atomic nature of the creation and initialization of `ready` to 0, but `sum` and `count`
can be initialized to any values.

Program 15.7 displays the shared count and sum when it receives a `SIGUSR1` signal.
The signal handler is allowed to use `fprintf` for output, even though it might not be
async-signal safe, since no output is done by the `main` program after the signal handler is
set up and the signal is unblocked.

Program 15.8 modifies Program 15.5 by copying information from a single file to
standard output and saving the number of bytes copied in a shared sum implemented by
Program 15.6. Program 15.8 has two command-line arguments: the name of the file; and
the key identifying the shared memory and its protecting semaphore. You can run multiple
copies of Program 15.8 simultaneously with different filenames and the same key. The
common shared memory stores the total number of bytes copied.

Program 15.7 ———————————————————— **showshared.c**

A program to display the shared count and sum when it receives a SIGUSR1 *signal.*

```c
#include <signal.h>
#include <stdio.h>
#include <stdlib.h>
#include <unistd.h>

int getcountandsum(int *countp, double *sump);
int initshared(int key);

/* ARGSUSED */
static void showit(int signo) {
   int count;
   double sum;
   if (getcountandsum(&count, &sum) == -1)
      printf("Failed to get count and sum\n");
   else
      printf("Sum is %f and count is %d\n", sum, count);
}

int main(int argc, char *argv[]) {
   struct sigaction act;
   int key;
   sigset_t mask, oldmask;

   if (argc != 2) {
      fprintf(stderr, "Usage: %s key\n", argv[0]);
      return 1;
   }
   key = atoi(argv[1]);
   if (initshared(key) == -1) {
      perror("Failed to initialize shared memory");
      return 1;
   }
   if ((sigfillset(&mask) == -1) ||
       (sigprocmask(SIG_SETMASK, &mask, &oldmask) == -1)) {
      perror("Failed to block signals to set up handlers");
      return 1;
   }
   printf("This is process %ld waiting for SIGUSR1 (%d)\n",
           (long)getpid(), SIGUSR1);

   act.sa_handler = showit;
   act.sa_flags = 0;
   if ((sigemptyset(&act.sa_mask) == -1) ||
       (sigaction(SIGUSR1, &act, NULL) == -1)) {
      perror("Failed to set up signal handler");
      return 1;
   }
   if (sigprocmask(SIG_SETMASK, &oldmask, NULL) == -1) {
      perror("Failed to unblock signals");
      return 1;
   }
   for ( ; ; )
      pause();
}
```

Program 15.7 ———————————————————— **showshared.c**

Program 15.8 ──────────────────────── **monitoroneshared.c**

A program to monitor one file and send the output to standard output. It keeps track of the number of bytes received by calling add *from Program 15.6.*

```c
#include <fcntl.h>
#include <stdio.h>
#include <stdlib.h>
#include <unistd.h>
#include "restart.h"

int add(double x);
int initshared(int key);

int main(int argc, char *argv[]) {
   int bytesread;
   int fd;
   int key;

   if (argc != 3) {
      fprintf(stderr,"Usage: %s file key\n",argv[0]);
      return 1;
   }
   if ((fd = open(argv[1],O_RDONLY)) == -1) {
      perror("Failed to open file");
      return 1;
   }
   key = atoi(argv[2]);
   if (initshared(key) == -1) {
      perror("Failed to initialize shared sum");
      return 1;
   }
   while ((bytesread = readwrite(fd, STDOUT_FILENO)) > 0)
      if (add((double)bytesread) == -1) {
         perror("Failed to add to count");
         return 1;
      }
   return 0;
}
```

Program 15.8 ──────────────────────── **monitoroneshared.c**

□ **Exercise 15.13**

Start Program 15.7 in one window, using key 12345, with the following command.

```
showshared 12345
```

Create a few named pipes, say, pipe1 and pipe2. Start copies of monitoroneshared in different windows with the following commands.

```
monitoroneshared pipe1 12345
monitoroneshared pipe2 12345
```

In other windows, send characters to the pipes (e.g., cat > pipe1). Periodically send SIGUSR1 signals to showshared to monitor the progress.

15.4 POSIX:XSI Message Queues

The message queue is a POSIX:XSI interprocess communication mechanism that allows a process to send and receive messages from other processes. The data structures for message queues are defined in `sys/msg.h`. The major data structure for message queues is `msqid_ds`, which has the following members.

```
struct ipc_perm msg_perm; /* operation permission structure */
msgqnum_t msg_qnum;       /* number of messages currently in queue */
msglen_t msg_qbytes;      /* maximum bytes allowed in queue */
pid_t msg_lspid;          /* process ID of msgsnd */
pid_t msg_lrpid;          /* process ID of msgrcv */
time_t msg_stime;         /* time of last msgsnd */
time_t msg_rtime;         /* time of last msgrcv */
time_t msg_ctime;         /* time of last msgctl */
```

The `msgqnum_t` data type holds the number of messages in the message queue; the `msglen_t` type holds the number of bytes allowed in a message queue. Both types must be at least as large as an `unsigned short`.

15.4.1 Accessing a message queue

The `msgget` function returns the message queue identifier associated with the `key` parameter. It creates the identifier if either the key is `IPC_PRIVATE` or `msgflg & IPC_CREAT` is nonzero and no message queue or identifier is already associated with `key`.

```
SYNOPSIS

   #include <sys/msg.h>

   int msgget(key_t key, int msgflg);
                                                    POSIX:XSI
```

If successful, `msgget` returns a nonnegative integer corresponding to the message queue identifier. If unsuccessful, `msgget` returns −1 and sets `errno`. The following table lists the mandatory errors for `msgget`.

errno	cause
EACCES	message queue exists for `key`, but permission denied
EEXIST	message queue exists for `key`, but
	`((msgflg & IPC_CREAT) && (msgflg & IPC_EXCL)) != 0`
ENOENT	message queue does not exist for `key`, but
	`(msgflg & IPC_CREAT) == 0`
ENOSPC	systemwide limit on message queues would be exceeded

■ **Example 15.14**

Create a new message queue.

```
#define PERMS (S_IRUSR | S_IWUSR)

int msqid;
if ((msqid = msgget(IPC_PRIVATE, PERMS)) == -1)
    perror("Failed to create new private message queue");
```

After obtaining access to a message queue with `msgget`, a program inserts messages into the queue with `msgsnd`. The `msqid` parameter identifies the message queue, and the `msgp` parameter points to a user-defined buffer that contains the message to be sent, as described below. The `msgsz` parameter specifies the actual size of the message text. The `msgflg` parameter specifies actions to be taken under various conditions.

SYNOPSIS

```
#include <sys/msg.h>

int msgsnd(int msqid, const void *msgp, size_t msgsz, int msgflg);
```
POSIX:XSI

If successful, `msgsnd` returns 0. If unsuccessful, `msgsnd` returns –1 and sets `errno`. The following table lists the mandatory errors for `msgsnd`.

errno	cause
EACCES	operation is denied to the caller
EAGAIN	operation would block the process, but
	`(msgflg & IPC_NOWAIT) != 0`
EIDRM	`msqid` has been removed from the system
EINTR	`msgsnd` was interrupted by a signal
EINVAL	`msqid` is invalid, the message type is < 1,
	or `msgsz` is out of range

The `msgp` parameter points to a user-defined buffer whose first member must be a `long` specifying the type of message, followed by space for the text of the message. The structure might be defined as follows.

```
struct mymsg{
    long mtype;        /* message type */
    char mtext[1];     /* message text */
} mymsg_t;
```

The message type must be greater than 0. The user can assign message types in any way appropriate to the application.

Here are the steps needed to send the string `mymessage` to a message queue.

1. Allocate a buffer, `mbuf`, which is of type `mymsg_t` and size
    `sizeof(mymsg_t) + strlen(mymessage)`.

2. Copy `mymessage` into the `mbuf->mtext` member.
3. Set the message type in the `mbuf->mtype` member.
4. Send the message.
5. Free `mbuf`.

Remember to check for errors and to free `mbuf` if an error occurs. Code for this is provided in Program 15.9, discussed later.

A program can remove a message from a message queue with `msgrcv`. The `msqid` parameter identifies the message queue, and the `msgp` parameter points to a user-defined buffer for holding the message to be retrieved. The format of `msgp` is as described above for `msgsnd`. The `msgsz` parameter specifies the actual size of the message text. The `msgtyp` parameter can be used by the receiver for message selection. The `msgflg` specifies actions to be taken under various conditions.

SYNOPSIS

```
#include <sys/msg.h>

ssize_t msgrcv(int msqid, void *msgp, size_t msgsz,
               long msgtyp, int msgflg);
```

POSIX:XSI

If successful, `msgrcv` returns the number of bytes in the text of the message. If unsuccessful, `msgrcv` returns `(ssize_t)-1` and sets `errno`. The following table lists the mandatory errors for `msgrcv`.

errno	cause
E2BIG	value of the `mtext` member of `msgp` is greater than `msgsize` and `(msgflg & MSG_NOERROR) == 0`
EACCES	operation is denied to the caller
EIDRM	`msqid` has been removed from the system
EINTR	`msgrcv` was interrupted by a signal
EINVAL	value of `msqid` is invalid
ENOMSG	queue does not contain a message of requested type and `(msgflg & IPC_NOWAIT) != 0`

Table 15.4 shows how `msgrcv` uses the `msgtyp` parameter to determine the order in which it removes messages from the queue.

Use `msgctl` to deallocate or change permissions for the message queue identified by `msqid`. The `cmd` parameter specifies the action to be taken as listed in Table 15.5. The `msgctl` function uses its `buf` parameter to write or read state information, depending on `cmd`.

msgtyp	action
0	remove first message from queue
> 0	remove first message of type `msgtyp` from the queue
< 0	remove first message of lowest type that is less than or equal to the absolute value of `msgtyp`

Table 15.4: The POSIX:XSI values for the `msgtyp` parameter determine the order in which `msgrcv` removes messages from the queue.

cmd	description
IPC_RMID	remove the message queue `msqid` and destroy the corresponding `msqid_ds`
IPC_SET	set members of the `msqid_ds` data structure from `buf`
IPC_STAT	copy members of the `msqid_ds` data structure into `buf`

Table 15.5: POSIX:XSI values for the `cmd` parameter of `msgctl`.

```
SYNOPSIS

    #include <sys/msg.h>

    int msgctl(int msqid, int cmd, struct msqid_ds *buf);

                                                              POSIX:XSI
```

If successful, `msgctl` returns 0. If unsuccessful, `msgctl` returns −1 and sets `errno`. The following table lists the mandatory errors for `msgctl`.

errno	cause
EACCES	cmd is IPC_STAT and the caller does not have read permission
EINVAL	msqid or cmd is invalid
EPERM	cmd is IPC_RMID or IPC_SET and caller does not have privileges

Program 15.9 contains utilities for accessing a message queue similar to that of Program 15.6, but simpler because no initialization or synchronization is needed. Each process should call the `initqueue` function before accessing the message queue. The `msgprintf` function has syntax similar to `printf` for putting formatted messages in the queue. The `msgwrite` function is for unformatted messages. Both `msgprintf` and `msgwrite` allocate memory for each message and free this memory after calling `msgsnd`. The `removequeue` function removes the message queue and its associated data structures.

The `msgqueuelog.h` header file contains the prototypes for these functions. If successful, these functions return 0. If unsuccessful, these functions return −1 and set `errno`.

Program 15.9 ——————————————————————— `msgqueuelog.c`

Utility functions that access and output to a message queue.

```c
#include <errno.h>
#include <stdio.h>
#include <stdarg.h>
#include <stdlib.h>
#include <string.h>
#include <sys/msg.h>
#include <sys/stat.h>
#include "msgqueuelog.h"
#define PERM (S_IRUSR | S_IWUSR)

typedef struct {
   long mtype;
   char mtext[1];
} mymsg_t;
static int queueid;

int initqueue(int key) {                      /* initialize the message queue */
   queueid = msgget(key, PERM | IPC_CREAT);
   if (queueid == -1)
      return -1;
   return 0;
}

int msgprintf(char *fmt, ...) {               /* output a formatted message */
   va_list ap;
   char ch;
   int error = 0;
   int len;
   mymsg_t *mymsg;

   va_start(ap, fmt);                         /* set up the format for output */
   len = vsnprintf(&ch, 1, fmt, ap);              /* how long would it be ? */
   if ((mymsg = (mymsg_t *)malloc(sizeof(mymsg_t) + len)) == NULL)
      return -1;
   vsprintf(mymsg->mtext, fmt, ap);                /* copy into the buffer */
   mymsg->mtype = 1;                          /* message type is always 1 */
   if (msgsnd(queueid, mymsg, len + 1, 0) == -1)
      error = errno;
   free(mymsg);
   if (error) {
      errno = error;
      return -1;
   }
   return 0;
}

int msgwrite(void *buf, int len) {     /* output buffer of specified length */
   int error = 0;
   mymsg_t *mymsg;
```

```
        if ((mymsg = (mymsg_t *)malloc(sizeof(mymsg_t) + len - 1)) == NULL)
            return -1;
        memcpy(mymsg->mtext, buf, len);
        mymsg->mtype = 1;                            /* message type is always 1 */
        if (msgsnd(queueid, mymsg, len, 0) == -1)
            error = errno;
        free(mymsg);
        if (error) {
            errno = error;
            return -1;
        }
        return 0;
    }

    int remmsgqueue(void) {
        return msgctl(queueid, IPC_RMID, NULL);
    }
```

Program 15.9 ── `msgqueuelog.c`

☐ Exercise 15.15

Why does the `msgprintf` function of Program 15.9 use `len` in `malloc` and
`len+1` in `msgsnd`?

Answer:

The `vsnprintf` function returns the number of bytes to be formatted, not including the string terminator, so `len` is the string length. We need one extra byte for
the string terminator. One byte is already included in `mymsg_t`.

Program 15.10, which outputs the contents of a message queue to standard output, can
save the contents of a message queue to a file through redirection. The `msgqueuesave`
program takes a key that identifies the message queue as a command-line argument and
calls the `initqueue` function of Program 15.9 to access the queue. The program then
outputs the contents of the queue to standard output until an error occurs. Program 15.10
does not deallocate the message queue when it completes.

Program 15.11 reads lines from standard input and sends each to the message queue.
The program takes a key as a command-line argument and calls `initqueue` to access the
corresponding message queue. Program 15.11 sends an informative message containing
its process ID before starting to copy from standard input.

You should be able to run multiple copies of Program 15.11 along with a single copy
of Program 15.10. Since none of the programs call `removequeue`, be sure to execute the
`ipcrm` command when you finish.

☐ Exercise 15.16

Why does Program 15.10 use `r_write` from the restart library even though the
program does not catch any signals?

Answer:

In addition to restarting when interrupted by a signal (which is not necessary here), r_write continues writing if write did not output all of the requested bytes.

☐ Exercise 15.17

How would you modify these programs so that messages from different processes could be distinguished?

Answer:

Modify the functions in Program 15.9 to send the process ID as the message type. Modify Program 15.10 to output the message type along with the message.

Program 15.10 ——————————————————————— `msgqueuesave.c`

A program that copies messages from a message queue to standard output.

```c
#include <stdio.h>
#include <stdlib.h>
#include <unistd.h>
#include <sys/msg.h>
#include "msgqueuelog.h"
#include "restart.h"
#define MAXSIZE 4096
typedef struct {
   long mtype;
   char mtext[MAXSIZE];
} mymsg_t;

int main(int argc, char *argv[]) {
   int id;
   int key;
   mymsg_t mymsg;
   int size;

   if (argc != 2) {
      fprintf(stderr, "Usage: %s key\n", argv[0]);
      return 1;
   }
   key = atoi(argv[1]);
   if ((id = initqueue(key)) == -1) {
      perror("Failed to initialize message queue");
      return 1;
   }
   for ( ; ; ) {
      if ((size = msgrcv(id, &mymsg, MAXSIZE, 0, 0)) == -1) {
         perror("Failed to read message queue");
         break;
      }
      if (r_write(STDOUT_FILENO, mymsg.mtext, size) == -1) {
         perror("Failed to write to standard output");
         break;
      }
   }
   return 1;
}
```

Program 15.10 ——————————————————————— `msgqueuesave.c`

Program 15.11 ——————————————————————————— `msgqueuein.c`

A program that sends standard input to a message queue.

```c
#include <stdio.h>
#include <stdlib.h>
#include <string.h>
#include <sys/msg.h>
#include <unistd.h>
#include "msgqueuelog.h"
#include "restart.h"
#define MAXLINE 1024

int main(int argc, char *argv[]) {
   char buf[MAXLINE];
   int key;
   int size;

   if (argc != 2) {
      fprintf(stderr, "Usage: %s key\n", argv[0]);
      return 1;
   }
   key = atoi(argv[1]);
   if (initqueue(key) == -1) {
      perror("Failed to initialize message queue");
      return 1;
   }
   if (msgprintf("This is process %ld\n", (long)getpid()) == -1) {
      perror("Failed to write header to message queue");
      return 1;
   }
   for ( ; ; ) {
      if ((size = readline(STDIN_FILENO, buf, MAXLINE)) == -1) {
         perror("Failed to read from standard input");
         break;
      }
      if (msgwrite(buf, size) == -1) {
         perror("Failed to write message to standard output");
         break;
      }
   }
   return 0;
}
```

Program 15.11 ——————————————————————————— `msgqueuein.c`

15.5 Exercise: POSIX Unnamed Semaphores

This exercise describes an implementation of POSIX:SEM-like unnamed semaphores in terms of semaphore sets. Represent the unnamed semaphore by a data structure of type `mysem_t`, which for this exercise is simply an `int`. The `mysem.h` header file should contain the definition of `mysem_t` and the prototypes for the semaphore functions.

```
int mysem_init(mysem_t *sem, int pshared, unsigned int value);
int mysem_destroy(mysem_t *sem);
int mysem_wait(mysem_t *sem);
int mysem_post(mysem_t *sem);
```

All these functions return 0 if successful. On error, they return −1 and set `errno` appropriately. Actually, the last point is a little subtle. It will probably turn out that the only statements that can cause an error are the semaphore set calls and they set `errno`. If that is the case, the functions return the correct `errno` value as long as there are no intervening functions that might set `errno`.

Assume that applications call `mysem_init` before creating any threads. The `mysem_t` value is the semaphore ID of a semaphore set. Ignore the value of `pshared`, since semaphore sets are sharable among processes. Use a key of `IPC_PRIVATE`.

Implement the `mysem_wait` and `mysem_post` directly with calls to `semop`. The details will depend on how `sem_init` initializes the semaphore. Implement `mysem_destroy` with a call to `semctl`.

Test your implementation with Programs 14.5 and 14.6 to see that it enforces mutual exclusion.

Before logging out, use `ipcs -s` from the command line. If semaphores still exist (because of a program bug), delete each of them, using the following command.

```
ipcrm -s n
```

This command deletes the semaphore with ID n. The semaphore should be created only once by the test program. It should also be deleted only once, not by all the children in the process chain.

15.6 Exercise: POSIX Named Semaphores

This exercise describes an implementation of POSIX:SEM-like named semaphores in terms of semaphores sets. Represent the named semaphore by a structure of type `mysem_t`. The `mysemn.h` file should include the definition of `mysem_t` and the prototypes of the following functions.

```
mysem_t *mysem_open(const char *name, int oflag, mode_t mode,
                    unsigned int value);
int mysem_close(mysem_t *sem);
int mysem_unlink(const char *name);
int mysem_wait(mysem_t *sem);
int mysem_post(mysem_t *sem);
```

The `mysem_open` function returns `NULL` and sets `errno` when there is an error. All the other functions return −1 and set `errno` when there is an error. To simplify the interface, always call `mysem_open` with four parameters.

Represent the named semaphore by an ordinary file that contains the semaphore ID of the semaphore set used to implement the POSIX semaphore. First try to open the file with open, using O_CREAT | O_EXCL. If you created the file, use fdopen to get a FILE pointer for the file. Allocate the semaphore set and store the ID in the file. If the file already exists, open the file for reading with fopen. In either case, return the file pointer. The mysem_t data type will just be the type FILE.

The mysem_close function makes the semaphore inaccessible to the caller by closing the file. The mysem_unlink function deletes the semaphore and its corresponding file. The mysem_wait function decrements the semaphore, and the mysem_post function increments the semaphore. Each function reads the semaphore ID from the file by first calling rewind and then reading an integer. It is possible to get an end-of-file if the process that created the semaphore has not yet written to the file. In this case, try again.

Put all the semaphore functions in a separate library and treat this as an object in which the only items with external linkage are the five functions listed above. Do not worry about race conditions in using mysem_open to create the file until a rudimentary version of the test program works. Devise a mechanism that frees the semaphore set after the last mysem_unlink but only after the last process closes this semaphore. The mysem_unlink cannot directly do the freeing because other processes may still have the semaphore open. One possibility is to have mysem_close check the link count in the inode and free the semaphore set if the link count becomes 0.

Try to handle the various race conditions by using an additional semaphore set to protect the critical sections for semaphore initialization and access. What happens when two threads try to access the semaphore concurrently? Use the same semaphore for all copies of your library to protect against interaction between unrelated processes. Refer to this semaphore by a filename, which you can convert to a key with ftok.

15.7 Exercise: Implementing Pipes with Shared Memory

This section develops a specification for a software pipe consisting of a semaphore set to protect access to the pipe and a shared memory segment to hold the pipe data and state information. The pipe state information includes the number of bytes of data in the pipe, the position of next byte to be read and status information. The pipe can hold at most one message of maximum size _POSIX_PIPE_BUF. Represent the pipe by the following pipe_t structure allocated in shared memory.

```
typedef struct pipe {
    int semid;                    /* ID of protecting semaphore set */
    int shmid;                    /* ID of the shared memory segment */
    char data[_POSIX_PIPE_BUF];      /* buffer for the pipe data */
    int data_size;                   /* bytes currently in the pipe */
    void *current_start;          /* pointer to current start of data */
    int end_of_file;           /* true after pipe closed for writing */
} pipe_t;
```

A program creates and references the pipe by using a pointer to `pipe_t` as a handle. For simplicity, assume that only one process can read from the pipe and one process can write to the pipe. The reader must clean up the pipe when it closes the pipe. When the writer closes the pipe, it sets the `end_of_file` member of `pipe_t` so that the reader can detect end-of-file.

The semaphore set protects the `pipe_t` data structure during shared access by the reader and the writer. Element zero of the semaphore set controls exclusive access to `data`. It is initially 1. Readers and writers acquire access to the pipe by decrementing this semaphore element, and they release access by incrementing it. Element one of the semaphore set controls synchronization of writes so that `data` contains only one message, that is, the output of a single `write` operation. When this semaphore element is 1, the pipe is empty. When it is 0, the pipe has data or an end-of-file has been encountered. Initially, element one is 1. The writer decrements element one before writing any data. The reader waits until element one is 0 before reading. When it has read all the data from the pipe, the reader increments element one to indicate that the pipe is now available for writing. Write the following functions.

`pipe_t *pipe_open(void);`

> creates a software pipe and returns a pointer of type `pipe_t *` to be used as a handle in the other calls. The algorithm for `pipe_open` is as follows.
>
> 1. Create a shared memory segment to hold a `pipe_t` data structure by calling `shmget`. Use a key of `IPC_PRIVATE` and owner read/write permissions.
> 2. Attach the segment by calling `shmat`. Cast the return value of `shmat` to a `pipe_t *` and assign it to a local variable p.
> 3. Set `p->shmid` to the ID of the shared memory segment returned by the `shmget`.
> 4. Set `p->data_size` and `p->end_of_file` to 0.
> 5. Create a semaphore set containing two elements by calling `semget` with `IPC_PRIVATE` key and owner read, write, execute permissions.
> 6. Initialize both semaphore elements to 1, and put the resulting semaphore ID value in `p->semid`.
> 7. If all the calls were successful, return p.
> 8. If an error occurs, deallocate all resources, set `errno`, and return a `NULL` pointer.

`int pipe_read(pipe_t *p, char *buf, int bytes);`

> behaves like an ordinary blocking `read` function. The algorithm for `pipe_read` is as follows.
>
> 1. Perform `semop` on `p->semid` to atomically decrement semaphore

element zero, and test semaphore element one for 0. Element zero provides mutual exclusion. Element one is only 0 if there is something in the buffer.

2. If `p->data_size` is greater than 0 do the following.

   a. Copy at most `bytes` bytes of information starting at position `p->current_start` of the software pipe into `buf`. Take into account the number of bytes in the pipe.

   b. Update the `p->current_start` and `p->data_size` members of the pipe data structure.

   c. If successful, set the return value to the number of bytes actually read.

3. Otherwise, if `p->data_size` is 0 and `p->end_of_file` is true, set the return value to 0 to indicate end-of-file.

4. Perform another `semop` operation to release access to the pipe. Increment element zero. If no more data is in the pipe, also increment element one unless `p->end_of_file` is true. Perform these operations atomically by a single `semop` call.

5. If an error occurs, return −1 with `errno` set.

`int pipe_write(pipe_t *p, char *buf, int bytes);`

behaves like an ordinary blocking `write` function. The algorithm for `pipe_write` is as follows.

1. Perform a `semop` on `p->semid` to atomically decrement both semaphore elements zero and one.

2. Copy at most `_POSIX_PIPE_BUF` bytes from `buf` into the pipe buffer.

3. Set `p->data_size` to the number of bytes actually copied, and set `p->current_start` to 0.

4. Perform another `semop` call to atomically increment semaphore element zero of the semaphore set.

5. If successful, return the number of bytes copied.

6. If an error occurs, return −1 with `errno` set.

`int pipe_close(pipe_t *p, int how);`

closes the pipe. The `how` parameter determines whether the pipe is closed for reading or writing. Its possible values are `O_RDONLY` and `O_WRONLY`. The algorithm for `pipe_close` is as follows.

1. Use the `semop` function to atomically decrement element zero of `p->semid`. If the `semop` fails, return −1 with `errno` set.

2. If `how & O_WRONLY` is true, do the following.

     a. Set `p->end_of_file` to true.

     b. Perform a `semctl` to set element one of `p->semid` to 0.

     c. Copy `p->semid` into a local variable, `semid_temp`.

     d. Perform a `shmdt` to detach `p`.

     e. Perform a `semop` to atomically increment element zero of `semid_temp`.

If any of the `semop`, `semctl`, or `shmdt` calls fail, return –1 immediately with `errno` set.

3. If `how & O_RDONLY` is true, do the following.

     a. Perform a `semctl` to remove the semaphore `p->semid`. (If the writer is waiting on the semaphore set, its `semop` returns an error when this happens.)

     b. Copy `p->shmid` into a local variable, `shmid_temp`.

     c. Call `shmdt` to detach `p`.

     d. Call `shmctl` to deallocate the shared memory segment identified by `shmid_temp`.

If any of the `semctl`, `shmdt`, or `shmctl` calls fail, return –1 immediately with `errno` set.

Test the software pipe by writing a main program that is similar to Program 6.4. The program creates a software pipe and then forks a child. The child reads from standard input and writes to the pipe. The parent reads what the child has written to the pipe and outputs it to standard output. When the child detects end-of-file on standard input, it closes the pipe for writing. The parent then detects end-of-file on the pipe, closes the pipe for reading (which destroys the pipe), and exits. Execute the `ipcs` command to check that everything was properly destroyed.

The above specification describes blocking versions of the functions `pipe_read` and `pipe_write`. Modify and test a nonblocking version also.

15.8 Exercise: Implementing Pipes with Message Queues

Formulate a specification of a software pipe implementation in terms of message queues. Implement the following functions.

```
pipe_t *pipe_open(void);
int pipe_read(pipe_t *p, char *buf, int chars);
int pipe_write(pipe_t *p, char *buf, int chars);
int pipe_close(pipe_t *p);
```

Design a `pipe_t` structure to fit the implementation. Test the implementation as described in Section 15.7.

15.9 Additional Reading

Most books on operating systems [107, 122] discuss the classical semaphore abstraction. *UNIX Network Programming* by Stevens [116] has an extensive discussion on System V Interprocess Communication including semaphores, shared memory and message queues.

Chapter 16

Project: Producer Consumer Synchronization

This chapter focuses on variations of producer-consumer synchronization using mutex locks, semaphores, condition variables and signals. Implementations for different types of stopping conditions are developed with careful attention to error handling and shutdown. The chapter describes two projects, a parallel file copy and a print server. The parallel file copy uses bounded buffers; the print server uses unbounded buffers.

Objectives

- Learn about producer-consumer synchronization
- Experiment with complex synchronization problems
- Explore how ending conditions affect synchronization
- Use a large number of threads in a realistic application
- Understand thread interaction and synchronization

16.1 The Producer-Consumer Problem

Producer-consumer problems involve three types of participants—producers, consumers and temporary holding areas called *buffer slots*. A *buffer* is a collection of buffer slots. Producers create items and place them in buffer slots. Consumers remove items from buffer slots and use the items in some specified way so that they are no longer available.

Producer-consumer synchronization is required because producers and consumers do not operate at exactly the same speed, hence the holding areas are needed. For example, many fast food restaurants precook food and place it under lights in a warming area to get ahead of the mealtime rush. The cooks are the producers, and the customers are the consumers. The buffer is the area that holds the cooked food before it is given to the customer. Similarly, airplanes line up on a holding runway before being authorized to take off. Here the control tower or the airline terminals (depending on your view) produce airplanes. The take-off runways consume them.

Producer-consumer problems are ubiquitous in computer systems because of the asynchronous nature of most interactions. Network routers, printer queues and disk controllers follow the producer-consumer pattern. Because buffers in computer systems have finite capacity, producer-consumer problems are sometimes called *bounded buffer* problems, but producer-consumer problems also occur with *unbounded buffers*.

Chapter 13 introduced reader-writer synchronization. Both reader-writer and producer-consumer synchronization involve two distinguished parties. In reader-writer synchronization, a writer may create new resources or modify existing ones. A reader, however, does not change a resource by accessing it. In producer-consumer synchronization, a producer creates a resource. In contrast to readers, consumers remove or destroy the resource by accessing it. Shared data structures that do not act as buffers generally should use reader-writer synchronization or simple mutex locks rather than producer-consumer synchronization.

Figure 16.1 shows a schematic of the producer-consumer problem. Producer and consumer threads share a buffer and must synchronize when inserting or removing items. Implementations must avoid the following synchronization errors.

- A consumer removes an item that a producer is in the process of inserting in the buffer.
- A consumer removes an item that is not there at all.
- A consumer removes an item that has already been removed.
- A producer inserts an item in the buffer when there is no free slot (bounded buffer only).
- A producer overwrites an item that has not been removed.

Two distinct time scales occur in synchronization problems—the short, bounded duration holding of resources, and the unbounded duration waiting until some event occurs. Producers should acquire a lock on the buffer only when a buffer slot is available and they

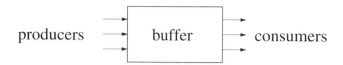

Figure 16.1: Schematic of the producer-consumer problem.

have an item to insert. They should hold the lock only during the insertion period. Similarly, consumers should lock the buffer only while removing an item and release the lock before processing the removed item. Both of these locking actions are of short, bounded duration (in virtual time), and mutex locks are ideal for these.

When the buffer is empty (no buffer slots are filled), consumer threads should wait until there are items to remove. In addition, if the buffer has fixed size (an upper bound for the number of slots), producers should wait for room to become available before producing more data. These actions are not of bounded duration, and you must take care that your producers and consumers do not hold locks when waiting for such events. Semaphores or condition variables can be used for waiting of this type.

More complicated producer-consumer flow control might include *high-water* and *low-water marks*. When a buffer reaches a certain size (the high-water mark), producers block until the buffer empties to the low-water mark. Condition variables and semaphores can be used to control these aspects of the producer-consumer problem.

This chapter explores different aspects of the producer-consumer problem, using a simple mathematical calculation. We begin by demonstrating that mutex locks are not sufficient for an efficient implementation, motivating the need for condition variables (Section 13.4) and semaphores (Section 14.3). The chapter then specifies two projects that have a producer-consumer structure. A parallel file copier project based on the program of Section 12.3.5 uses the bounded buffers developed in this chapter. A threaded print server project uses unbounded buffers.

16.2 Bounded Buffer Protected by Mutex Locks

Figure 16.2 shows a diagram of a circular buffer with eight slots that might be used as a holding area between producers and consumers. The buffer has three data items, and the remaining five slots are free. The `bufout` variable has the slot number of the next data item to be removed, and the `bufin` variable has the number of the next slot to be filled.

Program 16.1 is an initial version of a circular buffer implemented as a shared object. The data structures for the buffer have internal linkage because the `static` qualifier limits their scope. (See Appendix A.5 for a discussion of the two meanings of the `static`

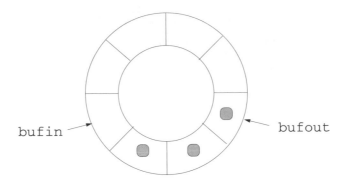

Figure 16.2: Circular buffer.

qualifier in C.) The code is in a separate file so that the program can access the buffer only through `getitem` and `putitem`. The header file, `buffer.h`, contains the definitions of `BUFSIZE` and `buffer_t`. The functions of Program 16.1 follow the preferred POSIX error-handling semantics and return 0 if successful or a nonzero error code if unsuccessful.

Program 16.1 ──────────────────────── **bufferbad.c**
A flawed circular buffer protected by mutex locks.

```c
#include <pthread.h>
#include "buffer.h"
static buffer_t buffer[BUFSIZE];
static pthread_mutex_t  bufferlock = PTHREAD_MUTEX_INITIALIZER;
static int bufin = 0;
static int bufout = 0;

int getitem(buffer_t *itemp) {  /* remove item from buffer and put in *itemp */
   int error;
   if (error = pthread_mutex_lock(&bufferlock))          /* no mutex, give up */
     return error;
   *itemp = buffer[bufout];
   bufout = (bufout + 1) % BUFSIZE;
   return pthread_mutex_unlock(&bufferlock);
}

int putitem(buffer_t item) {                      /* insert item in the buffer */
   int error;
   if (error = pthread_mutex_lock(&bufferlock))          /* no mutex, give up */
     return error;
   buffer[bufin] = item;
   bufin = (bufin + 1) % BUFSIZE;
   return pthread_mutex_unlock(&bufferlock);
}
```

Program 16.1 ──────────────────────── **bufferbad.c**

❑ Exercise 16.1

The following code segment uses the circular buffer defined in Program 16.1. What happens when it executes?

```
int myitem;
if (getitem(&myitem) == 0)
   printf("retrieved %d from the buffer\n", myitem);
```

Answer:

The result cannot be predicted. The `getitem` returns an error only when the locking fails, but it does not keep track of the number of items in the buffer. If a consumer executes this code before a producer calls `putitem`, the value retrieved for `myitem` will not be meaningful.

❑ Exercise 16.2

The following code segment uses the circular buffer defined in Program 16.1. What happens when it executes?

```
int i;
for (i = 0; i < 10; i++)
   if (putitem(i))
      break;
```

Answer:

The buffer has only 8 slots, but this code segment calls `putitem` 10 times. The `putitem` does not keep track of how many empty slots are available, so it does not report an error if full slots are overwritten. If a consumer does not call `getitem`, the code overwrites the first items in the buffer.

Program 16.1 is flawed because the code does not protect the buffer from overflows or underflows. Program 16.2 is a revised implementation that keeps track of the number of items actually in the buffer. If successful, `getitem` and `putitem` return 0. If unsuccessful, these functions return a nonzero error code. In particular, `getitem` returns `EAGAIN` if the buffer is empty, and `putitem` returns `EAGAIN` if the buffer is full.

■ Example 16.3

The following code segment attempts to retrieve at most 10 items from the buffer of Program 16.2.

```
int error;
int i;
int item;

for (i = 0; i < 10; i++) {
   while((error = getitem(&item)) && (error == EAGAIN)) ;
   if (error)                     /* real error occurred */
      break;
   printf("Retrieved item %d: %d\n", i, item);
}
```

Program 16.2 ───────────────────────────── `buffer.c`

A circular buffer implementation that does not allow overwriting of full slots or retrieval of empty slots.

```c
#include <errno.h>
#include <pthread.h>
#include "buffer.h"
static buffer_t buffer[BUFSIZE];
static pthread_mutex_t  bufferlock = PTHREAD_MUTEX_INITIALIZER;
static int bufin = 0;
static int bufout = 0;
static int totalitems = 0;

int getitem(buffer_t *itemp) {  /* remove item from buffer and put in *itemp */
   int error;
   int erroritem = 0;
   if (error = pthread_mutex_lock(&bufferlock))         /* no mutex, give up */
      return error;
   if (totalitems > 0) {                      /* buffer has something to remove */
      *itemp = buffer[bufout];
       bufout = (bufout + 1) % BUFSIZE;
       totalitems--;
   } else
       erroritem = EAGAIN;
   if (error = pthread_mutex_unlock(&bufferlock))
      return error;                   /* unlock error more serious than no item */
   return erroritem;
}

int putitem(buffer_t item) {                       /* insert item in the buffer */
   int error;
   int erroritem = 0;
   if (error = pthread_mutex_lock(&bufferlock))         /* no mutex, give up */
      return error;
   if (totalitems < BUFSIZE) {             /* buffer has room for another item */
      buffer[bufin] = item;
      bufin = (bufin + 1) % BUFSIZE;
      totalitems++;
   } else
      erroritem = EAGAIN;
   if (error = pthread_mutex_unlock(&bufferlock))
       return error;                   /* unlock error more serious than no slot */
   return erroritem;
}
```

Program 16.2 ───────────────────────────── `buffer.c`

The `while` loop of Example 16.3 uses busy waiting. The implementation is worse than you might imagine. Not only does busy waiting waste CPU time, but consumers executing this code segment block the producers, resulting in even more delay. Depending on the thread-scheduling algorithm, a busy-waiting consumer could prevent a producer from ever obtaining the CPU.

16.3 Buffer Implementation with Semaphores

A more efficient implementation uses POSIX:SEM semaphores (introduced in Section 14.3). Recall that POSIX:SEM semaphores are not part of the POSIX:THR Extension but can be used with threads. Semaphores differ in several operational respects from the POSIX thread functions. If unsuccessful, the semaphore functions return −1 and set `errno`. In contrast, the POSIX:THR thread functions return a nonzero error code. The blocking semaphore functions can be interrupted by a signal and are cancellation points for thread cancellation, so you must be careful to handle the effects of signals and cancellation when using semaphores.

The traditional semaphore solution to the producer-consumer problem uses two counting semaphores to represent the number of items in the buffer and the number of free slots, respectively. When a thread needs a resource of a particular type, it decrements the corresponding semaphore by calling `sem_wait`. Similarly when the thread releases a resource, it increments the appropriate semaphore by calling `sem_post`. Since the semaphore variable never falls below zero, threads cannot use resources that are not there. Always initialize a counting semaphore to the number of resources initially available.

Program 16.3 shows a bounded buffer that synchronizes its access with semaphores. The `semslots` semaphore, which is initialized to `BUFSIZE`, represents the number of free slots available. This semaphore is decremented by producers and incremented by consumers through the `sem_wait` and `sem_post` calls, respectively. Similarly, the `semitems` semaphore, which is initialized to 0, represents the number of items in the buffer. This semaphore is decremented by consumers and incremented by producers through the `sem_wait` and `sem_post` calls, respectively.

POSIX:SEM semaphores do not have a static initializer and must be explicitly initialized before they are referenced. The implementation assumes that the `bufferinit` function will be called exactly once before any threads access the buffer. Program 16.4 and Program 16.5 give alternative implementations of `bufferinit` that do not make these assumptions.

Program 16.3 illustrates several differences between semaphores and mutex locks. The `sem_wait` function is a cancellation point, so a thread that is blocked on a semaphore can be terminated. The `getitem` and `putitem` functions have no other cancellation points, so the threads cannot be interrupted while the buffer data structure is being modified. Since the mutex is not held very long, a canceled thread quickly hits another cancellation point. The semaphore operations, unlike the mutex operations, can also be interrupted by a signal. If we want to use Program 16.3 with a program that catches signals, we need to restart the functions that can return an error with `errno` set to `EINTR`. Because semaphore functions return −1 and set `errno` rather than returning the error directly, the error handling must be modified.

Program 16.3 ———————————————— **bufferseminit.c**

A bounded buffer synchronized by semaphores. Threads using these functions may be canceled with deferred cancellation without corrupting the buffer.

```c
#include <errno.h>
#include <pthread.h>
#include <semaphore.h>
#include "buffer.h"
static buffer_t buffer[BUFSIZE];
static pthread_mutex_t  bufferlock = PTHREAD_MUTEX_INITIALIZER;
static int bufin = 0;
static int bufout = 0;
static sem_t semitems;
static sem_t semslots;

int bufferinit(void) { /* call this exactly once BEFORE getitem and putitem  */
   int error;
   if (sem_init(&semitems, 0, 0))
      return errno;
   if (sem_init(&semslots, 0, BUFSIZE)) {
      error = errno;
      sem_destroy(&semitems);                     /* free the other semaphore */
      return error;
   }
   return 0;
}

int getitem(buffer_t *itemp) {   /* remove item from buffer and put in *itemp */
   int error;
   while (((error = sem_wait(&semitems)) == -1) && (errno == EINTR)) ;
   if (error)
      return errno;
   if (error = pthread_mutex_lock(&bufferlock))
      return error;
   *itemp = buffer[bufout];
   bufout = (bufout + 1) % BUFSIZE;
   if (error = pthread_mutex_unlock(&bufferlock))
      return error;
   if (sem_post(&semslots) == -1)
      return errno;
   return 0;
}

int putitem(buffer_t item) {                      /* insert item in the buffer */
   int error;
   while (((error = sem_wait(&semslots)) == -1) && (errno == EINTR)) ;
   if (error)
      return errno;
   if (error = pthread_mutex_lock(&bufferlock))
      return error;
   buffer[bufin] = item;
   bufin = (bufin + 1) % BUFSIZE;
   if (error = pthread_mutex_unlock(&bufferlock))
      return error;
   if (sem_post(&semitems) == -1)
      return errno;
   return 0;
}
```

Program 16.3 ———————————————— **bufferseminit.c**

Program 16.3 assumes that programs call `bufferinit` exactly once before referencing the buffer. Program 16.4 shows an alternative implementation that does not make these assumptions. The code assumes that programs call `bufferinitmutex` at least once before any thread accesses the buffer. The `bufferinitmutex` function can be called by each thread when the thread starts execution. The static initializer for the mutex ensures that `smutex` is initialized before any call. The `bufferinitmutex` can be called any number of times but initializes the semaphores only once.

Program 16.4 ──────────────────────────── **bufferinitmutex.c**

An initialization function for `bufferseminit.c` *that can be called more than once.*

```
#include <pthread.h>
static int seminit = 0;
static pthread_mutex_t smutex = PTHREAD_MUTEX_INITIALIZER;

int bufferinit(void);

int bufferinitmutex(void) {                    /* initialize buffer at most once */
    int error = 0;
    int errorinit = 0;
    if (error = pthread_mutex_lock(&smutex))
        return error;
    if (!seminit && !(errorinit = bufferinit()))
        seminit = 1;
    error = pthread_mutex_unlock(&smutex);
    if (errorinit)                 /* buffer initialization error occurred first */
        return errorinit;
    return error;
}
```

Program 16.4 ──────────────────────────── **bufferinitmutex.c**

☐ Exercise 16.4

How can we make the initialization of the semaphores completely transparent to the calling program?

Answer:

Make `bufferinitmutex` have internal linkage by adding the `static` qualifier. Now `getitem` and `putitem` should call `bufferinitmutex` before calling `sem_wait`. The initialization is now transparent, but we pay a price in efficiency.

Program 16.5 shows an alternative to `bufferinitmutex` for providing at-most-once initialization of the buffer in Program 16.3. The implementation uses `pthread_once`. Notice that `initerror` isn't protected by a mutex lock, because it will only be changed once and that modification occurs before any call to `bufferinitonce` returns. Call the `bufferinitonce` function from each thread when it is created, or just from the main thread before it creates the producer and consumer threads. You can make initialization transparent by calling `bufferinitonce` at the start of `getitem` and `putitem`.

Program 16.5 ———————————————————— **bufferinitonce.c**

An initialization function for bufferseminit.c *that uses* pthread_once *to ensure that initialization is performed only once.*

```
#include <pthread.h>
static int initerror = 0;
static pthread_once_t initonce = PTHREAD_ONCE_INIT;

int bufferinit(void);

static void initialization(void) {
   initerror = bufferinit();
   return;
}

int bufferinitonce(void) {                /* initialize buffer at most once */
   int error;
   if (error = pthread_once(&initonce, initialization))
      return error;
   return initerror;
}
```

Program 16.5 ———————————————————— **bufferinitonce.c**

Program 16.6 shows an alternative way of making the buffer initialization transparent without the overhead of calling the initialization routine from each putitem and getitem. The initdone variable is declared to be of type volatile sig_atomic_t. The volatile qualifier indicates that the value may change asynchronously to the running thread. The sig_atomic_t type is one that can be accessed atomically.

Program 16.6 ———————————————————— **buffersem.c**

A semaphore buffer implementation that does not require explicit initialization and has low initialization overhead.

```
#include <errno.h>
#include <pthread.h>
#include <semaphore.h>
#include <signal.h>
#include "buffer.h"
static buffer_t buffer[BUFSIZE];
static pthread_mutex_t  bufferlock = PTHREAD_MUTEX_INITIALIZER;
static int bufin = 0;
static int bufout = 0;
static volatile sig_atomic_t initdone = 0;
static int initerror = 0;
static pthread_once_t initonce = PTHREAD_ONCE_INIT;
static sem_t semitems;
static sem_t semslots;

static int bufferinit(void) { /* called exactly once by getitem and putitem  */
   int error;
   if (sem_init(&semitems, 0, 0))
      return errno;
   if (sem_init(&semslots, 0, BUFSIZE)) {
```

```
            error = errno;
            sem_destroy(&semitems);                 /* free the other semaphore */
            return error;
        }
        return 0;
    }

static void initialization(void) {
    initerror = bufferinit();
    if (!initerror)
        initdone = 1;
}

static int bufferinitonce(void) {          /* initialize buffer at most once */
    int error;
    if (error = pthread_once(&initonce, initialization))
        return error;
    return initerror;
}

int getitem(buffer_t *itemp) {  /* remove item from buffer and put in *itemp */
    int error;
    if (!initdone)
        bufferinitonce();
    while (((error = sem_wait(&semitems)) == -1) && (errno == EINTR)) ;
    if (error)
        return errno;
    if (error = pthread_mutex_lock(&bufferlock))
        return error;
    *itemp = buffer[bufout];
    bufout = (bufout + 1) % BUFSIZE;
    if (error = pthread_mutex_unlock(&bufferlock))
        return error;
    if (sem_post(&semslots) == -1)
        return errno;
    return 0;
}

int putitem(buffer_t item) {                         /* insert item in the buffer */
    int error;
    if (!initdone)
        bufferinitonce();
    while (((error = sem_wait(&semslots)) == -1) && (errno == EINTR)) ;
    if (error)
        return errno;
    if (error = pthread_mutex_lock(&bufferlock))
        return error;
    buffer[bufin] = item;
    bufin = (bufin + 1) % BUFSIZE;
    if (error = pthread_mutex_unlock(&bufferlock))
        return error;
    if (sem_post(&semitems) == -1)
        return errno;
    return 0;
}
```

Program 16.6 ————————————————————————————— **buffersem.c**

The `initdone` variable is statically initialized to 0. Its value changes only when the initialization has completed and the value is changed to 1. If the value of `initdone` is nonzero, we may assume that the initialization has completed successfully. If the value is 0, the initialization may have been done, so we use the `bufferinitonce` as in Program 16.5. Using `initdone` lowers the overhead of checking for the initialization once the initialization has completed. It does not require additional function calls once the initialization is complete.

The bounded buffer implementation of this section has no mechanism for termination. It assumes that producers and consumers that access the buffer run forever. The semaphores are not deleted unless an initialization error occurs.

16.4 Introduction to a Simple Producer-Consumer Problem

This section introduces a simple producer-consumer problem to test the buffer implementations; the problem is based on Programs 13.6 and 13.7 in Section 13.2.3. The programs approximate the average value of sin(x) on the interval from 0 to 1, using a probabilistic algorithm. The producers calculate random numbers between 0 and 1 and put them in a buffer. Each consumer removes a value x from the buffer and adds the value of sin(x) to a running sum, keeping track of the number of entries summed. At any time, the sum divided by the count gives an estimate of the average value. Simple calculus shows that the exact average value is 1 – cos(1) or about 0.4597. Using bounded buffers is not a particularly efficient way of solving this problem, but it illustrates many of the relevant ideas needed to solve more interesting problems.

Program 16.7 shows a threaded producer object that uses the bounded buffer defined by Program 16.6. Each producer of Program 16.7 generates random double values and places them in the buffer. The implementation uses the `globalerror` object of Program 13.4 on page 455 to keep the number of the first error that occurs and uses the thread-safe `randsafe` of Program 13.2 on page 454 to generate random numbers. The `initproducer` function, which creates a producer thread, can be called multiple times if multiple producers are needed.

Program 16.8 shows an implementation of a consumer object. The publicly accessible `initconsumer` function allows an application to create as many consumer threads as desired. In case of an error, the offending thread sets the global error and returns. The other threads continue unless they also detect that an error occurred.

Program 16.9 is a `main` program that can be used with the producer (Program 16.7) and consumer (Program 16.8) threads as well as the `buffersem` buffer implementation (Program 16.6). The implementation assumes that no explicit buffer initialization is required. Program 16.9 takes three command-line arguments; a sleeptime in seconds, the number of producer threads and the number of consumer threads. The `main` program starts the threads, sleeps for the indicated time, and displays the results so far. After sleeping again, the `main` program displays the results and returns, terminating all the threads. This application illustrates the producer-consumer problem when the threads run forever or until `main` terminates.

The `main` program of Program 16.9 can display errors by using `strerror` rather than `strerror_r` because it is the only thread making this call. Program 16.9 calls the `showresults` function of Program 13.8 on page 459 to display the statistics.

Program 16.7 ──────────────────────── **randproducer.c**

An implementation of a producer that generates random numbers and places them in a synchronized buffer, such as the one shown in Program 16.6.

```
#include <pthread.h>
#include "buffer.h"
#include "globalerror.h"
#include "randsafe.h"

/* ARGSUSED */
static void *producer(void *arg1) {          /* generate pseudorandom numbers */
   int error;
   buffer_t item;

   for ( ;  ;  ) {
      if (error = randsafe(&item))
         break;
      if (error = putitem(item))
         break;
   }
   seterror(error);
   return NULL;
}

/* --------------- Public functions --------------------------------------- */
int initproducer(pthread_t *tproducer) {                       /* initialize */
   int error;

   error = pthread_create(tproducer, NULL, producer, NULL);
   return (seterror(error));
}
```

Program 16.7 ──────────────────────── **randproducer.c**

☐ Exercise 16.5

What happens to the semaphores when Program 16.9 terminates?

Answer:

Since we are using POSIX:SEM unnamed semaphores with `pshared` equal to 0, the resources of the semaphores are released when the process terminates. If we had been using named semaphores or POSIX:XSI semaphores, they would still exist after the process terminated.

Program 16.8 ———————————————————————— `randconsumer.c`

*An implementation of a consumer that calculates the sine of double values removed
from a shared buffer and adds them to a running sum.*

```c
#include <math.h>
#include <pthread.h>
#include "buffer.h"
#include "globalerror.h"
#include "sharedsum.h"

/* ARGSUSED */
static void *consumer(void *arg) {                        /* compute partial sums */
   int error;
   buffer_t nextitem;
   double value;

   for ( ;  ;  ) {
      if (error = getitem(&nextitem))                     /* retrieve the next item */
         break;
      value = sin(nextitem);
      if (error = add(value))
         break;
   }
   seterror(error);
   return NULL;
}

/* --------------- Public functions -------------------------------------- */
int initconsumer(pthread_t *tconsumer) {                  /* initialize */
   int error;

   error = pthread_create(tconsumer, NULL, consumer, NULL);
   return (seterror(error));
}
```

Program 16.8 ———————————————————————— `randconsumer.c`

☐ Exercise 16.6

Suppose Program 16.9 runs on a machine with a single processor under preemptive priority scheduling. In what order are the items processed if `BUFSIZE` is 8 and one of the producers starts first?

Answer:

For preemptive priority scheduling, a thread with greater priority than the currently running thread preempts it. If the producer and consumers have the same priority, as in Program 16.9, a producer deposits eight items in the buffer and then blocks. The first consumer then retrieves the first eight items. One of the producers then produces the next 8 items, and so on. This alternation of blocks occurs because the producers and consumers are of equal priority. On the other hand, if the consumers have a higher priority, a consumer preempts the producer after the producer deposits a single item, so the producer and the consumers alternately process individual items. If the producer has higher priority, it fills the buffer with 8 items and then preempts the consumers after each slot becomes available.

Program 16.9 ———————————————————— **randpcforever.c**
   A main program that creates any number of producer and consumer threads.

```c
#include <pthread.h>
#include <stdio.h>
#include <stdlib.h>
#include <string.h>
#include <unistd.h>
#include "buffer.h"
#include "globalerror.h"
#include "sharedsum.h"

int initconsumer(pthread_t *tid);
int initproducer(pthread_t *tid);
int showresults(void);

int main(int argc, char *argv[]) {
   int error;
   int i;
   int numberconsumers;
   int numberproducers;
   int sleeptime;
   pthread_t tid;

   if (argc != 4) {
      fprintf(stderr, "Usage: %s sleeptime producers consumers\n", argv[0]);
      return 1;
   }

   sleeptime = atoi(argv[1]);
   numberproducers = atoi(argv[2]);
   numberconsumers = atoi(argv[3]);
   for (i = 0; i < numberconsumers; i++)             /* initialize consumers */
      if (error = initconsumer(&tid)) {
         fprintf(stderr, "Failed to create consumer %d:%s\n",
                           i, strerror(error));
         return 1;
      }
   for (i = 0; i < numberproducers; i++)             /* initialize producers */
      if (error = initproducer(&tid)) {
         fprintf(stderr, "Failed to create producer %d:%s\n",
                           i, strerror(error));
         return 1;
      }

   sleep(sleeptime);                                 /* wait to get the partial sum */
   if (showresults())
      return 1;
   sleep(sleeptime);                                 /* wait again before terminating */
   if (showresults())
      return 1;
   return 0;
}
```

Program 16.9 ———————————————————— **randpcforever.c**

16.5 Bounded Buffer Implementation Using Condition Variables

Program 16.10 gives a condition variable implementation of a bounded buffer that is similar to the semaphore implementation of Program 16.6.

Program 16.10 ──────────────────────── **buffercond.c**

Condition variable implementation of a bounded buffer.

```
#include <pthread.h>
#include "buffer.h"
static buffer_t buffer[BUFSIZE];
static pthread_mutex_t bufferlock = PTHREAD_MUTEX_INITIALIZER;
static int bufin = 0;
static int bufout = 0;
static pthread_cond_t items = PTHREAD_COND_INITIALIZER;
static pthread_cond_t slots = PTHREAD_COND_INITIALIZER;
static int totalitems = 0;

int getitem(buffer_t *itemp) { /* remove an item from buffer and put in itemp */
   int error;
   if (error = pthread_mutex_lock(&bufferlock))
      return error;
   while ((totalitems <= 0) && !error)
      error = pthread_cond_wait (&items, &bufferlock);
   if (error) {
      pthread_mutex_unlock(&bufferlock);
      return error;
   }
   *itemp = buffer[bufout];
   bufout = (bufout + 1) % BUFSIZE;
   totalitems--;
   if (error = pthread_cond_signal(&slots)) {
      pthread_mutex_unlock(&bufferlock);
      return error;
   }
   return pthread_mutex_unlock(&bufferlock);
}

int putitem(buffer_t item) {                    /* insert an item in the buffer */
   int error;
   if (error = pthread_mutex_lock(&bufferlock))
      return error;
   while ((totalitems >= BUFSIZE) && !error)
      error = pthread_cond_wait (&slots, &bufferlock);
   if (error) {
      pthread_mutex_unlock(&bufferlock);
      return error;
   }
   buffer[bufin] = item;
   bufin = (bufin + 1) % BUFSIZE;
   totalitems++;
   if (error = pthread_cond_signal(&items)) {
      pthread_mutex_unlock(&bufferlock);
      return error;
   }
   return pthread_mutex_unlock(&bufferlock);
}
```

Program 16.10 ──────────────────────── **buffercond.c**

Program 16.10 is simpler than the semaphore implementation because condition variables have static initializers. Test Program 16.10 on a producer-consumer problem by linking it with Programs 16.7, 16.8 and 16.9. It also needs Program 13.4 (`globalerror`), Program 13.2 (`randsafe`) and Program 13.5 (`sharedsum`).

16.6 Buffers with Done Conditions

The bounded buffer implementations of Section 16.3 and Section 16.5 do not have any mechanism for indicating that no more items will be deposited in the buffer. Unending producer-consumer problems occur frequently at the system level. For example, every network router has a buffer between incoming and outgoing packets. The producers are the processes that handle the incoming lines, and the consumers are the processes handling the outgoing lines. A web server is another example of an unending producer-consumer. The web server clients (browsers) are producers of requests. The web server acts as a consumer in handling these requests.

Things are not so simple when the producers or consumers are controlled by more complicated exit conditions. In a *producer-driven* variation on the producer-consumer problem, there is one producer and an arbitrary number of consumers. The producer puts an unspecified number of items in the buffer and then exits. The consumers continue until all items have been consumed and the producer has exited.

A possible approach is for the producer to set a flag signifying that it has completed its operation. However, this approach is not straightforward, as illustrated by the next exercise.

☐ **Exercise 16.7**

Consider the following proposed solution to a producer-driven problem. The `producer` thread produces only `numitem` values, calls `setdone` of Program 13.3 on page 454, and exits. The `consumer` calls `getdone` on each iteration of the loop to discover whether the `producer` has completed. What can go wrong?

Answer:

If the `producer` calls `setdone` while `consumer` is blocked on `getitem` with an empty buffer, the consumer never receives notification and it deadlocks, waiting for an item to be produced. Also, when `consumer` detects that `producer` has called `setdone`, it has no way of determining whether there are items left in the buffer to be processed without blocking.

Both the semaphore implementation of the bounded buffer in Program 16.6 and the condition variable implementation of the bounded buffer in Program 16.10 have no way of unblocking `getitem` after `setdone` is called. Program 16.11 shows an implementation that moves the `doneflag` into the buffer object. The `setdone` function not only sets the `doneflag` but also wakes up all threads that are waiting on condition variables. If `getitem` is called with an empty buffer after the producer has finished, `getitem` returns the error ECANCELED. The consumer then terminates when it tries to retrieve the next item.

Program 16.11 ———————————————————— **bufferconddone.c**

A buffer that uses condition variables to detect completion.

```c
#include <errno.h>
#include <pthread.h>
#include "buffer.h"
static buffer_t buffer[BUFSIZE];
static pthread_mutex_t  bufferlock = PTHREAD_MUTEX_INITIALIZER;
static int bufin = 0;
static int bufout = 0;
static int doneflag = 0;
static pthread_cond_t items = PTHREAD_COND_INITIALIZER;
static pthread_cond_t slots = PTHREAD_COND_INITIALIZER;
static int totalitems = 0;

int getitem(buffer_t *itemp) {/* remove an item from buffer and put in itemp */
   int error;
   if (error = pthread_mutex_lock(&bufferlock))
      return error;
   while ((totalitems <= 0) && !error && !doneflag)
      error = pthread_cond_wait (&items, &bufferlock);
   if (error) {
      pthread_mutex_unlock(&bufferlock);
      return error;
   }
   if (doneflag && (totalitems <= 0)) {
      pthread_mutex_unlock(&bufferlock);
      return ECANCELED;
   }
   *itemp = buffer[bufout];
   bufout = (bufout + 1) % BUFSIZE;
   totalitems--;
   if (error = pthread_cond_signal(&slots)) {
      pthread_mutex_unlock(&bufferlock);
      return error;
   }
   return pthread_mutex_unlock(&bufferlock);
}

int putitem(buffer_t item) {                    /* insert an item in the buffer */
   int error;
   if (error = pthread_mutex_lock(&bufferlock))
      return error;
   while ((totalitems >= BUFSIZE) && !error && !doneflag)
      error = pthread_cond_wait (&slots, &bufferlock);
   if (error) {
      pthread_mutex_unlock(&bufferlock);
      return error;
   }
   if (doneflag) {                 /* consumers may be gone, don't put item in */
```

```
          pthread_mutex_unlock(&bufferlock);
          return ECANCELED;
      }
      buffer[bufin] = item;
      bufin = (bufin + 1) % BUFSIZE;
      totalitems++;
      if (error = pthread_cond_signal(&items)) {
          pthread_mutex_unlock(&bufferlock);
          return error;
      }
      return pthread_mutex_unlock(&bufferlock);
}

int getdone(int *flag) {                              /* get the flag */
    int error;
    if (error = pthread_mutex_lock(&bufferlock))
        return error;
    *flag = doneflag;
    return pthread_mutex_unlock(&bufferlock);
}

int setdone(void) {       /* set the doneflag and inform all waiting threads */
    int error1;
    int error2;
    int error3;

    if (error1 = pthread_mutex_lock(&bufferlock))
        return error1;
    doneflag = 1;
    error1 = pthread_cond_broadcast(&items);              /* wake up everyone */
    error2 = pthread_cond_broadcast(&slots);
    error3 = pthread_mutex_unlock(&bufferlock);
    if (error1)
        return error1;
    if (error2)
        return error2;
    if (error3)
        return error3;
    return 0;
}
```

Program 16.11 ————————————————————— **bufferconddone.c**

☐ Exercise 16.8

Why did we use the same mutex to protect `doneflag` in `getdone` and `setdone` as we used to protect the buffer in `getitem` and `putitem`?

Answer:

The `getitem` function needs to access `doneflag` at a time when it owns the `bufferlock` mutex. Using the same mutex simplifies the program.

❏ Exercise 16.9

Can the mutex calls in `getdone` and `setdone` be eliminated?

Answer:

The lock around `doneflag` in `getdone` could be eliminated if we knew that access to an `int` was atomic. We can guarantee that accesses to `doneflag` are atomic by declaring it to have type `sig_atomic_t`. In `setdone`, it is best to do the condition variable broadcasts while owning the lock, and we need to make sure that the threads see that `doneflag` has been set to 1 when they wake up.

Program 16.12 and Program 16.13 show modifications of `producer` of Program 16.7 and `consumer` of Program 16.8 to account for termination. They are linked with Program 16.11, which provides `setdone`. They handle the error `ECANCELED` by terminating without calling `seterror`.

Program 16.12 ───────────────────────────── **`randproducerdone.c`**

A producer that detects whether processing should end.

```
#include <errno.h>
#include <pthread.h>
#include "buffer.h"
#include "globalerror.h"
#include "randsafe.h"

int getdone(int *flag);

/* ARGSUSED */
static void *producer(void *arg1) {          /* generate pseudorandom numbers */
   int error;
   buffer_t item;
   int localdone = 0;

   while (!localdone) {
      if (error = randsafe(&item))
         break;
      if (error = putitem(item))
         break;
      if (error = getdone(&localdone))
         break;
   }
   if (error != ECANCELED)
      seterror(error);
   return NULL;
}

/* --------------- Public functions -------------------------------------- */
int initproducer(pthread_t *tproducer) {                         /* initialize */
   int error;

   error = pthread_create(tproducer, NULL, producer, NULL);
   return (seterror(error));
}
```

Program 16.12 ───────────────────────────── **`randproducerdone.c`**

Program 16.13 ─────────────────────────── **randconsumerdone.c**

A consumer that detects whether the buffer has finished.

```
#include <errno.h>
#include <math.h>
#include <pthread.h>
#include "buffer.h"
#include "globalerror.h"
#include "sharedsum.h"

/* ARGSUSED */
static void *consumer(void *arg) {                    /* compute partial sums */
   int error;
   buffer_t nextitem;
   double value;

   for (  ;  ;  ) {
      if (error = getitem(&nextitem))                 /* retrieve the next item */
         break;
      value = sin(nextitem);
      if (error = add(value))
         break;
   }
   if (error != ECANCELED)
      seterror(error);
   return NULL;
}

/* --------------- Public functions ------------------------------------- */
int initconsumer(pthread_t *tconsumer) {                      /* initialize */
   int error;

   error = pthread_create(tconsumer, NULL, consumer, NULL);
   return (seterror(error));
}
```

Program 16.13 ─────────────────────────── **randconsumerdone.c**

Program 16.14 shows a `main` program that creates a specified number of the producer threads (Program 16.12) and consumer threads (Program 16.13). After creating the threads, `main` sleeps for a specified amount of time and then calls the `setdone` function of Program 16.11. The program joins with all the threads to make sure that they have finished their computations before calling `showresults` of Program 13.8 on page 459 to display the results.

☐ **Exercise 16.10**

What would happen if `randconsumerdone` of Program 16.13 called `seterror` when `getitem` returned `ECANCELED`?

Answer:

The results of the calculation would not be displayed. The `showresults` function only prints an error message if `geterror` returns a nonzero value.

Program 16.14 ──────────────────────────────── `randpcdone.c`

A `main` *program that creates producer threads of Program 16.12 and consumer threads of Program 16.13. After sleeping, it calls* `setdone`. *The program should use the buffer of Program 16.11.*

```c
#include <pthread.h>
#include <stdio.h>
#include <stdlib.h>
#include <string.h>
#include <unistd.h>
#include "buffer.h"
#include "doneflag.h"
#include "globalerror.h"

int initconsumer(pthread_t *tid);
int initproducer(pthread_t *tid);
int showresults(void);

int main(int argc, char *argv[]) {
   int error;
   int i;
   int numberconsumers;
   int numberproducers;
   int sleeptime;
   pthread_t *tidc;
   pthread_t *tidp;

   if (argc != 4) {
      fprintf(stderr, "Usage: %s sleeptime producers consumers\n", argv[0]);
      return 1;
   }
   sleeptime = atoi(argv[1]);
   numberproducers = atoi(argv[2]);
   numberconsumers = atoi(argv[3]);
   tidp = (pthread_t *)calloc(numberproducers, sizeof(pthread_t));
   if (tidp == NULL) {
     perror("Failed to allocate space for producer IDs");
     return 1;
   }
   tidc = (pthread_t *)calloc(numberconsumers, sizeof(pthread_t));
   if (tidc == NULL) {
     perror("Failed to allocate space for consumer IDs");
     return 1;
   }
   for (i = 0; i < numberconsumers; i++)              /* initialize consumers */
      if (error = initconsumer(tidc+i)) {
         fprintf(stderr, "Failed to create consumer %d:%s\n",
                         i, strerror(error));
         return 1;
      }
   for (i = 0; i < numberproducers; i++)              /* initialize producers */
      if (error = initproducer(tidp+i)) {
         fprintf(stderr, "Failed to create producer %d:%s\n",
                         i, strerror(error));
         return 1;
      }
```

```
      sleep(sleeptime);                     /* wait a while to get the partial sum */
      if (error = setdone()) {
         fprintf(stderr, "Failed to set done indicator:%s\n", strerror(error));
         return 1;
      }
      for (i = 0; i < numberproducers; i++)            /* wait for producers */
         if (error = pthread_join(tidp[i], NULL)) {
            fprintf(stderr, "Failed producer %d join:%s\n", i, strerror(error));
            return 1;
         }
      for (i = 0; i < numberconsumers; i++)            /* wait for consumers */
         if (error = pthread_join(tidc[i], NULL)) {
            fprintf(stderr, "Failed consumer %d join:%s\n", i, strerror(error));
            return 1;
         }
      if (showresults())
         return 1;
      return 0;
   }
```

Program 16.14 ——————————————————————————— **randpcdone.c**

Program 16.15 shows a second version of `main` that creates a signal thread of Program 13.14 on page 476 to wait on SIGUSR1. Program 13.14 should be linked to `bufferconddone.c` rather than `doneflag.c` so that it calls the correct `setdone`. As before, `main` creates a specified number of the producer and consumer threads of Program 16.12 and Program 16.13. After creating the threads, `main` waits for the threads to complete by executing `pthread_join` before displaying the results. The threads continue to compute until the user sends a SIGUSR1 signal from the command line. At this point, the `signalthread` calls `setdone`, causing the producers and consumers to terminate.

Program 16.15 ——————————————————————— **randpcsig.c**
A main *program that creates producer threads of Program 16.12 and consumer threads of Program 16.13. The threads detect done when the user enters* SIGUSR1.

```
#include <pthread.h>
#include <signal.h>
#include <stdio.h>
#include <stdlib.h>
#include <string.h>
#include <unistd.h>
#include "buffer.h"
#include "globalerror.h"
#include "sharedsum.h"
#include "signalthread.h"

int initconsumer(pthread_t *tid);
int initproducer(pthread_t *tid);
int showresults(void);

int main(int argc, char *argv[]) {
```

```c
    int error;
    int i;
    int numberconsumers;
    int numberproducers;
    pthread_t *tidc;
    pthread_t *tidp;

    if (argc != 3) {
       fprintf(stderr, "Usage: %s producers consumers\n", argv[0]);
       return 1;
    }
    numberproducers = atoi(argv[1]);
    numberconsumers = atoi(argv[2]);
    if (error = signalthreadinit(SIGUSR1)) {
       perror("Failed to start signalthread");
       return 1;
    }
    fprintf(stderr,"Process %ld will run until SIGUSR1 (%d) signal.\n",
                   (long)getpid(), SIGUSR1);
    tidp = (pthread_t *)calloc(numberproducers, sizeof(pthread_t));
    if (tidp == NULL) {
       perror("malloc producer IDs");
       return 1;
    }
    tidc = (pthread_t *)calloc(numberconsumers, sizeof(pthread_t));
    if (tidc == NULL) {
       perror("malloc consumer IDs");
       return 1;
    }
    for (i = 0; i < numberconsumers; i++)              /* initialize consumers */
       if (error = initconsumer(tidc + i)) {
          fprintf(stderr, "Failed to create consumer %d:%s\n",
                           i, strerror(error));
          return 1;
       }
    for (i = 0; i < numberproducers; i++)              /* initialize producers */
       if (error = initproducer(tidp + i)) {
          fprintf(stderr, "Failed to create producer %d:%s\n",
                           i, strerror(error));
          return 1;
       }
    for (i = 0; i < numberproducers; i++)               /* wait for producers */
       if (error = pthread_join(tidp[i], NULL)) {
          fprintf(stderr, "Failed producer %d join:%s\n", i, strerror(error));
          return 1;
       }
    for (i = 0; i < numberconsumers; i++)               /* wait for consumers */
       if (error = pthread_join(tidc[i], NULL)) {
          fprintf(stderr, "Failed consumer %d join:%s\n", i, strerror(error));
          return 1;
       }
    if (showresults())
       return 1;
    return 0;
}
```

Program 16.15 ——————————————————————————————————— `randpcsig.c`

16.7 Parallel File Copy

This section revisits the parallel file copy of Program 12.8 on page 427. The straightforward implementation of the parallel file copy creates a new thread to copy each file and each directory. When called with a large directory tree, this implementation quickly exceeds system resources. This section outlines a *worker pool* implementation that regulates how many threads are active at any time. In a worker pool implementation, a fixed number of threads are available to handle the load. The workers block on a synchronization point (in this case, an empty buffer) and one worker unblocks when a request comes in (an item is put in the buffer). Chapter 22 compares the performance of worker pools to other server threading strategies.

16.7.1 Parallel file copy producer

Begin by creating a producer thread function that takes as a parameter an array of size 2 containing the pathnames of two directories. For each regular file in the first directory, the producer opens the file for reading and opens a file of the same name in the second directory for writing. If a file already exists in the destination directory with the same name, that file should be opened and truncated. If an error occurs in opening either file, both files are closed and an informative message is sent to standard output. The two open file descriptors and the name of the file are put into the buffer. Use the `bufferconddone` implementation so that the threads can be terminated gracefully. The `buffer.h` file contains the definition of `buffer_t`, the type of a buffer entry. Use the following definition for this project.

```
typedef struct {
    int infd;
    int outfd;
    char filename[PATH_MAX];
} buffer_t;
```

Only ordinary files will be copied for this version of the program. The `filename` member should contain the name of the file only, without a path specification. Use the `opendir` and `readdir` functions described in Section 5.2 on page 152 to access the source directory. These functions are not thread-safe, but there will be only one producer thread and only this thread will call these functions. Use the `lstat` function described in Section 5.2.1 on page 155 to determine if the file is a regular file. The file is a regular file if the `S_ISREG` macro returns true when applied to the `st_mode` field of the `stat` structure. Program 16.16 shows a function that returns true if `filename` represents a regular file and false otherwise.

This is a producer-driven bounded buffer problem. When the producer is finished filling the buffer with filenames from the given directory, it calls `setdone` in Program 16.11 and exits.

Program 16.16 ─────────────────────────────── `isregular.c` ┐

A function that returns true if the filename parameter is a regular file.

```
#include <sys/stat.h>
#include <sys/types.h>

int isregular(const char *filename) {
   struct stat buf;

   if (lstat(filename, &buf) == -1)
      return 0;
   return S_ISREG(buf.st_mode);
}
```

└ **Program 16.16** ───────────────────────────── `isregular.c` ┘

16.7.2 Parallel file copy consumer

Each consumer thread reads an item from the buffer, copies the file from the source file descriptor to the destination file descriptor, closes the files, and writes a message to standard output giving the file name and the completion status of the copy.

Note that the producer and multiple consumers are writing to standard output and that this is a critical section that must be protected. Devise a method for writing these messages atomically.

The consumers should terminate when they detect that a done flag has been set and no more entries remain in the buffer, as in Program 16.13.

16.7.3 Parallel file copy `main` program

The `main` program should take the number of consumers and the source and destination directories as command-line arguments. The application always has exactly one producer thread.

The `main` program should start the threads and use `pthread_join` to wait for the threads to complete, as in Program 16.15. Use `gettimeofday` to get the time before the first thread is created and after the last join. Display the total time to copy the files in the directory.

Experiment with different buffer sizes and different numbers of consumer threads. Which combinations produce the best results? Be careful not to exceed the per-process limit on the number of open file descriptors. The number of open file descriptors is determined by the size of the buffer and the number of consumers. Make sure that the consumers close the file descriptors after copying a file and before removing another item from the buffer.

16.7.4 Parallel file copy enhancements

After the programs described above are working correctly, add the following enhancements.

1. Copy subdirectories as well as ordinary files, but do not (at this time) copy the contents of the subdirectories. (Just create a subdirectory in the destination directory for each subdirectory in the source directory.) You can either have the producer do this (and not put a new entry into the buffer) or add a field in `buffer_t` giving the type of file to be copied. Read item 3 below before deciding which method to use.

2. Copy FIFOs. For each FIFO in the source directory, make a FIFO with the same name in the destination directory. You can handle this as in item 1.

3. Recursively copy subdirectories. This part should just require modifying the producer if the producer creates the subdirectory. If the consumers create the subdirectories, you need to figure out how to avoid having the producer try to open a destination file before its directory has been created. Store the path of the file relative to the source directory in the buffer slots so that the consumers can print relevant messages.

4. Keep statistics about the number and types of files copied. Keep track of the total number of bytes copied. Keep track of the shortest and longest copy times.

5. Add a signal thread that outputs the statistics accumulated so far when the process receives a `SIGUSR1` signal. Make sure that the handler output is atomic with respect to the output generated by the producer and the consumers.

16.8 Threaded Print Server

This section develops a project based on producer-consumer synchronization that uses an unbounded buffer rather than a buffer of fixed size.

The `lp` command on most systems does not send a file directly to the specified printer. Instead, `lp` sends the request to a process called a *print server* or a *printer daemon*. The print server places the request in a queue and makes an identification number available to the user in case the user decides to cancel the print job. When a printer becomes free, the print server begins copying the file to the printer device. The file to be printed may not be copied to a temporary spool device unless the user explicitly specifies that it should be. Many implementations of `lp` try to create a hard link to the file while it is waiting to be printed, to prevent the file from being removed completely. It is not always possible for the `lp` command to link to the file, and the man page warns the user not to change the file until after it is printed.

■ **Example 16.11**

The following UNIX `lp` command outputs the file `myfile.ps` to the printer designated as `nps`.

```
lp -d nps myfile.ps
```

The `lp` command might respond with a request number similar to the following.

```
Request nps-358 queued
```

Use the `nps-358` in a `cancel` command to delete the print job.

Printers are slow devices relative to process execution times, and one print server process can handle many printers. Like the problem of handling input from multiple descriptors, the problems of print serving are natural for multithreading. Figure 16.3 shows a schematic organization of a threaded print server. The server uses a dedicated thread to read user requests from an input source. The request thread allocates space for the request and adds it to the request buffer.

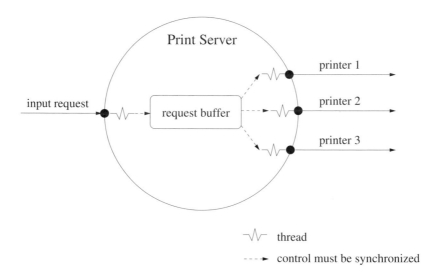

Figure 16.3: Schematic of a threaded print server.

The print server of Figure 16.3 has dedicated threads for handling its printers. Each printer thread removes a request from the request buffer and copies the file specified in the request to the printer. When the copying is complete, the printer thread frees the request and handles another request.

The threads within the print server require producer-consumer synchronization with a single producer (the request thread) and multiple consumers (the printer threads). The buffer itself must be protected so that items are removed and added in a consistent manner. The consumers must synchronize on the requests available in the buffer so that they do not attempt to remove nonexistent requests. The request buffer is not bounded because the request thread dynamically allocates space for requests as they come in. The request thread could also use a *high-water mark* to limit the number of requests that it buffers before blocking. In this more complicated situation, the request thread synchronizes on a predicate involving the size of the buffer.

Several aspects of the print server are simplified for this exercise. A real server may accept input from a network port or by remote procedure call. There is no requirement for printers to be identical, and realistic print requests allow a variety of options for users to specify how the printing is to be done. The system administrator can install default filters that act on files of particular types. The print server can analyze request types and direct requests to the best printer for the job. Printer requests may have priorities or other characteristics that affect the way in which they are printed. The individual printer threads should respond to error conditions and status reports from the printer device drivers.

This exercise describes the print server represented schematically in Figure 16.3. Keep pending requests in a request buffer. Synchronize the number of pending requests with a condition variable, called `items`, in a manner similar to the standard producer-consumer problem. This exercise does not require a condition variable for `slots`, since the request buffer can grow arbitrarily large. Represent print requests by a string consisting of an integer followed by a blank and a string specifying the full pathname of the file to be printed.

16.8.1 The request buffer

Represent the request buffer by a linked list of nodes of type `prcmd_t`. The following is a sample definition.

```
typedef struct pr_struct {
    int owner;
    char filename[PATH_MAX];
    struct pr_struct *nextprcmd;
} prcmd_t;
static prcmd_t *prhead = NULL;
static prcmd_t *prtail = NULL;
static int pending = 0;
static pthread_mutex_t prmutex = PTHREAD_MUTEX_INITIALIZER;
```

Put the request buffer data structure in a separate file and access it only through the following functions.

`int add(prcmd_t *node);`

> adds a node to the request buffer. The `add` function increments `pending` and inserts `node` at the end of the request buffer. If successful, `add` returns 0. If unsuccessful, `add` returns −1 and sets `errno`.

```
int remove(prcmd_t **node);
```
removes a node from the request buffer. The `remove` function blocks if the buffer is empty. If the buffer is not empty, the `remove` function decrements `pending` and removes the first node from the request buffer. It sets `*node` to point to the removed node. If `remove` successfully removes a node, it returns 0. If unsuccessful, `remove` returns −1 and sets `errno`.

```
int getnumber(void);
```
returns the size of the request buffer, which is the value of `pending`.

Use the synchronization strategy of Program 16.11, but eliminate the conditions for controlling the number of slots.

16.8.2 The producer thread

The producer thread, `getrequests`, inserts input requests in the buffer.

```
void *getrequests(void *arg);
```

The parameter `arg` points to an open file descriptor specifying the location where the requests are read. The `getrequests` function reads the user ID and the pathname of the file to be printed, creates a `prcmd_t` node to hold the information, and calls `add` to add the request to the printer request list. If `getrequests` fails to allocate space for `prcmd_t` or if it detects end-of-file, it returns after setting a global error flag. Otherwise, it continues to monitor the open file descriptor for the next request.

Write a `main` program to test `getrequests`. The `main` program creates the `getrequests` thread with `STDIN_FILENO` as the input file. It then goes into a loop in which it waits for `pending` to become nonzero. The main thread removes the next request from the buffer and writes the user ID and the filename to standard output. Run the program with input requests typed from the keyboard. Test the program with standard input redirected from a file.

16.8.3 The consumer threads

Each consumer thread, `printer`, removes a request from the printer request buffer and "prints" it. The prototype for `printer` is the following.

```
void *printer(void *arg);
```

The parameter `arg` points to an open file descriptor to which `printer` outputs the file to be printed. The `printer` function waits for the counter `pending` to become nonzero in a manner similar to `consumer` in Program 16.13. When a request is available, remove the request from the buffer, open the file specified by the `filename` member for reading, and copy the contents of the file to the output file. Then close the input file, free the space occupied by the request node, and resume waiting for more requests. If a consumer thread encounters an error when reading the input file, write an appropriate error message, close the input file, and resume waiting for more requests. Since the output file plays the role of the printer in this exercise, an output file error corresponds to a printer failure. If `printer` encounters an error on output, close the output file, write an appropriate error message, set a global error flag, and return.

16.8.4 The print server

Write a new `main` program to implement the print server. The server supports a maximum of `MAX_PRINT` printers. (Five should suffice for testing.) The `main` program takes two command-line arguments: the output file basename and the number of printers. The input requests are taken from standard input, which may be redirected to take requests from a file. The output for each printer goes to a separate file whose filename starts with the output file basename. For example, if the basename is `printer.out`, the output files are `printer.out.1`, `printer.out.2`, and so on. The `main` program creates a thread to run `get_requests` and a `printer` thread for each printer to be supported. It then waits for all the threads to exit before exiting itself. The `main` program should not exit just because an error occurred in one of the printer threads. Thoroughly test the print server.

16.8.5 Other enhancements

Add facilities so that each `printer` thread keeps track of statistics such as total number of files printed and total number of bytes printed. When the server receives a `SIGUSR1` signal, it writes the statistics for all the printers to standard error.

Add facilities so that the input now includes a command as well as a user ID and filename. The commands are as follows.

> `lp:`   Add the request to the buffer and echo a request ID to standard output.
>
> `cancel:` Remove the request from the buffer if it is there.
>
> `lpstat:` Write to standard output a summary of all pending requests and requests currently being printed on each printer.

Modify the synchronization mechanism of the buffer to use `highmark` and `lowmark` to control the size of the request buffer. Once the number of requests reaches the `highmark` value, `getrequests` blocks until the size of the request buffer is less than `lowmark`.

16.9 Additional Reading

Most classical books on operating systems discuss some variation of the producer-consumer problem. See, for example, [107, 122]. Unfortunately, in most classic treatments, producers and consumers loop forever, uninterrupted by signals or other complications that arise from a finite universe. "Experimentation with bounded buffer synchronization," by S. Robbins [96] introduces some simple models for estimating how long it takes for an error to show in an incorrectly synchronized bounded buffer program. An online simulator is available for experimentation.

Chapter 17

Project: The Not Too Parallel Virtual Machine

PVM (Parallel Virtual Machine) provides a high-level, but not transparent, system for a user to coordinate tasks spread across workstations on a network. This project describes a threaded implementation of the Not Too Parallel Virtual Machine (NTPVM) dispatcher, a simplified PVM system. The multithreaded implementation illustrates the interaction between threads and fork, providing a semirealistic application in which to explore complex thread interactions.

Objectives

- Learn about distributed processing
- Experiment with threads and I/O
- Explore the interaction of threads with `fork`
- Use threads to solve a real problem
- Understand the use of objects in thread design

17.1 PVM History, Terminology, and Architecture

Grace Murray Hopper, a vocal early advocate of parallel computing, was fond of reminding her audiences that the way to pull a heavier load was not to grow a bigger ox but to hitch more oxen to the load. Seymour Cray, a pioneer in computer architecture, is reported to have later countered, "If you were plowing a field, which would you rather use, two strong oxen or 1024 chickens?" The chickens versus oxen debate continues to rage. IBM's Blue Gene Project involves the building of a 64,000-processor machine with petaflop capabilities (a thousand trillion operations per second) based on relatively low-powered, embedded PowerPC chips [14]. On the other hand, the NEC Earth-Simulator, which was rated as the world's fastest computer in 2002, uses only 640 nodes. Each "NEC oxen node" consists of 8 tightly coupled vector processors [135].

Another important development in the parallel/distributed computing arena is the move to harness cheap workstations to solve large problems. Programming libraries, such as PVM (Parallel Virtual Machine) [118] and MPI (Message Passing Interface) [43], allow groups of heterogeneous, interconnected machines to provide a transparent parallel-computing environment by providing a cross-platform message-passing facility with higher-level services built on top. These systems allow users to solve large problems on networks of workstations by providing the illusion of a single parallel machine. PVM operates at the task level and presents a message-passing abstraction that hides the details of the network and individual machines that make up the *virtual machine*. PVM/MPI libraries have become the mainstay of distributed scientific computing because they allow researchers to develop platform-independent software. However, programs based on this paradigm are hard for nonexperts to debug and optimize.

A new notion of "computing as a utility" has recently emerged in the form of *grid computing* [38]. The Open Grid Services Architecture provides a higher-level layer of services built over message-passing libraries and native host runtime systems. These higher-level abstractions are quickly bringing distributed computing into the mainstream.

This chapter project develops a PVM-like library for managing tasks. We begin by introducing PVM terminology and providing an overview of the PVM architecture.

The basic unit of computation in PVM is called a *task* and is analogous to a UNIX process. A PVM program calls PVM library functions to create and coordinate tasks. The tasks can communicate by passing messages to other tasks through calls to PVM library functions. Tasks that cooperate, either through communication or synchronization, are organized into groups called *computations*. PVM supports direct communication, broadcast and barriers within a computation.

Figure 17.1 shows a logical view of a typical PVM system. A PVM application generally starts with an input and partitioning task that controls the problem solution. The user specifies in this task how other tasks cooperate to solve the problem. The input and partitioning task creates several computations. Tasks within each computation share data and

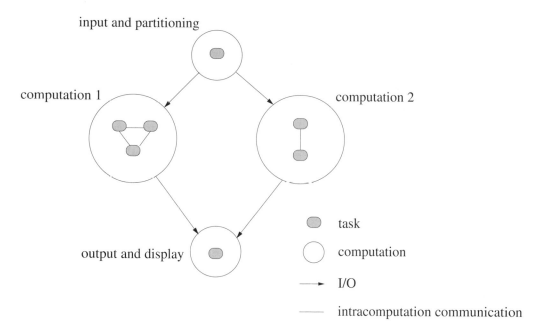

Figure 17.1: Logical view of an application running on a PVM virtual machine.

communicate with each other. The PVM application also has a dedicated task to handle output and user display. The other tasks in the PVM application forward their output to this task for display on the application's console.

To run a PVM application, a user first designates the pool of machines or *hosts* that make up the *virtual machine* and then starts the PVM control daemon, `pvmd`, on each of these hosts. The control daemon communicates with the user's console and handles communication and controls tasks on its machine. To send input to a particular task, PVM sends the data to the `pvmd` daemon on the destination host, which then forwards it to the appropriate task. Similarly, a task outputs by sending a message to its `pvmd`, which in turn forwards it to the console's `pvmd` and on to the application's output task. The underlying message passing is transparent, so the user sees only that a particular task has sent a message to the console.

Figure 17.2 shows how an application might be mapped onto the virtual machine. The tasks that make up a logical computation are not necessarily mapped to the same host but might be spread across all the hosts on the virtual machine. Host 1 of Figure 17.2 has three computations, one containing a single task, one with two tasks and one that is part of a computation that also has tasks on host 2.

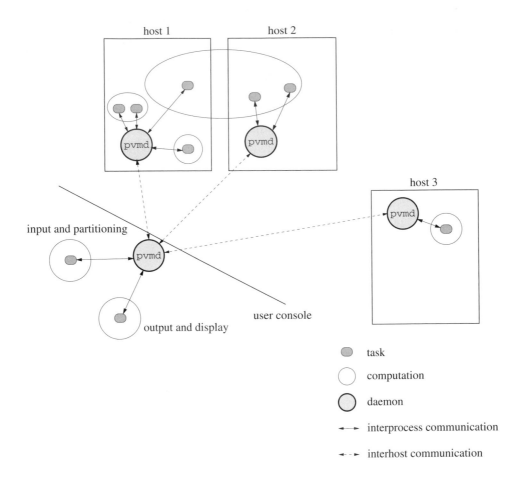

Figure 17.2: Schematic of a PVM.

17.2 The Not Too Parallel Virtual Machine

The Not Too Parallel Virtual Machine (NTPVM) is a dispatcher that shares many characteristics of a PVM control daemon, pvmd. The NTPVM dispatcher is responsible for creating and managing tasks on a single host, as shown schematically in Figure 17.3. The dispatcher receives requests through its standard input and responds through its standard output. (Later, standard input and standard output can be redirected to network communication ports.) The dispatcher might receive a request to create a task or to forward data to a task under its control.

A task is just a process that executes a specified program. Each task is identified by a computation ID and a task ID. When the dispatcher receives a request to create a task with a particular computation ID and task ID, it creates a pair of pipes and forks a child to execute the task. Figure 17.4 shows the communication layout between a task and its dispatcher. The pipe that carries communication from the dispatcher to the child task is labeled `writefd` on the dispatcher end. The child redirects its standard input to this pipe. Similarly, the pipe that carries communication from the child to the dispatcher is labeled `readfd` on the dispatcher end. The child redirects its standard output to this pipe.

The dispatcher supports delivery of input data to the tasks, delivery of output from the tasks and broadcast of data to tasks that have the same computation ID. The dispatcher also supports numbered barriers and cancellation for tasks with the same computation ID. NTPVM is simpler than the real PVM in several respects. PVM has in-order message delivery and allows any task to communicate with other tasks in its computation. It has a buffering mechanism for holding messages. PVM also provides sophisticated computation monitoring tools. NTPVM delivers messages whenever it gets them, does not support point-to-point task communication, and has primitive monitoring capabilities.

17.3 NTPVM Project Overview

The tasks in NTPVM are independent processes grouped into units called computations. The dispatcher is responsible for creating and managing tasks. In general, the tasks of a computation do not have to reside on the same machine, and the specification of the project is designed with this extension in mind. However, a single dispatcher controls all the computations for the project described in this chapter.

The dispatcher communicates with the outside world by reading packets from its standard input and writing packets to its standard output. The dispatcher might receive a packet requesting that it create a new task, or it might receive a data packet intended for a task under its control. The dispatcher forwards output generated by the tasks under its control to its own standard output in the form of packets. For the first four parts of the project, the tasks send ASCII data and the dispatcher wraps the data in a packet. Later, the tasks generate the packets themselves.

Program 17.1 shows the `ntpvm.h` header file that contains the relevant type definitions for the dispatcher. Include this file in all the programs in this project.

The dispatcher packets include a computation ID, a task ID, a packet type, a packet length and the packet information. The first four items make up a fixed-length *packet header* that is stored in a structure of type `taskpacket_t`. Assume that the information portion of the packet contains no more than `MAX_PACK_SIZE` bytes.

The dispatcher keeps information about each active task in a global `tasks` array of type `ntpvm_task_t`, which should be implemented as an object with appropriate functions for accessing and modifying it. When the description refers to "modifying" or "accessing" information in the `tasks` object, it means calling a public function in the file to

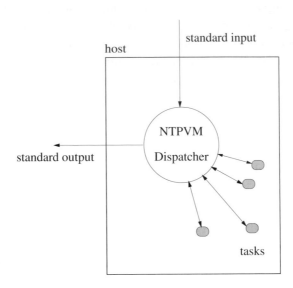

Figure 17.3: Schematic of the NTPVM dispatcher.

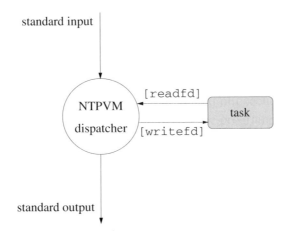

Figure 17.4: NTPVM dispatcher communicates with its children through pipes.

perform the action. Do not allow the dispatcher to execute more than MAX_TASKS simultaneous tasks. Initially, set the compid member of each element of the tasks array to −1 to indicate that the slot is empty.

Program 17.1 ———————————————————————————— **ntpvm.h**

The ntpvm.h *header file.*

```
#include <pthread.h>
#include <sys/types.h>
#define MAX_PACK_SIZE 1024
#define MAX_TASKS 10
#define NUMTYPES 6

typedef enum ptype {NEWTASK, DATA, BROADCAST, DONE,
                    TERMINATE, BARRIER} packet_t;

typedef struct {
    int compid;
    int taskid;
    packet_t type;
    int length;
} taskpacket_t;

typedef struct {
    int compid;                          /* computation ID for task */
    int taskid;                             /* task ID for the task */
    int writefd;                       /* holds dispatcher->child fd */
    int readfd;                        /* holds child->dispatcher fd */
    int recvbytes;
    int recvpacksets;
    int sentbytes;
    int sentpackets;
    pid_t taskpid;                 /* process ID of the forked task */
    pthread_t tasktid;          /* thread ID of task output thread */
    int barrier;         /* -1 if not at barrier, else barrier number */
    pthread_mutex_t mlock;            /* mutex lock for element */
    int endinput;                 /* true if no more input for task */
} ntpvm_task_t;
```

Program 17.1 ———————————————————————————— **ntpvm.h**

There are six types of dispatcher packets in all: NEWTASK, DATA, BROADCAST, DONE, TERMINATE and BARRIER. A packet consists of a header structure of type taskpacket_t followed by a data field that is an array whose size is specified by the length field of the header. The maximum value of length is MAX_PACK_SIZE. The dispatcher interprets the packet types as follows.

1. When the dispatcher receives a NEWTASK packet on standard input, it initiates a new task. The information portion of this packet gives the command line to be executed by the forked child task. The dispatcher creates two pipes and forks a child that calls execvp for the specified command.

2. The dispatcher treats the DATA packets that it receives on standard input as input data for the task identified by the computation ID and task ID members of the packet header. For the first four parts of the project, the dispatcher strips off the packet header and writes the actual packet data to writefd of the appropriate task.

3. When a task writes data to its standard output, the dispatcher forwards the data to standard output. The first four parts of this project run standard UNIX utilities as the tasks. Since these commands produce just ASCII text as output, the dispatcher packages the data into DATA packets before sending to standard output. Starting with part five, the tasks send DATA packets.

4. When the dispatcher receives a DONE packet on standard input, it closes the writefd file descriptor for the task identified by the computation ID and task ID members of the packet header. The corresponding task then detects end-of-file on its standard input.

5. When the dispatcher detects end-of-file on the readfd descriptor of a task, it performs the appropriate cleanup and sends a DONE packet on standard output to signify that the task has completed.

6. The dispatcher forwards any BROADCAST packets from standard input to all tasks in the specified computation.

7. If a task sends a BROADCAST packet to the dispatcher, the dispatcher forwards the request to all tasks in the same computation and also forwards the request on its standard output. In this way, all the tasks within a computation receive the message.

8. If the dispatcher receives a TERMINATE packet on its standard input, it kills the task identified by the packet's computation ID and task ID. If task ID is −1, the dispatcher kills all tasks in the specified computation. The dispatcher handles a TERMINATE packet received from readfd in a similar way. However, if no task ID matches the packet or if task ID is −1, the dispatcher also writes the TERMINATE packet to standard output.

9. The BARRIER packets synchronize tasks of a computation at a particular point in their execution.

The NTPVM project has the following parts:

Part I: Setup of I/O and testing [Section 17.4].

Part II: Single task with no input (handle NEWTASK and outgoing data) [Section 17.5].

Part III: One task at a time (handle NEWTASK, DATA and DONE packets) [Section 17.6].

Part IV: Multiple tasks and computations (handle NEWTASK, DATA and DONE packets) [Section 17.7].

Part V: Task synchronization (handle BROADCAST and BARRIER packets) [Section 17.8].

Part VI: Cleanup (handle TERMINATION packets and signals) [Section 17.9].

Part VII: Ordered message delivery [Section 17.10].

In the first four parts of the project, the child tasks do not communicate by using packets, and the dispatcher strips off the packet headers before writing to writefd. This format allows the dispatcher to run ordinary UNIX utilities such as cat or ls as tasks. In Part V, the tasks communicate with the dispatcher by using packets. At that point, the project requires specific task programs for NTPVM testing. The remainder of this section gives examples of different types of packets and methods the dispatcher uses to handle them.

17.3.1 NEWTASK packets

The dispatcher waits for a NEWTASK packet from standard input. Such a packet includes a computation ID, a task ID and a command-line string.

■ **Example 17.1**

The following NEWTASK packet requests that task 2 in computation 3 be created to execute ls -l.

Computation ID:	3
Task ID:	2
Packet Type:	NEWTASK
Packet Data Length:	5
Packet Information:	ls -l

The data in the packet of Example 17.1 is not null-terminated. The dispatcher must convert the data to such a string before handing it to makeargv or execvp.

The dispatcher asks the tasks array to find a free entry and to store the information about the new task. The dispatcher discards the packet and reports an error if it detects that a task with the same computation and task IDs is already in the tasks array. The new entry has sentpackets, sentbytes, recvpackets, recvbytes and endinput members of the tasks array entry set to 0 and the barrier member set to −1 to signify that the task is not waiting at a barrier.

The dispatcher then creates two pipes and uses two of the four resulting pipe file descriptors for communication with the child task. These descriptors are stored in the readfd and writefd members of the tasks array entry. The dispatcher forks a child and stores the child process ID in the taskpid member of the tasks entry. The dispatcher closes unused pipe file descriptors and then waits for I/O either from its standard input or from the readfd descriptors of its tasks.

The child task forked by the dispatcher redirects its standard input and output to the pipes and closes the unused file descriptors. The child then calls execvp to execute the command string. Use the makeargv function of Program 2.2 on page 37 to create an argument array for input to execvp.

17.3.2 DATA packets

When the dispatcher reads a DATA packet from standard input, it asks the tasks object to determine whether the packet's task ID and computation ID match those of any entry in the tasks array. The dispatcher discards the packet if no entry matches. Otherwise, the dispatcher updates the recvpackets and recvbytes members of the task's entry in the tasks array.

For the first four parts of the project, the tasks are standard UNIX utilities that accept ASCII input. The dispatcher forwards the information portion of the packet to the task on the task's writefd descriptor. In Parts V, VI and VII the tasks receive the full data packets directly.

■ **Example 17.2**

After receiving the following DATA packet, the dispatcher sends the words This is my data to task 2 in computation 3.

Computation ID:	3
Task ID:	2
Packet Type:	DATA
Packet Data Length:	15
Packet Data:	This is my data

The dispatcher also forwards data received from individual tasks to its standard output in the form of DATA packets. For the first four parts of the project, the dispatcher interprets input from readfd as raw output from the task. It creates a DATA packet with the task's computation ID and task ID and uses the information read from readfd as the information portion of the packet. The dispatcher then writes the DATA packet to its standard output. Starting with Section 17.8, each task reads and writes its data in packet format. In these sections, the dispatcher copies the DATA packets to its standard output.

17.3.3 DONE packets

When the dispatcher receives a DONE packet on standard input, it sets the corresponding task's endinput member in the tasks array and closes the writefd descriptor for the task. The dispatcher discards any subsequent DONE or DATA packets that arrive for the task.

■ **Example 17.3**

The following DONE packet specifies that there is no more input data for task 2 in computation 3.

Computation ID:	3
Task ID:	2
Packet Type:	DONE
Packet Data Length:	0
Packet Data:	

When the dispatcher receives an end-of-file indication on a readfd descriptor, it closes that descriptor and forwards a DONE packet on its standard output. If the writefd descriptor for the task is still open, the dispatcher closes it. The dispatcher must eventually call wait on the child task process and set the compid member of the tasks array entry to −1 so that the array entry can be reused.

If the dispatcher receives an end-of-file indication on its own standard input, it closes the writefd descriptors of all active tasks and sets the endinput member of the tasks array entry for each active task to 1. When it has received an end-of-file indication on the readfd descriptors for all active tasks, the dispatcher waits for each task and exits. The dispatcher should also periodically wait for all its completed children.

17.4 I/O and Testing of Dispatcher

This section develops dispatcher I/O functions and debugging layout. The dispatcher receives input data from standard input by calling getpacket and sends output data on standard output by calling putpacket, as shown in Figure 17.5. The data is always transferred in two parts. First, the dispatcher reads or writes a header of type taskpacket_t. Second, it uses the length member in the header to determine how many bytes of packet data to read or to write. Finally, it reads or writes the data portion of the packet. Assume that the packet data field contains no more than MAX_PACK_SIZE bytes so that the dispatcher can use a fixed-length buffer of MAX_PACK_SIZE bytes to hold the packet data during input and output.

The getpacket function has the following prototype.

```
int getpacket(int fd, int *compidp, int *taskidp,
              packet_t *typep, int *lenp, unsigned char *buf);
```

The getpacket function reads a taskpacket_t header from fd and then reads into buf the number of bytes specified by the length member. If successful, getpacket returns 0. If unsuccessful, getpacket returns −1 and sets errno. The getpacket function sets *compidp, *taskidp, *typep and *lenp from the compid, taskid, type and length members of the packet header, respectively. If getpacket receives an end-of-file while

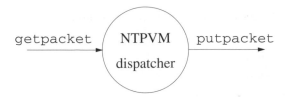

Figure 17.5: Basic dispatcher I/O.

trying to read a packet, it returns −1 and sets errno. Since errno will not automatically be set, you must pick an appropriate value. There is no standard error number to represent end-of-file. One possibility is to use EINVAL.

The putpacket function has the following prototype.

```
int putpacket(int fd, int compid, int taskid,
              packet_t type, int len, unsigned char *buf);
```

The putpacket function assembles a taskpacket_t header from compid, taskid, type and len. It then writes the packet header to fd followed by len bytes from buf. If successful, putpacket returns 0. If unsuccessful, putpacket returns −1 and sets errno.

■ **Example 17.4**

The following program uses getpacket and putpacket to copy packets from standard input to standard output.

```
#include <unistd.h>
#include "ntpvm.h"

int getpacket(int, int *, int *, packet_t *, int *, unsigned char *);
int putpacket(int, int, int, packet_t, int, unsigned char *);

int main(void) {
   unsigned char buf[MAX_PACK_SIZE];
   int compid;
   int taskid;
   int tdatalen;
   int tin, tout;
   packet_t type;

   tin = STDIN_FILENO;
   tout = STDOUT_FILENO;
   while (getpacket(tin, &compid, &taskid, &type, &tdatalen, buf) != -1) {
      if (putpacket(tout, compid, taskid, type, tdatalen, buf) == -1)
         break;
   }
   return 0;
}
```
—————————————————————————————————— **testpacket.c**

The specification for Part I of the project is as follows.

1. Write the `getpacket` and `putpacket` functions.
2. Compile and run `lint` on the program to make sure that there are no syntax errors.
3. Test the program, using one of the methods described below.
4. Add debugging messages to the loop of the `main` program to show what values are being read and written. All debugging messages should go to standard error.

The hardest part of the NTPVM project is the testing of the dispatcher. The dispatcher communicates with standard input and standard output, using packets that have non-ASCII components. During debugging, the dispatcher should produce messages on standard error reporting its progress. A small amount of work is needed to isolate the dispatcher output and input from the informative messages by directing the three types of I/O to appear in ASCII format on different screens.

Program 17.2 shows the `a2ts` filter that reads ASCII characters from standard input, constructs a task packet, and writes it to standard output. The `a2ts` program writes all prompt messages to standard error, so it can be run either with interactive prompts or with standard input redirected from a file. For interactive use, `a2ts` prompts for the required information, sending the prompts to standard error.

Program 17.2 ———————————————————— **a2ts.c**

The filter a2ts *prompts for information and writes a task packet to standard output. Some error checking is omitted.*

```
#include <string.h>
#include <stdio.h>
#include <stdlib.h>
#include <unistd.h>
#include "restart.h"
#include "ntpvm.h"
#define MAX_LINE_SIZE 100
#define TERMINATE_STRING "!!!!!\n"

static char *typename[] = {"Start Task", "Data", "Broadcast", "Done",
                           "Terminate", "Barrier"};

int main(void)  {
   char buf[MAX_PACK_SIZE + MAX_LINE_SIZE];
   char *bufptr;
   int i;
   int linelen;
   taskpacket_t pack;
   int tasktype;
   int wsize;

   wsize = sizeof(taskpacket_t);
   fprintf(stderr, "Ready for first packet\n");
   for( ; ; ) {                             /* loop with menu for interactive input */
      fprintf(stderr, "Enter compid:");
```

```
        if (scanf("%d", &pack.compid) == EOF)
           break;
        fprintf(stderr, "Enter taskid:");
        scanf("%d", &pack.taskid);
        fprintf(stderr, "Enter task type:\n");
        for (i=0; i< NUMTYPES; i++)
           fprintf(stderr, "    %d = %s\n", i, typename[i]);
        scanf("%d", &tasktype);
        pack.type = tasktype;
        pack.length = 0;
        bufptr = buf;
        *bufptr = 0;
        fprintf(stderr, "Enter first line of data (%.*s to end):\n",
           strlen(TERMINATE_STRING) - 1, TERMINATE_STRING);

        while ((linelen = readline(STDIN_FILENO, bufptr, MAX_LINE_SIZE)) != -1) {
           if (linelen == 0)
              break;
           if (strcmp(TERMINATE_STRING, bufptr) == 0)
              break;
           bufptr = bufptr + linelen;
           pack.length = pack.length + linelen;
           if (pack.length >= MAX_PACK_SIZE) {
              fprintf(stderr, "**** Maximum packet size exceeded\n");
              return 1;
           }
           fprintf(stderr, "Received %d, total=%d, Enter line (%.*s to end):\n",
               linelen, pack.length, strlen(TERMINATE_STRING) - 1,
               TERMINATE_STRING);
        }
        fprintf(stderr, "Writing packet header: %d %d %d %d\n",
            pack.compid, pack.taskid, (int)pack.type, pack.length);
        if (write(STDOUT_FILENO, &pack, wsize) != wsize) {
           fprintf(stderr, "Error writing packet\n");
           return 1;
        }
        fprintf(stderr, "Writing %d bytes\n", pack.length);
        if (write(STDOUT_FILENO, buf, pack.length) != pack.length) {
           fprintf(stderr,"Error writing packet\n");
           return 1;
        }
        fprintf(stderr, "Ready for next packet\n");
     }
     fprintf(stderr, "a2ts exiting normally\n");
     return 0;
  }
```

Program 17.2 ———————————————————————— **a2ts.c**

The `ts2a` filter of Program 17.3 reads a task packet from standard input and writes the contents of the packet to standard output in ASCII format. For this project, assume that the data portion of a task packet always contains ASCII information.

☐ Exercise 17.5

The `ts2a` program assumes that header and data will each be read with a single call to `read`. How would you make this more robust?

Answer:

Use the `readblock` function from the restart library described in Appendix B.

Program 17.3 ———————————————————————— `ts2a.c`

The ts2a *filter reads a packet from standard input and writes the header and data to standard output in ASCII format. Some error checking is omitted.*

```c
#include <stdio.h>
#include <stdlib.h>
#include <unistd.h>
#include "ntpvm.h"
#define MAX_LINE_SIZE 100

static char *typename[] = {"Start Task", "Data", "Broadcast", "Done",
                           "Terminate", "Barrier"};

int main(void) {
   char buf[MAX_PACK_SIZE + MAX_LINE_SIZE];
   int bytesread;
   taskpacket_t pack;
   int wsize;

   wsize = sizeof(taskpacket_t);
   fprintf(stderr, "***** Waiting for first packet\n");
   for( ; ; ) {
      bytesread = read(STDIN_FILENO, &pack, wsize);
      if (bytesread == 0) {
         fprintf(stderr, "End-of-file received\n");
         break;
      }
      if (bytesread != wsize) {
         fprintf(stderr, "Error reading packet header\n");
         return 1;
      }
      if ( (pack.type < 0) || (pack.type >= NUMTYPES) ) {
         fprintf(stderr, "Got invalid packet\n");
         return 1;
      }
      printf("Received packet header of type %s\n",typename[pack.type]);
      printf("   compid = %d, taskid = %d, length = %d\n",
             pack.compid, pack.taskid, pack.length);
      fflush(stdout);
      if (pack.length > MAX_PACK_SIZE) {
         fprintf(stderr, "Task data is too long\n");
         return 1;
      }
      if (read(STDIN_FILENO, buf, pack.length) != pack.length) {
         fprintf(stderr, "Error reading packet data\n");
         return 1;
      }
      write(STDOUT_FILENO, buf, pack.length);
      fprintf(stderr, "***** Waiting for next packet\n");
   }
   return 0;
}
```

Program 17.3 ———————————————————————— `ts2a.c`

■ **Example 17.6**

The following command prompts for the fields of a packet. It then echoes the packet to standard output in ASCII format.

```
a2ts | ts2a
```

The `a2ts` program of Example 17.6 interactively prompts for packet information and writes the information as a binary packet to its standard output. The standard output of `a2ts` is piped into standard input of `ts2a`. The `ts2a` program reads binary packets from its standard input and outputs them in ASCII format to its standard output. Input entered to `a2ts` will be interleaved with output from `ts2a`, but this should not be a problem since `ts2a` will not produce any output until `a2ts` has received an entire packet.

■ **Example 17.7**

The following command shows a possible method of testing the dispatcher inter-actively. For now, use the `testpacket` program of Example 17.4 instead of the dispatcher.

```
a2ts | dispatcher | ts2a
```

Example 17.7 pipes standard output of `a2ts` into standard input of the dispatcher and standard output of the dispatcher into `ts2a`. The command line of Example 17.7 allows a user to enter ASCII data and to display the task packet output in ASCII. Unfortunately, real tests produce too much data from different sources, making it difficult to distinguish information from different programs. Input to `a2ts` and output from `ts2a` will be inter-leaved with error messages sent to standard error. The next two subsections propose two different methods for handling this problem.

17.4.1 Testing with multiple windows

The first strategy for improving the usability of `a2ts` and `ts2a` in testing the dispatcher is to use separate windows, as shown in Figure 17.6. The dispatcher, which runs in the *dispatcher window*, redirects its standard input to the named pipe `inpipe` and its standard output to the named pipe `outpipe`. The output from the dispatcher's standard error still appears in the dispatcher window. The `a2ts` program reads from standard input in the *input window* and writes to its standard output, which is redirected to the named pipe `inpipe`. Enter packets in ASCII format in this window. The `ts2a` program redirects its standard input to the named pipe `outpipe`. As the dispatcher runs, `ts2a` displays dispatcher output in the output window.

Figure 17.6 shows the setup for the three windows. Be sure to use the same working directory for all three windows. The procedure for running the dispatcher is as follows.

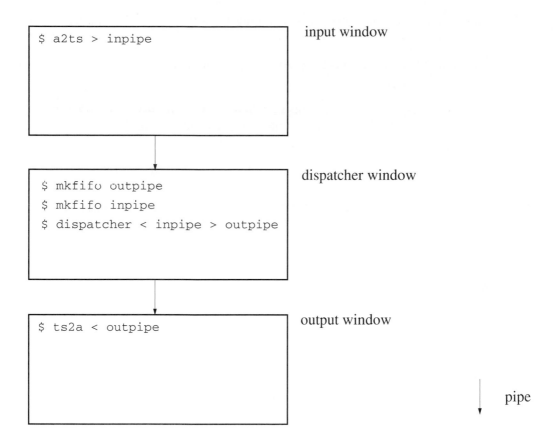

Figure 17.6: Use three windows to debug the NTPVM dispatcher.

1. Create two named pipes in the dispatcher window by executing the following commands.

   ```
   mkfifo outpipe
   mkfifo inpipe
   ```

2. Start the dispatcher in the dispatcher window by executing the following command.

   ```
   dispatcher < inpipe > outpipe
   ```

   This window displays only the messages that the dispatcher sends to standard error, since both standard input and standard output are redirected.

3. In the output window, execute the following command.

   ```
   ts2a < outpipe
   ```

This window displays the packets coming from the standard output of the dispatcher.

4. In the input window, execute the following command.

```
a2ts > inpipe
```

This window displays the prompts for the user to enter packets. The `a2ts` program converts the entered information from ASCII to packet format and writes it to the standard input of the dispatcher.

Figure 17.7 shows the layout of the windows for the debugging. If you do not have a workstation that supports multiple windows, try to persuade your system administrator to install a program such as `screen`, which supports multiple screens on an ASCII terminal.

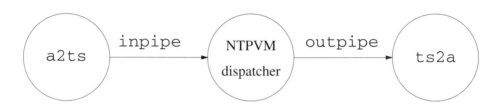

Figure 17.7: Logical process layout for debugging the dispatcher.

17.4.2 Testing with remote logging

The second strategy for testing the dispatcher uses the remote logging facility discussed in Section 10.3.4 and in Appendix D. Replace the `ts2a` program with the `ts2log` program of Program 17.4. The `ts2log` program uses the `r_readblock` function of the restart library described in Appendix B.

■ **Example 17.8**

The following command shows how to test the dispatcher by using remote logging.

```
a2ts | dispatcher | ts2log
```

The dispatcher should also log events. It could send the packets to standard output and have the `ts2log` program receive them through redirection. Alternatively, the dispatcher could log them directly.

Program 17.4 ———————————————————————— **ts2log.c**

A program that logs packets using the remote logging utilities. Some error checking is omitted.

```
#include <stdio.h>
#include <stdlib.h>
#include <unistd.h>
#include "ntpvm.h"
#include "restart.h"
#include "rlogging.h"
#define MAX_LINE_SIZE 100

static char *typename[] = {"Start Task", "Data", "Broadcast", "Done",
                           "Terminate", "Barrier"};

int main(void) {
   char buf[MAX_PACK_SIZE + MAX_LINE_SIZE];
   int bytesread;
   LFILE *lf;
   taskpacket_t pack;
   int wsize;

   wsize = sizeof(taskpacket_t);
   lf = lopen(NULL,0);
   if (lf == NULL)
      fprintf(stderr, "Failed to open remote logger.\n");
   for( ; ; ) {
      bytesread =  readblock(STDIN_FILENO, &pack, wsize);
      if (bytesread == 0) {
         lprintf(lf, "End-of-file received\n");
         break;
      }
      if (bytesread != wsize) {
         lprintf(lf, "Error reading packet header\n");
         return 1;
      }
      if ( (pack.type < 0) || (pack.type >= NUMTYPES) ) {
         fprintf(stderr, "Got invalid packet\n");
         return 1;
      }
      lprintf(lf, "%s %s\n   compid = %d\n   taskid = %d\n   length = %d\n",
             "Received packet header of type",
             typename[pack.type], pack.compid, pack.taskid, pack.length);
      if (pack.length > MAX_PACK_SIZE) {
         lprintf(lf, "Task data is too long\n");
         return 1;
      }
      if (readblock(STDIN_FILENO, buf, pack.length) != pack.length) {
         lprintf(lf, "Error reading packet data\n");
         return 1;
      }
      lprintf(lf, buf, pack.length);
   }
   return 0;
}
```

Program 17.4 ———————————————————————— **ts2log.c**

17.5 Single Task with No Input

This part of the project uses a single task that has no input to allow testing of the code to create the task and the pipes for communication without the added complication of monitoring multiple file descriptors for input. The task outputs ASCII text rather than packets.

The dispatcher reads a single NEWTASK packet from standard input, creates the appropriate pipes, and forks the child that executes the task. The dispatcher then monitors the readfd pipe file descriptor for output from the task and forwards what it reads as DATA packets on standard output. When the dispatcher encounters an end-of-file on readfd, it waits for the child task to exit and then exits.

Implement the NTPVM dispatcher as described above. The dispatcher does the following.

1. Read a packet from standard input, using getpacket. If the packet is not a NEWTASK packet, then exit after outputting an error message.

2. Create a pipe for communication with a child task.

3. Fork a child to execute the command given in the NEWTASK packet of step 1. The child should redirect standard input and output to the pipe and close all pipe file descriptors before executing the command. Use the makeargv function of Program 2.2 on page 37 to construct the argument array in the child. If an error occurs, the child just exits after printing an informative message.

4. Have the parent close all unneeded pipe descriptors so that the parent can detect end-of-file on readfd.

5. Wait for output from the child on readfd. For this part of the assignment, the child will be executing standard UNIX commands. Assume that the child outputs only text. The dispatcher reads the child task's output from readfd, wraps this output in a DATA packet, and sends the packet to standard output by calling putpacket.

6. If getpacket returns an error, assume that this is an end-of-file. Close the readfd and writefd descriptors for the task. Send a DONE packet to standard output identifying the task and exit.

The dispatcher should liberally use standard error or the remote logging facility to display informative messages about what it is doing. For example, when it receives something from readfd, the dispatcher should display information about the source task, the number of bytes read and the message read. It is worthwhile to invest time in designing a readable layout for the informative messages so that all the relevant information is available at a glance.

Test the program by using ls -l as the command to be executed.

17.6 Sequential Tasks

This section describes the behavior of the dispatcher when the child task has both input and output. Although the dispatcher handles only one task at a time, it must monitor two input file descriptors. Complete Section 17.5 before starting this part.

The dispatcher keeps information about the child task in the `tasks` array. For simplicity, the discussion refers to members of the `ntpvm_task_t` array such as `readfd` without their qualifying structure. Implement the `tasks` array as an object with appropriate access functions. The `tasks` array and its access functions should be in a file separate from the dispatcher `main` program. The array and its access functions are referred to as the `tasks` object, and an individual element of the `tasks` array is referred to as an entry of the `tasks` object. For this part, we only allow one task at a time, so the `tasks` object does not need an array of tasks.

Figure 17.8 suggests the structure of threaded NTPVM dispatcher. An *input thread* monitors standard input and processes the incoming packets. An *output thread* monitors the `readfd` descriptor for input from the child task and writes this information to standard output.

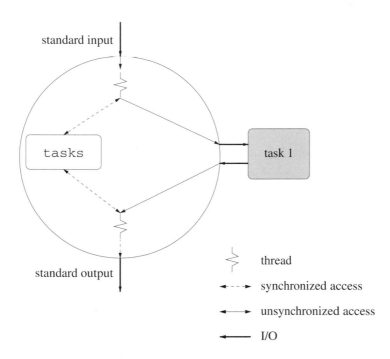

Figure 17.8: Schematic of a threaded NTPVM dispatcher for a single task.

The input and output threads share the `tasks` object and must synchronize their access to this structure. One possible approach for synchronizing threads is to use a mutex lock to protect the entire `tasks` object. This choice cuts down on the potential parallelism because only one thread at a time can access the `tasks` object. Since mutex locks are low cost, we use a mutex lock for each element of the `tasks` array.

17.6.1 The input thread

The input thread monitors standard input and takes action according to the input it receives. Write an `input` function that executes the following steps in a loop until it encounters an end-of-file on standard input.
1. Read a packet from standard input by using `getpacket`.
2. Process the packet.

After falling through the loop, close `writefd` and call `pthread_exit`.

Processing a packet depends on the packet type.

NEWTASK
1. If a child task is already executing, discard the packet and output an error message.
2. Otherwise, if no child task exists, create two pipes to handle the task's input and output.
3. Update the `tasks` object, and fork a child. The child should redirect its standard input and output to the pipes and use the `makeargv` function of Program 2.2 to construct the argument array before calling `execvp` to execute the command given in the packet.
4. Create a detached `output` thread by calling `pthread_create`. Pass a key for the `tasks` entry of this task as an argument to the `output` thread. The key is just the index of the appropriate `tasks` array entry.

DATA
1. If the packet's communication and task IDs don't match those of the executing task or if the task's `endinput` is true, output an error message and discard the packet.
2. Otherwise, copy the data portion to `writefd`.
3. Update the `recvpackets` and `recvbytes` members of the appropriate task entry of the `tasks` object.

DONE
1. If the packet's computation and task IDs do not match those of the executing task, output an error message and discard the packet.
2. Otherwise, close the `writefd` descriptor if it is still open.
3. Set the `endinput` member for this task entry.

BROADCAST, BARRIER or TERMINATE
1. Output an error message.
2. Discard the packet.

□ **Exercise 17.9**

When a process that contains multiple threads creates a child by calling fork, how many threads exist in the child?
Answer:
Although fork creates a copy of the process, the child does not inherit the threads of the parent. POSIX specifies that the child has only one thread of execution—the thread that called fork.

17.6.2 The output thread

The output thread handles input from the readfd descriptor of a particular task. The output thread receives a tasks object key to the task it monitors as a parameter. Write an output function that executes the following steps in a loop until it encounters an end-of-file on readfd.
1. Read data from readfd.
2. Call putpacket to construct a DATA packet and send it to standard output.
3. Update the sentpackets and sentbytes members of the appropriate task entry in the tasks object.

After falling through the loop because of an end-of-file or an error on readfd, the output thread does the following.
1. Close the readfd and writefd descriptors for the task.
2. Execute wait for the child task.
3. Send a DONE packet with the appropriate computation and task IDs to standard output.
4. Output information about the finished task to standard error or to the remote logger. Include the computation ID, the task ID, the total bytes sent by the task, the total packets sent by the task, the total bytes received by the task and the total packets received by the task.
5. Deactivate the task entry by setting the computation ID to −1.
6. Call pthread_exit.

Test the program by starting tasks to execute various cat and ls -l commands. Try other filters such as sort to test the command-line parsing. For this part you should not enter a new command until the previous command has completed.

17.7 Concurrent Tasks

Modify the program to allow multiple computations and tasks. Use a MAX_TASKS value of 10 for this part. A new NEWTASK packet may come in before the data from previous tasks has been completely transmitted.

When a new NEWTASK packet comes in, find an available slot in the tasks object, create a new set of pipes, and fork a new child to execute the command. Don't enter any duplicates in the tasks array.

Figure 17.9 shows a schematic of a threaded NTPVM dispatcher that supports multiple simultaneous tasks. When another request comes in, the input thread creates a new output thread. Since multiple output threads write to standard output, define an additional mutex lock to synchronize output on the dispatcher's standard output.

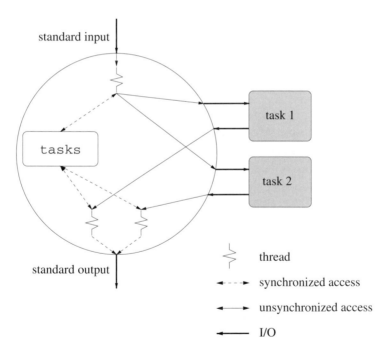

Figure 17.9: Schematic of a threaded NTPVM dispatcher.

17.8 Packet Communication, Broadcast and Barriers

Once the dispatcher handles multiple simultaneous tasks, implement the handling of the BROADCAST and BARRIER packets. The child tasks now have to communicate with the dispatcher in packet format so that the dispatcher and its tasks can distinguish control information (broadcast or barrier) from data information.

When the dispatcher receives a BROADCAST request from standard input, it forwards the packet on the writefd descriptors for each task whose computation ID matches that of the BROADCAST packet. If the dispatcher receives a BROADCAST request from one of the readfd descriptors, it forwards the packet on the writefd descriptors for each task whose computation ID matches that in the BROADCAST packet. Since, in a future extension, tasks from the computation may reside on other hosts, the dispatcher also forwards the packet on its standard output.

When the dispatcher receives a BARRIER packet from a task, it sets the barrier member for that task to the barrier number specified by the packet data. When all the tasks in a computation have reported that they are waiting for the barrier, the dispatcher sends a BARRIER message on standard output.

When the dispatcher reads a BARRIER packet for that barrier number from standard input, it resets the barrier member to −1 and sends a SIGUSR1 signal to all the tasks in the computation. The BARRIER packet from standard input signifies that all tasks in the computation are waiting at the designated barrier and that they can be released. Assume that the dispatcher never receives a second BARRIER packet from standard input before it has forwarded a corresponding BARRIER packet on standard output.

Implement the barrier on the task side by blocking the SIGUSR1 signal, writing a BARRIER packet to standard output, and then executing sigsuspend in a loop until the SIGUSR1 signal arrives. Example 8.26 shows how this is done.

Write a dummy task program to generate appropriate broadcast and barrier messages.

❑ Exercise 17.10

What complications do BROADCAST packets present from a synchronization point of view?

Answer:

Since BROADCAST packets may have to be forwarded to other tasks, the input and output threads now share the writefd descriptor associated with those tasks.

17.9 Termination and Signals

Implement signal handling so that the dispatcher shuts down gracefully when it receives Ctrl-C. Also add code to handle TERMINATE packets.

17.10 Ordered Message Delivery

Add a sequence number to the packet format and implement in-order delivery of packets from each source-destination pair.

17.11 Additional Reading

The PVM system was developed by Oak Ridge National Laboratory and Emory University. The paper "PVM: A framework for parallel distributed computing" by V. S. Sunderam [118] provides an overview of the development and implementation of the PVM system. Other articles of interest include "Visualization and debugging in a heterogeneous environment" by Beguelin et al. [10] and "Experiences with network-based concurrent computing on the PVM system" by Geist and Sunderam [41]. The PVM distribution is available electronically from `www.csm.ornl.gov/pvm`.

Part IV

Communication

Chapter 18

Connection-Oriented Communication

Most local-area networks have file servers that manage common disk space, making it easier to share files and perform backups for user clients. Standard UNIX network services such as mail and file transfer also use the client-server paradigm. This chapter discusses several common client-server models for providing services over existing network infrastructure. The models are implemented with the Universal Internet Communication Interface (UICI), a simplified API for connection-oriented communication that is freely available from the book web site. The UICI interface is then implemented in terms of stream sockets and TCP.

Objectives
- Learn about connection-oriented communication
- Experiment with sockets and TCP
- Explore different server designs
- Use the client-server model in applications
- Understand thread-safe communication

18.1 The Client-Server Model

Many network applications and services such as web browsing, mail, file transfer (`ftp`), authentication (Kerberos), remote login (`telnet`) and access to remote file systems (NFS) use the client-server paradigm. In each of these applications, a client sends a request for service to a server. A service is an action, such as changing the status of a remote file, that the server performs on behalf of the client. Often the service includes a response or returns information, for example by retrieving a remote file or web page.

The client-server model appears at many levels in computer systems. For example, an object that calls a method of another object in an object-oriented program is said to be a *client of the object*. At the system level, daemons that manage resources such as printers are servers for system user clients. On the Internet, browsers are client processes that request resources from web servers. The key elements of the client-server model are as follows.

- The client, not the service provider, initiates the action.
- The server waits passively for requests from clients.
- The client and server are connected by a communication channel that they access through communication endpoints.

Servers should robustly handle multiple simultaneous client requests in the face of unexpected client behavior. This chapter especially emphasizes the importance of catching errors and taking appropriate action during client-server interactions. You wouldn't want a web server to exit when a user mistypes a URL in the browser. Servers are long-running and must release *all* the resources allocated for individual client requests.

Although most current computer system services are based on the client-server model, other models such as event notification [4, 36] or peer-to-peer computing [90] may become more important in the future.

18.2 Communication Channels

A *communication channel* is a logical pathway for information that is accessed by participants through communication endpoints. The characteristics of the channel constrain the types of interaction allowed between sender and receiver. Channels can be shared or private, one-way or two-way. Two-way channels can be symmetric or asymmetric. Channels are distinguished from the underlying physical conduit, which may support many types of channels.

In object-orient programming, clients communicate with an object by calling a method. In this context, client and server share an address space, and the communication channel is the activation record that is created on the process stack for the call. The request consists of the parameter values that are pushed on the stack as part of the call, and the optional reply is the method's return value. Thus, the activation record is a private, asymmetric two-way communication channel. The method call mechanism of the object-oriented programming language establishes the communication endpoints. The system infrastructure for managing the process stack furnishes the underlying conduit for communication.

Many system services in UNIX are provided by server processes running on the same machine as their clients. These processes can share memory or a file system, and clients make requests by writing to such a shared resource.

Programs 6.7 and 6.8 of Chapter 6 use a named pipe as a communication channel for client requests. The named pipe is used as a shared one-way communication channel that can handle requests from any number of clients. Named pipes have an associated pathname, and the system creates an entry in the file system directory corresponding to this pathname when mkfifo executes. The file system provides the underlying conduit. A process creates communication endpoints by calling open and accesses these endpoints through file descriptors. Figure 18.1 shows a schematic of the communication supported in this example.

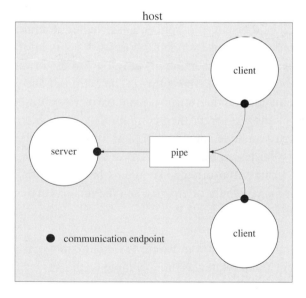

Figure 18.1: Multiple clients write requests to a shared one-way communication channel.

Named pipes can be used for short client requests, since a write of PIPE_BUF bytes or less is not interleaved with other writes to the same pipe. Unfortunately, named pipes present several difficulties when the requests are long or the server must respond. If the server simply opens another named pipe for responses, individual clients have no guarantee that they will read the response meant for them. If the server opens a unique pipe for each response, the clients and server must agree in advance on a naming convention. Furthermore, named pipes are persistent. They remain in existence unless their owners explicitly unlink them. A general mechanism for communication should release its resources when the interacting parties no longer exist.

Transmission Control Protocol (TCP) is a connection-oriented protocol that provides a reliable channel for communication, using a conduit that may be unreliable. *Connection-oriented* means that the initiator (the client) first establishes a connection with the destination (the server), after which both of them can send and receive information. TCP implements the connection through an exchange of messages, called a *three-way handshake*, between initiator and destination. TCP achieves reliability by using receiver acknowledgments and retransmissions. TCP also provides flow control so that senders don't overwhelm receivers with a flood of information. Fortunately, the operating system network subsystem implements TCP, so the details of the protocol exchanges are not visible at the process level. If the network fails, the process detects an error on the communication endpoint. The process should never receive incorrect or out-of-order information when using TCP.

Figure 18.2 illustrates the setup for connection-oriented communication. The server monitors a passive communication endpoint whose address is known to clients. Unlike other endpoints, passive or listening endpoints have resources for queuing client connection requests and establishing client connections. The action of accepting a client request creates a new communication endpoint for private, two-way symmetric communication with that client. The client and server then communicate by using handles (file descriptors) and do not explicitly include addresses in their messages. When finished, the client and server close their file descriptors, and the system releases the resources associated with the connection. Connection-oriented protocols have an initial setup overhead, but they allow transparent management of errors when the underlying conduits are not error-free.

☐ Exercise 18.1

Figure 18.3 illustrates a situation in which two clients have established connections with a server. What strategies are available to the server for managing the resulting private communication channels (each with its own file descriptor)?

Answer:

The server cannot make any assumptions about the order in which information will arrive on the file descriptors associated with the clients' private communication channels. Therefore, a solution to alternately read from one descriptor and then the other is incorrect. Section 12.1 outlines the available approaches for monitoring multiple file descriptors. The server could use `select` or `poll`, but the server would not be able to accept any additional connection requests while blocking on

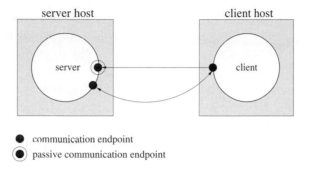

Figure 18.2: Schematic of connection-oriented client-server communication.

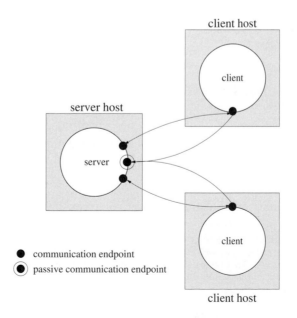

Figure 18.3: Many clients can request connections to the same communication endpoint.

these calls. Simple polling wastes CPU cycles. Asynchronous I/O is efficient, but complex to program. Alternatively, the server can fork a child process or create a separate thread to handle the client communication.

Both connectionless and connection-oriented protocols are considered to be low-level in the sense that the request for service involves visible communication. The programmer is explicitly aware of the server's location and must explicitly name the particular server to be accessed.

The naming of servers and services in a network environment is a difficult problem. An obvious method for designating a server is by its process ID and a host ID. However, the operating system assigns process IDs chronologically by process creation time, so the client cannot know in advance the process ID of a particular server process on a host.

The most commonly used method for specifying a service is by the address of the host machine (the IP address) and an integer called a port number. Under this scheme, a server monitors one or more communication channels associated with port numbers that have been designated in advance for a particular service. Web servers use port 80 by default, whereas `ftp` servers use port 21. The client explicitly specifies a host address and a port number for the communication. Section 18.8 discusses library calls for accessing IP addresses by using host names.

This chapter focuses on connection-oriented communication using TCP/IP and stream sockets with servers specified by host addresses and port numbers. More sophisticated methods of naming and locating services are available through object registries [44], directory services [129], discovery mechanisms [4] or middleware such as CORBA [104]. Implementations of these approaches are not universally available, nor are they particularly associated with UNIX.

18.3 Connection-Oriented Server Strategies

Once a server receives a request, it can use a number of different strategies for handling the request. The *serial server* depicted in Figure 18.2 completely handles one request before accepting additional requests.

■ Example 18.2

The following pseudocode illustrates the serial-server strategy.

```
for ( ; ; ) {
    wait for a client request on the listening file descriptor
    create a private two-way communication channel to the client
    while (no error on the private communication channel)
        read from the client
        process the request
        respond to the client
    close the file descriptor for the private communication channel
}
```

A busy server handling long-lived requests such as file transfers cannot use a serial-server strategy that processes only one request at a time. A *parent server* forks a child process to handle the actual service to the client, freeing the server to listen for additional requests. Figure 18.4 depicts the parent-server strategy. The strategy is ideal for services such as file transfers, which take a relatively long time and involve a lot of blocking.

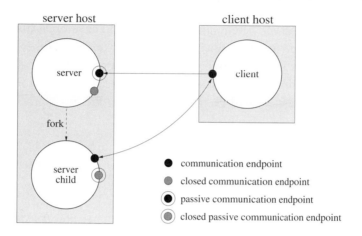

Figure 18.4: A parent server forks a child to handle the client request.

■ Example 18.3

The following pseudocode illustrates the parent-server strategy.

```
for( ; ; ) {
    wait for a client request on the listening file descriptor
    create a private two-way communication channel to the client
    fork a child to handle the client
    close file descriptor for the private communication channel
    clean up zombie children
}
```

The child process does the following.

```
close the listening file descriptor
handle the client
close the communication for the private channel
exit
```

Since the server's child handles the actual service in the parent-server strategy, the server can accept multiple client requests in rapid succession. The strategy is analogous to the old-fashioned switchboard at some hotels. A client calls the main number at the hotel (the connection request). The switchboard operator (server) answers the call, patches the connection to the appropriate room (the server child), steps out of the conversation, and resumes listening for additional calls.

☐ Exercise 18.4

What happens in Example 18.3 if the parent does not close the file descriptor corresponding to the private communication channel?

Answer:

In this case, both the server parent and the server child have open file descriptors to the private communication channel. When the server child closes the communication channel, the client will not be able to detect end-of-file because a remote process (the server parent) still has it open. Also, if the server runs for a long time with many client requests, it will eventually run out of file descriptors.

☐ Exercise 18.5

What is a zombie child? What happens in Example 18.3 if the server parent does not periodically wait for its zombie children?

Answer:

A *zombie* is a process that has completed execution but has not been waited for by its parent. Zombie processes do not release all their resources, so eventually the system may run out of some critical resource such as memory or process IDs.

The *threaded server* depicted in Figure 18.5 is a low-overhead alternative to the parent server. Instead of forking a child to handle the request, the server creates a thread in its own process space. Threaded servers can be very efficient, particularly for small or I/O intensive requests. A drawback of the threaded-server strategy is possible interference among multiple requests due to the shared address space. For computationally intensive services, the additional threads may reduce the efficiency of or block the main server thread. Per-process limits on the number of open file descriptors may also restrict the number of simultaneous client requests that can be handled by the server.

■ Example 18.6

The following pseudocode illustrates the threaded-server strategy.

```
for ( ; ; ) {
    wait for a client request on the listening file descriptor
    create a private two-way communication channel to the client
    create a detached thread to handle the client
}
```

☐ Exercise 18.7

What is the purpose of creating a detached (as opposed to attached) thread in Example 18.6?

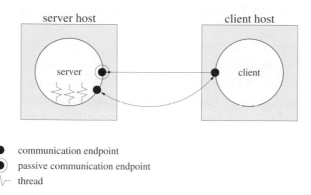

	communication endpoint
	passive communication endpoint
	thread

Figure 18.5: A threaded server creates threads to handle client requests.

Answer:
Detached threads release all their resources when they exit, hence the main thread
doesn't have to wait for them. The `waitpid` function with the `NOHANG` option
allows a process to wait for completed children without blocking. There is no
similar option for the `pthread_join` function.

❑ Exercise 18.8

What would happen if the main thread closed the communication file descriptor
after creating the thread to handle the communication?
Answer:
The main thread and child threads execute in the same process environment and
share the same file descriptors. If the main thread closes the communication file
descriptor, the newly created thread cannot access it. Compare this situation to
that encountered in the parent server of Example 18.3, in which the child process
receives a copy of the file descriptor table and executes in a different address
space.

Other strategies are possible. For example, the server could create a fixed number of
child processes when it starts and each child could wait for a connection request. This
approach allows a fixed number of simultaneous parallel connections and saves the overhead of creating a new process each time a connection request arrives. Similarly, another
threading strategy has a main thread that creates a pool of worker threads that each wait
for connection requests. Alternatively, the main thread can wait for connection requests
and distribute communication file descriptors to free worker threads. Chapter 22 outlines
a project to compare the performance of different server strategies.

18.4 Universal Internet Communication Interface (UICI)

The Universal Internet Communication Interface (UICI) library, summarized in Table 18.1, provides a simplified interface to connection-oriented communication in UNIX. UICI is not part of any UNIX standard. The interface was designed by the authors to abstract the essentials of network communication while hiding the details of the underlying network protocols. UICI has been placed in the public domain and is available on the book web site. Programs that use UICI should include the uici.h header file.

This section introduces the UICI library. The next two sections implement several client-server strategies in terms of UICI. Section 18.7 discusses the implementation of UICI using sockets, and Appendix C provides a complete UICI implementation.

When using sockets, a server creates a communication endpoint (a socket) and associates it with a well-known port (binds the socket to the port). Before waiting for client requests, the server sets the socket to be passive so that it can accept client requests (sets the socket to listen). Upon detection of a client connection request on this endpoint, the server generates a new communication endpoint for private two-way communication with the client. The client and server access their communication endpoints by using file descriptors to read and write. When finished, both parties close the file descriptors, releasing the resources associated with the communication channel.

UICI prototype	description (assuming no errors)
`int u_open(u_port_t port)`	creates a TCP socket bound to `port` and sets the socket to be passive returns a file descriptor for the socket

`int u_accept(int fd,`
`        char *hostn,`
`        int hostnsize)`
	waits for connection request on `fd`; on return, `hostn` has first `hostname-1` characters of the client's host name returns a communication file descriptor

`int u_connect(u_port_t port,` `        char *hostn)`	initiates a connection to server on port `port` and host `hostn`. returns a communication file descriptor

Table 18.1: The UICI API. If unsuccessful, UICI functions return −1 and set `errno`.

Figure 18.6 depicts a typical sequence of UICI calls used in client-server communication. The server creates a communication endpoint (u_open) and waits for a client to send a request (u_accept). The u_accept function returns a private communication file descriptor. The client creates a communication endpoint for communicating with the server (u_connect).

Once they have established a connection, a client and server can communicate over the network by using the ordinary read and write functions. Alternatively, they can use the

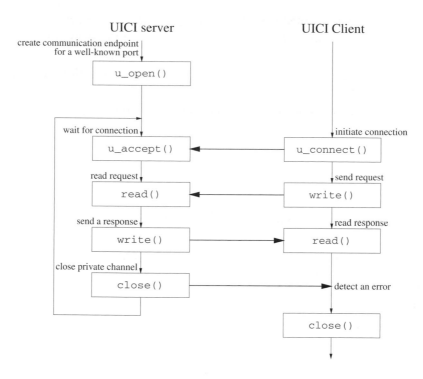

Figure 18.6: A typical interaction of a UICI client and server.

more robust `r_read` and `r_write` from the restart library of Appendix B. Either side can terminate communication by calling `close` or `r_close`. After `close`, the remote end detects end-of-file when reading or an error when writing. The diagram in Figure 18.6 shows a single request followed by a response, but more complicated interactions might involve several exchanges followed by `close`.

In summary, UICI servers follow these steps.

1. Open a well-known listening port (`u_open`). The `u_open` functions returns a *listening file descriptor*.
2. Wait for a connection request on the listening file descriptor (`u_accept`). The `u_accept` function blocks until a client requests a connection and then returns a *communication file descriptor* to use as a handle for private, two-way client-server communication.
3. Communicate with the client by using the communication file descriptor (`read` and `write`).
4. Close the communication file descriptor (`close`).

UICI clients follow these steps.

1. Connect to a specified host and port (u_connect). The connection request returns the communication file descriptor used for two-way communication with the server.
2. Communicate with the server by using the communication file descriptor (read and write).
3. Close the communication file descriptor (close).

18.4.1 Handling errors

A major design issue for UICI was how to handle errors. UNIX library functions generally report errors by returning –1 and setting errno. To keep the UICI interface simple and familiar, UICI functions also return –1 and set errno. None of the UICI functions display error messages. Applications using UICI should test for errors and display error messages as appropriate. Since UICI functions always set errno when a UICI function returns an error, applications can use perror to display the error message. POSIX does not specify an error code corresponding to the inability to resolve a host name. The u_connect function returns –1 and sets errno to EINVAL, indicating an invalid parameter when it cannot resolve the host name.

18.4.2 Reading and writing

Once they have obtained an open file descriptor from u_connect or u_accept, UICI clients and servers can use the ordinary read and write functions to communicate. We use the functions from the restart library since they are more robust and simplify the code.

Recall that r_read and r_write both restart themselves after being interrupted by a signal. Like read, r_read returns the number of bytes read or 0 if it encounters end-of-file. If unsuccessful, r_read returns –1 and sets errno. If successful, r_write returns the number of bytes requested to write. The r_write function returns –1 and sets errno if an error occurred or if it could not write all the requested bytes without error. The r_write function restarts itself if not all the requested bytes have been written. This chapter also uses the copyfile function from the restart library, introduced in Program 4.6 on page 100 and copy2files introduced in Program 4.13 on page 111.

The restart library supports only blocking I/O. That is, r_read or r_write may cause the caller to block. An r_read call blocks until some information is available to be read. The meaning of blocking for r_write is less obvious. In the present context, blocking means that r_write returns when the output has been transferred to a buffer used by the transport mechanism. Returning does not imply that the message has actually been delivered to the destination. Writes may also block if message delivery problems arise in the lower protocol layers or if all the buffers for the network protocols are full. Fortunately, the issues of blocking and buffering are transparent for most applications.

18.5 UICI Implementations of Different Server Strategies

Program 18.1 shows a serial-server program that copies information from a client to standard output, using the UICI library. The server takes a single command-line argument specifying the number of the well-known port on which it listens. The server obtains a listening file descriptor for the port with u_open and then displays its process ID. It calls u_accept to block while waiting for a client request. The u_accept function returns a communication file descriptor for the client communication. The server displays the name of the client and uses copyfile of Program 4.6 on page 100 to perform the actual copying. Once it has finished the copying, the server closes the communication file descriptor, displays the number of bytes copied, and resumes listening.

Program 18.1 ————————————————————— **server.c**

A serial server implemented using UICI.

```c
#include <limits.h>
#include <stdio.h>
#include <stdlib.h>
#include <unistd.h>
#include "restart.h"
#include "uici.h"

int main(int argc, char *argv[]) {
   int bytescopied;
   char client[MAX_CANON];
   int communfd;
   int listenfd;
   u_port_t portnumber;

   if (argc != 2) {
      fprintf(stderr, "Usage: %s port\n", argv[0]);
      return 1;
   }
   portnumber = (u_port_t) atoi(argv[1]);
   if ((listenfd = u_open(portnumber)) == -1) {
      perror("Failed to create listening endpoint");
      return 1;
   }
   fprintf(stderr, "[%ld]:waiting for the first connection on port %d\n",
                   (long)getpid(), (int)portnumber);
   for ( ; ; ) {
      if ((communfd = u_accept(listenfd, client, MAX_CANON)) == -1) {
         perror("Failed to accept connection");
         continue;
      }
      fprintf(stderr, "[%ld]:connected to %s\n", (long)getpid(), client);
      bytescopied = copyfile(communfd, STDOUT_FILENO);
      fprintf(stderr, "[%ld]:received %d bytes\n", (long)getpid(), bytescopied);
      if (r_close(communfd) == -1)
         perror("Failed to close communfd\n");
   }
}
```

Program 18.1 ————————————————————— **server.c**

◻ **Exercise 18.9**

Under what circumstances does a client cause the server in Program 18.1 to terminate?

Answer:

The server executes the first `return` statement if it is not started with a single command-line argument. The `u_open` function creates a communication endpoint associated with a port number. The `u_open` function fails if the port is invalid, if the port is in use, or if system resources are not available to support the request. At this point, no clients are involved. Once the server has reached `u accept`, it does not terminate unless it receives a signal. A client on a remote machine cannot cause the server to terminate. A failure of `u_accept` causes the server to loop and try again. Notice that I/O errors cause `copyfile` to return, but these errors do not cause server termination.

Program 18.2 implements the parent-server strategy. The parent accepts client connections and forks a child to call `copyfile` so that the parent can resume waiting for connections. Because the child receives a copy of the parent's environment at the time of the fork, it has access to the private communication channel represented by `communfd`.

◻ **Exercise 18.10**

What happens if the client name does not fit in the buffer passed to `u_accept`?

Answer:

The implementation of `u_accept` does not permit the name to overflow the buffer. Instead, `u_accept` truncates the client name. (See Section 18.7.6.)

◻ **Exercise 18.11**

What happens if after the connection is made, you enter text at standard input of the server?

Answer:

The server program never reads from standard input, and what you type at standard input is not sent to the remote machine.

◻ **Exercise 18.12**

Program 18.2 uses `r_close` and `r_waitpid` from the restart library. How does this affect the behavior of the program?

Answer:

Functions in the restart library restart the corresponding function when the return value is −1 and `errno` is `EINTR`. This return condition occurs when the signal handler of a caught signal returns. Program 18.2 does not catch any signals, so using the restarted versions is not necessary. We use the functions from the restart library to make it easier to add signal handling capability to the programs.

Program 18.2 ———————————————————————— `serverp.c`

A server program that forks a child to handle communication.

```c
#include <errno.h>
#include <limits.h>
#include <stdio.h>
#include <stdlib.h>
#include <string.h>
#include <unistd.h>
#include <sys/types.h>
#include <sys/wait.h>
#include "restart.h"
#include "uici.h"

int main(int argc, char *argv[]) {
   int bytescopied;
   pid_t child;
   char client[MAX_CANON];
   int communfd;
   int listenfd;
   u_port_t portnumber;

   if (argc != 2) {
      fprintf(stderr, "Usage: %s port\n", argv[0]);
      return 1;
   }
   portnumber = (u_port_t) atoi(argv[1]);
   if ((listenfd = u_open(portnumber)) == -1) {
      perror("Failed to create listening endpoint");
      return 1;
   }
   fprintf(stderr, "[%ld]: Waiting for connection on port %d\n",
                   (long)getpid(), (int)portnumber);
   for ( ; ; ) {
      if ((communfd = u_accept(listenfd, client, MAX_CANON)) == -1) {
         perror("Failed to accept connection");
         continue;
      }
      fprintf(stderr, "[%ld]:connected to %s\n", (long)getpid(), client);
      if ((child = fork()) == -1) {
         perror("Failed to fork a child");
         continue;
      }
      if (child == 0) {                               /* child code */
         if (r_close(listenfd) == -1) {
            fprintf(stderr, "[%ld]:failed to close listenfd: %s\n",
                            (long)getpid(), strerror(errno));
            return 1;
         }
         bytescopied = copyfile(communfd, STDOUT_FILENO);
         fprintf(stderr, "[%ld]:received %d bytes\n",
                         (long)getpid(), bytescopied);
         return 0;
      }
      if (r_close(communfd) == -1)                    /* parent code */
         fprintf(stderr, "[%ld]:failed to close communfd: %s\n",
                         (long)getpid(), strerror(errno));
      while (r_waitpid(-1, NULL, WNOHANG) > 0)  ;     /* clean up zombies */
   }
}
```

Program 18.2 ———————————————————————— `serverp.c`

18.6 UICI Clients

Program 18.3 shows the client side of the file copy. The client connects to the desired port on a specified host by calling u_connect. The u_connect function returns the communication file descriptor. The client reads the information from standard input and copies it to the server. The client exits when it receives end-of-file from standard input or if it encounters an error while writing to the server.

Program 18.3 ——————————————————————— `client.c`

A client that uses UICI for communication.

```
#include <stdio.h>
#include <stdlib.h>
#include <unistd.h>
#include "restart.h"
#include "uici.h"

int main(int argc, char *argv[]) {
    int bytescopied;
    int communfd;
    u_port_t portnumber;

    if (argc != 3) {
        fprintf(stderr, "Usage: %s host port\n", argv[0]);
        return 1;
    }
    portnumber = (u_port_t)atoi(argv[2]);
    if ((communfd = u_connect(portnumber, argv[1])) == -1) {
        perror("Failed to make connection");
        return 1;
    }
    fprintf(stderr, "[%ld]:connected %s\n", (long)getpid(), argv[1]);
    bytescopied = copyfile(STDIN_FILENO, communfd);
    fprintf(stderr, "[%ld]:sent %d bytes\n", (long)getpid(), bytescopied);
    return 0;
}
```

Program 18.3 ——————————————————————— `client.c`

☐ Exercise 18.13

How would you use Programs 18.1 and 18.3 to transfer information from one machine to another?

Answer:

Compile the server of Program 18.1 as `server`. First, start the server listening on a port (say 8652) by executing the following command.

```
server 8652
```

Compile Program 18.3 as `client`. If the server is running on `usp.cs.utsa.edu`, start the client on another machine with the following command.

```
client usp.cs.utsa.edu 8652
```

Once the client and server have established a connection, enter text on the standard input of the client and observe the server output. Enter the end-of-file character (usually Ctrl-D). The client terminates, and both client and server print the number of bytes transferred. Be sure to replace `usp.cs.utsa.edu` with the host name of your server.

❑ Exercise 18.14

How would you use Programs 18.1 and 18.3 to transfer the file `t.in` on one machine to the file `t.out` on another? Will `t.out` be identical to `t.in`? What happens to the messages displayed by the client and server?

Answer:

Use I/O redirection. Start the server of Program 18.1 on the destination machine (say, `usp.cs.utsa.edu`) by executing the following command.

```
server 8652 > t.out
```

Start the client of Program 18.3 on the source machine by executing the following command.

```
client usp.cs.utsa.edu 8652 < t.in
```

Be sure to substitute your server's host name for `usp.cs.utsa.edu`. The source and destination files should have identical content. Since the messages are sent to standard error, which is not redirected, these messages still appear in the usual place on the two machines.

The client and server programs presented so far support communication only from the client to the server. In many client-server applications, the client sends a request to the server and then waits for a response.

❑ Exercise 18.15

How would you modify the server of Program 18.1 to produce a server called `reflectserver` that echoes its response back to the client, rather than to standard output?

Answer:

The only modification needed would be to replace the reference to `STDOUT_FILENO` with `communfd`.

Program 18.4 is a client program that can be used with the server of Exercise 18.15. The `reflectclient.c` sends a fixed-length message to a server and expects that message to be echoed back. Program 18.4 checks to see that it receives exactly the same message that it sends.

Program 18.4 ──────────────────────────── `reflectclient.c`

A client that sends a fixed-length test message to a server and checks that the reply is identical to the message sent.

```c
#include <errno.h>
#include <stdio.h>
#include <stdlib.h>
#include <string.h>
#include <unistd.h>
#include "restart.h"
#include "uici.h"
#define BUFSIZE 1000

int main(int argc, char *argv[]) {
   char bufrecv[BUFSIZE];
   char bufsend[BUFSIZE];
   int bytesrecvd;
   int communfd;
   int i;
   u_port_t portnumber;
   int totalrecvd;

   if (argc != 3) {
      fprintf(stderr, "Usage: %s host port\n", argv[0]);
      return 1;
   }
   for (i = 0; i < BUFSIZE; i++)                    /* set up a test message */
      bufsend[i] = (char)(i%26 + 'A');
   portnumber = (u_port_t)atoi(argv[2]);
   if ((communfd = u_connect(portnumber, argv[1])) == -1) {
      perror("Failed to establish connection");
      return 1;
   }
   if (r_write(communfd, bufsend, BUFSIZE) != BUFSIZE) {
      perror("Failed to write test message");
      return 1;
   }
   totalrecvd = 0;
   while (totalrecvd < BUFSIZE) {
      bytesrecvd = r_read(communfd, bufrecv + totalrecvd, BUFSIZE - totalrecvd);
      if (bytesrecvd <= 0) {
         perror("Failed to read response message");
         return 1;
      }
      totalrecvd += bytesrecvd;
   }
   for (i = 0; i < BUFSIZE; i++)
      if (bufsend[i] != bufrecv[i])
         fprintf(stderr, "Byte %d read does not agree with byte written\n", i);
   return 0;
}
```

Program 18.4 ──────────────────────────── `reflectclient.c`

Many client-server applications require symmetric bidirectional communication between client and server. The simplest way to incorporate bidirectionality is for the client and the server to each fork a child to handle the communication in the opposite direction.

■ Example 18.16

To make the client in Program 18.3 bidirectional, declare an integer variable, `child`, and replace the line

```
bytescopied = copyfile(STDIN_FILENO, communfd);
```

with the following code segment.

```
if ((child = fork()) == -1) {
   perror("Failed to fork a child");
   return 1;
}
if (child == 0)                                    /* child code */
   bytescopied = copyfile(STDIN_FILENO, communfd);
else                                               /* parent code */
   bytescopied = copyfile(communfd, STDOUT_FILENO);
```

□ Exercise 18.17

Suppose we try to make a bidirectional serial server from Program 18.1 by declaring an integer variable called `child` and replacing the following line with the replacement code of Example 18.16.

```
bytescopied = copyfile(communfd, STDOUT_FILENO);
```

What happens?

Answer:

This approach has several flaws. Both the parent and child return to the `u_accept` loop after completing the transfer. While copying still works correctly, the number of processes grows each time a connection is made. After the first connection completes, two server processes accept client connections. If two server connections are active, characters entered at standard input of the server go to one of the two connections. The code also causes the process to exit if `fork` fails. Normally, the server should not exit on account of a possibly temporary problem.

■ Example 18.18

To produce a bidirectional serial server, replace the `copyfile` line in Program 18.1 with the following code.

```
int child;

child = fork();
if ((child = fork()) == -1)
   perror("Failed to fork second child");
else if (child == 0) {                             /* child code */
   bytescopied = copyfile(STDIN_FILENO, communfd);
   fprintf(stderr, "[%ld]:sent %d bytes\n", (long)getpid(), bytes_copied);
   return 0;
}
bytescopied = copyfile(communfd, STDOUT_FILENO);     /* parent code */
fprintf(stderr, "[%ld]:received %d bytes\n", (long)getpid(), bytescopied);
r_wait(NULL);
```

The child process exits after printing its message. The original process waits for the child to complete before continuing and does not accept a new connection until both ends of the transmission complete. If the fork fails, only the parent communicates.

❑ Exercise 18.19

The modified server suggested in Example 18.18 prints out the number of bytes transferred in each direction. How would you modify the code to print a single number giving the total number of bytes transferred in both directions?

Answer:

This modification would not be simple because the values for transfer in each direction are stored in different processes. You can establish communication by inserting code to create a pipe before forking the child. After it completes, the child could write to the pipe the total number of bytes transferred to the parent.

❑ Exercise 18.20

Suppose that the child of Example 18.18 returns the number of bytes transferred and the parent uses the return value from the status code to accumulate the total number of bytes transferred. Does this approach solve the problem posed in Exercise 18.19?

Answer:

No. Only 8 bits are typically available for the child's return value, which is not large enough to hold the number of bytes transferred.

Another way to do bidirectional transfer is to use `select` or `poll` as shown in Program 4.13 on page 111. The `copy2files` program copies bytes from `fromfd1` to `tofd1` and from `fromfd2` to `tofd2`, respectively, without making any assumptions about the order in which the bytes become available in the two directions. You can use `copy2files` by replacing the `copyfile` line in both server and client with the following code.

```
bytescopied = copy2files(communfd, STDOUT_FILENO, STDIN_FILENO, communfd);
```

Program 18.5 shows the bidirectional client.

❑ Exercise 18.21

How does using `copy2files` differ from forking a child to handle communication in the opposite direction?

Answer:

The `copy2files` function of Program 4.13 terminates both directions of communication if either receives an end-of-file from standard input or if there is an error in the network communication. The child method allows communication to continue in the other direction after one side is closed. You can modify `copy2files` to keep a flag for each file descriptor indicating whether the descriptor has encountered an error or end-of-file. Only active descriptors would be included in each iteration of `select`.

Program 18.5 ──────────────────────────── `client2.c`

A bidirectional client.

```c
#include <stdio.h>
#include <stdlib.h>
#include <unistd.h>
#include "uici.h"
#include "restart.h"

int main(int argc, char *argv[]) {
   int bytescopied;
   int communfd;
   u_port_t portnumber;

   if (argc != 3) {
      fprintf(stderr, "Usage: %s host port\n", argv[0]);
      return 1;
   }
   portnumber = (u_port_t)atoi(argv[2]);
   if ((communfd = u_connect(portnumber, argv[1])) == -1) {
      perror("Failed to establish connection");
      return 1;
   }
   fprintf(stderr, "[%ld]:connection made to %s\n", (long)getpid(), argv[1]);
   bytescopied = copy2files(communfd, STDOUT_FILENO, STDIN_FILENO, communfd);
   fprintf(stderr, "[%ld]:transferred %d bytes\n", (long)getpid(), bytescopied);
   return 0;
}
```

Program 18.5 ──────────────────────────── `client2.c`

18.7 Socket Implementation of UICI

The first socket interface originated with 4.1cBSD UNIX in the early 1980s. In 2001, POSIX incorporated 4.3BSD sockets and an alternative, XTI. XTI (X/Open Transport Interface) also provides a connection-oriented interface that uses TCP. XTI's lineage can be traced back to AT&T UNIX System V TLI (Transport Layer Interface). This book focuses on socket implementations. (See Stevens [115] for an in-depth discussion of XTI.)

This section introduces the main socket library functions and then implements the UICI functions in terms of sockets. Section 18.9 discusses a thread-safe version of UICI. Appendix C gives a complete unthreaded socket implementation of UICI as well as four alternative thread-safe versions. The implementations of this chapter use IPv4 (Internet

UICI	socket functions	action
u_open	socket	create communication endpoint
	bind	associate endpoint with specific port
	listen	make endpoint passive listener
u_accept	accept	accept connection request from client
u_connect	socket	create communication endpoint
	connect	request connection from server

Table 18.2: Overview of UICI API implementation using sockets with TCP.

Protocol version 4). The names of the libraries needed to compile the socket functions are not yet standard. Sun Solaris requires the library options -lsocket and -lnsl. Linux just needs -lnsl, and Mac OS X does not require that any extra libraries be specified. The man page for the socket functions should indicate the names of the required libraries on a particular system. If unsuccessful, the socket functions return −1 and set errno.

Table 18.2 shows the socket functions used to implement each of the UICI functions. The server creates a handle (socket), associates it with a physical location on the network (bind), and sets up the queue size for pending requests (listen). The UICI u_open function, which encapsulates these three functions, returns a file descriptor corresponding to a passive or listening socket. The server then listens for client requests (accept).

The client also creates a handle (socket) and associates this handle with the network location of the server (connect). The UICI u_connect function encapsulates these two functions. The server and client handles, sometimes called *communication* or *transmission endpoints*, are file descriptors. Once the client and server have established a connection, they can communicate by ordinary read and write calls.

18.7.1 The socket function

The socket function creates a communication endpoint and returns a file descriptor. The domain parameter selects the protocol family to be used. We use AF_INET, indicating IPv4. A type value of SOCK_STREAM specifies sequenced, reliable, two-way, connection-oriented byte streams and is typically implemented with TCP. A type value of SOCK_DGRAM provides connectionless communication by using unreliable messages of a fixed length and is typically implemented with UDP. (See Chapter 20.) The protocol parameter specifies the protocol to be used for a particular communication type. In most implementations, each type parameter has only one protocol available (e.g., TCP for SOCK_STREAM and UDP for SOCK_DGRAM), so protocol is usually 0.

```
SYNOPSIS

    #include <sys/socket.h>

    int socket(int domain, int type, int protocol);
                                                              POSIX
```

If successful, `socket` returns a nonnegative integer corresponding to a socket file descriptor. If unsuccessful, `socket` returns –1 and sets `errno`. The following table lists the mandatory errors for `socket`.

errno	cause
EAFNOSUPPORT	implementation does not support specified address family
EMFILE	no more file descriptors available for process
ENFILE	no more file descriptors available for system
EPROTONOSUPPORT	protocol not supported by address family or by implementation
EPROTOTYPE	socket type not supported by protocol

■ Example 18.22

The following code segment sets up a socket communication endpoint for Internet communication, using a connection-oriented protocol.

```
int sock;

if ((sock = socket(AF_INET, SOCK_STREAM, 0)) == -1)
    perror("Failed to create socket");
```

18.7.2 The `bind` function

The `bind` function associates the handle for a socket communication endpoint with a specific logical network connection. Internet domain protocols specify the logical connection by a port number. The first parameter to `bind`, `socket`, is the file descriptor returned by a previous call to the `socket` function. The `*address` structure contains a family name and protocol-specific information. The `address_len` parameter is the number of bytes in the `*address` structure.

```
SYNOPSIS

    #include <sys/socket.h>

    int bind(int socket, const struct sockaddr *address,
             socklen_t address_len);
                                                              POSIX
```

If successful, `bind` returns 0. If unsuccessful, `bind` returns –1 and sets `errno`. The following table lists the mandatory errors for `bind` that are applicable to all address families.

errno	cause
EADDRINUSE	specified address is in use
EADDRNOTAVAIL	specified address not available from local machine
EAFNOSUPPORT	invalid address for address family of specified socket
EBADF	socket parameter is not a valid file descriptor
EINVAL	socket already bound to an address, protocol does not support binding to new address, or socket has been shut down
ENOTSOCK	socket parameter does not refer to a socket
EOPNOTSUPP	socket type does not support binding to address

The Internet domain uses `struct sockaddr_in` for `struct sockaddr`. POSIX states that applications should cast `struct sockaddr_in` to `struct sockaddr` for use with socket functions. The `struct sockaddr_in` structure, which is defined in `netinet/in.h`, has at least the following members expressed in network byte order.

```
sa_family_t    sin_family;   /* AF_NET */
in_port_t      sin_port;     /* port number */
struct in_addr sin_addr;     /* IP address */
```

For Internet communication, `sin_family` is `AF_INET` and `sin_port` is the port number. The `struct in_addr` structure has a member, called `s_addr`, of type `in_addr_t` that holds the numeric value of an Internet address. A server can set the `sin_addr.s_addr` field to `INADDR_ANY`, meaning that the socket should accept connection requests on any of the host's network interfaces. Clients set the `sin_addr.s_addr` field to the IP address of the server host.

■ Example 18.23

The following code segment associates the port 8652 with a socket corresponding to the open file descriptor `sock`.

```
struct sockaddr_in server;
int sock;

server.sin_family = AF_INET;
server.sin_addr.s_addr = htonl(INADDR_ANY);
server.sin_port = htons((short)8652);
if (bind(sock, (struct sockaddr *)&server, sizeof(server)) == -1)
   perror("Failed to bind the socket to port");
```

Example 18.23 uses `htonl` and `htons` to reorder the bytes of `INADDR_ANY` and `8652` to be in network byte order. Big-endian computers store the most significant byte first; little-endian computers store the least significant byte first. Byte ordering of integers presents a problem when machines with different endian architectures communicate, since they may misinterpret protocol information such as port numbers. Unfortunately, both architectures are common—the SPARC architecture (developed by Sun Microsystems) uses big-endian, whereas Intel architectures use little-endian. The Internet protocols specify that big-endian should be used for *network byte order*, and POSIX requires that certain socket address fields be given in network byte order. The `htonl` function reorders a `long` from the host's internal order to network byte order. Similarly, `htons` reorders a `short` to network byte order. The mirror functions `ntohl` and `ntohs` reorder integers from network byte order to host order.

18.7.3 The `listen` function

The `socket` function creates a communication endpoint, and `bind` associates this endpoint with a particular network address. At this point, a client can use the socket to connect to a server. To use the socket to accept incoming requests, an application must put the socket into the passive state by calling the `listen` function.

The `listen` function causes the underlying system network infrastructure to allocate queues to hold pending requests. When a client makes a connection request, the client and server network subsystems exchange messages (the TCP *three-way handshake*) to establish the connection. Since the server process may be busy, the host network subsystem queues the client connection requests until the server is ready to accept them. The client receives an `ECONNREFUSED` error if the server host refuses its connection request. The `socket` value is the descriptor returned by a previous call to `socket`, and the `backlog` parameter suggests a value for the maximum allowed number of pending client requests.

```
SYNOPSIS

   #include <sys/socket.h>

   int listen(int socket, int backlog);
                                                              POSIX
```

If successful, `listen` returns 0. If unsuccessful, `listen` returns −1 and sets `errno`. The following table lists the mandatory errors for `listen`.

errno	cause
EBADF	`socket` is not a valid file descriptor
EDESTADDRREQ	socket is not bound to a local address and protocol does not allow listening on an unbound socket
EINVAL	socket is already connected
ENOTSOCK	`socket` parameter does not refer to a socket
EOPNOTSUPP	socket protocol does not support `listen`

Traditionally, the `backlog` parameter has been given as 5. However, studies have shown [115] that the `backlog` parameter should be larger. Some systems incorporate a fudge factor in allocating queue sizes so that the actual queue size is larger than `backlog`. Exercise 22.14 explores the effect of `backlog` size on server performance.

18.7.4 Implementation of u_open

The combination of socket, bind and listen establishes a handle for the server to monitor communication requests from a well-known port. Program 18.6 shows the implementation of u_open in terms of these socket functions.

┌─ **Program 18.6** ──────────────────────────────────── **u_open.c** ─┐

A socket implementation of the UICI u_open.

```c
#include <errno.h>
#include <netdb.h>
#include <stdio.h>
#include <unistd.h>
#include <sys/socket.h>
#include <sys/types.h>
#include "uici.h"

#define MAXBACKLOG 50

int u_ignore_sigpipe(void);

int u_open(u_port_t port) {
   int error;
   struct sockaddr_in server;
   int sock;
   int true = 1;

   if ((u_ignore_sigpipe() == -1) ||
       ((sock = socket(AF_INET, SOCK_STREAM, 0)) == -1))
     return -1;

   if (setsockopt(sock, SOL_SOCKET, SO_REUSEADDR, (char *)&true,
                  sizeof(true)) == -1) {
      error = errno;
      while ((close(sock) == -1) && (errno == EINTR));
      errno = error;
      return -1;
   }

   server.sin_family = AF_INET;
   server.sin_addr.s_addr = htonl(INADDR_ANY);
   server.sin_port = htons((short)port);
   if ((bind(sock, (struct sockaddr *)&server, sizeof(server)) == -1) ||
       (listen(sock, MAXBACKLOG) == -1)) {
      error = errno;
      while ((close(sock) == -1) && (errno == EINTR));
      errno = error;
      return -1;
   }
   return sock;
}
```

└─ **Program 18.6** ──────────────────────────────────── **u_open.c** ─┘

If an attempt is made to write to a pipe or socket that no process has open for reading, `write` generates a `SIGPIPE` signal in addition to returning an error and setting `errno` to `EPIPE`. As with most signals, the default action of `SIGPIPE` terminates the process. Under no circumstances should the action of a client cause a server to terminate. Even if the server creates a child to handle the communication, the signal can prevent a graceful termination of the child when the remote host closes the connection. The socket implementation of UICI handles this problem by calling `u_ignore_sigpipe` to ignore the `SIGPIPE` signal if the default action of this signal is in effect.

The `htonl` and `htons` functions convert the address and port number fields to network byte order. The `setsockopt` call with `SO_REUSEADDR` permits the server to be restarted immediately, using the same port. This call should be made before `bind`.

If `setsockopt`, `bind` or `listen` produces an error, `u_open` saves the value of `errno`, closes the socket file descriptor, and restores the value of `errno`. Even if `close` changes `errno`, we still want to return with `errno` reporting the error that originally caused the return.

18.7.5 The `accept` function

After setting up a passive listening socket (`socket`, `bind` and `listen`), the server handles incoming client connections by calling `accept`. The parameters of `accept` are similar to those of `bind`. However, `bind` expects `*address` to be filled in before the call, so that it knows the port and interface on which the server will accept connection requests. In contrast, `accept` uses `*address` to return information about the client making the connection. In particular, the `sin_addr` member of the `struct sockaddr_in` structure contains a member, `s_addr`, that holds the Internet address of the client. The value of the `*address_len` parameter of `accept` specifies the size of the buffer pointed to by `address`. Before the call, fill this with the size of the `*address` structure. After the call, `*address_len` contains the number of bytes of the buffer actually filled in by the `accept` call.

SYNOPSIS

```
#include <sys/socket.h>

int accept(int socket, struct sockaddr *restrict address,
           socklen_t *restrict address_len);
```
POSIX

If successful, `accept` returns the nonnegative file descriptor corresponding to the accepted socket. If unsuccessful, `accept` returns −1 and sets `errno`. The following table lists the mandatory errors for `accept`.

`errno`	cause
`EAGAIN` or `EWOULDBLOCK`	`O_NONBLOCK` is set for socket file descriptor and no connections are present to be accepted
`EBADF`	`socket` parameter is not a valid file descriptor
`ECONNABORTED`	connection has been aborted
`EINTR`	`accept` interrupted by a signal that was caught before a valid connection arrived
`EINVAL`	socket is not accepting connections
`EMFILE`	`OPEN_MAX` file descriptors are currently open in calling process
`ENFILE`	maximum number of file descriptors in system are already open
`ENOTSOCK`	`socket` does not refer to a socket
`EOPNOTSUPP`	socket type of specified socket does not support the accepting of connections

■ **Example 18.24**

The following code segment illustrates how to restart `accept` if it is interrupted by a signal.

```
int len = sizeof(struct sockaddr);
int listenfd;
struct sockaddr_in netclient;
int retval;

while (((retval =
       accept(listenfd, (struct sockaddr *)(&netclient), &len)) == -1) &&
       (errno == EINTR))
   ;
if (retval == -1)
   perror("Failed to accept connection");
```

18.7.6 Implementation of `u_accept`

The `u_accept` function waits for a connection request from a client and returns a file descriptor that can be used to communicate with that client. It also fills in the name of the client host in a user-supplied buffer. The socket `accept` function returns information about the client in a `struct sockaddr_in` structure. The client's address is contained in this structure. The socket library does not have a facility to convert this binary address to a host name. UICI calls the `addr2name` function to do this conversion. This function takes as parameters a `struct in_addr` from a `struct sockaddr_in`, a buffer and the size of the buffer. It fills this buffer with the name of the host corresponding to the address given. The implementation of this function is discussed in Section 18.8.

Program 18.7 implements the UICI `u_accept` function. The socket `accept` call waits for a connection request and returns a communication file descriptor. If `accept` is interrupted by a signal, it returns –1 with `errno` set to `EINTR`. The UICI `u_accept` function reinitiates `accept` in this case. If `accept` is successful and the caller has furnished a `hostn` buffer, then `u_accept` calls `addr2name` to convert the address returned by `accept` to an ASCII host name.

Program 18.7 ──────────────────────────────── **u_accept.c**

A socket implementation of the UICI `u_accept` function.

```
#include <errno.h>
#include <netdb.h>
#include <string.h>
#include <arpa/inet.h>
#include <sys/socket.h>
#include <sys/types.h>
#include "uiciname.h"

int u_accept(int fd, char *hostn, int hostnsize) {
   int len = sizeof(struct sockaddr);
   struct sockaddr_in netclient;
   int retval;

   while (((retval =
           accept(fd, (struct sockaddr *)(&netclient), &len)) == -1) &&
          (errno == EINTR))
      ;
   if ((retval == -1) || (hostn == NULL) || (hostnsize <= 0))
      return retval;
   addr2name(netclient.sin_addr, hostn, hostnsize);
   return retval;
}
```

Program 18.7 ──────────────────────────────── **u_accept.c**

☐ Exercise 18.25

Under what circumstances does `u_accept` return an error caused by client behavior?

Answer:

The conditions for `u_accept` to return an error are the same as for `accept` to return an error except for interruption by a signal. The `u_accept` function restarts `accept` when it is interrupted by a signal (e.g., `errno` is `EINTR`). The `accept` function may return an error for various system-dependent reasons related to insufficient resources. The `accept` function may also return an error if the client disconnects after the completion of the three-way handshake. A server that uses `accept` or `u_accept` should be careful not to simply exit on such an error. Even an error due to insufficient resources should not necessarily cause the server to exit, since the problem might be temporary.

18.7.7 The `connect` function

The client calls `socket` to set up a transmission endpoint and then uses `connect` to establish a link to the well-known port of the remote server. Fill the `struct sockaddr` structure as with `bind`.

```
SYNOPSIS

  #include <sys/socket.h>

  int connect(int socket, const struct sockaddr *address,
              socklen_t address_len);
                                                                    POSIX
```

If successful, `connect` returns 0. If unsuccessful, `connect` returns −1 and sets `errno`. The following table lists the mandatory errors for `connect` that are applicable to all address families.

errno	cause
EADDRNOTAVAIL	specified address is not available from local machine
EAFNOSUPPORT	specified address is not a valid address for address family of specified socket
EALREADY	connection request already in progress on socket
EBADF	`socket` parameter not a valid file descriptor
ECONNREFUSED	target was not listening for connections or refused connection
EINPROGRSS	O_NONBLOCK set for file descriptor of the socket and connection cannot be immediately established, so connection shall be established asynchronously
EINTR	attempt to establish connection was interrupted by delivery of a signal that was caught, so connection shall be established asynchronously
EISCONN	specified socket is connection mode and already connected
ENETUNREACH	no route to network is present
ENOTSOCK	`socket` parameter does not refer to a socket
EPROTOTYPE	specified address has different type than socket bound to specified peer address
ETIMEDOUT	attempt to connect timed out before connection made

18.7.8 Implementation of `u_connect`

Program 18.8 shows `u_connect`, a function that initiates a connection request to a server. The `u_connect` function has two parameters, a port number (`port`) and a host name (`hostn`), which together specify the server to connect to.

Program 18.8 ———————————————————————— **u_connect.c**

A socket implementation of the UICI u_connect *function.*

```c
#include <ctype.h>
#include <errno.h>
#include <netdb.h>
#include <stdio.h>
#include <string.h>
#include <unistd.h>
#include <arpa/inet.h>
#include <sys/select.h>
#include <sys/socket.h>
#include <sys/types.h>
#include "uiciname.h"
#include "uici.h"

int u_ignore_sigpipe(void);

int u_connect(u_port_t port, char *hostn) {
   int error;
   int retval;
   struct sockaddr_in server;
   int sock;
   fd_set sockset;

   if (name2addr(hostn,&(server.sin_addr.s_addr)) == -1) {
      errno = EINVAL;
      return -1;
   }
   server.sin_port = htons((short)port);
   server.sin_family = AF_INET;

   if ((u_ignore_sigpipe() == -1) ||
        ((sock = socket(AF_INET, SOCK_STREAM, 0)) == -1))
      return -1;

   if (((retval =
        connect(sock, (struct sockaddr *)&server, sizeof(server))) == -1) &&
        ((errno == EINTR) || (errno == EALREADY))) {          /* asynchronous */
      FD_ZERO(&sockset);
      FD_SET(sock, &sockset);
      while (((retval = select(sock+1, NULL, &sockset, NULL, NULL)) == -1)
            && (errno == EINTR)) {
         FD_ZERO(&sockset);
         FD_SET(sock, &sockset);
      }
   }
   if (retval == -1) {
       error = errno;
       while ((close(sock) == -1) && (errno == EINTR));
       errno = error;
       return -1;
   }
   return sock;
}
```

Program 18.8 ———————————————————————— **u_connect.c**

The first step is to verify that `hostn` is a valid host name and to find the corresponding IP address using `name2addr`. The `u_connect` function stores this address in a `struct sockaddr_in` structure. The `name2addr` function, which takes a string and a pointer to `in_addr_t` as parameters, converts the host name stored in the string parameter into a binary address and stores this address in the location corresponding to its second parameter. Section 18.8 discusses the implementation of `name2addr`.

If the `SIGPIPE` signal has the default signal handler, `u_ignore_sigpipe` sets `SIGPIPE` to be ignored. (Otherwise, the client terminates when it tries to write after the remote end has been closed.) The `u_connect` function then creates a `SOCK_STREAM` socket. If any of these steps fails, `u_connect` returns an error.

The `connect` call can be interrupted by a signal. However, unlike other library functions that set `errno` to `EINTR`, `connect` should not be restarted, because the network subsystem has already initiated the TCP 3-way handshake. In this case, the connection request completes asynchronously to program execution. The application must call `select` or `poll` to detect that the descriptor is ready for writing. The UICI implementation of `u_connect` uses `select` and restarts it if interrupted by a signal.

❏ Exercise 18.26

How would the behavior of `u_connect` change if

```
if ((u_ignore_sigpipe() != 0) ||
    ((sock = socket(AF_INET, SOCK_STREAM, 0)) == -1))
    return -1;
```

were replaced by the following?

```
if (((sock = socket(AF_INET, SOCK_STREAM, 0)) == -1) ||
    (u_ignore_sigpipe() != 0) )
    return -1;
```

Answer:

If `u_ignore_sigpipe()` fails, `u_connect` returns with an open file descriptor in `sock`. Since the calling program does not have the value of `sock`, this file descriptor could not be closed.

❏ Exercise 18.27

Does `u_connect` ever return an error if interrupted by a signal?

Answer:

To determine the overall behavior of `u_connect`, we must analyze the response of each call within `u_connect` to a signal. The `u_ignore_sigpipe` code of Appendix C only contains a `sigaction` call, which does not return an error when interrupted by a signal. The `socket` call does not return an `EINTR` error, implying that it either restarts itself or blocks signals. Also, `name2addr` does not return `EINTR`. An arriving signal is handled, ignored or blocked and the program continues (unless of course a handler terminates the program). The `connect` call can return if interrupted by a signal, but the implementation then calls `select` to wait for asynchronous completion. The `u_connect` function also restarts `select` if it is interrupted by a signal. Thus, `u_connect` should never return because of interruption by a signal.

18.8 Host Names and IP Addresses

Throughout this book we refer to hosts by name (e.g., `usp.cs.utsa.edu`) rather than by a numeric identifier. Host names must be mapped into numeric network addresses for most of the network library calls. As part of system setup, system administrators define the mechanism by which names are translated into network addresses. The mechanism might include local table lookup, followed by inquiry to domain name servers if necessary. The Domain Name Service (DNS) is the glue that integrates naming on the Internet [81, 82].

In general, a host machine can be specified either by its name or by its address. Host names in programs are usually represented by ASCII strings. IPv4 addresses are specified either in binary (in network byte order as in the `s_addr` field of `struct in_addr`) or in a human readable form, called the *dotted-decimal notation* or *Internet address dot notation*. The dotted form of an address is a string with the values of the four bytes in decimal, separated by decimal points. For example, 129.115.30.129 might be the address of the host with name `usp.cs.utsa.edu`. The binary form of an IPv4 address is 4 bytes long. Since 4-byte addresses do not provide enough room for future Internet expansion, a newer version of the protocol, IPv6, uses 16-byte addresses.

The `inet_addr` and `inet_ntoa` functions convert between dotted-decimal notation and the binary network byte order form used in the `struct in_addr` field of a `struct sockaddr_in`.

The `inet_addr` function converts a dotted-decimal notation address to binary in network byte order. The value can be stored directly in the `sin_addr.s_addr` field of a `struct sockaddr_in`.

SYNOPSIS

```
#include <arpa/inet.h>

in_addr_t inet_addr(const char *cp);
```

POSIX

If successful, `inet_addr` returns the Internet address. If unsuccessful, `inet_addr` returns `(in_addr_t)−1`. No errors are defined for `inet_addr`.

The `inet_ntoa` function takes a `struct in_addr` structure containing a binary address in network byte order and returns the corresponding string in dotted-decimal notation. The binary address can come from the `sin_addr` field of a `struct sockaddr_in` structure. The returned string is statically allocated, so `inet_ntoa` may not be safe to use in threaded applications. Copy the returned string to a different location before calling `inet_ntoa` again. Check the man page for `inet_ntoa` on your system to see if it is thread-safe.

```
SYNOPSIS

  #include <arpa/inet.h>

  char *inet_ntoa(const struct in_addr in);
                                                              POSIX
```

The `inet_ntoa` function returns a pointer to the network address in Internet standard dot notation. No errors are defined for `inet_ntoa`.

The different data types used for the binary form of an address often cause confusion. The `inet_ntoa` function, takes a `struct in_addr` structure as a parameter; the `inet_addr` returns data of type `in_addr_t`, a field of a `struct in_addr` structure. POSIX states that a `struct in_addr` structure must contain a field called `s_addr` of type `in_addr_t`. It is implied that the binary address is stored in `s_addr` and that a `struct in_addr` structure may contain other fields, although none are specified. It seems that in most current implementations, the `struct in_addr` structure contains only the `s_addr` field, so pointers to `sin_addr` and `sin_addr.s_addr` are identical. To maintain future code portability, however, be sure to preserve the distinction between these two structures.

At least three collections of library functions convert between ASCII host names and binary addresses. None of these collections report errors in the way UNIX functions do by returning −1 and setting `errno`. Each collection has advantages and disadvantages, and at the current time none of them stands out as the best method.

UICI introduces the `addr2name` and `name2addr` functions to abstract the conversion between strings and binary addresses and allow for easy porting between implementations. The `uiciname.h` header file shown in Program C.3 contains the following prototypes for `addr2name` and `name2addr`.

```
    int name2addr(const char *name, in_addr_t *addrp);
    void addr2name(struct in_addr addr, char *name, int namelen);
```

Link `uiciname.c` with any program that uses UICI.

The `name2addr` function behaves like `inet_addr` except that its parameter can be either a host name or an address in dotted-decimal format. Instead of returning the address, `name2addr` stores the address in the location pointed to by `addrp` to allow the return value to report an error. If successful, `name2addr` returns 0. If unsuccessful, `name2addr` returns −1. An error occurs if the system cannot determine the address corresponding to the given name. The `name2addr` function does not set `errno`. We suggest that when `name2addr` is called by a function that must return with `errno` set, the value `EINVAL` be used to indicate failure.

The `addr2name` function takes a `struct in_addr` structure as its first parameter and writes the corresponding name to the supplied buffer, `name`. The `namelen` value specifies the size of the `name` buffer. If the host name does not fit in `name`, `addr2name` copies the first `namelen - 1` characters of the host name followed by a string terminator. This function never produces an error. If the host name cannot be found, `addr2name` converts the host address to dotted-decimal notation.

We next discuss two possible strategies for implementing `name2addr` and `addr2name`. Section 18.9 discusses two additional implementations. Appendix C presents complete implementations using all four approaches. Setting the constant `REENTRANCY` in `uiciname.c` picks out a particular implementation. We first describe the default implementation that uses `gethostbyname` and `gethostbyaddr`.

A traditional way of converting a host name to a binary address is with the `gethostbyname` function. The `gethostbyname` function takes a host name string as a parameter and returns a pointer to a `struct hostent` structure containing information about the names and addresses of the corresponding host.

```
SYNOPSIS

  #include <netdb.h>

  struct hostent {
     char    *h_name;        /* canonical name of host */
     char    **h_aliases;    /* alias list */
     int     h_addrtype;     /* host address type */
     int     h_length;       /* length of address */
     char    **h_addr_list;  /* list of addresses */
  };

  struct hostent *gethostbyname(const char *name);

                                                            POSIX:OB
```

If successful, `gethostbyname` returns a pointer to a `struct hostent`. If unsuccessful, `gethostbyname` returns a `NULL` pointer and sets `h_errno`. Macros are available to produce an error message from an `h_errno` value. The following table lists the mandatory errors for `gethostbyname`.

h_errno	cause
HOST_NOT_FOUND	no such host
NO_DATA	server recognized request and name but has no address
NO_RECOVERY	unexpected server failure that cannot be recovered
TRY_AGAIN	temporary or transient error

The `struct hostent` structure includes two members of interest that are filled in by `gethostbyname`. The `h_addr_list` field is an array of pointers to network addresses used by this host. These addresses are in network byte order, so they can be used directly in the address structures required by the socket calls. Usually, we use only the first entry, `h_addr_list[0]`. The integer member `h_length` is filled with the number of bytes in the address. For IPv4, `h_length` should always be 4.

■ Example 18.28

The following code segment translates a host name into an IP address for the `s_addr` member of a `struct sockaddr_in`.

```
char *hostn = "usp.cs.utsa.edu";
struct hostent *hp;
struct sockaddr_in server;

if ((hp = gethostbyname(hostn)) == NULL)
    fprintf(stderr, "Failed to resolve host name\n");
else
    memcpy((char *)&server.sin_addr.s_addr, hp->h_addr_list[0], hp->h_length);
```

Often, a host has multiple names associated with it. For example, because `usp.cs.utsa.edu` is a web server for this book, the system also responds to the alias `www.usp.cs.utsa.edu`.

☐ Exercise 18.29

Use the `struct hostent` structure returned in Example 18.28 to output a list of aliases for `usp.cs.utsa.edu`.

Answer:

```
char **q;
struct hostent *hp;

for (q = hp->h_aliases; *q != NULL; q++)
    (void) printf("%s\n", *q);
```

☐ Exercise 18.30

Use the `struct hostent` structure returned in Example 18.28 to find out how many IP addresses are associated with `usp.cs.utsa.edu`.

Answer:

```
int addresscount = 0;
struct hostent *hp;
char **q;

for (q = hp->h_addr_list; *q != NULL; q++)
    addresscount++;
printf("Host %s has %d IP addresses\n", hp->h_name, addresscount);
```

Program 18.9 is one implementation of `name2addr`. The `name2addr` function first checks to see if `name` begins with a digit. If so, `name2addr` assumes that `name` is a dotted-decimal address and uses `inet_addr` to convert it to `in_addr_t`. Otherwise, `name2addr` uses `gethostbyname`.

Program 18.9 ———————————— `name2addr_gethostbyname.c`

An implementation of `name2addr` *using* `gethostbyname.`

```c
#include <ctype.h>
#include <netdb.h>
#include <string.h>
#include <unistd.h>
#include <arpa/inet.h>
#include <netinet/in.h>
#include <sys/socket.h>
#include <sys/types.h>

int name2addr(char *name, in_addr_t *addrp) {
   struct hostent *hp;

   if (isdigit((int)(*name)))
      *addrp = inet_addr(name);
   else {
      hp = gethostbyname(name);
      if (hp == NULL)
         return -1;
      memcpy((char *)addrp, hp->h_addr_list[0], hp->h_length);
   }
   return 0;
}
```

Program 18.9 ———————————————— `name2addr_gethostbyname.c`

The conversion from address to name can be done with `gethostbyaddr`. For IPv4, the `type` should be `AF_INET` and the `len` value should be 4 bytes. The `addr` parameter should point to a `struct in_addr` structure.

SYNOPSIS

```c
#include <netdb.h>

struct hostent *gethostbyaddr(const void *addr,
                              socklen_t len, int type);
```

POSIX:OB

If successful, `gethostbyaddr` returns a pointer to a `struct hostent` structure. If unsuccessful, `gethostbyaddr` returns a `NULL` pointer and sets `h_error`. The mandatory errors for `gethostbyaddr` are the same as those for `gethostbyname`.

■ Example 18.31

The following code segment prints the host name from a previously set `struct sockaddr_in` structure.

```c
struct hostent *hp;
struct sockaddr_in net;
int sock;

if (( hp = gethostbyaddr(&net.sin_addr, 4, AF_INET))
   printf("Host name is %s\n", hp->h_name);
```

Program 18.10 is an implementation of the `addr2name` function that uses the `gethostbyaddr` function. If `gethostbyaddr` returns an error, then `addr2name` uses `inet_ntoa` to convert the address to dotted-decimal notation. The `addr2name` function copies at most `namelen-1` bytes, allowing space for the string terminator.

Program 18.10 ———————————————— **addr2name_gethostbyaddr.c**

An implementation of addr2name *using* gethostbyaddr.

```c
#include <ctype.h>
#include <netdb.h>
#include <string.h>
#include <unistd.h>
#include <arpa/inet.h>
#include <netinet/in.h>
#include <sys/socket.h>
#include <sys/types.h>

void addr2name(struct in_addr addr, char *name, int namelen) {
   struct hostent *hostptr;
   hostptr = gethostbyaddr((char *)&addr, 4, AF_INET);
   if (hostptr == NULL)
      strncpy(name, inet_ntoa(addr), namelen-1);
   else
      strncpy(name, hostptr->h_name, namelen-1);
   name[namelen-1] = 0;
}
```

Program 18.10 ———————————————— **addr2name_gethostbyaddr.c**

When an error occurs, `gethostbyname` and `gethostbyaddr` return `NULL` and set `h_errno` to indicate an error. Thus, `errno` and `perror` cannot be used to display the correct error message. Also, `gethostbyname` and `gethostbyaddr` are not thread-safe because they use static data for storing the returned `struct hostent`. They should not be used in threaded programs without appropriate precautions being taken. (See Section 18.9.) A given implementation might use the same static data for both of these, so be careful to copy the result before it is modified.

A second method for converting between host names and addresses, `getnameinfo` and `getaddrinfo`, first entered an approved POSIX standard in 2001. These general functions, which can be used with both IPv4 and IPv6, are preferable to `gethostbyname` and `gethostbyaddr` because they do not use static data. Instead, `getnameinfo` stores the name in a user-supplied buffer, and `getaddrinfo` dynamically allocates a buffer to return with the address information. The user can free this buffer with `freeaddrinfo`. These functions are safe to use in a threaded environment. The only drawback in using these functions, other than the complication of the new structures used, is that they are not yet available on many systems.

```
SYNOPSIS

    #include <sys/socket.h>
    #include <netdb.h>

    void freeaddrinfo(struct addrinfo *ai);
    int getaddrinfo(const char *restrict nodename,
                    const char *restrict servname,
                    const struct addrinfo *restrict hints,
                    struct addrinfo **restrict res);
    int getnameinfo(const struct sockaddr *restrict sa,
                    socklen_t  salen, char *restrict node,
                    socklen_t nodelen, char *restrict service,
                    socklen_t servicelen, unsigned flags);
                                                            POSIX
```

If successful, `getaddrinfo` and `getnameinfo` return 0. If unsuccessful, these functions
return an error code. The following table lists the mandatory error codes for `getaddrinfo`
and `getnameinfo`.

error	cause
EAI_AGAIN	name cannot be resolved at this time
EAI_BADFLAGS	`flags` had an invalid value
EAI_FAIL	unrecoverable error
EAI_FAMILY	address family was not recognized or address length invalid for specified family
EAI_MEMORY	memory allocation failure
EAI_NONAME	name does not resolve for supplied parameters
EAI_SERVICE	service passed not recognized for socket (`getaddrinfo`)
EAI_SOCKTYPE	intended socket type not recognized (`getaddrinfo`)
EAI_SYSTEM	a system error occurred and error code can be found in `errno`
EAI_OVERFLOW	argument buffer overflow (`getaddrinfo`)

The `struct addrinfo` structure contains at least the following members.

```
int             ai_flags;      /* input flags */
int             ai_family;     /* address family */
int             ai_socktype;   /* socket type */
int             ai_protocol;   /* protocol of socket */
socklen_t       ai_addrlen;    /* length of socket address */
struct sockaddr *ai_addr;      /* socket address */
char            *ai_canonname; /* canonical service name */
struct addrinfo *ai_next;      /* pointer to next entry */
```

The user passes the name of the host in the `nodename` parameter of `getaddrinfo`.
The `servname` parameter can contain a service name (in IPv6) or a port number. For our
purposes, the `nodename` determines the address, and the `servname` parameter can be a
`NULL` pointer. The `hints` parameter tells `getaddrinfo` what type of addresses the caller
is interested in. For IPv4, we set `ai_flags` to 0. In this case, `ai_family`, `ai_socktype`

and `ai_protocol` are the same as in `socket`. The `ai_addrlen` parameter can be set to 0, and the remaining pointers can be set to `NULL`. The `getaddrinfo` function, using the `res` parameter, returns a linked list of `struct addrinfo` nodes that it dynamically allocates to contain the address information. When finished using this linked list, call `freeaddrinfo` to free the nodes.

Program 18.11 shows an implementation of `name2addr` that uses `getaddrinfo`. After calling `getaddrinfo`, the function copies the address and frees the memory that was allocated.

Program 18.11 ──────────────────────── **`name2addr_getaddrinfo.c`** ┐

An implementation of `name2addr` *using* `getaddrinfo`.

```c
#include <ctype.h>
#include <netdb.h>
#include <string.h>
#include <unistd.h>
#include <arpa/inet.h>
#include <netinet/in.h>
#include <sys/socket.h>
#include <sys/types.h>

int name2addr(char *name, in_addr_t *addrp) {
   struct addrinfo hints;
   struct addrinfo *res;
   struct sockaddr_in *saddrp;

   hints.ai_flags = 0;
   hints.ai_family = PF_INET;
   hints.ai_socktype = SOCK_STREAM;
   hints.ai_protocol = 0;
   hints.ai_addrlen = 0;
   hints.ai_canonname = NULL;
   hints.ai_addr = NULL;
   hints.ai_next = NULL;

   if (getaddrinfo(name,NULL,&hints,&res) != 0)
      return -1;

   saddrp = (struct sockaddr_in *)(res->ai_addr);
   memcpy(addrp, &saddrp->sin_addr.s_addr, 4);
   freeaddrinfo(res);
   return 0;
}
```

Program 18.11 ──────────────────────── **`name2addr_getaddrinfo.c`** ┘

To use `getnameinfo` to convert an address to a name, pass a pointer to a `sockaddr_in` structure in the first parameter and its length in the second parameter. Supply a buffer to hold the name of the host as the third parameter and the size of that buffer as the fourth parameter. Since we are not interested in the service name, the fifth parameter can be `NULL` and the sixth parameter can be 0. The last parameter is for flags, and it can be 0, causing the fully qualified domain name to be returned. The `sin_family` field of the `sockaddr_in` should be `AF_INET`, and the `sin_addr` field contains the addresses. If the name cannot be determined, the numeric form of the host name is returned, that is, the dotted-decimal form of the address.

Program 18.12 shows an implementation of `addr2name`. The `addr2name` function never returns an error. Instead, it calls `inet_ntoa` if `getnameinfo` produces an error.

Program 18.12 ──────────────────────── **addr2name_getnameinfo.c**
An implementation of `addr2name` *using* `getnameinfo`.

```
#include <ctype.h>
#include <netdb.h>
#include <string.h>
#include <unistd.h>
#include <arpa/inet.h>
#include <netinet/in.h>
#include <sys/socket.h>
#include <sys/types.h>

void addr2name(struct in_addr addr, char *name, int namelen) {
   struct sockaddr_in saddr;
   saddr.sin_family = AF_INET;
   saddr.sin_port = 0;
   saddr.sin_addr = addr;
   if (getnameinfo((struct sockaddr *)&saddr, sizeof(saddr), name, namelen,
         NULL, 0, 0) != 0) {
      strncpy(name, inet_ntoa(addr), namelen-1);
      name[namelen-1] = 0;
   }
}
```

Program 18.12 ──────────────────────────── **addr2name_getnameinfo.c**

18.9 Thread-Safe UICI

The UNIX functions that use `errno` were originally unsafe for threads. When `errno` was an external integer shared by all threads, one thread could set `errno` and have another thread change it before the first thread used the value. Multithreaded systems solve this problem by using thread-specific data for `errno`, thus preserving the syntax for the standard UNIX library functions. This same problem exists with any function that returns values in variables with static storage class.

The TCP socket implementation of UICI in Section 18.7 is thread-safe provided that the underlying implementations of `socket`, `bind`, `listen`, `accept`, `connect`, `read`, `write` and `close` are thread-safe and that the name resolution is thread-safe. The POSIX standard states that all functions defined by POSIX and the C standard are thread-safe, except the ones shown in Table 12.2 on page 432. The list is short and mainly includes functions, such as `strtok` and `ctime`, that require the use of static data.

The `gethostbyname`, `gethostbyaddr` and `inet_ntoa` functions, which are used in some versions of UICI name resolution, appear on the POSIX list of functions that might not be thread-safe. Some implementations of `inet_ntoa` (such as that of Sun Solaris) are thread-safe because they use thread-specific data. These possibly unsafe functions are used only in `name2addr` and `addr2name`, so the issue of thread safety of UICI is reduced to whether these functions are thread-safe.

Since `getnameinfo` and `getaddrinfo` are thread-safe, then if `inet_ntoa` is thread-safe, the implementations of `name2addr` and `addr2name` that use these are also thread-safe. Unfortunately, as stated earlier, `getnameinfo` and `getaddrinfo` are not yet available on many systems.

On some systems, thread-safe versions of `gethostbyname` and `gethostbyaddr`, called `gethostbyname_r` and `gethostbyaddr_r`, are available.

```
SYNOPSIS

   #include <netdb.h>

   struct hostent *gethostbyname_r(const char *name,
       struct hostent *result, char *buffer, int buflen,
       int *h_errnop);
   struct hostent *gethostbyaddr_r(const char *addr,
       int length, int type, struct hostent *result,
       char *buffer,  int buflen, int *h_errnop);
```

These functions perform the same tasks as their unsafe counterparts but do not use static storage. The user supplies a pointer to a `struct hostent` in the `result` parameter. Pointers in this structure point into the user-supplied `buffer`, which has length `buflen`. The supplied `buffer` array must be large enough for the generated data. When the `gethostbyname_r` and `gethostbyaddr_r` functions return `NULL`, they supply an error code in the integer pointed to by `*h_errnop`. Program 18.13 shows a thread-safe implementation of `addr2name`, assuming that `inet_ntoa` is thread-safe. Section C.2.2 contains a complete implementation of UICI, using `gethostbyname_r` and `gethostbyaddress_r`.

Unfortunately, `gethostbyname_r` and `gethostbyaddress_r` were part of the X/OPEN standard, but when this standard was merged with POSIX, these functions were omitted. Another problem associated with Program 18.13 is that it does not specify how large the user-supplied buffer should be. Stevens [115] suggests 8192 for this value, since that is what is commonly used in the implementations of the traditional forms.

An alternative for enforcing thread safety is to protect the sections that use static storage with mutual exclusion. POSIX:THR mutex locks provide a simple method of doing this. Program 18.14 is an implementation of `addr2name` that uses mutex locks. Section C.2.3 contains a complete implementation of UICI using mutex locks. This implementation does not require `inet_ntoa` to be thread-safe, since its static storage is protected also.

Program 18.13 ──────────────────── **addr2name_gethostbyaddr_r.c**
              A version of addr2name *using* gethostbyaddr_r.

```
#include <ctype.h>
#include <netdb.h>
#include <string.h>
#include <unistd.h>
#include <arpa/inet.h>
#include <netinet/in.h>
#include <sys/socket.h>
#include <sys/types.h>
#define GETHOST_BUFSIZE 8192

void addr2name(struct in_addr addr, char *name, int namelen) {
    char buf[GETHOST_BUFSIZE];
    int h_error;
    struct hostent *hp;
    struct hostent result;

    hp = gethostbyaddr_r((char *)&addr, 4, AF_INET, &result, buf,
                         GETHOST_BUFSIZE, &h_error);
    if (hp == NULL)
        strncpy(name, inet_ntoa(addr), namelen-1);
    else
        strncpy(name, hp->h_name, namelen-1);
    name[namelen-1] = 0;
}
```

Program 18.13 ──────────────────────────── **addr2name_gethostbyaddr_r.c**

Program 18.14 ──────────────────────── **addr2name_mutex.c**
            A thread-safe version of addr2name *using POSIX mutex locks.*

```
#include <ctype.h>
#include <netdb.h>
#include <pthread.h>
#include <string.h>
#include <unistd.h>
#include <arpa/inet.h>
#include <netinet/in.h>
#include <sys/socket.h>
#include <sys/types.h>

static pthread_mutex_t mutex = PTHREAD_MUTEX_INITIALIZER;

void addr2name(struct in_addr addr, char *name, int namelen) {
    struct hostent *hostptr;

    pthread_mutex_lock(&mutex);
    hostptr = gethostbyaddr((char *)&addr, 4, AF_INET);
    if (hostptr == NULL)
        strncpy(name, inet_ntoa(addr), namelen-1);
    else
        strncpy(name, hostptr->h_name, namelen-1);
    pthread_mutex_unlock(&mutex);
    name[namelen-1] = 0;
}
```

Program 18.14 ──────────────────────────── **addr2name_mutex.c**

18.10 Exercise: Ping Server

The ping command can be used to elicit a response from a remote host. The default for some systems is to just display a message signifying that the host responded. On other systems the default is to indicate how long it took for a reply to be received.

■ Example 18.32

The following command queries the usp.cs.utsa.edu host.

```
ping usp.cs.utsa.edu
```

The command might output the following message to mean that the host usp.cs.utsa.edu is responding to network communication.

```
usp.cs.utsa.edu is alive
```

This section describes an exercise that uses UICI to implement myping, a slightly fancier version of the ping service. The myping function responds with a message such as the following.

```
usp.cs.utsa.edu: 5:45am up 12:11, 2 users, load average: 0.14, 0.08, 0.07
```

The myping program is a client-server application. A myping server running on the host listens at a well-known port for client requests. The server forks a child to respond to the request. The original server process continues listening. Assume that the myping well-known port number is defined by the constant MYPINGPORT.

Write the code for the myping client. The client takes the host name as a command-line argument, makes a connection to the port specified by MYPINGPORT, reads what comes in on the connection and echoes it to standard output until end-of-file, closes the connection, and exits. Assume that if the connection attempt to the host fails, the client sleeps for SLEEPTIME seconds and then retries. After the number of failed connection attempts exceeds RETRIES, the client outputs the message that the host is not available and exits. Test the program by using the bidirectional server discussed in Example 18.18.

Implement the myping server. The server listens for connections on MYPINGPORT. If a client makes a connection, the server forks a child to handle the request and the original process resumes listening at MYPINGPORT. The child closes the listening file descriptor, calls the process_ping function, closes the communication file descriptor, and exits.

Write a process_ping function with the following prototype.

```
int process_ping(int communfd);
```

For initial testing, process_ping can just output an error message to the communication file descriptor. For the final implementation, process_ping should construct a message consisting of the host name and the output of the uptime command. An example message is as follows.

```
usp.cs.utsa.edu: 5:45am up 13:11, 2 users, load average: 0.14, 0.08, 0.07
```

Use `uname` to get the host name.

SYNOPSIS

```
#include <sys/utsname.h>

int uname(struct utsname *name);
```

POSIX

If successful, `uname` returns a nonnegative value. If unsuccessful, `uname` returns −1 and sets `errno`. No mandatory errors are defined for `uname`.

The `struct utsname` structure, which is defined in `sys/utsname.h`, has at least the following members.

```
char sysname[];    /* name of this OS implementation */
char nodenamep[]; /* name of this node within communication network */
char release[];    /* current release level of this implementation */
char version[];    /* current version level of this release */
char machine[];    /* name of hardware type on which system is running */
```

18.11 Exercise: Transmission of Audio

This section extends the UICI server and client of Program 18.1 and Program 18.3 to send audio information from the client to the server. These programs can be used to implement a network intercom, network telephone service, or network radio broadcasts, as described in Chapter 21.

Start by incorporating audio into the UICI server and client as follows.

- Run Programs 18.1 and 18.3 with redirected input and output to transfer files from client to server, and vice versa. Use `diff` to verify that each transfer completes correctly.

- Redirect the input to the client to come from the audio device (microphone) and redirect the output on the server to go to the audio device (speakers). You should be able to send audio across the network. (See Section 6.6 for information on how to do this.)

- Modify the bidirectional server and client to call the audio functions developed in Section 6.6 and Section 6.7 to transmit audio from the microphone of the client to the speaker of the server. Test your program for two-way communication.

The program sends even if no one is talking because once the program opens the audio device, the underlying device driver and interface card sample the audio input at a fixed rate until the program closes the file. The continuous sampling produces a prohibitive amount of data for transmission across the network. Use a filter to detect whether a packet contains voice, and throw away audio packets that contain no voice. A simple method of filtering is to convert the u-law (μ-law) data to a linear scale and reject packets that fall below a threshold. Program 18.15 shows an implementation of this filter for Solaris. The `hasvoice` function returns 1 if the packet contains voice and 0 if it should be thrown away. Incorporate `hasvoice` or another filter so that the client does not transmit silence.

Program 18.15 ────────────────────────────── `hasvoice.c`

A simple threshold function for filtering data with no voice.

```
#include <stdio.h>
#include <stdlib.h>
#include "/usr/demo/SOUND/include/multimedia/audio_encode.h"
#define THRESHOLD 20   /* amplitude of ambient room noise, linear PCM */

            /* return 1 if anything in audiobuf is above THRESHOLD */
int hasvoice(char *audiobuf, int length) {
   int i;

   for (i = 0; i < length; i++)
      if (abs(audio_u2c(audiobuf[i])) > THRESHOLD)
         return 1;
   return 0;
}
```

Program 18.15 ────────────────────────────── `hasvoice.c`

Write the following enhancements to the basic audio transmission service.
1. Develop a calibration function that allows the threshold for voice detection to be adjusted according to the current value of the ambient room noise.
2. Use more sophisticated filtering algorithms in place of simple thresholds.
3. Keep track of the total number of packets and the actual number of those that contain voice data. Display the information on standard error when the client receives a SIGUSR1 signal.
4. Add volume control options on both client and server sides.
5. Design an interface for accepting or rejecting connections in accordance with sender information.
6. Devise protocols analogous to caller ID and call-waiting.
7. Add an option on the server side to record the incoming audio to a file for later playback. Recording is easy if the client is sending all the packets. However, since the client is sending only packets with voice, straight recording does not sound right on playback because all silences are compressed. Keep timing information as well as the audio information in the recorded data.

18.12 Additional Reading

Computer Networks, 4th ed. by Tanenbaum [123] is a standard reference on computer networks. The three-volume set *TCP/IP Illustrated* by Stevens and Wright [113, 134, 114] provides details of the TCP/IP protocol and its implementation. The two volumes of *UNIX Network Programming* by Stevens [115, 116] are the most comprehensive references on UNIX network programming. *UNIX System V Network Programming* by Rago [92] is an excellent reference book on network programming under System V. The standard for network services was incorporated into POSIX in 2001 [49].

Chapter 19

Project: WWW Redirection

The World Wide Web has a client-server architecture based on a resource identification scheme (URI), a communication protocol (HTTP) and a document format (HTML), which together allow easy access and exchange of information. The decentralized nature of the Web and its effectiveness in making information accessible have led to fundamental social and cultural change. Every product, from breakfast cereal to cars, has a presence on the Web. Businesses and other institutions have come to regard the Web as an interface, even the primary interface, with their customers. By providing ubiquitous access to information, the Web has reduced barriers erected by geographic and political borders in a profound way.

Objectives
- Learn the basic operation of the HTTP protocol
- Experiment with a ubiquitous distributed system
- Explore the operation of the World Wide Web
- Use client-server communication
- Understand the roles of tunnels, proxies and gateways

19.1 The World Wide Web

Electronic hypertext contains links to expanded or related information embedded at relevant points in a document. The links are analogous to footnotes in a traditional paper document, but the electronic nature of these documents allows easier physical access to the links. As early as 1945, Vannevar Bush proposed linked systems for documents on microfiche [18], but electronic hypertext systems did not take hold until the 1960s and 1970s.

In 1980, Tim Berners-Lee wrote a notebook program for CERN called ENQUIRE that had bidirectional links between nodes representing information. In 1989, he proposed a system for browsing the CERN Computer Center's documentation and help service. Tim Berners-Lee and Robert Cailliau developed a prototype GUI browser-editor for the system in 1990 and coined the name "World Wide Web." The initial system was released in 1991. At the beginning of 1993 there were 50 known web servers, a number that grew to 500 by the end of 1993 and to 650,000 by 1997. Today, web browsers have become an integral interface to information, and the Internet has millions of web servers.

The World Wide Web is a collection of clients and servers that have agreed to interact and exchange information in a certain format. The *client* (an application such as a browser) first establishes a connection with a *server* (an application that accepts connections and responds). Once it has established a connection, the client sends an initial request asking for service. The server responds with the requested information or an error.

As described so far, the World Wide Web is a simple client-server architecture, no different from many others. Its attractiveness lies in the simplicity of the rules for locating resources (URIs), communicating (HTTP) and presenting information (HTML). The next section describes URLs, the most common format for resource location on the Web. Section 19.3 gives an overview of HTTP, the web communication protocol. HTML, the actual format for web pages, is not within the scope of this book. Section 19.4 discusses tunnels, gateways and caching. The chapter project explores various aspects of tunnels, proxies and gateways. Sections 19.5 and 19.6 guide you through the implementation of a tunnel that might be used in a firewall. Section 19.7 describes a driver for testing the programs. Section 19.8 discusses the HTTP parsing needed for the proxy servers. Sections 19.9 and 19.10 describe a proxy server that monitors the traffic generated by the browsers that use it. Sections 19.12 and 19.13 explore the use of gateways for firewalls and load balancing, respectively.

19.2 Uniform Resource Locators (URLs)

A Uniform Resource Locator (URL) has the form *scheme : location*. The *scheme* refers to the method used to access the resource (e.g., HTTP), and the *location* specifies where the resource resides.

■ **Example 19.1**

The URL `http://www.usp.cs.utsa.edu/usp/simple.html` specifies that the resource is to be accessed with the HTTP protocol. This particular resource, `usp/simple.html`, is located on the server `www.usp.cs.utsa.edu`.

While `http` is not the only valid URL scheme, it is certainly the most common one. Other schemes include `ftp` for file transfer, `mailto` for mail through a browser or other web client, and `telnet` for remote shell services. The syntax for `http` URLs is as follows.

```
http_URL = "http:" "//" host [ ":" port ] [abs_path [ "?" query]]
```

The optional fields are enclosed in brackets. The `host` field should be the human-readable name of a host rather than a binary IP address (Section 18.8). The client (often a browser) determines the server location by obtaining the IP address of the specified host. If the URL does not specify a port, the client assumes port 80. The `abs_path` field refers to a path that is relative to the web root directory of the server. The optional query is not discussed here.

■ **Example 19.2**

The URL `http://www.usp.cs.utsa.edu:8080/usp/simple.html` specifies that the server for the resource is listening on port 8080 rather than default port 80. The URL's absolute path is `/usp/simple.html`.

When a user opens a URL through a browser, the browser parses the server's host name and makes a TCP connection to that host on the specified port. The browser then sends a request to the server for the resource, as designated by the URL's absolute path using the HTTP protocol described in the next section.

■ **Example 19.3**

Figure 19.1 shows the location of a typical web server root directory (`web`) in the host file system. Only the part of the file system below the `web` directory root is visible and accessible through the web server. If the host name is `www.usp.cs.utsa.edu`, the image `title.gif` has the URL `http://www.usp.cs.utsa.edu/usp/images/title.gif`.

The specification of a resource location with a URL ties it to a particular server. If the resource moves, web pages that refer to the resource are left with bad links. The Uniform Resource Name (URN) gives more permanence to resource names than does the URL alone. The owner of a resource registers its URN and the location of the resource with a service. If the resource moves, the owner just updates the entry with the registration service. URNs are not in wide use at this time. Both URLs and URNs are examples of Uniform Resource Identifiers (URIs). Uniform Resource Identifiers are formatted strings that identify a resource by name, location or other characteristics.

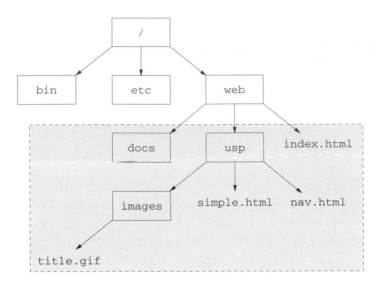

Figure 19.1: The root directory for the web server running on this host is /web. Only the boxed subtree is accessible through the Web.

19.3 HTTP Primer

Clients and web servers have a specific set of rules, or *protocol*, for exchanging information called HyperText Transfer Protocol (HTTP). HTTP is a request-reply protocol that assumes that messages are delivered reliably. For this reason, HTTP communication usually uses TCP, and that is what we assume in this discussion. We also restrict our initial discussion to HTTP 1.0 [53].

Figure 19.2 presents a schematic of a simple HTTP transaction. The client sends a request (e.g., a message that starts with the word GET). The server parses the message and responds with the status and possibly a copy of the requested resource.

19.3.1 Client requests

HTTP client requests begin with an *initial line* that specifies the kind of request being made, the location of the resource and the version of HTTP being used. The initial line ends with a carriage return followed by a line feed. In the following, <CRLF> denotes a carriage return followed by a line feed, and <SP> represents a white space character. A white space character is either a blank or tab.

■ **Example 19.4**

The following HTTP 1.0 client request asks a server for the resource

GET /usp/simple.html HTTP/1.0

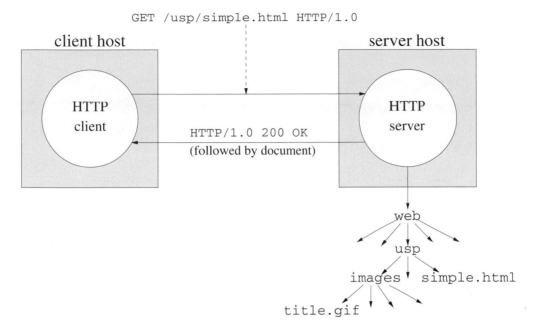

Figure 19.2: Schematic of an HTTP 1.0 transaction.

/usp/simple.html.

```
GET <SP> /usp/simple.html <SP> HTTP/1.0 <CRLF>
User-Agent:uiciclient <CRLF>
<CRLF>
```

The first or initial line of HTTP client requests has the following format.

```
Method <SP> Request-URI <SP> HTTP-Version <CRLF>
```

Method is usually GET, but other client methods include POST and HEAD.

The second line of the request in Example 19.4 is an example of a *header line* or *header field*. These lines convey additional information to the server about the request. Header lines are of the following form.

```
Field-Name:Field-Value <CRLF>
```

The last line of the request is empty. That is, the last header line just contains a carriage return and a line feed, telling the server that the request is complete. Notice that the HTTP request of Example 19.4 does not explicitly contain a server host name. The request of Example 19.4 might have been generated by a user opening the URL http://www.usp.cs.utsa.edu/usp/simple.html in a browser. The browser parses the URL into a server location `www.usp.cs.utsa.edu` and a location within that server `/usp/simple.html`. The browser then opens a TCP connection to port 80 of the server `www.usp.cs.utsa.edu` and sends the message of Example 19.4.

19.3.2 Server response

A web server responds to a client HTTP request by sending a *status line*, followed by any number of optional header lines, followed by an empty line containing just `<CRLF>`. The server then may send a resource. The status line has the following format.

```
HTTP-Version <SP> Status-Code <SP> Reason-Phrase <CRLF>
```

Table 19.1 summarizes the status codes, which are organized into groups by the first digit.

code	category	description
1xx	informational	reserved for future use
2xx	success	successful request
3xx	redirection	additional action must be taken (e.g., object has moved)
4xx	client error	bad syntax or other request error
5xx	server error	server failed to satisfy apparently valid request

Table 19.1: Common status codes returned by HTTP servers.

■ Example 19.5

When the request of Example 19.4 is sent to `www.usp.cs.utsa.edu`, the web server running on port 80 might respond with the following status line.

```
HTTP/1.0 <SP> 200 <SP> OK <CRLF>
```

After sending any additional header lines and an empty line to mark the end of the header, the server sends the contents of the requested file.

19.3.3 HTTP message exchange

HTTP presumes reliable transport of messages (in order, error-free), usually achieved by the use of TCP. Figure 19.3 shows the steps for the exchange between client and server, using a TCP connection. The server listens on a well-known port (e.g., 80) for a connection request. The client establishes a connection and sends a `GET` request. The server responds and closes the connection. HTTP 1.0 allows only a single request on a connection, so the client can detect the end of the sending of the resource by the remote closing of the connection. HTTP 1.1 allows the client to pipeline multiple requests on a single connection, requiring the server to send resource length information as part of the response.

☐ Exercise 19.6

How could you use Program 18.5 (`client2`) on page 629 to access the web server that is running on `www.usp.cs.utsa.edu`?

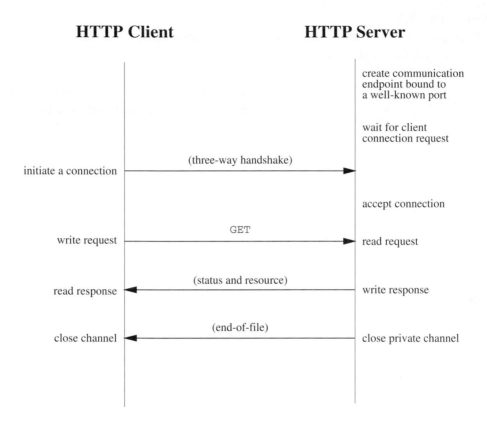

Figure 19.3: Sequence of steps in HTTP 1.0 communication.

Answer:

Start `client2` with the following command.

```
client2 www.usp.cs.utsa.edu 80
```

Type the HTTP request of Example 19.4 at the keyboard. The third line of the request is just an empty line. The host `www.usp.cs.utsa.edu` runs a web server that listens on port 80. The server interprets the message as an HTTP request and responds. The server then closes the connection.

❏ Exercise 19.7

What message does `client2` send to the host when you enter an empty line?

Answer:

The `client2` program sends a single byte, the line feed character with ASCII code 10 (the newline character).

◻ **Exercise 19.8**

Why does the web server still respond if you enter only a line feed and not a <CRLF> for the empty line?

Answer:

Although the HTTP specification [53] says that request lines should be terminated by <CRLF>, it also recommends that applications (clients and servers) be tolerant in parsing. Specifically, HTTP parsers should recognize a simple line feed as a line terminator and ignore the leading carriage return. It also recommends that parsers allow any number of space or tab characters between fields. Almost all web servers and browsers follow these guidelines.

◻ **Exercise 19.9**

Run Program 18.5 in the same way as in Exercise 19.6, but enter the following.

```
GET <SP> /usp/badref.html <SP> HTTP/1.0 <CRLF>
<CRLF>
```

What happens?

Answer:

The server responds with the following initial line.

```
HTTP/1.1 <SP> 404 <SP> Not <SP> Found <CRLF>
```

The server response may contain additional header lines before the blank line marking the end of the header. After sending the header, the server closes the connection. Note that the server is using HTTP version 1.1, but it sends a response that can be understood by the client, which is using HTTP version 1.0.

◻ **Exercise 19.10**

Run Program 18.5, using the following command to redirect the client's standard output to t.out.

```
client2 www.usp.cs.utsa.edu 80 > t.out
```

Enter the following at standard input of the client. What will t.out contain?

```
GET <SP> /usp/images/title.gif <SP> HTTP/1.0 <CRLF>
<CRLF>
```

Answer:

The t.out contains the server response, which consists of an ASCII header followed by a binary file representing an image. You can view the file by first removing the header and then opening the result in your browser. Use the UNIX more command to see how many header lines are there. If the file has 10 lines, use the following command to save the resources.

```
tail +11 t.out > t.gif
```

You can then use your web browser to display the result.

To summarize, an HTTP transaction consists of the following components.

- An initial line (GET, HEAD or POST for clients and a status line for servers).
- Zero or more header lines (giving additional information).
- A blank line (contains only <CRLF>).
- An optional message body. For the server response, the message body is the requested item, which could be binary.

The initial and header lines are tokenized ASCII separated by linear white space (tabs and spaces).

19.4 Web Communication Patterns

According to HTTP terminology [133], a *client* is an application that establishes a connection, and a *server* is an application that accepts connections and responds. A *user agent* is a client that initiates a request for service. Your browser is both a client and a user agent according to this terminology.

The *origin server* is the server that has the resource. Figure 19.2 on page 661 shows communication between a client and an origin server. In the current incarnation of the World Wide Web, firewalls, proxy servers and content distribution networks have changed the topology of client-server interaction. Communication between the user agent and the origin server often takes place through one or more intermediaries. This section covers four fundamental building blocks of this more complex topology: tunnels, proxies, caches and gateways.

19.4.1 Tunnels

A *tunnel* is an intermediary that acts as a blind relay. Tunnels do not parse HTTP, but forward it to the server. Figure 19.4 shows communication between a user agent and an origin server with an intermediate tunnel.

The tunnel of Figure 19.4 accepts an HTTP connection from a client and establishes a connection to the server. In this scenario, the tunnel acts both as a client and as a server according to the HTTP definition, although it is neither a user agent nor an origin server. The tunnel forwards the information from the client to the server. When the server responds, the tunnel forwards the response to the client. The tunnel detects closing of connections by either the client or server and closes the other end. After closing both ends, the tunnel ceases to exist. The tunnel of Figure 19.4 always connects to the web server running on the host www.usp.cs.utsa.edu.

Sometimes a tunnel does not establish its own connections but is created by another entity such as a firewall or gateway after the connections are established. Figure 19.5 illustrates one such situation in which a client connects to www.usp.cs.utsa.edu, a host running outside of a firewall. The firewall software creates a tunnel for the connection

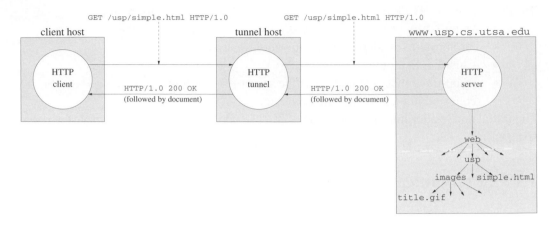

Figure 19.4: Communication between a user agent and an origin server through a tunnel.

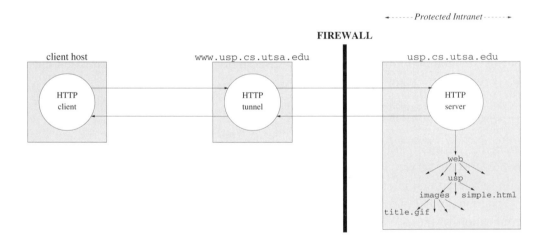

Figure 19.5: Tunnels provide a controlled portal through a firewall.

to a machine `usp.cs.utsa.edu` that is behind the firewall. Clients behind the firewall connect directly to `usp.cs.utsa.edu`, but `usp` is not visible outside of the firewall. As far as the client is concerned, the content is on the machine `www.usp.cs.utsa.edu`. The client knows nothing of `usp.cs.utsa.edu`.

19.4.2 Proxies

A *proxy* is an intermediary between clients and servers that makes requests on behalf of its clients. Proxies are addressed by a special form of the GET request and must parse HTTP. Like tunnels, proxies act both as clients and servers. However, a proxy is generally long-lived and often acts as an intermediary for many clients. Figure 19.6 shows an example in which a browser has set its proxy to org.proxy.net. The HTTP client (e.g., a browser) makes a connection to the HTTP proxy (e.g., org.proxy.net) and writes its HTTP request. The HTTP proxy parses the request and makes a separate connection to the HTTP origin server (e.g., www.usp.cs.utsa.edu). When the origin server responds, the HTTP proxy copies the response on the channel connected to the HTTP client.

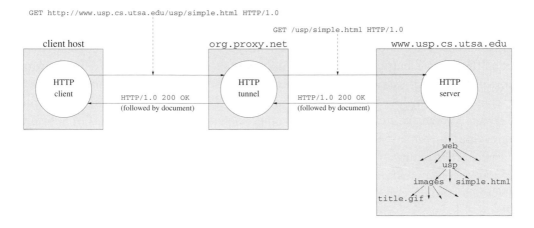

Figure 19.6: A proxy accesses any server on behalf of a client.

The GET request of Example 19.4 uses an *absolute path* to specify the resource location. Clients use an alternative form, the *absolute URI*, when directing requests to a proxy. The absolute URI contains the full HTTP address of the destination server. In Figure 19.6, the http://www.usp.cs.utsa.edu/usp/simple.html is an absolute URI; /usp/simple.html is an absolute path.

■ Example 19.11

This HTTP request contains an absolute URI rather than an absolute path.

```
GET <SP> http://www.usp.cs.utsa.edu/usp/simple.html <SP> HTTP/1.0 <CRLF>
User-Agent:uiciclient <CRLF>
<CRLF>
```

The proxy server parses the GET line and initiates an HTTP request to www.usp.cs.utsa.edu for the resource /usp/simple.html.

When directing a request through a proxy, user agents use the absolute URI form of the GET request and connect to the proxy rather than directly to the origin server. When a server receives a GET request containing an absolute URI, it knows that it should act as a proxy rather than as the origin server. The proxy reconstructs the GET line so that it contains an absolute path, such as the one shown in Example 19.4, and makes the connection to the origin server. Often, the proxy adds additional header lines to the request. The proxy itself can use another proxy, in which case it forwards the original GET to its designated proxy. Most browsers allow a user option of setting a proxy rather than connecting directly to the origin server. Once set up, the browser's operation with a proxy is transparent to the user, other than a performance improvement or degradation.

19.4.3 Caching and Transparency

A *transparent proxy* is one that does not modify requests or responses beyond what is needed for proxy identification and authentication. *Nontransparent proxies* may perform many other types of services on behalf of their clients (e.g., annotation, anonymity filtering, content filtering, censorship, media conversion). Proxies may keep statistics and other information about their clients. Search engines such as Google are proxies of a different sort, caching information about the content of pages along with the URLs. Users access the cached information by keywords or phrases. Clients that use proxies assume that the proxies are correct and trustworthy.

The most important service that proxies perform on behalf of clients is caching. A *cache* is a local store of response messages. Browsers usually cache recent response messages on disk. When a user opens a URL, the browser checks first to see if the resource can be found on disk and only initiates a network request if it didn't find the object locally.

❏ Exercise 19.12

Examine the current settings and contents of the cache on your browser. Different browsers allow access to this information in different ways. The local cache and proxies are accessible under the Advanced option of the Preferences submenu on the Edit menu in Netscape 6. In Internet Explorer 6, you can access the information from the Internet Options submenu under the Tools menu. The cache is designated under Temporary Internet Files on the General menu. Proxies are designed under LAN Settings on the Connections submenu of Internet Options. Look at the files in the directory that holds your local browser cache. Your browser should offer an option for clearing the local cache. Use the option to clear your local cache, and examine the directory again. What is the effect? Why does the browser keep a local cache and how does the browser use this cache?

Answer:
Clearing the cache should remove the contents of the local cache directory. When the user opens a page in the browser, the browser first checks the local disk for the requested object. If the requested object is in the local cache, the browser can retrieve it locally and avoid a network transfer. Browsers use local caches to speed access and reduce network traffic.

A *proxy cache* stores resources that it fetches in order to more effectively service future requests for those resources. When the proxy cache receives a request for an object from a client, it first checks its local store of objects. If the object is found in the proxy's local cache (Figure 19.7), the proxy can retrieve the object locally rather than by transferring it from the origin server.

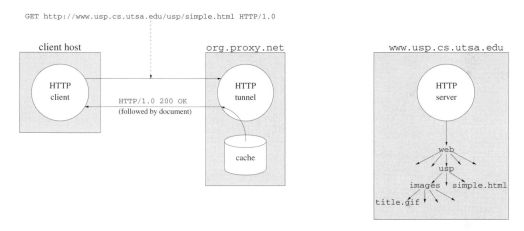

Figure 19.7: If possible, a proxy cache retrieves requested resources from its local store.

If the proxy cache does not find an object in its local store (Figure 19.8), it retrieves the object from the origin server and decides whether to save it locally. Some objects contain headers indicating they cannot be cached. The proxy may also decide not to cache an object for other reasons, for example, because the object is too large to cache or because the proxy does not want to remove other, frequently accessed, objects from its cache.

Often, proxy caches are installed at the gateways to local area networks. Clients on the local network direct all their requests through the proxy. The objects in the proxy cache's local store are responses to requests from many different users. If someone else has already requested the object and the proxy has cached the object, the response to the current request will be much faster.

You are probably wondering what happens if the object has changed since the cache stored the object. In this case, the proxy may return an object that is out-of-date, or *stale*,

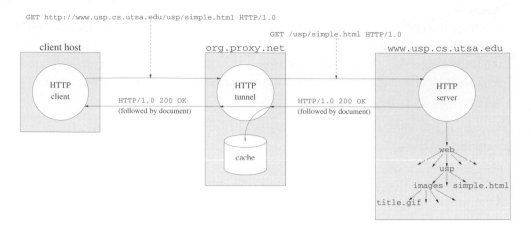

Figure 19.8: When a proxy cannot locate a requested resource locally, it requests the object from the origin server and may elect to add the object to its local cache.

a situation that can be mitigated by expiration strategies. Origin servers often provide an expiration time as part of the response header. Proxy caches also use expiration policies to keep old objects from being cached indefinitely. Finally, the proxy (or any client) can execute a conditional GET by including an If-Modified-Since field as a header line. The server only returns objects that have changed since the specified modification date. Otherwise, the server returns a 304 Not Modified response, and the proxy can use the copy from its cache.

19.4.4 Gateways

While a proxy can be viewed as a client-side intermediary, a *gateway* is a server-side mechanism. A gateway receives requests as though it is an origin server. A gateway may be located at the boundary router for a local area network or outside a firewall protecting an intranet. Gateways provide a variety of services such as security, translation and load balancing. A gateway might be used as the common interface to a cluster of web servers for an organization or as a front-end portal to a web server that is behind a firewall.

Figure 19.9 shows an example of how a gateway might be configured to provide a common access point to resources inside and outside a firewall. The server www.usp.cs.utsa.edu acts as a gateway for usp.cs.utsa.edu, a server that is behind the firewall. If a GET request accesses a resource in the usp directory, the gateway creates a tunnel to usp.cs.utsa.edu. For other resources, the gateway creates a tunnel to the www.cs.utsa.edu server outside the firewall.

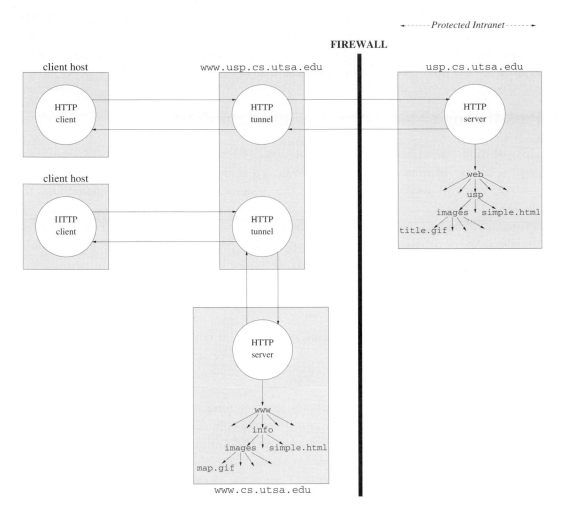

Figure 19.9: The server `www.usp.cs.utsa.edu` acts as a gateway for servers inside and outside the firewall.

☐ Exercise 19.13

How does a gateway differ from a tunnel?

Answer:

A tunnel is a conduit that passes information from one point to another without change. A gateway acts as a front end for a resource, perhaps a cluster of servers.

This chapter explores various aspects of tunnels, proxies and gateways. Sections 19.5 and 19.6 guide you through the implementation of a tunnel that might be used in a firewall.

Section 19.7 describes a driver for testing the programs. Section 19.8 discusses the HTTP parsing needed for the proxy servers. Sections 19.9 and 19.10 describe a proxy server that monitors the traffic generated by the browsers that use it. Sections 19.12 and 19.13 explore the use of gateways for firewalls and load balancing, respectively.

19.5 Pass-through Monitoring of Single Connections

This section describes an implementation of a simple pass-through monitor, `passmonitor`, similar to the tunnel illustrated in Figure 19.4. The `passmonitor` program takes its listening port number, the destination web server host name and an optional destination web server port number as command-line arguments. If the last argument is omitted, `passmonitor` assumes that the destination web server uses port 80. The monitor listens at the specified port for TCP connection requests (using the UICI `u_accept` function). When it accepts a client connection, `passmonitor` initiates a TCP connection to the destination server (using `u_connect`) and calls the `tunnel` function described below. After control returns from `tunnel`, `passmonitor` resumes listening for another client connection request.

The `tunnel` function, which handles one session between a client and the origin server, has the following prototype.

```
int tunnel(int clientfd, int serverfd);
```

Here, `clientfd` is the open file descriptor returned after acceptance of the client's connection request. The `serverfd` parameter is an open file descriptor for a TCP connection between the monitor and the destination server. The `tunnel` function forwards all messages received from `clientfd` to `serverfd`, and vice versa. If either the client or the destination server closes a connection (`clientfd` or `serverfd`, respectively), `tunnel` closes its connections and returns the total number of bytes that were forwarded in both directions.

After control returns from `tunnel`, `passmonitor` writes status information to standard error, reporting the total number of bytes written for this communication and the time the communication took. The monitor then resumes listening for another client connection request.

To correctly implement `passmonitor`, you cannot assume that the client and the server strictly alternate responses. The `passmonitor` program reads from two sources (the client and the server) and must allow for the possibility that either could send next. Use `select` or `poll` as in Program 4.13 to monitor the two file descriptors. A simple implementation of `tunnel` is given in Example 19.14. Be sure to handle all errors returned by library functions. Under what circumstances should `passmonitor` exit? What other strategies should `passmonitor` use when errors occur?

■ **Example 19.14**

The `tunnel` function can easily be implemented in terms of the `copy2files` function of Program 4.13 on page 111.

```
int tunnel(int fd1, int fd2) {
   int bytescopied;

   bytescopied = copy2files(fd1, fd2, fd2, fd1);
   close(fd1);
   close(fd2);
   return bytescopied;
}
```

Recall that `copy2files` returns if either side closes a file descriptor.

□ **Exercise 19.15**

Use Program 18.5 on page 629 to test `passmonitor` by having it connect to web servers through `passmonitor`. Why doesn't `passmonitor` have to parse the client's request before forwarding it to the destination server?

Answer:

The `passmonitor` program uses only the destination server that is passed to it on the command line.

□ **Exercise 19.16**

Suppose you start `passmonitor` on machine `os1.cs.utsa.edu` with the following command.

```
passmonitor 15000 www.usp.cs.utsa.edu
```

Start `client2` on another machine with the following command.

```
client2 os1.cs.utsa.edu 15000
```

If you then enter the following request (on `client2`), the `passmonitor` sends the request to port 80 of www.usp.cs.utsa.edu.

```
GET <SP> /usp/simple.html <SP> HTTP/1.0 <CRLF>
User-Agent:uiciclient <CRLF>
<CRLF>
```

How does the reply differ from the one received by having `client2` connect directly as in Example 19.4?

Answer:

The replies should be the same in the two cases if `passmonitor` is correct.

□ **Exercise 19.17**

Test `passmonitor` by using a web browser as the client. Start `passmonitor` as in Exercise 19.16. To access `/usp/simple.html`, open the URL as follows.

```
http://os1.cs.utsa.edu:15000/usp/simple.html
```

Notice that the browser treats the host on which `passmonitor` is running as the origin server with port number 15000. What happens when you don't specify a port number in the URL?

Answer:
The browser makes the connection to port 80 of the host running `passmonitor`.

□ **Exercise 19.18**

Suppose that you are using a browser and have started `passmonitor` as in Exercise 19.16. What series of connections are initiated when you open the URL as specified in Exercise 19.17?

Answer:
Your browser makes a connection to port 15000 on `os1.cs.utsa.edu` and sends a request similar to the one in Example 19.4 on page 660. The `passmonitor` program receives the request, establishes a connection to port 80 on `www.usp.cs.utsa.edu`, and forwards the browser's request. The `passmonitor` program returns `www.usp.cs.utsa.edu`'s response to the browser and closes the connections.

19.6 Tunnel Server Implementation

A tunnel is a blind relay that ceases to exist when both ends of a connection are closed. The `passmonitor` program of Section 19.5 is technically not a tunnel because it resumes listening for another connection request after closing its connections to the client and the destination server. It acts as a server for the `tunnel` function. One limitation of `passmonitor` is that it handles only one communication at a time.

Modify the `passmonitor` program of Section 19.5 to fork a child to handle the communication. The child should call the `tunnel` function and print to standard output a message containing the total number of bytes written. Call the new program `tunnelserver`.

The parent, which you can base on Program 18.2 on page 623, should clean up zombies by calling `waitpid` with the WNOHANG option and resume listening for additional requests.

□ **Exercise 19.19**

How would you start `tunnelserver` on port 15002 to service the web server `www.usp.cs.utsa.edu` running on port 8080 instead of port 80?

Answer:

```
tunnelserver 15002 www.usp.cs.utsa.edu 8080
```

☐ Exercise 19.20

Why can't the child process of `tunnelserver` return the total number of bytes processed to the parent process in its return value?

Answer:

Only 8 bits of the process return value can be stored in the status value from `wait`.

19.7 Server Driver for Testing

Modify Program 18.3 (`client`) on page 624 to create a test program for the `tunnelserver` program and call it `servertester`. The test program should take four command-line arguments: the tunnel server host name, the tunnel server port number, the number of children to fork and the number of requests each child should make. The parent process forks the specified number of children and then waits for them to exit. Wait for the children by calling `wait(NULL)` a number of times equal to the number of children created. (See, for example, Example 3.15 on page 73.) Each child executes the `testhttp` function described below and examines its return value. The `testhttp` function has the following prototype.

```
int testhttp(char *host, int port, int numTimes);
```

The `testhttp` function executes the following in a loop for `numTimes` times.
  1. Make a connection to `host` on `port` (e.g., `u_connect`).
  2. Write the `REQUEST` string to the connection. `REQUEST` is a string constant containing the three lines of a `GET` request similar to that of Example 19.4 on page 660. Use a `REQUEST` string appropriate for the host you plan to connect to.
  3. Read from the connection until the remote end closes the connection or until an error occurs. Keep track of the total number of bytes read from this connection.
  4. Close the connection.
  5. Add the number of bytes to the overall total.

If successful, `testhttp` returns the total number of bytes read from the network. If unsuccessful, `testhttp` returns –1 and sets `errno`.

Begin by writing a simple version of `servertester` that calls `testhttp` with `numTimes` equal to 1 and saves and prints the number of bytes corresponding to one request.

After you have debugged the single request case, modify `servertester` to fork children after the first call to `testhttp`. Each child calls `testhttp` and displays an error message if the number of bytes returned is not `numTimes` times the number returned by the call made by the original parent process.

Add statements in the `main` program to read the time before the first fork and after the last child has been waited for. Output the difference in these times. Make sure there is no output to the screen between the two statements that read the time. Use conditional compilation to include or not include the print statements of `tunnelserver`. The `tunnelserver` program should not produce any output after its initial startup unless an error occurs.

Start testing `servertester` by directly accessing a web server. For example, access `www.usp.cs.utsa.edu`, using the following command to estimate how long it takes to directly access the web server.

```
servertester www.usp.cs.utsa.edu 80 10 20
```

Then, do some production runs of `tunnelserver` and compare the times. You can also run `servertester` on multiple machines to generate a heavier load.

☐ Exercise 19.21

Suppose, as in Exercise 19.19, that `tunnelserver` was started on port 15002 of host `os1.cs.utsa.edu` to service the web server `www.usp.cs.utsa.edu` on port 8080. How would you start `servertester` to make 20 requests from each of 10 children?

Answer:

```
servertester os1.cs.utsa.edu 15002 10 20
```

☐ Exercise 19.22

How do you expect the elapsed time for `servertester` to complete in Exercise 19.21 to compare with that of directly accessing the origin server?

Answer:

If both programs are run under the same conditions, Exercise 19.21 should take longer. The difference in time is an indication of the overhead incurred by going through the tunnel.

19.8 HTTP Header Parsing

In contrast to tunnels, proxies and gateways are party to the HTTP communication and must parse at least the initial line of the client request. This section discusses a `parse` function that parses the initial request line. The `parse` function has the following prototype.

```
int parse(char *inlin, char **commandp, char **serverp,
                char **pathp, char **protocolp, char **portp);
```

The `inlin` parameter should contain the initial line represented as an array terminated by a line feed. Do not assume in your implementation of `parse` that `inlin` is a string, because it may not have a string terminator. The `parse` function parses `inlin` in place so that no additional memory needs to be allocated or freed.

The `parse` function returns 1 if the initial line contains exactly three tokens, or 0 otherwise. On a return of 1, `parse` sets the last five parameters to strings representing the command, server, path, protocol and port, respectively. These strings should not contain any blanks, tabs, carriage returns or line feeds.

The server and port pointers may be `NULL`. If an absolute path rather than an absolute URI is given, the server pointer is `NULL`. If the optional port number is not given, the port pointer is `NULL`. Allow any number of blanks or tabs at the start of `inlin`, between tokens, or after the last token. The `inlin` buffer may have an optional carriage return right before the line feed.

■ Example 19.23

Figure 19.10 shows the result of calling `parse` on a line containing an absolute path form of the URI. The line has two blanks after `GET` and two blanks after the path. The carriage return and line feed directly follow the protocol. The `parse` function sets the first blank after `GET` and the first blank after the path to the null character (i.e., `'\0'`). The `parse` function also replaces the carriage return by the null character. The `NULL` value of the `*serverp` parameter signifies that no host name was present in the initial `inlin`, and the `NULL` value of `*portp` signifies that no port number was specified.

■ Example 19.24

Figure 19.11 shows the result of `parse` for a line that contains an absolute URI distinguished by the leading `http://` after `GET`. Notice that `parse` moves the host name one character to the left so that it can insert a null character between the host name and the path. There is always room to do this, since the leading `http://` is no longer needed.

Implement `parse` in stages. Start by skipping the leading blanks and tabs, and check that there are exactly three tokens before the first line feed. If `inlin` does not have exactly three tokens, return 0. Then break these tokens into three strings, setting the command, path and protocol pointers. Consider the second token to be an absolute URI if it starts with `http://` and contains at least one additional `/` character. The server and port pointers should be set to `NULL`. After successful testing, handle the server pointer. When this is working, check for the port number.

You should write the code to break the input line into strings yourself. Do not use `strtok`, since it is not thread-safe. Be careful not to assume that the input line is terminated by a string terminator. Do not modify any memory before or after the input line. Test `parse` by writing a simple driver program. Remember not to assume that the first parameter to `parse` is a string.

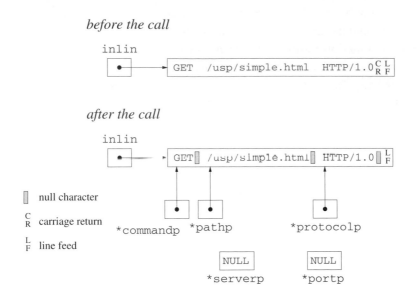

Figure 19.10: The `parse` function parses an absolute path form of the initial line in place.

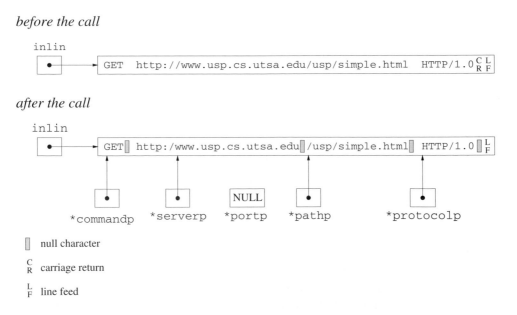

Figure 19.11: The `parse` function parses the absolute URI form of the initial line by moving the server name to the left.

19.9 Simple Proxy Server

This section describes a modification of the `tunnelserver` program of Section 19.6 so that it acts like a proxy rather than a tunnel. A proxy must parse the initial request line (unless the proxy happens to be using a proxy, too).

■ Example 19.25

When a proxy server receives the following `GET` line, it knows that it is to act as a proxy because the absolute URI form of the request is given.

```
GET http://www.usp.cs.utsa.edu/usp/simple.html  HTTP/1.0
```

The proxy knows that the origin server is `www.usp.cs.utsa.edu` and replaces the initial line with the following initial line.

```
GET  /usp/simple.html  HTTP/1.0
```

The proxy then makes a connection to port 80 of `www.usp.cs.utsa.edu`.

Make a new directory with a copy of the files for `tunnelserver` of Section 19.6. Rename `tunnelserver` to `proxyserver`. The `proxyserver` program takes a single command-line argument, the port number at which it listens for requests. The `proxyserver` program does not need the destination web server as a command-line argument because it parses the initial HTTP request from the client, as in Example 19.25. Write a `processproxy` function that has the following prototype.

```
int processproxy(int clientfd);
```

The `clientfd` parameter is the file descriptor returned when the server accepts the client's connection request.

The `processproxy` function reads in the first line from `clientfd` and calls `parse` to parse the initial request. If `parse` is successful and the line contains an absolute URI (the server pointer is not `NULL`), `processproxy` establishes a connection to the destination server. Then `processproxy` writes to the destination server an initial line containing a command with an absolute path and calls the `tunnel` function to continue the communication. If the port parameter of `parse` is not `NULL`, use the indicated port. Otherwise use port 80.

If successful, `processproxy` returns the total number of bytes transferred, which is the return value from `tunnel` plus the length of the initial line read from the client and the corresponding line sent to the server. If unsuccessful, `processproxy` returns −1 and sets `errno`.

Assume a maximum line length of 4096 bytes for the initial command from the client so that you need not do dynamic memory allocation. This means that a longer request is considered invalid, but you must not let a long request overflow the buffer. To read the first line from the client, you must read one byte at a time until you get a newline.

If `parse` returns an error, `processproxy` should treat the connection request as an error. In this case, `processproxy` writes the following message on `clientfd`, closes the connection, and returns −1 with `errno` set.

```
HTTP/1.0 <SP> 400 <SP> Bad <SP> Request <CRLF>
<CRLF>
```

The `proxyserver` program listens for connection requests on the given port, and for each request it forks a child that calls `processproxy` and prints the number of bytes transferred.

Copy your `servertester.c` into `proxytester.c` and modify the request to contain an absolute URI instead of an absolute path. Use `proxytester` to test `proxyserver`.

☐ Exercise 19.26

How would you test `proxyserver` through your browser?

Answer:

Set your browser to use `proxyserver` as its proxy. Suppose that `proxyserver` is running on machine `os1.cs.utsa.edu` using port 15000. Set your browser proxy to be `os1.cs.utsa.edu` on port number 15000. You should be able to use your browser with no noticeable difference.

19.10 Proxy Monitor

Make a copy of `proxyserver` from Section 19.9 and call it `proxymonitor`. Modify `proxymonitor` to take an optional command-line argument, `pathname`, giving the name of a log file. All header traffic and additional information should be dumped to this file in a useful format. Modify `processproxy` to take an additional parameter, the name of the log file. Do no logging if this additional parameter is NULL. Log the following information.

1. Client host name and destination host name
2. Process ID of the process running `processproxy`
3. Initial request line from the client to the proxy
4. Initial request line sent by the proxy to the server
5. All additional header lines from the client
6. All additional header lines from the server
7. The following byte counts
    a. Length of the initial request from the client
    b. Length of the initial request from the proxy

c. Length of the additional header lines from the client

d. Length of the additional header lines from the server

e. Number of additional bytes sent by the server

f. Number of additional bytes sent by the client

g. Total number of bytes sent from the client to the proxy

h. Total number of bytes sent from the proxy to the server

i. Total number of bytes sent from the server to the proxy

All this information should be stored in a convenient readable format. All header lines should be labeled to indicate their source. Logging must be done atomically so that the log produced by one child running `processsproxy` is not interleaved with another. You can do this by opening the log file with the `O_APPEND` flag and doing all logging with a single call to `write`. A simpler way would be to use the atomic logging facility described in Section 4.9. Section D.1 provides the complete code for this facility.

You will not be able to use `tunnel` for your implementation because sometimes `proxymonitor` reads lines and sometimes it reads binary content that is not line oriented. After sending the initial request to the host, as in the `proxyserver`, the client sends line-oriented data that the proxy logs until the client sends a blank line. The client may then send arbitrary data until the connection is closed. The `proxymonitor` needs to log only the number of bytes of this additional data. Similarly, the server sends line-oriented header information that `proxymonitor` logs until the server sends a blank line. The server may then send arbitrary data until the connection is closed, but the `proxymonitor` logs only the number of bytes the server sent for this portion.

❏ Exercise 19.27

What is wrong with the following strategy for implementing `proxymonitor`?

- Read the initial header line from the client and send the corresponding line to the server (as in the `proxyserver`).
- Read, log and send client header lines until encountering a blank line.
- Read, log and send server header lines until encountering a blank line.
- Handle binary data between the client and the server as in `tunnel`, keeping track of the number of bytes sent in each direction for logging.

Answer:

This should work for GET and HEAD, but it will fail for POST. For a POST command, the client sends its content before the server sends back a header, so the process blocks while waiting for the server header when in fact it should be reading the client content.

One method of implementing `proxymonitor` is to keep track of the states of the client and server. Each sends headers until a blank line and then sends content. Use `select` to determine which descriptor is ready and then process either a header line or content, depending on the state of the source. If `proxymonitor` encounters a blank header line, it changes the state of the respective client or server from header to content.

◻ **Exercise 19.28**

What happens if several copies of `proxymonitor` run concurrently using the same log file?

Answer:

As long as the different copies run on different ports, there should not be a problem, provided that logging is atomic. In this case, you might also want to log the port number with each transaction.

◻ **Exercise 19.29**

Why don't we log the total number of bytes sent from the proxy to the client?

Answer:

This should be the same as the total number of bytes sent from the server to the proxy.

◻ **Exercise 19.30**

The last three numbers logged are the byte totals for a given transaction. How would you keep track of and log the total number of bytes for each of these items for all transactions processed by `proxymonitor`?

Answer:

This requires some work, since the different transactions are handled by different processes. One possibility is to convert the program to use threads rather than children. The total could then be kept in global variables and updated by each thread. The routines to update these totals would have to be protected by a synchronization construct such as a semaphore or a mutex lock.

To do this without using threads, `proxymonitor` could create an additional child process to keep track of the totals. This process could communicate with the children by running `processproxy` with two pipes, one to send the new values to this process and one to receive the new totals from this process. Create the two pipes and this child before doing any other processing. The server processes can store the integers in a structure and output them to the pipe in raw form with a single `write` operation. You need not worry about byte ordering, since the communication is on the same machine. You still need to worry about synchronization to guarantee that the totals received by the children include the values of the current transaction.

❑ Exercise 19.31

Explain the last sentence of the answer to the previous exercise.

Answer:

Suppose we keep track of only one number. The child running `processproxy` sends the number corresponding to a transaction on one pipe and then reads the new total on the other pipe. Consider the case in which the proxy has just started up and so the current total is 1000. Child A is running a small transaction of 100 bytes, and child B is running a larger transaction of 100,000 bytes. Child A sends 100 on the first pipe and reads the new total on the second pipe. Child B sends 100,000 on the first pipe and reads the new total on the second pipe. If the sending and receiving for each process is not done atomically, The following ordering is possible.

- Child A sends 100 on the first pipe.
- 1100 (the new total) is written to the second pipe.
- Child B sends 100,000 on the first pipe.
- 101,100 (the new total) is written to the second pipe.
- Child B reads 1100 from the second pipe.
- Child A reads 101,100 from the second pipe.

At this pipe, Child B will have completed a transaction of 100,000 bytes and report that the total so far (including this transaction) is 1100 bytes. To fix this problem, make the writing to the first pipe and the reading from the second pipe be atomic. You can do this by using a POSIX:XSI semaphore set shared by all the child processes.

19.11 Proxy Cache

Proxy caches save resources in local storage so that requests can be satisfied locally. The cache can be in memory or on disk.

Starting with the `proxymonitor` of Section 19.10, write a program called `proxycache` that stores all the resources from the remote hosts on disk. Each unique resource must be stored in a unique file. One way to do this is to use sequential file names like cache00001, cache00002, etc., and keep a list containing host name, resource name and filename. Most proxy implementations use some type of hashing or digest mechanism to efficiently represent and search the contents of the cache for a particular resource.

Start by just storing the resources without modifying the communication. If the same resource is requested again, update the stored value rather than create a new entry. Keep track of the number of hits on each resource.

The child processes must coordinate their access to the list of resources, and they must coordinate the generation of unique file names. Consider using threads, shared memory or message passing to implement the coordination.

Once you have the coordination working, implement the code to satisfy requests for cached items locally. Keep track of the total number of bytes transferred from client to proxy, proxy to server, server to proxy and proxy to client. Now the last two of these should be different. Remember that when you are testing with a browser, the browser also does caching, so some requests will not even go to the proxy server. Either turn off the browser's caching or force a remote access in the browser (usually by holding down the SHIFT key and pressing reload or refresh).

Real proxy caches need to contend with a number of issues.

- Real caches are not infinite.
- Caches should not store items above a certain size. The optimal size may vary dynamically with cache content.
- The cache should have an expiration policy so that resources do not stay in the cache forever.
- The cache should respect directives from the server stating that certain items should not be cached.
- The cache should check whether an item has been modified before using a local copy.

How many of the above issues can you resolve in your implementation? What else could be added to this list?

19.12 Gateways as Portals

A gateway receives requests as though it were the origin server and acts as an intermediary for other servers. This section discusses a server program, `gatewayportal`, which implements a gateway as shown in Figure 19.9. In this configuration, `gatewayportal` directs certain requests to a web server that is inside a firewall and directs the remaining requests to a server outside the firewall. The `gatewayportal` program has three command-line arguments: the port number that it listens on, the default server host name and the default server port number. Start by copying `proxyserver.c` of Section 19.9 to `gatewayportal.c`. The `gatewayportal` program parses the initial line. If the line contains an absolute URI, `gatewayportal` returns an HTTP error response to the client. If the absolute path of the initial line is for a resource that starts with `/usp`, then `gatewayportal` creates a tunnel to `www.usp.cs.utsa.edu`. The `gatewayportal` program directs all other requests to the default server through another tunnel.

19.13 Gateway for Load Balancing

This section describes a gateway, called gatewaymonitor, used for load balancing. Start with tunnelserver of Section 19.6. The gatewaymonitor program takes two ports as command-line arguments: a listening port for client requests and a listening port for server registration requests. The gatewaymonitor program acts like tunnelserver of Section 19.6 except that instead of directing all requests to a particular server, it maintains a list of servers with identical resources and can direct the request to any of those servers. The gatewaymonitor program keeps track of how many requests it has directed to each of the servers. If a connection request to a particular server fails, gatewaymonitor outputs an error message to standard error, reporting which server failed and providing usage statistics for that server. The gatewaymonitor program removes the failed server from its list and sends the request to another server. If the server list is empty, gatewaymonitor sends an HTTP error message back to the client.

A server can add itself to gatewaymonitor's list of servers by making a connection request to the server listening port of gatewaymonitor. The server then registers itself by sending its host name and its request listening port number. The gatewaymonitor program monitors the client listening port as before but also monitors the server request listening port. (Use select here.) If a request comes in on the server listening port, gatewaymonitor accepts the connection, reads the port information from the server, adds the host and port number to the server list, and closes the connection. The server should send the port number as a string to avoid byte-ordering problems.

Write a server program called registerserver that registers a server with gatewaymonitor as described above. The registerserver takes three or four command-line arguments. The first two arguments are the host name and server registration port number of the gatewaymonitor. The third parameter is the port number that the registered server will listen on for client requests. The optional fourth command-line argument is the name of a host to register. When called with four command-line arguments, registerserver exits after registering the specified host. The four-argument version of registerserver can be used to register an existing web server. If only three command-line arguments are given, registerserver registers itself and waits for requests.

The registerserver should have a canned HTTP response (with a resource) to send in response to all requests. The host name and process ID should be embedded in the resource so that you can tell how the request to the gateway monitor was serviced. Test your program by using a browser with as many as five servers registering with the gateway. Kill various servers and make sure that gatewaymonitor responds correctly.

19.14 Postmortem

This section describes common pitfalls and mistakes that we have observed in student implementations of the servers described in this chapter.

19.14.1 Threading and timing errors

Most timing errors for this type of program result from an incorrect understanding of TCP. Do not assume that an entire request can be read in a single read, even if you provide a large enough buffer. TCP provides an abstraction of a stream of bytes without packet or message boundaries. You have no control over how much will be delivered in a single read operation because the amount depends on how the message was encapsulated into packets and how those packets were delivered through an unreliable channel. Unfortunately, a program that makes this assumption works most of the time when tested on a fast local area network.

Whether writing a tunnel, proxy or gateway, do not assume that a client first sends its entire request and then the server responds. A program that reads from the client until it detects the end of the HTTP request does not follow the specification. Your program should simultaneously monitor the incoming file descriptors for both the client and the origin server. (See Sections 12.1 and 12.2 for approaches to do this.)

According to the specification, `passmonitor` should measure the time it takes to process each client request. How you approach this depends, to some extent, on your method of handling multiple file descriptors. In any case, do not measure the start time before the `accept` call because doing so incorporates an indefinite client "think" time. Do not measure the end time right after the `fork` call if you are using multiple processes, right after `pthread_create` if you are using multiple threads, or right after `select` if you are monitoring multiple descriptors in a single thread of execution. Why not?

Be sure that the time values you measure are reasonable. Most time-related library functions return seconds and milliseconds, seconds and microseconds, or seconds and nanoseconds. A common mistake is to confuse the units of the second element. Another common mistake is to subtract the start and end times without allowing for wrap-around. If you come out with a time value in days or months, you know that you made a mistake.

Do not use `sleep` to "cover up" incorrectly synchronized code. These programs should not need `sleep` to work correctly, and the presence of a `sleep` call in the code is a tip-off that something is seriously wrong.

Logging of headers also presents a timing problem. If you write one header line at a time to the log file, it is possible that headers for responses and requests will be interleaved. Accumulate each header in a buffer and write it by using a single `write` function when your program detects that the header is complete.

Do not connect to the destination web server in the tunnel programs before accepting a client connection. If you type fast enough during testing, you might not detect a problem. However, most web servers disconnect after a fairly short time when no incoming request appears.

19.14.2 Uncaught errors and bad exits

If you did not seriously or correctly address how your servers react to errors and when they should exit, your running programs may represent a system threat, particularly if they run with heightened privileges.

A server usually should run until the system reboots, so think about exit strategies. Do not exit from any functions except the `main` function. In general, other functions should either handle the error or return an error code to the caller. Do not exit if the proxy fails to connect to the destination web server—the problem may be temporary or may just be for that particular server. In general, a client should *not* be able to cause a server to exit. The server should exit only if there is an unrecoverable error due to lack of resources (memory, descriptors, etc.) that would jeopardize future correct execution. Remember the Mars Pathfinder (see page 483)! For these programs, a server should exit only when it fails to create a socket for listening to client requests. You should think about what actions to take in other situations.

Programs in C continue to execute even when a library function returns an error, possibly causing a fatal and virtually untrackable error later in the execution. To avoid this type of problem, check the return value for *every* library function that can return an error.

Releasing resources is always important. In servers, it is critical. Close all appropriate file descriptors when the client communication is finished. If a function allocates buffers, be sure to free them somewhere. Check to see that resources are freed on all paths through each function, paying particular attention to what happens when an error occurs.

Decide when a function should output an error message as well as return an error code. Use conditional compilation to leave informational messages in the source without having them appear in the released application. Remember that in the real world those messages have to go somewhere—probably to some unfortunate console log. Write messages to standard error, not to standard output. Usually, standard error is redirected to a console log—where someone might actually read the message. Also, the system does not buffer standard error, so the message appears when the error occurs.

19.14.3 Writing style and presentation

Most significant projects have an accompanying report or auxiliary documentation. Here are some things to think about in producing such a report.

Clean up the spelling and grammar. No one is going to believe that the code is debugged if the report isn't. Using (and paying attention to) a grammar checker won't make you a great writer, but it will help you avoid truly awful writing. Be consistent in your style, typeface, numbering scheme and use of bullets. Not only does this attention to detail result in a more visually pleasing report, but it helps readers who may use style as a cue to meaning. Put some thought into the layout and organization of your report. Use section titles and subsection titles to make the organization of the report clear. Use paragraph divisions that are consistent with meaning. If your report contains single-spaced paragraphs that are a third of a page or longer, you probably need more paragraphs or more conciseness. Avoid excessive use of code in the report. Use outlines, pseudocode or block diagrams to convey implementation details. If readers want to see code, they can look at the programs.

Pay attention to the introduction. Be sure that it has enough information for readers to understand the project. However, irrelevant information is sometimes worse than no information at all.

Diagrams are useful and can greatly improve the clarity of the presentation, but a diagram that conveys the wrong idea is worse than no diagram. Ask yourself what information you are trying to convey by the diagram, and distinguish that information with carefully chosen and consistent symbols. For example, don't use the same style box to represent both a process and a port, or the same type of arrow to represent a connection request and a thread.

Use architectural diagrams to convey overall structure and differences in design. For example, if contrasting the implementations of the tunnel and the proxy, give separate architectural diagrams for each that are clearly distinct. Alternatively, you could give one diagram for both (not two copies of the same diagrams) and emphasize that the two implementations have the same communication structure but differ in other ways.

On your final pass, verify that the report agrees with the implementation. For example, you might describe a resource-naming scheme in the report and then modify it in the program during testing. It is easy to forget to change the documentation to reflect the modifications. Section 22.12 gives some additional discussion about technical reports.

19.14.4 Poor testing and presentation of results

Each of the tunnel and proxy programs should be tested in a controlled environment before being tested with browsers and web servers. Otherwise, you are contending with three linked systems, each with unknown behavior. This configuration is impossible to test in a meaningful way.

A good way to start is to test the tunnel programs with simple copying programs such as Programs 18.1 and 18.3 to be sure that `tunnel` correctly transfers all of the information. Be sure that ordinary and binary files are correctly transmitted for all versions. Testing that the program transmitted data is not the same as testing to see that it transmitted correctly. Use `diff` or other utilities to make sure that files were exactly transmitted.

Avoid random test syndrome by organizing the test cases before writing the programs. Think about what factors might affect program behavior—different types of web pages, different types of servers, different network connections, different times of day, etc., and clearly organize the tests.

State clearly in the report what tests were performed, what the results were, and what aspect of the program these tests were designed to exercise. The typical beginner's approach to test reporting is to write a short paragraph saying the program worked and then append a large log file of test results to the report. A better approach might be to organize the test results into a table with annotations of the outcomes and a column with page numbers in the output so that the reader can actually find the tests.

Always record and state the conditions under which tests or performance experiments were run (machines, times of day, etc.). These factors may not appear to be important at the time, but you usually can't go back later and reconstruct these details accurately. Include in your report an analysis of what you expected to happen and what actually did happen.

19.14.5 Programming errors and bad style

Well-written programs are always easier to debug and modify. If you try to produce clean code from the initial design, you will usually spend less time debugging.

Avoid large or inconsistent indentation—it generally makes complicated code difficult to follow. Also avoid big loops—use functions to reduce complexity. For example, parsing the GET line of an HTTP request should be done in a function and tested separately.

Don't reinvent the wheel. Use libraries if available. Consolidate common code. For example, in the proxy, call the same function for each direction once the GET line is parsed. Do not assume that a header or other data will never exceed some arbitrary, predetermined size. It is best to include code to resize arrays (by realloc) when necessary. Be careful of memory leaks. Alternatively, you could use a fixed-size buffer and report longer requests as invalid. Be sure your buffer size is large enough. In no circumstance should you write past the end of an array. However, be cognizant of when a badly behaved program (e.g., a client that tries to write an infinitely long HTTP request) might cause trouble and be prepared to take appropriate action.

Always free allocated resources such as buffers, but don't free them more than once because this can cause later allocations to fail. Good programming practice suggests setting the pointer argument of free to NULL after the call, since the free function ignores NULL pointers. Often, a function will correctly free a buffer or other resource when successful but will miss freeing it when certain error conditions occur.

Do not use numeric values for buffer sizes and other parameters within the program. Use predefined constants for default and initial values so that you know what they mean and only have to modify them in one place. Be careful about when to use a default value and when not to. Mistakes here can be difficult to detect during testing. For example, the absolute URL contains an optional port number. You should not assume port 80 if this optional number is present. Be sure that all command-line arguments meet their specifications.

Parsing the HTTP headers is quite difficult. If you implement robust parsing, you need to assume that lines can end in a carriage return followed by a line feed, by just a line feed, or by just a carriage return. The line feed is the same as the newline character. If you did this parsing inline in the main loop, you probably didn't test parsing very well—how could you?

Headers in HTTP are in ASCII format, but resources may be in binary format. You will need to switch strategies in the middle of handling input.

19.15 Additional Reading

You can obtain more information about current developments on the World Wide Web by visiting the web site of the World Wide Web Consortium (W3C) [132], an organization that serves as a forum for development of new standards and protocols for the Web. The Internet Engineering Task Force (IETF) [55] is an open community of researchers, engineers and network operators concerned with the evolution and smooth operation of the Internet. Many important architectural developments and network designs appear in some form as IETF RFCs (Request for Comments). The specifications of HTTP/1.0 [53] and HTTP/1.1 [54] are of particular interest for this project. Both W3C and IETF maintain extensive web sites with much technical documentation. An excellent general reference on networking and the Internet can be found in *Computer Networking: A Top-Down Approach Featuring the Internet* by Kurose and Ross [68]. *Web Protocols and Practice: HTTP/1.1, Networking Protocols, Caching, and Traffic Measurement* [66] gives a more technical discussion of web performance and HTTP/1.1. "The state of the art in locally distributed web-server systems," by Cardellini et al. [21] reviews different architectures for web server clusters.

Chapter 20

Connectionless Communication and Multicast

In unreliable connectionless communication, single messages are transmitted between sender and receiver. A message may or may not arrive correctly at its destination. While such communication has low overhead, it requires that the application manage errors. This chapter expands the UICI library to include facilities for connectionless communication with timeouts and error checking. The chapter develops applications of the simple-request and request-reply protocols based on the connectionless interface. The UICI connectionless interface is then implemented with sockets, using UDP. UICI UDP also includes functions for multicast communication.

Objectives

- Learn about connectionless communication
- Experiment with sockets and UDP
- Explore simple-request and request-reply protocols
- Use timeouts in an application
- Understand invocation semantics

20.1 Introduction to Connectionless Communication

Connectionless communication is an abstraction based on transmission of single messages or datagrams between sender and receiver. A *datagram* is a unit of data transferred from one endpoint to another. Connectionless communication makes no association between the endpoints, and a process can use a single connectionless endpoint to send messages to or receive messages from many other endpoints.

Figure 20.1 illustrates connectionless communication among four processes running on different hosts. Process A receives messages from several different sources on the same communication endpoint. Process A uses this communication endpoint both to reply to the message from C and to send a message to D. Process C uses its connectionless communication endpoint to send messages to both A and D. Since each message includes the sender's return address, the receiver knows where to send the response.

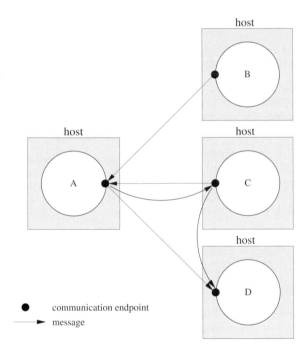

Figure 20.1: Four processes with connectionless communication endpoints.

This chapter develops a model for connectionless communication based on UDP, the User Datagram Protocol. UDP is used in many common Internet applications and protocols, including DNS (name service), NFS (distributed file system), NTP (time protocol), RTP (realtime transfer protocol) and SNMP (network management).

A UDP communication endpoint is identified by host IP address and port number. The receiver can extract the address of the sender's communication endpoint and use the information as a return address in replying to the message. Because no connection is involved, connectionless communication might not follow the client-server model. However, the client-server communication pattern holds for many applications, with clients sending request messages to servers on well-known ports (e.g., NFS servers use port 2049).

While the connection-oriented TCP protocol provides an error-free byte stream, UDP is unreliable. A UDP datagram might not arrive at its destination, or it might arrive before a message that was sent earlier. The sender has no information about the success or failure of the transmission. Even if the datagram arrives at the destination host, the network subsystem might drop the message before delivering it to the application because the endpoint buffers are full. Thus, while UDP has very low overhead, the application must handle considerably more complex errors than with TCP.

UDP datagrams are transmitted atomically, that is, a given datagram either arrives in its entirety at the destination endpoint or it does not arrive at all. To achieve this, modern network subsystems assemble UDP datagrams and verify UDP checksums. If a checksum is not correct, the subsystem discards the packet. Unfortunately, the computation of UDP checksums in IPv4 is optional, and some older systems disable checking by default. The UDP checksum guards against transmission errors, but not against malicious attackers. Such an attacker could modify both the data and the checksum in a consistent way. UDP does not authenticate what was sent and so has no way of detecting that an attack has occurred. Authentication must take place in a higher-level layer or in the application itself.

As with connection-oriented protocols, we introduce a simplified interface for connectionless communication, based on a socket implementation with UDP. Section 20.2 describes the UICI UDP interface. Sections 20.3 and 20.4 use this interface to implement the simple-request and the request-reply protocols, respectively. Section 20.5 adds timeouts and retries to the request-reply protocol. Section 20.6 outlines the implementation of request-reply-acknowledge protocols. Section 20.7 describes the implementation of each function in the UICI UDP interface in terms of sockets and UDP. Section 20.8 compares the UDP and TCP protocols. Section 20.9 discusses multicast communication and adds two functions to UICI UDP to support multicast communication.

20.2 Simplified Interface for Connectionless Communication

Connectionless communication using UDP is based on the `sendto` and `recvfrom` functions. The UICI UDP connectionless communication interface has `u_sendto`, `u_sendtohost`, `u_recvfrom` and `u_recvfromtimed` that provide the same functionality, but with simpler parameters. Also, unlike the underlying UDP functions, the UICI

UDP functions restart themselves after being interrupted by signals. Table 20.1 summarizes the UICI UDP interface to connectionless communication. To use these functions, you must compile your programs with both the UICI name and the UICI UDP libraries. Include both `uiciname.h` and `uiciudp.h` in your source files. Section 20.2.2 discusses error handling with the UICI UDP functions.

UICI UDP	description
`int u_openudp(u_port_t port)`	creates a UDP socket and if `port > 0`, binds socket to `port` returns the socket file descriptor

`ssize_t u_recvfrom(int fd,`
 `        void *buf, size_t nbytes,`
 `        u_buf_t *ubufp)`
	waits for up to `nbytes` from socket `fd`
	 returns number of bytes received
	 on return `buf` has received bytes
	 and `ubufp` points to sender address

`ssize_t u_recvfromtimed(int fd,`
 `        void *buf, size_t nbytes,`
 `        u_buf_t *ubufp, double time)`
	waits at most `time` seconds for up to `nbytes` from socket `fd`
	 returns the number of bytes received
	 on return `buf` has received bytes
	 and `ubufp` points to sender address

`ssize_t u_sendto(int fd, void *buf,`
 `        size_t nbytes,`
 `        u_buf_t *ubufp)`
	sends `nbytes` of `buf` on socket `fd`
	 to the receiver specified by `ubufp`
	 returns number of bytes actually sent

`ssize_t u_sendtohost(int fd,`
 `        void *buf, size_t nbytes,`
 `        char *hostn, u_port_t port)`
	sends `nbytes` of `buf` on socket `fd` to
	 receiver specified by `hostn` and `port`
	 returns number of bytes actually sent

`void u_gethostname(u_buf_t *ubufp,` `        char *hostn, int hostnsize)`	copies host name specified by `ubufp` into buffer `hostn` of size `hostnsize`
`void u_gethostinfo(u_buf_t *ubufp,` `        char *info, inf infosize)`	copies printable string containing host name and port specified by `ubufp` into user-supplied buffer `info` of size `infosize`.
`int u_comparehost(u_buf_t *ubufp,` `        char *hostn, u_port_t port)`	returns 1 if host and port specified by `ubufp` match given host name and port number, or else returns 0

Table 20.1: Summary of UICI UDP calls.

The `u_openudp` function returns a file descriptor that is a handle to a UDP socket. This function takes a single integer parameter, `port`, specifying the port number to bind to. If `port` is zero, the socket does not bind to a port. Typically, a server binds to a port and a client does not.

The `u_recvfrom` function reads up to `nbytes` from the file descriptor `fd` into the user-provided buffer `buf` and returns the number of bytes read. The `u_recvfrom` function fills in the user-supplied u_buf_t structure pointed to by ubufp with the address of the sender.

The u_recvfromtimed function is similar to u_recvfrom, but it takes an additional time parameter that specifies the number of seconds that u_recvfromtimed should wait for a message before returning with an error. The time parameter is a double, allowing fine-grained time values. Because messages may be lost, robust receivers call u_recvfromtimed to avoid blocking indefinitely.

The u_sendto function transmits nbytes from buf through the socket fd to the destination pointed to by ubufp. The u_sendto function requires a destination parameter because the communication endpoint is capable of sending to any host or receiving from any host. Use a u_buf_t value set by u_recvfrom to respond to a particular sender.

The u_sendtohost function is similar to u_sendto, but it requires a host name and port number rather than a pointer to a u_buf_t structure to specify the destination. Clients use u_sendtohost to initiate a communication with a server on a well-known port.

20.2.1 Host names and the **u_buf_t** structure

To be implementation-independent, applications that use UICI UDP should treat u_buf_t objects as opaque and use them in u_sendto without parsing. Appendix C provides an implementation of UICI UDP with IPv4, but it is also possible to implement UICI UDP with IPv6. The u_buf_t structure would be different for the two implementations. Three UICI UDP functions provide access to the information in the u_buf_t structure in an implementation-independent way. The u_gethostname function returns the host name encoded in a u_buf_t structure. The u_gethostinfo function returns a printable string containing a u_buf_t structure's information about host name and port number and can be used for debugging. The u_comparehost function returns 1 if the information in u_buf_t matches the specified host name and port number. Use u_comparehost to verify the identity of a sender.

20.2.2 UICI UDP return errors

The u_gethostname and u_gethostinfo functions return information in user-supplied buffers and cannot return an error code. The u_comparehost function returns 1 (true) if the hosts and ports match and 0 (false) if they do not. The other UICI UDP functions return −1 on error and set errno. If u_recvfromtimed times out, it sets errno to ETIME. If u_sendtohost cannot resolve the host name, it sets errno to EINVAL. Other errno settings match the underlying socket settings, as explained in Section 20.7. When a UICI UDP function returns an error and sets errno, you can use perror or strerror to display an appropriate error message, as long as you take into account these functions' lack of thread-safety.

20.2.3 UDP buffer size and UICI UDP

Messages sent under UDP are received atomically, meaning that a message sent with `u_sendto` or `u_sendtohost` is either transmitted entirely or not at all. A given implementation of UDP has a maximum message size. If you attempt to send a message that is too large, `u_sendto` or `u_sendtohost` returns –1 and sets `errno` to `EMSGSIZE`.

The `u_recvfrom` function reads exactly one message. If the message is smaller than `nbytes`, `u_recvfrom` returns the number of bytes actually read and its `buf` contains the entire message. If the message is larger than `nbytes`, `u_recvfrom` fills `buf` and truncates the message. In this case, `u_recvfrom` does not generate an error and returns the number of bytes put in the buffer (e.g., the size of the buffer).

Care must be taken to ensure that the receive buffer is large enough for the message, since UICI UDP truncates the message rather than generating an error when the buffer is too small. One way to handle this is to make the buffer one byte larger than the size expected and have the calling program generate an error if the buffer is completely filled.

Each UDP datagram is passed to the lower layers of the network protocol and encapsulated as a packet (header + data) in an IP datagram for transmission on the network. The network also imposes size limitations that affect transmission of datagrams. Each link in a path on the network has an MTU (maximum transmission unit), the largest chunk of information that a link can transmit. A datagram may be broken up into pieces (fragments) so that it can be physically transmitted along a link. These fragments are reassembled only when they reach the destination host. If any fragment is missing, the entire datagram is lost. While most UDP implementations allow datagrams of 8192 bytes, the typical network link has an MTU considerably smaller (e.g., 1500 bytes for Ethernet). As of this writing, most hosts and routers on the Internet use the IPv4 protocol for exchanging information. Under IPv4, hosts are not required to receive IP datagrams larger than 576 bytes, so many applications that use UDP limit their message size to fit in a datagram of this size, i.e., 576 – 20(IP header) – 8(UDP header) = 548 bytes.

◻ Exercise 20.1

How would you modify `u_recvfrom` so that it detects messages that are too large for the buffer?

Answer:
Use `malloc` to modify `u_recvfrom` to accommodate a buffer size one byte larger than the buffer passed in. Receive the message into this larger buffer. If the number of bytes received is equal to this buffer size, `u_recvfrom` should return –1 and set `errno` to an appropriate value. One possible value to use is `EMSGSIZE`. Otherwise, `u_recvfrom` should copy the message into `buf`, the buffer that was passed as a parameter by the caller. In either case, `u_recvfrom` must free the temporary buffer.

20.3 Simple-Request Protocols

A *protocol* is a set of rules that endpoints follow when they communicate. Simple request [110] is a client-server protocol in which a client sends a request to the server but expects no reply. Figure 20.2 shows a schematic of the steps involved in implementing a simple-request protocol using UICI UDP.

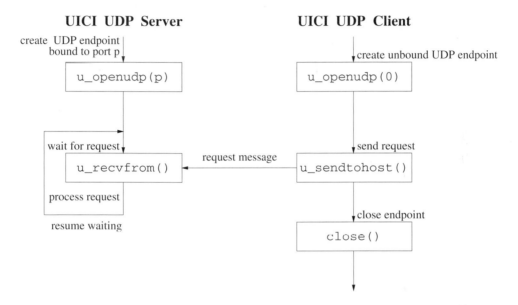

Figure 20.2: Interaction of a UICI UDP client and server using a simple-request protocol.

Programs 20.1 and 20.2 illustrate the simple-request protocol. The server creates a UDP socket associated with a well-known port (u_openudp) and then waits for a request from any sender (u_recvfrom). The server blocks on u_recvfrom until receiving a message. The server responds by writing the remote host name and received message to standard output and then waits in a loop for another message.

❑ Exercise 20.2

Under what conditions does the server of Program 20.1 exit?

Answer:

The server exits if it is given the wrong number of command-line arguments or if u_openudp fails. After that, the server will not exit unless it receives a signal. No transmission by a client can cause the server to exit.

Program 20.1 ─── `server_udp.c`

A server program writes sender information and the received message to its standard output.

```c
#include <stdio.h>
#include <stdlib.h>
#include <string.h>
#include <unistd.h>
#include "restart.h"
#include "uiciudp.h"
#define BUFSIZE 1024

int main(int argc, char *argv[]) {
   char buf[BUFSIZE];
   ssize_t bytesread;
   char hostinfo[BUFSIZE];
   u_port_t port;
   int requestfd;
   u_buf_t senderinfo;

   if (argc != 2) {
      fprintf(stderr, "Usage: %s port\n", argv[0]);
      return 1;
   }
   port = (u_port_t) atoi(argv[1]);         /* create communication endpoint */
   if ((requestfd = u_openudp(port)) == -1) {
      perror("Failed to create UDP endpoint");
      return 1;
   }
   for ( ; ; ) {                                    /* process client requests */
      bytesread = u_recvfrom(requestfd, buf, BUFSIZE, &senderinfo);
      if (bytesread < 0) {
         perror("Failed to receive request");
         continue;
      }
      u_gethostinfo(&senderinfo, hostinfo, BUFSIZE);
      if ((r_write(STDOUT_FILENO, hostinfo, strlen(hostinfo)) == -1) ||
          (r_write(STDOUT_FILENO, buf, bytesread) == -1)) {
         perror("Failed to echo reply to standard output");
      }
   }
}
```

Program 20.1 ─── `server_udp.c`

The client of Program 20.2 creates a UDP socket by calling `u_openudp` with a parameter of 0. In this case, `u_openudp` does not bind the socket to a port. The client initiates a request by calling `u_sendtohost`, specifying the host name and the well-known port of the server. Since the client has not bound its socket to a port, the first send on the socket causes the network subsystem to assign a private port number, called an *ephemeral port*, to the socket. The client of Program 20.2 sends a single request and then calls `r_close` to release the resources associated with the communication endpoint. Notice that the server does not detect an error or end-of-file when the client closes its socket, because there is no connection between the endpoints in the two applications.

Program 20.2 ———————————————————————— `client_udp.c`

A client program that sends a request containing its process ID.

```
#include <limits.h>
#include <stdio.h>
#include <stdlib.h>
#include <string.h>
#include <unistd.h>
#include "restart.h"
#include "uiciudp.h"
#define BUFSIZE 1024

int main(int argc, char *argv[]) {
   ssize_t byteswritten;
   char request[BUFSIZE];
   int requestfd;
   int rlen;
   u_port_t serverport;

   if (argc != 3) {
      fprintf(stderr, "Usage: %s servername serverport\n", argv[0]);
      return 1;
   }
   serverport = (u_port_t) atoi(argv[2]);
   if ((requestfd = u_openudp(0)) == -1) {      /* create unbound UDP endpoint */
      perror("Failed to create UDP endpoint");
      return 1;
   }
   sprintf(request, "[%ld]\n", (long)getpid());           /* create a request */
   rlen = strlen(request);
    /* use  simple-request protocol to send a request to (server, serverport) */
   byteswritten = u_sendtohost(requestfd, request, rlen, argv[1], serverport);
   if (byteswritten == -1)
      perror("Failed to send");
   if (r_close(requestfd) == -1 || byteswritten == -1)
      return 1;
   return 0;
}
```

Program 20.2 ———————————————————————— `client_udp.c`

◻ Exercise 20.3

Compile Programs 20.1 and 20.2.   Start the server on one machine (say, `yourhost`) with the following command.

```
server_udp 20001
```

Run clients on different hosts by executing the following on several machines.

```
client_udp yourhost 20001
```

Observe the assignment of ephemeral port numbers. What output does the server produce? How about the clients?

Answer:

Ephemeral ports are assigned in a system-dependent way. If all goes well, the clients do not produce output. For each message sent by a client, the server produces a line of output. If a client with process ID 2345 runs on machine `myhost` and uses ephemeral port 56525, the following message appears on standard output of the server.

```
port number is 56525 on host myhost[2345]
```

Figure 20.3 uses a time line to depict a sequence of events produced by the simple-request protocol. The diagram assumes that the client and the server have created their communication endpoints before the time line starts. Black dots represent event times relative to the same clock. For functions, the dots indicate the times at which the function returns to the caller. Remember that the clock times observed by the client and server are usually not synchronized unless the client and server are on the same machine.

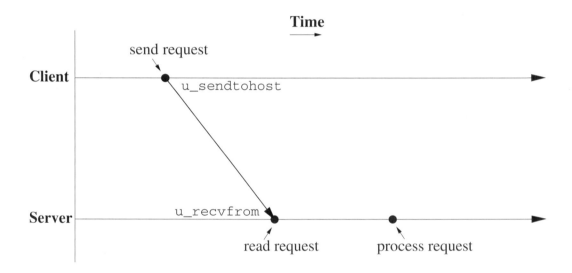

Figure 20.3: Time line illustrating the sequence of events for the simple-request protocol.

The `u_sendtohost` function is nonblocking in the sense that it returns after copying the message to the network subsystem of the local machine. The `u_recvfrom` function blocks until it receives a message or an error occurs. The `u_recvfrom` function restarts itself after receiving a signal, in contrast to the underlying library function `recvfrom`, as explained in Section 20.7.

☐ **Exercise 20.4**
Run Program 20.2 without starting the corresponding server. What happens?

Answer:

UDP does not determine whether the receiver host and its server program exist, so the client cannot detect whether the server has errors. A client generates an error only if it cannot resolve the server host name.

◻ Exercise 20.5

Figure 20.3 assumes that the server has been started before the client and is ready to receive when the message arrives. What happens if the client's message arrives before the server has created its communication endpoint? What happens if the client's message arrives after the server has created its endpoint but before it has called `u_recvfrom`?

Answer:

If the client's message arrives before the server has created its endpoint, the message is lost. In the second case, the result depends on how much buffer space has been allocated for the endpoint and how many messages have already arrived for that endpoint. If the endpoint's buffer has room, the network subsystem of the server host stores the message in the endpoint's buffer. The server calls `u_recvfrom` to remove the message. Communication is an asynchronous process, and a major role of the communication endpoint is for the network and I/O subsystems to provide buffering for incoming messages until user processes are ready for them.

◻ Exercise 20.6

Modify the client in Program 20.2 to send 1000 requests, and modify the server in Program 20.1 to sleep for 10 seconds between the `u_openudp` call and the `while` loop. Start the server and immediately start the client. How many messages are received by the server?

Answer:

The answer depends on the size of the endpoint buffers. You might see about 100 messages delivered. If all of the messages are delivered, try increasing the number of messages sent by the client to 10,000.

Figure 20.3 illustrates the ideal scenario, in which the client's message successfully arrives at the server and is processed. In reality, today's network infrastructure provides no guarantee that all messages actually arrive. Figure 20.4 illustrates a scenario in which the message is lost because of a network error. The server has no knowledge of the message's existence.

◻ Exercise 20.7

Draw a timing diagram similar to those of Figures 20.3 and 20.4 that illustrates a scenario in which the server receives a client request and then crashes before processing the request.

Answer:
Relabel the second event dot on the server's time line in Figure 20.3 as a crash event.

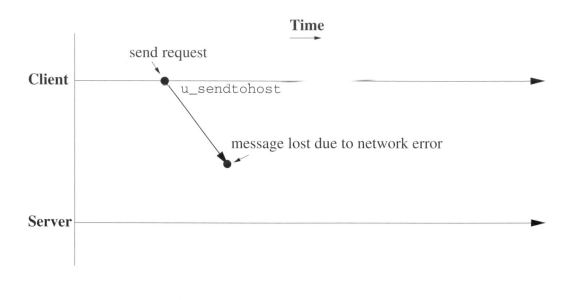

● event completion time

Figure 20.4: Time line illustrating a lost request for the simple-request protocol.

20.4 Request-Reply Protocols

In the simple-request protocol, the client cannot distinguish the scenario of Figure 20.3 from those of Figure 20.4 and Exercise 20.7 because it does not receive an acknowledgment of its request or any results produced by the request. A request-reply protocol handles this problem by requiring that the server respond to the client. Figure 20.5 shows a sequence of steps, using UICI UDP, to implement a simplified request-reply protocol. If no errors occur, the server's reply message notifies the client that the transmission was successful. The server reply message can contain actual results or just a flag reporting the status of the request.

Program 20.3 shows the server-side implementation of the request-reply protocol of Figure 20.5. The server receives a request and uses u_gethostinfo to extract the identity of the client. After printing the client's name and request to STDOUT_FILENO, the server

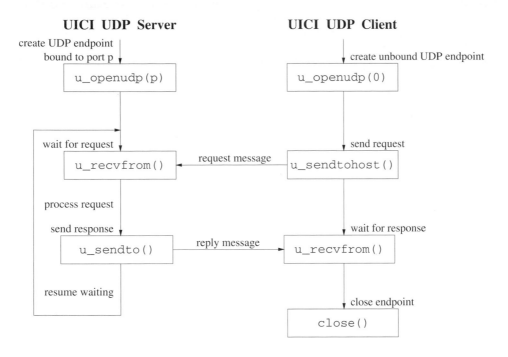

Figure 20.5: Sequence of steps in an error-free request-reply protocol.

uses `u_sendto` with the `u_buf_t` structure (`senderinfo`) returned from `u_recvfrom` to respond to that client. The UICI UDP `u_sendto` function uses the `u_buf_t` structure as the destination address to ensure that the reply is directed to the correct client. The server shown here replies with a copy of the request it received.

◻ **Exercise 20.8**

An important consideration in writing a server is to decide which conditions should cause the server to exit, which conditions should be ignored, which conditions should be logged and which conditions should trigger a recovery procedure. The server of Program 20.3 never exits on its own once its port is bound to the socket. You can terminate the server by sending it a signal. Under what conditions would it be reasonable for a server such as an ftp server to exit?

Answer:

You could argue that an ftp server should never exit because it should be running at all times. Certainly, an error caused by a client should not terminate the server. Even if system resources are not available to handle a connection, the problem might be temporary and the server would continue to work after the problem is resolved. Errors should be logged so the administrator has a record of any problems.

Program 20.3 ───────────────── `server_udp_request_reply.c`

A server program that implements a request-reply protocol.

```c
#include <stdio.h>
#include <stdlib.h>
#include <string.h>
#include <unistd.h>
#include "restart.h"
#include "uiciudp.h"
#define BUFSIZE 1024

int main(int argc, char *argv[]) {
   char buf[BUFSIZE];
   ssize_t bytesread;
   char hostinfo[BUFSIZE];
   u_port_t port;
   int requestfd;
   u_buf_t senderinfo;

   if (argc != 2) {
      fprintf(stderr, "Usage: %s port\n", argv[0]);
      return 1;
   }
   port = (u_port_t) atoi(argv[1]);           /* create UDP endpoint for port */
   if ((requestfd = u_openudp(port)) == -1) {
      perror("Failed to create UDP endpoint");
      return 1;
   }
   for ( ; ; ) {                    /* process client requests and send replies */
      bytesread = u_recvfrom(requestfd, buf, BUFSIZE, &senderinfo);
      if (bytesread == -1) {
         perror("Failed to receive client request");
         continue;
      }
      u_gethostinfo(&senderinfo, hostinfo, BUFSIZE);
      if ((r_write(STDOUT_FILENO, hostinfo, strlen(hostinfo)) == -1) ||
          (r_write(STDOUT_FILENO, buf, bytesread) == -1)) {
         perror("Failed to echo client request to standard output");
      }
      if (u_sendto(requestfd, buf, bytesread, &senderinfo) == -1) {
         perror("Failed to send the reply to the client");
      }
   }
}
```

Program 20.3 ───────────────── `server_udp_request_reply.c`

Program 20.4 shows a client that uses the request-reply protocol of Figure 20.5. The request is just a string containing the process ID of the requesting process. The protocol is implemented in the `request_reply` function shown in Program 20.5. The client sends the initial request and then waits for the reply. Since anyone can send a message to an open port, the client checks the host/port information against the sender information supplied in `senderinfo` to make sure that it received the reply from the same host that it sent to.

Program 20.4 ————————————— `client_udp_request_reply.c`

A client program that sends a request containing its process ID and reads the reply.

```
#include <stdio.h>
#include <stdlib.h>
#include <string.h>
#include <unistd.h>
#include "restart.h"
#include "uiciudp.h"
#define BUFSIZE 1024

int request_reply(int requestfd, void* request, int reqlen,
                  char* server, int serverport, void *reply, int replen);

int main(int argc, char *argv[]) {
   ssize_t bytesread, byteswritten;
   char reply[BUFSIZE];
   char request[BUFSIZE];
   int requestfd;
   u_port_t serverport;

   if (argc != 3) {
      fprintf(stderr, "Usage: %s servername serverport\n", argv[0]);
      return 1;
   }
   serverport = (u_port_t) atoi(argv[2]);
   if ((requestfd = u_openudp(0)) == -1) {      /* create unbound UDP endpoint */
      perror("Failed to create UDP endpoint");
      return 1;
   }
   sprintf(request, "[%ld]\n", (long)getpid());            /* create a request */
                              /* use request-reply protocol to send a message */
   bytesread = request_reply(requestfd,  request, strlen(request)+1,
                        argv[1], serverport, reply, BUFSIZE);
   if (bytesread == -1)
      perror("Failed to do request_reply");
   else {
      byteswritten = r_write(STDOUT_FILENO, reply, bytesread);
      if (byteswritten == -1)
        perror("Failed to echo server reply");
   }
   if ((r_close(requestfd) == -1) || (bytesread  == -1) || (byteswritten == -1))
      return 1;
   return 0;
}
```

Program 20.4 ————————————— `client_udp_request_reply.c`

❏ Exercise 20.9

What happens when the scenario of Figure 20.4 occurs for the request-reply protocol of Figure 20.5?

Answer:

The client hangs indefinitely on the blocking `u_recvfrom` call.

Program 20.5 ─────────────────────────────── `request_reply.c`

Request-reply implementation A—assumes error-free delivery.

```c
#include <sys/types.h>
#include "uiciudp.h"

int request_reply(int requestfd, void* request, int reqlen,
                  char* server, int serverport, void *reply, int replen) {
    ssize_t nbytes;
    u_buf_t senderinfo;
                                                  /* send the request */
    nbytes = u_sendtohost(requestfd, request, reqlen, server, serverport);
    if (nbytes == -1)
        return (int)nbytes;
                            /* wait for a response, restart if from wrong server */
    while ((nbytes = u_recvfrom(requestfd, reply, replen, &senderinfo)) >= 0 )
        if (u_comparehost(&senderinfo, server, serverport))   /* sender match */
            break;
    return (int)nbytes;
}
```

Program 20.5 ─────────────────────────────── `request_reply.c`

☐ **Exercise 20.10**

Compile Programs 20.3 and 20.4. Start the server on one machine (say, `yourhost`) with the following command.

```
server_udp_request_reply 20001
```

Run clients on different hosts by executing the following on several machines.

```
client_udp_request_reply yourhost 20001
```

Put timing statements in Program 20.4 to measure how long it takes for the client to send a request and receive a response. (See Example 9.8.) Run the client program several times. Do any of the instances hang? Under what circumstances would you expect the client to hang?

Answer:

The client blocks indefinitely on `u_recvfrom` if it does not receive the reply from the server. Modern networks have become so reliable that if the client and server are running on the same local area network (LAN), it is unlikely that either the request or the reply messages will be lost because of errors along particular wires. In high-congestion situations, packets may be dropped at LAN switches. If many clients are making simultaneous requests, the network subsystem of the server host might discard some packets because the communication endpoint's buffers are full. Messages from clients and servers on different LANs generally follow paths consisting of many links connected by routers. Congested routers drop messages that they can't handle, increasing the likelihood that a message is not delivered.

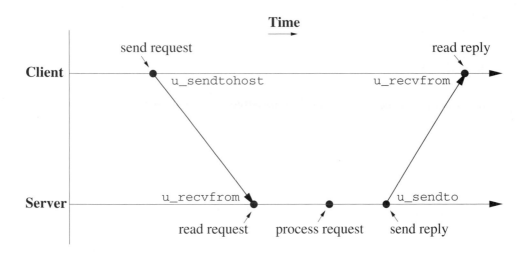

● event completion time

Figure 20.6: Timing diagram of the request-reply protocol.

☐ **Exercise 20.11**

Figure 20.6 illustrates the timing for the request-reply protocol when there are no errors. When errors are possible, the nine events listed in the following table can occur in various orders.

event	description
A	client sends request message
B	server receives request message
C	server processes request
D	server sends reply message
E	client receives reply message
F	request message is lost
G	reply message is lost
H	client crashes
I	server crashes

The event sequence ABCDE represents the scenario of Figure 20.6. For the five event sequences listed below, state whether each represents a physically realizable scenario. If the scenario is realizable, explain the outcome and draw a timing diagram similar to that shown in Figure 20.6. If the scenario is not realizable, explain why.

1. ABCED
2. ABCDG
3. ABCI
4. ABCGD
5. ABCDIE

What other event sequences represent possible scenarios for request-reply?

Answer:

1. ABCED is not realizable, since the client cannot receive a message before the server sends it. This assumes that no other process on the server host has guessed the ephemeral port number used by the client and sent a bogus reply. It also assumes that another host has not spoofed the IP address of the server. We do not consider these scenarios here.
2. ABCDG is realizable and represents a situation in which the client does not receive a response even though the server has processed the request.
3. ABCI is realizable and represents a situation in which the server receives the request and processes it but crashes before it sends the response.
4. ABCGD is not realizable, since a message cannot be lost before it is sent.
5. ABCDIE is possible. If the server crashes after it sends the reply, the reply can still be received.

Many other event sequences represent realizable scenarios.

20.5 Request-Reply with Timeouts and Retries

The client of Program 20.4 can hang indefinitely if either the request message or the reply message is lost or if the server crashes. The client can use timeouts to handle these potential deadlocks. Before making a blocking call, the process sets a timer that generates a signal to interrupt the call after a certain length of time. If the interrupt occurs, the process can try again or use a different strategy.

You can implement a timeout directly by setting a software timer or by using timeout facilities included as options to calls such as `select`. Sockets themselves have some options for setting timeouts. Section 20.7 discusses the pros and cons of different timeout strategies.

The `u_recvfromtimed` function of UICI UDP provides a simple interface to these timeout facilities. The `u_recvfromtimed` function is similar to `u_recvfrom`, but it takes an additional `double` parameter, `time`, indicating the number of seconds to block, waiting for a response. After blocking for `time` seconds without receiving a response on the specified endpoint, `u_recvfromtimed` returns –1 and sets `errno` to `ETIME`. For other errors, `u_recvfromtimed` returns –1 and sets the `errno` as `u_recvfrom` does.

Program 20.6 modifies Program 20.4 to call the function `request_reply_timeout`, shown in Program 20.7, instead of calling `request_reply`. A third command-line argument to this program specifies the number of seconds to wait before timing out.

Program 20.6 ———————— **`client_udp_request_reply_timeout.c`**
A client program that uses timeouts with request-reply.

```c
#include <stdio.h>
#include <stdlib.h>
#include <string.h>
#include <unistd.h>
#include "restart.h"
#include "uiciudp.h"
#define BUFSIZE 1024

int request_reply_timeout(int requestfd, void* request, int reqlen,
                char* server, int serverport, void *reply, int replen,
                double timeout);

int main(int argc, char *argv[]) {
   ssize_t bytesread, byteswritten;
   char reply[BUFSIZE];
   char request[BUFSIZE];
   int requestfd;
   u_port_t serverport;
   double timeout;

   if (argc != 4) {
      fprintf(stderr, "Usage: %s servername serverport timeout\n", argv[0]);
      return 1;
   }
   serverport = (u_port_t) atoi(argv[2]);
   timeout = atof(argv[3]);
   if ((requestfd = u_openudp(0)) == -1) {      /* create unbound UDP endpoint */
      perror("Failed to create UDP endpoint");
      return 1;
   }
   sprintf(request, "[%ld]\n", (long)getpid());    /* create a request string */
                /* use request-reply protocol with timeout to send a message */
   bytesread = request_reply_timeout(requestfd, request, strlen(request) + 1,
                     argv[1], serverport, reply, BUFSIZE, timeout);
   if (bytesread == -1)
      perror("Failed to complete request_reply_timeout");
   else {
      byteswritten = r_write(STDOUT_FILENO, reply, bytesread);
      if (byteswritten == -1)
         perror("Failed to echo server reply");
   }
   if ((r_close(requestfd) == -1) || (bytesread == -1) || (byteswritten == -1))
      return 1;
   return 0;
}
```

Program 20.6 ———————— **`client_udp_request_reply_timeout.c`**

Program 20.7 ──────────────────── **request_reply_timeout.c**
                    Request-reply implementation with timeout.

```
#include <sys/types.h>
#include "uiciudp.h"

int request_reply_timeout(int requestfd, void* request, int reqlen,
                  char* server, int serverport, void *reply, int replen,
                  double timeout) {
   ssize_t nbytes;
   u_buf_t senderinfo;

                                                /* send the request */
   nbytes = u_sendtohost(requestfd, request, reqlen, server, serverport);
   if (nbytes == -1)
      return -1;
      /* wait timeout seconds for a response, restart if from wrong server */
   while ((nbytes = u_recvfromtimed(requestfd, reply, replen,
                                 &senderinfo, timeout)) >= 0 &&
          (u_comparehost(&senderinfo, server, serverport) == 0)) ;
   return (int)nbytes;
}
```

Program 20.7 ──────────────────── **request_reply_timeout.c**

Figure 20.7 shows a state diagram for the request-reply logic of Program 20.7. The circles represent functions calls that implement the major steps in the protocol, and the arrows indicate outcomes.

The request_reply_timeout function of Program 20.7 returns an error if the server does not respond after an interval of time. Either the request was not serviced or it was serviced and the reply was lost or never sent. The client cannot distinguish between a lost message and a server crash.

Another potential problem is that Program 20.7 resets the timeout each time it encounters an incorrect responder. In a *denial-of-service attack*, offenders continually send spurious packets to ports on the attacked machine. Program 20.7 should limit the number of retries before taking some alternative action such as informing the user of a potential problem.

☐ **Exercise 20.12**

Request-reply protocols can also be implemented over TCP. Why are these implementations usually simpler than UDP implementations? Are there disadvantages to a TCP implementation?

Answer:

Since TCP provides an error-free stream of bytes, the application can use the error-free request-reply protocol shown in Figure 20.5. Another advantage of TCP implementations is that the client has a connection to the server and can signal that it is finished by closing this connection. The server can then release resources

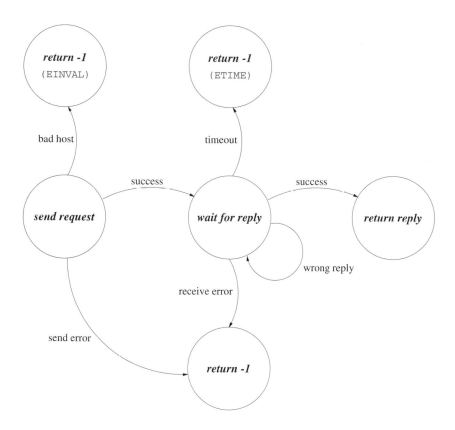

Figure 20.7: State diagram of the client for request-reply with simple timeout.

that it has allocated to servicing that client's requests. The client can also detect a server crash while it is waiting for a reply. On the downside, TCP implementations incur overhead in setting up the connection.

Usually, implementations of request-reply with timeout have a mechanism for retrying the request a certain number of times before giving up. The state diagram of Figure 20.8 summarizes this approach. The user specifies a maximum number of retries. The application retries the entire request-reply sequence each time a timeout occurs until the number of retries exceeds the specified maximum.

Program 20.8 implements the request-reply protocol of Figure 20.8 for use in a client similar to Program 20.6.

□ **Exercise 20.13**

How would the client in Program 20.6 need to be modified to use the protocol in Program 20.8?

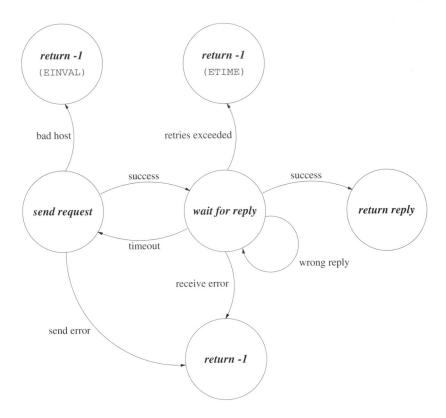

Figure 20.8: Request-reply with timeouts.

Answer:

The client would have to take an extra command-line argument for the number of retries and call `request_reply_timeout_retry` instead of `request_reply_timeout`.

❑ Exercise 20.14

Propose a more sophisticated method of handling timeouts than that of Program 20.8. How might a potential infinite loop due to wrong host be handled?

Answer:

The selection of a timeout value is somewhat arbitrary. If the timeout value is large, the application may wait too long before recognizing a problem. However, timeout values that are too short do not account for natural delays that occur in transit over a network. A more sophisticated timeout strategy would lengthen the timeout value on successive retries and perhaps keep statistics about response times to use in setting future timeout values. Often, the timeout value is doubled for each successive timeout. The potential infinite loop for the wrong host might be handled by incorporating a counter for the wrong host condition and returning an error if this condition occurs more than a certain number of times.

Program 20.8 ———————————— `request_reply_timeout_retry.c`
Request-reply implementation with timeout and retries.

```
#include <stdio.h>
#include <errno.h>
#include "uiciudp.h"

int request_reply_timeout_retry(int requestfd, void* request, int reqlen,
                 char* server, int serverport, void *reply, int replen,
                 double timeout, int maxretries) {
   ssize_t nbytes;
   int retries;
   u_buf_t senderinfo;

   retries = 0;
   while (retries < maxretries) {
                               /* send process ID to (server, serverport) */
      nbytes = u_sendtohost(requestfd, request, reqlen, server, serverport);
      if (nbytes == -1)
        return -1;                                       /* error on send */
       /* wait timeout seconds for a response, restart if from wrong server */
      while (((nbytes = u_recvfromtimed(requestfd, reply, replen,
                                   &senderinfo, timeout)) >= 0) &&
           (u_comparehost(&senderinfo, server, serverport) == 0)) ;
      if (nbytes >= 0)
         break;
      retries++;
   }
   if (retries >= maxretries) {
      errno = ETIME;
      return -1;
   }
   return (int)nbytes;
}
```

Program 20.8 ———————————— `request_reply_timeout_retry.c`

With the request-reply with timeouts and retries of Program 20.8, the server may execute the same client request multiple times, with multiple repeats being reflected in the logs produced by the server of Program 20.3. Sometimes reexecution of a request produces invalid results, for example, in banking when a client request to credit an account should not be performed multiple times. On the other hand, a client request for information from a static database can be repeated without ill effect. Operations that can be performed multiple times with the same effect are called *idempotent operations*. The next section introduces a strategy for handling nonidempotent operations.

20.6 Request-Reply-Acknowledge Protocols

The *invocation semantics* describe the behavior of a request protocol.   The `request_reply` function of Program 20.5 implements *maybe semantics*.   The request may or may not be executed. In the limit as the maximum number of allowed retries becomes large, Program 20.8 approximates *at-least-once semantics*. Unless the request represents an idempotent operation, at-least-once semantics may result in incorrect behavior if a particular request is executed more than once.

An alternative is *at-most-once semantics*, which can be implemented by having the server save the results of previous requests. If a duplicate request comes, the server retransmits the reply without reexecuting the request. To recognize that a request is a duplicate, the client and server must agree on a format for uniquely identifying requests. The server also must save all replies from all requests until it is sure that the respective clients have received the replies. In the request-reply-acknowledge protocol of Figure 20.9, the client sends an acknowledgment to the server after receiving a reply. The server can safely discard the reply after receiving the acknowledgment.

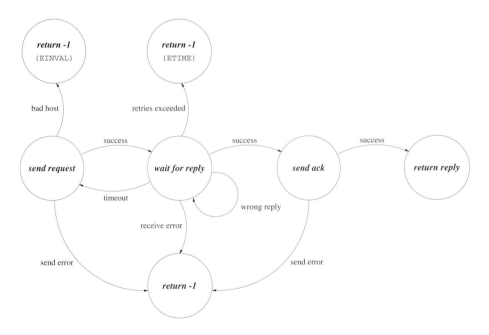

Figure 20.9: State diagram of the client side of a request-reply-acknowledge protocol.

☐ Exercise 20.15

Devise a format for a message containing a process ID that could be used in the request-reply-acknowledge protocol of Figure 20.9.

Answer:
One possibility is to use a structure containing the process ID and a sequence number. The client initializes the sequence number to 1 and increments it for each new request. This approach works as long as the sequence numbers and process IDs do not wrap around. Since we are sending the process ID as a string rather than in raw binary form, we can send the sequence number in the same way. The string sent consists of the sequence number followed by a blank followed by the process ID. The server parses this string to separate the two values. If data is sent in raw form rather than as a string, care must be taken to handle differences in byte ordering (big-endian vs. little-endian) between the client and server if the values are used for anything other than uniqueness.

The server side of the request-reply-acknowledge protocol is more complicated. The server must keep a copy of each reply until it receives the corresponding acknowledgment. If the client fails to send an acknowledgment, say, because of a crash, the server may keep the information forever. Connection-oriented communication is more suitable for this type of communication. TCP implements reliable communication by using a request-reply-acknowledge protocol, including negative acknowledgments and flow control, that is optimized for good performance.

20.7 Implementation of UICI UDP

UICI UDP functions use the same name resolution functions, `addr2name` and `name2addr`, as the UICI TCP functions. Program C.4 shows implementations of these functions. Compile your source with `uiciname.c` when using UICI UDP.

20.7.1 Implementation of `u_openudp`

The UICI UDP function `u_openudp` takes a port number as its parameter and creates a connectionless socket for communication using UDP. The `u_openudp` function returns a file descriptor if the communication endpoint was successfully created. Servers call `u_openudp` with their well-known port as a parameter. Clients generally call `u_openudp` with a parameter of 0, meaning that they will allow the system to choose an ephemeral port when it becomes necessary. The `u_openudp` function returns −1 and sets `errno` if an error occurs.

Program 20.9 implements `u_openudp`. The `u_openudp` function uses the `socket` function discussed on page 631 to create the communication endpoint. As in the case of TCP, the `domain` is `AF_INET` and the `protocol` is 0. The `type` is `SOCK_DGRAM` rather than `SOCK_STREAM`.

If the port number parameter is greater than 0, u_openudp associates the newly created socket with this port number by calling bind, a library function described on page 631.

Program 20.9 ———————————————————————————— **u_openudp.c**

An implementation of u_openudp.

```
#include <errno.h>
#include <unistd.h>
#include <sys/socket.h>
#include "restart.h"
#include "uiciudp.h"

int u_openudp(u_port_t port) {
    int error;
    int one = 1;
    struct sockaddr_in server;
    int sock;

    if ((sock = socket(AF_INET, SOCK_DGRAM, 0)) == -1)
        return -1;
    if (setsockopt(sock, SOL_SOCKET, SO_REUSEADDR, &one, sizeof(one)) == -1) {
        error = errno;
        r_close(sock);
        errno = error;
        return -1;
    }
    if (port > 0) {
        server.sin_family = AF_INET;
        server.sin_addr.s_addr = htonl(INADDR_ANY);
        server.sin_port = htons((short)port);
        if (bind(sock, (struct sockaddr *)&server, sizeof(server)) == -1) {
            error = errno;
            r_close(sock);
            errno = error;
            return -1;
        }
    }
    return sock;
}
```

Program 20.9 ———————————————————————————— **u_openudp.c**

Comparing u_openudp with u_open on page 634, we see that bind is called only when the port number is greater than 0. Only a server needs to bind the socket to a particular port. Also, it is not necessary to worry about SIGPIPE. A write to a pipe (or a TCP socket) generates a SIGPIPE signal when there are no active readers. In contrast, UDP provides no information about active receivers. A UDP datagram is considered to be sent correctly when it is successfully copied into the buffers of the network subsystem. UDP does not detect an error when an application sends a datagram to a destination that is not waiting to receive it, so sending does not generate a SIGPIPE.

20.7.2 The `sendto` function

The POSIX `sendto` function transmits data as a single datagram and returns the number of transmitted bytes if successful. However, `sendto` checks only local errors, and success does not mean that the receiver actually got the data.

The first three parameters for `sendto` have the same meaning as for `read` and `write`. The `socket` parameter holds a file descriptor previously opened by a call to `socket`. The `message` parameter has the data to be sent, and `length` is the number of bytes to send. The `flags` parameter allows special options that we do not use, so this value is always zero. The `dest_addr` parameter points to a structure filled with information about the destination, including the remote host address and the remote port number. Since we are using the Internet domain, `*dest_addr` is a `struct sockaddr_in` structure. The `dest_len` is the size of the `struct sockaddr_in` structure.

```
SYNOPSIS

    #include <sys/socket.h>

    ssize_t sendto(int socket, const void *message, size_t length,
                   int flags, const struct sockaddr *dest_addr,
                   socklen_t dest_len);
                                                                  POSIX
```

If successful, `sendto` returns the number of bytes sent. If unsuccessful, `sendto` returns −1 and sets `errno`. The following table lists the mandatory errors for `sendto` with unconnected sockets.

errno	cause
EAFNOSUPPORT	address family cannot be used with this socket
EAGAIN or EWOULDBLOCK	O_NONBLOCK is set and operation would block
EBADF	socket parameter is not a valid file descriptor
EINTR	sendto interrupted before any data was transmitted
EMSGSIZE	message too large to be sent all at once as required by socket
ENOTSOCK	socket does not refer to a socket
EOPNOTSUPP	specified flags not supported for this type of socket

The `sendto` function can be used with sockets connected to a particular destination host and port. However, `sendto` still determines the destination host and port number by the information in the `*dest_addr` structure, independently of this connection.

If `sendto` is used on a socket that is not yet bound to a source port, the network subsystem assigns an unused ephemeral port to bind with the socket. Datagrams originating from this socket include the port number and the source host address along with the data so that the remote host can reply.

20.7.3 Implementation of `u_sendto` and `u_sendtohost`

The UICI UDP library provides two functions for sending messages, u_sendto and u_sendtohost, shown in Program 20.10. The u_sendtohost takes the destination host name and port number as parameters. It is meant to be used when initiating a communication with a remote host. The u_sendto function uses a u_buf_t structure that was filled by a previous call to u_recvfrom. The u_buf_t structure is meant to be used in a reply.

```
Program 20.10 ──────────────────────────────── u_sendto.c
                  An implementation of u_sendto and u_sendtohost.

#include <errno.h>
#include <sys/socket.h>
#include "uiciname.h"
#include "uiciudp.h"

ssize_t u_sendto(int fd, void *buf, size_t nbytes, u_buf_t *ubufp) {
   int len;
   struct sockaddr *remotep;
   int retval;

   len = sizeof(struct sockaddr_in);
   remotep = (struct sockaddr *)ubufp;
   while (((retval = sendto(fd, buf, nbytes, 0, remotep, len)) == -1) &&
           (errno == EINTR)) ;
   return retval;
}

ssize_t u_sendtohost(int fd, void *buf, size_t nbytes, char *hostn,
                     u_port_t port) {
   struct sockaddr_in remote;

   if (name2addr(hostn, &(remote.sin_addr.s_addr)) == -1) {
      errno = EINVAL;
      return -1;
   }
   remote.sin_port = htons((short)port);
   remote.sin_family = AF_INET;
   return u_sendto(fd, buf, nbytes, &remote);
}
```
Program 20.10 ──────────────────────────────── u_sendto.c

The u_sendto function is almost identical to sendto except that u_sendto restarts if interrupted by a signal. The u_buf_t data type is defined in uiciudp.h by a typedef that sets it to be equivalent to struct sockaddr_in. This allows a u_buf_t pointer to be cast to a struct sockaddr pointer in the implementation of u_sendto. The user does not need to know anything about the internal representation of the u_buf_t structure, provided that its value was set by u_recvfrom or u_recvfromtimed.

The u_sendtohost function uses name2addr from uiciname.c to convert the host name to an address. If the host name begins with a digit, name2addr assumes that it is an IP address in dotted form and calls inet_addr to decode it. Otherwise, name2addr resolves the host name and fills struct sockaddr_in with the remote host address. The u_sendtohost function fills in the port number and address family and calls u_sendto. Since name2addr does not set errno when an error occurs, the u_sendtohost sets errno to EINVAL when name2addr returns an error.

20.7.4 The `recvfrom` function

The POSIX recvfrom function blocks until a datagram becomes available on file descriptor representing an open socket. While it is possible to use recvfrom with TCP sockets, we consider only UDP SOCK_DGRAM sockets. Be sure to associate socket with a port, either by explicitly calling bind or by calling sendto, which forces a binding to an ephemeral port. A call to recvfrom on a socket that has not been bound to a port may hang indefinitely.

The buffer parameter of recvfrom points to a user-provided buffer of length bytes that receives the datagram data. The amount of data received is limited by the length parameter. If the datagram is larger than length, recvfrom truncates the message to size length and drops the rest of the datagram. In either case, recvfrom returns the number of bytes of data placed in buffer.

The *address structure is a user-provided struct sockaddr structure that recvfrom fills in with the address of the sender. If address is NULL, recvfrom does not return sender information. The address_len parameter is a pointer to a value-result parameter. Set *address_len to the length of address before calling recvfrom. On return, recvfrom sets *address_len to the actual length of *address. The address_len parameter prevents buffer overflows because recvfrom truncates the sender information to fit in *address. It is not considered an error if the information put in *address is truncated, so be sure to make the buffer is large enough. For our purposes, the buffer should be able to hold a struct sockaddr_in structure.

SYNOPSIS

```
#include <sys/socket.h>

ssize_t recvfrom(int socket, void *restrict buffer, size_t length,
                 int flags, struct sockaddr *restrict address,
                 socklen_t *restrict address_len);
```
POSIX

If successful, recvfrom returns the number of bytes that were received. If unsuccessful, recvfrom returns −1 and sets errno. The following table lists the mandatory errors for recvfrom with an unconnected socket.

errno	cause
EAGAIN or EWOULDBLOCK	O_NONBLOCK is set and no data is waiting to be received, or MSG_OOB is set and no out-of-band data is available and either O_NONBLOCK is set or socket does not support blocking with out-of-band data
EBADF	socket is not a valid file descriptor
EINTR	recvfrom interrupted by a signal before any data was available
EINVAL	MSG_OOB is set and no out-of-band data is available
ENOTSOCK	socket does not refer to a socket
EOPNOTSUPP	specified flags not supported for this type of socket

20.7.5 Implementation of `u_recvfrom` and `u_recvfromtimed`

Program 20.11 implements `u_recvfrom`. It is similar to `recvfrom` except that it restarts `recvfrom` if interrupted by a signal. The returned sender information is encapsulated in the `u_buf_t` parameter, which is used as an opaque object for a reply, using `u_sendto`, to the sender. If successful, `u_recvfrom` returns the number of bytes received. If unsuccessful, `u_recvfrom` returns −1 and sets `errno`. Since UDP datagrams of length 0 are valid, a return value of 0 indicates a datagram of length 0 and should not be interpreted as end-of-file.

Program 20.11 ———————————————————— `u_recvfrom.c`

An implementation of u_recvfrom.

```
#include <errno.h>
#include <sys/socket.h>
#include "uiciudp.h"

ssize_t u_recvfrom(int fd, void *buf, size_t nbytes, u_buf_t *ubufp) {
   int len;
   struct sockaddr *remote;
   int retval;

   len = sizeof (struct sockaddr_in);
   remote = (struct sockaddr *)ubufp;
   while ((((retval = recvfrom(fd, buf, nbytes, 0, remote, &len)) == -1) &&
           (errno == EINTR)) ;
   return retval;
}
```

Program 20.11 ———————————————————— `u_recvfrom.c`

Since UDP is not reliable, a datagram can be lost without generating an error for either the sender or the receiver. More reliable protocols based on UDP use some form of request-reply or request-reply-acknowledge protocol discussed in Sections 20.4 through 20.6. These protocols require that the receiver not block indefinitely waiting for messages or replies. The `u_recvfromtimed` function returns after a specified time if it does not receive a datagram. If successful, `u_recvfromtimed` returns the number of bytes written in *buf. If a timeout occurs, `u_recvfromtimed` returns –1 and sets `errno` to `ETIME`. For other errors, `u_recvfromtimed` returns –1 and sets `errno` to the same values as `u_recvfrom` does.

Strategies for implementing timeouts include socket options for timeout, signals or `select`. Unfortunately, the socket options supporting timeouts are not universally available. The signal strategy uses a timer to generate a signal after a specified time. When a signal is caught, `recvfrom` returns with the error `EINTR`. The use of signals may interfere with other timers that a program might be using.

Program 20.12 implements `u_recvfromtimed` with the `waitfdtimed` function from the restart library. The implementation of `waitfdtimed` using `select` is shown in Program 4.15 on page 114. The `waitfdtimed` function takes two parameters: a file descriptor and an ending time. The `add2currenttime` function from the restart library converts the timeout interval into an ending time. Using the ending time rather than directly using the time interval allows `waitfdtimed` to restart if interrupted by a signal and still retain the same ending time for the timeout.

Program 20.12 ─────────────────────────── **u_recvfromtimed.c**

An implementation of u_recvfromtimed.

```
#include <errno.h>
#include <sys/socket.h>
#include <sys/time.h>
#include "restart.h"
#include "uiciudp.h"

ssize_t u_recvfromtimed(int fd, void *buf, size_t nbytes, u_buf_t *ubufp,
                        double seconds) {
   int len;
   struct sockaddr *remote;
   int retval;
   struct timeval timedone;

   timedone = add2currenttime(seconds);
   if (waitfdtimed(fd, timedone) == -1)
      return (ssize_t)(-1);
   len = sizeof (struct sockaddr_in);
   remote = (struct sockaddr *)ubufp;
   while (((retval = recvfrom(fd, buf, nbytes, 0, remote, &len)) == -1) &&
          (errno == EINTR)) ;
   return retval;
}
```

Program 20.12 ─────────────────────────── **u_recvfromtimed.c**

◻ Exercise 20.16

Suppose you call u_recvfromtimed with a timeout of 2 seconds and 10 signals come in 1 second apart. When does u_recvfromtimed time out if no data arrives?

Answer:

It still times out 2 seconds after it is called. The reason is that waitfdtimed times out at a given ending time, independently of the number of times it needs to restart.

20.7.6 Host names and u_buf_t

The UICI UDP library also provides three functions for examining receiver information. The u_gethostname function, which can be called after u_recvfrom or u_recvfromtimed, creates a string that corresponds to the name of a host. The first parameter of u_gethostname is a u_buf_t structure previously set, for example, by u_recvfrom. The u_gethostname function returns a null-terminated string containing the name of the host in the user-supplied buffer hostn. The third parameter of u_gethostname is the length of hostn. The u_gethostname function truncates the host name so that it fits.

The implementation of u_gethostname in Program 20.13 just calls addr2name and sets its *hostn buffer to the result. Recall that if addr2name cannot convert the address to a host name, it sets *hostn to the dotted-decimal representation of the host address. The addr2name function never returns an error.

Program 20.13 ──────────────────────────── **u_gethostname.c**

An implementation of u_gethostname.

```
#include "uiciname.h"
#include "uiciudp.h"

void u_gethostname(u_buf_t *ubufp, char *hostn, int hostnsize) {
    struct sockaddr_in *remotep;

    remotep = (struct sockaddr_in *)ubufp;
    addr2name(remotep->sin_addr, hostn, hostnsize);
}
```

Program 20.13 ──────────────────────────── **u_gethostname.c**

The u_gethostinfo function is similar to u_gethostname but is meant primarily for debugging. The u_gethostinfo function fills in a printable string with both the host name and port number corresponding to a u_buf_t structure. Program 20.14 implements u_gethostinfo.

Program 20.14 ──────────────────────────── **u_gethostinfo.c** ┐

An implementation of u_gethostinfo.

```
#include <stdio.h>
#include "uiciudp.h"
#define BUFSIZE 1024

void u_gethostinfo(u_buf_t *ubufp, char *info, int infosize) {
   int len;
   int portnumber;

   portnumber = ntohs(ubufp->sin_port);
   len = snprintf(info, infosize, "port number is %d on host ", portnumber);
   info[infosize-1] = 0;                         /* in case name did not fit */
   if (len >= infosize) return;
   u_gethostname(ubufp, info+len, infosize-len);
}
```

Program 20.14 ──────────────────────────────── **u_gethostinfo.c** ┘

The function u_comparehost returns 1 if the given host name and port number match the information given in a u_buf_t structure, *ubufp, and 0 otherwise. The u_comparehost function first checks that the port numbers agree and returns 0 if they do not. Otherwise, u_comparehost calls name2addr to convert the host name to an address and compares the result to the address stored in ubufp. Program 20.15 implements u_comparehost.

Program 20.15 ──────────────────────────── **u_comparehost.c** ┐

An implementation of u_comparehost.

```
#include <string.h>
#include <sys/socket.h>
#include "uiciname.h"
#include "uiciudp.h"

int u_comparehost(u_buf_t *ubufp, char *hostn, u_port_t port) {
   in_addr_t addr;
   struct sockaddr_in *remotep;

   remotep = (struct sockaddr_in *)ubufp;
   if ((port != ntohs(remotep->sin_port)) ||
       (name2addr(hostn, &addr) == -1) ||
       (memcmp(&(remotep->sin_addr.s_addr), &addr, sizeof(in_addr_t)) != 0))
      return 0;
   return 1;
}
```

Program 20.15 ──────────────────────────────── **u_comparehost.c** ┘

20.8 Comparison of UDP and TCP

Both UDP and TCP are standard protocols used by applications to send information over a network. The choice of which to use for a given application depends on the design goals of the application. This section summarizes the main differences between UDP and TCP from the viewpoint of the application.

1. *TCP is connection-oriented and UDP is not.* To send over a TCP communication endpoint, a client first makes a connection request and the server accepts it. Once the client and server have established the connection, they can enjoy symmetric bidirectional communication with standard read and write functions. The endpoints are associated with the client and server pair. Either side can close the connection, in which case the other side finds out about it when it tries to read or write. Thus, applications communicating with TCP can tell when the other side is done. In contrast, an application can use a UDP communication endpoint to send to or receive from anyone. Each message must include the destination address (usually an IP address and port number). UDP does not provide an application with knowledge about the status of the remote end.

2. *UDP is based on messages, and TCP is based on byte streams.* If an application sends a UDP message with a single `sendto`, then (if the buffer is large enough) a call to `recvfrom` on the destination endpoint either retrieves the entire message or nothing at all. (Remember that we only consider unconnected UDP sockets.) In contrast, an application that sends a block of data with a single TCP write has no guarantee that the receiver retrieves the entire block in a single read. A single read retrieves a contiguous sequence of bytes in the stream. This sequence may contain all or part of the block or may extend over several blocks.

3. *TCP delivers streams of bytes in the same order in which they were sent.* UDP can deliver messages out of order, even if no errors occur anywhere in the network. UDP delivers messages to the application in the order they are received. Since individual UDP packets may travel different routes on the Internet, they may not arrive in the order they were sent. In contrast, the network subsystem of the receiving host buffers TCP packets and uses sequence numbers to deliver bytes to the application in the order they were sent.

4. *TCP is reliable and UDP is unreliable.* If TCP cannot deliver data to the remote host, it eventually reports the failure by returning an error. UDP is unreliable. The network might drop UDP packets and never deliver them to the remote host. UDP does not notify either the sender or the receiver that an error has occurred.

5. *The UDP `sendto` and the TCP `write` functions return after successfully copying their message into a buffer of the network subsystem.* The point of return for UDP does not depend in any way on the status of the receiver. For TCP, the point

of return depends indirectly on the status of the receiver and the network. The TCP network subsystem may hold outgoing data in its buffers because the receiving host has no available buffers, the receiver has not acknowledged packets, or the network is congested. The held data may cause subsequent TCP `write` calls to block. *Although TCP has flow control, you should not interpret a return from a TCP* `write` *call as an indication that data has arrived at the destination host.*

20.9 Multicast

The connectionless protocols that we have been discussing thus far are *unicast* or point-to-point, meaning that each message is sent to a single communication endpoint. In *multicast*, by contrast, a single send call can cause the delivery of a message to multiple communication endpoints.

Multicasting, which is usually implemented over an existing network structure, supports the abstraction of a group of processes that receive the same messages. Reliable multicast delivers messages exactly once to the members of the group. Ordered multicast delivers messages to each group member in the same order.

This section focuses on low-level IP multicasting available to applications through UDP sockets. Unlike unicast operations, several processes on the same host can receive messages on communication endpoints bound to the same multicast port.

IP multicast groups are identified by a particular IP address. A process joins a multicast group by binding a UDP socket (`SOCK_DGRAM`) to its multicast address and by setting appropriate socket options. The socket options inform the network interface that incoming messages for the indicated multicast address should be forwarded to the socket. If several processes on the same machine have joined a multicast group, the network interface duplicates each incoming message for all group members. The socket options also cause the host to inform LAN routers that processes on this host have joined the group. If a multicast message arrives at a LAN router, the router forwards the message on all LANs that have at least one host with a member process.

20.9.1 Multicast Addressing

This book discusses only IPv4 multicast. IPv4 multicast addresses are in the range `224.0.0.0` through `239.255.255.255`. IPv4 hosts and routers are not required to support multicasting. Hosts that support multicasting must join the *all-hosts* group `224.0.0.1`. Routers that support multicasting must join the *all-routers* group `224.0.0.2`. The addresses used to specify multicast groups are divided into four groups according to the scope of the group. The *multicast scope* refers to how far from the source multicast messages should be distributed.

Link-local multicast addresses are in the range `224.0.0.0` through `224.0.0.255`. Link-local addresses are only for machines connected at the lowest level of topology of the network. Multicast messages with these addresses are not forwarded by a multicast router.

Global multicast addresses are in the range `224.0.1.0` to `238.255.255.255`. Global addresses should be forwarded by all multicast routers. Currently, multicast is not truly global because some routers do not support multicast and many router administrators have disabled global multicast for security reasons. Also, there is no political mechanism for reserving a global multicast address and port.

Addresses in the rest of the range, `239.0.0.0` to `239.255.255.255`, are called *administratively scoped multicast addresses*. These addresses are meant to be used inside an organization. They should not be forwarded outside the administrative control of the organization, since they are not guaranteed to be unique.

Table 20.2 gives the prototypes of the two UICI UDP functions needed to support multicast communication. The `u_join` function creates a UDP socket and calls the socket options needed for the socket to join a particular multicast group. The `u_leave` function calls a socket option to leave the multicast group. After `u_leave` returns, the socket is still open and bound to the same port, but it can no longer receive multicast messages.

UICI UDP	description

`int u_join(char *IP_address,`
`        u_port_t port,`
`        u_buf_t *mcast_info)`
	creates UDP socket for multicast and binds socket to `port` returns the socket file descriptor

`int u_leave(int fd, u_buf_t *mcast_info)`	leaves multicast group

Table 20.2: Summary of UICI UDP multicast calls.

The `IP_address` parameter of `u_join` holds a string representing the multicast address in dotted form. The `port` parameter is the multicast port number. The `mcast_info` parameter points to a user-supplied `u_buf_t` structure. If successful, `u_join` returns the file descriptor of the newly created socket and fills in the user-supplied `u_buf_t` structure with the multicast address for later use with `u_sendto` or `u_leave`. If successful, `u_leave` returns 0. If unsuccessful, `u_join` and `u_leave` return −1 and set `errno`.

The `u_join` function sets up a socket that can both send to and receive from the multicast group, but *a socket does not have to belong to a multicast group to send to it*. The simple UDP client in Program 20.2 can be used for sending. All that is necessary is for `sendto` to use a valid multicast destination address.

Program 20.16 shows a program that receives multicast messages. It takes two command-line arguments: the multicast IP address in dotted form and the multicast port number. The program first joins the multicast group with `u_join` and then echoes what it receives to standard output along with the name of the sending host.

Program 20.16 ————————————————— `multicast_receiver.c`
A multicast receiver that echoes what it receives to standard output.

```c
#include <stdio.h>
#include <stdlib.h>
#include <string.h>
#include <unistd.h>
#include "restart.h"
#include "uiciudp.h"
#define BUFSIZE 1024

int main(int argc, char *argv[]) {
   char buf[BUFSIZE];
   ssize_t bytesread;
   char hostinfo[BUFSIZE];
   int mcastfd;
   u_buf_t mcastinfo;
   u_port_t mcastport;
   u_buf_t senderinfo;

   if (argc != 3) {
      fprintf(stderr, "Usage: %s multicast-address multicast-port\n", argv[0]);
      return 1;
   }

   mcastport = (u_port_t)atoi(argv[2]);          /* join the multicast group */
   if ((mcastfd = u_join(argv[1], mcastport, &mcastinfo)) == -1) {
      perror("Failed to join multicast group");
      return 1;
   }

   u_gethostinfo(&mcastinfo, buf, BUFSIZE);
   fprintf(stderr, "Info: %s\n", buf);
   fprintf(stderr, "mcastfd is %d\n", mcastfd);

                 /* read information from multicast, send to standard output */
   while ((bytesread = u_recvfrom(mcastfd, buf, BUFSIZE, &senderinfo)) > 0) {
      u_gethostinfo(&senderinfo, hostinfo, BUFSIZE);
      if ((r_write(STDOUT_FILENO, hostinfo, strlen(hostinfo)) == -1) ||
         (r_write(STDOUT_FILENO, buf, bytesread) == -1)) {
         perror("Failed to echo message received to standard output");
         break;
      }
   }
   return 0;
}
```

Program 20.16 ————————————————— `multicast_receiver.c`

20.9.2 Implementation of `u_join`

Program 20.17 implements the `u_join` function. The application first creates a UDP socket. Next, the application joins the multicast group by using `setsockopt` with level `IPPROTO_IP`, option name `IP_ADD_MEMBERSHIP`, and an option value specifying the multicast address. These options instruct the link layer of the host's network subsystem to forward multicast packets from that address to the application. The application can then use `u_sendto` and `u_recvfrom` (and the underlying `sendto` and `recvfrom`) as before.

Program 20.17 ——————————————————————————— **u_join.c**

An implementation of `u_join`.

```
#include <arpa/inet.h>
#include <sys/socket.h>
#include "uiciudp.h"

int u_join(char *IP_address, u_port_t port, u_buf_t *ubufp) {
   int mcastfd;
   struct ip_mreq tempaddress;

   if ((mcastfd = u_openudp(port)) == -1)
      return mcastfd;

   tempaddress.imr_multiaddr.s_addr = inet_addr(IP_address);
   tempaddress.imr_interface.s_addr = htonl(INADDR_ANY);

       /* join the multicast group; let kernel choose the interface */
   if (setsockopt(mcastfd, IPPROTO_IP, IP_ADD_MEMBERSHIP,
                  &tempaddress, sizeof(tempaddress)) == -1)
      return -1;

   ubufp->sin_family = AF_INET;
   ubufp->sin_addr.s_addr = inet_addr(IP_address);
   ubufp->sin_port = htons((short)port);
   return mcastfd;
}
```

Program 20.17 ——————————————————————————— **u_join.c**

20.9.3 Implementation of `u_leave`

Program 20.18 implements the `u_leave` function. The `u_leave` function informs the network subsystem that the application is no longer participating in the multicast group by calling by `setsockopt` with the `IP_DROP_MEMBERSHIP` option. Since `u_leave` does not close it, the `mcast` socket can still send multicast messages and receive non-multicast messages.

Program 20.18 ———————————————————————————————— **u_leave.c**

An implementation of u_leave.

```
#include <string.h>
#include <sys/socket.h>
#include "uiciudp.h"

int u_leave(int mcastfd, u_buf_t *ubufp) {
   struct ip_mreq tempaddress;

   memcpy(&(tempaddress.imr_multiaddr),
          &(ubufp->sin_addr), sizeof(struct in_addr));
   tempaddress.imr_interface.s_addr = htonl(INADDR_ANY);
   return setsockopt(mcastfd, IPPROTO_IP, IP_DROP_MEMBERSHIP,
                     &tempaddress, sizeof(tempaddress));
}
```

Program 20.18 ———————————————————————————————— **u_leave.c**

20.10 Exercise: UDP Port Server

This exercise describes a server that uses UDP to provide information about the services that are available on the host on which it is running. Start by reading the man page for getservbyname if this function is available on your system. Also, get a copy of the netdb.h header file. If your system does not support getservbyname, your server should use a table of your own construction.

Design a "service server" that allows clients to find out which services are available on a host. The client sends a UDP request containing the following.

- Sequence number (an integer in network byte order)
- Protocol name (a null-terminated string)
- Name of the service (a null-terminated string)

The server returns a response containing the following information.

- Same sequence number as in the request
- Integer port number (in network byte order)
- Set of null-terminated strings giving aliases of the service

If the host does not support the service, the server should return −1 for the port number. For simplicity, use the following structure for both the request and the response.

```
#define NAMESIZE 256
struct service {
    int sequence;
    int port;
    char names[NAMESIZE];
} hostsev;
```

Write a UDP test client that prompts the user for host information, protocol and service name. The client chooses a sequence number at random, marshals the request (puts it in the form of the preceding structure), and sends it to the server.

The UDP client should take three command-line arguments: the name of the host running the service server, the UDP port number for this service and the timeout value by the client. The client either waits until it receives a response from the server or times out before prompting the user for another request. If the sequence number of a received response does not match the sequence number of the most recent request, the client should print the response, noting the mismatch, and resume waiting for the server to respond. As part of your testing, set a very short timeout in the client and insert a delay in the server between the receipt of the request and the response. The delay will cause a previous packet to be received on the next request. During testing, run several servers on different machines and have multiple clients accessing different servers in turn.

20.11 Exercise: Stateless File Server

This exercise describes the implementation of a simple stateless file server based on UDP. A *stateless server* is one for which client requests are completely self-contained and leave no residual state information on the server. Not all problems can be cast in stateless form, but there are some well-known examples of stateless servers. Sun NFS (Network File System) is implemented as a stateless client-server system based on unreliable remote procedure calls (RPCs).

Program 20.19 shows a `putblock` function that writes a block of data to a specified file. Although the normal `write` function assumes an open file descriptor and manipulates a file pointer, the `putblock` function is stateless. The stateless form of file access does not assume that a file descriptor has been previously opened and does not leave file descriptors open after servicing the request.

☐ Exercise 20.17

An *idempotent operation* is an operation that can be performed multiple times with the same effect. Is the `putblock` operation of Program 20.19 idempotent?
Answer:
Although the contents of the file will not change if `putblock` is called multiple times with the same parameters, `putblock` is not strictly idempotent because the modification date changes.

☐ Exercise 20.18

Write a `getblock` function that is similar to `putblock`. Is `getblock` idempotent?
Answer:
POSIX specifies that the `struct stat` structure have a `time_t st_atime` field giving the time that a file was last accessed. Thus, `getblock` is not strictly idempotent.

Program 20.19 ──────────────────────────────── `putblock.c`

Implementation of a stateless write to a file.

```c
#include <errno.h>
#include <fcntl.h>
#include <unistd.h>
#include <sys/stat.h>
#include "restart.h"
#define BLKSIZE 8192
#define PUTBLOCK_PERMS (S_IRUSR | S_IWUSR)

int putblock(char *fname, int blknum, char *data) {
   int error = 0;
   int file;

   if ((file = open(fname, O_WRONLY|O_CREAT, PUTBLOCK_PERMS)) == -1)
      return -1;
   if (lseek(file, blknum*BLKSIZE, SEEK_SET) == -1)
      error = errno;
   else if (r_write(file, data, BLKSIZE) == -1)
      error = errno;
   if ((r_close(file) == -1) && !error)
      error = errno;
   if (!error)
      return 0;
   errno = error;
   return -1;
}
```

Program 20.19 ──────────────────────────────── `putblock.c`

20.11.1 Remote File Services

A simple remote file service can be built from the `getblock` of Exercise 20.18 and `putblock` of Program 20.19. A server running on the machine containing the file system listens for client requests. Clients can send a request to read or write a block from a file. The server executes `getblock` or `putblock` on their behalf and returns the results. The client software translates user requests for reading and writing a file into requests to read and write specific blocks and makes the requests to the server.

This is a simplification of the strategy pursued by remote file services such as NFS. Real systems have caching at both ends—the client and the server keep blocks for files that have been accessed recently in memory, to give better performance. File servers often bypass the file system table and use low-level device operations to read from and write to the disk. Of course, both sides must worry about authorization and credentials for making such requests.

A typical file service might provide the following services.
1. Read a particular block from a specified remote file.
2. Write a particular block to a specified remote file.

3. Create or delete a new remote file.
4. Create or delete a special remote file such as a directory.
5. Get the `struct stat` equivalent for a specified remote file.
6. Access or modify the permissions for a specified file.

Based on the file services that you might want to implement, devise a format for the client request and the server response. Discuss your strategy for handling errors and for dealing with network byte order.

Implement and test the portion of the remote file service for getting and putting single file blocks, using UDP with a request-reply-acknowledge for the client side. Discuss how you would implement client-side libraries that would allow reading and writing a stream of bytes based on these single-block functions.

20.12 Additional Reading

UNIX Network Programming Networking APIs: Sockets and XTI by Stevens [115] has an in-depth discussion of programming with UDP. *TCP/IP Illustrated:The Protocols, Volume 1* by Stevens explains the inner workings of the UDP protocol.

Chapter 21

Project: Internet Radio

Broadcast, telephone and network technologies are converging rapidly, blurring the distinction between telephone and television. Software for video and telephone conferencing on the Internet is widely available, and most cable companies now offer high-speed Internet connections. Telephone companies have entered the entertainment business with video-on-demand and content services. The final resolution of these competing forces will probably be determined by politics and regulatory decisions as well as by technical merit. Whatever the outcome, more computers will handle voice, audio and video streams in addition to data. This chapter explores how well network communication protocols such as UDP, multicast and TCP support streaming media applications. The chapter outlines a project to send audio streams over a network under various conditions. The project explores timing, buffering and packet loss, as well as synchronization and a dynamic number of receivers.

Objectives
- Learn about streaming media
- Experiment with UDP, multicast and TCP
- Explore timing strategies for multimedia
- Use audio in a real application
- Understand synchronization with multiple receivers

21.1 Project Overview

Historically, Internet Talk Radio was an outgrowth of the rapid expansion of multimedia facilities on the Internet. Professionally produced audio broadcasts of interest to travelers on the *Information Highway* were encoded in Sun .au format and spooled to regional servers. Once a show was distributed to regional spool sites, users could listen to the show through a multicast program called radio.

The first Internet Talk Radio program was *Geek of the Week*, in which leading "network researchers, engineers, implementers, and a wide variety of other troublemakers" were interviewed in 1993 and 1994. Geek of the Week broadcasts have been archived and are available on the Internet for download [40]. A decade later over 3000 radio stations broadcast over the Internet. Some radio stations broadcast the same programming as they do over traditional airwaves; others broadcast solely on the Internet. Most of the Internet-only stations broadcast music, and the survival of these will depend on how royalties are assessed.

This chapter develops both point-to-point and multicast systems for distributing audio to multiple destinations based on the concept of streaming audio. In streaming audio (or video), the receiver plays the data as it receives the information, rather than waiting for the entire broadcast. Both audio and video data must be played at a fixed rate that is independent of network traffic. To compensate for the uneven flow through the network, streaming media receivers buffer a small amount of data, corresponding to a few seconds of a broadcast. Video streams require a much higher data rate than audio streams and generally require more CPU power for decompression. Video streams can also tolerate greater loss before the user perceives a degradation.

As an alternative to streaming, the receiver can save the entire broadcast and play it back later. A 30-minute audio program might contain several megabytes of data. A video program might require several gigabytes, even in a highly compressed format.

The main strategies for handling streaming data to multiple receivers are either to have an independent sending source for each receiver or to have one sending source with receivers that join a program in progress. Live Internet radio broadcasts sometimes use the latter strategy; audio archives use the first strategy.

This chapter compares implementations of streaming Internet audio broadcasts using UDP, multicast and TCP. We examine the need for buffering in the sender and receiver in addition to the buffering that occurs in the network and I/O subsystems.

This chapter assumes that the audio files and the audio device use 8K bytes per second of audio. If this is not the case for your system, you will need to modify various buffer and timing parameters. Section 21.2 shows how to do this project without an audio device. We evaluate the designs from this chapter, using the following tests to compare how the solutions behave.

Test Case 1: Start one receiver and then suspend the receiver process in the middle of the transmission by entering Ctrl-Z in the console window of the receiver. After a few seconds, resume the process by executing `fg`. Is any of the transmission lost?

Test Case 2: Start one receiver and direct the output to a file rather than to the audio device. Is the received file identical to the input file? Does it take less time for the transmission than it did when outputting to the audio device?

Test Case 3: Start two receivers and suspend one receiver in the middle of the transmission by entering Ctrl-Z in the console window of that receiver. Does the suspension affect the other receiver?

Test Case 4: Start two receivers and direct the output from one receiver to a file rather than to the audio device. Is the received file identical to the input file? Does this affect what the other receiver gets?

This chapter specifies several progressive variations of the sender and the receiver, which are summarized in Table 21.1. Most of the programs are created by modification of previous variations of the sender or receiver as specified in the "start from" column of the table.

21.2 Audio Device Simulation

If you do not have access to an audio device on your machine, you can send ordinary text to a simulated audio device. The simulated audio device consists of a named pipe that replaces the `/dev/audio` device and a program, `slowreader`, that reads from the pipe at a fixed rate. In this project replace all references to `/dev/audio` with your named pipe and run the `slowreader` program with input redirected to the pipe.

The `slowreader` program is a filter. Eight times a second it reads a 1000-byte block from standard input and writes it to standard output. Use a timer that generates a signal 8 times a second. To see what happens when no data is available, set standard input to nonblocking. Attempt to read 1000 bytes. Output the bytes read. If fewer than 1000 bytes were available, output a message reporting how many bytes were missing.

21.3 UDP Implementation with One Program and One Receiver

This section discusses an Internet Radio implementation using UDP. UDP is an unreliable protocol in which messages may be delivered out of order. Start by assuming that the protocol is reliable with in-order delivery (UDP approximately satisfies these assumptions on a LAN) and then modify the programs to take into account the behavior of UDP on the Internet.

program name	text section	start from	description
server_udp	20.3		basic UDP server
client_udp	20.3		basic UDP client
UDPSend	21.3.1	server_udp	simple sender of messages
UDPRecv	21.3.1	client_udp	simple receiver of messages
UDPSendEnd	21.3.2	UDPSend	sender transmits end marker
UDPRecvEnd	21.3.2	UDPRecv	receiver detects transmission end
UDPRecvSelect	21.3.3	UDPRecvEnd	buffer with read/write select
UDPRecvThread	21.3.3	UDPRecvEnd	buffer with read/write threads
UDPRecvShared	21.3.3	UDPRecvEnd	shared buffer with child
UDPSendSeq	21.3.4	UDPSendEnd	messages with sequence numbers
UDPSendSeqTest	21.3.4	UDPSendSeq	out-of-order sequence numbers
UDPRecvSeq	21.3.4	UDPRecvSelect	receive messages with
		UDPRecvThread	sequence numbers
		UDPRecvShared	
UDPSendProg	21.4.1	UDPSendSeq	send a program listing on request
UDPRecvProg	21.4.1	UDPRecvSeq	handle a program listing
UDPSendMult	21.4.2	UDPSendProg	send to multiple receivers
UDPSendBcast	21.5	UDPSendSeq	broadcast in progress
UDPRecvBcast	21.5	UDPRecvSeq	join broadcast in progress
UDPSendMcast	21.6	UDPSendBcast	multicast in progress
UDPRecvMcast	21.6	UDPRecvBcast	join multicast in progress
TCPSend	21.7.1	serverp.c	parent-server transmission
TCPRecv	21.7.1	client.c	simple transmission receiver
TCPSendProg	21.7.2	TCPSend	send a program listing
TCPRecvProg	21.7.2	TCPRecv	get a program listing
TCPSendBcast	21.7.3	TCPSend	send to multiple receivers
TCPRecvMime	21.8.1	TCPRecv	receive stream through a browser

Table 21.1: Summary of Internet Radio project variations.

21.3.1 Simple implementation

Copy Program 20.2 (client_udp.c) on page 699 into UDPRecv.c and compile it as UDPRecv. UDPRecv sends a message to a server and reads a response. Modify UDPRecv to receive messages of at most 1000 bytes after sending the initial message. The program should take an optional third command-line argument, the name of a file. If called with three command-line arguments, UDPRecv writes the received information to the specified file. Otherwise, UDPRecv writes the received information to /dev/audio.

Copy Program 20.1 (server_udp) on page 698 into UDPSend.c and compile it as UDPSend. Modify UDPSend to take two command-line arguments: a port number and a file name. The UDPSend listens on the specified port for client requests. When UDPSend receives a request (any message), it opens the file and copies the file contents to the requesting host in 1000-byte messages. Since the Internet Radio application sends 8000 byte/second audio, UDPSend should sleep for one second after sending each eight messages. After sending the entire file, UDPSend waits for another request. For each of these programs remember to change the value of BUFSIZE from 1024 to 1000.

☐ Exercise 21.1

How would the message size, number of messages per block and sleep time between blocks change for a file containing CD-quality audio rather than voice-quality audio?

Answer:

CD-quality audio consists of two channels of 16-bit values played at a rate of 44.1 kHz, which translates to a throughput of 176,400 bytes/sec or 1.4112 Mbps. With a 1000-byte message size, the sender must write an average of 176.4 packets per second. Sending 176 packets per second can result in underflow for long transmissions, whereas sending 177 packets per second can result in receiver buffer overflow. A packet size of 1225 bytes evenly divides the data rate and still fits within a typical Ethernet packet. In this case, the sender should send 144 packets per second.

☐ Exercise 21.2

How does UDPRecv open the output file?

Answer:

The UDPRecv function opens the file by calling open with three parameters: the pathname, flags and permissions. The flags are O_WRONLY, O_CREAT and O_TRUNC. Set the permissions appropriately.

☐ Exercise 21.3

How can you use UDPSend to send the file myaudio.au to remote receivers?

Answer:

Decide on a port number to use, say, 16001, and start the program with the following command.

```
UDPSend 16001 myaudio.au
```

◻ **Exercise 21.4**

Suppose the program from Exercise 21.3 is running on os1.cs.utsa.edu. How should you start UDPRecv to receive the transmission?

Answer:

```
UDPRecv os1.cs.utsa.edu 16001
```

◻ **Exercise 21.5**

What happens if you omit the call to sleep from UDPSend?

Answer:

The program sends the file as fast as it can, limited by the speed of the network, the speed of disk access and the size of the network buffers. A client like UDPRecv does not buffer its input and the audio device can only handle eight messages a second. Once the buffers of the audio device are full, UDPRecv blocks while outputting to the audio device and may miss some of the transmission from the server.

◻ **Exercise 21.6**

Suppose that as in Exercise 21.5 the input file contains a 30-minute radio program. How many bytes of buffer space does the receiver need to fully buffer the transmission?

Answer:

For 8000 byte per second audio, the receiver needs 30*60*8K = 14 megabytes.

◻ **Exercise 21.7**

Modify UDPSend so that it sleeps for one second after every nine messages instead of eight. What does the output of UDPRecv sound like? What if it sleeps after every seven messages? Which is more annoying?

Answer:

If UDPSend sleeps after nine messages, it sends about nine messages a second. Since the receiver can only process eight messages a second, it misses about 1/8-second of sound every second over a long transmission, causing jumps in the audio. If UDPSend sleeps after only seven messages, the receiver sometimes blocks while waiting for input from the network and cannot keep the local audio buffer full. There would be pauses in the audio, sometimes in the middle of a word. The loss of 1/8 second of audio every second is annoying, but understandable for spoken audio. The brief pauses caused by sending the audio too slowly is sometimes more annoying. Of course, this judgment is subjective and you may judge differently.

☐ Exercise 21.8

What drawbacks does sleeping for 1 second after every eight messages have in controlling flow?

Answer:

This sleep strategy does not take into account the overhead in transmitting the messages or the scheduling delays caused by other processes in the system. For example, if these delays average 100 ms for every eight messages, the server sends 1 second of audio every 1.1 seconds, causing slight pauses in the audio at the receiver. The POSIX description of `sleep` states that the suspension time may be longer than requested because of scheduling or other activity by the system.

☐ Exercise 21.9

How could you fix the problem of an inaccurate data rate because of the inaccuracy of `sleep`?

Answer:

Use a timer that generates an interrupt every second. Each time the interrupt occurs, send the required messages. You should avoid sending the information from the interrupt service routine. Have the interrupt server routine set a flag, and use `sigsuspend` to wait for the interrupt, as in Example 8.26. Consider using absolute time as discussed in Section 9.6.

☐ Exercise 21.10

How would the original implementation behave under Test Case 1 and Test Case 2?

Answer:

Under Test Case 1, the receiver loses some of the transmission if it is delayed long enough. The amount lost depends on the amount of time the process is suspended, the size of the receiver buffers and the size of the network subsystem buffers on the receiver host. Under Test Case 2, the output file at the receiver is usually identical to the input file for senders and receivers on the same uncongested local area network. It takes the same time to write the data to a file as to the audio device because the sender limits the rate at which it transmits the data.

21.3.2 Termination of the receiver

Connectionless communication protocols such as UDP do not indicate when the transmission is complete, so the receiver does not know when to terminate. There are several ways to handle the termination problem.

The sender can transmit a special message reporting that it has sent all of the data. The special message must be distinguishable from audio data. Since in most audio formats, any data is possible, the special message might be embedded in the audio data.

Alternatively, the receiver can use the timeout capability of UICI. If it receives no data in a certain length of time, say, 5 seconds, the receiver assumes that the transmission has ended and terminates. Receivers using this approach could terminate prematurely unless they use a very large timeout value.

Another method relies on the atomic nature of UDP messages—a UDP message is either received in its entirety or is not received at all. The receiver assumes that all messages except the last one are exactly 1000 bytes. If the size of the file is not a multiple of 1000 bytes, the last message has fewer than 1000 bytes and the receiver knows that this is the last message. If the file is a multiple of 1000 bytes, the sender transmits a message of length 0 after the last message.

Copy `UDPSend.c` into `UDPSendEnd.c`, and copy `UDPRecv.c` into `UDPRecvEnd.c`. Modify these programs to transmit a zero-length message to signify the end of the transmission.

❏ Exercise 21.11

Propose another method of termination that uses the atomicity of UDP messages.
Answer:
The receiver uses a receive buffer of size 1001 instead of 1000. The sender transmits a message of size 1001 after the last message containing data. If the receiver reads a message of size 1001, it knows that the transmission has completed.

❏ Exercise 21.12

Under what circumstances does the solution proposed in Exercise 21.11 cause the receiver to not terminate? How can you fix this?
Answer:
UDP is an unreliable protocol, so the receiver never terminates if the last message never arrives. You can handle this problem by using `u_recvfrom_timed` with a very long value of the timeout, say, 30 seconds.

21.3.3 Buffering by the receiver to handle network latency

One of the problems with streaming audio (or video) is that the transmission time may not be constant. Periods of heavy network traffic cause messages to be delayed or lost. For now we assume that the messages are received in order and never lost, but there may be short periods (equivalent to the time to play a few messages) in which no messages are received. The receiver can compensate for this uneven transmission by allocating buffers and filling many of the buffers before starting to play the first message. The receiver must fill the buffers from incoming network messages concurrently with the emptying and playing of the buffers.

☐ Exercise 21.13

A naive approach to handling the buffers is for the receiver to alternate between reading from the network and writing to the audio device. What is wrong with this idea?

Answer:

Depending on the rate at which messages arrive, there may be times when a network message is available but the receiver blocks while waiting to write to the audio device. At other times, the audio device buffers may be empty and the receiver blocks while waiting for input from the network, even though there are process buffers containing data for the audio device.

☐ Exercise 21.14

How would you implement a solution in which the receiver forks a child process that reads only from the network, filling the process buffers. The parent receiver process empties the process buffers, sending to the audio device.

Answer:

The process buffers must reside in shared memory, and the receiver parent and child must use interprocess synchronization mechanisms to access the shared memory.

The receiver buffer problem is a standard producer-consumer problem involving two file descriptors that must be monitored concurrently. We discuss three possible solutions to this problem—select, multiple threads and parent-child processes.

In the first solution, the receiver calls select to determine which file descriptor is ready. The receiver has one descriptor for reading and one for writing in contrast to Program 4.12, which monitors two file descriptors for reading.

Copy UDPRecvEnd.c into UDPRecvSelect.c and compile it as UDPRecvSelect. Modify the program to call select to monitor the two file descriptors. Preallocate NUMBUF buffers. Use a value of NUMBUF that corresponds to about 10 seconds of audio, and do not start sending anything to the audio device until at least half the process buffers are filled.

☐ Exercise 21.15

What is a buffer overflow and what is a buffer underflow? How would you handle these conditions?

Answer:

A buffer overflow means that the network has available data but the receiver does not have a free buffer. Overflows occur when the sender produces data faster than the receiver uses it. A buffer underflow means that the audio device requires data but the receiver does not have any filled buffers. Underflows occur when the audio device uses data faster than the sender transmits it or when the network incurs heavy packet loss.

When `select` reports that data is available from the network but no buffer is free, the receiver should block on writing to the audio device until a buffer can be freed. If this does not happen soon enough, the network subsystem may drop messages because its buffers are full. Similarly, when `select` reports that a write to the audio device would not block but there is no data to write, the receiver should block while waiting for data from the network.

Since only a single process accesses the process buffers, the receiver does not have a critical section in the `select` implementation. However, the programming is still tricky, since the program can be in one of three states: only reading from the network (initially and when the buffers are empty), only writing to the audio device (when the buffers are full), and using `select`.

The threaded solution uses a producer thread responsible for reading from the network and a consumer thread responsible for outputting to the audio device. Each thread just blocks when its input or output is not ready. Use Program 16.14 and Program 16.11 as models for your solution. Take care that the producer thread does not obtain exclusive access to the buffer before blocking for network input. Similarly, the consumer thread should not hold exclusive access to the buffer before waiting for audio output to return from its previous write. Copy `UDPRecvEnd.c` into `UDPRecvThread.c` and compile it as `UDPRecvThread`. Modify `UDPRecvThread` so that it implements the threaded solution.

A third solution uses a child process to output to the audio device while the parent reads from the network. The process buffers can be implemented with shared memory, as described in Section 15.3. As in the threaded implementation, the critical sections that access the shared buffer must be protected. Copy `UDPRecvEnd.c` into `UDPRecvShared.c` and compile it as `UDPRecvShared`. Modify `UDPRecvShared` so that it implements the parent-child solution. The child process terminates when it has finished reading from the network. The parent terminates when the process buffers are empty and the child has terminated.

◻ Exercise 21.16

How can the parent determine whether the child process has terminated?

Answer:

The parent checks to see if the child has terminated only when the process buffers are empty. A simple `wait` call blocks until the child finishes, leading to a deadlock when the buffers fill. Use `waitpid` with the `NOHANG` option, or catch the `SIGCHLD` signal and set a flag when the child terminates.

◻ Exercise 21.17

What happens when the process that is sending to the audio device terminates while the audio device still has data in its buffer?

Answer:

The outcome depends on the system you are using. On some systems, if you exit while the audio buffer contains data, the audio stops. An explicit call to `close` on the audio device may block until the audio device buffers are empty.

☐ Exercise 21.18

How would the three implementations of the buffered receiver behave under Test Case 1 and Test Case 2?

Answer:

All three implementations behave similarly under Test Case 1 and Test Case 2. Under Test Case 1, the receiver loses some of the transmission if it is delayed long enough; however, the amount lost would be decreased by the amount stored in the input buffer. Under Test Case 2, the output file should usually be identical to the input file if run on a local area network that was not too busy. Because the rate is determined by the sender, it takes about the same time to save the data to a file as to write it to the audio device.

21.3.4 Buffering by the receiver to handle out-of-order delivery

The UDP protocol does not force in-order delivery of packets. Out-of-order packets are seldom observed on a LAN in which there is only one path between sender and receiver, but UDP packets are often delivered out of order on the Internet.

The usual way to handle out-of-order transmission is with sequence numbers. Each message starts with a header containing a sequence number that is incremented by the sender for each message sent. For this part of the project, we assume that a 32-bit sequence number is sufficient.

☐ Exercise 21.19

Suppose an 8000 byte per second audio stream uses 1000-byte messages. How long does it take for the audio stream to overflow a 32-bit sequence number?

Answer:

A 32-bit unsigned sequence number representation has 2^{32} possible values. Since the audio stream sends one message every 1/8 second, it takes 2^{29} seconds (approximately 17 years) to wrap around.

☐ Exercise 21.20

Suppose a 2-gigabyte per hour stream of video uses 1000-byte messages. How long does it take for the video stream to overflow a 32-bit sequence number?

Answer:

Using unsigned 32-bit integers, the video stream takes about 2100 hours (about 3 months) to overflow its sequence number.

❏ Exercise 21.21

How would you design a message to contain a sequence number and 1000 bytes of audio?

Answer:

Prepend a 4-byte header to the message body so that messages are now 1004 bytes. The header represents the message sequence number in network byte order.

❏ Exercise 21.22

The code segment below reads 1000 bytes of audio from the open file descriptor `filefd` and sends it along with a 32-bit sequence number to a remote host as a single UDP message. Aside from the lack of error checking, what is wrong with this implementation?

```
#define BUFSIZE 1000
char buf[BUFSIZE+4];
uint32_t seq;

r_read(filefd, buf+4, BUFSIZE);
*(uint32_t *)buf = htonl(seq++);
u_sendtohost(sendfd, buf, BUFSIZE+4, hostn, port);
```

Answer:

Some systems force integers to be aligned on word boundaries, and the declaration of `buf` does not guarantee word alignment. You can fix the alignment problem by using `memcpy` rather than statement assignment, as illustrated by the following code.

```
uint32_t seqn;
seqn = htonl(seq++);
memcpy(buf, &seqn, 4);
```

❏ Exercise 21.23

What happens if the sequence number is sent in one 4-byte message followed immediately by a 1000-byte message containing the audio data?

Answer:

This approach does not solve the out-of-order delivery problem. Even assuming the receiver reads a 4-byte message followed by a 1000-byte message, the sequence number in the first message might not correspond to the audio data in the second message.

❏ Exercise 21.24

Design a buffer scheme for a receiver to store messages that might arrive out of order.

Answer:

A receiver with `NUMBUF` buffers places message number `n` into buffer slot `n % NUMBUF`. Each buffer slot has a flag, `filled`, that specifies whether the corresponding buffer slot contains unsent audio data. The receiver must prevent the following errors.

- Insert an item into a filled buffer slot.
- Remove an item from an empty or previously consumed buffer slot.

◻ Exercise 21.25

How should you modify the synchronization of a threaded implementation to support the buffer scheme described in Exercise 21.24?

Answer:

A typical threaded implementation based on Program 16.11 blocks the producer if no buffer slots are available. Modify this code so that the producer blocks after reading an item from the network if the corresponding buffer is not available. The consumer no longer blocks when `totalitems` is 0, but instead blocks if the next buffer slot is empty.

◻ Exercise 21.26

The solution described in Exercise 21.25 has a potential deadlock. How could this deadlock happen and how could it be avoided?

Answer:

Suppose there are eight buffers. Sequence numbers 0 and 1 have been processed by the producer and the consumer . The producer receives messages with sequence numbers 3, 4, 5, 6, 7, 8, 9, and 11, missing both 2 and 10. The consumer blocks while waiting for message number 2 from slot 2 to be filled. The producer blocks while waiting for slot 3 to be emptied so that it can insert sequence number 11. The consumer should time out and move on to the next slot if the current item is not available when it is time to send the next packet to the audio device. For the scenario described in this exercise, the consumer removes message number 3, allowing the writer to put message 11 in the buffer.

Copy `UDPSendEnd.c` into `UDPSendSeq.c` and compile it as `UDPSendSeq`. Modify `UDPSendSeq` to send 1004-byte messages with sequence numbers. Copy one of your implementations from Section 21.3.3 into `UDPRecvSeq` and compile it as `UDPRecvSeq`. Modify `UDPRecvSeq` to handle out-of-order delivery of messages. Test these together.

◻ Exercise 21.27

How does the termination criterion change when sequence numbers are used?

Answer:

The receiver knows that the last message has been received if the message length is not 1004. A message of length 4 specifies the end, with no audio data in the message. The receiver terminates after reading this message once the buffer is empty. The receiver should also terminate under a long timeout condition when the buffers are empty.

☐ **Exercise 21.28**

How does the synchronization in the threaded implementation of the receiver change when messages can be received out of order?

Answer:

The synchronization of the consumer is almost the same. The consumer now blocks when the filled flag of the next slot is clear rather than when `nitems` is 0. The producer does not know which slot is needed until it reads the message. One solution is to have the producer read a message into a local buffer, check the sequence number, and block if the corresponding slot is not available. Be sure to implement producer and consumer blocking in a loop that checks whether the blocking condition has changed.

Testing the out-of-order receiver on a LAN is difficult since programs rarely receive out-of-order UDP messages. To test receiver handling of out-of-order messages usually requires that the messages actually be sent out of order. Copy `UDPSendSeq.c` into `UDPSendSeqTest.c` and compile it as `UDPSendSeqTest`.

Modify `UDPSendSeqTest` to occasionally delay a message for 1, 2 or 3 messages. Use a separate buffer for a delayed message and an integer counter specifying how long to delay. You should also pick a threshold value between 0 and 1. If the threshold is 0, the sender transmits packets in order. For thresholds greater than 0, the sender transmits a greater fraction of the packets out of order. The sender sets the counter to 0 when it starts and checks the counter each time it is ready to send a message. A nonzero counter indicates that a delayed message exists. If the counter is greater than 1, the sender decrements it and sends the current message. If the counter is equal to 1, the sender decrements it and sends the current message followed by the delayed message in the buffer. If the counter is 0, the sender picks a pseudorandom number between 0 and 1. If the value is not below the threshold, the sender transmits the current message. If the value is less than the threshold, the sender places the message in the buffer and sets the counter to 1, 2 or 3 (at random).

21.4 UDP Implementation with Multiple Programs and Receivers

This section describes an implementation that allows both multiple programs and multiple receivers.

21.4.1 Multiple programs and one receiver

Copy `UDPSendSeq.c` into `UDPSendProg.c` and compile it as `UDPSendProg`. Modify `UDPSendProg` to interpret the filename command-line argument as a program listing of available audio files. Each line of the program listing has the name of an audio file and a description. When the sender receives a request message consisting of a 0 byte, the sender transmits the contents of the program listing file to the receiver as a single message. (Assume that the listing file is small enough to be sent as a single UDP message.) When the sender receives a message containing a single nonzero integer in network byte order, the sender begins to transmit the audio file identified by that integer. A value of 1 represents the first file in the program listing. Any value out of range causes the sender to ignore the request message and resume listening for another request.

Copy `UDPRecvSeq.c` into `UDPRecvProg.c` and compile it as `UDPRecvProg`. `UDPRecvProg` begins by sending a single 0 byte to the sender and reading the program listing. `UDPRecvProg` presents the listing to the user and prompts for the user's selection. `UDPRecvProg` then sends the request number to the sender and plays the audio file as before.

◻ Exercise 21.29

What happens if `UDPRecvProg`'s initial 0 byte is lost? How can you modify `UDPRecvProg` to deal with the possibility of such a loss? What other types of loss are possible?

Answer:

If the initial 0 byte is lost (or the program listing returned by the sender is lost), `UDPRecvProg` hangs while waiting for the sender's reply. You can modify `UDPRecvProg` to time out and retry the initial byte a specified number of times before giving up. Similarly, the request number may be lost. Again, `UDPRecvProg` should time out and retry a specified number of times. `UDPRecvProg` should ignore loss of individual audio packets. However, if `UDPRecvProg` detects that the audio packet loss rate is too high, it should probably inform the user of a problem.

21.4.2 Multiple programs and multiple receivers

Copy `UDPSendProg.c` into `UDPSendMult.c` and compile it as `UDPSendMult`. Modify the program to work with multiple copies of the receiver. This modification is similar to changing a serial server into a parallel server.

◻ Exercise 21.30

How does `UDPSendMult` behave under Test Case 3 and Test Case 4?

Answer:

In this implementation the receivers are independent and receive independently generated data streams. One receiver does not affect another.

21.5 UDP Implementation of Radio Broadcasts

The simplest strategy for handling multiple receivers of the same audio program is to treat them as completely independent, as described in Section 21.4.2. An alternative strategy, used by some radio stations on the Internet, is to multicast the program in a single stream. Listeners "tune in" at any time and receive the program as it is being broadcast on the air. A third strategy, used by video-on-demand (VOD) providers, broadcasts multiple copies of the same stream (a movie). Each copy starts a few minutes later than the previous one. Customers tune in to the stream that starts next so that they don't miss anything.

Copy `UDPSendSeq.c` into `UDPSendBcast.c` and compile it as `UDPSendBcast`. Modify `UDPSendBcast` to begin "sending" the file when it starts up. At first the sender has no receivers, so it just reads from the file and sleeps after reading each eight blocks. If the sender has receivers, it sends each message to every receiver. As receiver requests come in, the sender adds these receivers to its list. When a receiver requests the broadcast, the sender responds with a message containing a description of the audio broadcast (in this case, just the name of the file) and the elapsed time (in minutes and seconds) since program transmission started.

Logically, the sender consists of two distinct operations. One operation accepts new requests, and the other transmits the audio program. A possible implementation of both operations with a single process (or thread) generates a signal once per second. The signal handler sends eight messages to all of the receiving hosts, and the `main` program handles new receivers. The `main` program and the signal handler share the list of receiving hosts. A correct implementation with signals is only possible if the socket calls and name resolution calls that UICI uses are async-signal-safe or if the `main` program blocks signals at appropriate points.

❑ Exercise 21.31

Describe an appropriate data structure for the list of receivers.

Answer:

The data type of a receiver could be a `u_buf_t` structure that holds all the information needed to describe a receiver of a UDP message. (See Section 20.2 for a description.) If the sender sets a maximum number of receivers, it can use an array. Otherwise, the sender can use a linked list of `u_buf_t` items.

An implementation that does not require the async-signal safety of the UICI calls and that does not use threads has a parent process receiving connection requests and a child process sending the audio stream to a list of remote hosts. The parent process could send `u_buf_t` messages through a pipe to its child to keep it informed about receivers. The child can set the pipe for nonblocking reads and could attempt to read new receivers from the pipe each time it is awakened by the periodic signals for transmitting messages. The algorithm is as follows.

1. While the pipe is not empty, do a nonblocking read of a `u_buf_t` item and update the list of receivers.
2. Read eight blocks from the audio file and send them to all receivers.
3. Suspend until the next signal.

☐ Exercise 21.32

How can the parent process determine how far along the child's transmission is so that it can send the information to the requesting receiver?

Answer:

The sender can record the time it starts and calculate the difference between the current time and the start time of the broadcast.

Copy `UDPRecvSeq` into `UDPRecvBcast.c` and compile it as `UDPRecvBcast`. Modify `UDPRecvBcast` to receive audio from `UDPSendBcast`. The `UDPRecvBcast` program displays the initial message from the sender (rather than sending the message to the audio device) and adjusts its state to start in the middle of a broadcast.

☐ Exercise 21.33

Describe a strategy for initially partially filling the receive buffer before sending audio.

Answer:

Care must be taken so that the receiver does not wait for a message that has previously been sent. Since messages can be received out of order, the message after the one with the lowest sequence number may never arrive. Record the first sequence number that comes in and start filling the receive buffer according to the sequence numbers until a message comes in that would overflow the buffer. Then throw away the earliest half of the receive buffer. This should make room for the message just received.

☐ Exercise 21.34

What happens if the sender's first message giving the description of the broadcast is lost?

Answer:

The first message received contains binary audio data. The result of the receiver outputting this type of information to a terminal is unpredictable. The receiver should do a sanity check on the first message and display the message only if it consists of printing characters.

☐ Exercise 21.35

How does the UDP implementation of the radio broadcast behave under the four basic test cases?

Answer:

`UDPRecvBcast` behaves similarly to the other implementations. The receiver loses data if it is suspended long enough, and the receivers are independent.

21.6 Multicast Implementation of Radio Broadcasts

Copy `UDPSendBcast.c` into `UDPSendMcast.c` and compile it as `UDPSendMcast`. Modify `UDPSendMcast` to take a multicast address as an additional command-line argument. The `port` argument is now the multicast port for sending. The sender does not need to know anything about the receivers and does not have any direct contact with them. The sender's only responsibility is to send.

Copy `UDPRecvBcast.c` into `UDPRecvMcast.c` and compile it as `UDPRecvMcast`. Modify `UDPRecvMcast` to receive audio from `UDPSendMcast`. The first command-line argument of `UDPRecvMcast` is a multicast address, and the second command-line argument is a multicast port. The `UDPRecvMcast` program now only receives messages and does not send anything over the network.

❑ Exercise 21.36

How would you incorporate into the receiver the ability to display a message indicating how far along the audio transmission is when it joins?

Answer:

The receiver can estimate the time from first sequence number of the first audio packet that it receives, given that eight sequence numbers corresponds to one second of audio.

❑ Exercise 21.37

How does `UDPRecvMcast` behave under the four basic test cases?

Answer:

`UDPRecvMcast` behaves as the other UDP implementations did. The receiver loses data if it is suspended long enough, and the receivers are independent.

21.7 TCP Implementation Differences

All the differences between UDP and TCP discussed in Section 20.8 factor into the implementation of Internet Radio. The main drawback of the UDP implementation is its unreliability. Messages can be lost or delivered out of order. While the problem of out-of-order receipt of messages can be solved simply by buffering at the receiver end, message loss is more difficult to handle with UDP. TCP handles this automatically.

The case of a single sender and a single receiver is simpler in TCP because TCP already ensures that information will be received in order. Sequence numbers are not needed. Since the receiver can send information to the audio device no faster than 8000 bytes/second on average, the receiver cannot read faster than this rate on average. Because TCP has flow control, the sender's network subsystem automatically forces the sender to slow down if it tries to send too quickly. The sender, therefore, does not have to sleep to limit the rate at which it sends, as in Section 21.3.1. Also, because of the connection-oriented nature of TCP, the sender can close the connection when finished, and the receiver can detect this. The issues discussed in Sections 21.3.2– 21.3.4 are all either irrelevant or are easily handled with TCP, though the receiver may still want to buffer the data to handle variation in network latency.

Multiple programs with a single receiver can be handled in a simple way, as in Section 21.4.2, with the server sending the list of programs to the receiver. However, because TCP provides byte streams rather than messages or datagrams, the receiver may not receive the entire list with a single read, even if the buffer is large enough and the sender sends the list with a single write. The information must contain a well-defined terminator, such as a blank line. The receiver must keep reading until it receives this terminator. Once the sender and receiver agree on an audio file to transmit, the implementation reduces to the single-program case.

With multiple receivers and multiple audio files, the transmissions can be considered independent and can be done by separate processes or threads.

Implementing the capacity to tune in while the transmission is in progress, as in Section 21.5, makes TCP more complicated to use, even with a single program and multiple receivers. With UDP, the sender just sends to all the receivers, one after another. This works because a problem with the network connection to a given receiver does not affect the sender's ability to send to other receivers. With TCP, if a server is sending audio to more than one host, network congestion or a busy receiver can cause `write` to block, delaying transmission to subsequent receivers. To handle this, use `select`, multiple processes, or multiple threads. In any of these cases, different receivers might be receiving at a temporarily different rate, and so the audio data must be buffered at the sender. Sender buffering is different from the buffering done by a receiver to account for network latency or out-of-order receipt. The following sections discuss these issues in more detail.

21.7.1 TCP implementation of one program and one receiver

Copy `serverp.c` from Program 18.2 on page 623 to `TCPSend.c` and compile it as `TCPSend`. Modify `TCPSend` to take a second command-line argument, the name of an audio file. After the sender accepts a network connection, it forks a child that opens the audio file and transmits its contents to the remote host. Since the child transmits the file and the parent resumes waiting for another request, `TCPSend` can handle multiple receiver requests for the same file. Note that the original program transfers data from the network to standard output, whereas this program transfers information from a file to the network.

Copy `client.c` from Program 18.3 on page 624 into `TCPRecv.c` and compile it as `TCPRecv`. Modify `TCPRecv` to take an optional third command-line argument. When called with two command-line arguments, `TCPRecv` copies data from the network to the audio device. When called with three command-line arguments, `TCPRecv` copies data from the network to the file named by the third argument. Open the output file as in Exercise 21.2.

TCPSend and TCPRecv can be used together to transfer audio from the sender machine to the receiver machine.

☐ **Exercise 21.38**

How does TCPRecv behave under Test Case 1 and Test Case 2?

Answer:

If the receiver is suspended, the sender eventually blocks. No data is lost. If the receiver writes the data to a file, the file should be identical to the input audio file. If the network and the disk drive are faster than the audio device (a likely occurrence), transmission to a file completes much more rapidly than transmission to an audio device.

☐ **Exercise 21.39**

What happens if the parent of TCPSend opens the audio file before forking any children?

Answer:

In this case, all children share the same file descriptor and have the same offset into the file for reading. The children would transmit mutually disjoint pieces of the audio file rather than each transmitting the complete file.

21.7.2 TCP implementation of multiple programs with one receiver

Copy TCPSend.c into TCPSendProg.c and compile it as TCPSendProg. Modify TCPSendProg to send multiple audio files. Now, as in UDPSendProg, the file command-line argument specifies the name of a file containing the program listing. Each line of the program listing has the name of an audio file and a description of the file. When the sender accepts a connection from the receiver, it sends the program listing to the receiver, followed by an empty line. The sender waits for another message from the receiver containing the number of the audio file in network byte order. The value 1 represents the first file. Any value out of range causes the sender to close the connection.

Copy TCPRecv.c into TCPRecvProg.c and compile it as TCPRecvProg. Modify TCPRecvProg to be used with TCPSendProg. After reading the list of audio files from the sender, TCPRecvProg presents the information to the user as a numbered list and prompts the user to make a selection by entering a number. TCPRecvProg sends the user's selection to the sender and plays the audio file as before. The sender terminates its initial message by an empty line. Do not assume that the receiver can receive the entire list with a single read.

☐ **Exercise 21.40**

How can you test that TCPRecvProg correctly handles the initial message?

Answer:

Temporarily modify the sender so that it sends the initial message in two pieces with a sleep in between.

21.7.3 TCP implementation of radio broadcasts

With TCP and a single receiver per process, the sender can rely on TCP flow control to regulate the rate at which it sends data. A receiver that malfunctions and cannot read from the network does not delay the other receivers. Similarly, a receiver that just throws away data rather than writing to the audio device can still receive data at the rate of the network, which may be much faster than the audio devices of other receivers. In this case, too, the faulty receiver does not affect the other receivers because the sending to different receivers is independent.

When broadcasts can be joined in progress, only one process or thread is reading from the audio file and the data must be sent to all receivers. Different receivers may be able to handle the data at slightly different rates, at least over short time intervals. The sender can handle the uneven rates by using a shared buffer that contains blocks of the file. In a threaded implementation, the sender's writer fills the buffer at the rate of the audio device and the various reader threads access the buffer to transmit audio. If a reader thread reads too quickly, it must wait for the buffer to be filled. If a reader thread reads too slowly, then buffer slots are overwritten before being read by that reader thread.

Copy `TCPSend.c` into `TCPSendBcast.c` and compile it as `TCPSendBcast`. Modify `TCPSendBcast` to use multiple threads. The main thread starts by creating a writer thread to handle the filling of the buffer. The main thread is responsible for accepting connections. For each connection, the main thread creates a reader thread that is responsible for sending the data from the buffer to a particular remote host. The writer fills the buffer at a rate corresponding to the audio device. Use a timer that generates a signal at a given rate compensated for timer drift (Section 9.6). The simplest implementation has all threads blocking the signal while the writer uses `sigwait` to wait for the particular signal. No signal handler is necessary for this implementation. If no buffer slots are available, the writer writes over the oldest buffer slot.

Reader threads do not remove items from the buffer since each reader should be able to read all of the data. Each reader thread attempts to send data as fast as possible, blocking only on the write to the network and after it has accessed all items currently in the buffer.

❑ Exercise 21.41

What type of synchronization should `TCPSendBcast` use to protect its buffer?

Answer:

Since audio is time critical, writers should have priority. Each buffer slot should have reader/writer synchronization with *strong writer preference*.

◻ **Exercise 21.42**

How can the individual readers keep track of which packets they have already accessed?

Answer:

It is not sufficient to just keep track of which slots have been accessed, since the writer writes new items over existing ones. Each buffer slot keeps the sequence number of the packet it currently holds. Each reader keeps track of the sequence number of the last packet it sent and blocks if the sequence number in the next buffer slot is not greater than this value. TCPSendBcast does not need to send the sequence numbers to remote receivers. TCP handles missing packets and out-of-order delivery on transmission, and the sender controls the rate of play.

◻ **Exercise 21.43**

Which buffer entry should a new reader thread send when it starts?

Answer:

If the reader thread sends the item with the lowest sequence number, it may have some of the next buffers overwritten before it can access them. If the newly created reader thread starts eight items later, it is guaranteed that the writer will sleep for at least one second before overwriting any of the next buffers. Assuming a buffer size of at least 16, starting halfway through the buffers would be a reasonable choice.

◻ **Exercise 21.44**

How should you modify TCPRecv to work with TCPSendBcast?

Answer:

TCPRecv works without modification. Since sequence numbers are not attached to the data, the receiver does not care that it is receiving from the middle of the broadcast.

◻ **Exercise 21.45**

What is wrong with the following scheme for having a reader thread of the sender protect the buffers?

    1. Obtain a read lock for the slot buffer.

    2. Copy the data from the appropriate buffer slot to the network.

    3. Unlock the buffer slot.

Answer:

With TCP, writing to the network can block if the remote receiver is slow in processing the data. The reader's lock would prevent the writer from accessing the shared buffer.

■ **Example 21.46**

A correct method for the reader thread to access the shared buffer is as follows.

1. Obtain a read lock for the buffer slot.
2. Copy the data from the appropriate buffer into a local memory.
3. Unlock the buffer slot.
4. Write the data from the local memory to the network.

This implementation ensures that the buffers will only be locked for a short time and that a remote receiver cannot affect access to the buffer by the writer thread.

□ **Exercise 21.47**

Suppose each buffer slot holds 1000 bytes and that it takes 10 ns to copy a byte from one memory location to another. Estimate the maximum time that a reader would have the buffer locked for a single transfer.

Answer:

The nominal answer is 10 microseconds plus the time for locking and unlocking. However, since the thread may lose the CPU during the transfer, the actual time may be longer.

□ **Exercise 21.48**

How does `TCPRecv` behave under the four test conditions of Section 21.1?

Answer:

The maximum rate of output is independent of whether the result goes to a file or to the audio device since the rate is controlled by the sender. Suspending a receiver may cause the reader thread for this receiver to skip packets, but the suspension should not affect the other receivers if the synchronization at the sender is correct.

21.8 Receiving Streaming Audio Through a Browser

This section discusses how to run the Internet Radio programs from a browser. Create a web page containing a list of links to the broadcasts that are available. When a user clicks on a link, the browser launches a receiver helper program to receive and play the audio program.

21.8.1 Using browser helper applications

You may have noticed that when you click on certain links, the corresponding file does not appear in your browser window, but rather the browser launches a separate program, called a *helper application*, to handle the data sent by the server. For example, if you have a Real Audio Player installed on your machine and have set your browser to use this application, clicking on a link for a file with extension `ram` causes the browser to store the corresponding file as a temporary file on the local machine. The browser then launches the Real Audio Player application, passing the temporary file name to the application as a command-line argument. The file contains the information the Real Audio Player needs to locate the audio program.

Browsers use one of two methods to identify the type of resource being sent and the application that should handle this resource. Some browsers use the file extension to determine the type of resource; others rely on a `Content-Type` header line in the server response. Browsers that use file extensions store the correspondence between resource types and filename extensions in a file, typically named `mime.types`. The word *MIME* is an acronym for Multipurpose Internet Mail Extensions and was originally intended for mail attachments. Applications now interpret mime types more generally to associate an application type with a file extension. Web server responses often include a header line that describes the type of resource being sent.

■ **Example 21.49**

For an ordinary text document in HTML format, a server might send the following header line.

```
Content-Type: text/html
```

For a file with the `ram` extension, the server might send the following.

```
Content-Type: audio/x-pn-realaudio
```

When the browser receives this header line, it checks to see if a helper application has been set up with type `audio/x-pn-realaudio`, and if so, it puts the resource sent by the web server in a temporary file and calls that application with the name of the temporary file as a command-line argument.

When classifying resources on the basis of file extensions, the browser looks for an entry in its `mime.types` file corresponding to the `ram` extension such as the following.

```
audio/x-pn-realaudio    ram rm
```

The preceding command specifies that both the `ram` and `rm` extensions should be associated with audio applications of type `x-pn-realaudio`.

Start with one of your receiver programs, say, `TCPRecv.c` from Section 21.7.1 and copy it into `TCPRecvMime.c`. Modify `TCPRecvMime` to take one command-line argument, the name of a file containing the host name and port number of the sender.

□ **Exercise 21.50**

Suppose `TCPRecvMime` uses the following to read the host name and port tokens from the file specified on its command line.

```
scanf("%s %d", hostname, &port);
```

What problems might occur, assuming that `hostname` is an array of `char` and that `port` is an integer?

Answer:

The `TCPRecvMime` program has no way of telling in advance how long the host name is. Although valid host names cannot be too long, anything can appear in the resource file referenced on a web page. A bad resource file could generate a buffer overflow with potentially serious security implications. One solution is to allocate a buffer of prespecified size, say, 80 bytes, for the host name and use the following line.

```
scanf("%79s %d", hostname, &port);
```

The numerical qualifier on `%s` prevents `scanf` from filling `hostname` with more than 79 characters and the string terminator.

Test `TCPRecvMime` with `TCPSend` by creating a file containing the host and port number. Setting `TCPRecvMime` to be launched through a browser requires the following three steps that are described in the subsections below.

1. Set the web server to handle a new mime type and send the appropriate `Content-Type` line. (This step needs a system administrator and is necessary for browsers that use this line to determine the application type.)
2. Set your browser to handle the new mime type by launching `TCPRecvMime` when it receives a resource of the appropriate type.
3. Create a web page for testing.

21.8.2 Setting a new mime type in your web server

Setting up your web server to handle a new mime type requires that you have administrative access to the web server. If you do not have administrative access, ask your system administrator to do this step for you. Alternatively, you can use one of the mime types already set up for your browser. We discuss this option in Section 21.8.5.

Depending on your web server, you can set a new server mime type by modifying a file of mime types or by modifying the configuration file. For example, if your web server configuration directory has a file with a name similar to `mime.types`, add the following line to this file.

```
application/uspir      uspir
```

The preceding line allows the web server to associate an application type called `application/uspir` with the file extension `.uspir`. Alternatively, you might be able to just add the following line to the web server configuration file, possibly a file called `httpd.conf`.

```
AddType application/uspir      uspir
```

You must restart the web server after changing this file.

You can use the `client2` program from Program 18.5 on page 629 to verify that your web server is set correctly for this mime type. Create a small file called `test.uspir` in a directory accessible to the web server. If the web server is running on host `webhost` and this file is in the directory `mydir` relative to the web root directory, start `client2` with the following command.

```
client2 webhost 80
```

Type the following line terminated by an empty line.

```
GET /mydir/test.uspir HTTP/1.0
```

You should see the file after a few header lines. A correct response should have a header line similar to the following.

```
Content-Type: application/uspir
```

21.8.3 Setting your browser to handle a new mime type

The method for setting a new mime type for a browser depends on which browser you are using. For Netscape 6 or 7, go to Edit → Preferences → Navigator → Helper Applications. Click on New Type and fill in the information requested. The Description can be any phrase. The File extension should be `uspir` and the MIME type should be `application/uspir`. For the application, put the full pathname for your `TCPRecvMime` program.

21.8.4 Creating a web page

Create a file with extension `.uspir` containing the host name and port number of your `TCPSend` program. The values should specify a server that is distinct from the web server. Make the file accessible to your web server and create a web link to the file. Start `TCPSend`. When you click on the link, you should start hearing the audio program.

21.8.5 Using a predefined mime type

If you cannot add a new mime type to your web server, you can use one of the predefined types that your browser is not using or does not use often. Some suggested extensions to try are `ez`, `hqx`, `cpt`, `oda`, `smi` and `mif`. You can test these by creating a file with the appropriate extension in a place accessible to your web server and issuing the appropriate `GET` command from `client2`. You should get back a `Content-Type` line giving the corresponding application type.

Set your browser to call your `TCPRecvMime` program for this application type. Follow the procedure in Section 21.8.3. If the application type is already defined for your web browser, click EDIT and modify the values.

21.9 Additional Reading

Many radio and television stations now support streaming archives of their programming. A favorite of ours is the National Public Radio Archive that can be accessed at `www.npr.org`. The Web page of Internet Talk Radio is `http://town.hall.org/radio`. We often use the *Geek of the Week* programs to test our projects. Historical streaming media are freely available in many areas. For example, the Oyez Project of Northwestern University maintains the *US Supreme Court Multimedia Database* at `http://oyez.nwu.edu`. The site archives original recordings of famous cases as well oral arguments and oral opinions in streaming audio format.

Understanding networked multimedia applications and technology by Fluckiger [37] is dated but gives a good overview of terminology and applicable standards. *The Technology of Video and Audio Streaming* by Austerberry and Starks [8] and *Streaming Media Bible* by Mack [75] are newer guides to actually using streaming media with current products. For a technical guide to multicast and multicast applications, see *Multicast Communication: Protocols, Programming, and Applications* by Wittmann and Zitterbart [131].

Many of the current streaming media tools use RTSP (Realtime Streaming Protocol) built over RTP (Realtime Transport Protocol). You can find a good overview of RTP and its enhancements in the article "Timer reconsideration for enhanced RTP scalability," by Rosenberg and Schulzrinne [100]. The Multiparty Multimedia Session Control (mmusic) Working Group [84] of the IETF (Internet Engineering Task Force) [55] is in charge of maintaining and revising the RTSP and RTP specifications. This working group also oversees the development of the Session Initiation Protocol (SIP) for supporting voice over IP (VOIP) applications.

Chapter 22

Project: Server Performance

Large-scale client-server architecture is ubiquitous on the Internet. Web sites may service thousands of simultaneous clients, with individual servers processing hundreds of clients. Parallelism can be achieved by multiple processes, by multiple threads within a process, by asynchronous I/O and events within a single process thread or by combinations of these approaches. This chapter explores the interaction of threading, forking, network communication and disk I/O on the performance of servers.

Objectives

- Learn to measure times and control timing errors
- Experiment with server disk I/O performance
- Explore tradeoffs between threads and processes
- Use the POSIX thread libraries
- Understand different threaded-server architectures

22.1 Server Performance Costs

Effective deployment of high-performance web servers has become an increasingly important commercial enterprise. Nearly every organization has a web site that serves as an important access point for customers or members. Commercial sites are particularly concerned with handling peak loads and with fault tolerance.

The administrator of a single web server must decide how to distribute data across available disks as well as how many separate processes and separate threads within server processes to create. The effectiveness of different strategies depends on processor and system architecture as well as on the offered load.

Early web servers created a new process to handle each HTTP request. Later web servers, such as Squid [130] and Zeus [137], used a single-process approach to reduce context-switch and synchronization costs. Process creation costs considerably more than thread creation, but thread creation also has some associated costs. Kernel-level thread creation usually costs more than user-level thread creation, but user-level threads must share the kernel resources allocated for a single process.

Creation costs can be offset by preliminary creation of either processes or threads and causing them to wait at a synchronization point until activated. When the process or thread completes its task, it executes another blocking call and resumes waiting. Overhead with this approach depends on the efficiency and scalability of the blocking calls.

Synchronization costs also factor into the efficiency of cache and disk accesses. A single process/single thread architecture that uses asynchronous I/O can be more effective than multiple threads for certain types of cached workloads. Remember that user threads are implemented by a software layer that uses jackets around system calls and manages asynchronous I/O. Sometimes the overhead for this layer is greater than a carefully optimized implementation that directly uses asynchronous I/O. However, event-driven asynchronous I/O is usually more complex to program.

Context-switch costs are another factor in server performance. A switch between user threads within the same process does not incur the overhead of a kernel context switch and can therefore be done quite efficiently. Context switches and synchronization are generally more expensive at the process level than at the thread level.

22.2 Server Architectures

Chapter 18 introduced three models of client-server communication: the serial-server (Example 18.2), the parent-server (Example 18.3), and the threaded-server (Example 18.6), respectively. Because the parent-server strategy creates a new child process to handle each client request, it is sometimes called *process-per-request*. Similarly, the threaded-server strategy creates a separate thread to handle each incoming request, so it is often called the *thread-per-request* strategy.

An alternative strategy is to create processes or threads to form a *worker pool* before accepting requests. The workers block at a synchronization point, waiting for requests to arrive. An arriving request activates one thread or process while the rest remain blocked. Worker pools eliminate creation overhead, but may incur extra synchronization costs. Also, performance is critically tied to the size of the pool. Flexible implementations may dynamically adjust the number of threads or processes in the pool to maintain system balance.

■ Example 22.1

In the simplest worker-pool implementation, each worker thread or process blocks on the `accept` function, similar to a simple serial server.

```
for (  ;  ;  ) {
   accept request
   process request
}
```

Although POSIX specifies that `accept` be thread-safe, not all operating systems currently support thread safety. Alternatively, workers can block on a lock that provides exclusive access to `accept`, as the next example shows.

■ Example 22.2

The following worker-pool implementation places the `accept` function in a protected critical section so that only one worker thread or process blocks on `accept` at a time. The remaining workers block at the lock or are processing a request.

```
for (  ;  ;  ) {
   obtain lock (semaphore or mutex)
      accept request
   release lock
   process request
}
```

POSIX provides semaphores for interprocess synchronization and mutex locks for synchronization within a process.

☐ Exercise 22.3

If a server uses N workers, how many simultaneous requests can it process? What is the maximum number of simultaneous client connections?

Answer:

The server can process N requests simultaneously. However, additional client connections can be queued by the network subsystem. The `backlog` parameter of the `listen` function provides a hint to the network subsystem on the maximum number of client requests to queue. Some systems multiply this hint by a fudge factor. If the network subsystem sets its maximum backlog value to B, a maximum of N + B clients can be connected to the server at any one time, although only N clients may be processed at any one time.

Another worker-pool approach for threaded servers uses a standard producer-consumer configuration in which the workers block on a bounded buffer. A master thread blocks on `accept` while waiting for a connection. The `accept` function returns a communication file descriptor. Acting as the producer, the master thread places the communication file descriptor for the client connection in the bounded buffer. The worker threads are consumers that remove file descriptors and complete the client communication.

The buffer implementation of the worker pool introduces some interesting measurement issues and additional parameters. If connection requests come in bursts and service time is short, buffering can smooth out responses by accepting more connections ahead than would be provided by the underlying network subsystem. On the other hand, if service time is long, accepted connections languish in the buffer, possibly triggering timeouts at the clients. The number of additional connections that can be accepted ahead depends on the buffer size and the order of the statements synchronizing communication between the master producer and the worker consumers.

■ **Exercise 22.4**

How many connections ahead can be accepted for a buffer of size M with a master and N workers organized as follows?

```
Master:
    for ( ; ; ) {
        obtain a slot
        accept connection
        copy the file descriptor to slot
        signal item
    }

Worker:
    for ( ; : ) {
        obtain an item (the file descriptor)
        process the communication
        signal slot
    }
```

Answer:
If N ≥ M, then each worker holds a slot while processing the request, and the master cannot accept any connections ahead. For N < M the master can process M − N connections ahead.

■ **Exercise 22.5**

How does the following strategy differ from that of Exercise 22.4? How many connections ahead can be accepted for a buffer of size M with a master and N workers organized as follows?

```
Master:
   for ( ; ; ) {
      accept connection
      obtain a slot
      copy the file descriptor to slot
      signal item
   }

Worker:
   for ( ; ; ) {
      obtain an item (a file descriptor)
      signal slot
      process the communication
   }
```

Answer:

The strategy here differs from that of Exercise 22.4 in two respects. First, the master accepts a connection before getting a slot. Second, each worker thread immediately releases the slot (signal slot) after copying the communication file descriptor. In this case, the master can accept up to M+1 connections ahead.

☐ Exercise 22.6

In what way do system parameters affect the number of connections that are made before the server accepts them?

Answer:

The `backlog` parameter set by `listen` determines how many connections the network subsystem queues. The TCP flow control mechanisms limit the amount that the client can send before the server calls `accept` for that connection. The `backlog` parameter is typically set to 100 or more for a busy server, in contrast to the old default value of 5 [115].

☐ Exercise 22.7

What a priori advantages and disadvantages do worker-pool implementations have over thread-per-request implementations?

Answer:

For short requests, the overhead of thread creation and buffer allocation can be significant in thread-per-request implementations. Also, these implementations do not degrade gracefully when the number of simultaneous connections exceeds system capacity—these implementations usually just keep accepting additional connections, which can result in system failure or thrashing. Worker-pool implementations save the overhead of thread creation. By setting the worker-pool size appropriately, a system administrator can prevent thrashing and crashing that might occur during busy times or during a denial-of-service attack. Unfortunately, if the worker-pool size is too low, the server will not run to full capacity. Hence, good worker-pool deployments need the support of performance measurements.

☐ **Exercise 22.8**

Can the buffer-pool approach be implemented with a pool of child processes?
Answer:
The communication file descriptors are small integer values that specify position in the file descriptor table. These integers only have meaning in the context of the same process, so a buffer-pool implementation with child processes would not be possible.

In *thread-per-request* architectures, the master thread blocks on accept and creates a thread to handle each request. While the size of the pool limits the number of concurrent threads competing for resources in worker pool approaches, thread-per-request designs are prone to overallocation if not carefully monitored.

☐ **Exercise 22.9**

What is a *process-per-request* strategy and how might it be implemented?
Answer:
A *process-per-request* strategy is analogous to a *thread-per-request* strategy. The server accepts a request and forks a child (rather than creating a thread) to handle it. Since the main thread does not fork a child to handle the communication until the communication file descriptor is available, the child inherits a copy of the file descriptor table in which the communication file descriptor is valid.

The designs thus far have focused on the communication file descriptor as the principal resource. However, heavily used web servers are often limited by their disks, I/O subsystems and memory caches. Once a thread receives a communication file descriptor and is charged with handling the request, it must locate the resource on disk. This process may require a chain of disk accesses.

■ **Example 22.10**

The client request to retrieve /usp/exercises/home.html may require several disk accesses by the OS file subsystem. First, the file subsystem locates the inode corresponding to usp by reading the contents of the web server's root directory and parsing the information to find usp. Once the file subsystem has retrieved the inode for usp, it reads and parses data blocks from usp to locate exercises. The process continues until the file subsystem has retrieved the actual data for home.html. To eliminate some of these disk accesses, the operating system may cache inodes indexed by pathname.

To avoid extensive disk accesses to locate a resource, servers often cache the inode numbers of the most popular resources. Such a cache might be effectively managed by a single thread or be controlled by a monitor.

Disk accesses are usually performed through the I/O subsystem of the operating system. The operating system provides caching and prefetching of blocks. To eliminate the inefficiency of extra copying and blocking through the I/O subsystem, web servers sometimes cache their most popular pages in memory or in a disk area that bypasses the operating system file subsystem.

22.3 Project Overview

This project explores the performance tradeoffs of several server designs and examines the interaction of the implementations during disk I/O and cache access. Section 22.4 describes a test client that standardizes the offered load for different test architectures. Section 22.5 explores the use of multiple client drivers to load a single server. Sections 22.6-22.9 outline a project to compare efficiency of thread-per-request versus process-per-request implementations for different offered loads. Section 22.10 looks at the effect of disk I/O. Later sections discuss how to design experiments and how to write up the results.

22.4 Single-Client Driver

This section describes a `singleclientdriver` program that can be used to present controlled offered loads to servers and to gather statistics. The `singleclientdriver` program forks a specified number of processes, each of which makes a specified number of connections to a server that is listening on a specified host and port. The `singleclientdriver` program takes the following command-line arguments.

1. Hostname of the server
2. Port number of the server
3. Number of processes to fork
4. Number of connections per process
5. Number of requests per connection
6. Smallest response size in bytes
7. Largest response size in bytes

Each process of `singleclientdriver` sequentially creates a connection, performs the specified communication, and then closes the connection. The communication consists of a specified number of request-response pairs. The process sends a request specifying the size of the desired response and then does a blocking read to wait for that response. The process picks a desired response size that is a random integer between the smallest and largest response size.

22.4.1 Processing a connection

The client driver algorithm for processing a connection consists of the following.

1. Get the time.
2. Connect to the specified server.
3. For the number of requests per connection do the following.
   a) Get the time.
   b) Send a request (that includes the desired length of the response).
   c) Read the response.
4. Get the time.
5. Close the connection.
6. Update and save the statistics.

Each request message from a client process consists of a 4-byte message containing the length of the response in network byte order. Each time a client process sends a request, it increments its client message number. After closing a connection, the client increments its connection count and resets the request count to zero. Write your program so that it allows the saving of different levels of detail depending on a `loglevel` flag. The level can range from only keeping statistics (as described below) to full logging that includes saving the response header information. Take care not to do any output or string processing (e.g., `sprintf`) between the starting and ending timing statements, since these operations may be comparable in time to the operations that you are timing.

The algorithm glosses over the possibility of a failed connection attempt, which may occur if the server or network experiences congestion. The client should keep track of the number of failed connections. You can handle failed connections by retrying, by continuing, or by aborting the client. Each of these approaches introduces subtle problems for keeping correct statistics. Be sure to think carefully about this issue and devise and document a strategy.

22.4.2 Programming the response

Write a test server program that waits for connection requests from the client driver. After accepting a connection, the test server calls a `handleresponse` function that takes the communication file descriptor returned from `accept` as a parameter. The function reads requests from the socket designated by the communication file descriptor and sends response messages. When the function detects that the remote end has closed the socket, it closes the socket and returns. The response message consists of a response identification followed by response data of the specified length. The response identification contains the following three 32-bit integers in network byte order.

1. Process ID of server process.
2. Thread number of the thread that processes the message (or 0 for an unthreaded implementation). The thread number is a value that is unique for each thread of the process. The main thread passes this unique identifier to each thread on creation.
3. Message number. (Messages processed by a particular thread or process are numbered consecutively.)

This simple test server avoids disk accesses by using a previously created buffer with a dummy message to send as a response. The server may need to send the dummy message multiple times to fulfill the length requirement of the request. Think about how large a buffer the server requires and how this might affect the timing of the result. You can pass the address and size of the buffer to the `handleresponse` function.

22.4.3 Gathering statistics

Your `singleclientdriver` program should gather statistics about mean, standard deviation and median of both the connection times and the response times. The sample mean $\bar{x}$ for a sample of size n is given by the following formula.

$$\bar{x} = \frac{\sum_{i=1}^{n} x_i}{n}$$

The sample standard deviation is given by the following formula.

$$s = \sqrt{\frac{\sum_{i=1}^{n} x_i^2 - n\bar{x}^2}{n-1}}$$

For evaluation, combine the statistics of the processes. Calculating combined statistics for the mean and standard deviation is straightforward—just accumulate the number of values, the sum of the values, and the total of the squares of the values.

The median of a distribution is the value in the middle position of the sorted distribution values. (For distributions with an even number of values, the median is the mean of the middle two values.) When distributions are skewed, median times often better reflect behavior than do mean times. Finding the median of combined distributions typically requires that all the values be kept and sorted.

An alternative method of estimating the median of a combined distribution is to keep a histogram of the values for each distribution and then combine the histograms and estimate the median from these. A histogram is an array of counts of the number of times a value falls in a given interval. For unbounded distributions, the last histogram entry accumulates the number of values larger than a specified value. Combine histograms by adding corresponding entries. Estimate the median by accumulating the counts in the bins, starting with the bin representing the smallest value, until the sum reaches $\frac{n}{2}$, where n is the number of values in the distribution. The median can be estimated as the midpoint of the range of values corresponding to the bin. You can also use linear interpolation on the range of values counted by the bin containing the median value. You may wish to use histogram approximation for calculating the median in the short form of logging.

22.4.4 Testing the client

Test the `singleclientdriver` for different values of the command-line arguments. You should devise tests in which 5, 10 and 20 simultaneous connections are maintained for a reasonable length of time.

☐ **Exercise 22.11**

What parameters determine the number of simultaneous connections that `singleclientdriver` offers to the test server?

Answer:

The nominal number of simultaneous connections is the same as the number of child processes. However, during the initial setup period when processes are forked and during the final shutdown period when processes are completing and exiting, the number of connections is unstable. Hence, the individual processes of `singleclientdriver` should be active long enough to offset these unstable phases. Also, if the number of requests per connection multiplied by the number of bytes per request is too small, each connection will be of short duration and client processes will spend most of their time trying to establish connections rather than communicating. Finally, a given host can only effectively support a limited number of processes performing these activities. To effectively load a server under test conditions, you should run `singleclientdriver` programs on several hosts at the same time.

☐ **Exercise 22.12**

What parameters describe the offered load?

Answer:

The offered load is determined by the rate of connection attempts, the duration of each connection once established and the amount of I/O required to service the request.

☐ **Exercise 22.13**

What external factors might influence the presentation of offered load?

Answer:
Network traffic, processor load and disk load from sources external to the web server and client drivers could have a significant impact on the results.

22.5 Multiple-Client Driver

A single host, even though it is running multiple threads or processes, may not be able to offer a large enough load to a web server to measure its capacity. Your implementation should have the following features to support running multiple loading clients.

- Be able to coordinate the clients to send at the same time.
- Be able to collect and analyze combined statistics from all clients.
- Be sure that the traffic generated by the clients for synchronization and statistics does not interfere with the traffic being measured.

This section discusses a client-driver design that can be used to put a coordinated load on a server and gather statistics with minimal interference with the measurements.

The design involves two programs: a control driver and a client driver. The control driver controls multiple copies of the client driver and gathers and analyzes statistics from them. The client driver takes an optional port number in addition to the command-line arguments specified in Section 22.4. Without the optional port number, the multiple-client driver behaves like the single-client driver. If the optional port is given, the client communicates with the control driver through this port. The client starts by listening for a connection request on the optional port before loading the server and sends statistical data back over the connection. A synchronization mechanism is set up so that all clients start almost simultaneously and do not send their statistics over the network until all other clients have completed communication with the server.

Copy your `singleclientdriver.c` into `multipleclientdriver.c` and compile it as `multipleclientdriver`. Modify `multipleclientdriver` to take an additional optional control port number as a command-line argument. If this optional argument is present, `multipleclientdriver` does the following.

1. Wait for a connection request from the control host on the control port.
2. When this request arrives, send the number of child processes to the control host as a 32-bit integer in network byte order.
3. Create the child processes to load the host.
4. When loading completes, send a single byte to the control host and wait for a 1-byte response.
5. When a response from the control host arrives, forward data to the control host in an appropriate format and exit. A format for the data is given below; it includes a special record to indicate that all the data has been sent.

Notice that `multipleclientdriver` acts as both a client of the server being tested and a server for the control host.

Write a program called `controldriver.c` to control `multipleclientdriver`. The first command-line argument of `controldriver` specifies the port number for communicating with `multipleclientdriver`. This is followed by one or more command-line arguments specifying the names of the hosts running `multipleclientdriver`.

The `controldriver` program does the following.

1. Establish a connection to each of the hosts specified on the command line, using the given port number. Keep the file descriptors for these connections in an array.

2. Read a 4-byte integer in network byte order from each connection. Each integer specifies the number of child processes on the corresponding host. Save the integers in an array.

3. For each connection, read a byte for each process corresponding to that connection. (When all the bytes have been read, all the processes have finished loading the server.)

4. After receiving all the bytes from all connections, do the following for each process on each connection,

   a) Send a single byte. (This tells a process to start sending its data.)

   b) Read data until no more data is available from that process. The event type `EVENT_TYPE_DATA_END` can be used to signify the end of data from a single process.

5. After receiving all data, analyze and report the results.

One of the important design decisions is the format for the data that `multipleclientdriver` sends to `controldriver`. If `multipleclientdriver` sends raw data, then `controldriver` can dump the data to a single file for later processing or it can perform analysis itself.

Since `controldriver` does not necessarily know how much information will be sent from each process, it is simplest if the data is sent in fixed-length records. The `controldriver` program can store these in a linked list as they come in or write the data to a file. A possible format for a data record is the following.

```
typedef struct {
    int_32 time_sec;
    int_32 time_nsec;
    int_32 con;
    int_32 req;
    int_32 pid;
    int_32 serv_pid;
    int_32 serv_tid;
    int_32 serv_msgnum;
    int_32 event;
} con_time_t;
```

All the values in this structure are 4-byte integers in network byte order. Each record represents an event that occurred at one of the `multipleclientdriver` processes. The first two fields represent the time at which the event took place. These values represent wall clock times on the individual `multipleclientdriver` hosts, and only differences are relevant since the clocks on these hosts are not assumed to be synchronized. The `con` and `req` fields represent the connection number and request number for a given process of `multipleclientdriver`. Different processes are distinguished by the `pid` field, which gives the process ID of the process generating the data. The value here is important only in distinguishing data from different processes, since all the processes of a given `multipleclientdriver` send concurrently. The next three fields are the values returned to the `multipleclientdriver` from the server being tested. The last field is an indicator of the event. Some possible types include the following.

```
#define EVENT_TYPE_PROCESS_START 0
#define EVENT_TYPE_CONNECTION_START 1
#define EVENT_TYPE_CONNECTION_END 2
#define EVENT_TYPE_SERVER_LOAD_DONE 3
#define EVENT_TYPE_CLIENT_ALL_DONE 4
#define EVENT_TYPE_CLIENT_FIRST_DATA_SENT 5
#define EVENT_TYPE_CLIENT_LAST_DATA_SENT 6
#define EVENT_TYPE_SERVER_DATA_REQUEST_START 7
#define EVENT_TYPE_SERVER_DATA_REQUEST_END 8
#define EVENT_TYPE_DATA_END 9
```

The `controldriver` process can either keep a linked list of events for each `multipleclientdriver` process or it can store information about which connection the data came from in a single linked list.

22.5.1 Alternative multiple-client design

An alternative design puts all the parameters in the control program. The `multipleclientdriver` program takes a single command-line argument: the port number for communicating with the control driver. After establishing the connections, the control driver sends its command-line arguments to each `multipleclientdriver`. Since both string (hostname) and numeric data (everything else) are to be communicated, a format for this information would need to be specified. If all machines were ASCII-character based, a string that the client would read one character at a time could be sent. An alternative would be to send all data in numeric form (network-byte-ordered integers) by sending the IP address of the server rather than its name.

Since the control driver knows the number of processes on each client, the client driver does not need to send any information back to the control driver until it is ready to send statistics.

The control driver would need more command-line arguments or a configuration file containing the name and port number of the server as well as the number of processes, connections, requests and request size. A configuration file could have one line for each client driver, specifying the name and port number of the client driver as well as the number of processes, connections, requests and connection size. The control program takes the server name, port and configuration file name as command-line arguments. The same configuration file can be used to put loads on different servers.

22.6 Thread-per-request and Process-per-request Implementations

This section specifies programs to compare the performance of *thread-per-request* and *process-per-request* server implementations when disk I/O is not a factor. Write two server programs, `thread_per_request` and `process_per_request`, that are to be tested under the same offered load.

The `thread_per_request` server takes the port number on which to accept connections as a command-line argument. The main thread listens for connection requests and creates a detached thread to handle the communication. The detached thread is passed an array containing the communication file descriptor and a thread number. The thread calls `handle_request` of Section 22.4.2 and then exits.

Implement a program that uses child processes instead of threads to handle the requests. The `process_per_request` program is similar to `thread_per_request` except that the `main` program waits for completed children (e.g., Example 3.13). Be sure to use the `WNOHANG` option when waiting so that the server can process concurrent children. Compare the performance of these two approaches as a function of the offered load. Present your results with graphics and a written discussion.

22.7 Thread-worker-pool Strategy

A thread-worker-pool strategy creates a fixed number of workers at the beginning of execution instead of creating a new thread each time a connection is made. Thread-worker-pool implementations have several advantages over thread-per-request implementations.

- The cost of creating worker threads is incurred only at startup and does not grow with the number of requests serviced.
- Thread-per-request implementations do not limit the number of simultaneous active requests, and the server could run out of file descriptors if requests come in rapid succession. Thread-worker-pool implementations limit the number of open file descriptors based on the number of workers.
- Because thread-worker-pool implementations impose natural limits on the number of simultaneous active requests, they are less likely to overload the server when a large number of requests come in.

Write a `thread_worker_pool` server that takes the listening port number and the number of worker threads as command-line arguments. Create the specified number of worker threads before accepting any connections. Each worker thread calls u_accept and handles the connection directly.

Although POSIX specifies that accept be thread-safe, some systems have not yet complied with this requirement. One way to handle this problem is to do your own synchronization. Use a single statically initialized mutex to protect the call to u_accept. Each thread locks the mutex before calling u_accept and unlocks it when u_accept returns. In this way, at most one thread at a time can be waiting for a connection request. As soon as a request comes in, the worker thread unlocks the mutex, and another thread can begin waiting.

22.8 Thread-worker Pool with Bounded Buffer

This section describes an implementation of a thread-worker pool that synchronizes on a bounded buffer containing client communication file descriptors. (See, for example, Section 16.5.) The server is a producer that places communication file descriptors in a circular buffer. The worker threads are consumers that wait for the communication file descriptors to become available in the buffer.

Write a worker_pool_buffer server that takes three command-line arguments: the listening port number, the size of the bounded buffer and the number of worker threads in the pool. The threads call the handle_request function to process the communication. Design and run experiments to answer the following questions.

1. How does the connection time depend on the size of the bounded buffer? What factors influence the result?
2. How does the number of worker threads influence the server response byte rate?
3. How sensitive is overall performance to the number of worker threads?
4. When does worker pool perform better than thread-per-request?

Before running the experiments, write a discussion of how different experimental parameters might influence the results in each case.

22.9 Process-worker Pool

Implement a process-worker pool, whereby each worker process blocks on accept. The server takes two command-line arguments: the listening port number and the number of worker processes to fork.

Compare connection times for the process-worker pool with those for the thread pool of Section 22.7. Explore performance as a function of offered load. Explore hybrid designs in which a pool of threaded process workers blocks on accept. Each threaded process maintains a pool of worker threads as in Section 22.7.

□ Exercise 22.14

How would you determine whether the backlog value set by `listen` affects server performance?

Answer:

The backlog is set in UICI to the value of the MAXBACKLOG constant defined near the top of `uici.c` in Program C.2. Pick parameters that put a moderate load on the server and recompile with different values of the backlog. UICI uses the default value of 50 if MAXBACKLOG is not defined. You can use the `-D` option on the compile line to define MAXBACKLOG. Start with this value and then modify it and see if smaller or larger values affect the performance of the server.

22.10 Influence of Disk I/O

Disk accesses can be a million times slower than memory accesses. This section explores the effect of disk I/O on server performance.

To measure this performance, modify the various servers to access the disk rather than a memory buffer to satisfy requests. If your server selects from a small number of request files, your measurements may not be accurate because the operating system buffers file I/O and most of the requests may be satisfied from memory rather than from disk.

One possibility is to create a large number of files whose names are numeric, say, 00000, 00001, 00002, etc. When a request comes in, the server could pick one of these files at random and access it to satisfy the request. Some users might not have enough free disk space to implement this solution.

Another possibility is to use the system files that already exist. The idea is to create a list of the files on the server for which the user has read access. When a request comes in, the server randomly selects one of the files that is large enough to satisfy that request. Care must be taken to ensure that the process of selecting the file does not significantly burden the server.

Program 22.1 illustrates one method of ensuring careful file selection. To enable easy access, the program creates lists of files of different sizes by organizing entries according to the logarithm of their sizes. Each list consists of records that each contain the full pathname and size of a file that is of at least a given size but less than 10 times the given size. The first list contains files of at least 10 bytes, the second has files of at least 100 bytes, etc. Each list contains files 10 times the size of the previous list. If a server receives a request for a resource of size 1234 bytes, it should select at random one of the files from the list of files containing at least 10,000 bytes and transmit the required number of bytes from the selected file. Since each list is an array rather than a linked list, the server uses a random index to directly access the name of the file.

Program 22.1 creates NUMRANGES lists. For NUMRANGES equal to 5, the lists contain files of sizes at least 10, 100, 1000, 10,000 and 100,000 bytes, so makefileinfo can satisfy access requests of up to 100,000 bytes. The makefileinfo program stores the full pathname and size of each file in a record of type fileinfo. Only files whose full pathname is of size at most MAXPATH are inserted in the list. A value of 100 for MAXPATH picks up almost all files on most systems. We avoid using the system value PATH_MAX, which may be 1024 or greater, because this choice takes too much space.

Program 22.1 takes two command-line arguments, the first specifying the base path of the directory tree under which to search for files and the second specifying the number of files to find for each list. The program uses the nftw system function to step through the file system. Each time makefileinfo visits a file, it calls insertfile with the full pathname and other parameters that give information about the file. This function keeps track of how many of the lists are full and returns 1 when all are full. The function nftw stops stepping through the directory tree when insertfile returns a nonzero value.

The function insertfile first checks that it was passed a file rather than a directory by checking the info parameter against FTW_F. It also verifies that the path fits in the list and uses the stat information to make sure that the file is a regular file. If all these conditions are satisfied, insertfile attempts a nonblocking open of the file for reading to make sure that the current process has read access to that file. A nonblocking open guarantees that the attempt does not block. If all these operations are successful, insertfile calls whichlist to determine which list the file should go into. The size of each list is kept in the array filecounts, and the function keeps track of the number of these entries that are equal to the maximum size of the list.

After the list is created, makefileinfo displays a list of counts and then calls showfiles to display the sizes and names of the files in each list. Comment out the call to showfiles after you are convinced that the program is working.

Modify Program 22.1 to make it usable by your servers. Replace the main function with a create_lists function that takes two parameters—the same values as the two command-line arguments of Program 22.1. This function creates the lists. Write an additional function, openfile, that takes a size as a parameter. The openfile function chooses one of the files that is at least as large as the size parameter, opens the file for reading, and returns the open file descriptor. If an error occurs, openfile returns −1 with errno set.

Modify one of the servers from Section 22.6, 22.7, 22.8 or 22.9 so that it satisfies requests from the disk rather than from a memory buffer. The server now takes two additional command-line arguments like those of Program 22.1 and creates the lists before accepting any connection requests. The server should display a message after creating the lists so that you can tell when to start your clients. Compare the results with those of the corresponding server that did not access the disk.

Program 22.1 ———————————————— **makefileinfo.c**
A program that creates a list of files by walking through a directory tree.

```c
#include <fcntl.h>
#include <ftw.h>
#include <limits.h>
#include <stdio.h>
#include <stdlib.h>
#include <string.h>
#include <unistd.h>
#include "restart.h"
#define MAXPATH 100
#define NUMRANGES 5

typedef struct {
   off_t filesize;
   char path[MAXPATH+1];
} fileinfo;

static int filecounts[NUMRANGES];
static fileinfo *files[NUMRANGES];
static int maxnum;

static int whichlist(off_t size) {
   int base = 10;
   int limit;
   int lnum;

   if (size < base)
      return -1;
   for (lnum = 0, limit = base*base;
         lnum < NUMRANGES - 1;
         lnum++, limit *= 10)
      if (size < limit)
         break;
   return lnum;
}

static int insertfile(const char *path, const struct stat *statbuf,
         int info, struct FTW *ftwinfo) {
   int fd;
   int lnum;
   static int numfull = 0;

   if (info != FTW_F)
      return 0;
   if (strlen(path) > MAXPATH)
      return 0;
   if ((statbuf->st_mode & S_IFREG) == 0)
      return 0;
   if ((fd = open(path, O_RDONLY | O_NONBLOCK)) == -1)
      return 0;
   if (r_close(fd) == -1)
      return 0;
   lnum = whichlist(statbuf->st_size);
```

```
      if (lnum < 0)
         return 0;
      if (filecounts[lnum] == maxnum)
         return 0;
      strcpy(files[lnum][filecounts[lnum]].path, path);
      files[lnum][filecounts[lnum]].filesize = statbuf->st_size;
      filecounts[lnum]++;
      if (filecounts[lnum] == maxnum) numfull++;
      if (numfull == NUMRANGES)
         return 1;
      return 0;
   }

   void showfiles(int which) {
      int i;
      fprintf(stderr, "List %d contains %d entries\n", which, filecounts[which]);
      for (i = 0; i < filecounts[which]; i++)
         fprintf(stderr, "%*d: %s\n",which + 6,files[which][i].filesize,
                          files[which][i].path);
   }

   int main(int argc, char *argv[]) {
      int depth = 10;
      int ftwflags = FTW_PHYS;
      int i;

      if (argc != 3) {
         fprintf(stderr, "Usage: %s directory maxnum\n", argv[0]);
         return 1;
      }
      maxnum = atoi(argv[2]);
      for (i = 0; i < NUMRANGES; i++) {
         filecounts[i] = 0;
         files[i] = (fileinfo *)calloc(maxnum, sizeof(fileinfo));
         if (files[i] == NULL) {
            fprintf(stderr,"Failed to allocate memory for list %d\n", i);
            return 1;
         }
      }
      fprintf(stderr, "Max number for each range is %d\n", maxnum);
      if (nftw(argv[1], insertfile, depth, ftwflags) == -1) {
         perror("Failed to execute nftw");
         return 1;
      }
      fprintf(stderr, "**** nftw is done\n");
      fprintf(stderr, "Counts are as follows with sizes at most %d\n", maxnum);
      for (i = 0; i < NUMRANGES; i++)
         fprintf(stderr, "%d:%d\n", i, filecounts[i]);
      for (i = 0; i < NUMRANGES; i++)
         showfiles(i);
      return 0;
   }
```

Program 22.1 ──────────────────────────────────── **makefileinfo.c**

22.11 Performance Studies

This section provides guidelines for doing a performance study and points out common pitfalls. We focus on the problem of comparing the performance of thread-per-request and worker-pool implementations for servers that do no disk I/O. You are asked to evaluate connection time and response times for the two approaches and to assess the influence of message size on the results. While this book is about UNIX, not performance evaluation, performance-based tuning is often necessary in such systems. In our experience, many excellent programmers do not have a good sense of what to measure, how to measure it, and what they have actually measured after doing the performance study.

22.11.1 Baseline measurements

All real computer performance studies face the same problem—a large number of hard-to-control variables whose influence on the result is highly nonlinear. Therefore, it is essential to understand the factors that might affect the results before starting to measure.

The first rule of performance measurement is to establish a baseline before varying any parameters. Do you expect the results to be on the order of seconds? Milliseconds? Microseconds? How much will the results vary from measurement to measurement? What influences variability besides the experimental parameters that you are explicitly varying?

Since you are trying to measure the difference in performance between two different strategies, a natural baseline is the time for exchanging a single message stream of the same type as will be used in testing the threaded servers. For example, you might take the `reflectclient.c` of Program 18.4 and the `reflectserver.c` of Exercise 18.15 as a starting point for your preliminary measurements. Measure the connection times and times to send and receive messages of different sizes in order to establish the baseline or *control* for comparing threaded servers. These measurements give a lower bound on the times and the variability of the measurements in the environment that you are working in. Establishing the baseline is an important step in understanding your measurements.

◻ Exercise 22.15

We modified the reflecting client of Program 18.4 to measure the time to establish a connection to the reflection server of Exercise 18.15 and to send and receive a 1K message. The client and server were running on two Sun Microsystems Ultra-10 machines with 440 MHz processors that were connected by 100 Mbit/sec Ethernet through a switch. The first run gave a connect time of 120 ms and a round trip response time of 152 ms. Subsequent runs gave connect times of around 3 ms and round trip times of about 1 ms. Can you explain these results?

Answer:
A quick look at `u_connect` and `u_accept` suggested that DNS lookup was probably the culprit in the long first initial times. The `u_connect` function calls

name2addr before calling connect. After return from accept, u_accept also contacts DNS to obtain the hostname of the client. Once the names are in the local DNS cache, retrieval is much faster. These results suggest that UICI should probably be modified for measuring timing.

22.11.2 Sources of variability

Clearly, the underlying system variability that you observe in single-threaded measurements confounds your ability to distinguish performance differences between the two threading approaches. You can reduce variability by carefully selecting the conditions under which you take measurements. If you have control over the machines in question, you can make sure that no one else is using those machines during your measurements. In many situations, however, you do not have sufficient control of the resources to restrict access. Two other steps are essential in obtaining meaningful answers. First, you should record the conditions under which you performed the measurements and make sure that they did not change significantly over the course of the experiments. Second, when the confounding factors vary significantly over time or you can't quantify how much they are varying, you need to take many more measurements over extended periods to be sure that your numbers are valid.

☐ Exercise 22.16

How might system load contribute to the variability of single-threaded client server communication?

Answer:

Relevant system load parameters are CPU usage, memory usage and network subsystem usage. If the virtual memory system does not have enough pages to accommodate the working sets of the processes running on the system, the system will spend a lot of time swapping disk pages in and out. All network communication on a host passes through the same subsystems, so other processes that are doing network I/O or disk I/O compete for subsystem resources.

☐ Exercise 22.17

Investigate the tools for measuring system load on your system. How can you use these tools to characterize the environment for your measurements?

Answer:

System load is hard to control unless you have control over the machines on which the clients and server are running. At a minimum, you should record the system loads immediately before and after your measurements. For long-running measurements, you should periodically record the system load during the run. The

UNIX `uptime` command supplies information about system load. You might also investigate vendor-specific tools such as Sun Microsystems' `perfmeter`. The `rstatd(1M)` service allows remote access to system performance information.

22.11.3 Measurement errors

Measurement errors result from side effects whose times are significant compared with the event times that are to be measured (e.g., printing in the timing loop).

◻ Exercise 22.18

We measured the time to execute a single

```
fprintf(stderr, "this is a test");
```

displaying to the screen in unbuffered form on the system described in Exercise 22.15. The single `fprintf` took about .25 ms, while an `fprintf` that outputted five `double` values took about .4 ms. However, we found that the time for 10,000 executions of the first print statement was highly variable, ranging from 1 to 10 seconds. Give possible explanations for the variability.

Answer:
Although standard error is not buffered from the user perspective, the actual screen device driver buffers output to match the speed of the output device, as the buffer fills up and empties, the time to return from `fprintf` varies significantly.

Given that the request-response cycle for a 1K packet is about 1 ms for the system and that we are trying to measure additional overhead incurred by threading, the time to execute extraneous print statements can be significant. The `sprintf` statements may also incur significant overhead for formatting strings. To do careful measurements, you should avoid all printing in timing loops. The next two examples show two common timing-loop errors.

◻ Exercise 22.19

What timing errors occur in the following pseudocode for measuring the connection and response times of a server? What happens if you omit the last assignment statement?

```
get time1
connect to the server
get time 2
output time2 - time1
loop
    write request to the server
    read response from the server
    get time3
    output time3 - time2
    time2 = time3
```

Answer:

The output of `time3 - time2` occurs between the measurement of two successive `time3` values, hence this statement is in the timing loop. The program should also not output `time2 - time1` between the connect and the first write. A better approach would be to save the times in an array and output them after the measurements are complete. If you omit the `time2 = time3` statement, all times are measured from the beginning of the session. The estimates for the request-response cycle won't mean anything. If you want to measure the time for the total response, move the statement to get the ending time outside the loop.

▢ Exercise 22.20

Would outputting to disk during the timing be better or worse than outputting to screen?

Answer:

The outcome is a little hard to predict, but either way it cannot be good. Disk access times are on the order of 10 ms. However, a disk write does not actually go directly to the disk but is usually buffered or cached. If the disk is not local but mounted through NFS, the output introduces network traffic as well as delay. For I/O that must be done during the measurements in such an environment, it is better to use `/tmp`, which is likely to be located on a local disk.

▢ Exercise 22.21

What is wrong with measuring the sending of the request and the receiving of the response individually, such as in the following?

```
get time1
write request
get time2
read response
get time3
sendtime = time2 - time1
receivetime = time3 - time2
```

Answer:

The `sendtime` is not the time for the message to reach its destination, but the time to copy the information from the user's variable to system buffers so that the network subsystem can send it. This copying time is usually not meaningful in the context of client-server performance.

Printing inside the timing loop can also occur in the server, as illustrated by the pseudocode in the next example. Direct screen output by the threads has the effect of synchronizing all the threads (the effect gets worse when there are a lot of threads) on each request-response, eliminating parallelism. Use flags and conditional compilation to handle debugging statements.

❑ Exercise 22.22

Why does the following pseudocode for a server thread using thread-per-request present a problem for timing measurements?

```
loop until error:
    read request
    write response
    output a message summarizing the response
close connection
```

Answer:

The output statement, although executed by the server, is effectively in the client's timing loop. Print statements on the server side have the added problem of implicitly synchronizing the threads on a shared device.

Another inefficiency that can affect timing is the use of an unnecessary `select` statement in the worker threads. You do not need to use `select` for request-response situations unless you must control timeouts.

❑ Exercise 22.23

What is wrong with the following code segment for writing a block of size `BLKSIZE` followed by reading a block of the same size?

```
if (r_write(communfd, buf, BLKSIZE)) < 0)
    perror("Failed to write");
else if (r_read(communfd, buf, BLKSIZE) < 0)
    perror("Failed to read");
```

Answer:

The `r_write` function calls `write` in a loop until the entire `BLKSIZE` buffer is written. The `r_read` function only executes one successful `read`, so the entire `BLKSIZE` response may not be read. Thus, a client driver that uses a single `r_read` call may not correctly time this request-response, particularly for large packets on a wide area network. Worse, the next time the client times a request-response for the connection, it will read the response from the previous request.

22.11.4 Synchronization

The thread-per-request server does not require explicit synchronization, so in theory synchronization isn't an issue for this server. However, implicit synchronization can occur even for thread-per-request whenever threads share a common resource, such as the screen. Avoid print statements in your server except for debugging or for warning of a serious error condition. Debugging statements should always be enclosed in a conditional compilation clause.

■ Example 22.24

The following statement is compiled in the program because `DEBUG` has been defined.

```
#define DEBUG 1

#ifdef DEBUG
   fprintf(stderr, "Sending the message....\n");
#endif
```

To eliminate `fprintf`, comment out the `#define` statement or remove it entirely. In the latter case, you can redefine `DEBUG` by using the `-D` option on compilation.

The synchronization issues for the worker pool are more complex. The three common implementations for the worker-pool model have different synchronization characteristics. In the most straightforward implementation, each worker thread blocks on `accept`. This mechanism relies on the availability of a thread-safe `accept` function with synchronization handled by the library function itself. POSIX specifies that `accept` should be thread-safe, but not all OS implementations provide a reliable thread-safe `accept`. A second implementation of worker pool protects `accept` with a mutex lock, as illustrated schematically in Example 22.25.

■ Example 22.25

In the following pseudocode for a worker-pool implementation, the mutex lock effectively forms a barrier allowing one thread at a time to pass through and block on `accept`.

```
loop
   mutex lock (if error, output message to log, clean up and exit)
   accept (if error, release lock and continue)
   mutex unlock (if error, output message to log, clean up and exit)
   process request (if error, output message to log, clean up and continue)
```

The pseudocode of Example 22.25 indicates what to do in case of error. A common problem occurs in not releasing the lock properly if an error occurs on `accept`. In this case, the system deadlocks because no other worker can acquire the mutex lock.

The buffer implementation of the worker pool is prone to other performance bottlenecks. For example, if the master producer thread executes `pthread_cond_broadcast` rather than `pthread_cond_signal` when it puts an item in the buffer, all waiting threads will be awakened and have to contend for the mutex that controls the items. This implementation puts a significant synchronization load on the server, even for moderate numbers of workers. Producers should avoid broadcasting on slots, and consumers should avoid broadcasting on items.

22.11.5 Just plain errors

You can't rely on timing results from a program that doesn't work correctly. It is important to catch return values on *all* library functions, including thread calls. Use the `lint` utility on your source and pay attention to the output. In particular, do not ignore the *implicitly assumed to return int* message, suggesting that you are missing header files.

Because the threads are executing in the environment of their parent, threaded servers are prone to memory leaks that are not a problem for servers that fork children. If a thread calls `pthread_exit` without freeing buffers or closing its communication file descriptor, the server will be saddled with the remnants for the remainder of its lifetime.

❑ Exercise 22.26

What memory leaks are possible in the following code?

```
loop
    malloc space for communfd
    if malloc fails
        quit
    accept a client connection
    if accept fails
        continue
    create a thread to handle the communication
    if the thread create fails,
        continue
```

Answer:

If `accept` fails, the space for the communication file descriptor leaks. If the thread create fails, the server leaves an open file descriptor as well as allocated memory.

❑ Exercise 22.27

What assumptions does the following code make in casting `communfd`?

```
int communfd
if ((communfd = u_accept(listenfd, client, MAX_CANON)) == -1)
    return -1;
if (pthread_create(&tid, null, process_request, (void *)communfd))
    return -1;
```

Answer:

The code implicitly assumes that an `int` can be correctly cast to `void *`, an assumption that may not be true for all machines.

Memory leaks for threaded servers can occur if any path of execution doesn't free resources. The thread-per-request threads must free any space that they allocated or that was allocated on their behalf by their parent thread before creation. In addition, they must close the communication file descriptor even if an error occurred.

The worker-pool implementations do not need to allocate memory space for the communication file descriptors, and often they allocate buffers only once. However, the explicit synchronization introduces its own quagmire of error possibilities. Using a single mutex lock for mutual exclusion on the buffer and for tracking items and slots can result in incorrect or extremely delayed synchronization. Failure to synchronize empty slots can result in the server overwriting file descriptors before they are consumed.

Another resource management problem can occur in thread-per-request. When a thread exits, it leaves state and must be waited for unless it is a detached thread. These "zombie" threads are a leak for a long-running server. Finally, you should think seriously about the legitimate causes for a server to exit. In general, a client should *not* be able to cause a server to exit. The server should only exit if an irrecoverable error due to resources (memory, descriptors, etc.) would jeopardize future correct execution. Remember the Mars Pathfinder!

22.11.6 What to measure?

In most computer performance studies there are too many parameters to vary simultaneously—so usually you can't run exhaustive tests. If you could, the results would be hard to handle and make sense of. The specific problem that we are considering here has relatively few variables for a performance problem, but even it is complex. Random testing of such a problem generally does not produce insight, and you should avoid it except for debugging. As a first step in formulating testable hypotheses, you should write down the factors that might influence the performance, their probable effect, plausible limits for their sizes, and how these tests should compare with baseline tests.

■ Example 22.28

The performance of the thread-per-request server without disk I/O depends on the number of simultaneous requests, the duration of these requests, and the I/O that must be performed during the processing of the request and the response. While the I/O costs probably depend on both the number of messages that are exchanged and their sizes, to first order the total number of bytes exchanged is probably the most important cost. Plausible limits are just that—guesses. One might guess that a server should be able to handle 10 simultaneous streams without a problem. Whether it could handle 100 or a 1000 simultaneous streams is anyone's guess, but these ranges give a starting point for the measurements.

□ Exercise 22.29

Give performance factors for the worker pool implemented with a mutex lock protecting `accept`.
Answer:
The factors specified in Example 22.28 are relevant. In addition, the number of threads in the worker pool relative to the number of simultaneous connections should also be important.

The preceding examples and exercises suggest that the most important control variable is the number of simultaneous connections that a server can handle. To measure the

server capacity, you will need to be able to control the number of simultaneous connections offered by your driver programs. The client-driver program of Section 22.4 offers
parallel loads. Such a client driver running on a single machine might reasonably offer 5
or 10 parallel streams, but is unlikely to sustain 100 parallel streams. Suppose you want
to test your server with 10 and 100 parallel streams. A reasonable approach to generating the 100 parallel streams might be to have 10 different hosts generate 10 streams
each.

☐ Exercise 22.30

Describe the load offered by the client-driver program of Section 22.4 if it forks
10 children that each make 10 connections. Suppose each connection consists of
10 request/response pairs of 100 bytes each.

Answer:

The number of connections per child is far too low to offer a sustained load of
10 simultaneous streams. Forking the 10 children takes sufficiently long and the
request streams are sufficiently short that some of the first children will finish or
nearly finish before the later children start execution.

Many beginning analysts typically do not take enough measurements to make their
studies meaningful and do not account for transient behavior. One approach to eliminating
transients is for the loading programs to sustain the load longer than needed and discard
the beginning and the end of the record. You can decrease or eliminate the amount that
needs to be discarded by synchronizing the children before starting. Children of a single
parent can call `sigsuspend`. The parent can then send a wake-up signal to the process
group. For clusters of driver processes running on different machines, the parents can
listen for a synchronization server, whose sole job is to initiate connections to the parent
drivers. Section 22.5 describes the approach in detail.

To pick parameter values that make sense, you must understand the relationship of the
processes/connections/messages values. The number of processes roughly corresponds
to the number of parallel connections that are established. However, this assumes steady
state. If each client process makes only two connections and sends two messages on
each connection, some client processes will probably complete before the client finishes
forking all the child processes. The actual length of a run needed to accurately estimate
performance is a statistical question beyond the scope of this text. Roughly, the larger the
variability in the values, the more measurements you need.

Generally, if the number of threads in the worker pool is greater than the number of request streams, you would expect a worker pool to consistently outperform
thread-per-request because it should have less overhead. If the number of request
streams exceeds the number of workers, thread-per-request might do better, provided
that the system has enough resources. Therefore, if the main variable is offered load,

be sure to vary the number of simultaneous request streams from 1 to a value well beyond the number of worker-pool threads. Look, too, for discontinuities in behavior as the number of request streams approaches and exceeds the number of worker-pool threads.

For parameters that influence the system in a highly nonlinear way, it is often useful to measure a few widely separated values. For example, to understand the influence of message size on the performance, you might decide to measure the response as a function of offered load for two different message sizes. Choosing message sizes of 32 bytes and 64 bytes to compare does not give meaningful results because each of these messages always fits into a single physical packet. Although one message is twice as big as the other, the messages are essentially the same size as far as the network is concerned. The network headers on these messages might be comparable to the data in size. You would get more useful information by picking message sizes of 512 bytes and 20 kilobytes, typical sizes for a simple web page and an image, respectively. In addition to being physically meaningful, these sizes exercise different characteristics of the underlying network protocols. A 512-byte message should traverse the network in a single packet even on a wide area network. The 20K message is larger than the typical 8K slow-start limit for TCP, so its transmission should experience some congestion control, at least on a wide area network.

22.11.7 Data analysis and presentation

Simple statistical measures such as the mean, median and standard deviation are useful characterizations of behavior. The median is less sensitive to outliers and is often used in network measurements. In general, medians should be smaller and more stable than means for these distributions. If your medians don't reflect this, you probably are not computing the statistics correctly. If your medians and means are consistently different by an order of magnitude, you should worry! Also, when combining results from multiple clients, don't take the median of the medians and present that as the median.

Think about how to analyze the data before designing an output format. If you plan to import the data into a spreadsheet, your output format should be spreadsheet-friendly so that you don't have to manually edit the data before analysis. You may want to output the results in multiple formats, for example, as tables without intermediate text so that the values fall into columns. Combine the numbers from all the client processes for final analysis. Standard deviation or quartiles are good indications of data variability.

You should also consider whether a table of results conveys the message better than a graph. Tables work well when the test consists of a few measurements or if some results are close together while others vary significantly, You can present more than one version if the results are meaningful.

22.12 Report Writing

Performance studies are often presented in a technical report. This section describes the key elements of a good technical report and mentions common mistakes. Poor presentation undermines your work, so it pays to put some effort into this aspect of a project. It goes without saying that you should use spelling- and grammar-checking tools. You should also pay attention to the typography and layout, separating sections with subtitles and consistent spacing. No one will have confidence that you have done the technical work correctly if your report is riddled with errors.

Technical reports generally have an abstract that gives an overview of the work and summarizes the principal results. More extensive reports may have a table of contents, a list of figures and an index. Most technical reports include a list of references at the end. Typically, the body of a technical report has an introduction followed by sections describing the design or system architecture, the implementation, the testing or experiments, the results and the conclusions.

22.12.1 Introduction

The introduction should provide an overview of the topic, without becoming mired in irrelevant detail. You should describe the particular problem being addressed and why it is important. The introduction should also present terminology and background material needed to understand the rest of the report. For example, if you are asked to write a report comparing server performance using thread-per-request and worker-pool implementations, your introduction should explain thread-per-request and worker-pool architectures, but should probably not provide an extensive description of the POSIX thread libraries. After all, the report is about these server strategies, not about POSIX threads. To emphasize the relevance of the topic, you might name well-known software that uses one strategy or the other.

Sometimes a technical report's introduction includes a review of other work on the topic, comparing results or approaches with those done by others. Other technical papers discuss related works in a separate section after the introduction or after the results, depending on the emphasis of the paper. The introduction usually ends with a paragraph describing the organization of the rest of the report.

22.12.2 Design, implementation and testing

The design section of your report should review the implementation of the various parts of the project. Architectural diagrams convey fundamental structure, but badly done diagrams introduce more confusion than clarity. If the architectures are different, the diagrams should not look exactly the same. Use consistent symbols in each diagram and across diagrams in the report. For example, use the same symbol for a thread in each diagram. Don't use a circle to represent a process in one diagram and a rectangle in another (or, worse, in the same diagram). Don't use the same symbol to represent a process and a library function. Eliminate unnecessary detail and be sure to provide a legend identifying the symbols.

An implementation details section should not include code—if code is necessary, put it in an appendix. You might include pseudocode or algorithms, if relevant. For example, for a worker-pool implementation using a circular buffer, the placement of the synchronization influences the behavior of the program, so it should be documented in the report.

The testing section should present a detailed description of how you tested the program. (No, "I tested the program and it works" is not an acceptable testing section!) A table of tests keyed to sample output in an appendix makes testing clearer and more convincing. Detail unusual behavior or other problems that you encountered during the development of the program. Explain known bugs that your program has. If you encountered unexpected problems during development, describe these here.

For a technical report that emphasizes performance rather than the development of a system, the description of the design, implementation and testing are often combined into a single section.

22.12.3 Experiments

Performance studies often have a separate section detailing the procedures used to conduct the performance measurements. The section details the specific conditions under which the program was tested, including the characteristics of the test machines, such as machine architecture, operating system version, type of network, etc. The section should explain the setup for the experiment and the ambient conditions such as the time of day and the network and machine loads. The procedures section should report how the load was established and sustained for the different experiments. The section might also describe how you assembled the measurement data during the computation.

22.12.4 Results and analysis

The presentation of the results is the centerpiece of a performance study. Present a clear description of what happened and what was expected to happen. Use graphs and bar charts to compare results from different experiments. For example, if you are comparing thread-per-request and worker-pool implementations, you should plot the corresponding response times for the two architectures on the same graph. Your figures should be labeled, captioned and referred to by number in the text discussion. You should give enough details in your report that someone else could reproduce your results.

Use meaningful units to plot the results. For the server comparison, milliseconds would be good. Don't use nanoseconds (huge numbers) or seconds (tiny numbers) just because the timer call you happened to use produced those units. Plot consecutive graphs with the same units. Avoid axis labels that contain a large number of digits—change the units. Avoid labeling every tightly spaced tick mark, and use consistent labeling of tick marks. Also plot your graphs in units that are understandable. If you are plotting several curves on the same graph, make sure that the symbols used for the different graphs are clearly distinguishable. Avoid using color if your report will not be printed or viewed in color unless the curves can still be distinguished if reproduced in greyscale. Use legends and in-graph labels to identify the curves and important features.

For this project, plotting response time or connection time versus presented load would be a good starting point for a performance comparison. Plotting response time versus process ID or thread ID displays the variability of the data, but these plots do not show a performance relationship. Variability might be better characterized by the standard deviation.

22.12.5 Conclusion

Often, authors run out of gas before the conclusion section. However, after the abstract, this is the section that many people read first and most carefully. Summarize the overall results of the project, including the principal performance findings. Discuss the strengths and weaknesses of your implementation and experiments. Point out problems that you encountered but did not address, and suggest how this project might be expanded or used in other situations. For course reports, explain what you learned and what you are still confused about. Do not overstate your achievements in the conclusion—let your work stand on its merits. Readers will ascribe more credibility to your conclusions if you are straightforward about the strengths and weaknesses of the study.

22.12.6 Bibliography

The bibliography lists the references that you used. Specify them in a consistent format. You should explicitly reference all the items that appear in the text of the report. The IEEE, the ACM and other professional societies have style files available for most word processors. Pick one of the standard styles.

22.13 Additional Reading

A classic text in the field of performance analysis is *The Art of Computer Systems Performance Analysis: Techniques for Experimental Design, Measurement, Simulation, and Modeling* by Jain [59]. Another excellent book is *The Practical Performance Analyst* by Gunther [45]. *Performance Evaluation and Benchmarking with Realistic Applications* by Eigenmann [35] emphasizes the collection and analysis of data from standard benchmarks. *Web Protocols and Practice* by Krishnamurthy and Rexford [66] has some excellent performance case studies characterizing web traffic and web server workload. *Capacity Planning for Web Services: Metrics, Models and Methods* by Menasce and Almeida devotes an entire book to web server modeling and performance analysis. Finally, *Probability and Statistics with Reliability, Queuing and Computer Science Applications, 2nd ed.* by Trivedi [126] is an invaluable statistical reference if you plan to go beyond mean and standard deviation in your analysis. For current examples of excellent work in performance evaluation, look at recent proceedings of the ACM Sigmetrics Conferences or the IEEE/ACM Transactions on Networking. "Performance issues of enterprise level web proxies," by Maltzahn et al. [77] and "Performance issues in WWW servers," by Nahum et al. [85] are examples of recent articles.

Appendices

Appendix A

UNIX Fundamentals

A.1 Manual Pages

The programs in this book are based on the Single UNIX Specification, Version 3. We refer to this specification by its IEEE name, POSIX. Essentially identical documents have been published by three standards organizations, the IEEE [49, 50, 51, 52], ISO/IEC [57], and the Open Group [89]. The IEEE and ISO/IEC publish print and electronic versions of the standard that are available for a fee. The Open Group publishes the standard on CD-ROM, but this organization also makes the standard freely available on their web site, `http://www.UNIX-systems.org/single_unix_specification/`. You must register the first time you enter the web site, but it is open to the public at no charge. The standard is organized into the following four parts.

1. Base Definitions: general terms and concepts, header files
2. System Interfaces: definitions of functions
3. Shell and Utilities: definitions of commands
4. Rationale: discussion of historical information and why features were or were not included in the standard

Use section 2 of the standard to find out about system calls and library functions such as `pipe` and `socket`. Look in section 3 for information about commands, such as `ls` and `cat`, that can be executed from the shell.

Most UNIX systems have online documentation called the *man pages*. Here, "man" stands for "manual" as in system manual. The `man` utility displays these pages of online documentation in a readable format.

SYNOPSIS

```
man [-k] name
```

POSIX:Shell and Utilities

797

Unfortunately, the standard does not require much functionality from the manual facility. If `name` is a standard utility, the standard requires only that a message describing its syntax, options and operands be displayed. The `-k` option lists the summaries of manual entries that contain `name`.

Most UNIX implementations divide the manual pages into sections, with typical section numbers shown in Table A.1. The first three sections are of most interest to us. Most implementations of `man` display only the information about the first occurrence of an entry. For example, `write` of section 1 is a command that can be executed from the shell to send a message to a terminal of another user. Users of this book would probably be more interested in the `write` description of section 2, which is the library function described in Section 4.2. Most implementations of `man` provide an option called `-a` to display all manual entries and an option called `-s` or `-S` to display only entries from a given section for the manual.

section	contents
1	user commands
2	system calls
3	C library functions
4	devices and network interfaces
5	file formats
6	games and demos
7	environments, tables and `troff` macros
8	system maintenance

Table A.1: Typical sections numbers for UNIX man pages.

■ Example A.1

The following command can be used under Solaris to display the manual entry for `write` from section 2.

```
man -s 2 write
```

Under Linux or Mac OS X the corresponding command is the following.

```
man -S 2 write
```

Figure A.1 shows the typical output of the `man` utility when the `man tee` command executes. The first line or header line of the man page gives the name of the command followed in parentheses by the man page section number. The `tee(1)` in Figure A.1 refers to the `tee` command described in section 1 of the man pages. Do not try to execute `tee(1)`. The (1) suffix is not part of the command name, rather it is a man page section indicator.

```
tee(1)                    User Commands                    tee(1)

NAME
     tee - duplicate standard output

SYNOPSIS
     tee [ -ai ]  [ file ... ]

DESCRIPTION
     The tee  utility  shall  copy  standard  input  to  standard
     output, making a copy in zero or more files. The tee utility
     shall not  buffer  output.  The  options  determine  if  the
     specified files are overwritten or appended to.

OPTIONS
     The following options shall be supported.

     -a    Append the output to the files rather than overwriting
           them.

     -i    Ignore the SIGINT signal.

OPERANDS
     The following operands are supported:

     file  A pathname of an output file.  Processing of at least
           13 file operands shall be supported.

ENVIRONMENT VARIABLES
     ...

EXIT STATUS
     The following exit values are returned:

     0     The standard input was successfully copied to all out-
           put files.

     >0    The number of files that could not be opened or whose
           status could not be obtained.

APPLICATION USAGE
     The tee utility is usually used in a pipeline, to make a
     copy of the output of some utility.

     The file operand is technically optional, but tee is no more
     useful than cat when none is specified.

EXAMPLES
     Save an unsorted intermediate form of the data in a pipeline:
     ... | tee unsorted | sort > sorted

SEE ALSO
     cat(1), attributes(5), environ(5)
```

Figure A.1: Typical man page listing for the tee command.

Each man page covers some aspect of UNIX (e.g., a command, a utility, a library call). The individual man pages are organized into sections like the `tee` man page of Figure A.1. Some common section titles are given in Table A.2.

section title	contents
HEADER	title for the individual man page
NAME	one-line summary
SYNOPSIS	description of usage
EXIT STATUS	values returned on exit from a command
DESCRIPTION	discussion of what the command or function does
RETURN VALUES	possible return values
ERRORS	summary of `errno` values and conditions for errors
FILES	list of the system files that the command or function uses
SEE ALSO	list of related commands or additional sections of the manual
ENVIRONMENT	list of relevant environment variables
NOTES	information on unusual usage or implementation features
BUGS	list of known bugs and caveats

Table A.2: Typical sections of a UNIX man page.

The name section of a man page lists the names of the items described on that man page. The man pages contain information about many types of items. The man page on `write(1)` describes a command, and the man page on `write(2)` describes a library function. The two `write` entries have completely different purposes. Look at the synopsis section to determine which `write` you want. The synopsis summarizes how a command or function is invoked. The synopsis for a library function has function prototypes along with the required header files. The `write(2)` function is called from a C program. In contrast, `write(1)` is executed from the command prompt or from a shell script.

In addition to the standard documents and manual pages, many UNIX vendors make detailed documentation accessible through the Web. Sun provides documentation at `http://docs.sun.com`. The Linux Documentation Project web page, `http://tldp.org/`, has the Linux manual pages, HOWTO guides and other information. Apple provides documentation for Mac OS X on their developer's web site, `http://developer.apple.com`.

A.2 Compilation

The C compiler, `cc`, translates a collection of C source programs and object files into either an executable file or an object file. On your system, the compiler may have another name, such as `gcc`. The `cc` command may be a symbolic link to another executable.

Compilation proceeds in stages. In the first stage, a preprocessor expands macros and includes header files. The compiler then makes several passes to translate the code, first to the assembly language of the target machine and then into machine code. The result is an *object module*, which has machine code and tables of unresolved references. The final stage of compilation links a collection of object modules together to form the executable module with all references resolved. An *executable file* is ready to be loaded and run. The executable contains exactly one `main` function.

■ Example A.2

The following command compiles `mine.c` and produces the executable `mine`.

```
cc -o mine mine.c
```

If the `-o mine` option is omitted, the C compiler produces an executable called `a.out`. Use the `-o` option to avoid the noninformative default name.

■ Example A.3

The following `mine.c` source file contains an undefined reference to the `serr` function.

```
void serr(char *msg);

int main(void) {
    serr("This program does not do much\n");
    return 0;
}
```

When `mine.c` of Example A.3 is compiled as in Example A.2, the C compiler displays a message indicating that `serr` is an unresolved reference and does not produce an executable.

Programs are usually organized into multiple source files that must be linked together. You can compile all the source files with a single `cc` command. Alternatively, you can compile the source into separate object modules and link these object modules to form an executable module in a separate step.

■ Example A.4

Suppose that the `serr` function is contained in the source file `minelib.c`. The following command compiles the `mine.c` source file of Example A.3 with `minelib.c` to produce an executable module called `mine`.

```
cc -o mine mine.c minelib.c
```

The `-c` option of `cc` causes the C compiler to produce an object module rather than an executable. An object module cannot be loaded into memory or executed until it is linked to libraries and other modules to resolve references. The C compiler does not complain about unresolved references in object modules. A misspelled variable or missing library function might not be detected until that object module is linked into an executable.

■ Example A.5

The following command produces the object module `mine.o`.

```
cc -c mine.c
```

When the `-c` option is used, the C compiler produces an object module named with the `.o` extension. The `mine.o` produced by the `cc` command of Example A.5 can later be linked with another object file (e.g., `minelib.o`) to produce an executable.

■ Example A.6

The following command links the object modules `mine.o` and `minelib.o` to produce the executable `mine`.

```
cc -o mine mine.o minelib.o
```

A.2.1 Header files

Before a function such as `serr` in Example A.3 is referenced, it should either be defined or have a prototype. Often, prototypes are contained in header files.

Before compilation, the C preprocessor copies the header files specified by `#include` statements into the source. By convention, header files have a `.h` extension. Put declarations of constants, types and functions in header files. *Do not put variable declarations in header files, because this can result in multiply-defined variables.* The next exercise illustrates the difficulties caused by placing variable declarations in header files.

□ Exercise A.7

What happens if you execute the following commands?

```
cc -o mystuff my.c mylib.c
mystuff
```

The file `myinc.h` contains the following segment.

```
#include <stdio.h>
static int num;
void changenum(void);
```

The file `my.c` contains the following `main` program.

```
#include "myinc.h"
int main (void) {
   num = 10;
   changenum();
   printf("num is %d\n", num);
   return 0;
}
```

The file `mylib.c` contains the following function.

```
#include "myinc.h"
void changenum(void) {
   num = 20;
}
```

Answer:

Both `my.c` and `mylib.c` contain a `num` variable because its definition appears in `myinc.h`. The call by the `main` program to `changenum` does not affect the value of the variable `num` defined in `my.c`. The `mystuff` program outputs `10` rather than `20`.

Enclose system-defined header files in angle brackets (as in `#include <stdio.h>`) since the compiler then looks in the standard place for the file. The standard place depends on the system, but the man page for `cc` usually describes how the standard search occurs. The `/usr/include` directory holds many of the standard header files. The files in this directory often include other `.h` files from subdirectories beneath `/usr/include`. The `/usr/include/sys` directory is a standard location for many of the `.h` files needed for this book. Be sure to include the header files specified by the man page synopsis when using a library function. Enclose personal header filenames in double quotes as follows.

```
#include "myinc.h"
```

The quotes tells the compiler to look for the header file in the directory containing the source file before looking in the standard place.

☐ Exercise A.8

A program uses the error symbol `EAGAIN` in conjunction with a call to `write`. The compiler complains that `EAGAIN` is not defined. Now what?

Answer:

Try the following steps to solve the problem.

- Make sure to include all the header files mentioned in the synopsis for `write`. The man page specifies the header file `<unistd.h>`.
- Buried somewhere in the man pages is a statement mentioning that `errno.h` must be included in programs that refer to error symbols. If the program includes `errno.h`, the problem is solved.
- If the `errno.h` statement in the man page escapes your notice, look for the symbol `EAGAIN` directly in the system header files by using

  ```
  cd /usr/include
  grep EAGAIN *
  ```

  The `grep` command searches for the string `EAGAIN` in all of the files in the directory `/usr/include`. Unfortunately, the `EAGAIN` symbol is not in any of the files in `/usr/include`.
- Change to the `/usr/include/sys` directory and try `grep` again. The following is a typical response to `grep`.

  ```
  errno.h:#define EAGAIN 11
  errno.h:#define EWOULDBLOCK      EAGAIN
  ```

It might be tempting to eliminate the problem by including the file sys/errno.h in the source, but what the compiler really wants is errno.h. Using errno.h directly is better because it includes sys/errno.h and also contains additional definitions.

A.2.2 Linking and libraries

Just because a program has the right header files does not mean that your troubles are over. A header file gives symbol declarations and function prototypes, but it does not supply the actual code for the function call.

☐ Exercise A.9

The mylog.c source file calculates the logarithm of a value. After including math.h in that source file, the user compiles the program and receives an error message that the log function could not be found. Why not?

Answer:

The math.h header file just tells the C compiler what the form (prototype) of the log function is. It does not actually supply the function.

Compilation takes place in two distinct phases. In the first phase, the compiler translates each C source file into object code. The cc -c option stops at this point. Object code is not ready to execute because the program may reference outside items that have not been located. To produce an executable module, the compile must find all the undefined symbols (*unresolved external references*). The cc compiler calls the link editor, ld, to accomplish this task.

■ Example A.10

The following command compiles the mylog.c source file with the system math library to produce an executable called mylog.

```
cc -o mylog mylog.c -lm
```

To use C mathematics library functions, put #include <math.h> in the source file and also specify that the program should be linked with the math library (-lm) when it is compiled.

The names of libraries are specified by the -l option. The object files are processed in the order in which they appear on the cc command line, so the location of -l on the cc line is significant. It should come after the object files because only those entries that match unresolved references are loaded. By default, the link editor automatically searches the standard C library.

☐ Exercise A.11

What happens if the math library in Example A.10 is linked, but the header file math.h is not included in the source?

Answer:
The compiler assumes that `log` has a return value of type `int` rather than `double`. If the program calls the `log` function, the calculation produces an incorrect numerical result. The compiler may not produce an error or warning message. However, `lint` (Section A.4) reports that `log` *has been implicitly declared to return* `int`.

■ Example A.12
The following linking command processes the object files in the order `my.o`, the math library, and then `mylib.o`.

```
cc  -o my my.o -lm mylib.o
```

The link editor includes only those objects in the library that correspond to unresolved references. Thus, if `mylib.o` contains a reference to the math library, that reference is not resolved by this command.

The `-lx` option is short for either `libx.a` (a *library archive*) or `libx.so` (a *shared library*). Which is the default depends on how the system is set up. Many compilers allow you to specify `-Bstatic -lx` in the `cc` command for a library archive and `-Bdynamic -lx` for a shared library. The compiler scans the *shared libraries* for references, but it does not actually put the functions in the executable output file. Instead, the runtime system loads them by dynamic loading and binding.

Several versions of a particular library may coexist on a system—at least one for each version of the C compiler. A typical search order for libraries is the following.
- `-L` directories specified on the `cc` line
- Directories in the `LD_LIBRARY_PATH` environment variable
- Standard library directories (e.g., `/usr/lib`)

The `-L` option of `cc` explicitly specifies pathnames for directories to be searched for libraries. The `LD_LIBRARY_PATH` environment variable specifies default pathnames for searching for load libraries. Generally, `LD_LIBRARY_PATH` includes pathnames for the directories in which the compilers are installed, as well as directories such as `/usr/local/lib`. Your system administrator has probably set up the `LD_LIBRARY_PATH` variable for using the standard compilers.

A.2.3 Macros and conditional compilation

Before the Single UNIX Specification, there were several incompatible UNIX standards, and vendors would use conditional compilation to adjust for these differences. The preprocessor can produce different code for the compiler from a single source file through the use of the `#if`, `#ifdef` and `#ifndef` preprocessor statements. Such *conditional compilation* can be used to allow a program to be compiled under different implementations or in different environments.

■ Example A.13

The UICI restart library sets `errno` to `ETIME` when the function `waitfdtimed` times out. Some systems do not define `ETIME` but instead use the error `ETIMEDOUT`. The file `restart.h` solves this problem with the following.

```
#ifndef ETIME
#define ETIME ETIMEDOUT
#endif
```

If `ETIME` is not already defined, it is defined as `ETIMEDOUT`.

`ETIME` and `ETIMEDOUT` are examples of simple macros specified by a `#define` statement. The preprocessor replaces these defined constants with their values before passing the code to the C compiler.

Most C compilers have a `-D` option that allows the setting of macros at compile time.

■ Example A.14

The Linux header files provide a number of options to support different standards and implementations. Linux uses the constant `_GNU_SOURCE` for many of the features that are now part of the Single UNIX Specification. If this constant is defined, then these features are turned on. Some of the programs in this book require this constant to be defined when the programs are compiled under Linux. To compile the program `myprog.c` with this constant defined, use the following command.

```
cc -D_GNU_SOURCE -o myprog myprog.c
```

This causes the constant `_GNU_SOURCE` to be defined with the default value of 1, as if the following statement appeared as the first line of the source file.

```
#define _GNU_SOURCE 1
```

■ Example A.15

The UICI name library in Section C.2 gives four implementations of the function `addr2name` and `name2addr`, using conditional compilation to choose one of the implementations. The general format of the code is as follows.

```
#ifndef REENTRANCY
#define REENTRANCY_NONE
#endif

#if REENTRANCY==REENTRANT_NONE
    /* default code using gethostbyname and gethostbyaddr */
#elif REENTRANCY==REENTRANT_R
    /* code using gethostbyname_r and gethostbyaddr_r */
#elif REENTRANCY==REENTRANT_MUTEX
    /* code using mutex locks */
#elfi REENTRANCY==REENTRANT_POSIX
    /* code using getnameinfo and getaddrinfo */
#endif
```

The first three lines guarantee that REENTRANCY has its default value if it is not otherwise defined.

■ Example A.16

Execute the following command to compile the program client.c with the restart library, the UICI library, and the UICI name library. Use the getnameinfo and getaddrinfo functions.

```
cc -DREENTRANCY=REENTRANT_POSIX -o client client.c restart.c uiciname.c uici.c
```

Additional libraries may be needed on your system.

A.3 Makefiles

The make utility, which allows users to incrementally recompile a collection of program modules, is convenient and helps avoid mistakes. To use make, you must specify dependencies among modules in a *description file*. The make utility uses the description file to see if anything needs updating.

The description file specifies dependency relationships that exist between *targets* and other components. Lines starting with # are comments. The dependencies in the description file have the following form.

```
target:         components
TAB             rule
```

The first line is called a *dependency*, and the second line is called a *rule*. *The first character on a rule line in a description file must be the TAB character.* A dependency may be followed by one or more rule lines.

The default description filenames are makefile and Makefile. When the user types make with no additional arguments, the make utility looks for makefile or Makefile in the current directory to use as its description file.

■ Example A.17

In Example A.6, the executable mine depends on the object files mine.o and minelib.o. The following description specifies that dependency relationship.

```
mine:   mine.o minelib.o
        cc -o mine mine.o minelib.o
```

The dependency relationship specifies that the target mine should be updated by executing the rule cc -o mine mine.o minelib.o if either mine.o or minelib.o has been modified since mine was last changed.

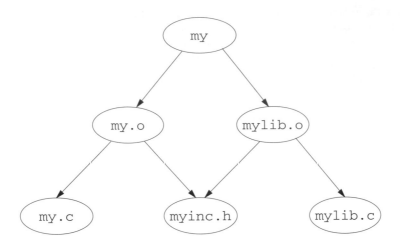

Figure A.2: A dependency graph for the `makefile` of Example A.18.

■ **Example A.18**

A makefile target may depend on components that are themselves targets. The following `makefile` description file has three targets.

```
my:      my.o mylib.o
         cc -o my my.o mylib.o

my.o:    my.c myinc.h
         cc -c my.c

mylib.o: mylib.c myinc.h
         cc -c mylib.c
```

The target `my` depends on the targets `my.o` and `mylib.o`. Just type `make` to do the required updates.

Sometimes it is helpful to visualize the dependencies of a description file by a directed graph. Use graph nodes (with no duplicates) to represent the targets and components. Draw a directed arc from node A to node B if target A depends on B. A proper description file's graph should have no cycles. Figure A.2 shows the dependency graph for the description file of Example A.18.

Description files can also contain *macro definitions* of the following form.

```
NAME = value
```

Whenever `$(NAME)` appears in the description file, `make` substitutes `value` before processing. Do not use tabs in macros.

■ Example A.19

The following description file uses a macro to represent the compiler options. With this definition, the compiler options need only be changed in a single place rather than in the entire file.

```
OPTS = -g

my:     my.c  my.h
        cc $(OPTS) -o my my.c
```

The `make` command also allows the name of a target to be specified on the command line. In this case, `make` updates only the specified target. When developing multiple targets in the same directory (e.g., send and receive programs), use this feature to debug one target at a time. If no targets are explicitly specified on the command line, `make` checks only the first target in the description file. Often, a description file has a first target called `all` that depends on all the other targets.

■ Example A.20

The following command causes `make` to update only the target `my`.

```
make my
```

The command of Example A.20 does not interpret `my` as a description file but as a target within the default description file (either `makefile` or `Makefile` in the current directory).

Use the `-f` option with `make` for description files with names other than `makefile` or `Makefile`.

■ Example A.21

The following command updates `target1` from the description file `mymake`.

```
make -f mymake target1
```

A.4 Debugging Aids

This section discusses the `lint` utility, debuggers, the `truss` utility and profiling.

A.4.1 The `lint` utility

The `lint` utility finds errors and inconsistencies in C source files. The `lint` program performs type checking, tries to detect unreachable statements, and points out code that might be wasteful or nonportable; `lint` also detects a variety of common errors, such as using = instead of == or omitting & in arguments of `scanf`. You should call `lint` for all programs. Pay attention to the resulting warning messages, since `lint` is pickier than the C compiler in many areas. The C compiler presumes that programs have already been linted and is usually implemented to be fast rather than fussy.

❑ Exercise A.22

Add the following lines to the description file of Example A.18 to lint the sources.

```
lintall:
           lint my.c mylib.c > my.lint
```

Type `make lintall` to lint the programs. The output of `lint` is in `my.lint`.

❑ Exercise A.23

How should the following `lint` message be interpreted?

```
implicitly declared to return int:
    (14) strtok
```

Answer:

This `lint` message warns that the program did not include the `string.h` header file associated with `strtok` appearing on line 14 of the source file. Lacking information to the contrary, the compiler assumes that `strtok` returns `int`. Unfortunately, `strtok` returns `char*`. The lack of header can lead to disastrous results at execution time.

❑ Exercise A.24

How should the following `lint` message be interpreted?

```
(5) warning: variable may be used before set: p
```

Answer:

This message usually appears when the program uses a pointer before setting its value, as in the following code segment.

```
char *p;
scanf("%s", p);
```

The pointer `p` is not pointing to an appropriate character buffer. The code may compile, but the program will probably produce a segmentation error when executed.

A.4.2 Debuggers

Debuggers are runtime programs that monitor and control the execution of other programs. Common debuggers found in UNIX environments are `dbx`, `adb`, `sdb` and `debug`. Debuggers allow a user to single-step through a program and monitor changes to specified variables. To use a debugger, compile the program with the `-g` option.

❑ Exercise A.25

Compile the program `my.c` with the `-g` option as follows to instrument the executable for debugger control.

```
cc -g -o my my.c
```

Run `my` under the `dbx` debugger by typing the following command.

```
dbx my
```

The debugger responds with the following prompt.

```
(dbx)
```

Respond with `help` for a list of commands or `run` to run the program. Set a stopping point with `stop`, or turn on tracing when a variable changes, by typing `trace` before typing `run`.

Many programmers, especially beginning programmers, find debuggers useful for pointer problems. Some debuggers have graphical user interfaces that make them easier to use. Standard debuggers are less useful in a concurrent environment, in which processes interact or timing can change the behavior of a program. Thread debuggers are also available on a limited basis. Debuggers may help you find a particular execution error, but using a debugger is no substitute for having a program test plan. Good error trapping for function calls is probably the most valuable debugging strategy to follow.

A.4.3 The `truss` utility

For runtime debugging, the `truss` command is useful if it is available. The `truss` command produces a trace of system calls that are made and the signals delivered while a particular process is running. Use the `-f` option with `truss` to trace the calls of all children of the process. The `truss` command is not part of POSIX and is not available on all systems.

☐ Exercise A.26

Suppose that a program called `dvips` is installed on a system and that this program accesses the `psfonts.map` file. You have placed a copy of `psfonts.map` in the `bin` subdirectory of your home directory. When you run the program, you receive the following error message.

```
unable to open file
```

How can you figure out how to correct the problem?

Answer:

Try executing the following command (from a C shell).

```
truss dvips -f t.dvi |& grep psfonts.map
```

The `truss` program runs the command `dvips -f t.dvi`, and `grep` displays the output lines containing `psfonts.map`. The `|&` argument causes both the standard output and the standard error of `truss` to be piped to the standard input of `grep`. The output might appear as follows.

```
open("./psfonts.map", O_RDONLY, 0666)          Err#2 ENOENT
open("/usr/local/tex/dvips/psfonts.map", O_RDONLY, 0666) Err#2 ENOENT
```

The output reports that the program first looked for `psfonts.map` in the current directory and then in the directory `/usr/local/tex/dvips`. Copy the `psfonts.map` to `/usr/local/tex/dvips` and everything should be ready to go!

A.4.4 Profilers

Most C compilers have options for profiling programs. Profilers accumulate statistical information such as execution times for basic blocks and frequency of calls. Consult the man pages for `prof`, `gprof`, `monitor`, `profil` and `tcov` as well as for `cc` to obtain additional information about profiling.

A.5 Identifiers, Storage Classes and Linkage Classes

Programmers are often confused about the meaning of the keyword `static`, in part because C uses the word two different ways. The main points to remember are the following.

1. If `static` is applied to a function, that function can only be called from the file in which it is defined.
2. If a variable definition appears outside any block, the variable exists for the duration of the program. If `static` is applied, the variable can only be accessed from within the file containing the definition. Otherwise, the variable can be accessed anywhere in the program.
3. If a variable is defined inside a block, it can only be accessed within the block. If `static` is applied, the variable exists for the duration of the program and it retains its value when execution leaves the block. Otherwise, the variable is created when the block is entered, and it is destroyed when execution leaves the block. Such a variable needs to be explicitly initialized before it can be used.

These rules are based on C's notion of *scope of an identifier* and *linkage*, which we now discuss.

According to the ISO C standard, "An identifier can denote an object; a function; a tag or member of a structure, union, or enumeration; a typedef name; a label name; a macro name; or a macro parameter." [56, section 6.2.1] Here, we mainly discuss identifiers that are associated with variables and functions.

An identifier can be used only in a region of program text called its *scope*. If two different entities are designated by the same identifier, their scopes must be disjoint, or one scope must be completely contained in the other. In the inner scope, the other entity is hidden and cannot be referenced by that identifier.

The scope begins at the identifier declaration. If the declaration occurs inside a block, the identifier has *block scope* and the scope ends at the end of the block. If the declaration occurs outside any block, the identifier has *file scope*, and the scope ends at the end of the file in which it is declared.

Identifiers declared more than once may refer to the same object because of linkage. Each identifier has a *linkage class* of external, internal or none. Declarations in a program of a particular identifier with *external linkage* refer to the same entity. Declarations in a file of a particular identifier with *internal linkage* represent the same entity. Each declaration of an identifier with *no linkage* represents a unique entity.

An identifier representing a function has external linkage by default. This means that it can be referenced in any file of the program. Referencing it in a file other than the one in which it is defined requires a function prototype. You can hide a function from other files by giving it internal linkage, using the `static` qualifier.

An identifier representing an object (such as a variable) has a linkage class related to its *storage class*, also called *storage duration*. The storage duration determines the *lifetime* of the object, the portion of the program execution for which storage is guaranteed to be reserved for the object. There are three storage durations: static, automatic and allocated. Allocated objects have a lifetime that begins with a successful `malloc` or related function and ends when the object is explicitly freed or the program terminates. The lifetimes of other objects are determined by the declaration of the corresponding identifier.

An identifier of an object declared outside any block has static storage class. Objects with static storage class have a lifetime that is the duration of the program. They are initialized once and retain their last stored value. If no explicit initialization is given in the declaration, they are initialized to 0. As with functions, these identifiers have external linkage by default but can be given internal linkage by means of the `static` qualifier.

An identifier of an object declared inside a block has no linkage. Each identifier denotes a unique object. These identifiers have automatic storage duration by default. Objects with automatic storage class have a lifetime that begins when execution enters the block and ends when execution exits the block. These objects are not initialized by default and do not necessarily retain their last stored value after execution exits the block. If the block is entered through recursion or with multiple threads, each entry into the block creates a distinct object. A variable with automatic storage class is called an automatic variable.

An identifier of an object declared inside a block can be given static storage duration with the `static` qualifier. The object then has a lifetime that is the duration of the program and retains its last stored value. If the block is entered through recursion or multiple threads, the same object is used.

Objects with identifiers having static storage duration are often called static variables; those with identifiers having automatic storage duration are called automatic variables.

As described above, the `static` qualifier can affect either the storage class or linkage class of an object depending on the context. When `static` is applied to a function, it always changes its linkage class from the default of external to internal. Functions do not have a storage duration. For objects declared inside a block, the linkage class is always none and `static` changes the storage class from automatic to static. For objects declared outside any block, the storage class is always static and the `static` specifier changes the linkage class from external to internal. These rules are summarized in Table A.3.

where declared	`static` modifies	`static` applied?	storage class	linkage class
inside a block	storage class	yes	static	none
inside a block	storage class	no	automatic	none
outside any block	linkage class	yes	static	internal
outside any block	linkage class	no	static	external

Table A.3: Effect of using the `static` keyword modifier on an object in a C program.

A.6 Additional Reading

UNIX SYSTEM V: A Practical Guide, 3rd ed., by Sobell [108] is an up-to-date reference on using the UNIX utilities. *UNIX System Administration Handbook*, 3rd ed., by Nemeth et al. [86] is an excellent and readable introduction to many of the configuration issues involved in setting up UNIX systems. O'Reilly Press has individual books on many of the topics in this appendix including `emacs` [20], the libraries [27], `lint` [28], `make` [120], and `vi` [69].

Appendix B

Restart Library

The *restart library* is a collection of functions that restart themselves when they have not completed because of a possibly temporary event. We use functions from the restart library throughout the book to simplify programs that must deal with the effects of signals and incomplete I/O. The source code for the restart library is available on the book web site. We have included only those functions that are needed in the book. You can easily add other functions, if necessary.

The restart library addresses two main types of events: interruption by a signal and incomplete I/O. For example, many library functions, including read and write, return −1 and set errno to EINTR when interrupted by a signal before any I/O takes place. This interruption is not a real error but a natural event that occurs when the program handles a signal in the presence of blocking I/O. The library functions restart when the function they wrap returns −1 with errno set to EINTR.

Some functions such write might return before a full request is satisfied. When a request is made to write n bytes, the write call is considered successful when any number of bytes greater than zero has been written. A write function could return a positive value less than n if a signal is caught before the requested amount has been written or if an I/O buffer is full, such as when writing to a pipe or network connection. Typically, the program must handle this case and write the remaining bytes. The functions in the restart library simplify the user code by writing the remaining bytes. Table B.1 gives a complete list of the functions in the restart library.

The restart library includes two types of functions. The functions whose names start with r_ are restarted versions of traditional library functions. These functions have the same prototypes as the corresponding traditional functions. For example, the r_read function takes the same parameters as read, but restarts read if the read function returns −1 with errno set to EINTR. For these functions, the table describes only the differences between the function and its traditional counterpart.

prototype	description
`int r_close(int fildes)`	similar to `close`
`int r_dup2(int fildes,` `    int fildes2)`	similar to `dup2`
`int r_open2(const char *path,` `    int oflag)`	similar to `open` called with two parameters
`int r_open3(const char *path,` `    int oflag, mode_t mode)`	similar to `open` called with three parameters
`int r_read(int fd, void *buf,` `    size_t size)`	similar to `read`
`pid_t r_wait(int *stat_loc)`	similar to `wait`
`pid_t r_waitpid(pid_t pid,` `    int *stat_loc, int options)`	similar to `waitpid`
`int r_write(int fd, void *buf,` `    size_t size)`	similar to `write` but restarts if fewer than `size` bytes are written (The only possible return values are `size` and −1.)

`struct timeval`
`    add2currenttime(`
`    double seconds)`
	returns a `struct timeval` structure
	corresponding to the current time
	plus `seconds` seconds

`int copyfile(int fromfd,` `    int tofd)`	copies bytes from one open file descriptor to another until the end of the file or an error
`int readblock(int fd,` `    void *buf, size_t size)`	reads exactly `size` bytes into the buffer or returns an error
`int readline(int fd,` `    char *buf, int nbytes)`	reads a line into `buf`, which has size `nbytes`
`int readwrite(int fromfd,` `    int tofd)`	copies at most `PIPE_BUF` bytes from one open file descriptor to another

`int readwriteblock(int fromfd,`
`    int tofd, char *buf,`
`    int size)`
	copies exactly `size` bytes from one
	open file descriptor to another,
	using the given buffer and size

`int waitfdtimed(int fd,` `    struct timeval end)`	waits for data to be available on given file descriptor or until time `end`

Table B.1: The functions in the restart library. The first part of the table shows the functions that correspond to traditional functions. All functions in the restart library restart when interrupted by a signal. None of these functions return −1 with `errno` set to `EINTR`.

The functions shown in the second part of Table B.1 do not correspond to any traditional library functions. For example, `readline` handles restarting when a signal occurs and continues reading until the end of a line or the end of the buffer. The `readblock` function restarts when the requested number of bytes has not yet been read.

The following is a more complete description of the functions in the restart library.

`struct timeval add2currenttime(double seconds);`
> returns a `struct timeval` corresponding to the current time plus `seconds` seconds. The implementation calls `gettimeofday` to get the current time, converts the `seconds` parameter to integer values representing seconds and microseconds, and adds these values to the current time.

`int copyfile(int fromfd, int tofd);`
> copies bytes from open file descriptor `fromfd` to open file descriptor `tofd` until either end-of-file or an error occurs. If successful, `copyfile` returns the number of bytes copied. If unsuccessful, `copyfile` returns −1 and sets `errno`. The `copyfile` function does not return an error if any bytes are successfully copied, even if an error occurs on a subsequent write that follows a successful read.

`int r_close(int fildes);`
> closes `fildes`. If successful, `r_close` returns 0. If unsuccessful, `r_close` returns −1 and sets `errno`. The implementation calls `close` in a loop, restarting if `close` returns −1 with `errno` set to `EINTR`.

`int r_dup2(int fildes, int fildes2);`
> closes `fildes2` if it was open and causes `fildes2` to refer to the same file as `fildes`. If successful, `r_dup2` returns `fildes2`. If unsuccessful, `r_dup2` returns −1 and sets `errno`. The implementation calls `dup2` in a loop, restarting if `dup2` returns −1 with `errno` set to `EINTR`.

`int r_open2(const char *path, int oflag);`
> opens a file descriptor for `path`. The `oflag` should not have the `O_CREAT` bit set. If successful, `r_open2` returns an open file descriptor. If unsuccessful, `r_open2` returns −1 and sets `errno`. The implementation calls `open` in a loop, restarting if `open` returns −1 with `errno` set to `EINTR`.

`int r_open3(const char *path, int oflag, mode_t mode);`
> opens a file descriptor for `path`. The `oflag` should have the `O_CREAT` bit set. If successful, `r_open3` returns an open file descriptor. If unsuccessful, `r_open3` returns −1 and sets `errno`. The implementation calls `open` in a loop, restarting if `open` returns −1 with `errno` set to `EINTR`.

```
ssize_t r_read(int fd, void *buf, size_t size);
```
reads at most `size` bytes from the open file descriptor `fd` into `buf`. If successful, `r_read` returns the number of bytes read. If unsuccessful, `r_read` returns −1 and sets `errno`. The implementation calls `read` in a loop, restarting if `read` returns −1 with `errno` set to `EINTR`.

```
pid_t r_wait(int *stat_loc);
```
suspends execution of the calling thread until status information for one of its terminated children is available. If successful, `r wait` returns the process ID of a terminated child process. If unsuccessful, `r_wait` returns −1 and sets `errno`. The implementation calls `wait` in a loop, restarting if `wait` returns −1 with `errno` set to `EINTR`.

```
pid_t r_waitpid(pid_t pid, int *stat_loc, int options);
```
suspends execution of the calling thread until status information is available for a specified child process. If successful, `r_waitpid` returns the process ID of a child process. If unsuccessful, `r_waitpid` returns −1 and sets `errno`. The implementation calls `waitpid` in a loop, restarting if `waitpid` returns −1 with `errno` set to `EINTR`.

```
ssize_t r_write(int fd, void *buf, size_t size);
```
attempts to write exactly `size` bytes from `buf` to the open file descriptor `fd`. If successful, `r_write` returns `size`. If unsuccessful, `r_write` returns −1 and sets `errno`. The only possible return values are `size` and −1. The implementation calls `write` in a loop, restarting if `write` returns −1 with `errno` set to `EINTR`. If `write` does not output all the requested bytes, `r_write` continues to call `write` until all the bytes have been written or an error occurs.

```
ssize_t readblock(int fd, void *buf, size_t size);
```
attempts to read exactly `size` bytes from the open file descriptor `fd` into the `buf`. If `readblock` reaches end-of-file before reading any bytes, it returns 0. If exactly `size` bytes are read, `readblock` returns `size`. If unsuccessful, `readblock` returns −1 and sets `errno`. If `readblock` encounters end-of-file after some but not all of the needed bytes, the function returns −1 and sets `errno` to `EINVAL`.

```
int readline(int fd, void *buf, size_t size);
```
attempts to read a line from the open file descriptor `fd` into `buf`, a buffer of size `size`. If `readline` reaches end-of-file before reading any bytes, it returns 0. If successful, `buf` contains a string ending with a newline. The `readline`

function returns the length of the string. If unsuccessful, `readline` returns −1 and sets `errno`. Two errors are possible other than an error reading from `fd`: end-of-file before newline or `size-1` bytes read before newline. Both errors cause `readline` to set `errno` to `EINVAL`.

```
ssize_t readtimed(int fd, void *buf, size_t nbyte,
                  double seconds);
```
attempts to read at most `nbyte` bytes from the open file descriptor `fd` into the buffer `buf`. The `readtimed` function behaves the same as `r_read` unless no bytes are available in a number of seconds given by `seconds`. If no bytes are available within the timeout period, `readtimed` returns −1 and sets `errno` to `ETIME`. If interrupted by a signal, `readtimed` restarts but maintains the original ending timeout.

```
int readwrite(int fromfd, int tofd);
```
reads at most `PIPE_BUF` bytes from open file descriptor `fromfd` and writes the bytes read to the open file descriptor `tofd`. If successful, `readwrite` returns the number of bytes copied. If `readwrite` reaches end-of-file on `fromfd`, it returns 0. If unsuccessful, `readwrite` returns −1 and sets `errno`.

```
int readwriteblock(int fromfd, int tofd, char *buf, int size);
```
reads exactly `size` bytes from the open file descriptor `fromfd` and writes them to the open file descriptor `tofd`. The `buf` parameter is a buffer of size `size`. If successful, `readwriteblock` returns `size` and the bytes read are in `buf`. If `readwriteblock` reaches end-of-file on `fromfd` before any bytes are read, it returns 0. If unsuccessful, `readwriteblock` returns −1 and sets `errno`.

```
int waitfdtimed(int fd, struct timeval end);
```
waits until data is available to be read from file descriptor `fd` or until the current time is later than the time in `end`. If a read on `fd` will not block, `waitfdtimed` returns 0. If unsuccessful, `waitfdtimed` returns −1 and sets `errno`. If `fd` will still block when time `end` occurs, `waitfdtimed` sets `errno` to `ETIME`. If `fd` is negative or greater than or equal to `FD_SETSIZE`, `waitfdtimed` sets `errno` to `EINVAL`.

Program B.1 is the header file containing the prototype for these functions. Program B.2 gives the complete code for the restart library.

Program B.1 ———————————————————————— `restart.h`

The header file containing the prototypes for the restart library.

```
#include <fcntl.h>
#include <unistd.h>
#include <sys/time.h>
#include <sys/types.h>

#ifndef ETIME
#define ETIME ETIMEDOUT
#endif

struct timeval add2currenttime(double seconds);
int copyfile(int fromfd, int tofd);
int r_close(int fildes);
int r_dup2(int fildes, int fildes2);
int r_open2(const char *path, int oflag);
int r_open3(const char *path, int oflag, mode_t mode);
ssize_t r_read(int fd, void *buf, size_t size);
pid_t r_wait(int *stat_loc);
pid_t r_waitpid(pid_t pid, int *stat_loc, int options);
ssize_t r_write(int fd, void *buf, size_t size);
ssize_t readblock(int fd, void *buf, size_t size);
int readline(int fd, char *buf, int nbytes);
ssize_t readtimed(int fd, void *buf, size_t nbyte, double seconds);
int readwrite(int fromfd, int tofd);
int readwriteblock(int fromfd, int tofd, char *buf, int size);
int waitfdtimed(int fd, struct timeval end);
```

Program B.1 ———————————————————————— `restart.h`

Program B.2 ———————————————————————— `restart.c`

The restart library.

```
#include <errno.h>
#include <fcntl.h>
#include <limits.h>
#include <string.h>
#include <sys/select.h>
#include <sys/time.h>
#include <sys/wait.h>
#include "restart.h"
#define BLKSIZE PIPE_BUF
#define MILLION 1000000L
#define D_MILLION 1000000.0

/* Private functions */

static int gettimeout(struct timeval end,
                             struct timeval *timeoutp) {
   gettimeofday(timeoutp, NULL);
   timeoutp->tv_sec = end.tv_sec - timeoutp->tv_sec;
   timeoutp->tv_usec = end.tv_usec - timeoutp->tv_usec;
   if (timeoutp->tv_usec >= MILLION) {
      timeoutp->tv_sec++;
      timeoutp->tv_usec -= MILLION;
   }
```

```
       if (timeoutp->tv_usec < 0) {
          timeoutp->tv_sec--;
          timeoutp->tv_usec += MILLION;
       }
       if ((timeoutp->tv_sec < 0) ||
           ((timeoutp->tv_sec == 0) && (timeoutp->tv_usec == 0))) {
          errno = ETIME;
          return -1;
       }
       return 0;
    }

    /* Restart versions of traditional functions */

    int r_close(int fildes) {
       int retval;
       while (retval = close(fildes), retval == -1 && errno == EINTR) ;
       return retval;
    }

    int r_dup2(int fildes, int fildes2) {
       int retval;
       while (retval = dup2(fildes, fildes2), retval == -1 && errno == EINTR) ;
       return retval;
    }


    int r_open2(const char *path, int oflag) {
       int retval;
       while (retval = open(path, oflag), retval == -1 && errno == EINTR) ;
       return retval;
    }

    int r_open3(const char *path, int oflag, mode_t mode) {
       int retval;
       while (retval = open(path, oflag, mode), retval == -1 && errno == EINTR) ;
       return retval;
    }

    ssize_t r_read(int fd, void *buf, size_t size) {
       ssize_t retval;
       while (retval = read(fd, buf, size), retval == -1 && errno == EINTR) ;
       return retval;
    }

    pid_t r_wait(int *stat_loc) {
       pid_t retval;
       while (((retval = wait(stat_loc)) == -1) && (errno == EINTR)) ;
       return retval;
    }

    pid_t r_waitpid(pid_t pid, int *stat_loc, int options) {
       pid_t retval;
       while (((retval = waitpid(pid, stat_loc, options)) == -1) &&
               (errno == EINTR)) ;
       return retval;
    }
```

```
ssize_t r_write(int fd, void *buf, size_t size) {
   char *bufp;
   size_t bytestowrite;
   ssize_t byteswritten;
   size_t totalbytes;

   for (bufp = buf, bytestowrite = size, totalbytes = 0;
        bytestowrite > 0;
        bufp += byteswritten, bytestowrite -= byteswritten) {
      byteswritten = write(fd, bufp, bytestowrite);
      if ((byteswritten) == -1 && (errno != EINTR))
         return -1;
      if (byteswritten == -1)
         byteswritten = 0;
      totalbytes += byteswritten;
   }
   return totalbytes;
}

/* Utility functions */

struct timeval add2currenttime(double seconds) {
   struct timeval newtime;

   gettimeofday(&newtime, NULL);
   newtime.tv_sec += (int)seconds;
   newtime.tv_usec += (int)((seconds - (int)seconds)*D_MILLION + 0.5);
   if (newtime.tv_usec >= MILLION) {
      newtime.tv_sec++;
      newtime.tv_usec -= MILLION;
   }
   return newtime;
}

int copyfile(int fromfd, int tofd) {
   int bytesread;
   int totalbytes = 0;

   while ((bytesread = readwrite(fromfd, tofd)) > 0)
      totalbytes += bytesread;
   return totalbytes;
}

ssize_t readblock(int fd, void *buf, size_t size) {
   char *bufp;
   ssize_t bytesread;
   size_t bytestoread;
   size_t totalbytes;

   for (bufp = buf, bytestoread = size, totalbytes = 0;
        bytestoread > 0;
        bufp += bytesread, bytestoread -= bytesread) {
      bytesread = read(fd, bufp, bytestoread);
      if ((bytesread == 0) && (totalbytes == 0))
         return 0;
      if (bytesread == 0) {
```

```
            errno = EINVAL;
            return -1;
         }
      if ((bytesread) == -1 && (errno != EINTR))
         return -1;
      if (bytesread == -1)
         bytesread = 0;
      totalbytes += bytesread;
   }
   return totalbytes;
}

int readline(int fd, char *buf, int nbytes) {
   int numread = 0;
   int returnval;

   while (numread < nbytes - 1) {
      returnval = read(fd, buf + numread, 1);
      if ((returnval == -1) && (errno == EINTR))
         continue;
      if ((returnval == 0) && (numread == 0))
         return 0;
      if (returnval == 0)
         break;
      if (returnval == -1)
         return -1;
      numread++;
      if (buf[numread-1] == '\n') {
         buf[numread] = '\0';
         return numread;
      }
   }
   errno = EINVAL;
   return -1;
}

ssize_t readtimed(int fd, void *buf, size_t nbyte, double seconds) {
   struct timeval timedone;

   timedone = add2currenttime(seconds);
   if (waitfdtimed(fd, timedone) == -1)
      return (ssize_t)(-1);
   return r_read(fd, buf, nbyte);
}

int readwrite(int fromfd, int tofd) {
   char buf[BLKSIZE];
   int bytesread;

   if ((bytesread = r_read(fromfd, buf, BLKSIZE)) < 0)
      return -1;
   if (bytesread == 0)
      return 0;
   if (r_write(tofd, buf, bytesread) < 0)
      return -1;
   return bytesread;
}
```

```c
int readwriteblock(int fromfd, int tofd, char *buf, int size) {
   int bytesread;

   bytesread = readblock(fromfd, buf, size);
   if (bytesread != size)            /* can only be 0 or -1 */
      return bytesread;
   return r_write(tofd, buf, size);
}

int waitfdtimed(int fd, struct timeval end) {
   fd_set readset;
   int retval;
   struct timeval timeout;

   if ((fd < 0) || (fd >= FD_SETSIZE)) {
      errno = EINVAL;
      return -1;
   }
   FD_ZERO(&readset);
   FD_SET(fd, &readset);
   if (gettimeout(end, &timeout) == -1)
      return -1;
   while (((retval = select(fd+1, &readset, NULL, NULL, &timeout)) == -1)
          && (errno == EINTR)) {
      if (gettimeout(end, &timeout) == -1)
         return -1;
      FD_ZERO(&readset);
      FD_SET(fd, &readset);
   }
   if (retval == 0) {
      errno = ETIME;
      return -1;
   }
   if (retval == -1)
      return -1;
   return 0;
}
```

Program B.2 ─── `restart.c`

Appendix C

UICI Implementation

This appendix contains source code for the UICI implementation. UICI has three parts: TCP, UDP and name resolution. The TCP and UDP UICI are implemented with sockets. Several different implementations of the name resolution functions are given. The name resolution functions are used by both UICI TCP and UICI UDP, but UICI TCP and UICI UDP are independent of each other. Section C.1 gives the UICI TCP implementation, Section C.2 gives the name resolution implementations, and Section C.3 gives the UICI UDP implementation.

C.1 Connection-Oriented UICI TCP Implementation

This section gives a complete implementation of the UICI TCP functions in terms of sockets.

Program C.1 shows the header file containing the prototypes for the UICI TCP functions. This file should be included in all application code that calls any of the public UICI functions.

Program C.1 ——————————————————————————— **uici.h**
The header file containing prototypes of the UICI functions.

```
/********************************* uici.h *************************/
/*    Prototypes for the three public UICI functions             */
/****************************************************************/
#define UPORT
typedef unsigned short u_port_t;
int u_open(u_port_t port);
int u_accept(int fd, char *hostn, int hostnsize);
int u_connect(u_port_t port, char *hostn);
```
Program C.1 ——————————————————————————— **uici.h**

The `u_accept` and `u_connect` functions call the name resolution functions `addr2name` and `name2addr`, respectively. Several implementations of these name resolution functions are discussed in Sections C.2.1, C.2.2 and C.2.3.

Writing to a network socket that has no readers generates a `SIGPIPE` signal. If an application does not handle this signal, the remote host can cause the application to terminate by prematurely closing the connection. Both `u_open` and `u_connect` call `u_ignore_sigpipe`, which ignores the `SIGPIPE` signal if the default action for `SIGPIPE` (termination of the process) is in effect.

The `u open` function also sets the `SO REUSEADDR` option of the socket so that a server can immediately reuse a port number when it is not in use. This option is useful during debugging, for otherwise after terminating a server, you must wait (possibly several minutes) before starting the server listening again on the same port. The maximum backlog is set to 50 by default, but you can change this value either by modifying the `uici.c` file or by setting a compiler option (usually `-D`).

The `u_accept` function calls `addr2name` with three parameters. The first parameter is an address of type `struct in_addr`, which is converted to an ASCII string. The second parameter is a pointer to a buffer for storing the string, and the third parameter is the length of the buffer. If the buffer is not long enough to contain the host name string, `addr2name` silently truncates the string without producing an error. If `name2addr` cannot determine the host name, it uses the dotted-decimal notation address.

The `u_connect` function calls `name2addr` to convert an ASCII host name to an Internet address. If the `name2addr` call is not successful, `u_connect` returns −1 with `errno` set to `EINVAL`. The ASCII host name can be either a traditional name or an address in dotted-decimal notation. In the latter case, all the implementations of `name2addr` use `inet_addr` to convert the name to an address. The `u_connect` function must be handled in a special way when it is interrupted by a signal. If interrupted by a signal, `u_connect` continues to establish the connection asynchronously and it should not be called again. Instead, `u_connect` calls `select` to wait until the socket is available for writing. At this point the connection is established.

Program C.2 ──────────────────────────────────── `uici.c`

The complete uici library.

```
/* uici.c  sockets implementation */

#include <errno.h>
#include <signal.h>
#include <string.h>
#include <unistd.h>
#include <sys/select.h>
#include <sys/socket.h>
#include "uici.h"
#include "uiciname.h"
```

```
#ifndef MAXBACKLOG
#define MAXBACKLOG 50
#endif

/*
 *                              u_igniore_sigpipe
 * Ignore SIGPIPE if the default action is in effect.
 *
 * returns: 0 if successful
 *          -1 on error and sets errno
 */
static int u_ignore_sigpipe() {
   struct sigaction act;

   if (sigaction(SIGPIPE, (struct sigaction *)NULL, &act) == -1)
      return -1;
   if (act.sa_handler == SIG_DFL) {
      act.sa_handler = SIG_IGN;
      if (sigaction(SIGPIPE, &act, (struct sigaction *)NULL) == -1)
         return -1;
   }
   return 0;
}

/*
 *                              u_open
 * Return a file descriptor, which is bound to the given port.
 *
 * parameter:
 *       s = number of port to bind to
 * returns:  file descriptor if successful
 *           -1 on error and sets errno
 */
int u_open(u_port_t port) {
   int error;
   struct sockaddr_in server;
   int sock;
   int true = 1;

   if ((u_ignore_sigpipe() == -1) ||
       ((sock = socket(AF_INET, SOCK_STREAM, 0)) == -1))
      return -1;

   if (setsockopt(sock, SOL_SOCKET, SO_REUSEADDR, (char *)&true,
                  sizeof(true)) == -1) {
      error = errno;
      while ((close(sock) == -1) && (errno == EINTR));
      errno = error;
      return -1;
   }

   server.sin_family = AF_INET;
   server.sin_addr.s_addr = htonl(INADDR_ANY);
   server.sin_port = htons((short)port);
   if ((bind(sock, (struct sockaddr *)&server, sizeof(server)) == -1) ||
```

```
                (listen(sock, MAXBACKLOG) == -1)) {
        error = errno;
        while ((close(sock) == -1) && (errno == EINTR));
        errno = error;
        return -1;
    }
    return sock;
}

/*
 *                              u_accept
 * Wait for a connection request from a host on a specified port.
 *
 * parameters:
 *      fd = file descriptor previously bound to listening port
 *      hostn = a buffer that will hold the name of the remote host
 *      hostnsize = size of hostn buffer
 * returns:  a communication file descriptor on success
 *                hostn is filled with the name of the remote host.
 *            -1 on error with errno set
 *
 * comments: This function is used by the server to wait for a
 * communication.  It blocks until a remote request is received
 * from the port bound to the given file descriptor.
 * hostn is filled with an ASCII string containing the remote
 * host name.  It must point to a buffer of size at least hostnsize.
 * If the name does not fit, as much of the name as is possible is put
 * into the buffer.
 * If hostn is NULL or hostnsize <= 0, no hostname is copied.
 */
int u_accept(int fd, char *hostn, int hostnsize) {
    int len = sizeof(struct sockaddr);
    struct sockaddr_in netclient;
    int retval;

    while (((retval =
             accept(fd, (struct sockaddr *)(&netclient), &len)) == -1) &&
           (errno == EINTR))
        ;
    if ((retval == -1) || (hostn == NULL) || (hostnsize <= 0))
        return retval;
    addr2name(netclient.sin_addr, hostn, hostnsize);
    return retval;
}

/*
 *                              u_connect
 * Initiate communication with a remote server.
 *
 * parameters:
 *      port = well-known port on remote server
 *      hostn = character string giving the Internet name of remote host
 * returns:  a communication file descriptor if successful
 *            -1 on error with errno set
 */
```

```c
int u_connect(u_port_t port, char *hostn) {
   int error;
   int retval;
   struct sockaddr_in server;
   int sock;
   fd_set sockset;

   if (name2addr(hostn,&(server.sin_addr.s_addr)) == -1) {
      errno = EINVAL;
      return -1;
   }
   server.sin_port = htons((short)port);
   server.sin_family = AF_INET;

   if ((u_ignore_sigpipe() == -1) ||
       ((sock = socket(AF_INET, SOCK_STREAM, 0)) == -1))
      return -1;

   if (((retval =
        connect(sock, (struct sockaddr *)&server, sizeof(server))) == -1) &&
        ((errno == EINTR) || (errno == EALREADY))) {
      FD_ZERO(&sockset);
      FD_SET(sock, &sockset);
      while ( ((retval = select(sock+1, NULL, &sockset, NULL, NULL)) == -1) &&
              (errno == EINTR) ) {
         FD_ZERO(&sockset);
         FD_SET(sock, &sockset);
      }
   }
   if (retval == -1) {
      error = errno;
      while ((close(sock) == -1) && (errno == EINTR));
      errno = error;
      return -1;
   }
   return sock;
}
```

Program C.2 ———————————————————————————— `uici.c`

C.2 Name Resolution Implementations

The socket functions are both standardized and generally available. Unfortunately, several options are available for converting between host name and address, and none is optimal for all situations. The functions that are robust and thread-safe are not yet readily available on all systems. We offer several options controlled by compile-time definitions. The two UICI name resolution functions are `addr2name` and `name2addr`. Prototypes for these are in `uiciname.h`, shown in Program C.3.

Program C.3 ——————————————————————— `uiciname.h`

The header file for the UICI name resolution functions.

```
/* uiciname.h   name resolution functions */

#include <netinet/in.h>
#define REENTRANT_NONE 0
#define REENTRANT_R 1
#define REENTRANT_MUTEX 2
#define REENTRANT_POSIX 3

int name2addr(char *name, in_addr_t *addrp);
void addr2name(struct in_addr addr, char *name, int namelen);
```

Program C.3 ——————————————————————— `uiciname.h`

The `addr2name` function never returns an error. If the name cannot be resolved, the address is converted to a dotted-decimal notation format. The `name2addr` function returns 0 on success and −1 on failure. The UICI TCP and UDP functions that call the name resolution functions handle this error by returning −1 and setting `errno` to `EINVAL`.

Program C.4 contains four implementations of the name resolution functions `addr2name` and `name2addr`. Conditional compilation enables the constant `REENTRANCY` to determine which implementation is picked. If this constant is not defined, the default value of `REENTRANT_NONE` is used, giving an implementation with `gethostbyname` and `gethostbyaddr`. The value of `REENTRANCY` can be set either by adding a `#define` in the `uiciname.h` file or with a compile-time option.

C.2.1 Implementation with `gethostbyaddr` and `gethostbyname`

The first implementation of name resolution presented here uses `gethostbyname` and `gethostbyaddr`. These functions should be available on all UNIX implementations. Their main drawback is that they are not thread-safe, so they cannot be directly used by more than one thread. These implementations are used by default or when the constant `REENTRANCY` is set to `REENTRANT_NONE`.

C.2.2 Reentrant versions of name resolution functions

If `REENTRANCY` is equal to `REENTRANT_R`, the implementations use `gethostbyaddr_r` and `gethostbyname_r`. These functions were part of the X/OPEN standard, but when this standard was merged with POSIX, these functions were omitted. However, they are still available on some systems. These functions require a user-supplied buffer, but the documentation does not specify how large this buffer should be. Stevens [115] suggests 8192 for this value, since that is what is commonly used in the implementations of the non-thread-safe forms.

If REENTRANCY is equal to REENTRANT_POSIX, then the implementation uses the newer getnameinfo and getaddrinfo functions. These thread-safe functions can also be used with IPv6. Unfortunately, they are not yet available on many systems. Section 18.8 describes getnameinfo and getaddrinfo.

C.2.3 Reentrant name resolution with mutex locks

If neither group of reentrant name resolution functions is available, you can use gethostbyname and gethostbyaddr by protecting them with mutex locks. Set REENTRANCY to REENTRANT_MUTEX to use this implementation. The implementation uses a single mutex lock to protect calls to gethostbyname and gethostbyaddr.

Program C.4 ———————————————————————— **uiciname.c**

Four implementations of the UICI name resolution functions.

```
/* uiciname.c  name resolution functions */

#include <ctype.h>
#include <netdb.h>
#include <string.h>
#include <arpa/inet.h>
#include <sys/socket.h>
#include "uiciname.h"

#ifndef REENTRANCY
#define REENTRANCY REENTRANT_NONE
#endif

#if REENTRANCY==REENTRANT_MUTEX
#include <pthread.h>
static pthread_mutex_t mutex = PTHREAD_MUTEX_INITIALIZER;
#endif

#if REENTRANCY==REENTRANT_NONE
/* Convert struct in_addr to a host name */
void addr2name(struct in_addr addr, char *name, int namelen) {
   struct hostent *hostptr;
   hostptr = gethostbyaddr((char *)&addr, 4, AF_INET);
   if (hostptr == NULL)
      strncpy(name, inet_ntoa(addr), namelen-1);
   else
      strncpy(name, hostptr->h_name, namelen-1);
   name[namelen-1] = 0;
}

/* Return -1 on error, 0 on success */
int name2addr(char *name, in_addr_t *addrp) {
   struct hostent *hp;

   if (isdigit((int)(*name)))
      *addrp = inet_addr(name);
   else {
      hp = gethostbyname(name);
      if (hp == NULL)
```

```
         return -1;
      memcpy((char *)addrp, hp->h_addr_list[0], hp->h_length);
   }
   return 0;
}
#elif REENTRANCY==REENTRANT_R
#define GETHOST_BUFSIZE 8192
void addr2name(struct in_addr addr, char *name, int namelen) {
   char buf[GETHOST_BUFSIZE];
   int h_error;
   struct hostent *hp;
   struct hostent result;

   hp = gethostbyaddr_r((char *)&addr, 4, AF_INET, &result, buf,
                        GETHOST_BUFSIZE, &h_error);
   if (hp == NULL)
      strncpy(name, inet_ntoa(addr), namelen-1);
   else
      strncpy(name, hp->h_name, namelen-1);
   name[namelen-1] = 0;
}

/* Return -1 on error, 0 on success */
int name2addr(char *name, in_addr_t *addrp) {
   char buf[GETHOST_BUFSIZE];
   int h_error;
   struct hostent *hp;
   struct hostent result;

   if (isdigit((int)(*name)))
      *addrp = inet_addr(name);
   else {
      hp = gethostbyname_r(name, &result, buf, GETHOST_BUFSIZE, &h_error);
      if (hp == NULL)
         return -1;
      memcpy((char *)addrp, hp->h_addr_list[0], hp->h_length);
   }
   return 0;
}
#elif REENTRANCY==REENTRANT_MUTEX
/* Convert struct in_addr to a host name */
void addr2name(struct in_addr addr, char *name, int namelen) {
   struct hostent *hostptr;

   if (pthread_mutex_lock(&mutex) == -1) {
      strncpy(name, inet_ntoa(addr), namelen-1);
      name[namelen-1] = 0;
      return;
   }
   hostptr = gethostbyaddr((char *)&addr, 4, AF_INET);
   if (hostptr == NULL)
      strncpy(name, inet_ntoa(addr), namelen-1);
   else
      strncpy(name, hostptr->h_name, namelen-1);
   pthread_mutex_unlock(&mutex);
   name[namelen-1] = 0;
}
```

```c
/* Return -1 on error, 0 on success */
int name2addr(char *name, in_addr_t *addrp) {
   struct hostent *hp;

   if (isdigit((int)(*name)))
      *addrp = inet_addr(name);
   else {
      if (pthread_mutex_lock(&mutex) == -1)
         return -1;
      hp = gethostbyname(name);
      if (hp == NULL) {
         pthread_mutex_unlock(&mutex);
         return -1;
      }
      memcpy((char *)addrp, hp->h_addr_list[0], hp->h_length);
      pthread_mutex_unlock(&mutex);
   }
   return 0;
}
#elif REENTRANCY==REENTRANT_POSIX
/* Convert struct in_addr to a host name */
void addr2name(struct in_addr addr, char *name, int namelen) {
   struct sockaddr_in saddr;
   saddr.sin_family = AF_INET;
   saddr.sin_port = 0;
   saddr.sin_addr = addr;
   if (getnameinfo((struct sockaddr *)&saddr, sizeof(saddr), name, namelen,
         NULL, 0, 0) != 0) {
      strncpy(name, inet_ntoa(addr), namelen-1);
      name[namelen-1] = 0;
   }
}

/* Return -1 on error, 0 on success */
int name2addr(char *name, in_addr_t *addrp) {
   struct addrinfo hints;
   struct addrinfo *res;
   struct sockaddr_in *saddrp;

   hints.ai_flags = AI_PASSIVE;
   hints.ai_family = PF_INET;
   hints.ai_socktype = SOCK_STREAM;
   hints.ai_protocol = 0;
   hints.ai_addrlen = 0;
   hints.ai_canonname = NULL;
   hints.ai_addr = NULL;
   hints.ai_next = NULL;

   if (getaddrinfo(name, NULL, &hints, &res) != 0)
      return -1;
   saddrp = (struct sockaddr_in *)(res->ai_addr);
   memcpy(addrp, &saddrp->sin_addr.s_addr, 4);
   freeaddrinfo(res);
   return 0;
}

#endif
```

Program C.4 ———————————————————————————————— **uiciname.c**

C.3 Connectionless UICI UDP Implementation

Program C.5 shows the header file containing the prototypes for the UICI UDP functions. This file should be included in all applications that call any of these public functions. The details of the implementation have already been given in Section 20.7, so we just present the complete code in Program C.6.

Program C.5 ——————————————————————————— `uiciudp.h`

The header file for the UICI UDP functions.

```
#include <netinet/in.h>

#ifndef UPORT
typedef unsigned short u_port_t;
#endif
#define UPORT

#ifndef ETIME
#define ETIME ETIMEDOUT
#endif

typedef struct sockaddr_in u_buf_t;
int u_openudp(u_port_t port);
void u_gethostname(u_buf_t *ubufp, char *hostn, int hostnsize);
void u_gethostinfo(u_buf_t *ubufp, char *info, int infosize);
int u_comparehost(u_buf_t *ubufp, char *hostn, u_port_t port);
ssize_t u_sendtohost(int fd, void *buf, size_t nbyte, char *hostn,
                     u_port_t port);
ssize_t u_sendto(int fd, void *buf, size_t nbyte, u_buf_t *ubufp);
ssize_t u_recvfrom(int fd, void *buf, size_t nbyte, u_buf_t *ubufp);
ssize_t u_recvfromtimed(int fd, void *buf, size_t nbyte, u_buf_t *ubufp,
                        double time);
int u_join(char *IP_address, u_port_t port, u_buf_t *ubufp);
int u_leave(int mcastfd, u_buf_t *ubufp);
```

Program C.5 ——————————————————————————— `uiciudp.h`

Program C.6 ——————————————————————————— `uiciudp.c`

An implementation of UICI UDP using sockets.

```
/* uiciudp.c udp sockets implementation */

#include <errno.h>
#include <stdio.h>
#include <string.h>
#include <unistd.h>
#include <arpa/inet.h>
#include <sys/socket.h>
#include <sys/time.h>
#include "restart.h"
#include "uiciname.h"
#include "uiciudp.h"
```

```
/*
 *                              u_openudp
 * Return a file descriptor.
 *  It is bound to the given port if the port is positive.
 *
 * parameter:
 *        port = number of port to bind to
 * returns:  file descriptor if successful
 *            -1 on error and sets errno
 */
int u_openudp(u_port_t port) {
   int error;
   int one = 1;
   struct sockaddr_in server;
   int sock;

   if ((sock = socket(AF_INET, SOCK_DGRAM, 0)) == -1)
      return -1;

   if (setsockopt(sock, SOL_SOCKET, SO_REUSEADDR, &one, sizeof(one)) == -1) {
      error = errno;
      r_close(sock);
      errno = error;
      return -1;
   }

   if (port > 0) {
      server.sin_family = AF_INET;
      server.sin_addr.s_addr = htonl(INADDR_ANY);
      server.sin_port = htons((short)port);

      if (bind(sock, (struct sockaddr *)&server, sizeof(server)) == -1) {
         error = errno;
         r_close(sock);
         errno = error;
         return -1;
      }
   }
   return sock;
}


/*
 *                              u_recvfrom
 *
 * Retrieve information from a file descriptor.
 *
 * parameters:
 *        fd = socket file descriptor
 *        buf = buffer that receives the data
 *        nbytes = number of bytes to retrieve
 *        ubufp = a pointer to a buffer of type u_buf_t
 * returns:
 *        the number of bytes read if successful.
 *           ubufp is filled with information about the sending host and port
 *        -1 on error and sets errno
 */
```

```c
ssize_t u_recvfrom(int fd, void *buf, size_t nbytes, u_buf_t *ubufp) {
    int len;
    struct sockaddr *remote;
    int retval;

    len = sizeof (struct sockaddr_in);
    remote = (struct sockaddr *)ubufp;
    while (((retval = recvfrom(fd, buf, nbytes, 0, remote, &len)) == -1) &&
            (errno == EINTR)) ;
    return retval;
}

/*
 *                          u_recvfromtimed
 *
 * Retrieve information from a file descriptor with a timeout.
 *
 * parameters:
 *        fd = socket file descriptor
 *        buf = buffer to receive the data
 *        nbytes = number of bytes to retrieve
 *        ubufp = a pointer to a buffer of type u_buf_t
 *        seconds = timeout in seconds
 * returns:
 *        number of bytes received if successful
 *        -1 on error and sets errno
 */

ssize_t u_recvfromtimed(int fd, void *buf, size_t nbytes, u_buf_t *ubufp,
                        double seconds) {
    int len;
    struct sockaddr *remote;
    int retval;
    struct timeval timedone;

    timedone = add2currenttime(seconds);
    if (waitfdtimed(fd, timedone) == -1)
       return (ssize_t)(-1);
    len = sizeof (struct sockaddr_in);
    remote = (struct sockaddr *)ubufp;
    while (((retval = recvfrom(fd, buf, nbytes, 0, remote, &len)) == -1) &&
            (errno == EINTR)) ;
    return retval;
}

/*
 *                          u_gethostname
 *
 * Get the host name from a buffer of type u_buf_t
 *
 * parameters:
 *        ubufp = a pointer to a buffer of type u_buf_t that was
 *            filled by u_recvfrom
 *        hostn = a buffer of size hostnsize
 *        hostsize = the size of the hostn buffer
 * returns:
 *        hostn is filled with the name of the host, possibly truncated.
```

```
 */

void u_gethostname(u_buf_t *ubufp, char *hostn, int hostnsize) {
   struct sockaddr_in *remotep;

   remotep = (struct sockaddr_in *)ubufp;
   addr2name(remotep->sin_addr, hostn, hostnsize);
}

/*
 *                         u_gethostinfo
 *
 * Get a printable string containing the host name and port
 *
 * parameters:
 *       ubufp = a pointer to a buffer of type u_buf_t that was
 *         filled by u_recvfrom
 *       info = a buffer to hold the returned string
 *       infosize = the size of the info buffer
 * returns:
 *      a string is put in info, possibly truncated
 */
void u_gethostinfo(u_buf_t *ubufp, char *info, int infosize) {
   int len;
   int portnumber;

   portnumber = ntohs(ubufp->sin_port);
   len = snprintf(info, infosize, "port number is %d on host ", portnumber);
   info[infosize-1] = 0;                             /* in case name not fit */
   if (len >= infosize) return;
   u_gethostname(ubufp, info+len, infosize-len);
}


/*
 *                         u_comparehost
 *
 * Compare the given host and port with the info in a u_buf_t structure
 *
 * parameters:
 *       ubufp = a pointer to a buffer of type u_buf_t that was
 *         filled by u_recvfrom
 *       hostn = a string representing the host name
 *       port  = a port number
 * returns:
 *      1 if match
 *      0 if no match
 */

int u_comparehost(u_buf_t *ubufp, char *hostn, u_port_t port) {
   in_addr_t addr;
   struct sockaddr_in *remotep;

   remotep = (struct sockaddr_in *)ubufp;
   if ((port != ntohs(remotep->sin_port)) ||
       (name2addr(hostn, &addr) == -1) ||
       (memcmp(&(remotep->sin_addr.s_addr), &addr, sizeof(in_addr_t)) != 0))
```

```
      return 0;
   return 1;
}


/*
 *                         u_sendto
 *
 * Send information atomically to a remote host, using the buffer filled in
 * by recvfrom
 *
 * This is almost the same as sendto except that
 *   it retries if interrupted by a signal and
 *   the length of the buffer indicating the destination is not passed
 *
 * parameters:
 *      fd = file descriptor
 *      buf = buffer to be output
 *      nbytes = number of bytes to send
 *      ubufp = a pointer to a buffer of type u_buf_t that was
 *          filled by u_recvfrom
 * returns:
 *      the number of bytes that were sent (may not have been received)
 *      -1 on error and sets errno
 */

ssize_t u_sendto(int fd, void *buf, size_t nbytes, u_buf_t *ubufp) {
   int len;
   struct sockaddr *remotep;
   int retval;

   len = sizeof(struct sockaddr_in);
   remotep = (struct sockaddr *)ubufp;
   while (((retval = sendto(fd, buf, nbytes, 0, remotep, len)) == -1) &&
          (errno == EINTR)) ;
   return retval;
}


/*
 *                         u_sendtohost
 *
 * Send information atomically to a remote host given the host name and port
 *
 * parameters:
 *      fd = file descriptor
 *      buf = buffer to be output
 *      nbyte = number of bytes to send
 *      port = the port number to send to
 *      hostn = a string containing the name of the destination host
 * returns:
 *      the number of bytes that were sent (may not have been received)
 *      -1 on error and sets errno
 */

ssize_t u_sendtohost(int fd, void *buf, size_t nbytes, char *hostn,
                     u_port_t port) {
   struct sockaddr_in remote;
```

```
   if (name2addr(hostn, &(remote.sin_addr.s_addr)) == -1) {
      errno = EINVAL;
      return -1;
   }
   remote.sin_port = htons((short)port);
   remote.sin_family = AF_INET;
   return u_sendto(fd, buf, nbytes, &remote);
}


/*
 *                            u_join
 *
 * Join a multicast group
 *
 * parameters:
 *        IP_address = string representing the IP address of the group
 *        port = port number of multicast group
 *        ubufp = buffer to be filled in u_join
 * returns:
 *        a file descriptor on success
 *        -1 on error and sets errno
 */
int u_join(char *IP_address, u_port_t port, u_buf_t *ubufp) {
   int mcastfd;
   struct ip_mreq tempaddress;

   if ((mcastfd = u_openudp(port)) == -1)
      return mcastfd;

   tempaddress.imr_multiaddr.s_addr = inet_addr(IP_address);
   tempaddress.imr_interface.s_addr = htonl(INADDR_ANY);

       /* Join the multicast group. Let kernel choose the interface */
   if (setsockopt(mcastfd, IPPROTO_IP, IP_ADD_MEMBERSHIP,
                  &tempaddress, sizeof(tempaddress)) == -1)
      return -1;
   ubufp->sin_family = AF_INET;
   ubufp->sin_addr.s_addr = inet_addr(IP_address);
   ubufp->sin_port = htons((short)port);
   return mcastfd;
}

/* This version leaves the group but keeps the file descriptor open and
   still bound to the same port.  It can still receive messages on the port,
   but only those addressed directly to the given host.
*/
/*
 *                            u_leave
 *
 * Leave a multicast group.  Messages can still be received on the port
 * if they are directly addressed to the host.
 *
 * parameters:
 *        mcastfd = previously opened file descriptor returned by u_join
 *        ubufp = buffer filled in by previous u_join
 * returns:
```

```
 *       0 on success
 *       -1 on error with errno set
 */
int u_leave(int mcastfd, u_buf_t *ubufp) {
   struct ip_mreq tempaddress;

   memcpy(&(tempaddress.imr_multiaddr),
          &(ubufp->sin_addr), sizeof(struct in_addr));
   tempaddress.imr_interface.s_addr = htonl(INADDR_ANY);
   return setsockopt(mcastfd, IPPROTO_IP, IP_DROP_MEMBERSHIP,
                     &tempaddress, sizeof(tempaddress));
}
```

Program C.6 ——————————————————————————————— `uiciudp.c`

Appendix D

Logging Functions

D.1 Local Atomic Logging

The local atomic logging library is described in Section 4.9.1. This library allows messages to be atomically written to a file descriptor. A message may be made up of pieces, which are assembled by the logging library and sent atomically. There are no a priori limits to the sizes of the pieces, the number of pieces, or the total size of the message. However, the logger reports an error if the total amount to be logged with a single call to `atomic_log_send` cannot be written with a single call to `write`. Multiple processes may concurrently log data to the same file or different files. The library uses static data and should not be used by concurrent threads.

Programs that use this library include the `atomic_logger.h` file shown in Program D.1 and are linked with `atomic_logger.c` shown in Program D.2. All the public functions in the library return 0 if successful or –1 on error. A program uses the logging facility as follows.

1. Call `atomic_log_open` with the name of the log file as the parameter.
2. Call any of the functions `atomic_log_array`, `atomic_log_printf` and `atomic_log_string` to create pieces of the message.
3. Call `atomic_log_send` to log the message. This logging deletes the pieces of the message that have been saved in the logger.
4. Repeat steps 2 and 3 as often as you like.
5. The program can use the `atomic_log_clear` function to discard the pieces of the message generated so far without sending them.
6. Call `atomic_log_close` when logging to this file is complete.

Each piece that is logged is put in a linked list. The function `atomic_log_send` allocates a contiguous block large enough to hold all the pieces, copies the pieces into this block, and sends them to the log file with a single call to `write`. The `atomic_log_send` function returns 0 only if `write` actually writes all the requested bytes.

When strings are logged with `atomic_log_printf` or `atomic_log_string`, the facility saves the string terminator with each piece. These functions call the `insert_new_entry` function with `extra` equal to 1. The logger allocates space for the string terminator but does not count the terminator in the length field and does not send the terminator to the log file.

Program D.1 ————————————————————— `atomic_logger.h`
The header file for the atomic logging module.

```
int atomic_log_array(char *s, int len);
int atomic_log_clear();
int atomic_log_close();
int atomic_log_open(char *fn);
int atomic_log_printf(char *fmt, ...);
int atomic_log_send();
int atomic_log_string(char *s);
```

Program D.1 ————————————————————— `atomic_logger.h`

Program D.2 ————————————————————— `atomic_logger.c`
An implementation of the atomic logging module.

```c
#include <errno.h>
#include <fcntl.h>
#include <stdarg.h>
#include <stdio.h>
#include <stdlib.h>
#include <string.h>
#include <unistd.h>
#include <sys/stat.h>

#define FILE_PERMS (S_IRUSR | S_IWUSR| S_IRGRP | S_IROTH)
#define OPEN_FLAGS (O_WRONLY|O_APPEND|O_CREAT)
typedef struct list {
   char *entry;
   int len;
   struct list *next;
} list;

static int fd = -1;
static list *first = NULL;
static list *last = NULL;


/* ---------------------------------------------------------------
   Private Functions
*/
```

```c
/* This is the same as write, but restarts if interrupted by a signal */
static ssize_t my_write(int fd, void *buf, size_t size) {
   ssize_t bytes;

   while (((bytes = write(fd, buf, size)) == -1) && (errno == EINTR));
   return bytes;
}

/* Insert an entry with the given len field, but allocate extra bytes.*/
/* Return a pointer to the new entry on success or NULL on failure.   */
static list *insert_new_entry(int len, int extra) {
   char *new_str;
   list *new_entry;

   new_entry = (list *)malloc(sizeof(list)+len+extra);
   if (new_entry == NULL)
      return NULL;
   new_str = (char *)new_entry+sizeof(list);
   new_entry->entry = new_str;
   new_entry->next = NULL;
   new_entry->len = len;
   if (last == NULL)
      first = new_entry;
   else
      last->next = new_entry;
   last = new_entry;
   return new_entry;
}

/* Return the sum of the lengths of all the entries.                  */
static int get_length() {
   int len = 0;
   list *current;

   current = first;
   while (current != NULL) {
      len += current->len;
      current = current->next;
   }
   return len;
}

/* Clear the list and free all the space.                             */
static void clear() {
   list *current;
   list *free_entry;

   current = first;
   while (current != NULL) {
      free_entry = current;
      current = current->next;
      free(free_entry);
   }
   first = NULL;
   last = NULL;
}
```

```
/* ------------------------------------------------------------
   Public Functions
*/

/* Open the given file for logging.                            */
/* If successful, return 0.  Otherwise, return -1 with errno set.  */
int atomic_log_open(char *fn) {
   while (fd = open(fn, OPEN_FLAGS, FILE_PERMS), fd == -1 && errno == EINTR);
   if (fd < 0)
      return -1;
   return 0;
}

/* Insert the given array with given size in the list.         */
/* If successful, return 0.  Otherwise, return -1 with errno set.  */
int atomic_log_array(char *s, int len) {
   list *new_entry;

   if (fd < 0) {
      errno = EINVAL;
      return -1;
   }
   new_entry = insert_new_entry(len, 0);
   if (new_entry == NULL)
      return -1;
   (void)memcpy(new_entry->entry, s, len);
   return 0;
}

/* Insert the given string in the list.                        */
/* Do not include the string terminator.                       */
/* If successful, return 0.  Otherwise, return -1 with errno set.  */
int atomic_log_string(char *s) {
   return atomic_log_array(s, strlen(s));
}

/* Insert an entry in the list.                                */
/* The syntax is similar to printf.                            */
/* Include the string terminator but do not count it in the length.  */
/* If successful, return 0.  Otherwise, return -1 with errno set.  */
int atomic_log_printf(char *fmt, ...) {
   va_list ap;
   char ch;
   int len;
   list *new_entry;

   if (fd < 0) {
      errno = EINVAL;
      return -1;
   }
   va_start(ap, fmt);
   len = vsnprintf(&ch, 1, fmt, ap);
   new_entry = insert_new_entry(len, 1);
   if (new_entry == NULL)
      return -1;
```

```
        vsprintf(new_entry->entry, fmt, ap);
        return 0;
}

/* Attempt to log the entire list with a single write.          */
/* Clear the list if successful.                                */
/* If successful, return 0.  Otherwise, return -1 with errno set. */
/* If the entire list cannot be logged with a single write, this is */
/*    considered a failure.                                     */
int atomic_log_send() {
    char *buf;
    list *current;
    int len;

    if (fd < 0) {
        errno = EINVAL;
        return -1;
    }
    len = get_length();
    if (len == 0)
        return 0;
    buf = (char *)malloc(len);
    if (buf == NULL)
        return -1;
    current = first;
    len = 0;
    while (current != NULL) {
        (void)memcpy(buf+len, current->entry, current->len);
        len += current->len;
        current = current->next;
    }
    if (my_write(fd, buf, len) != len) {
        free(buf);
        errno = EAGAIN;
        return -1;
    }
    free(buf);
    clear();
    return 0;
}

/* Clear the list and free all the space without logging anything.    */
int atomic_log_clear() {
    clear();
    return 0;
}

/* Close the log file.  Any data not yet logged is lost.          */
int atomic_log_close() {
    int retval;
    clear();
    while (retval = close(fd), retval == -1 && errno == EINTR) ;
    return retval;
}
```

Program D.2 ───────────────────────────────── `atomic_logger.c`

D.2 Remote Logging

The local logging facility discussed in Section D.1 is useful when the message to be logged is created in pieces that need to be logged together. However, the local logging facility can be used only by collections of single-threaded processes on the same host. The remote logging facility is meant to be used in a multithreaded environment or one in which processes on multiple machines are cooperating or communicating.

Programs that depend on concurrency (primarily those that fork children, create multiple threads, or that depend on communicating processes) are often difficult to understand and debug. Debuggers for multithreaded programs are not generally available, let alone ones that can unify the debugging of communicating processes running on different machines, possibly on incompatible hardware.

The logging facility described here allows for instrumenting code in a simple way to log events. The logged events are sent to a possibly remote machine and gathered for analysis. Events are timestamped according to when they arrive at the receiving machine. If the variance of network delays are small compared with the granularity of the logging, these times acceptably indicate the sequence of events that occur in logged programs. Optionally, messages can be timestamped with the time they were generated. This is useful if all messages are logged from the same host or from hosts with synchronized clocks.

The underlying philosophy of the logging facility is to provide a simple, familiar C-language-based interface that can be mastered in a few minutes. Most of the complication is moved to the receiving end, which has a GUI for ease of use.

The facility is thus broken into two independent parts, the C language interface which runs in a UNIX environment, and a Java-based GUI receiving module that can be run on any system having a Java runtime environment.

The C language interface is modeled on the C language `FILE` pointer I/O interface and has functions corresponding to `fopen`, `fclose` and `fprintf`. These are called `lopen`, `lclose` and `lprintf`, respectively. Three other functions, `lprintfg`, `lgenerator` and `lsendtime`, allow more control over how the logged data is labeled.

The logging functions return `NULL` (`lopen`) or −1 (all others) on error. Do not use `errno` with any of the functions in the library. By default, these functions do not print error messages. To simplify debugging, they send error messages to standard error if in debugging mode. You can enter debugging mode by calling `ldebug(1)` and exit debugging mode by calling `ldebug(0)`. Alternatively, you can turn on debugging by compiling with `LDEBUGGING` defined.

To use the logging facility, include `rlogging.h`, shown in Program D.3, and compile with `rlogging.c`, shown in Program D.4. The former file contains the typedefs and prototypes, and the latter contains the code. The program must also be linked with `restart.c`, described in Appendix B, and with `uici.c` and `uiciname.c`, described in Appendix C. If the program is used in a multithreaded environment, the constant LUSETHREAD should be defined. The simplest way to do this is with a compiler option. Many compilers support the use of –DLUSETHREAD option to define LUSETHREAD at compile time.

Program D.3 ———————————————————— `rlogging.h`

The header file for the remote logging module.

```
#define LFILE_GENLENGTH 16
typedef struct LFILE {
   int id;
   int fd;
   int tmode;
   char gen[LFILE_GENLENGTH];
} LFILE;

LFILE *lopen(char *host, int port);
int lclose(LFILE *mf);                        /* not thread safe */
void ldebug(int debug);
int lprintf(LFILE *mf, char *fmt, ...);
int lprintfg(LFILE *mf, char *gen, char *fmt, ...);
int lgenerator(LFILE *mf, char *gen);
int lsendtime(LFILE *mf);
```

Program D.3 ———————————————————— `rlogging.h`

Program D.4 ———————————————————— `rlogging.c`

C source for the logging module.

```
#include <errno.h>
#include <limits.h>
#include <stdio.h>
#include <stdlib.h>
#include <stdarg.h>
#include <string.h>
#include <time.h>
#include <unistd.h>
#include <sys/time.h>
#ifdef LUSETHREAD
#include <pthread.h>
#endif
#include "restart.h"
#include "rlogging.h"
#include "uici.h"

#define DEFAULT_HOST "localhost"
#define DEFAULT_PORT 20100

#define LOGGING_BUFSIZE PIPE_BUF
#define LOGGING_GENMAX 50

/* Note: LOGGING_BUFSIZE must be at most PIPE_BUF */
```

```
static int nextID = 0;
#ifdef LDEBUGGING
static int ldebug_flag = 1;
#else
static int ldebug_flag = 0;
#endif

#ifdef LUSETHREAD
static pthread_mutex_t ctime_mutex = PTHREAD_MUTEX_INITIALIZER;
static pthread_mutex_t generator_mutex = PTHREAD_MUTEX_INITIALIZER;
static pthread_mutex_t ID_mutex = PTHREAD_MUTEX_INITIALIZER;
#endif

/* Turn on debugging if debug = 1                                    */
void ldebug(int debug) {
   ldebug_flag = debug;
}

static long get_threadid() {
#ifdef NOTHREADID
   return 0L;
#else
#ifdef LUSETHREAD
   return (long)pthread_self();
#else
   return 1L;
#endif
#endif
}

/* Expand the generator, gen_fmt, into the buffer gen that has size gensize.
 * return 0 if fits, 1 if it does not.
 * %p is converted to process ID.
 * %t is converted to thread ID.
 * if (gen_fmt[0] == 0) then just then pid.tid is used.
 * at most one %p and one %t are allowed.
*/
static int expand_gen(const char *gen_fmt, char *gen, int gensize) {
   int needed;
   char *pp;
   char *pt;
   pp = strstr(gen_fmt, "%p");
   pt = strstr(gen_fmt, "%t");
   if (gen_fmt[0] == 0) {                            /* Use default generator */
#ifdef NOTHREADID
      needed = snprintf(gen, gensize, "%ld", (long)getpid());
#else
#ifdef LUSETHREAD
      needed = snprintf(gen, gensize, "%ld.%ld", (long)getpid(),
                        get_threadid());
#else
      needed = snprintf(gen, gensize, "%ld", (long)getpid());
#endif
#endif
   }
   else if ((pt == NULL) && (pp == NULL))
      needed = snprintf(gen, gensize, "%s", gen_fmt);
```

```
    else if (pt == NULL)
        needed = snprintf(gen, gensize, "%.*s%ld%s", (int)(pp-gen_fmt), gen_fmt,
                         (long)getpid(), pp+2);
    else if (pp == NULL) {
        needed = snprintf(gen, gensize, "%.*s%ld%s", (int)(pt-gen_fmt), gen_fmt,
                         get_threadid(), pt+2);
    }
    else if (pp < pt) {
        needed = snprintf(gen, gensize, "%.*s%ld%.*s%ld%s",
                         (int)(pp-gen_fmt), gen_fmt, (long)getpid(),
                         (int)(pt-pp-2), pp+2, get_threadid(), pt+2);
    }
    else {
        needed = snprintf(gen, gensize, "%.*s%ld%.*s%ld%s", (int)(pt-gen_fmt),
                         gen_fmt, get_threadid(), (int)(pp-pt-2), pt+2,
                         (long)getpid(), pp+2);
    }
    if (needed >= gensize)
        return 1;
    return 0;
}

#define RWBUFSIZE PIPE_BUF
/* Read from infd and write to outfd until an error or end-of-file occurs */
static void readwriteall(int infd, int outfd) {
    char buf[RWBUFSIZE];
    int bytes_read;

    while ((bytes_read = r_read(infd, buf, RWBUFSIZE)) > 0) {
        if (r_write(outfd, buf, bytes_read) != bytes_read) {
            if (ldebug_flag)
                fprintf(stderr, "Pipe write error\n");
            close(infd);
            close(outfd);
            return;
        }
    }
    if (bytes_read < 0) {
        if (ldebug_flag)
            fprintf(stderr, "Pipe read error\n");
    }
    close(infd);
    close(outfd);
}

/* Create a pipe and a child process.
 * All output is sent to the pipe.
 * The child process reads from the pipe and outputs to the network.
 */
static void go_through_pipe(LFILE *mf) {
    int childpid;
    int fds[2];

    if (pipe(fds) < 0) {
        if (ldebug_flag)
            fprintf(stderr, "Pipe creation failed\n");
        return;
```

```
      }
      childpid = fork();
      if (childpid < 0) {
         if (ldebug_flag)
            fprintf(stderr, "Fork failed\n");
         close(fds[0]);
         close(fds[1]);
         return;
      }
      if (childpid == 0) {                                    /* child code */
         close(fds[1]);
         readwriteall(fds[0], mf->fd);
         exit(0);
      }
      close(fds[0]);
      close(mf->fd);
      mf->fd = fds[1];
   }

/* Set the parameters to the current time
 * return 0 on success and 1 on failure.
 */
static int set_times(unsigned long *secp, unsigned long *usecp) {
   struct timeval tp;

   if (gettimeofday(&tp, NULL))
      return 1;
   *secp = (unsigned long)tp.tv_sec;
   *usecp = (unsigned long)tp.tv_usec;
   return 0;
}

/* Create a string representing the time given by sec and usec in the
 *    buffer buf.  This assumes that buf is large enough.
 * Return 0 on success and 1 on failure.
 */
static int make_time_string(char *buf, unsigned long sec, unsigned long usec) {
   time_t clock;
   double fract;
   char *tm;

   clock = (time_t)sec;
   fract = usec/1000000.0;
   sprintf(buf+7, "%5.3f", fract);
#ifdef LUSETHREAD
   if (pthread_mutex_lock(&ctime_mutex))
      return 1;
#endif
   tm = ctime(&clock);
   strncpy(buf,tm+11,8);
#ifdef LUSETHREAD
   if (pthread_mutex_unlock(&ctime_mutex))
      return 1;
#endif
   return 0;
}
```

```
/* Log the string given by the last two parameters.
 * Use the given generator.
 * Return 0 on success and -1 on failure.
 */
static int lprintfgen(LFILE *mf, char *gen, char *fmt, va_list ap) {

    int blen;                                       /* size of data buffer */
    char buf[LOGGING_BUFSIZE];
    char buftemp[LOGGING_BUFSIZE];
    char genbuf[LOGGING_GENMAX];
    int ret;
    unsigned long sec;
    char timebuf[13];
    char *timep;
    char timesbuf[20];                      /* holds seconds and microseconds */
    unsigned long usec;
    int written;

    if (mf==NULL) {
        if (ldebug_flag)
            fprintf(stderr, "lprintf called with NULL first parameter\n");
        return -1;
    }
    if ( (mf->tmode) || (strstr(fmt, "%t") != NULL) )
        if (set_times(&sec, &usec) != 0) {
            if (ldebug_flag)
                fprintf(stderr, "Error getting current time\n");
            return -1;
        }
    if (mf->tmode)
        sprintf(timesbuf, "%lu;%lu;", sec, usec);
    else
        timesbuf[0] = 0;
    timep = strstr(fmt, "%t");
    if (timep != NULL) {
        if (make_time_string(timebuf, sec, usec) != 0) {
            if (ldebug_flag)
                fprintf(stderr, "Error making time string in lprintf\n");
            return -1;
        }
        if (strlen(fmt) + 13 >= LOGGING_BUFSIZE) {
                fprintf(stderr, "Format string is too long\n");
            return -1;
        }
        sprintf(buf, "%.*s%s%s", (int)(timep-fmt), fmt, timebuf, timep+2);
        ret = vsnprintf(buftemp, LOGGING_BUFSIZE, buf, ap);
    }
    else
        ret = vsnprintf(buftemp, LOGGING_BUFSIZE, fmt, ap);
    if ((ret < 0) || (ret >= LOGGING_BUFSIZE)) {
         if (ldebug_flag)
            fprintf(stderr, "Error in lprintf format string\n");
         return -1;
    }
    if (expand_gen(gen, genbuf, LOGGING_GENMAX) != 0) {
         if (ldebug_flag)
            fprintf(stderr, "Generator info does not fit\n");
```

```
        }
    blen = strlen(buftemp) + strlen(genbuf) + strlen(timesbuf);
    ret = snprintf(buf, LOGGING_BUFSIZE, "%d:%s%s;%s", blen+1,
                    timesbuf, genbuf, buftemp);
    if (ret >= LOGGING_BUFSIZE) {
        if (ldebug_flag)
            fprintf(stderr, "Error in lprintf: size too large to fit\n");
        return -1;
    }
    while (written = write(mf->fd, buf, ret), written == -1 && errno == EINTR) ;
    if (written != ret) {
        if (ldebug_flag)
            fprintf(stderr, "lprintf error writing to pipe\n");
        return -1;
    }
    return 0;
}

/* Open a connection to the given host and port for logging.
 * If host is NULL, use the environment variable LOGGINGHOST if it is set;
 *      otherwise, use the host "localhost".
 * If port is 0, use the environment variable LOGGINGPORT if it is set;
 *      otherwise, use the default port DEFAULT_PORT.
 * Return a pointer to an LFILE if successful, or NULL if unsuccessful.
 */
LFILE *lopen(char *host, int port) {
    int fd;
    LFILE *mf;
    char *portstr;

    if (host == NULL) {
        host = getenv("LOGGINGHOST");
        if (host == NULL)
            host = DEFAULT_HOST;
    }
    if (port <= 0) {
        portstr = getenv("LOGGINGPORT");
        if (portstr == NULL)
            port = DEFAULT_PORT;
        else
            port = atoi(portstr);
    }
    fd = u_connect(port, host);
    if (fd < 0) {
        if (ldebug_flag)
            fprintf(stderr, "Connection failed to host %s on port %d\n",
                    host,port);
        return NULL;
    }
    mf = (LFILE *)malloc(sizeof(LFILE));
    if (mf == NULL) {
        if (ldebug_flag)
            fprintf(stderr, "Memory allocation error for lopen\n");
        return NULL;
    }
#ifdef LUSETHREAD
    if (pthread_mutex_lock(&ID_mutex))
```

```
        return NULL;
#endif
    mf->id = nextID++;
#ifdef LUSETHREAD
    if (pthread_mutex_unlock(&ID_mutex))
        return NULL;
#endif
    mf->fd = fd;
    mf->tmode = 0;
    mf->gen[0] = 0;
    go_through_pipe(mf);
#ifdef LSENDTIME
    lsendtime(mf);
#endif
    return mf;
}

/* Close the connection corresponding to mf.
 * Return 0 on success and -1 on failure.
 */
int lclose(LFILE *mf) {

    if (mf == NULL) {
        if (ldebug_flag)
            fprintf(stderr, "lclose called with NULL parameter\n");
        return -1;
    }
    if (close(mf->fd) == -1) {
        if (ldebug_flag)
            fprintf(stderr, "lclose failed to close the connection\n");
    }
    free(mf);
    return 0;
}

/* Log the given string, using the default generator.
 * The parameters are similar to those of printf.
 * Return 0 on success and -1 on failure.
 */
int lprintf(LFILE *mf, char *fmt, ...) {
    char genbuf[LFILE_GENLENGTH];
    va_list ap;

    if (mf==NULL) {
        if (ldebug_flag)
            fprintf(stderr, "lprintf called with NULL first parameter\n");
        return -1;
    }
    va_start(ap, fmt);
#ifdef LUSETHREAD
    if (pthread_mutex_lock(&generator_mutex))
        return -1;
#endif
    strcpy(genbuf, mf->gen);
#ifdef LUSETHREAD
    if (pthread_mutex_unlock(&generator_mutex))
        return -1;
```

```
#endif
   return lprintfgen(mf, genbuf, fmt, ap);
}

/* Log the given string, using the given generator.
 * The parameters are similar to those of printf.
 * Return 0 on success and -1 on failure.
 */
int lprintfg(LFILE *mf, char *gen, char *fmt, ...) {
   va_list ap;
   if (mf==NULL) {
      if (ldebug_flag)
         fprintf(stderr, "lprintf called with NULL first parameter\n");
      return -1;
   }
   va_start(ap, fmt);
   return lprintfgen(mf, gen, fmt, ap);
}

/* Set the default generator to the given one.
 * Return 0 on success and -1 on failure.
 */
int lgenerator(LFILE *mf, char *gen) {
   if (mf == NULL)
      return -1;
   if (gen == NULL)
      mf->gen[0] = 0;
   if (strlen(gen) >= LFILE_GENLENGTH)
      return -1;
#ifdef LUSETHREAD
   if (pthread_mutex_lock(&generator_mutex))
      return -1;
#endif
   strcpy(mf->gen,gen);
#ifdef LUSETHREAD
   if (pthread_mutex_unlock(&generator_mutex))
      return -1;
#endif
   return 0;
}

/* Send the local time with each logged message.
 * Return 0 on success and -1 on failure.
 */
int lsendtime(LFILE *mf) {
   if (mf == NULL)
      return -1;
   mf->tmode = 1;
   if (r_write(mf->fd, "-", 1) < 0) {
      if (ldebug_flag)
         fprintf(stderr, "Pipe write error\n");
      return -1;
   }
   return 0;
}
```

Program D.4 ———————————————————————————— `rlogging.c`

D.2.1 Use of the remote logging facility

This section briefly describes how to use the remote logging facility. For a more detailed discussion, see [98]. A complete user's guide and all the programs are available online [99].

The logging GUI must be started first. It can be run on any host with a Java runtime environment. The GUI listens for connections using TCP. If no port number is specified on the command line, the GUI takes the port number from the environment variable LOGGINGPORT or uses a default port number if this environment variable is not defined.

The program that is being logged must be linked with the restart library, the UICI library, the UICI name resolution library and the logging library. The only functions that need to be directly accessed are given in Program D.3.

First, make a connection to the GUI by using lopen. The parameters are a host name and a port number. If the host name is NULL or the port number is less than or equal to zero, lopen uses the values of the environment variables (LOGGINGPORT and LOGGINGHOST). If these environment variables are undefined, lopen uses default values. The lopen function returns a pointer of type LFILE that is used as a parameter to the other logging functions. You can then set optional behavior with the lsendtime and lgenerator functions. Logging is done with the lprintf and lprintfg functions, which have syntax similar to that of fprintf.

The implementation assumes that the thread ID can be cast to a long in a meaningful way. If this is not the case, the function get_threadid might have to be changed. Alternatively, when using the remote logger with threads, compile with NOTHREADID defined, and the thread ID will not be used as part of the generator.

Details of these functions are given below.

```
LFILE *lopen(char *host, int port);
```
> open a connection to the logging GUI. The host parameter is the name of the host on which the GUI is running, and port is the port number that the GUI is using. If host is NULL, lopen takes the host name from the environment variable LOGGINGHOST. If LOGGINGHOST is not set, lopen uses the default host name localhost. If port is less than or equal to 0, lopen takes the port number from the environment variable LOGGINGPORT. If LOGGINGPORT is not set, lopen uses a default port number of 20100. The GUI uses the same default port number. If successful, lopen returns a pointer of type LFILE that is used by other logging functions. If unsuccessful, lopen returns NULL.

```
int lclose(LFILE *mf);
```
> close the connection to the GUI. If successful, lclose returns 0. If unsuccessful, lclose returns −1. The lclose function is not thread-safe. Do not close the connection while other threads can send messages to the GUI. Making this

function thread-safe would add considerable overhead to the logging functions and it was decided that thread safety was not necessary.

`int lsendtime(LFILE *mf);`

automatically send the local time with each message. The time is sent as two integer values giving the number of seconds since the Epoch and an additional number of microseconds. If successful, `lsendtime` returns 0. If unsuccessful, `lsendtime` returns –1. The design of `lsendtime` allows the GUI to optionally display the time that the message was sent rather than the time it was received. Call `lsendtime` before sending any messages to the GUI. When the GUI is set to display send times rather than receive times, messages sent before this call are displayed without a time. Displaying send times is useful when all messages are sent from the same host or from hosts with synchronized clocks. Otherwise, the receive times are more useful. The `lsendtime` function returns 0 if successful and –1 if unsuccessful. The `lsendtime` function is not thread-safe. Do not call `lsendtime` while other threads of the same process are concurrently logging.

`int lgenerator(LFILE *mf, char *gen);`

set the generator string to be `gen`. The generator string appears in the `gen` column of the GUI to identify the output. If successful, `lgenerator` returns 0. If unsuccessful, `lgenerator` returns –1. Failure can occur only if the `gen` string is longer than `LFILE_GENLENGTH` or if mutex locking fails in a threaded environment. The generator string follows a format specification. The `gen` parameter is a string that will be the new generator. The generator string specifies a format for the generator sent to the remote GUI. The first occurrence of `%p` in the generator string is replaced with the process ID of the process sending the message. In a threaded environment, the first occurrence of `%t` is also replaced by the thread ID. If `LUSETHREAD` is defined, compiling with `NOTHREADID` defined causes `%t` to be replaced by 0. The specified generator overrides the default generator that is equivalent to `%p` in a nonthreaded environment and to `%p.%t` in a threaded environment (`LUSETHREAD` defined). The default generator can be restored by a call to `lgenerator` with a `NULL` value of the `gen` parameter.

`int lprintf(LFILE *mf, char *fmt, ...);`
`int lprintfg(LFILE *mf, char *gen, char *fmt, ...);`

output a string to the logger. The `lprintf` and `lprintfg` functions are identical with one exception: the latter uses `gen` for the generator of this message only and the former uses the default generator. If successful, these functions return 0. If unsuccessful, these functions return –1. The syntax and parameters are similar to `fprintf`. The `fmt` parameter specifies a format string, and the remaining parameters are values to be included in the message. These functions allow one additional format specification, `%t`, which is replaced by the current time with a precision of milliseconds. If the message automatically includes the time (because of a previous call to lsendtime), the same time is used for both.

D.2.2 Implementation details

The logging facility can be used in a threaded or nonthreaded environment. The additional code for threaded operation is included if the constant LUSETHREAD is defined. The program uses mutex locks for synchronization. When LUSETHREAD is defined, all the functions are thread-safe except for lclose and lsendtime. Making these thread-safe would require additional synchronization every time the LFILE structure is accessed, adding considerable overhead and serializing much of the program being logged. The intention is that lopen and lsendtime be called before the threads are created and that lclose be called only when all logging has been completed. Optionally, you can avoid lclose completely by allowing the process exit to close the connection. Compiling with LSENDTIME defined causes the sending of the time to be the default.

To allow for maximum concurrency, separate mutexes are used to protect calls to the ctime function, calls to the lgenerator function, and access to the nextID variable.

Each connection to the GUI has an associated pipe. A call to lopen reserves three file descriptors: one for the connection to the GUI and two for the pipe. A new process is created to transfer anything written to the pipe to the GUI. This is done with a forked process rather than a thread so that the facility can be used in a nonthreaded environment. Also, some thread-scheduling mechanisms might not give sufficient priority to this thread when it is used with other CPU-bound threads.

The maximum-size message (including the message header) that can be sent is given by PIPE_BUF. This choice allows all messages sent through one connection to be passed atomically to the GUI by having them go through a single pipe shared by processes or threads. Messages sent through different connections are sorted by the GUI. POSIX specifies that PIPE_BUF must be at least _POSIX_PIPE_BUF, which has the value of 512. Typical values of PIPE_BUF may be 10 times this value, but even the minimum is suitable for logging simple error or status information.

Appendix E

POSIX Extensions

The programs in the book are based on the combined UNIX standard (POSIX) as published by the IEEE in 2001 [50]. The POSIX standard consists of a base specification containing mandatory requirements and several optional extensions. Implementations that comply with this standard have the symbol _POSIX_VERSION defined in unistd.h as 200112L.

At the time this book was written, none of our test systems claimed to be fully compliant with even the base of this version of this POSIX standard. Table 1.3 on page 19 shows the POSIX extensions that seem to be supported by our test systems. That is, the documentation agrees with the POSIX standard and the programs from the book behave correctly. Until these systems claim compliance, we must take this on faith.

An implementation that defines _POSIX_VERSION as 200112L must support the base standard. These systems support a particular extension if the corresponding symbol is defined in that implementation's unistd.h header file. Table E.1 lists the different extensions. The first column gives the code used by the POSIX manuals when describing a feature of an extension. The code appears in the margin of the manual. The second column gives the relevant symbol in unistd.h, when appropriate. If this symbol is defined and is not equal to –1, then the corresponding extension is supported. The last column of the table describes the extension.

The proper way to check the values of these symbols is to use the sysconf function described in Section 5.1. Call sysconf with a name derived from the symbol by replacing POSIX with SC. For example, to test the value of _POSIX_THREADS, call sysconf with parameter _SC_THREADS.

POSIX code	symbol	extension description
ADV	_POSIX_ADVISORY_INFO	advisory information
AIO	_POSIX_ASYNCHRONOUS_IO	asynchronous input and output
BAR	_POSIX_BARRIERS	barriers
BE	_POSIX2_PBS	batch environment services and utilities
CD	_POSIX2_C_DEV	C-language development utilities
CPT	_POSIX_CPUTIME	process CPU-time clocks
CS	_POSIX_CLOCK_SELECTION	clock selection
CX		extension to the ISO C standard (required)
FD	_POSIX2_FORT_DEV	FORTRAN development utilities
FR	_POSIX2_FORT_RUN	FORTRAN runtime utilities
FSC	_POSIX_FSYNC	file synchronization
IP6		IPV6
MC1		shorthand for ADV and either MF or SHM
MC2		shorthand for MF, SHM or MPR
	_POSIX_JOB_CONTROL	job control (required)
MF	_POSIX_MAPPED_FILES	memory mapped files
ML	_POSIX_MEMLOCK	process memory locking
MLR	_POSIX_MEMLOCK_RANGE	range memory locking
MON	_POSIX_MONOTONIC_CLOCK	monotonic clock
MPR	_POSIX_MEMORY_PROTECTION	memory protection
MSG	_POSIX_MESSAGE_PASSING	message passing
MX		IEC 60559 floating-point option
OB		obsolescent
OF		output format incompletely specified
OH		optional header
PIO	_POSIX_PRIORITIZED_IO	prioritized input and output
PS	_POSIX_PRIORITY_SCHEDULING	processing scheduling
RTS	_POSIX_REALTIME_SIGNALS	realtime signals
SD	_POSIX2_SW_DEV	software development utilities
	_POSIX_SAVED_IDS	process has saved set-user-ID (required)
SEM	_POSIX_SEMAPHORES	semaphores
SHM	_POSIX_SHARED_MEMORY_OBJECTS	shared memory objects
SIO	_POSIX_SYNCHRONIZED_IO	synchronized input and output
SPI	_POSIX_SPIN_LOCKS	spin locks
SPN	_POSIX_SPAWN	spawn
SS	_POSIX_SPORADIC_SERVER	process sporadic server
TCT	_POSIX_THREAD_CPUTIME	thread CPU-time clocks
TEF	_POSIX_TRACE_EVENT_FILTER	trace event filter
THR	_POSIX_THREADS	threads
TMO	_POSIX_TIMEOUTS	timeouts
TMR	_POSIX_TIMERS	timers
TPI	_POSIX_PRIO_INHERIT	thread priority inheritance
TPP	_POSIX_PRIO_PROTECT	thread priority protection
TPS	_POSIX_PRIORITY_SCHEDULING	thread execution scheduling
TRC	_POSIX_TRACE	trace
TRI	_POSIX_TRACE_INHERIT	trace inherit
TRL	_POSIX_TRACE_LOG	trace log
TSA	_POSIX_THREAD_ATTR_STACKADDR	thread stack address attribute
TSF	_POSIX_THREAD_SAFE_FUNCTIONS	thread-safe functions
TSH	_POSIX_THREAD_PROCESS_SHARED	thread process-shared synchronization
TSP	_POSIX_THREAD_SPORADIC_SERVER	thread sporadic server
TSS	_POSIX_THREAD_ATTR_STACKSIZE	thread stack address size
TYM	_POSIX_TYPED_MEMORY_OBJECTS	typed memory objects
UP	_POSIX2_UPE	user portability utilities
XSI	_XOPEN_UNIX	XSI
XSR	_XOPEN_STREAMS	XSR streams

Table E.1: POSIX extensions. If the symbol is defined in `unistd.h`, the system supports the corresponding POSIX extension.

Bibliography

[1] M. Accetta, R. Baron, D. Golub, R. Rashid, A. Tevanian and M. Young, "Mach: A new kernel foundation for UNIX development," *Proc. Summer 1986 USENIX Conference*, 1986, pp. 93–112.

[2] T. Anderson, B. Bershad, E. Lazowska and H. Levy, "Scheduler activations: Efficient kernel support for the user-level management of parallelism," *Proc. 13th ACM Symposium on Operating Systems Principles*, 1991, pp. 95–109.

[3] G. Andrews and F. Schneider, "Concepts and notations for concurrent programming," *ACM Computing Surveys*, vol. 15, No. 1, 1983, pp. 3–43.

[4] K. Arnold, B. O'Sullivan, R. Scheifler, J. Waldo and A. Wollrath, *The Jini Specification*, Addison-Wesley, 1999.

[5] M. Aron and P. Druschel, "Soft timers: Efficient microsecond software timer support for network processing," *Proc. 17th ACM Symposium on Operating Systems Principles*, 1999, pp. 232–246.

[6] L. J. Arthur, *UNIX Shell Programming*, John Wiley & Sons, 1990.

[7] H. Attiya, M. Snir and M. Warmuth, "Computing on an anonymous ring," *Journal of the ACM*, vol. 35, no. 4, 1988, pp. 845–875.

[8] D. Austerberry and G. Starks, *The Technology of Video and Audio Streaming*, Focal Press, 2002.

[9] M. Bach, *The Design of the UNIX Operating System*, Prentice Hall, 1986.

[10] A. Beguelin, J. Dongarra, A. Geist and V. Sunderam, "Visualization and debugging in a heterogeneous environment," *Computer*, vol. 26, no. 6, 1993, pp. 88–95.

[11] A. Black, N. Hutchinson, E. Jul, H. Levy and L. Carter, "Distribution and abstract types in Emerald," *IEEE Trans. Software Engineering*, vol. SE-13, no. 1, 1987, pp. 65–76.

[12] D. Black, "Scheduling support for concurrency and parallelism in the Mach operating system," *IEEE Computer*, vol. 23, no. 5, 1990, pp. 35–43.

[13] B. Blinn, *Portable Shell Programming*, Prentice Hall, 1995.

[14] BlueGene/L Team and Collaborators (115 authors), "An overview of the BlueGene/L supercomputer," *Supercomputing*, 2002.

[15] M. Bolsky and D. Korn, *The New KornShell Command and Programming Language*, 2nd ed., Prentice Hall, 1995.

[16] D. Bovet and M. Cesati, *Understanding the LINUX Kernel: From I/O Ports to Process Management*, O'Reilly & Associates, 2000.

[17] P. Buhr, M. Fortier and M. Coffin, "Monitor classification," *ACM Computing Surveys*, vol. 27, no. 1, 1995, pp. 63–107.

[18] V. Bush, "As we may think," *The Atlantic Monthly*, vol. 176, no. 1, 1945, pp. 101–108.

[19] D. Butenhof, *Programming with POSIX(R) Threads*, Addison Wesley, 1997.

[20] D. Cameron and B. Rosenblatt, *Learning GNU Emacs*, O'Reilly & Associates, 1991.

[21] V. Cardellini, E. Casalicchio, M. Colanjanni and P. Yu, "The state of the art in locally distributed web-server systems," *ACM Computing Surveys*, vol. 34, no. 2, 2002, pp. 263–311.

[22] E. Chang and R. Roberts, "An improved algorithm for decentralized extrema-finding in circular configurations of processes," *Communications of the ACM*, vol. 22, no. 5, 1979, pp. 281–283.

[23] A. Chou, J. Yang, B. Chelf, S. Hallem and D. Engler, "An empirical study of operating system errors," *Proc. 18th ACM Symposium on Operating Systems Principles*, 2001, pp. 73–88.

[24] Computer Emergency Response Team Coordination Center, http://www.cert.org.

[25] T. Cormen, C. Leiserson and R. Rivest, *An Introduction to Algorithms*, 2nd ed., MIT Press, 2001.

[26] G. Coulouris, J. Dollimore and T. Kindberg, *Distributed Systems: Concepts and Design*, 3rd ed., Addison-Wesley, 2001.

[27] D. Curry, *Using C on the UNIX System*, O'Reilly & Associates, 1989.

[28] I. Darwin, *Checking C Programs with* `lint`, O'Reilly & Associates, 1988.

[29] P. Dasgupta, R. LeBlanc, Jr., M. Ahamad and U. Ramachandran, "The Clouds distributed operating system," *IEEE Computer*, vol. 24, no. 11, 1991, pp. 34–44.

[30] E. Dijkstra, "Co-operating sequential processes," in *Programming Languages*, F. Genuys (ed.), Academic Press, 1968, pp. 43–112.

[31] L. Dowdy and C. Lowery, *P.S. to Operating Systems*, Prentice Hall, 1993.

[32] R. Draves, B. Bershad, R. Rashid and R. Dean, "Using continuations to implement thread managment and communication in operating systems," *Proc. 13th ACM Symposium on Operating Systems Principles*, 1991, pp. 122–136.

[33] P. DuBois, *Using* `csh` *and* `tsch`, O'Reilly & Associates, 1995.

[34] T. Durkin, "The Vx_files: What the media couldn't tell you about Mars Pathfinder," *Robot Science and Technology*, vol. 1, 1998, pp. 1–3.

[35] R. Eigenmann, ed. *Performance Evaluation and Benchmarking with Realistic Applications*, MIT Press, 2001.

[36] J. Farley, *Java Distributed Computing*, O'Reilly & Associates, 1998.

[37] F. Fluckiger, *Understanding Networked Multimedia Applications and Technology*, Prentice Hall, 1995.

[38] I. Foster, C. Kesselman, J. Nick and S. Tuecke, "Grid services for distributed system integration," *Computer*, vol. 35, no. 6, 2002, pp. 37–46.

[39] B. Gallmeister, *POSIX.4: Programming for the Real World*, O'Reilly & Associates, 1995.

[40] Geek of the Week Homepage, http://town.hall.org/radio/Geek/.

[41] G. Geist and V. Sunderam, "Experiences with network-based concurrent computing on the PVM system," *Concurrency: Practice and Experience*, vol. 4, no. 4, 1992, pp. 392–311.

[42] W. Golding, *Lord of the Flies*, Faber and Faber, London, 1954.

[43] B. Gropp, R. Lusk and A. Skjellum, *Using MPI*, 2nd ed., MIT Press, 1999.

[44] W. Grosso, *Java RMI*, O'Reilly & Associates, 2001.

[45] N. Gunther, *The Practical Performance Analyst*, Authors Choice Press and Mc-Graw Hill, 2000.

[46] S. Harbison and G. Steele, Jr., *C: A Reference Manual*, 5th ed., Prentice Hall, 2002.

[47] G. Held, *Data Communications Networking Devices*, 2nd ed., John Wiley & Sons, 1989.

[48] The Honeynet Project (ed.), Lance Spitzner (Preface), Bruce Schneier and the Honeynet Project, *Know Your Enemy: Revealing the Security Tools, Tactics, and Motives of the Blackhat Community*, Addison Wesley, 2001.

[49] IEEE, "Standard for Information Technology—Portable Operating System Interface (POSIX) System Interfaces," Issue 6, IEEE Std 1003.1-2001, 2001.

[50] IEEE, "Standard for Information Technology—Portable Operating System Interface (POSIX) Base Definitions," Issue 6, IEEE Std 1003.1-2001, 2001.

[51] IEEE, "Standard for Information Technology—Portable Operating System Interface (POSIX) Rationale (Informative)," IEEE Std 1003.1-2001, 2001.

[52] IEEE, "Standard for Information Technology—Portable Operating System Interface (POSIX) Shell and Utilities," IEEE Std 1003.1-2001, 2001.

[53] IETF/RFC: T. Berners-Lee, R. Fielding and H. Frystyk, *Hypertext Transfer Protocol – HTTP/1.0*, IETF Network Working Group RFC 1945, May 1996.

[54] IETF/RFC: R. Fielding, J. Gettys, J. Mogul, H. Frystyk, L. Masinter, P. Leach and T. Berners-Lee, *Hypertext Transfer Protocol – HTTP/1.1*, IETF Network Working Group RFC 2616, June 1999.

[55] Internet Engineering Task Force Homepage, http://www.ietf.org.

[56] ISO/IEC International Standard 9899: 1999, Programming Languages—C.

[57] ISO/IEC International Standard 9945: 2002, Information Technology—Portable Operating System Interface (POSIX), Part 2, 1-4.

[58] A. Itai and M. Rodeh, "Symmetry breaking in distributive networks," *Proc. 22nd Annual IEEE Symposium on the Foundations of Computer Science*, 1981, pp. 150–158.

[59] R. Jain, *The Art of Computer Systems Performance Analysis: Techniques for Experimental Design, Measurement, Simulation, and Modeling*, John Wiley & Sons, 1991.

[60] M. Johnson and E. Troan, *Linux Application Development*, Addison-Wesley, 1998.

[61] M. Jones, "Mars Pathfinder debugging," http://research.microsoft.com/~mbj/Mars_Pathfinder/Mars_Pathfinder.html.

[62] B. Kernighan and D. Ritchie, *The C Programming Language*, 2nd ed., Prentice Hall, 1988.

[63] S. Kleiman and J. Eykholt, "Interrupts as threads," *ACM SIGOPS Operating Systems Review*, vol. 29, no. 2, April 1995, pp. 21–26.

[64] S. Kochan and P. Wood, *UNIX Shell Programming*, revised ed., SAMS Publishing, 1989.

[65] L. Kontothanassis, R. Wisniewski and M. Scott, "Schedule-conscious synchronization," *ACM Trans. on Computer Systems*, vol. 15, no. 1, 1997, pp. 3–40.

[66] B. Krishnamurthy and J. Rexford, *Web Protocols and Practice: HTTP/1.1, Networking Protocols, Caching, and Traffic Measurement*, Addison Wesley, 2001.

[67] V. Kumar, A. Grama, A. Gupta and G. Karypis, *Introduction to Parallel Computing: Design and Analysis of Algorithms*, Benjamin-Cummings, 1994.

[68] J. Kurose and K. Ross, *Computer Networking: A Top-Down Approach Featuring the Internet*, Addison Wesley, 2000.

[69] L. Lamb, *Learning the* vi *Editor*, 5th ed., O'Reilly & Associates, 1990.

[70] S. J. Leffler, M. McKusick, M. Karels and J. Quarterman, *The Design and Implementation of the 4.3 BSD UNIX Operating System*, Addison-Wesley, 1989.

[71] N. Leveson and C. Turner, "An investigation of the Therac-25 accidents," *IEEE Computer*, vol. 26, no. 7, 1993, pp. 18–41.

[72] B. Lewis and D. Berg, *Multithreaded Programming with Pthreads*, Sun Microsystems Press, Prentice Hall, 1998.

[73] T. Lewis, "Where is computing heading?" *Computer*, vol. 27, no. 8, 1994, pp. 59–63.

[74] B. Liskow, "Distributed programming in Argus," *Communications of the ACM*, vol. 31, no. 3, 1988, pp. 300–312.

[75] S. Mack, *Streaming Media Bible*, John Wiley & Sons, 2002.

[76] M. Maekawa, A. Oldehoeft and R. Oldehoeft, *Operating Systems: Advanced Concepts*, Benjamin/Cummings, 1987.

[77] C. Maltzahn, K. Richardson and D. Grunwald, "Performance issues of enterprise level web proxies," *Proc. 1997 Sigmetrics Conference on Measurement and Modeling of Computer Systems*, 1997, pp. 13–23.

[78] B. Marsh, M. Scott, T. LeBlanc and E. Markatos, "First-class user-level threads," *Proc. 13th ACM Symposium on Operating Systems Principles*, 1991, pp. 110–121.

[79] J. Mauro and R. McDougall, *Solaris Internals: Core Kernel Architecture*, Prentice Hall, 2000.

[80] D. McNamee, J. Walpole, C. Pu, C. Cowen, C. Krasic, A. Goel, P. Wagle, C. Consel, G. Muller and R. Marlet, "Specialization tools and techniques for systematic optimization of system software," *ACM Transactions on Computer Systems*, vol. 19, no. 2, 2001, pp. 217–251.

[81] P. Mockapetris, *Domain Names—Concepts and Facilities*, IETF Network Working Group RFC 1034, 1987.

[82] P. Mockapetris, *Domain Names—Implementation and Specification*, IETF Network Working Group RFC 1035, 1987.

[83] D. Mossberger, S. Eranian and B. Perens, *IA-64 Linux Kernel: Design and Implementation*, Prentice Hall, 2002.

[84] Multiparty Multimedia Session Control (mmusic) Working Group Web Site, http://www.ietf.org/html.charters/mmusic-charter.html.

[85] E. Nahum, T. Barzilai and D. Kandlur, "Performance issues in WWW servers," *IEEE/ACM Transactions on Networking*, vol. 10, no. 1, 2002, pp. 2–11.

[86] E. Nemeth, G. Snyder, S. Seebass and T. Hein, *UNIX System Administration Handbook*, 3rd ed., Prentice Hall, 2000.

[87] B. Nichols, D. Buttlar and J. Farrell, *Pthreads Programming: A POSIX Standard for Better Multiprocessing*, O'Reilly & Associates, 1996.

[88] S. Nishio, K. Li and E. Manning, "A resilient mutual exclusion algorithm for computer networks," *IEEE Transactions on Parallel and Distributed Systems*, vol. 1, no. 3, 1990, pp. 344–355.

[89] "Open Group Single UNIX Specification V3," http://www.UNIX-systems.org/single_unix_specification/.

[90] A. Oram, ed., *Peer-To-Peer: Harnessing the Benefits of a Disruptive Technology*, O'Reilly & Associates, 2001.

[91] P. Plauger, *The Standard C Library*, Prentice Hall, 1992.

[92] S. Rago, *UNIX System V Network Programming*, Addison-Wesley, 1993.

[93] G. Reeves, "What really happened on Mars?" http://research.microsoft.com/~mbj/Mars_Pathfinder/Authoritative_Account.html.

[94] A. Robbins and D. Gilly, *UNIX in a Nutshell: A Desktop Quick Reference for SVR4 and Solaris 7*, 3rd ed., O'Reilly & Associates, 1999.

[95] K. Robbins, N. Wagner and D. Wenzel, "Virtual rings: An introduction to concurrency," *Proc. 21st SIGCSE Technical Symposium on Computer Science Education*, 1989, pp. 23–28.

[96] S. Robbins, "Experimentation with bounded buffer synchronization," *Proc. 31st SIGCSE Technical Symposium on Computer Science Education*, 2000, pp. 330–334.

[97] S. Robbins, "Exploration of process interaction in operating systems: A pipe-fork simulator," *Proc. 33rd SIGCSE Technical Symposium on Computer Science Education*, 2002, pp. 351–355.

[98] S. Robbins, "Using remote logging for teaching concurrency," *Proc. 34rd SIGCSE Technical Symposium on Computer Science Education*, 2003, pp. 177–181.

[99] S. Robbins, *Remote Logging User's Guide*, http://vip.cs.utsa.edu/nsf/logging.html.

[100] J. Rosenberg and H. Schulzrinne, "Timer reconsideration for enhanced RTP scalability," *Proc. Infocom*, 1998.

[101] B. Rosenblatt, *Learning the Korn Shell*, 2nd ed., O'Reilly & Associates, 2002.

[102] A. Rubini and J. Corbet, *Linux Device Drivers*, 2nd ed., O'Reilly & Associates, 2001.

[103] C. Schimmel, *UNIX Systems for Modern Architectures: Symmetric Multiprocessing and Caching for Kernel Programmers*, Addison-Wesley, 1994.

[104] K. Seetharamanan, Special Issue: The CORBA connection, *Communications of the ACM*, vol. 41, no. 10, 1998.

[105] L. Sha, R. Rajkumar and J. Lehoczky, "Priority inheritance protocols: An approach to real-time synchronization," *IEEE Transactions on Computers*, vol. 39, 1990, pp. 1175–1185.

[106] S. Shrivastava, G. Dixon and G. Parrington, "An overview of the Arjuna distributed programming system," *IEEE Software*, January 1991, pp. 66–73.

[107] A. Silberschatz, P. Galvin and G. Gagne, *Operating Systems Concepts*, 6th ed., Addison-Wesley Publishing, 2002.

[108] M. Sobell, *A Practical Guide to the UNIX System*, 3rd ed., Addison-Wesley, 1994.

[109] *Solaris Multithreaded Programming Guide*, SunSoft Incorporated, 1995.

[110] A. Spector, "Performing remote operations efficiently on a local computer network," *Communications of the ACM*, vol. 25, no. 4, 1982, pp. 246–260.

[111] W. Stallings, *Local and Metropolitan Area Networks*, 6th ed., Prentice Hall, 2000.

[112] W. Stevens, *Advanced Programming in the UNIX Environment*, Addison-Wesley, 1992.

[113] W. Stevens, *TCP/IP Illustrated: The Protocols*, Volume 1, Addison-Wesley, 1994.

[114] W. Stevens, *TCP/IP Illustrated: TCP for Transactions, HTTP, NNTP, and the UNIX(R) Domain Protocols*, Volume 3, Addison-Wesley, 1996.

[115] W. Stevens, *UNIX Network Programming, Volume 1, Networking APIs: Sockets and TLI*, 2nd ed., Prentice Hall, 1997.

[116] W. Stevens, *UNIX Network Programming, Volume 2, Interprocess Communications*, 2nd ed., Prentice Hall, 1998.

[117] R. Stones and N. Matthew, *Beginning Linux Programming*, 2nd ed., Wrox Press, 1999.

[118] V. Sunderam, "PVM: A framework for parallel distributed computing," *Journal of Concurrency: Practice and Experience*, vol. 2, no. 4, 1990, pp. 315–339.

[119] *Sun OS5.3 Writing Device Drivers*, SunSoft Incorporated, 1993.

[120] S. Talbott, *Managing Projects with* `make`, O'Reilly & Associates, 1991.

[121] A. Tanenbaum, *Distributed Operating Systems*, Prentice Hall, 1995.

[122] A. Tanenbaum, *Modern Operating Systems*, 2nd ed., Prentice Hall, 2001.

[123] A. Tanenbaum, *Computer Networks*, 4th ed., Prentice Hall, 2002.

[124] A. Tanenbaum, R. van Renesse, H. van Staveren, G. Sharp, S. Mullender, J. Jansen and G. van Rossum, "Experiences with the Amoeba distributed operating system," *Communications of the ACM*, vol. 33, no. 12, 1990, pp. 46–63.

[125] A. Tanenbaum and A. Woodhull, *Operating Systems: Design and Implementation*, 2nd ed., Prentice Hall, 1997.

[126] K. Trivedi, *Probability and Statistics with Reliability, Queuing and Computer Science Applications*, 2nd ed., John Wiley & Sons, 2002.

[127] M. Van Steen and A. Tanenbaum, *Distributed Systems: Principles and Paradigms*, Prentice Hall, 2002.

[128] G. Varghese and T. Lauck, "Hashed and hierarchical timing wheels: Data structures for efficient implementation of a timer facility," *Proc. 11th ACM Symposium on Operating Systems Principles*, 1987, pp. 25–38.

[129] M. Wahl, T. Howes and S. Kille, *The Lightweight Directory Access Protocol (v3)*, Internet RFC 2251, 1997, http://www.ietf.org/rfc/rfc2251.

[130] D. Wessels, "Squid Internet object cache," http://www.squid-cache.org.

[131] R. Wittmann and M. Zitterbart, *Multicast Communication: Protocols, Programming, and Applications*, Morgan Kaufmann, 2000.

[132] World Wide Web Consortium, Homepage, http://www.w3.org.

[133] World Wide Web Consortium RFC 1945: Hypertext Transfer Protocol—HTTP/1.0, http:/www.w3.org/Protocols/rfc1945/rfc1945.

[134] G. Wright and W. Stevens, *TCP/IP Illustrated: The Implementation*, Volume 2, Addison-Wesley, 1995.

[135] M. Yokokawa, K. Itakura, A. Uno, T. Ishihara and Y. Kaneda, "16.4 Tflops direct numerical simulation of turbulence by Fourier spectral method on the Earth Simulator," *Supercomputing*, 2002.

[136] F. Zabatta and K. Ying, "A thread performance comparison: Windows NT and Solaris on a symmetric multiprocessor," *Proc. 2nd USENIX Windows NT Symposium*, August, 1998.

[137] Zeus web site, http://www.zeus.co.uk.

Program Index

Entries refer to page numbers in the text.

Index

Entries refer to page numbers in the text. **Boldface** is used for the most important references.

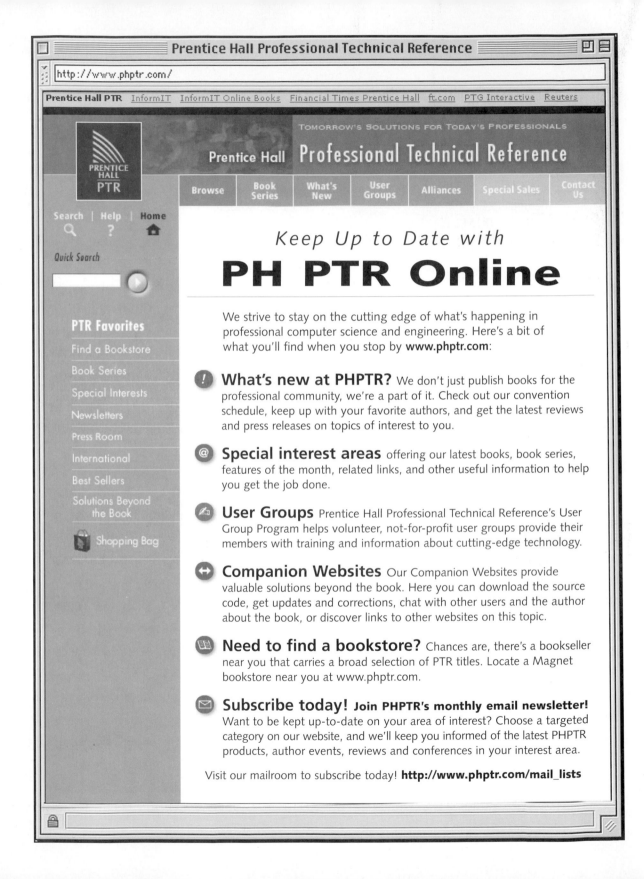